FOURTH EDITION

The Applied Psychology of
WORK BEHAVIOR

A Book of Readings

DENNIS W. ORGAN

Indiana University

IRWIN

Homewood, IL 60430
Boston, MA 02116

Sponsoring editor: Karen L. Johnson
Developmental editor: Elizabeth J. Rubenstein
Project editor: Karen Smith
Production manager: Ann Cassady
Designer: Laurie Entringer
Compositor: Better Graphics, Inc.
Typeface: 10/12 Caledonia
Printer: R. R. Donnelley & Sons Company

Library of Congress Cataloging-in-Publication Data

The Applied psychology of work behavior : a book of readings / [edited
    by] Dennis W. Organ. —4th ed.
        p.   cm.
    Includes bibliographical references.
    ISBN 0-256-08275-8
    1. Psychology, Industrial.   2. Organizational behavior.
I. Organ, Dennis W.
HF5548.8.A72   1991
158.7—dc20   90-22187

Printed in the United States of America

1 2 3 4 5 6 7 8 9 0 DOC 8 7 6 5 4 3 2 1

Preface

Users of previous editions of *The Applied Psychology of Work Behavior: A Book of Readings* will find much the same structure and major content areas in this version. Past users will also recognize the retention of a number of selections of longstanding significance in the field of organizational behavior. One of the more interesting processes incidental to revising a book of readings is noting which articles continue to command attention through the years, and I trust that my subjective assessment in this regard is not idiosyncratic.

Perhaps the most obvious—and important—difference between this edition and previous ones is the care taken to provide more international coverage of the major areas. Three new selections focus specifically on cultural discontinuities in the dynamics of organizational behavior, and several other articles were picked because they found some way of including the theme of globalism in their discussion.

On balance, my own judgment is that the present set of readings tilts somewhat more in the direction of the "real world" context of clinical richness than did prior editions. To be sure, several selections still grapple with matters of theory, and I suppose some reviewers feel that this version gives a heftier weight to theoretical concepts than do most books of readings. Nonetheless, users should now find an abundance of nontechnical material drawn from periodicals directed at broad readerships. These selections provide graphic illustrations, trend reports, lessons of experience, more than a little sage advice, and controversial points of view that should elicit lively discussions.

Retrospectively, I believe I discern in the final selection of articles the continuation of a trend I saw in the Third Edition—increased linkage from organizational behavior to human resource management. I consider this quite appropriate, as it reflects the growing interest of both academics and managers in the strategic relevance of selection, compensation, performance appraisal, and training.

As has been true of previous revisions, I felt twinges of regret at having to drop some of my favorite pieces to make room for new selections.

I wish to express my unrestrained appreciation to the authors who have given permission to reprint their work and to colleagues at Indiana University and elsewhere who pointed me to some valuable additions to this volume. Special thanks go to Artegal R. Camburn, Debra Steele Johnson, and Abdullah Pooyan for craftsmanlike and professional reviews of prior editions and for insightful suggestions for how to improve on them.

Dennis W. Organ

Contents

---

* Denotes new selection for this edition.

Section One

Organizational Behavior: Scope and Method

INTRODUCTION

In the beginning, there was Management. Those who pondered over the nature of organizations were bound, however loosely, by one discipline or quasi discipline called the *study of administration or management.* Whether the concern was with the motivation of individual performance, group decisions, the structural design of organizations, or leadership, one was thought to be studying management.

The loose bonds of this quasi discipline endured through most of the first half of this century. Since then, most of the substantive areas within management have been "co-opted" by professions outside management. Economics, mathematics, psychology, sociology, political science, and anthropology, to name a few, have staked the claim of their particular methods and conceptual approaches upon topics formerly considered the exclusive province of Management. Instead of one discipline, we now have several, including organizational behavior, operations research, organization theory, and business strategy. Management, as a discipline, is not so much a distinctive and ongoing enterprise now as it is simply a title of a holding company (for a more complete account of the fractionation of management as a discipline, see Charles Perrow, "The short and glorious history of organizational theory," *Organizational Dynamics* (Summer 1973), 2–15).

The first selection in this book should help the reader understand how organizational behavior (or, as some call it, *organizational psychology*) stands in relation to the larger sphere of what was once management. The article by Organ notes some of the historically significant events that served as catalysts to accelerate the process by which organizational behavior became a distinctive discipline.

The contribution by Porter and McKibbin to this section comes from a recently published report on the strengths and weaknesses of business school curricula, as seen by business school deans, faculty, alumni, and corporate managers. We might well anticipate that this report—and the

1

reactions to it—will affect both tone and substance of the study of organizational behavior in the 1990s, just as the earlier Gordon and Howell and the Pierson reports of the late 1950s did much to shape the discipline in the past three decades. Noteworthy in Porter and McKibbin's findings is that corporate leaders overwhelmingly endorse an increased emphasis on behavioral topics in academic business programs. Equally noteworthy is that our discipline is vulnerable to a number of more general criticisms of current programs: The failure to stimulate a "vision" among students, the absence of concerns with the "real problems of managing people," the lack of a thoroughgoing global perspective, and the tendency to skirt many of the ethical dilemmas of management. It remains to be seen whether, to what extent, or how organizational behavior scholars will address these issues in their theories and research.

As other disciplines have preempted the concerns of management, they have generally sought to impose upon these concerns the philosophy and methods of science. Armchair theorizing from informal observation gave way to the experiment, the survey, the mathematical model, statistical analysis, and life under the rule of the 0.05 level of significance. The article by Scott provides a more detailed description of how rigorous methods of research bear on the pursuit of knowledge about behavior in organizations.

Recently, a growing number of voices in our profession have expressed skepticism about the wisdom of a fixation with the natural science model of studying organizational behavior. The fear is that a narrowly construed definition of legitimate approaches will prevent us from learning about the more important aspects of organizations. Lawler, in the selection concluding this part of the book, addresses the question of how we can generate knowledge about organizations that is both valid and useful.

The reader will probably, and rightfully, conclude from the readings in Section One that organizational behavior as a discipline reflects an ongoing state of tension. This tension has various origins and has to do with striking the proper balance between description and prescription, between rigor and relevance, between objectivity and humanism, between the status quo and change. Unanimity is the exception, rather than the rule, among those who study this field. Yet it is precisely this tension that maintains the interest of its practitioners. And, in the final analysis, it is a tension that faithfully reflects its own subject of discourse: behavior in organizations.

Organizational Behavior as an Area of Study: Some Questions and Answers*

Dennis W. Organ

Q: What is "organizational behavior"?

A: The precise answer depends on which specific textbook or authority you consult. The consensual core of most definitions, however, would run something like this: "Organizational Behavior (OB), as a field of study, represents the application of behavioral science concepts and methods to the study of human behavior in the organizational environment."

Q: Is organizational behavior simply the "human" side of management or a "behavioral approach" to management?

A: No, although it might be fair to say that OB started out that way.

In the late 1920s and early 1930s, some experiments in illumination, pay systems, work breaks, and other job conditions took place at the Western Electric Hawthorne plant in Chicago. The results made little sense, at first, because productivity in an experimental group of female operators seemed to hold steady at a fairly high level regardless of the particular set of working conditions arranged. Finally the experimenters, after bringing in some outside consultants, realized that they had unwittingly altered supervisory styles (toward being more considerate of the individual workers and allowing them to make more job decisions) and allowed the operators to become a cohesive work group. These findings, plus others that emerged from an intensive interviewing program and close observation of a work group in action, made it clear that traditional management thinking up to that time was deficient. Previous approaches to administration had concentrated on the mechanics of getting things coordinated and controlled, without due consideration of the complexity of the human element. After the publication of *Management and the Worker* (which reported the Hawthorne findings and probed their implications) in 1938, the "behavioral" aspects of work organization were elevated to a much more serious status. Management thinking began to accord much greater emphasis to

---

* Prepared especially for this book.

worker feelings, motives, and the social forces in the "informal organiza-tion" not covered by the organization chart.

While these developments spurred a new interest in the relevance of behavioral sciences for management, they hardly resulted in a new disci-pline or field of knowledge. It was sometime later, near the end of the 1950s, that OB began to jell as a discipline.

In 1956, the Ford Foundation commissioned two economists, Professors R. A. Gordon and J. E. Howell, to undertake a comprehensive survey and assessment of business education at the college and university level. In their report, published in 1959, Gordon and Howell stated the view that business administration is the "enlightened application" of the behavioral sciences, among other things, to business problems. They felt, however, that business schools at the time were providing too little exposure in their curricula to basic conceptual material in the behavioral sciences.

Gordon and Howell noted approvingly that, at a number of the leading business schools, psychologists, sociologists, and political scientists were finding full-time positions on the faculty and encouraged other schools to consider this possibility. They urged, too, more cooperation between busi-ness schools and departments of psychology and sociology on behavioral research—basic as well as applied—of interest to the business community and aspiring students of management and administration.

The Gordon and Howell report had an enormous impact on the design of business school curricula and recruitment of faculty in the 1960s. The trickle of behavioral scientists, especially psychologists, into business schools became, if not a flood, certainly a sizable stream. As they increased in numbers, they began to share an emerging professional kinship, devel-oping their own national associations and doctoral programs within business schools. They, along with their intellectual offspring, gradually defined a coalescing discipline of OB. The discipline had reached a stage of consider-able maturity by the mid-to-late 1960s, although it is, of course, still evolving, like all fields of knowledge, and not locked into a rigid scheme of development or a fixed set of topics.

Q: Is OB, then, just the *application* of psychology and other behavioral sciences to the study of behavior in organizations?

A: Not exactly. It is certainly more than the mere mechanical process of fitting known facts, laws, findings, and so forth, from psychology to work organiza-tions. We *have* found it useful not to "reinvent the wheel." Where underly-ing disciplines, such as psychology and sociology, offer readily available concepts and methods of study that "fit" the organizational context, we do not hesitate to adopt them. Increasingly, however, we sometimes find it worth our while to develop our own constructs, theories, measuring instru-ments, and so on, when we address problems or issues unique to the organizational setting that have not been attended to by other behavioral sciences.

In any case, OB is not solely concerned with "application" in the narrow sense of the word. True, much of our effort is guided by the hope that we can contribute to pressing, urgent problems in work organizations, such as increasing the productivity and quality of work life in organizations. However, truly valid and lasting contributions will in some instances have to await a thorough testing and "thinking out" stage of our ideas, theories, and findings. Finally, as an intellectual discipline, OB, like any other, prizes knowledge and understanding as a goal in itself. Ultimately, knowledge is a seamless whole piece, and so any advance in our understanding of work behavior is worthwhile as well as intrinsically gratifying.

Q: How do developments in OB reach the practicing manager?

A: It might help, in answering this question, to look at the diagram of overlapping circles shown in Figure 1. At the far left, we have those behavioral

FIGURE 1

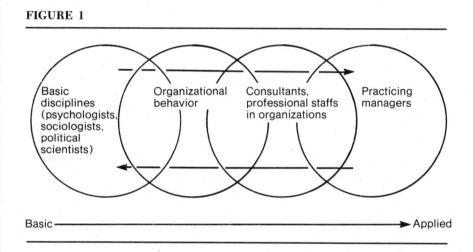

scientists (usually on the faculties of psychology or sociology departments) who teach and do basic research in such areas as human motivation, learning, attitude change, group dynamics, social stratification, and the like. Some of them have particular interests in organizations, most of them do not. Let us say a number of social psychologists conduct research showing that people's attitudes and opinions have little correspondence to their actual behavior. Now, people in OB, most of whom are affiliated with schools of business and administration, find out about this. They find out because many of them keep in touch with what people in the basic disciplines are doing; in fact, since the circles overlap, some of the organizational behavior types may be as much involved in the basic disciplines as anyone else. They ponder the implications of this finding about attitudes not jibing with behavior. Satisfaction with one's job is a type of attitude; productivity is a type of behavior. Maybe job satisfaction and productivity aren't too closely related, then. In any case, it's something to think about and investigate. So research is undertaken by organizational behaviorists, generally confirming that job satisfaction and productivity are not closely correlated.

These findings stimulate new thinking about the links between satisfaction and performance (see Section Two-A in this book). Later it turns up that social psychologists have found that certain factors determine whether attitudes and behavior are related. *If* the attitude is sufficiently specific (not general or vague) and not linked to powerful opposing attitudes, and if the behavior is not constrained by other forces, there may be a reasonably close correspondence between attitudes and behavior. So we may find that certain specific facets of job satisfaction *are* related to certain kinds of performance.

Many of the people who teach, write, and do research in OB also act as consultants to private firms and other organizations. In fact, some of them do part-time work in their own outside consulting firms, and a few do not belong to university faculties but work full-time on the professional staffs (e.g., in industrial relations, planning, personnel) of corporations. All of these people draw from their expertise and knowledge in teaching students (who later become managers), advising client managers, teaching in management development programs, or writing in popular periodicals, magazines, or trade publications.

Throughout the history of science, lines of influence have sometimes run from the practical problem-solving arena back to basic theory and research, as well as in the other direction. OB is no exception. In the late 1950s, an issue of immediate concern among executives was whether groups made more cautious, conservative decisions than individuals acting alone. A master's thesis (Stoner, 1961) research project by a student in industrial management produced evidence that groups actually make *riskier* decisions. The implications of this finding soon rocked academic social psychology to its foundation and influenced more than a decade of research in social psychology.

Q: Doesn't it take a long time for this communication process to operate?

A: The problem more frequently has been that it operates too quickly. In an address to the Academy of Management in 1974, Professor Lyman Porter reminded the organizational behaviorists that often we have been too quick to offer prescriptions to managers on the basis of premature, tentative, sometimes downright invalid findings. One result is that, by promising too much with a hard-sell approach, we have damaged our credibility with practitioners. We have foisted programs upon them that were attractive in package but weak in substance, and the implied payoffs were not realized.

Part of the problem is that OB, like any science, is a system or collection of "technologies" as well as a field of study. Professor L. L. Cummings (1977) of Wisconsin identifies OB techniques for training leaders, designing tasks, evaluating performance, and designing reward systems. Technologies have their market appeal even when they are based on untested or oversimplified representations of reality.

Q: How can premature prescribing be minimized?

A: Only by the discipline of the scientific method. As Cummings points out, OB is becoming more "influenced by the norms of skepticism, caution, replication of findings, and public exposure of knowledge based on facts."

Q: Doesn't the cold-blooded posture of "scientism" put a damper on the genuine and immediate concern for people?

A: Actually, as Cummings observes, "there is a distinctly humanistic tone within OB." That is, as much as anything else, we want to contribute a knowledge basis for designing organization environments that foster self-development, psychological growth, choice, and fulfillment of individuals—yet do it in a way that also makes organizations more effective in serving the larger society. As Cummings puts it, this is a "humanism without softness." OB is performance-oriented, as well as people-oriented; its orientation toward both is circumscribed by intellectual and scientific honesty, lest we delude ourselves into thinking we have already reached the promised land for which we strive (and will never reach, since it really exists only as a guiding ideal).

Q: What has OB accomplished? What is its track record?

A: To date, our major contribution has been, in a sense, negative. We have been more successful in challenging and overturning previous conceptions about behavior in organizations than we have been creative in providing alternative conceptions. Nowhere is this better illustrated than in the study of leadership. As Professor H. Joseph Reitz (1977) remarks, "the study of leadership is interesting and yet confusing. We seem to have been more proficient at discovering the misconceptions of leadership than the principles of leadership." We realize now that effective leaders cannot be picked on the basis of personality traits, that democratic leadership is not necessarily more effective than autocratic leadership, and that leader behavior is as much or more affected by subordinate performance than vice versa.

Q: Isn't this discouraging?

A: It is certainly cause for humility on our part. We realize now that grand theories which will explain any and every thing are not in the offing. If we can't endorse a particular style of leader behavior that is optimal for all situations, maybe we can find a style that at least seems to work reasonably well in a very limited set of situations.

Q: In the final analysis, what does OB have to offer the student?

A: It can help the student become, in the words of Professor R. J. House of the University of Toronto, a "good crap-detector." It can provide a basic framework for evaluating the assertions, conclusions, programs, and slogans that the manager is bombarded with from all sides. It can help the student recognize fallacies in his or her own thinking about work behavior. It can help one avoid painting oneself into a logical corner. It can provide a basis for informal, intelligent observation of behavior in organizations.

UPDATE: JULY 1986

Q: What developments have occurred in the last decade in OB?

A: Probably the most positive development for those of us who teach OB has been a livelier popular interest in the subject. Corporation presidents, business school deans, and public officials have recently been quoted in magazines, newspapers, and business periodicals to the effect that more emphasis should be accorded OB in business education and management development. (The Porter-McKibbin contribution that follows documents this trend in convincing detail.) And it is my impression that undergraduate and MBA students these days are also more receptive to behavioral concepts.

Q: How do you account for this development?

A: I attribute it in part to the suddenly increased awareness people have of Japanese management. In the late 1970s and early 1980s, numerous writers drew attention to the success of Japanese management in global markets, especially the auto industry. Meanwhile our own economy was not performing so well, as productivity lagged and unsold inventories of cars and steel mounted. People wanted to know what the Japanese "secret" was, and scholars responded with an outpouring of books and articles on Japanese management. Most of these publications expounded at length on the effectiveness with which Japanese managers developed team spirit, worker commitment, and constructive participation by all ranks of employees. Of course, perceptive readers learned that numerous other differences exist between their system and ours, that no one could guarantee that their system could be exported to our culture, and that the Japanese had some problems of their own. But out of all this discussion came the idea that American management had much to learn in the areas of worker motivation and group performance.

Q: Can you think of any other reasons for increased popular interest in OB?

A: Well, somewhat related to the interest in Japanese management was the emergence in the early 1980s of what Frank Freeman (1985) called the "management book as best-seller." The most noteworthy example of this was *In Search of Excellence* (Peters and Waterman, 1982). The authors of this book, which sold millions of copies, searched for the common characteristics of large American companies that had consistently competed very well, the Japanese onslaught notwithstanding. Peters and Waterman found the answers not in elaborate financial controls, complex formal structures, or technological advantages, but rather in the type of environment that fosters employee dedication to the customer, pride in product quality, and a pervasive sense of proprietorship in nurturing new ideas and small experiments. Furthermore, the authors were able to relate these findings to a fairly sophisticated discussion of concepts and theories from OB and related fields of study. Other top-selling management books, such as *Theory Z* (Ouchi, 1981), *Megatrends* (Naisbitt, 1982), and *The One Minute Manager* (Blanchard and Johnson, 1982) also contributed to an increased popular interest in OB.

Q: How has the field of OB responded to this popular interest?

A: Ironically, the effect has not been to unify the discipline but, apparently, to intensify some of the differences between various camps and perspectives within OB. Cummings (1981), in a fairly accurate prophecy of how OB would develop in the 1980s, noted the differences between "conservatives" and "radicals" within OB. Conservatives push for more and more rigor in our measurement tools, research designs, and statistical analysis. Radicals, on the other hand, are afraid that OB will become sterile and lacking in relevance if it exalts scientific rigor above substance. Conservatives argue that worthwhile contributions to the management of organizations can come only from sound research practices that offer reliable and valid findings; radicals contend that slavish imitation of the physical sciences leads to a widening gap between what is researched in OB and what managers need to know and can usefully apply.

Q: Are you saying that OB has to make a choice between what is rigorous but not relevant and what is relevant but not valid?

A: Actually, I think we are not locked into quite such a painful dilemma; neither, apparently, does Lawler (see Reading 4 in this section), who continues to hold hope for valid and useful research in OB. One promising role for loose, even downright unscientific, methods is that of sparking bold new theoretical advances. The last 10 years or so have not seen much of that in OB; the advances in research methods have been put to good use in assessing the theories and models that were already around but did little to provide fresh, reinvigorating perspectives.

Q: Are you expressing dissatisfaction with existing theories in OB?

A: No. Current OB frameworks have made and will continue to make their contributions. Just as early OB research had a contribution that was more negative than positive, in that it worked mainly to question and refute conventional wisdom, so has recent OB research been more impressive in its ability to find the weak spots in the theories first put forth to replace conventional wisdom. We cannot afford to throw out what we have; neither can we in good conscience junk what we know to be proper methods of research. Instead, we may have to be more patient with theories that do not readily yield to rigorous quantitative research. And, undoubtedly, if we in OB wish to influence what happens in the work environment, we need to devote as much ingenuity and care to the selection of *what* we study as we do in regard to *how* we study it.

REFERENCES

Blanchard, K., and S. Johnson. *The one minute manager.* New York: Morrow, 1982.

Cummings, L. L. "Organizational behavior in the 1980s." *Decision Sciences* (1981) *12*, 365–77.

Cummings, L. L. "Toward organizational behavior." *Academy of Management Review* (1977).

Freeman, F. H. "Books that mean business: The management best sellers." *Academy of Management Review* (1985) *10*, 345–50.

Gordon, R. A., and J. E. Howell. *Higher education for business.* New York: Columbia University Press, 1959.

Naisbitt, J. *Megatrends: Ten new directions transforming our lives.* New York: Warner, 1982.

Ouchi, W. G. *Theory Z: How American business can meet the Japanese challenge.* Reading, Mass.: Addison-Wesley Publishing, 1981.

Peters, T. J., and R. H. Waterman. *In search of excellence: Lessons from America's best-run companies.* New York: Harper & Row, 1982.

Porter, L. W. Presidential address, Academy of Management meeting, Seattle, 1974.

Reitz, H. J. *Behavior in organizations.* Homewood, Ill.: Richard D. Irwin, 1977, p. 535.

Roethlisberger, F. J., and W. J. Dickson. *Management and the worker.* New York: John Wiley & Sons, Science Editions, 1964.

Stoner, J. A. F. *A comparision of individual and group decisions including risk.* Unpublished master's thesis, School of Industrial Management, Massachusetts Institute of Technology, 1961.

Current Criticisms of Business School Curricula*

Lyman W. Porter

Lawrence E. McKibbin

The curriculum of business schools that has evolved over the past two decades or so has recently come in for sharp criticism from a number of sources, both in the academic community and in the world of business. Space does not permit an exhaustive listing and discussion of these critiques, but we will attempt to characterize them in general and to group them into what seem to be five or six major categories.

NATURE OF CURRENT CRITICISMS

Collectively, the current criticisms of business school curricula at both the undergraduate and master's degree levels represent a wide array, something of a "laundry list" as it were. That is, particular critics focus on particular deficiencies of commission or omission in the curriculum; but there is not always a high degree of agreement from one observer to another. What may seem like a vital weakness to one critic is sometimes given only minor consideration or is even omitted by another. This is not to say that there is no consensus at all across often perceptive commentators, because that would clearly be incorrect, but only that the criticisms as a group are not concentrated in just one or two areas but instead constitute a fairly diverse and broad list.

The total set of criticisms includes concerns about both what subject matter is overemphasized in today's business schools as well as, especially, what is underemphasized. Thus, an examination of a large sample of critical

* From "Curriculum," chapter 3 of L. W. Porter and L. E. McKibbin, *Management education and development: Drift or thrust into the 21st century?* (New York: McGraw-Hill, 1988), 64–74, 82–87.

articles and comments would seem to point to more concern with what is left out of the curriculum or not given sufficient attention as compared with what is given too much emphasis. However, some of the critics who point to various "sins" of omission do not then go on to give much consideration to how adding topics and subjects will affect the total length of the curriculum. The critical issue of how to fit an ever-expanding list of seemingly important subject matter areas into a curriculum program of finite length seldom gets addressed head on. A few suggestions (as noted below) have been made in this regard, but generally, the task of finding what to cut from the curriculum often seems to be left to business school deans and faculty—the very individuals usually held responsible by the critics for creating the problems in the first place.

MAJOR TYPES OF CRITICISMS

General Criticisms

There appear to be two general types of criticisms of business school curricula:

1. *Insufficient emphasis on generating "vision" in students.* This criticism typically takes the form of stating that current business school courses focus more on problem solving than on problem finding, more on analyzing solutions than on creating novel approaches, and more on locating safe or acceptable courses of action than on taking prudent or moderate risks. Obviously, considered most broadly, this criticism goes beyond a concern only with curriculum matters to include, also, problems with instructional methods, faculty and student attitudes, and the like. Nevertheless, the curriculum, in terms of the types of courses offered, is viewed as one of the chief culprits responsible for this state of affairs.

2. *Insufficient emphasis on integration across functional areas.* The Foundation reports strongly came out in favor of a "capstone" type of course in business policy/strategy that would be designed to show how knowledge from the various functional areas could be combined in addressing real-world business problems. The need for such an integrative approach (but not the necessity of confining it to a single course) was subsequently put into the AACSB Standards as one of the five required CBK (common body of knowledge) areas. The issue, from the perspective of some critics, is, does the typical business school curriculum—particularly at the undergraduate level—provide sufficient attention to both the need to and the means to use specialized functional knowledge in an integrated approach to the increasingly complex, fast-changing, and multidimensional problems of contemporary business?

Criticisms Addressed to Specific Topic Areas

1. *Too much emphasis on quantitative analytical techniques.* If there is one area that many critics seem to agree receives *too much* attention and emphasis in the modern business school, it is quantitatively based analytical techniques. The focus of such criticism is that, while it may be useful for students to learn many of these sophisticated techniques, the amount of time spent on them is too much relative to what could be spent on other, more useful areas, and also that too much attention to these techniques reinforces undesirable tendencies in students to believe that all business problems are amenable to quantitative solutions. Frequently, this supposed curriculum imbalance is linked by critics to the previously mentioned issue of students' lack of vision.

2. *Insufficient attention to managing people.* This is not a new concern. In fact, the point that some critics make is exactly this: Business schools, for all their changes in the last 25 years, have not made much progress in developing students' leadership and interpersonal skills. The curriculum, coupled with other elements in the total degree program, is seen as a major avenue for doing so if business schools and their faculty were inclined to use it in this way. The problem, say at least some critics, is that they (the faculty) by and large are not oriented in this direction and hence tend to ignore this problem or at best give it only passing attention in the curriculum.

3. *Insufficient attention to communication skills.* Here again, this is a long-standing criticism of business schools and was mentioned as a common complaint by respondents in the Gordon and Howell and Pierson studies. This type of criticism usually contains the observation that many business executives and managers complain that the students they hire out of business schools are not good communicators, either orally or in writing. If this is accepted as fact, then the presumption is usually made that the business school curriculum did not provide sufficient opportunities for students to develop their skills in this area.

4. *Insufficient attention to the external (legal, social, political) environment.* This criticism voices the concern that business schools have been overly concentrated on the internal operations and management of business—the traditional functional areas such as accounting, finance, production, etc.—and have generally tended (except in the area of marketing) to neglect the necessity for coping effectively with the external environment. It is mismanaged relationships with various aspects of the social, political, and legal environment, say the critics, that have caused some of the most serious problems for American business firms in the last decade. Business schools, so the reasoning goes, have contributed to these problems by not modifying their curric-

ula to keep up with important developments in the external context in which modern-day business organizations must operate.

5. *Insufficient attention to the international dimension of business.* As is glaringly obvious to any observer (especially American observers) of today's business world, the international aspects of business have grown increasingly crucial in recent years. The need to pay attention to the international as well as domestic aspects of business was recognized officially by AACSB in 1974 when the first paragraph of its Curriculum Standard was modified by adding the phrase "domestic and worldwide" to the statement about the purpose of the curriculum. This element of the Curriculum Standard was further emphasized by the addition of an "interpretation" in 1980 that stated that "every student should be exposed to the international dimension through one or more elements of the curriculum." Thus, in recent years (and before that in certain business schools), the international component of the curriculum has received emphasis both from the organization of business schools (i.e., AACSB) and from individual schools. The issue, for some of the critics, again, is: is there enough emphasis being put on the international area? Does actual curriculum practice strongly (not weakly) support the stated intention of the above-cited Standard interpretation?

6. *Insufficient attention to entrepreneurism.* This criticism, briefly stated, is that business schools traditionally have been far too much oriented toward preparing students for working within large, already established organizations rather than also encouraging and teaching students how organizations can be started and how small organizations operate.

7. *Insufficient attention to ethics.* Unethical behavior in all walks of life has, unfortunately, always been with us. However, in the eyes of some critics, examples of such inappropriate conduct in business have been on the rise in recent years, and business schools are given some of the blame for this. The charge is that in the typical business curriculum ethics is seldom given direct, explicit attention in either separate courses or as designated parts of other courses. The net result, say critics, is that business schools, while certainly not solely to blame for any increase in unethical business behavior, have not sensitized their students sufficiently to the ethical components of business problems and issues.

THE UNDERGRADUATE (BBA) CURRICULUM

In this section we review the findings from our interviews and questionnaire surveys in both the university and corporate communities regarding a number of facets of the undergraduate degree (BBA) curriculum: the general education part of the degree program, breadth/specialization within the business portion of the curriculum, quantitative/behavioral emphases, the need for change in the required (CBK) core curriculum, specific content areas, emphases on skills and personal characteristics, emphases on preparation for coping with change, and the future of the undergraduate business degree. In each case, differences across groups of respondents will be highlighted as well as the general trends of their viewpoints.

General Education (Liberal Arts) Components of the BBA Degree Program

Deans and faculty were asked whether they believed that the non-business (liberal arts) component of the undergraduate degree program in their respective schools ought to be increased, decreased, or remain about the same. The results showed that while the majority favored the current situation, almost a third (29 and 32 percent, respectively) of the deans and faculty members in the survey think that this component should be *increased* and only about 10 percent (6 and 13 percent, respectively) think that it should be decreased. These percentages, however, varied significantly (statistically) by type of school: The percentage of deans in Category I schools who believe that this component ought to be increased (56 percent) is almost double that of Category II school deans (31 percent) and more than double that of Category III deans (23 percent). The faculty responses showed a similar pattern by type of school.

Breadth/Specialization within the Business Curriculum

The issue of whether there should be more or less breadth in the undergraduate business curriculum was investigated with four of the university-based groups of respondents in the survey: deans, faculty members, graduating BBA students, and BBA alumni. (Although the word *business* was not specifically included as a modifier of the term *curriculum* in the particular questionnaire items, the context of the surrounding questions clearly implied that they referred to the business school portion of the total undergraduate curriculum.) Views across these four groups differed. Some 27 percent of deans think that the curriculum needs to be "significantly broadened," while only 8 percent think that the curriculum should "emphasize specialization to a significantly greater extent." The comparable figures for faculty members, however, are 23 and 21 percent. Thus, for those deans who think that there should be a change from the status quo, considerably more want increased breadth rather than specialization; faculty members wanting change, on the other hand, are about equally split between these two alternatives. (There was some tendency for Category I deans and faculty to be more strongly in favor of increased breadth compared to those from the other two categories of schools, but the differences were not statistically significant.) Of course, it should be emphasized that a clear majority—about 60 to 65 percent—of both groups, deans and faculty, prefer the present balance of breadth versus specialization.

The majority of undergraduate students and alumni also feel that the present breadth/depth balance is about right. However, of those who do not in both groups, more believe that there is "too much breadth" (31 percent of undergraduates and 34 percent of alumni) compared to those who believe there is "too much depth in a particular specialized area" (7 and 13 percent, respectively). These findings would appear to show that student and alumni opinions on this matter differ rather decisively from those of deans and somewhat from those of their faculty mentors.

Quantitative and Behavioral Emphases in the Curriculum

As indicated earlier, one set of major issues that has emerged in recent years is the degree of emphasis that business schools currently give to two broad dimensions of the curriculum: quantitative methods and behaviorally oriented subject matter. Certain critics have been especially concerned about what they regard as an overemphasis on the former. The less frequently expressed concerns about the behavioral side, if raised at all, have been addressed more to the issue of whether there is enough such emphasis in the curriculum. Each of these themes—the quantitative and behavioral— appear in curricula in at least two ways: as separate courses in their own right and as important elements of other courses (e.g., quantitative aspects of finance and behavioral aspects of marketing).

Our survey questions on these issues did not pit the two emphases against each other in an either/or choice, since we do not regard them as in any way antithetical to each other. A particular business school curriculum can be relatively strong in both, in neither, or in one and not the other. Also, the current AACSB Curriculum Standard virtually ensures that accredited schools will give more than minimal attention to each. Both academic and corporate respondents were asked whether they believe that the current emphasis on quantitatively (behaviorally) oriented subject matter is "too much," "about right," or "too little." (The particular questions in our surveys on this matter did not ask separately about master's degree and undergraduate curricula. They used the phrasing ". . . the emphasis in the current curricula in your school"; ". . . in business schools" in the corporate survey forms.)

Quantitatively Oriented Subject Matter.   Table 1 presents the results for the question concerning quantitatively oriented subject matter for both sets of respondents (academic and corporate). As can be seen, deans and the two sets of alumni generally regard the current emphasis as about right, with the remainder splitting fairly evenly between too much and too little. The

TABLE 1 Views Concerning the Amount of Quantitative Emphasis in the Business School Curriculum

	Deans	Faculty	BBA Alumni	MBA Alumni	CEOs	SCEs	VPHRs
Too much	16%	14%	14%	14%	35%	33%	42%
About right	70	59	68	73	57	57	54
Too little	15	27	17	13	8	9	4

Note: All columns total 100%, with rounding.

majority of faculty agree that the current amount of emphasis on quantitative material is about right, but about twice as many of the remainder think the emphasis is too little instead of too much. (It is also worth noting, however, that the views of both deans and faculty members differ significantly by category of school: Thirty percent of all Category I deans and 25 percent of Category I faculty think the emphasis is too much, while only 10 percent of Category III deans and faculty hold that same view. The percentages of Category II deans and faculty are intermediate at 19 and 12 percent, respectively.)

The views of corporate respondents on this issue are markedly different from those of the faculty and most of the deans (especially deans from Category II and III schools) and business school alumni. Just over half of chief executive officers (CEOs), senior corporate executives (SCEs), and vice presidents for human resources (VPHRs) in our sample (57, 57, and 54 percent, respectively) believe that the current level of quantitative emphasis in the curriculum is about right, but of the remainder, about 80 percent (i.e., 35 percent of the total sample) believe that such emphasis is too much. As will be seen next, these figures are decisively reversed when the question concerns the amount of *behavioral* emphasis in present-day business schools.

Behaviorally Oriented Subject Matter. The distribution of responses regarding the degree of emphasis on behaviorally oriented subject matter in current business school curricula is presented in Table 2. As can be seen, again the majority of deans and faculty believe that the current curricula in their schools give this type of subject matter about the right degree of emphasis. Those who have any qualms about this tend slightly more (faculty) or somewhat more (deans) to say that the current emphasis should be increased. On the other hand, as Table 2 clearly demonstrates, all three sets of high-level corporate respondents do *not* believe that the amount of current emphasis is correct and by sizable margins indicate that this area receives too little rather than too much attention. The contrast between the

TABLE 2   Views Concerning the Amount of Behavioral Emphasis in the Business
School Curriculum

	Deans	Faculty	BBA Alumni	MBA Alumni	CEOs	SCEs	VPHRs
Too much	11%	17%	6%	8%	9%	4%	7%
About right	68	60	48	62	24	30	21
Too little	21	23	46	30	67	66	72

Note: All columns total 100%, with rounding.

percentages of CEOs and SCEs (67 and 66 percent, respectively) who
believe that this area is given too little emphasis and the percentages of these
two groups (9 and 4 percent) who think that it gets too much emphasis
represents one of the most dramatic trends in the findings obtained in this
entire study. Even the similar contrast between the two percentages for
undergraduate alumni (46 and 6 percent) and MBA alumni (30 and 8 percent) of business school programs is quite pronounced.

Perceived Need for Change in the Required (Business) Curriculum

The question of whether deans and faculty see a need for a change in
their school's required undergraduate business curriculum was addressed by
two parallel survey items as well as by interview queries. The survey items
asked about whether new topic areas "need to be introduced into the
required curriculum" and whether "major topic areas need to be deleted or
greatly deemphasized." Based on both the survey findings and our interview
results, we would conclude that there was *not* a strong mandate for major
systemic changes in the basic core curriculum on the part of either deans or
faculty, although there was some sentiment in favor of specific changes.
About half the deans and faculty (46 and 50 percent, respectively) did answer
"yes" to the survey question about whether new topic areas should be
introduced into the required curriculum, but the other half preferred the
status quo. (There were no significant differences in these percentages by
category of school, either for deans or faculty members.) Members of both
groups made varied suggestions about which particular areas they thought
should receive more emphasis (see next section), and some deans and a few
faculty members in interviews expressed concern about the need for more
integration in the curriculum across functional areas. When the question
turned to whether or not (any) particular topic areas should be dropped from
the required core, about 7 of 10 individuals in both groups said "no" (with
this percentage being significantly greater for Category III deans).

Specific Content Areas of the Curriculum

For those deans and faculty members who believe that some changes are needed in the required undergraduate curriculum, survey and interview questions explored which specific topics or areas should be emphasized *more* and which should be emphasized *less*. (The survey questions presented some 14 listed options of topic areas, plus the opportunity for checking "no area" or to write in the names of areas not listed.) Deans and faculty showed strong agreement about which particular areas they think should receive increased emphasis: The top four for both groups are business communications (first for both groups), entrepreneurship (second for deans and fourth for faculty), international business/management (third for both), and management information systems (fourth for deans and second for faculty). (Our interview findings, incidentally, strongly reinforced the survey findings regarding these four topic areas.) BBA alumni, on the other hand, showed no consensus on which areas they think should receive more emphasis in the curriculum. Their survey responses were widely dispersed across the dozen or more listed alternatives. However, they did show more consensus in response to a question that asked them to indicate the areas that had been of most use in their careers to date. The three areas ranked highest were (1) accounting, (2) general management, and (3) marketing.

The survey question regarding which areas should receive less attention in the required undergraduate curriculum showed the strongest plurality (50 percent of the deans and 48 percent of the faculty) by far for "no topic should be emphasized less." Of those deans who thought at least one or more topics should be deemphasized, the highest percentages went to quantitative analysis (15 percent), general management (11 percent), and economics (10 percent). The areas receiving the largest faculty votes were general management (17 percent), organizational behavior (11 percent), and quantitative analysis, economics, and accounting (all tied at 10 percent).

Emphases on Skills and Personal Characteristics (SAPCs)

An issue that received special attention in our study, in part, at least, because of a recent extended project by AACSB that focused heavily on this general domain, was the extent to which the curriculum should emphasize the development of various skills and personal characteristics (SAPCs). Both deans and faculty were asked how much each of nine particular SAPCs were currently emphasized in the curriculum and how much each should be emphasized. The results are presented in Tables 3 (for deans) and 4 (for faculty). The first of these tables shows that deans perceive wide gaps between the current situation in the curricula of their own schools and what they think should be the situation. As can be seen, analytical skills and planning/organizing are the only SAPCs where there is even a semblance of

TABLE 3   Deans' Views of the Emphasis That Is Currently Given and Should Be
Given to the Development of Various Skills and Personal Characteristics
(SAPCs) in BBA Programs in Their Own Schools (percent checking
"emphasized very much")

	Current	Should Be
Analytical	50%	76%
Computer	32	65
Decision making	33	71
Initiative	14	53
Leadership/interpersonal skills	18	68
Oral communication	16	75
Planning/organizing	20	47
Risk taking	3	30
Written communication	24	84

TABLE 4   Faculty Views of the Emphasis That Is Currently Given and Should Be
Given to the Development of Various Skills and Personal Characteristics
(SAPCs) in BBA Programs in Their Own Schools (percent checking
"emphasized very much")

	Current	Should Be
Analytical	28%	78%
Computer	18	52
Decision making	20	68
Initiative	7	48
Leadership/interpersonal skills	11	52
Oral communication	8	71
Planning/organizing	12	42
Risk taking	3	27
Written communication	12	81

comparable percentages (and these are not closer than 25 percent) checking
that the skill/characteristic both should be emphasized very much and is in
fact being emphasized to this degree in the curriculum. All the other seven
SAPCs showed considerable discrepancies between perceptions of current
reality and beliefs about what ought to be taking place. Interestingly, for two
of the SAPCs (analytical skills and computer skills) a statistically significant
higher percentage of strong current emphasis was reported by deans of
higher category schools, and in two other SAPC areas (initiative and oral
communication) a significantly higher percentage of Category III deans

reported that the areas receive strong emphasis. For the remaining SAPCs, there were no significant differences by categories of schools. Overall, then, neither the reported amount of attention currently being given to these nine skills and personal characteristics nor the amount that deans think should be given to them seemed to vary systematically by type of school. Put another way, the large gap perceived by deans between what is and what "should be" the amount of emphasis given to the development of SAPCs is relatively consistent across schools with quite different types of missions, programs, and circumstances.

Faculty views about how much emphasis is and should be given to these same SAPCs are shown in Table 4. As with the deans, the differences in percentages checking that a particular SAPC is currently emphasized very much and checking that it should be emphasized to this extent in the curriculum are quite large. Also, again, differences across categories of schools are not consistent for perceptions of the current situation, although there is a tendency for Category I faculty to have somewhat smaller percentages checking that the various SAPCs should be emphasized strongly in the curricula in their own schools. (While the percentages checking "should be emphasized very much" are statistically significant across categories of schools for most of the SAPCs because of the large number—about 2,000— of faculty respondents involved, the practical differences tend to be mostly moderate or small; for example, for initiative, the relevant figures for the three categories of schools are 36, 50, and 51 percent, and for oral communication, they are 66, 71, and 76 percent.)

One other group of respondents in our sample that provided their views on the extent to which the typical BBA program is emphasizing the development of these skills and personal characteristics was comprised of undergraduate business students themselves. Specifically, they were asked "to what degree" each of the SAPCs was "currently emphasized in your school's . . . program." Table 5 shows the percentages of BBA undergraduates checking "currently emphasized very much" (out of three alternatives that also included "very little" and "somewhat"). Somewhat surprisingly, perhaps, these percentages are higher than are those of deans (Table 3) or faculty (Table 4) for seven of the nine SAPCs. Only on analytical skills and computer skills were the BBA students' percentages about equal to or lower than those of the deans. Apparently, undergraduate students are not as critical as deans and, especially, faculty concerning the amount of emphasis placed on these skills and personal attributes in the contemporary business school curriculum. Of course, as will become evident in the following chapter, skeptics may argue that BBA students do not have a very realistic baseline—because of a general lack of work experience—for gauging whether the emphasis they perceive represents in fact a lot or a little. Nevertheless, the divergence of their views from those of their mentors is noticeable.

TABLE 5   BBA Students' Views of the Emphasis That Is Currently Given to the Development of Various Skills and Personal Characteristics (SAPCs) in Their Own Schools (percent checking "emphasized very much")

Analytical	51%
Computer	18
Decision making	55
Initiative	28
Leadership/interpersonal skills	35
Oral communication	38
Planning/organizing	46
Risk taking	11
Written communication	44

TABLE 6   Views of VPHRs and MSBs Regarding the Emphasis That Should Be Given to the Development of Various Skills and Personal Characteristics (SAPCs) in BBA Programs (percent checking "emphasized very much")

	VPHRs	*MSBs*
Analytical	73%	59%
Computer	38	47
Decision making	61	65
Initiative	67	71
Leadership/interpersonal skills	78	76
Oral communication	76	76
Planning/organizing	56	59
Risk taking	29	18
Written communication	76	71

Corporate views on the extent to which SAPCs *should* be emphasized in business school undergraduate programs were obtained only from human resource executives (VPHRs) and the small sample of managers of small businesses (MSBs). (SAPC items were not included in the survey forms for other sets of corporate respondents only because of the paramount necessity to keep the survey instruments as short as possible.) The percentages checking "very much" for both groups are shown in Table 6, where it can be seen that there is strong agreement between these two samples. Except for computer skills and risk taking, high percentages of both the VPHRs and small business executives endorsed the idea that the undergraduate business program should strongly emphasize the development of these skills and characteristics.

Emphases on Preparation for Coping with Change

Three groups of respondents, deans and faculty members on the university side and VPHRs from the corporate side, were asked to rate, on a 10-point scale, how well business/management schools prepare graduates to cope with change. (*Note:* This question was not specific either to undergraduate or to MBA programs.) The results showed that deans were definitely more positive than either faculty or human resource executives on this issue. The former gave a mean rating of 7.3, while the mean ratings of both the latter two groups were below the scale midpoint (5.5) at 5.1. It would appear that important constituent groups in both the academic and corporate sectors are not convinced about the effectiveness of business school programs in this seemingly important aspect of preparation for a management career.

*   *   *   *   *

Curriculum Content Issues

There are a number of particular curriculum issues that deserve discussion, most of them dealing with curriculum content and most of them revolving around the various criticisms that have been leveled by observers in both the corporate and academic communities. These were summarized and outlined previously, and the commentary that follows will be organized around that set of general and specific criticisms. We will provide our appraisals of them in light of the data collected for this project and reported in the earlier results sections of this chapter.

Vision.   In our view, this criticism—that there is an insufficient emphasis on generating vision in graduates of business school programs—has as much or more to do with the way various courses are conducted and taught as it does with the content of the curriculum. While curriculum content is not irrelevant, it is only one factor affecting how much problem-finding/ creative-solution-generating vision students emerge with when they complete a BBA or MBA program. In any event, we were not able to obtain very much reliable data on this important issue in relation to the curriculum and its content. Our impression, subjective as it is, is that there is some validity to this concern and that it is not often enough discussed in relation to curriculum objectives in business school settings. One thing is certain: We did not find it spontaneously raised as an issue in those parts of our campus interviews which pertained to the curriculum. . . .

Integration across Functional Areas.   Unfortunately, for today's business school graduates, let alone those who will be graduating in coming years, the modern world of business is not very accommodating; it does not present problems and decisions neatly packaged and exclusively within a marketing, finance, accounting, or some other single functional box. The implication is clear: The manager of the future must understand more than a narrow discipline or functional area. Yet, our interview data indicated that many schools, perhaps most, are relying on the single "capstone" business policy course to cope with this all too obvious fact of business life by having it carry the major integrative load across functional areas. This raises several subissues: Is this enough, is this the only way to provide integration, and should such integration occur only at the very end of a (BBA and MBA) degree program? Our own answer to each of these questions would be "no," but we do not have quick solutions to suggest. Again, as with the vision issue, we believe that our interview soundings strongly support the assertion that cross-functional integration is not receiving the attention it deserves from business schools. To put this somewhat differently, we encountered a large degree of casual acceptance of the single business policy course placed at the finale of the program as sufficient, and this attitude seemed to be coupled with the view that any alternative approaches were either not feasible or not worth the bother of trying to implement them. Should and can more effective integration be provided within the limits of the total time available in BBA and MBA programs? This is a question worth attempting to answer.

The issue of integration across functional areas also is not unrelated to the issue of the balance between breadth and specialization in the curriculum. Most (not all) deans, faculty, and business school alumni are satisfied with the current balance. However, our findings, especially at the MBA level, suggest that those who want any change at all prefer the balance tipped toward more specialization. If this were to become a stronger trend of opinion—at the present time it is difficult to predict whether it will be, but there are signs that it may be somewhat likely—one can ask how this would affect the need for increased integration across functional specializations. On the surface, at least, it would appear that the two ideas are in conflict. Our own preference is for more of the one (integration) than there is now and no more of the other (specialization) than there is now, because we think that this is the type of curriculum that will best prepare students for the uncertain future. Our *prediction*, however, is that both issues—how much integration to build into the curriculum and how much specialization to allow students to take within the curriculum—will be continuing major battlegrounds and never definitively settled within business schools in the foreseeable future. . . .

Quantitative Emphasis in the Curriculum.   Has the Foundation reports-inspired revolution that urged the insertion of much toughened and more rigorous quantitative requirements into the curriculum gone too far? As documented in the survey findings presented earlier, most academic and corporate respondents do not think so. There was a preponderance of opinion among all parties—deans, faculty members, BBA and MBA alumni, and senior corporate executives—that the present amount of emphasis on quantitative-oriented subject matter throughout the business school curriculum is about right. However, there were enough corporate executives who disagreed to warrant further examination of the issue. Most (by a factor of about 4:1) of those in the corporate sector who think the amount of present emphasis is not appropriate want it decreased. Our interview findings, however, seemed to corroborate the majority opinion among corporate survey respondents, namely, that the present degree of emphasis is approximately correct. While we almost never found anyone in the corporate world in our interviews who wanted the quantitative aspects of the curriculum increased, most, when pressed on this issue, also thought it should not be decreased. In other words, whatever else they thought about the curriculum and what might be emphasized more, there was virtually no call for less quantitative emphasis. To the contrary, we found a general level of admiration and appreciation of the level of quantitative skills that business school graduates possessed as part of their overall strong mastery of analytical skills. . . . In short, based on our total set of data, both survey and interviews, we find little or no basis for recommending any major change—up or down—in how much quantitative analysis should be emphasized in the curriculum. This is, however, decidedly not the case with the next curriculum area.

Behavioral Emphasis in the Curriculum.   The Foundation reports were also insistent in recommending that business schools give far more attention to the behavioral science aspects of their curriculum than they ever had before. This, as noted earlier, was accomplished beginning in the 1960s by most schools requiring students to take courses in areas such as organizational behavior and organizational theory and by the inclusion of a relevant element in the CBK part of the revised AACSB Curriculum Standard adopted in 1969. As reported previously in this chapter, our survey findings point to a relatively high degree of concern in the corporate sector that behaviorally oriented subject matter is *not* being emphasized enough in the curriculum. This view represented two thirds of all senior corporate respondents and significant percentages of BBA and MBA alumni and, furthermore, was strongly reinforced in our corporate interviews (which included members of middle and lower management as well as upper-level executives).[1] Deans and faculty, on the other hand, on both the surveys and in interviews were mostly of the opinion that the present degree of emphasis was about right. Clearly, there are substantial differences of opinion between academia and the corporate world on this score (as will be further elaborated in the following chapter) which need to be explored and analyzed in greater depth than has been true to date.

All our data relating to SAPCs presented in this and the next chapter highlight a perceived gap in the corporate world between (1) the extent to which behavioral skills are seen as being emphasized currently in the curriculum and demonstrated by business school graduates and (2) the extent to which the curriculum and other elements of the total program *should* emphasize such skills. Either the expectations of the business community in this area are too high and unrealistic, or business schools are not placing enough attention on this area. We suspect there is truth to both these assertions; but as with most important educational matters, there are no simple, quick solutions that go much beyond the level of rhetoric or gimmicks. . . .

Communication.   This has been an area of criticism aimed at business schools for many years. Our survey findings strongly indicate that most deans and faculty think that communication is still not sufficiently emphasized in the curriculum. . . .

The External Environment.   The external legal/social/political environment, as an area of the curriculum, did not elicit especially strong concern in our interviews of either academic or corporate officials, although there was a moderate level of sentiment in both sets of respondents in the surveys in favor of placing more emphasis on this area. We believe that, because of the increasingly complex environment in which business operates, business schools must give more consideration to whether they have the appropriate balance between an internal and an external focus. (This is also related to the previously discussed issue of the need for integration across functional areas.) We were somewhat surprised that this did not seem to be as salient an issue as we thought it should be. Part of the reason may be that it is more of a subtle and diffuse issue than some other curriculum issues, but that does not mean it is any less important. In our opinion, failure

---

[1] Since one of the codirectors of this project is himself from the behavioral area, we were acutely conscious in interviews about the possibility of leading the interviewee into making statements about this area that he or she did not intend or would not have made otherwise. Although we would have a hard time proving that we did not do this, we made every effort to try to guard against this possibility. In point of fact, both of us were struck by how often respondents offered spontaneous comments about the behavioral area even when we were discussing other topics.

to address it in a more head-on fashion now will likely generate more pressure to do so in the not too distant future. However, that pressure does not appear to have developed very much to date.

International. This is an area of the curriculum where we found a considerable amount of, at worst, lip service, and, at best, serious concern on the part of deans and faculty (but, we should point out, *not* on the part of most corporate-sector respondents). It was, as we reported earlier in the chapter, one of the four specific areas most often mentioned in both interviews and on the surveys as needing more emphasis in the curriculum. The problem, as most acknowledged, is how to implement this—whether to do it through adding more specific courses on international business, international finance, international marketing, and the like or by putting more emphasis on international issues in courses already in the curriculum. This whole area has been the object of much discussion within the business school community, and we probably cannot shed much additional light on the curriculum aspects of the matter except to say this: Although there seems to be an increasing awareness among business school deans and faculty that more ought to be done to emphasize this area, this awareness or sensitivity so far does not appear to us to have been translated into a great deal of action. More is being done now than 10 years ago, and this seems clearly demonstrable by an examination of curricula and in interviews with knowledgeable observers, but much more needs to be done.

Entrepreneurism. This area, as did the international area, received a relatively high degree of endorsement as a topic needing more attention in the curriculum. Clearly, some schools have in recent years added specific programs in this area and have given it considerable attention already. Others have not addressed this subject to any great extent at all. Since we seem to be in an era of the downsizing of large corporations and a corresponding increase in emphasis on "intrapreneuring" within them and on starting new firms and related entrepreneurial activities, this would appear to be an area that will be given more attention in the typical business school curriculum in the future than it has in the past. More than likely, however, there will be a wide variance in how much attention it will receive from school to school. To allocate it more emphasis in the curriculum will, as with other such expanding areas, require consideration of what will be given less attention. Futhermore, as with the international area, schools will have to decide whether to spread the topic throughout the curriculum or give it separate, discrete treatment.

Ethics. This is an area somewhat like the international area insofar as the curriculum is concerned, because the issue is whether to treat this as a specific topic (like marketing, finance, etc.) or as an important consideration in any course. Because our own view is that ethics should receive attention throughout the total business school program (including the entire curriculum), we did not list it as a specific item in our survey question dealing with topic areas needing more (or less) emphasis. It was, however, viewed as such by some (not a large number of) deans and faculty respondents. It was listed more frequently than any other area as an open-ended response to "other areas needing more emphasis." Our interviews uncovered some general concern about how to achieve a stronger emphasis on ethics in the curriculum, but also an accompanying uncertainty about how best to do this. No reasonable person, in our opinion, could argue that business schools should ignore ethical aspects of business behavior and business decisions or should emphasize this less than currently, but how best to implement an increased emphasis is the challenge. Even more difficult is the question of how to make a concerted focus on ethics in the business curriculum have an impact on graduates' subsequent behavior, to go beyond merely making faculty and students "feel better" because they have discharged their obligations by giving consideration in their courses to moral standards and principles of conduct.

Future of the BBA and MBA Degrees

Although there have been a relatively large number of criticisms directed against business schools in general and aspects of the curriculum in particular in recent years, our survey and interview findings among corporate respondents did not point to any great disenchantment with either the BBA or MBA degrees as preparation for careers in the world of business and management. As we noted in reporting our findings earlier in the chapter, senior corporate executives are at least as positive as (and in the case of the MBA degree, slightly more positive than) deans and faculty members about the future of these degrees—in terms of their importance to the business world. This will no doubt disappoint some critics who are inclined to paint a more gloomy picture about the current condition of business education, but it appears to testify to the positive impacts of the generally strengthened curricula that business schools individually and collectively have put into place during the past two decades. However, to return to a point made earlier: Too much self-satisfaction with this current level of acceptance of business school degrees can—as has perhaps been the case with much of U.S. industry—lead to unpleasant consequences if "eternal vigilance" is not given to the challenge of making continuing changes and improvements. As we have attempted to point out elsewhere in this chapter, there appear to be certain curriculum issues and areas that need more monitoring and concerted attention than they are now receiving. . . .

The Development of Knowledge
in Organizational Behavior
and Human Performance*

W. E. Scott, Jr.

Within the past few years, researchers have been able to develop useful knowledge about the behavior of individuals in organizations to replace the human relations saws of an earlier time. It is comprised of a body of theory as well as empirical generalizations which possess sufficient reliability and generality to be worthy of critical study. While our knowledge of organizational behavior is incomplete, it is clear that we are no longer required to rely upon anecdotal evidence and speculation as our primary source of information. Rather, it is empirical knowledge based upon systematic study and experimentation which needs to be emphasized. That being the case, it may prove helpful to consider the nature and function of knowledge and the methods by which it is produced.

A number of practical benefits are gained from a study and development of knowledge of organizational behavior and human performance. First, systematic studies of this subject are being conducted at a rapidly increasing rate. Administrators and educators will soon become outdated unless they equip themselves to read, understand, and evaluate the reports of these studies. Second, interest in sponsoring research of all kinds of organizations has been increasing. Specialized research units in many large organizations have presented a number of unresolved, difficult organizational problems. Perhaps, an improved understanding of scientific goals and methods would lead to more satisfactory solutions to these problems. Finally, more interaction between researchers and practitioners is needed. The researcher who seeks to establish relationships between organizational variables and behavior under controlled settings also seeks to apply his findings to an expanding set of conditions. Administrators sensitive to the goals and methods of the behavioral scientist can provide feedback to researchers about the generality

* Abridged from *Decision Sciences* (1975) 6, no. 1, 142–65.

of these relationships in complex organizations. This feedback often can raise additional questions which are significant from both a practical and scientific viewpoint. While the popular misconceptions that research is simply a way of solving problems or that the so-called scientific method is applicable to all or most of the complex problems facing the administrator must be rejected, a better understanding of empirical knowledge and its development would enhance the administrator's ability to use and to contribute to the systematic study or organizational behavior.

CHARACTERISTICS OF KNOWLEDGE

An individual may acquire knowledge about objects and events in his environment through direct encounter or firsthand experience. Nearly all of us have observed the behavior of others in complex organizations. However, knowledge based solely on direct encounters with natural phenomena is limited. Some insist that these encounters cannot make the individual knowledgeable at all unless he is able to verbally describe or represent that experience to himself and to others. This is a complex psychological issue not to be pursued here, but raising the issue does provide an opportunity to emphasize two points. First, most of our scientific knowledge is received from significant others by means of conversation, lectures, newspapers, books, and other such media. Second, this process is so ubiquitous that we often forget that verbal symbols, concepts, or terms are different from that to which they refer. The term *organizational behavior*, for example, is a verbal stimulus distinguishable from the phenomena which it signifies. Unfortunately, some concepts from the everyday vernacular signify different meanings to different individuals. To avoid confusion and misunderstanding, the researcher is typically forced to develop a specialized vocabulary which employs precise and invariant meanings, but which lacks appeal until the user gains familiarity with it.

This paper focuses on that knowledge which enables an individual to describe objects and events specifically and to state relationships between objects and events. Several advantages accrue to those who possess this knowledge. First, the knowledgeable individual gains a viewpoint by which to examine and assess behavioral events, especially those in which the significance is not obvious. He is also sensitive to antecedent or causal variables which might not otherwise be perceived either because they are embedded in a complex setting or because they are not a part of the current stimulus field. Second, this kind of knowledge provides the individual with a set of expectancies regarding behavioral outcomes, given the occurrence of or variations in certain environmental and individual difference variables. Therefore, when one has possession of empirical propositions reflecting relationships between antecedent events and behavioral outcomes, that person understands and is able to predict organizational behavior, thereby avoiding uncertainty, surprises, and frustration. Finally, if an individual knows propositions stating relationships between behavior and environmental events which can be changed or varied, then he is able to influence behavior.

BELIEFS AND OPERATING ASSUMPTIONS
OF THE RESEARCHER

The researcher believes in reality. Unlike the solipsist,[1] the scientist assumes that the objects and events which he observes do exist apart from himself.

The researcher also believes that organizational behavior, like other natural phenomena, shows certain consistencies which can be anticipated and explained. He believes that organizational behavior is determined, but he does not assume that there is a single determinant or cause. Rather, he believes that there are multiple determinants which act alone and with other determinants to produce behavior. Yet, he posits *finite* causality. He does not believe that *all* events in nature can influence all other events.

The researcher is an empiricist. He believes reliable knowledge of organizational behavior can best be developed by means of firsthand, controlled observations. He would disagree with the philosophical doctrine which advocates that knowledge may be acquired or developed *solely* through reasoning processes and intuition. For the modern empiricist, reasoning is required for purposes of organizing knowledge and is indispensable to the process of inductive generalization, but the emphasis is upon direct observation and experimentation as the source of knowledge.

The researcher has learned to be skeptical, for he has learned that man, as an observer, is subject to error. Consequently, he does not readily agree with a propositional statement simply because it was uttered by a person of recognized status or because it appears intuitively to be true. He does not reject such statements as necessarily false since an empirical test may ultimately lead him to conclude otherwise. He merely asks (1) whether or not they are true, and (2) how could one go about demonstrating their truth or falsity (6, p. 9).

THE RESEARCHER AND HIS LANGUAGE

As stated above, the researcher believes that organizational behavior is a reality apart from himself and that reliable knowledge can be developed about it by means of direct encounter. However, he is aware of the so-

---

[1] One who subscribes to the philosophical view that nothing exists or is "real" except the self. [Editor's note.]

ciolinguistic nature of all scientific endeavor. While linguistic symbols can be distinguished from the objects and events they are meant to represent, few observations of any consequence can be communicated to others without the use of symbols. Direct experience is private and of little social value until it is communicated to others.

The researcher, sensitive to the problems of conceptualization and communication, sets about to construct an objective language which will accurately convey his observations. This language will never be totally independent of the vernacular. Nor should it be. Many terms in the common, everyday language are reasonably precise and unambiguous, in which case they are taken over by the researcher without modification. However, there are also terms in the common language which do not always refer to something out there, or, if they do, the "something" is so vague and amorphous that confusion and misunderstanding are rampant. In these cases the researcher is confronted with the necessity of either reconstructing the common language or coining new terms. He will often do both by defining his concepts operationally.

To define a concept operationally means to specify precisely the procedures or operations which are associated with its use. In making a concept synonymous with a set of concrete, reproducible operations, the researcher is able to clarify the phenomenon under investigation and to communicate his observations in an unambiguous manner. For example, to test the proposition that democratic leadership results in (is functionally related to, produces, causes) higher productivity than autocratic leadership, the researcher will have to develop a set of operations defining the terms *democratic leadership, autocratic leadership,* and *productivity.* How will the researcher do this?

First of all, the terms are taken from the common language and may require some logical explications[2] before operational definitions can be developed. Upon reflection, the researcher might conclude that the terms *autocratic* and *democratic* leadership refer to specific behavioral patterns exhibited by leaders in formal organizations. But what is the nature of these patterns and how do they differ? Further analysis might lead to the conclusion that autocratic leadership can be characterized by an individual who (1) unilaterally decides what tasks are to be performed by each subordinate, (2) directs subordinates to perform those tasks without deviation, and (3) makes punishment or threats of punishment contingent on not performing those tasks as directed. The researcher may also decide that democratic leadership can be characterized by an individual who (1) consults with and takes into account the suggestions and preferences of his subordinates in

---

[2] Mandler and Kessen (3, pp. 98–104) describe logical explication as a process by which terms in the common language are more precisely defined or redefined.

deciding what tasks are to be performed, (2) does not specifically direct his subordinates to perform the tasks, or, having elicited task performance, permits deviations in the manner in which they are performed, and (3) makes rewards or promises of rewards contingent upon successful task accomplishment.

If the researcher has not become discouraged at this point, he may attempt to develop a set of operations which he hopes will be somewhat reflective of the explicated concepts. For example, he might develop a behavioral questionnaire which requires organizational leaders to describe how they typically behave with regard to task decisions, methods of eliciting task performance, deviations from task performance, and administration of rewards and punishment. Several analyses and refinements of the questionnaire might enable him to set up a continuum and to classify high scorers on the questionnaire as democratic leaders and low scorers as autocratic leaders. This public and repeatable set of operations is synonymous with and defines the two concepts.[3] After analyzing and defining productivity in the same manner, the researcher is able to investigate the relationship between leadership syles and productivity to be operationally defined in a similar way.

Many concepts in the common, everyday language are rendered less vague and ambiguous by the use of the foregoing procedure. New concepts are also introduced by making them equivalent to a set of operations which others can reproduce. However, the operational analysis of the concepts must not be considered a panacea. Spence (9) points out that the formulation of operational definitions is merely one faltering step in building a body of empirical knowledge. If the operationally defined concept is not subsequently found to be related to other concepts, then, it has no scientific significance and should be discarded. The number of digits on the left foot multiplied by the number of freckles on the face divided by two is a perfectly acceptable set of operations defining a concept we shall label Welles, but it is highly improbable this would be of any interest to the behavioral scientist.

Another consideration of the researcher is the complexity or "size" of a concept. He may choose to work with concepts referring to a complex of empirical events treated as a syndrome, or he may prefer to work with molecular, unidimensional concepts. Yet, more important than the size or complexity of concepts is the continued persistence of the researcher in conducting research which utilizes a variety of conceptual approaches and

---

[3] Perhaps the defining operations should be referred to as "ZIZ" and "ZAZ." Democratic and autocratic leadership are common terms which have already acquired a variety of meanings. It is doubtful that the reader will readily dismiss those ingrained meanings in favor of the defining operations described here. It is for this reason that it is often a good idea to coin new terms to represent operational definitions.

which establishes systematic relationships between a syndrome of environmental events and behavioral variables. If these relationships are not found to hold up in every instance, the researcher should break up the syndrome in search of the one or a more limited subset of characteristics which may be responsible for the relationship.

RESEARCH VARIABLES IN ORGANIZATIONAL BEHAVIOR AND HUMAN PERFORMANCE

Most concepts contained in empirical propositions refer to things which vary or can be varied in amount, degree, or kind. The researcher seeks to establish relationships between *independent* and *dependent variables.*

A dependent variable is anything which is changed or modified as a consequence of a change or a modification in something else. The dependent variable is nearly always some observable aspect of behavior or the consequences of behavior. For example, a researcher may be interested in learning why individuals become members of an organization or *do not* become members, why they remain as members for a long period of time or leave the organization. He may be interested in learning why some individuals or groups are more creative than others, or why some individuals appear to be more satisfied with their jobs than others. He may be interested in learning why some individuals cooperate with each other, while others conflict; why some individuals often contribute far more than is prescribed, while others perform their jobs in the prescribed manner but rarely go beyond that; and, why some individuals engage in behavior that is judged to be organizationally disruptive.

Obviously, there are a number of dependent variables which are interesting and significant not only because they are functionally related to organizational success but also because they remain as scientific curiosities, not yet fully explained or predictable. The lives of researchers and managers would be considerably less complicated if they could say that dependent variables were all related and that those factors which lead to high productivity also produce satisfaction, cooperation, and creative contributions. Unfortunately, such is not the case. At least, the relationship between satisfaction and productivity is obscure. Moreover, it is possible that, under certain circumstances, such behavior variables as individual productivity and interpersonal cooperation are inversely related. The researcher will frequently direct his attention to these complexities to investigate the relationships between behavioral variables or to search for more basic dependent variables.

The independent variable is anything which when changed or modified induces a change or a modification in some aspect of organizational behavior. When a person seeks explanations for turnover, variations in productivity, cooperation, satisfaction, and so on, he is really inquiring about those factors (independent variables) which are functionally related to or cause variations in behavior.

Independent variables in organizational behavior may be viewed as falling into one of two broadly defined classes. There are *environmental* variables, such as task design, magnitude or quality of rewards and punishments and the manner in which they are scheduled, the presence and behavior of significant others, temperature, noise, illumination, group size, and variations in organizational structure. The second class of independent variables is known as *subject* or *individual-difference* variables. These are relatively enduring behavioral characteristics of the individual and include intelligence, aptitudes, propensity to take risks, characteristic energy level, motor skills, and motives.

OBSERVATIONAL STRATEGIES

Empirical propositions depend upon firsthand observation for their development, but past experience has made it quite clear that all humans are subject to a variety of observational errors. Consequently, researchers have developed strategies for observing phenomena so that such errors are reduced to a minimum.

Observational strategies may be viewed as falling on a continuum between naturalistic observation and experimentation. As a researcher progresses along the continuum, he exerts increasingly greater control over the phenomena which he is observing.

Naturalistic Observation

Utilizing this strategy, the researcher observes the behavior of individuals as it occurs in a natural setting—namely, in formal organizations. He does not control and manipulate independent variables in order to note their effects on behavior. Rather, he attends to behavior as it ordinarily occurs, watching for apparent covariation between environmental events and behavioral episodes. The researcher may attempt to record these events which seem to be relevant, and he emerges from his study with a verbal description of his observations.

Because naturalistic observation has a number of limitations, a researcher should maintain a cautious attitude toward knowledge based solely upon this strategy. Significant behavioral events may not occur frequently, and, since the researcher exerts no control over those events, he may not be prepared to observe them when they do occur. More important, the observer makes few attempts to reduce the sources of human error that are attributable to his own act of perceiving. He would not worry much about this source of error if he could depend on the fact that his sense organs furnish the brain with exact replicas of the real world. However, such is not the case. Illusions are common. Unaided perceptions of physical objects rarely correspond exactly with those resulting from a direct encounter with the object by means of various kinds of measurement techniques.

When the events observed are behavioral, and thus more variable and ambiguous than physical objects, the emotions, expectancies, and past experiences of the observer may become as prominent in determining what is perceived as the behavioral events themselves. Similarly, our perceptions of cause and effect relationships are often inaccurate, especially when the cause and the effect do not always occur together or when the effect does not immediately follow the cause in time (2). Temporal contiguity between events *is* a compelling factor in drawing cause and effect conclusions (11). However, there are a number of events occurring concomitantly with behavior when we observe it in a natural setting. Perhaps the observer could logically dismiss the fly unobtrusively crawling along the sill in another building as a determiner of the behavior of an operative employee on a production line. Yet, which of the several events that are present *will be* selectively attended to? The answer to the question is that the observer will usually arrive on the scene with certain preconceived notions or tentative ideas about what are the relevant and irrelevant factors, and he will direct his attention to those factors which he believes to be relevant. If he observes a relationship between those events he chooses to concentrate upon, does he do so because there is a relationship which could be confirmed by others, or is the observed relationship attributable to the fact that he expected to find one? Suppose, for example, that the observer suspected that the group productivity is higher when the supervisor is physically present than when he is physically absent. Let us further assume (1) that group productivity did not invariably change with the presence or absence of the supervisor, (2) that the supervisor was more often present than absent, (3) that there is *no* inherent relationship between the supervisor's presence and group productivity, and (4) that the observer could accurately discriminate between high and low group productivity and between supervisory presence and nonpresence.[4]

Figure 1 shows a record of a series of observations that might have been made under these circumstances.

---

[4] Point four is not a very valid assumption. Changes in group productivity are not easily discernible, and, in the absence of an objective means of assessing significant variations in group output, the observer may "see" changes in the direction of his expectations. Naturalistic observers attempt to sharpen the definitions of the concepts they use in reporting their observations, but they rarely define their dependent and independent variables in terms of a reproducible set of measurement operations. An attempt to develop operational definitions of the terms *supervisory presense* and *group productivity* could prove to be humorous, if not enlightening for the reader.

FIGURE 1　　A Record of Observations Made in Organization X Group Productivity

		High	Low	
Supervisor	Present	10 (a)	5 (b)	15
	Absent	4 (c)	2 (d)	6
		14	7	21

The naturalistic observer in this situation might perceive only a limited set of instances which would tend to verify his expectation. For example, Figure 1 shows that group productivity was high during 10 of the 15 times the supervisor was present and that group productivity was low only 5 of the 15 times he was present. Alternatively, the supervisor was present during 10 of the 14 times that group productivity was observed to be high and was absent only 4 times during which group productivity was observed to be high. In the event the observer was astute enough to look for *all* confirming and discomfirming cases during the observational period, he would note that there was a total of 12 confirming cases (cells *a* and *d*) and only 9 discomfirming ones (cells *b* and *c*). Again, however, the observer might erroneously conclude that the supervisor's presence enhances group productivity since his expectation is verified more than it is not.

Only the observer who has an abstract appreciation of correlation (2, pp. 14–15) would come to the correct conclusion. He would do so by comparing the probability of high group productivity given the supervisor's presence (10/15 or 0.67) with the probability of high group productivity given his absence (4/6 or 0.67). Since the probabilities are identical, he would conclude that in this situation variations in group productivity appear to be independent of the presence or absence of the supervisor.

Let us assume that all the conditions described above are the same except that the observations were made in a different organization in where there *is* a relationship between supervisory presence and group productivity. An example of a series of observations made under these circumstances is shown in Figure 2.

This set of observations would reinforce the observer's expectations in the same manner as those made in Organization X. In this case, however, the probability of high group productivity when the supervisor is present is 0.67, while the probability of high group productivity when he is not present is only 0.33.

Although the conclusion that the supervisor's presence caused higher group productivity seems to be supported by the observations made in

FIGURE 2   A Record of Observations Made in Organization Y Group Productivity

		High		Low	
Present		10		5	15
		(a)		*(b)*	
Supervisor					
Absent		2		4	6
		(c)		*(d)*	
		12		9	21

Organization Y, we must consider the possibility that *other* events were operating in this situation to cause the changes in group productivity. While repeated observations would rule out some of them on the basis that they were never present or always present (and nonvarying) when changes in group productivity occurred, perhaps not all of them could be so readily dismissed. Several events may occur together so that it is difficult to say which one is the cause of higher productivity. For example, suppose that the supervisor tended to appear only when production pressure was intense. Then, increased productivity could have resulted because of the varying backlog of visible materials, partially completed assemblies, work orders, etc., rather than the supervisor's presence. The above is an example of *confounding,* a situation in which any variable other than the dependent variable changes along with the independent variable of primary concern. Confounding is always a danger no matter what the observational strategy, but it is most likely to occur when the observer exercises little control over the events he observes.

One often hears that knowledge stemming from naturalistic observation is more relevant to real-life behavior, and hence more valuable to the administrator. But the possibility of confounding places limitations on this knowledge. Different supervisors may not show up only during those times when production pressure increases. Therefore, the results of this study would be of limited generality and quite erroneous if it could be established by more rigorous methods that production pressure rather than supervisory presence was the cause of changes in group productivity.

Despite the limitations of naturalistic observation, a researcher should remain open to knowledge that comes from observers utilizing this strategy. A significant portion of what we know or what we think we know about organizational behavior has been generated by astute individuals who have spent their lives observing behavior as it naturally occurs in formal organizations. Oppenheimer, the physicist, (5) has made a plea not to treat too harshly those who tell a story without having established the completeness or the generality of that story. That plea should not go unheard. In many cases, an observation that has been made in the field has been verified in the laboratory where the observer can exercise the necessary controls over the independent variable and other potentially confounding variables.

Systematic Assessment

In all probability, the individuals in the production departments of organizations X and Y were not responding as one. Some were undoubtedly producing more than others during the presence *and* absence of the supervisors. Furthermore, both the direction and amount of change may have varied from one individual to another as the supervisors were alternately present and absent. Behavioral scientists have grown to expect significant differences in behavior when several individuals are placed in a common environmental setting, and have approached the problem of explaining those differences by postulating that they are attributable to certain enduring characteristics of the individual. This postulate has led to the development of a wide variety of individual-difference measures, the most common of which are standardized tests. Thus, the term *systematic assessment* has come to be applied to that observational strategy in which events existing in varying degrees in nature are operationally defined, and the relationships between events, so defined, are investigated. The observer does not purposefully manipulate the independent variable as in the experimental strategy, but he typically exercises greater control than the naturalistic observer. An example will serve to illustrate the kinds of control that are exercised when the systematic assessment strategy is employed.

Noting that some employees are consistently more productive than others in the same situation, the observer might hypothesize that the differences are due to variations in aptitude.

The first step in testing the hypothesis is to select or construct operational definitions of the aptitudes which are important in determining productivity. In this case, let us assume that a researcher selects rather than constructs a measure of Closure Flexibility.[5] Then, he assembles all the employees in a room in which noise levels, illumination, and other features of the environment are held constant, and administers the test according to the instructions specified by the test manual. Since the observer has controlled environmental stimulation, he assumes that individual scores are representative of the ability which is measured rather than a function of environmental events. If the observer finds reliable differences in scores, he is ready for the next important step. He must now devise an operational

---

[5] The Closure Flexibility Test is a standardized measure of the ability to hold a configuration in mind despite distraction. This aptitude has been found to be related to certain personality traits and has also been found to differentiate among individuals in various occupational groups.

definition of productivity so that he might investigate the relationship between the attribute presumably measured by his test and productivity back at the work site. He may decide to define productivity as the number of acceptable units completed by each individual during a specified period of time. He might also choose to introduce some *additional controls* such as having the supervisor always present and holding the quality and quantity of materials constant for each individual during the observing period.

Having observed and recorded the output of each individual, the researcher is now ready to assess the relationship between scores on the Closure Flexibility Test and productivity. A relationship that might have been obtained is depicted by the scatter diagram in Figure 3.

Utilizing the Pearson product-moment correlation coefficient, one of several techniques for assessing relationships between variables, the observer finds a statistically significant correlation of .49. He concludes, therefore, that there is a functional relationship between scores achieved on the Closure Flexibility Test and the level of individual productivity in this situation.

There is a curious mixture of inference and empiricism in this and in all studies utilizing the systematic assessment strategy. It is empirical in the sense that the variables are operationally defined. Since concepts refer to observable events, the observations are capable of being repeated by another individual. Also, the proposition asserting the relationship between Closure Flexibility Test scores and productivity is relatively clear and unambiguous. However, it seems absurd to remain at a strictly empirical level and

FIGURE 3   The Relationship between Scores on the Closure Flexibility Test and Individual Productivity

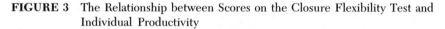

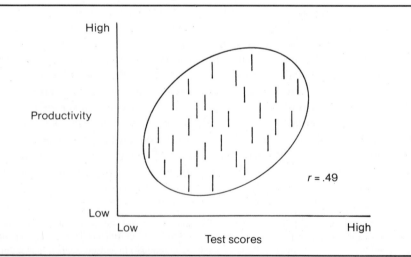

state that the individual's responses in the test-taking situation caused his subsequent behavior on the production line. Rather, a researcher *infers* some sort of characteristic from the score, and it is that characteristic which is believed to determine the behavioral outcome. In addition to finding that the inferred characteristic is somewhat obscure, a researcher has difficulty specifying and defending the direction of causality. In the above case, it was implicitly assumed that the characteristic measured by the test determined the level of productivity, but variations in task behavior *preceding* the test administration may have determined the score achieved on the test.

The observer utilizing the systematic assessment strategy takes advantage of differences which already exist in nature rather than deliberately creating those differences. As a consequence, the observer does not provide very convincing evidence for causal relationships, whatever the direction. While knowing that individuals differ with regard to closure flexibility, researchers do not know in what other respects the subjects might differ. Perhaps, those who score high on this test also have higher needs for achievement, and the latter characteristic, rather than a high degree of closure flexibility, results in high levels of productivity. The now-familiar problem of confounding is evident here as in every study in which systematic assessment is used.

Nevertheless, functional relationships established by means of systematic assessment can be very useful. Our Closure Flexibility Test, for example, could be used to select from an applicant population those who are most likely to be high producers. However, the possibility of confounding makes it difficult to understand why the relationship exists and places limitations on the generality of the relationship. If the tasks were different and were performed by a different group of individuals in another organization, the same relationship might not hold.

The use of the systematic assessment strategy is not restricted to psychological tests and individual differences. One can also establish operational definitions of organizational characteristics, and then investigate the relationships between differences in those characteristics and behavioral variables. Indik (1), for example, has reviewed a number of studies in which organizational size was found to be related to member satisfaction, absenteeism, and individual output. Size was operationally defined as the number of individuals who are members of the organization, and size was systematically assessed rather than deliberately manipulated as in the experimental strategy. Interestingly enough, Indik offered a set of theoretical postulates to account for the observed relationships between organizational size and behavior (and to account for contradictory findings as well). He speculated that as size increases, communications problems among members tend to increase, task complexity tends to decrease, the need for supervision and coordination increases, and the use of impersonal controls tend to increase. What Indik has done is to ask the reader to consider a variety of *confounding* variables which may be the real causes of dissatisfaction, absenteeism, and productivity. In other words, he seems to be saying that communications problems, task complexity, etc., may often, though not necessarily, vary concomitantly with size to cause the behavior. When they do not vary with size, the relationships will not be observed.

Experimentation

The observer who utilizes the experimental strategy deliberately produces the event he wishes to observe. He systematically varies one event (the independent variable), while controlling the influence of others (potentially confounding variables). Then he notes the effects of the varied event on behavior (the dependent variable). The experimental strategy is by no means a foolproof procedure for producing reliable and generalizable knowledge, but it does provide more convincing evidence for cause-and-effect relationships than other approaches.

Weick (12) prefers to discuss the experimental strategy without reference to a distinction between settings. However, there is some merit in distinguishing between *field experiments* and *laboratory experiments*. The observer may utilize the experimental strategy to study behavior in an ongoing organization, or he may choose to bring behavior into the laboratory where more control can be exercised. Seashore (7) has described the problems which an observer may encounter in conducting a field experiment. They arise primarily because the experiment is incidental to the pursuit of organizational goals and because some loss of control over the appropriate experimental variables is inevitable.

Assume that the observer has decided to conduct a field experiment in order to test the hypothesis that the supervisor's physical presence has a significant effect on group productivity. His first problem is to find an organization which will allow him to conduct the experiment. Having gained entry into an organization, the observer is now faced with a series of experimental design decisions. The experimental strategy, whether employed in the field or in the laboratory, requires at least two different values of the independent variable. Therefore, the observer's first decision is whether to have one group perform the task while the supervisor is present and the other group perform while he is absent (the between-subjects design), or to have *all* employees perform the task under *both* conditions (the within-subjects design). Should the former course of action be chosen, the observer must take care in assigning the subjects to each group so that both groups are approximately equal with respect to confounding variables. He may accomplish this goal by randomly assigning individuals to each group, and then tossing a coin to decide which group will perform with the supervisor present.

FIGURE 4   The Relationship between Supervisory Presence and Group
Productivity

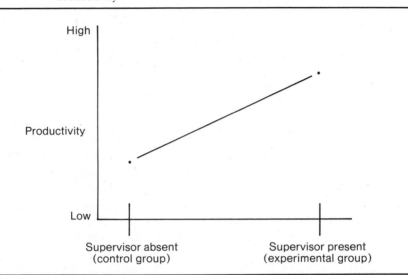

A series of observations in which both groups performed the task under
identical conditions except the presence and absence of the supervisor may
have yielded the data shown in Figure 4.

As the data indicate, the presence of the supervisor seems to affect
group productivity. This conclusion assumes that other variables were controlled either by holding them constant or by randomization. If, for example,
those who score high on the Closure Flexibility Test are typically the most
productive, the random assignment of individuals to the experimental and
control groups tends to insure that the average test scores of both groups will
be approximately equal before the observations are begun.

The various organizational constraints are likely to prevent the observer
from randomly assigning individuals to either the experimental or the control group. Furthermore, it would be nearly impossible to achieve a "pure"
condition of supervisory absence for any length of time in a formal organization. A consideration of these and other problems with the implementation
of a between-subjects design might have led the observer to adopt the
within-subjects design.

The observer is faced with a different kind of problem when he adopts
the within-subjects design. He must anticipate the possibility of a progressive error (11, p. 32), a change in behavior that may occur as a function of
performing the task over time. In this case, it would not be wise to have the
supervisor present during the first four hours of the day and absent during

the remaining hours because fatigue effects may confound the results. While there are a number of methods for controlling progressive error, probably the most appropriate one in this experiment would be randomization. The observer would have the supervisor appear at random times throughout the observing period.

The results of the within-subjects experiment may have been quite similar to those obtained from between-subjects design. However, in both cases, the conclusion that the supervisor's presence enhances group productivity may only hold true in this isolated situation. The observer is dealing with a specific supervisor and a specific work group, and neither is likely to be representative of supervisors and work groups in general. The patterns of interaction between the workers and the relationships between this supervisor and the work group have developed over a period of time. The nature of the interaction history peculiar to this group may be determined by the effects of the supervisor's presence. Moreover, production pressure, which may have affected group productivity and which could not be easily controlled by the observer, may have been significantly higher or lower when the supervisor was present than when he was absent.

The lack of control and the attendant probability of confounding may lead the observer to choose the laboratory as the site for conducting his observations. Here, he might be able to repeat his observations, using different supervisors and different work groups while holding interaction histories, production pressure, and other factors constant. Under these circumstances, the observer is most likely to be able to make a general causal statement about the effect of the supervisor's presence on productivity. However, he is also most likely to be criticized by the laymen on the grounds that the knowledge he has provided is too "theoretical" or has no relevance for the administrator. After all, work groups in organizations have an interaction history. They are not *ad hoc* groups who have never seen each other before, nor are they inexperienced at the task. Furthermore, supervisors come and go at will, and production pressures are variable rather than constant. What the critic really means in this case is that he is not likely to comprehend the influence of the supervisor's presence on behavior in a natural setting because there are other determining factors operating simultaneously there. The effect of the supervisor's physical presence observed in the laboratory may not be observed in the formal organization because that effect is swamped by the effects of other factors which could be controlled in the laboratory. But a researcher will never know whether a supervisor's presence has an effect on behavior until he observes it when the influences of other factors are controlled. If the effect *is* swamped by other variables in a natural setting, then they, too, need to be observed under controlled conditions.

As we have seen, the observer, suspecting that production pressure has an effect on behavior, could have controlled its influence either by holding it constant at some value or by allowing it to vary randomly. He could just as well have investigated its effects at the same time that he observed the effects of the supervisor's presence. This possibility brings us to a discussion of the *factorial* experiment in which the simultaneous effects of *two* or *more* independent variables are observed.

If production pressure could be defined in a manner that permitted the observer to systematically vary it from a normal value to a high value, the *main* effects of each of the two independent variables could then be examined. The primary influence of the supervisor's presence could be ascertained by contrasting average group productivity when he is present with average group productivity when he is absent, the average being obtained in both cases by summing across both levels of production pressure. This result is shown in Figure 5.

The main effect of variations in production pressure could be examined in a similar fashion, as shown in Figure 6.

The most significant feature of the factorial experiment is that it allows the observer to investigate the *interaction* effects on the independent variables. An interaction effect is said to exist when the relationship between the dependent variable (productivity) and one independent variable (super-

FIGURE 5   The Main Effect of the Supervisor's Presence on Group Productivity

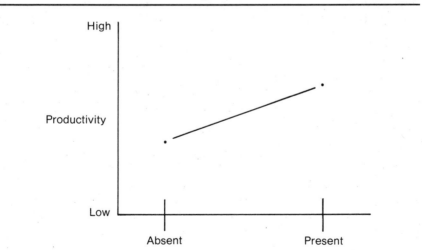

FIGURE 6 The Main Effect of Production Pressure on Group Productivity

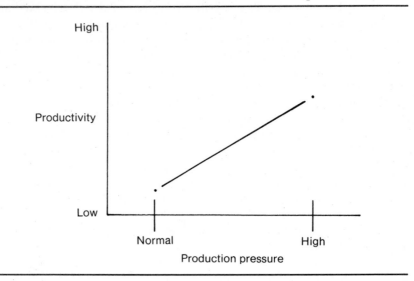

FIGURE 7 The Effects of Production Pressure and Supervisor's Presence on Group Productivity

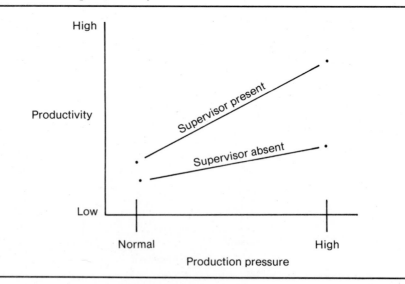

visor's presence) varies as a function of the value of another independent variable (production pressure). To clarify the notion of interaction effects, let us assume that the results of the observer's factorial experiment were as illustrated in Figure 7.

The data suggest[6] that the main effect of production pressure is significant since both lines slope upward. The main effect of the supervisor's presence also appears to be significant since group productivity is generally higher when he is present than when he is absent. However, there appears to be a significant interaction effect as well. That is, the effect of the supervisor's presence on group productivity varies with the value of production pressure. At normal levels of production pressure, the supervisor's presence does not seem to have a large effect on group productivity, but, when production pressure is high, his presence has a considerable effect.

One is now able to understand the negative attitude toward knowledge that is produced by the experimental strategy in which the influence of all variables except one is controlled. One observer might have unwittingly or deliberately observed the effects of the supervisor's presence only when production pressure was high, in which case he would have concluded that the physical presence of the supervisor has a very significant effect on group productivity. The response that this bit of knowledge is either irrelevant or theoretical is undoubtedly based upon the subjective feeling that the relationship would only hold under certain conditions which are not typically obtained in nature.

Further observations might support the critic's premise, but such support does not mean that the single factor experiment produced knowledge that is irrelevant or theoretical. That the supervisor's presence has an effect on productivity under certain specifiable circumstances represents a bit of knowledge which we did not possess before the experiment was conducted. Furthermore, researchers seek to extend the generality of their findings by repeating their observations under different conditions. A failure to observe the same relationship under different conditions inevitably stimulates speculation and additional studies until the contradictory findings are resolved. Finally, interaction effects are not always found. If the two productivity lines shown in Figure 7 were parallel or approached that condition, one would have to conclude that the effects of the supervisor's presence were similar whether production pressure was normal or high.

The experimental strategy is most frequently employed by those who seek to establish behavioral propositions which hold for all individuals.

---

[6] Needless to say, we cannot discern significant differences in productivity merely by inspection of the data. There are available a number of statistical tests for determining the significance of main and interaction effects.

Individual differences are deliberately masked or treated as experimental error when changes in behavior, if they occur as a consequence of a change in an environmental event, are shown as changes in group averages. The attempt to establish general behavioral laws is a perfectly legitimate and useful enterprise. However, researchers often observe the behavior of two individuals to be both quantitatively and qualitatively different at the same value of the independent variable. The attempt to explain individual differences in response to constant environmental events and to change in environmental events has led to the development of a factorial experiment in which at least one of the independent variables is an individual-difference variable systematically assessed (4).

As an example, let us assume that the observer administered the Closure Flexibility Test to his group of subjects and then observed the effects of the supervisor's presence on the productivity of those who scored high and those who scored low on the test. If the observer programmed the supervisor to appear in a randomized sequence, the influence of variations in production pressure would tend to be randomized, and progressive error would similarly be controlled. The results of this hypothetical experiment are shown in Figure 8.

The main effects of both independent variables appear to be significant, but there is also an interaction effect. In this case, the degree to which the supervisor's presence affects productivity depends upon the level of closure flexibility inherent in an individual.

FIGURE 8   The Effects of Closure Flexibility and the Supervisor's Presence on Productivity

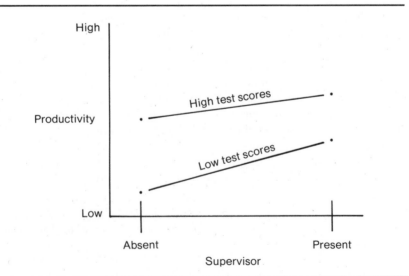

Since behavior is widely held to be a function of the *interaction* between the individual and his environment, the observational approach which combines systematic assessment and experimental manipulation is perhaps the most appropriate one yet devised.

REFERENCES

1. Indik, B. P. "Some effects of organizational size on member attitudes and behavior." *Human Relations* (1963) *16*, 369–84.
2. Jenkins, H. M., and W. C. Ward. "Judgment of contingency between responses and outcomes." *Psychological Monographs: General and Applied* (1965) *79*, 1–17.
3. Mandler, G., and W. Kessen, *The language of psychology.* New York: John Wiley & Sons, 1959.
4. McGuigan, F. J. *Experimental psychology: A methodological approach.* 2nd ed. Englewood Cliffs, N.J.: Prentice-Hall, 1968.
5. Oppenheimer, R. "Analogy in science." *American Psychologist* (1956) *11*, 127–35.
6. Scott, W., and M. Wertheimer, *Introduction to psychological research.* New York: John Wiley & Sons, 1962.
7. Seashore, S. E. "Field experiments with formal organizations." *Human Organization* (1964) *23*, 164–70.
8. Skinner, B. F. "Are theories of learning necessary?" *Psychological Review* (1950) *57*, 193–216.
9. Spence, K. W. "The nature of theory constructions in contemporary psychology." *Psychological Review* (1944) *51*, 47–68.
10. Turner, M. B. *Philosophy and the science of behavior.* New York: Appleton-Century-Crofts, 1967.
11. Underwood, B. J. *Experimental psychology.* 2nd ed. New York: Appleton-Century-Crofts, 1966.
12. Weick, K. E. "Laboratory experimentation with organizations." In *Handbook of organizations,* ed. J. G. March, Skokie, Ill.: Rand McNally, 1965.
13. Zajonc, R. B. "Social facilitation." *Science* (1965) *149*, 269–74.

Challenging Traditional Research Assumptions*

Edward E. Lawler III

Research on organizations has increased over its 50-year history. Starting in the 1950s, the volume has grown dramatically to the point where, today, we find ourselves overwhelmed with research on organizations. New journals are appearing regularly, books are being produced at an increasing rate, and Ph.D. programs are turning out researchers at a high rate.

As the research on organizational behavior has developed and increased in volume, a relatively well-codified set of principles about what constitutes "good" research has emerged. Indeed, today most people in the field can agree on what constitutes a well-designed research study and what represents a good application of the scientific method to research on organizational behavior. This agreement is clearly exemplified by the increasing use of quantitative methods in the field and by the greater sophistication of recent studies with respect to principles of experimental design. To many, the path toward further knowledge about organizational behavior is clear. It leads to more rigorous research with better designs, larger samples, and more sophisticated statistical analysis. But is this indeed the best route to lead us toward better understanding of organizations?

Before we can answer this question, we need to ask what constituencies are relevant for research on organizations. Unlike some fields of scientific research, research on organizations has a large, well-defined constituency of practitioners. Indeed, it is this feature of the field, along with the consideration of how data can best be gathered in organizations, that raises the question whether the "traditional" way of doing research is the way most likely to produce useful knowledge about organizations and their management.

This book assumes that research on organizations can serve not only the scientific research community but also those in the society who are generally

* From Edward E. Lawler III, Allan M. Mohrman, Jr., Susan A. Mohrman, Gerald E. Ledford, Jr., and Thomas G. Cummings and Associates, *Doing research that is useful for theory and practice*, pp. 1–17. Copyright © 1985 by Jossey-Bass, Inc., Publishers.

responsible for and interested in the effectiveness of organizations. In short, it assumes that the research agenda is one that should contribute to both theory and practice. This is an important point because it raises the standard; or perhaps a better way to phrase it is to say that it creates two standards that any research project must meet. The project must help practitioners understand organizations in a way that will improve practice, and it must contribute to a theoretically and scientifically useful body of knowledge about organizations.

USEFULNESS OF RESEARCH FOR THEORY AND PRACTICE

Traditionally, researchers of organizational behavior have not focused on the issue of usefulness. We have assumed that, if a research project is methodologically sound, it will contribute to scientific knowledge and ultimately to practice. Indeed, many researchers seem to have found comfort and justification for their basic position in Kurt Lewin's statement that nothing is so practical as a good theory. This comfort has often led to their doing studies that focus only on contributing to theory and justifying research that is far removed from practice.

Perhaps because it is not focused on the goal of usefulness, a considerable amount of the research done in organizational behavior has in fact not had an impact on practice. The belief that good scientific research will ultimately win out often turns out to be naive and misleading. For example, the best-known research on organization effectiveness is contained in the book *In Search of Excellence* (Peters and Waterman, 1983). From a methodological point of view, that book is a disaster (no control group, measures not specified, and so forth).

The suggestion here is that, if research is to jointly contribute to theory and practice, it must be designed to accomplish this objective. It cannot simply be taken as a matter of faith that adhering to certain scientific research principles will lead to jointly useful research. Indeed, it may be that adhering to principles that were designed to produce research that contributes to scientific knowledge will make it certain that this research will not contribute to practice.

At this point, I need to expand on my earlier statement about how data can best be gathered. Organizational behavior research has numerous characteristics that make it different from research in the physical and biological sciences. The study of organizations and people in them is a much more complex interactive process than the study of most physical and biological phenomena. People in organizations do not become subjects in the same sense that animals, neutrons, and chemical substances become subjects. They are an active part of the research process, and as such, they influence it very directly. Given this difference, it seems quite possible that what is a good research approach for contributing to theory and scientific knowledge in traditional fields of science may not be a good research approach in dealing with organizations.

Indeed, in the case of organizational behavior research there seems to be a particular danger that we will do research that is more a product of the methodology than of the phenomenon being studied. Taken to its extreme, this tendency could lead to a series of theories and findings that meet the test of traditional scientific validity but that are not useful to the practitioner and, indeed, may not be useful to the theorist either, because they do not describe actual organizational behavior. They may fail to be useful because they do not inform the practitioner or the theorist about the realities of the organizational environment. Instead, they frame the issues in such a way, and report on data so far removed from the realities of the complex, interactive, ever-changing world of organization, that they are not useful as a guide to either theory or practice.

It thus seems possible that a whole series of "scientifically acceptable" findings or theories could be developed that would have little or nothing to say about the realities of organizational behavior. How can this be avoided? The argument here is that it can best be avoided by doing research designed to influence both theory and practice.

Theory and practice are not competing mistresses. Indeed, research that is useless to either the theoretician or the practitioner is suspect. If it is useful to the practitioner but not the theoretician, then one must wonder whether it is a valid finding and whether it has addressed the correct issue. If it is useful to the theoretician but not to the practitioner, then one must wonder whether the research is capturing a critical issue. Indeed, it can be argued that we should always ask two questions about research: Is it useful for practice, and does it contribute to the body of scientific knowledge that is relevant to theory? If it fails either of these tests, then serious questions should be raised. It is a rare research study that can inform practice but not theory, or vice versa.

Research on organizations presents the researcher with a series of dilemmas. Hard choices need to be made and value judgments reached about the best way to design research. At this point I would like to raise some of the critical issues that need to be considered in designing research. I will consider how each of them is traditionally resolved and how each might be resolved if the desire is to be sure that the research produces scientifically and practically useful results.

DOES PRACTICE LAG BEHIND THEORY?

Traditional wisdom in most scientific disciplines says that practice lags behind theory and research, that improvements in practice follow, often by decades, breakthroughs in research and theory. In many areas of organizational behavior the same principle holds. In a number of research and theoretical breakthroughs that have led to changes in practice (e.g., the studies on job enrichment and on cafeteria fringe benefit plans), often the lag has been as long as 15 years between research findings and the changes in practice. But it does not necessarily follow that in all or even in most cases theory leads practice.

Virtually everyone is an observer and theorist with respect to organizations. Many people hold organizational positions that call for them to make organizational design decisions, policy decisions, and practice decisions. Quite a few of them are bright, perceptive people, capable of developing insights into practice without the help of theory and empirical research. So in some areas it is quite possible for practice to lead or at least precede theory. Innovative work designs, policies, and procedures can and do exist before there is a theoretical understanding of why they might work and empirical support for their effectiveness. Skill-based pay is an example, as are high-involvement new plants (see, for example, Lawler, 1978, 1981). Instances in which practice is ahead of theory have some important implications for the kind of research that is done. They suggest that, unless scholars and researchers are aware of practice, they may miss out on some important breakthroughs that are relevant to theory and research. Indeed, staying in touch with what is happening in the world of practice may be one of the best ways to develop new theory and to discover new research issues.

In short, what is being suggested is that advances in theory and practice are likely to come about not necessarily as a result of theory leading practice or practice leading theory. Either of these can happen and, therefore, research ought to focus not only on developing new theory and findings that will guide practice but also on studying practice that can guide theory and new research.

Researchers are prone to ask, "Why don't managers use what we know?" This is a good question, but so is its reverse, "Why don't researchers use what managers know?"

WHERE IS THE EXPERTISE?

In traditional scientific research the assumption is that expertise about the phenomenon being studied rests with the research scientist, not with the subject of the research. In most cases this is a safe assumption. But is it a safe assumption with respect to organizations and individual behavior in organizations? As already suggested, often managers and organization members are astute observers of the situation they are in, and their innovations in practice often precede theory. The clear implication is that any research targeted at improving both theory and practice needs to be guided by both practitioners and researchers. To ignore theory is to court rejection from the scientific community, and to ignore what managers already know and are doing runs the very definite risk of producing research that lags behind practice and, therefore, will not be useful to the practitioner.

The view that practitioners have knowledge about organizations has significant implications for research design. It suggests that in many cases members of an organization must be treated as coresearchers; that is, they must have a role in defining the types of research issues that are going to be looked at, and they must be informed of the scientific research issues involved. In short, the argument is that research that is to contribute to both theory and practice needs to be scrutinized by experts in both. Clearly the researcher ought to offer expertise about theory, past research, and methodology, but in many cases he or she has to rely on the members of the organization being studied to provide expertise about practice. For this to happen, the practitioner has to be involved in the study at more than a superficial level and, indeed, has to influence both the kind of topic studied and the methods used.

ROLE OF RESEARCH SUBJECTS

Traditional research design is very clear about defining the role of research subjects. It recommends what might be called an "experimental set" in which the subject, or respondent, is given a minimal amount of information about the study. The subject is told that the data will be used for research purposes only and that there is, therefore, no need to be concerned about how the data will affect his or her worklife. This research set clearly puts the subject in a dependent passive role with respect to the research study. It has some advantages, but it may not be the one that produces the best data for determining practice or developing research data that lead to valid theory.

The major problem with this approach is that it assumes people will conscientiously provide data simply because they are asked to and that these data will represent the best information that can be gathered about the subject being studied. An alternative view is that with this approach people might not care very much about giving valid data because doing so is not going to affect their lives and that they have other valid and important data that they could contribute to the study if they knew its focus. The latter would be particularly true if, as suggested earlier, people in organizations have expertise on organizations, just as researchers do. This point raises an interesting challenge for the researcher interested in doing theoretically and practically relevant research. It suggests that a researcher may want to rethink the relationship between the subject and the research so that it becomes a more balanced one in which the subject has knowledge of the key research issues. It also suggests, as discussed later, that better data are produced when the subjects know the study will affect practice in their organizations.

USEFULNESS OF COUNTERINTUITIVE FINDINGS

Social science researchers seem to love nothing better than a counterintuitive finding. Proving that "common sense" is wrong seems to produce a great deal of satisfaction and is highly rewarded in the research community. This is hardly surprising. Counterintuitive findings tend to justify the field because they show that social science theory and research can produce things that are otherwise nondiscoverable. There are numerous examples of counterintuitive findings in the organizational behavior literature, and they are often featured in the textbooks of the field. Indeed, they are used to justify study of organizational behavior because they point out clearly that there is something to be learned here that cannot be learned from the everyday experience of practitioners. And to a degree this characteristic has led us to value counterintuitive findings more highly than research findings that support common sense, elaborate on it, or put it in a more comprehensive package.

It is hard to argue against the importance of counterintuitive findings and the theories that support and explain them. They are an important part of scientific research, but it is also possible that our search for respect, esteem, and credibility has led us to overvalue them compared with less spectacular findings and theory. Often the theory or finding that simply confirms common sense, organizes it better, and allows it to be communicated more effectively is the most useful theory. All too often it seems that the counterintuitive theories on which we focus produce long sequences of research projects that explain relatively few of the phenomena that actually occur in the real world. They end up being artifacts of a particular set of conditions that produce the phenomena we studied. In short, they are catchy, but they do not explain many of the situations that occur in the day-to-day operation of organizations. In my own field of research, for example, the work on effects of overpayment and effects of pay on intrinsic motivation produced catchy findings but ones that in fact seem very limited in the situations where they occur (Adams, 1965; Deci, 1975).

What all this suggests is that, if we are to do research that is relevant to both theory and practice, we may have to value highly research that does not produce nonobvious findings but that produces confirmation of "common sense." This follows rather directly from the point that managers can be rather astute observers of common sense and, as such, they know something about organizations.

PROJECT SIZE

A great deal of the research in organizational behavior can be characterized as small-scale research. It is usually done on a small budget, involves a few researchers, and covers a short time period. There are a number of reasons for the frequency of such research, including the kind of funding available for organizational behavior research and the career considerations present in most universities. All too often this combination of factors leads to organizational behavior research dealing with issues that can be easily studied and works against investigation of major issues that can be studied only in large-scale research projects.

Reliance on small-scale studies may not have hindered the field so much from a theoretical perspective as it has from a practical one. Organizational behaviorists have been able to study a number of interesting theoretical issues without engaging in large-scale research undertakings. However, many practical questions concerning what works and does not work in influencing productivity, organizational effectiveness, and so on seem to demand large-scale, multivariable, complex research. For example, in order to know how such things as self-managing work teams, quality circles, Scanlon plans, and other new management practices work, when they work, and where they work, large-scale studies seem a necessity. Thus the traditional wisdom that says that a small, "doable" project is better than a large one may need to be changed if research that is relevant to both theory and practice is to be done. Researchers may need to think big, not small, in future research activities.

RESEARCHABLE QUESTIONS

Closely related to the issue of thinking big versus thinking small is the issue of the degree to which available methodology should drive the kind of research question that is addressed. I have often heard the distinction made between interesting questions and researchable questions. As the statement goes, in the field of organizational behavior there are interesting questions and there are researchable questions, and often the two are different.

Often a question is interesting because it is of practical importance. Consequently, to the degree that the field limits its research to researchable questions, it runs the danger of doing research that does not have practical importance. The implication of this point is clear. If we are to do research that is relevant to both theory and practice, we need to have a definition of "acceptable" or "good" methodology that is driven by the type of question being researched as well as by "traditional" scientific standards of what constitutes good research.

This may sound like a radical point of view, but it is not. It merely suggests that different approaches to data gathering, data analysis, and learning need to be used for different kinds of research problems. This follows rather directly from the view that not all problems can be solved with the same research strategy. The research question needs to drive the kind of data collected, and, because methods and questions interact in important ways, the kind of data needed to answer certain questions simply cannot be gathered with traditional research methods. Similarly, traditional research methods produce the best kind of data to answer certain kinds of questions.

DO PRACTITIONERS NEED FACTS OR FRAMES?

The field of organizational behavior is perhaps best at producing facts. The justification for this endeavor is that facts are ultimately a useful product because they allow theory testing, theory construction, and, of course, the improvement of practice.

It is quite possible, however, that the best way to improve practice is not by producing facts but by producing frames, or ways of organizing and thinking about the world. A good case can be made that the most important products of the field of organizational behavior are simple, elegant frames, not findings or hugely complex, ugly, inelegant frames.

The problem with saying we need frames is that it is difficult to identify where they come from and to determine the implication of their source for research strategy. However, drawing from some of my earlier points, at least one possibility is that frames come best from interaction between practitioners and researchers in which the researchers learn from the practitioners and vice versa. Frames, however, may come directly from the insights and research data of the researcher. The point here is not that there is one prescribed, clear-cut, best way to develop frames. It is merely that if part of the research agenda is to influence practice, frames may be the most important outcome of research.

BROAD-BRUSH VERSUS FINE-GRAINED RESEARCH

A number of the early important studies in organizational behavior were fine-grained research. They looked in depth at a particular interaction or small part of a work organization. The Western Electric studies (Roethlisberger and Dickson, 1939) were of this nature, as was much of the earlier work by William F. Whyte (e.g., Whyte, 1955). These studies included dialogue and intensive study of the behavior of small groups and individuals. This type of research has accounted for a smaller and smaller percentage of the total work in the field. Instead we have moved to more and more broad-brush studies that analyze organizations from a distance, either through questionnaires or through secondary data. Organizations are studied by researchers who never see them! The result is rather antiseptic descriptions of organizations and the development of theories from these. To a degree, broad-brush research is the enemy of research that influences practice. Broad-brush research often deals with only a few variables across a large number of people and as a result lacks, in the eyes of many practitioners, a truly comprehensive understanding of the workplace. It tends to lead to simple theories that ignore many of the factors the practitioner must take into account in managing the work organization.

It may be that the most useful research is that which takes a more fine-grained approach to data gathering, but there are problems with this kind of research as well. The challenge with fine-grained research is, of course, to extract from it some general conclusions, insights, and frames that contribute to theory. There is also the problem of gathering data in such a way that it is replicable and meets most people's standards for scientifically valid research.

CERTAINTY VERSUS USEFULNESS

Traditional science places great emphasis on establishing how certain we are of the validity of a particular relationship or finding. Indeed, most of the research in organizational behavior focuses on validating, extending, and establishing the conditions under which a certain finding holds. This focus reflects the high value placed on certainty in scientific research. But to a degree, certainty may be the enemy of usefulness.

The effort to establish certainty almost always leads to large numbers of studies being done on a single small topic and to more and more careful specification of the phenomenon. Once the phenomenon has been subjected to all the tests of certainty, it often ends up so complex that it is no longer useful to the practitioner. Establishing certainty presents a difficult challenge for the researcher who wishes to do research that is useful for both theory and practice. Somehow the researcher has to satisfy the scientific need to establish that the phenomenon is real and, at the same time, not lose sight of the usefulness issue. Often the conflict between these two demands leads the researcher who is concerned with usefulness and theory to stop doing research on a topic before others would say that the necessary level of certainty has been reached. In the researcher's eyes, however, certainty may have been established because of the kind of data that the researcher has gathered. A practice- and theory-oriented researcher, for example, may place more emphasis on observational data, reports by practitioners, and sense-making insights than would a researcher who is concerned with confidence levels, reliability estimates, and research design.

STUDY OF CHANGE

Assessing organizational change is difficult and often creates conditions that violate traditional views of what constitutes good scientific research. It typically requires a long-term involvement with an organization, an adaptive research design in which methods and questions change over time, and a close working relationship with the organization. All these conditions lead many to argue that it is hard to do "good" research on change. However, many of the most interesting practical questions concern change. Managers and practitioners constantly want to know what happens to Y if they do X, and they also want to know the best way to change organizations toward a particular kind of culture or strategy. Hence there is little doubt that if research is going to be practically useful, it needs to deal with the issue of organizational change.

Although there seems to be some reason for believing that doing good research and studying change are mutually exclusive, a good counterargument can be made. If, as stated earlier, good research is often fine-grained and large-scale, the study of change offers an excellent opportunity to do research that meets these conditions. Members of organizations are often very concerned about and interested in research on change, particularly if it can help inform and direct the change in constructive ways. Consequently, in the study of change there is often a natural alliance between the researcher who wants to do long-term, fine-grained research on an important organizational change issue and practitioners who want to understand the change and make it effective. Thus, the study of change may be a particularly good opportunity to do research that is useful both practically and theoretically.

If researchers are to do research on change, they need a set of skills often lacking in organizational behavior researchers. Not only do they need to be familiar with and capable of using a variety of research methods, they need to relate to organizations in a way that allows the research relationship to survive over a long period and, perhaps, even to support the change activities going on in the organization. In short, they need to have both research skills and certain consulting skills. If a researcher has these skills and is able to engage the organization in a study of the change process, the probability of studying significant problems in a comprehensive way is high.

Indeed, the key question may be: Is it possible to do good research *without* studying change? Given that the key issues in understanding organizations are not static and . . . are not the kinds that lend themselves to tightly controlled field experiments, studying change may be the only way.

CONSULTING AND RESEARCH

Many researchers take care to separate consulting and research. The two are seen as competing activities because they demand a different relationship with the organization and its members. This is clearly true in the traditional scientific model of what constitutes good research, but it is not so clear if the research agenda is targeted toward influencing both theory and practice.

It can be argued that testing many important theoretical concepts and developing improved practice depends on having some researchers who can engage in consulting relationships with organizations. It is only through this type of consulting relationship that organizations can actually try new ideas and breakthroughs in practice.

Some new practices and some new theories can be adequately tested only by putting them in place in an organization. This implies an intervention into an organization's actual operating procedures. Alternatively, one can simply wait for an organization to try something and then capitalize on it as a naturally occurring field experiment or a *post hoc* study of change. This is often done in the field of organizational behavior, but reliance on this technique places a severe limitation on the development of the field. It requires that new practices be tried by somebody else before the field can progress. A much more attractive alternative is for researchers to help in instituting innovations so that they can study issues that are likely to push the state of theory and practice forward.

SUMMARY

Taken in combination, the points made so far suggest that research that is likely to contribute to both theory and practice can be done but that it may look different from much of the research traditionally done in organizational behavior. To mention just a few points, it is more likely, for example, to involve change, to be large-scale, and to be fine-grained in the depth with which it looks at organizations. This is not to argue that traditional research is to be discontinued or that there is only one right way to do research; rather, there are multiple valid ways to do research on organizations, and the field needs to be eclectic in the approaches it includes. In short, the argument is that there is more than one way of establishing theory and fact. There are multiple ways, and these all need to be used if research that contributes to both theory and practice is to be conducted. . . . The best approach for a particular situation clearly reflects not only the topic to be studied but the skills of the researcher and the strengths and weaknesses of different methods of data gathering.

Figure 1 elaborates on this point by showing a possible relationship between data and the confidence one has in a finding about how organizations operate. The data gathered may vary from traditional scientific data to no data at all, and confidence can vary from high to low. Where few facts exist but confidence is high, we have entered the arena of value-driven decision making. At the other extreme, when scientific data exist, confidence will be high from a data-based perspective. Yet even where there is a great deal of data, the figure suggests that value contributes to reaching the highest level of confidence. Finally, it suggests that we should have the most "scientific" confidence when we have good traditional data.

Based on the arguments presented in this chapter, it is reasonable to question the nature of the confidence line separating value-driven and data-driven decision making in Figure 1. Figure 1 assumes that the best data are

FIGURE 1 Possible Relationship between Data and Confidence

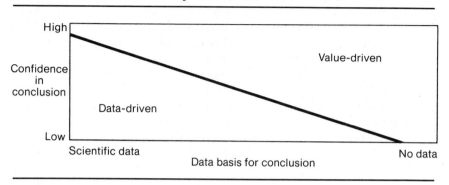

FIGURE 2 Alternative Relationship between Data and Confidence

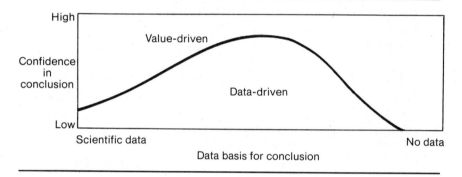

traditionally gathered scientific data. If we assume they are not, then we might draw the line as shown in Figure 2. Ultimately, it is up to each researcher to develop his own relationship between data and confidence in the decisions about what findings to believe and how strongly to believe them.

*   *   *   *   *

A Nobel Prize-winning economist has observed that the best current research and theory rarely inform contemporary practice in the field of economics (Stigler, 1976). He argues that the kind of data that economists need and the kind of theories they state are so obscure that they bear almost no relation to practice. At first glance, this might seem to be in contrast to Lewin's statement about the usefulness of theory, but I wonder whether Lewin would consider the theoretical work done in economics today good. In fact, I doubt that he would.

There is an interesting possible variant of Lewin's statement about the usefulness of theory: "Nothing is so useful as research that informs both theory and practice." If, indeed, research informs practice, then it is likely to have something to say about the reality of the workplace and to deal with issues that are relevant to practitioners. If it also informs theory, then it must describe more than just an isolated phenomenon or a nonreplicable phenomenon. It must state something that is generalizable across situations and issues. Unfortunately, much of the research on organizational behavior may be better at informing theory than practice. As a result, we end up with many theories that are not useful to the practitioner. We have many theories, but perhaps we have few good theories.

REFERENCES

Adams, J. S. Injustice in social exchange. In *Advances in experimental social psychology.* vol. 2, ed. L. Berkowitz. New York: Academic Press, 1965.

Deci, E. L. *Intrinsic motivation.* New York: Plenum Press, 1975.

Lawler, E. E., III. "The new plant revolution." *Organizational Dynamics* (1978) 6, no. 3, 2–12.

Lawler, E. E., III. *Pay and organization development.* Reading, Mass.: Addison-Wesley Publishing, 1981.

Peters, T., and R. Waterman. *In search of excellence.* New York: Harper & Row, 1983.

Roethlisberger, F. J., and W. J. Dickson. *Management and the worker.* Cambridge, Mass.: Harvard University Press, 1939.

Stigler, G. J. "Do economists matter?" *Southern Economic Journal* (1976) 42, 347–54.

Whyte, W. F. *Money and motivation: An analysis of incentives in industry.* New York: Harper & Row, 1955.

The Motivational Basis of Behavior in Organizations

INTRODUCTION

Except for the infirm and the heirs to family riches, people have to work at a job to attain a standard of living and creature comforts much beyond mere survival. And most of these people must work in organizations. However, these considerations provide only a beginning to understanding the motivational basis of individual behavior at work. We know that other goals and motives become adjoined to the vocational imperative, but what is the nature of these motives? We know that we work harder and better under some condition than others, but what accounts for this variability in our performance? What motives drive us into behavior that sometimes disrupts performance—sometimes our own as well as others'? Would the answers to these questions enable us to design work organizations that yield both member satisfaction and effective institutions?

These questions raise both theoretical and applied issues. The first six readings in Section Two tackle the basic conceptual problems attendant to the analysis of work motivation. These are followed by descriptions and assessments of several approaches to applying theories of job motivation.

Part A   Theoretical Issues

INTRODUCTION

To seek an understanding of the motivation of behavior at work is to ask "what?" and "how?" The question of *what* asks about the *content* or substance of motivation: What are the important goals that people seek to reach through work? What do they hope to *hold on to* throughout the course of work experience? What are the rewards, incentives, ends, and driving forces? What do people really want—especially once they can take for granted some reasonable success in meeting material and security needs?

Aronson argues that we strive to maintain and project some semblance of rationality and consistency in both thought and action. Henry Clay once said that he would rather "be right than be President"; most of us, according to Aronson, would often rather be consistent than right. Unfortunately, otherwise astute administrators underestimate and underappreciate the importance of this motive, both in themselves and others, and therein lies the potential for serious misreading of many acts and utterances.

Kerr turns us from the content to the process dimension of motivation (i.e., the question of *how* motives have their effects). Whatever the stated aims of organizations, people pursue those courses of action that traverse paths to valued goals. Unfortunately, organizations all too often arrange valued goal objects at the ends of paths that run away from, even opposite to, the paths that would lead to officially espoused objectives. Kerr provides several telling illustrations of this phenomenon and offers some explanations for why it happens.

Lawler and Porter likewise address primarily the process questions of motivation. In particular, they discuss the issue of how performance becomes part of this process. They argue that the process is *not*, as many would like to believe, one of satisfaction giving rise to subsequent performance. Rather, performance enters into the process only if it is conceived by members as the relevant path to extrinsic rewards (such as pay) or more intangible rewards (such as feelings of achievement and pride in work).

Organ suggests that job satisfaction has a more "subtle significance," to be found not in its effects on in-role productivity but rather in those spontaneous and discretionary contributions comprising organizational "citizenship behavior." Organ goes on to note that managing job satisfaction probably has not so much to do with "keeping people happy" as it does with meeting pervasive and deep-seated—though often competing—notions of what is fair. Thus, whatever other motives actuate behavior in organizations, we must reckon with fairness or justice as an omnipresent motive force at work.

Discussions of job motivation nowadays almost invariably touch upon the concept of "intrinsic motivation." Pinder provides an analysis of this concept, its origins and causes, and the intriguing question of how it interacts with the effects of extrinsic incentives.

We conclude this section with Hofstede's penetrating examination of whether work motivation theories developed in the United States have relevance abroad. Hofstede, drawing from the findings of his ambitious study of work cultures in over 40 different nations, argues persuasively that some of the major concepts and models of work motivation developed in the U.S.A. do not take adequate account of cultural differences in individualism and the need to avoid uncertainty. These cultural differences have profound implications not only for models of job motivation but also for ideas about leadership and organization structure that necessarily follow from assumptions about basic motivational premises of work behavior. As work organizations continue to reflect an increasingly international dimension, we might well anticipate a studied reexamination of the cultural bias built into mainstream models of job motivation.

The Rationalizing Animal*

Elliot Aronson

Man likes to think of himself as a rational animal. However, it is more true that man is a *rationalizing* animal, that he attempts to appear reasonable to himself and to others. Albert Camus even said that man is a creature who spends his entire life in an attempt to convince himself that he is not absurd.

Some years ago a woman reported that she was receiving messages from outer space. Word came to her from the planet Clarion that her city would be destroyed by a great flood on December 21. Soon a considerable number of believers shared her deep commitment to the prophecy. Some of them quit their jobs and spent their savings freely in anticipation of the end.

On the evening of December 20, the prophet and her followers met to prepare for the event. They believed that flying saucers would pick them up, thereby sparing them from disaster. Midnight arrived, but no flying saucers. December 21 dawned, but no flood.

What happens when prophecy fails? Social psychologists Leon Festinger, Henry Riecken, and Stanley Schachter infiltrated the little band of believers to see how they would react. They predicted that persons who had expected the disaster, but awaited it alone in their homes, would simply lose faith in the prophecy. But those who awaited the outcome in a group, who had thus admitted their belief publicly, would come to believe even more strongly in the prophecy and turn into active proselytizers.

That is exactly what happened. At first the faithful felt despair and shame because all their predictions had been for naught. Then, after waiting nearly five hours for the saucers, the prophet had a new vision. The city had been spared, she said, because of the trust and faith of her devoted group. This revelation was elegant in its simplicity, and the believers accepted it enthusiastically. They now sought the press that they had previously avoided. They turned from believers into zealots.

---

* Reprinted from *Psychology Today*, May 1973, by permission of Psychology Today Magazine. Copyright © 1973 Ziff-Davis Publishing Company.

LIVING ON THE FAULT

In 1957, Leon Festinger proposed his theory of *cognitive dissonance,* which describes and predicts man's rationalizing behavior. Dissonance occurs whenever a person simultaneously holds two inconsistent cognitions (ideas, beliefs, opinions). For example, the belief that the world will end on a certain day is dissonant with the awareness, when the day breaks, that the world has not ended. Festinger maintained that this state of inconsistency is so uncomfortable that people strive to reduce the conflict in the easiest way possible. They will change one or both cognitions so that they will "fit together" better.

Consider what happens when a smoker is confronted with evidence that smoking causes cancer. He will become motivated to change either his attitudes about smoking or his behavior. And as anyone who has tried to quit knows, the former alternative is easier.

The smoker may decide that the studies are lousy. He may point to friends ("If Sam, Jack, and Harry smoke, cigarettes can't be all that dangerous"). He may conclude that filters trap all the cancer-producing materials. Or he may argue that he would rather live a short and happy life with cigarettes than a long and miserable life without them.

The more a person is committed to a course of action, the more resistant he will be to information that threatens that course. Psychologists have reported that the people who are least likely to believe the dangers of smoking are those who tried to quit—and failed. They have become more committed to smoking. Similarly, a person who builds a $100,000 house astride the San Andreas Fault will be less receptive to arguments about imminent earthquakes than would a person who is renting the house for a few months. The new homeowner is committed; he doesn't want to believe that he did an absurd thing.

When a person reduces his dissonance, he defends his ego and keeps a positive self-image. But self-justification can reach startling extremes; people will ignore danger in order to avoid dissonance, even when that ignorance can cause their deaths. I mean that literally.

Suppose you are Jewish in a country occupied by Hitler's forces. What should you do? You could try to leave the country; you could try to pass as "Aryan"; you could do nothing and hope for the best. The first two choices are dangerous: If you are caught you will be executed. If you decide to sit tight, you will try to convince yourself that you made the best decision. You may reason that, while Jews are indeed being treated unfairly, they are not being killed unless they break the law.

Now suppose that a respected man from your town announces that he has seen Jews being butchered mercilessly, including everyone who has recently been deported from your village. If you believe him, you might have a chance to escape. If you don't believe him, you and your family will be slaughtered.

Dissonance theory would predict that you will not listen to the witness, because to do so would be to admit that your judgment and decisions were wrong. You will dismiss his information as untrue, and decide that he was lying or hallucinating. Indeed, Elie Wiesel reported that this happened to the Jews in Sighet, a small town in Hungary, in 1944. Thus people are not passive receptacles for the deposit of information. The manner in which they view and distort the objective world in order to avoid and reduce dissonance is entirely predictable. But one cannot divide the world into rational people on one side and dissonance reducers on the other. While people vary in their ability to tolerate dissonance, we are all capable of rational or irrational behavior, depending on the circumstances—some of which follow.

DISSONANCE BECAUSE OF EFFORT

Judson Mills and I found that if people go through a lot of trouble to gain admission to a group, and the group turns out to be dull and dreary, they will experience dissonance. It is a rare person who will accept this situation with an "Oh, pshaw. I worked hard for nothing. Too bad." One way to resolve the dissonance is to decide that the group is worth the effort it took to get admitted.

We told a number of college women that they would have to undergo an initiation to join a group that would discuss the psychology of sex. One third of them had severe initiation: They had to recite a list of obscene words and read some lurid sexual passages from novels in the presence of a male experimenter (in 1959, this really was a "severe" and embarrassing task). One third went through a mild initiation in which they read words that were sexual but not obscene (such as "virgin" and "petting"); and the last third had no initiation at all. Then all of the women listened to an extremely boring taped discussion of the group they had presumably joined. The women in the severe initiation group rated the discussion and its drab participants much more favorably than those in the other groups.

I am not asserting that people enjoy painful experiences, or that they enjoy things that are associated with painful experiences. If you got hit on the head by a brick on the way to a fraternity initiation, you would not like that group any better. But if you volunteered to get hit with a brick *in order to join* the fraternity, you definitely would like the group more than if you had been admitted without fuss.

After a decision—especially a difficult one that involves much time, money, or effort—people almost always experience dissonance. Awareness of defects in the preferred object is dissonant with having chosen it; awareness of positive aspects of the unchosen object is dissonant with having rejected it.

Accordingly, researchers have found that, *before* making a decision, people seek as much information as possible about the alternatives.

Afterward, however, they seek reassurance that they did the right thing, and do so by seeking information in support of their choice or by simply changing the information that is already in their heads. In one of the earliest experiments on dissonance theory, Jack Brehm gave a group of women their choice between two appliances, such as a toaster or a blender, that they had previously rated for desirability. When the subjects reevaluated the appliances after choosing one of them, they increased their liking for the one they had chosen and downgraded their evaluation of the rejected appliance. Similarly, Danuta Ehrlich and her associates found that a person about to buy a new car does so carefully, reading all ads and accepting facts openly on various makes and models. But after he buys his Volvo, for instance, he will read advertisements more selectively, and he will tend to avoid ads for Volkswagens, Chevrolets, and so on.

THE DECISION TO BEHAVE IMMORALLY

Your conscience, let us suppose, tells you that it is wrong to cheat, lie, steal, seduce your neighbor's husband or wife, or whatever. Let us suppose further that you are in a situation in which you are sorely tempted to ignore your conscience. If you give in to temptation, the cognition "I am a decent, moral person" will be dissonant with the cognition "I have committed an immoral act." If you resist, the cognition "I want to get a good grade (have that money, seduce that person)" is dissonant with the cognition "I could have acted so as to get that grade, but I chose not to."

The easiest way to reduce dissonance in either case is to minimize the negative aspects of the action one has chosen, and to change one's attitude about its immorality. If Mr. C. decides to cheat, he will probably decide that cheating isn't really so bad. It hurts no one; everyone does it; it's part of human nature. If Mr. D. decides not to cheat, he will no doubt come to believe that cheating is a sin, and deserves severe punishment.

The point here is that the initial attitudes of these men are virtually the same. Moreover, their decisions could be a hair's breadth apart. But once the action is taken, their attitudes diverge sharply.

Judson Mills confirmed these speculations in an experiment with sixth-grade children. First he measured their attitudes toward cheating, and then put them in a competitive situation. He arranged the test so that it was impossible to win without cheating, and so it was easy for the children to cheat, thinking they would be unwatched. The next day, he asked the children again how they felt about cheating. Those who had cheated on the test had become more lenient in their attitudes; those who had resisted the temptation adopted harsher attitudes.

The data are provocative. They suggest that the most zealous crusaders are not those who are removed from the problem they oppose. I would hazard to say that the people who are most angry about "the sexual promiscuity of the young" are *not* those who have never dreamed of being promiscuous. On the contrary, they would be persons who had been seriously tempted by illicit sex, who came very close to giving in to their desires, but who finally resisted. People who almost live in glass houses are the ones who are most likely to throw stones.

INSUFFICIENT JUSTIFICATION

If I offer George $20 to do a boring task and offer Richard $1 to do the same thing, which one will decide that the assignment was mildly interesting? If I threaten one child with harsh punishment if he does something forbidden and threaten another child with mild punishment, which one will transgress?

Dissonance theory predicts that, when people find themselves doing something and they have neither been rewarded adequately for doing it nor threatened with dire consequences for not doing it, they will find *internal* reasons for their behavior.

Suppose you dislike Woodrow Wilson and I want you to make a speech in his favor. The most efficient thing I can do is to pay you a lot of money for making the speech, or threaten to kill you if you don't. In either case, you will probably comply with my wish, but you won't change your attitude toward Wilson. If that were my goal, I would have to give you a *minimal* reward or threat. Then, in order not to appear absurd, you would have to seek additional reasons for your speech—this could lead you to find good things about Wilson and, hence, to conclude that you really do like Wilson after all. Lying produces great attitude change only when the liar is undercompensated.

Festinger and J. Merrill Carlsmith asked college students to work on boring and repetitive tasks. Then the experimenters persuaded the students to lie about the work, to tell a fellow student that the task would be interesting and enjoyable. They offered half of their subjects $20 for telling the lie, and they offered the others only $1. Later they asked all subjects how much they had really liked the tasks.

The students who earned $20 for their lies rated the work as deadly dull, which it was. They experienced no dissonance: they lied, but they were well paid for that behavior. By contrast, students who got $1 decided that the tasks were rather enjoyable. The dollar was apparently enough to get them to tell the lie but not enough to keep them from feeling that lying for so paltry a sum was foolish. To reduce dissonance, they decided that they hadn't lied after all; the task was fun.

Similarly, Carlsmith and I found that mild threats are more effective than harsh threats in changing a child's attitude about a forbidden object, in this case a delightful toy. In the severe-threat condition, children refrained from playing with the toys and had a good reason for refraining—the very severity of the threat provided ample justification for not playing with the toy. In the mild-threat condition, however, the children refrained from playing with the toy but, when they asked themselves, "How come I'm not playing with the toy?" they did not have a superabundant justification (because the threat was not terribly severe). Accordingly, they provided additional justification in the form of convincing themselves that the attractive toy was really not very attractive and that they didn't really want to play with it very much in the first place. Jonathan Freedman extended our findings and showed that severe threats do not have a lasting effect on a child's behavior. Mild threats, by contrast, can change behavior for many months.

Perhaps the most extraordinary example of insufficient justification occurred in India, where Jamuna Prasad analyzed the rumors that were circulated after a terrible earthquake in 1950. Prasad found that people in towns that were *not* in immediate danger were spreading rumors of impending doom from floods, cyclones, or unforeseeable calamities. Certainly the rumors could not help people feel more secure; why then perpetrate them? I believe that dissonance helps explain this phenomenon. The people were terribly frightened—after all, the neighboring villages had been destroyed—but they did not have ample excuse for their fear, since the earthquake had missed them. So they invented their own excuse; if a cyclone is on the way, it is reasonable to be afraid. Later, Durganand Sinha studied rumors in a town that had actually been destroyed. The people were scared, but they had good reason to be; they didn't need to seek additional justification for their terror. And their rumors showed no predictions of impending disaster and no serious exaggerations.

THE DECISION TO BE CRUEL

The need for people to believe that they are kind and decent can lead them to say and do unkind and indecent things. After the National Guard killed four students at Kent State, several rumors quickly spread: The slain girls were pregnant, so their deaths spared their families from shame; the students were filthy and had lice on them. These rumors were totally untrue, but the townspeople were eager to believe them. Why? The local people were conservative and infuriated at the radical behavior of some of the students. Many had hoped that the students would get their comeuppance. But death is an awfully severe penalty. The severity of this penalty outweighs and is dissonant with the "crimes" of the students. In these circumstances, any information that put the victims in a bad light reduces dissonance by implying, in effect, that it was good that the young people died. One high school teacher even avowed that anyone with "long hair, dirty clothes, or [who goes] barefooted deserves to be shot."

Keith Davis and Edward Jones demonstrated the need to justify cruelty. They persuaded students to help them with an experiment, in the course of which the volunteers had to tell another student that he was a shallow, untrustworthy, and dull person. Volunteers managed to convince themselves that they didn't like the victim of their cruel analysis. They found him less attractive than they did before they had to criticize him.

Similarly, David Glass persuaded a group of subjects to deliver electric shocks to others. The subjects, again, decided that the victim must deserve the cruelty; they rated him as stupid, mean, etc. Then Glass went a step further. He found that a subject with high self-esteem was most likely to derogate the victim. This led Glass to conclude, ironically, that it is precisely because a person thinks he is nice that he decides that the person he has hurt is a rat. "Since nice guys like me don't go around hurting innocent people," Glass's subjects seemed to say, "you must have deserved it." But individuals who have *low* self-esteem do not feel the need to justify their behavior and derogate their victims; it is *consonant* for such persons to believe they have behaved badly. "Worthless people like me do unkind things."

Ellen Berscheid and her colleagues found another factor that limits the need to derogate one's victim: the victim's capacity to retaliate. If the person doing harm feels that the situation is balanced, that his victim will pay him back in coin, he had no need to justify his behavior. In Berscheid's experiment, which involved electric shocks, college students did not derogate or dislike the persons they shocked if they believed the victims could retaliate. Students who were led to believe that the victims would not be able to retaliate *did* derogate them. Her work suggests that soldiers may have a greater need to disparage civilian victims (because they can't retaliate) than military victims. Lt. William L. Calley, who considered the "gooks" at My Lai to be something less than human, would be a case in point.

DISSONANCE AND THE SELF-CONCEPT

On the basis of recent experiments, I have reformulated Festinger's original theory in terms of the self-concept. That is, dissonance is most powerful when self-esteem is threatened. Thus, the important aspect of dissonance is not "I said one thing and I believe another," but "I have misled people—and I am a truthful, nice person." Conversely, the cognitions, "I believe the task is dull," and "I told someone the task was interesting," are not dissonant for a psychopathic liar.

David Mettee and I predicted in a recent experiment that persons who had low opinions of themselves would be more likely to cheat than persons with high self-esteem. We assumed that if an average person gets a temporary blow to his self-esteem (by being jilted, say, or not getting a promotion), he will temporarily feel stupid and worthless, and hence do any number of stupid and worthless things—cheat at cards, bungle an assignment, break a valuable vase.

Mettee and I temporarily changed 45 female students' self-esteem. We gave one third of them positive feedback about a personality test they had taken (we said that they were interesting, mature, deep, etc.); we gave one third negative feedback (we said that they were relatively immature, shallow, etc.); and one third of the students got no information at all. Then all the students went on to participate in what they thought was an unrelated experiment, in which they gambled in a competitive game of cards. We arranged the situation so that the students could cheat and thereby win a considerable sum of money, or not cheat, in which case they were sure to lose.

The results showed that the students who had received blows to their self-esteem cheated far more than those who had gotten positive feedback about themselves. It may well be that low self-esteem is a critical antecedent of criminal or cruel behavior.

The theory of cognitive dissonance has proved useful in generating research; it has uncovered a wide range of data. In formal terms, however, it is a very sloppy theory. Its very simplicity provides both its greatest strength and its most serious weakness. That is, while the theory has generated a great deal of data, it has not been easy to define the limits of the theoretical statement, to determine the specific predictions that can be made. All too often researchers have had to resort to the very unscientific rule of thumb, "If you want to be sure, ask Leon."

LOGIC AND PSYCHOLOGIC

Part of the problem is that the theory does not deal with *logical* inconsistency, but *psychological* inconsistency. Festinger maintains that two cognitions are inconsistent if the opposite of one follows from the other. Strictly speaking, the information that smoking causes cancer does not make it illogical to smoke. But these cognitions produce dissonance because they do not make sense psychologically, assuming that the smoker does not want cancer.

One cannot always predict dissonance with accuracy. A man may admire Franklin Roosevelt enormously and discover that throughout his marriage FDR carried out a clandestine affair. If he places a high value on fidelity and he believes that great men are not exempt from this value, then he will experience dissonance. Then I can predict that he will either change his attitudes about Roosevelt or soften his attitudes about fidelity. But, he may believe that marital infidelity and political greatness are totally unrelated; if this were the case, he might simply shrug off these data without modifying his opinions either about Roosevelt or about fidelity.

Because of the sloppiness in the theory, several commentators have criticized a great many of the findings first uncovered by dissonance theory. These criticisms have served a useful purpose. Often, they have goaded us to perform more precise research, which in turn has led to a clarification of some of the findings which, ironically enough, has eliminated the alternative explanations proposed by the critics themselves.

For example, Alphonse and Natalia Chapanis argued that the "severe initiation" experiment could have completely different causes. It might be that the young women were not embarrassed at having to read sexual words, but rather were aroused, and their arousal in turn led them to rate the dull discussion group as interesting. Or, to the contrary, the women in the severe-initiation condition could have felt much sexual anxiety, followed by relief that the discussion was so banal. They associated relief with the group, and so rated it favorably.

So Harold Gerard and Grover Mathewson replicated our experiment, using electric shocks in the initiation procedure. Our original findings were supported—subjects who underwent severe shocks in order to join a discussion group rated that group more favorably than subjects who had undergone mild shocks. Moreover, Gerard and Mathewson went on to show that merely linking an electric shock with the group discussion (as in a simple conditioning experiment) did not produce greater liking for the group. The increase in liking for the group occurred only when subjects volunteered for the shock *in order* to gain membership in the group—just as dissonance theory would predict.

ROUTES TO CONSONANCE

In the real world there is usually more than one way to squirm out of inconsistency. Laboratory experiments carefully control a person's alternatives, and the conclusions drawn may be misleading if applied to everyday situations. For example, suppose a prestigious university rejects a young Ph.D. for its one available teaching position. If she feels that she is a good scholar, she will experience dissonance. She can then decide that members of that department are narrow-minded and senile, sexist, and wouldn't recognize talent if it sat on their laps. Or she could decide that, if they could reject someone as fine and intelligent as she, they must be extraordinarily brilliant. Both techniques will reduce dissonance, but note that they leave this woman with totally opposite opinions about professors at the university.

This is a serious conceptual problem. One solution is to specify the conditions under which a person will take one route to consonance over another. For example, if a person struggles to reach a goal and fails, he may decide that the goal wasn't worth it (as Aesop's fox did) or that the effort was justified anyway (the fox got a lot of exercise in jumping for the grapes). My own research suggests that a person will take the first means when he has expended relatively little effort. But when he has put in a great deal of effort, dissonance will take the form of justifying the energy.

This line of work is encouraging. I do not think that it is very fruitful to demand to know what *the* mode of dissonance reduction is; it is more instructive to isolate the various modes that occur, and determine the optimum conditions for each.

IGNORANCE OF ABSURDITY

No dissonance theorist takes issue with the fact that people frequently work to get rewards. In our experiments, however, small rewards tend to be associated with greater attraction and greater attitude change. Is the reverse ever true?

Jonathan Freedman told college students to work on a dull task after first telling them (*a*) their results would be of no use to him, since his experiment was basically over, or (*b*) their results would be of great value to him. Subjects in the first condition were in a state of dissonance, for they had unknowingly agreed to work on a boring chore that apparently had no purpose. They reduced their dissonance by deciding that the task was enjoyable.

Then Freedman ran the same experiment with one change. He waited until the subjects finished the task to tell them whether their work would be important. In this study he found incentive effects: students told that the task was valuable enjoyed it more than those who were told that their work was useless. In short, dissonance theory does not apply when an individual performs an action in good faith without having any way of knowing it was absurd. When we agree to participate in an experiment we naturally assume that it is for a purpose. If we are informed afterward that it *had* no purpose, how were we to have known? In this instance we like the task better if it had an important purpose. But if we agreed to perform it *knowing* that it had no purpose, we try to convince ourselves that it is an attractive task in order to avoid looking absurd.

MAN CANNOT LIVE BY CONSONANCE ALONE

Dissonance reduction is only one of several motives, and other powerful drives can counteract it. If human beings had a pervasive, all-encompassing need to reduce all forms of dissonance, we would not grow, mature, or admit to our mistakes. We would sweep mistakes under the rug or, worse, turn the mistakes into virtues; in neither case would we profit from error.

But obviously people do learn from experience. They often do tolerate dissonance because the dissonant information has great utility. A person cannot ignore forever a leaky roof, even if that flaw is inconsistent with having spent a fortune on the house. As utility increases, individuals will come to prefer dissonance-arousing but useful information. But as dissonance increases, or when commitment is high, future utility and information tend to be ignored.

It is clear that people will go to extraordinary lengths to justify their actions. They will lie, cheat, live on the San Andreas Fault, accuse innocent bystanders of being vicious provocateurs, ignore information that might save their lives, and generally engage in all manner of absurd postures. Before we write off such behavior as bizarre, crazy, or evil, we would be wise to examine the situations that set up the need to reduce dissonance. Perhaps our awareness of the mechanism that makes us so often irrational will help turn Camus' observation on absurdity into a philosophic curiosity.

On the Folly of Rewarding A, while Hoping for B*

Steven Kerr

Whether dealing with monkeys, rats, or human beings, it is hardly controversial to state that most organisms seek information concerning what activities are rewarded, and then seek to do (or at least pretend to do) those things, often to the virtual exclusion of activities not rewarded. The extent to which this occurs, of course, will depend on the perceived attractiveness of the rewards offered, but neither operant nor expectancy theorists would quarrel with the essence of this notion.

Nevertheless, numerous examples exist of reward systems that are fouled up in that behaviors which are rewarded are those which the rewarder is trying to *discourage,* while the behavior he desires is not being rewarded at all.

In an effort to understand and explain this phenomenon, this paper presents examples from society, from organizations in general, and from profit-making firms in particular. Data from a manufacturing company and information from an insurance firm are examined to demonstrate the consequences of such reward systems for the organizations involved, and possible reasons why such reward systems continue to exist are considered.

SOCIETAL EXAMPLES

Politics

Official goals are "purposely vague and general and do not indicate . . . the host of decisions that must be made among alternative ways of achieving official goals and the priority of multiple goals . . ." (8, p. 66). They usually may be relied on to offend absolutely no one, and in this sense can be considered high-acceptance, low-quality goals. An example might be "build better schools." Operative goals are higher in quality but lower in

---

* Reprinted from *Academy of Management Journal* (1975) *18*, 769–83.

acceptance, since they specify where the money will come from, what alternative goals will be ignored, etc.

The American citizenry supposedly wants its candidates for public office to set forth operative goals, making their proposed programs "perfectly clear," specifying sources and uses of funds, etc. However, since operative goals are lower in acceptance, and since aspirants to public office need acceptance (from at least 50.1 percent of the people), most politicians prefer to speak only of official goals, at least until after the election. They, of course, would agree to speak at the operative level if "punished" for not doing so. The electorate could do this by refusing to support candidates who do not speak at the operative level.

Instead, however, the American voter typically punishes (withholds support from) candidates who frankly discuss where the money will come from, rewards politicians who speak only of official goals, but hopes that candidates (despite the reward system) will discuss the issues operatively. It is academic whether it was moral for Nixon, for example, to refuse to discuss his 1968 "secret plan" to end the Vietnam War, his 1972 operative goals concerning the lifting of price controls, the reshuffling of his cabinet, etc. The point is that the reward system made such refusal rational.

It seems worth mentioning that no manuscript can adequately define what is "moral" and what is not. However, examination of costs and benefits, combined with knowledge of what motivates a particular individual, often will suffice to determine what for him is "rational."[1] If the reward system is so designed that it is irrational to be moral, this does not necessarily mean that immorality will result. But is this not asking for trouble?

War

If some oversimplification may be permitted, let it be assumed that the primary goal of the organization (Pentagon, Luftwaffe, or whatever) is to win. Let it be assumed further that the primary goal of most individuals on the front lines is to get home alive. Then there appears to be an important conflict in goals—personally rational behavior by those at the bottom will endanger goal attainment by those at the top.

But not necessarily! It depends on how the reward system is set up. The Vietnam War was indeed a study of disobedience and rebellion, with terms such as "fragging" (killing one's own commanding officer) and "search and evade" becoming part of the military vocabulary. The difference in subordinates' acceptance of authority between World War II and Vietnam is

---

[1] In Simon's (10, pp. 76–77) terms, a decision is "subjectively rational" if it maximizes an individual's valued outcomes so far as his knowledge permits. A decision is "personally rational" if it is oriented toward the individual's goals.

reported to be considerable, and veterans of the Second World War often have been quoted as being outraged at the mutinous actions of many American soldiers in Vietnam.

Consider, however, some critical differences in the reward system in use during the two conflicts. What did the GI in World War II want? To go home. And when did he get to go home? When the war was won! If he disobeyed the orders to clean out the trenches and take the hills, the war would not be won and he would not go home. Furthermore, what were his chances of attaining his goal (getting home alive) if he obeyed the orders compared to his chances if he did not? What is being suggested is that the rational soldier in World War II, *whether patriotic or not*, probably found it expedient to obey.

Consider the reward system in use in Vietnam. What did the man at the bottom want? To go home. And when did he get to go home? When his tour of duty was over! This was the case *whether or not* the war was won. Furthermore, concerning the relative chance of getting home alive by obeying orders compared to the chance if they were disobeyed, it is worth noting that a mutineer in Vietnam was far more likely to be assigned rest and rehabilitation (on the assumption that fatigue was the cause) than he was to suffer any negative consequence.

In his description of the "zone of indifference," Barnard stated that "a person can and will accept a communication as authoritative only when . . . at the time of his decision, he belives it to be compatible with his personal interests as a whole" (1, p. 165). In light of the reward system used in Vietnam, would it not have been personally irrational for some orders to have been obeyed? Was not the military implementing a system which *rewarded* disobedience, while *hoping* that soldiers (despite the reward system) would obey orders?

Medicine

Theoretically, a physician can make either of two types of error, and intuitively one seems as bad as the other. A doctor can pronounce a patient sick when he is actually well, thus causing him needless anxiety and expense, curtailment of enjoyable foods and activities, and even physical danger by subjecting him to needless medication and surgery. Alternately, a doctor can label a sick person well, and thus avoid treating what may be a serious, even fatal, ailment. It might be natural to conclude that physicians seek to minimize both types of error.

Such a conclusion would be wrong.[2] It is estimated the numerous Americans are presently afflicted with iatrogenic (physician-*caused*) illnesses

---

[2] In one study (4) of 14,867 films for signs of tuberculosis, 1,216 positive readings turned out to be clinically negative; only 24 negative readings proved clinically active, a ratio of 50 to 1.

(9). This occurs when the doctor is approached by someone complaining of a few stray symptoms. The doctor classifies and organizes these symptoms, gives them a name, and obligingly tells the patient what further symptoms may be expected. This information often acts as a self-fulfilling prophecy, with the result that from that day on the patient for all practical purposes is sick.

Why does this happen? Why are physicians so reluctant to sustain a type 2 error (pronouncing a sick person well) that they will tolerate many type 1 errors? Again, a look at the reward system is needed. The punishments for a type 2 error are real: guilt, embarassment, and the threat of lawsuit and scandal. On the other hand, a type 1 error (labeling a well person sick) "is sometimes seen as sound clinical practice, indicating a healthy conservative approach to medicine" (9, p. 69). Type 1 errors also are likely to generate increased income and a stream of steady customers who, being well in a limited psychological sense, will not embarrass the doctor by dying abruptly.

Fellow physicians and the general public, therefore, are really *rewarding* type 1 errors and at the same time *hoping* fervently that doctors will try not to make them.

GENERAL ORGANIZATIONAL EXAMPLES

Rehabilitation Centers and Orphanages

In terms of the prime beneficiary classification (2, p. 42) organizations such as these are supposed to exist for the "public-in-contact," that is, clients. The orphanage, therefore, theoretically is interested in placing as many children as possible in good homes. However, often orphanages surround themselves with so many rules concerning adoption that it is nearly impossible to pry a child out of the place. Orphanages may deny adoption unless the applicants are a married couple, both of the same religion as the child, without history of emotional or vocational instability, with a specified minimum income and a private room for the child, etc.

If the primary goal is to place children in good homes, then the rules ought to constitute means toward that goal. Goal displacement results when these "means become ends-in-themselves that displace the original goals" (2, p. 229).

To some extent these rules are required by law. But the influence of the reward system on the orphanage's management should not be ignored. Consider, for example that the:

1. Number of children enrolled often is the most important determinant of the size of the allocated budget.

2. Number of children under the director's care will also affect the size of his staff.

3. Total organizational size will determine largely the director's prestige at the annual conventions, in the community, etc.

Therefore, to the extent that staff size, total budget, and personal prestige are valued by the orphanage's executive personnel, it becomes rational for them to make it difficult for children to be adopted. After all, who wants to be the director of the smallest orphanage in the state?

If the reward system errs in the opposite direction, paying off only for placements, extensive goal displacement again is likely to result. A common example of vocational rehabilitation in many states, for example, consists of placing someone in a job for which he has little interest and few qualifications, for two months or so, and then "rehabilitating" him again in another position. Such behavior is quite consistent with the prevailing reward system, which pays off for the number of individuals placed in any position for 60 days or more. Rehabilitation counselors also confess to competing with one another to place relatively skilled clients, sometimes ignoring persons with few skills who would be harder to place. Extensively disabled clients find that counselors often prefer to work with those whose disabilities are less severe.[3]

Universities

Society *hopes* that teachers will not neglect their teaching responsibilities but *rewards* them almost entirely for research and publications. This is most true at the large and prestigious universities. Clichés such as "good research and good teaching go together" notwithstanding, professors often find that they must choose between teaching and research-oriented activities when allocating their time. Rewards for good teaching usually are limited to outstanding teacher awards, which are given to only a small percentage of good teachers and which usually bestow little money and fleeting prestige. Punishments for poor teaching also are rare.

Rewards for research and publications, on the other hand, and punishments for failure to accomplish these, are commonly administered by universities at which teachers are employed. Furthermore, publication-orientation résumés usually will be well received at other universities, whereas teaching credentials, harder to document and quantify, are much less transferable. Consequently it is rational for university teachers to concentrate on research, even if to the detriment of teaching and at the expense of their students.

By the same token, it is rational for students to act based upon the goal displacement which has occurred within universities concerning what they

---

[3] Personal interviews conducted during 1972–73.

are rewarded for. It is assumed that a primary goal of a university is to transfer knowledge from teacher to student, then grades become identifiable as a means toward that goal, serving as motivational, control, and feedback devices to expedite the knowledge transfer. Instead, however, the grades themselves have become much more important for entrance to graduate school, successful employment, tuition refunds, parental respect, etc., than the knowledge or lack of knowledge they are supposed to signify.

It, therefore, should come as no surprise that information has surfaced in recent years concerning fraternity files for examinations, term-paper writing services, organized cheating at the service academies, and the like. Such activities constitute a personally rational response to a reward system which pays off for grades rather than knowledge.

BUSINESS-RELATED EXAMPLES

Ecology

Assume that the president of XYZ Corporation is confronted with the following alternatives:

1. Spend $11 million for antipollution equipment to keep from poisoning fish in the river adjacent to the plant; or

2. Do nothing, in violation of the law, and assume a 1 in 10 chance of being caught, with a resultant $1 million fine plus the necessity of buying the equipment

Under this not unrealistic set of choices it requires no linear program to determine that XYZ Corporation can maximize its probabilities by flouting the law. Add the fact that XYZ's president is probably being rewarded (by creditors, stockholders, and other salient parts of his task environment) according to criteria totally unrelated to the number of fish poisoned, and his probable course of action becomes clear.

Evaluation of Training

It is axiomatic that those who care about a firm's well-being should insist that the organization get fair value for its expenditures. Yet it is commonly known that firms seldom bother to evaluate a new GRID, MBO, job-enrichment program, or whatever, to see if the company is getting its money's worth. Why? Certainly it is not because people have not pointed out that this situation exists; numerous practitioner-oriented articles are written each year to just this point.

The individuals (whether in personnel, manpower planning, or wher-ever) who normally would be responsible for conducting such evaluations are the same ones often charged 'with introducing the change effort in the first place. Having convinced top management to spend the money, they usually are quite animated afterward in collecting rigorous vignettes and anecdotes about how successful the program was. The last thing many desire is a formal, systematic, and revealing evaluation. Although members of top management may actually *hope* for such systematic evaluation, their reward systems continue to *reward* ignorance in this area. And if the personnel department abdicates its responsibility, who is to step into the breach? The change agent himself? Hardly! He is likely to be too busy collecting anecdotal "evidence" of his own, for use with his next client.

Miscellaneous

Many additional examples could be cited of systems which in fact are rewarding behaviors other than those supposedly desired by the rewarder. A few of these are described briefly below.

Most coaches disdain to discuss individual accomplishments, preferring to speak of teamwork, proper attitude, and a one-for-all spirit. Usually, however, rewards are distributed according to individual performance. The college basketball player who feeds his teammates instead of shooting will not compile impressive scoring statistics and is less likely to be drafted by the pros. The ballplayer who hits to right field to advance the runners will win neither the batting nor home run titles and will be offered smaller raises. It, therefore, is rational for players to think of themselves first and the team second.

In business organizations where rewards are dispensed for unit performance or for individual goals achieved, without regard for overall effectiveness, smiliar attitudes often are observed. Under most management by objectives (MBO) systems, goals in areas where quantification is difficult often go unspecified. The organization, therefore, often is in a position where it *hopes* for employee effort in the areas of team building, interpersonal relations, creativity, etc., but it formally *rewards* none of these. In cases where promotions and raises are formally tied to MBO, the system itself contains a paradox in that it "asks employees to set challenging, risky goals, only to face smaller paychecks and possibly damaged careers if these goals are not accomplished" (5, p. 40).

It is *hoped* that administrators will pay attention to long-run costs and opportunities and will institute programs which will bear fruit later on. However, many organizational reward systems pay off for short-run sales and earnings only. Under such circumstances it is personally rational for officials to sacrifice long-term growth and profit (by selling off equipment and property or by stifling research and development) for short-term advantages. This probably is most pertinent in the public sector, with the result that many public officials are unwilling to implement programs which will not show benefits by election time.

As a final, clear-cut example of a fouled-up reward system, consider the cost-plus contract or its next of kin, the allocation of next year's budget as a direct function of this year's budget as a direct function of this year's expenditures. It probably is conceivable that those who award such budgets and contracts really hope for economy and prudence in spending. It is obvious, however, that adopting the proverb "to him who spends shall more be given" rewards not economy but spending itself.

TWO COMPANIES' EXPERIENCES

A Manufacturing Organization

A Midwest manufacturer of industrial goods had been troubled for some time by aspects of its organizational climate it believed dysfunctional. For research purposes, interviews were conducted with many employees and a questionnaire was administered on a companywide basis, including plants and offices in several American and Canadian locations. The company strongly encouraged employee participation in the survey, and made available time and space during workday for completion of the instrument. All employees in attendance during the day of the survey completed the questionnaire. All instruments were collected directly by the researcher, who personally administered each session. Since no one employed by the firm handled the questionnaires, and since respondent names were not asked for, it seems likely that the pledge of anonymity given was believed.

A modifed version of the Expect Approval scale (7) was included as part of the questionnaire. The instrument asked respondents to indicate the degree of approval or disapproval they could expect if they performed each of the described actions. A 7-point Likert scale was used, with 1 indicating that the action would probably bring strong disapproval and 7 signifying likely strong approval.

Although normative data for this scale from studies of other organizations are unavailable, it is possible to examine fruitfully the data obtained from this survey in several ways. First, it may be worth noting that the questionnaire data corresponded closely to information gathered through interviews. Furthermore, as can be seen from the results summarized in Table 1, sizable differences between various work units, and between employees at different job levels within the same work unit, were obtained. This suggests that response bias effects (social desirability in particular loomed as a potential concern) are not likely to be severe.

Most important, comparisons between scores obtained on the Expect Approval scale and a statement of problems which were the reason for the survey revealed that the same behaviors which managers in each division thought dysfunctional were those which lower level employees claimed were rewarded. As compared to job levels 1 to 8 in Division B (see Table 1), those in Division A claimed a much higher acceptance by management of

TABLE 1 Summary of Two Divisions' Data Relevant to Conforming and Risk-Avoidance Behaviors (extent to which subjects expect approval)

Dimension	Item	Division and Sample	Total Responses	Percentage of Workers Responding		
				1, 2, or 3 (Disapproval)	4	5, 6, or 7 (Approval)
Risk-avoidance	Making a risky decision based on the best information available at the time, but which turns out wrong.	A, levels 1–4 (lowest)	127	61%	25%	14%
		A, levels 5–8	172	46	31	23
		A, levels 9 and above	17	41	30	30
		B, levels 1–4 (lowest)	31	58	26	16
		B, levels 5–8	19	42	42	16
		B, levels 9 and above	10	50	20	30
Risk	Setting extremely high and challenging standards and goals and then narrowly failing to make them.	A, levels 1–4	122	47	28	25
		A, levels 5–8	168	33	26	41
		A, levels 9 +	17	24	6	70

Setting goals that are extremely easy to make and then making them.	B, levels 1–4	31	48	23	29
	B, levels 5–8	18	17	33	50
	B, levels 9+	10	30	0	70
	A, levels 1–4	124	35	30	35
	A, levels 5–8	171	47	27	26
	A, levels 9+	17	70	24	6
	B, levels 1–4	31	58	26	16
	B, levels 5–8	19	63	16	21
Being a "yes man" and always agreeing with the boss.	B, levels 9+	10	80	0	20
	A, levels 1–4	126	46	17	37
	A, levels 5–8	180	54	14	31
	A, levels 9+	17	88	12	0
	B, levels 1–4	32	53	28	19
	B, levels 5–8	19	68	21	11
	B, levels 9+	10	80	10	10

TABLE 1 (concluded)

Dimension	Item	Division and Sample	Total Responses	1, 2, or 3 (Disapproval)	4	5, 6, or 7 (Approval)
						Percentage of Workers Responding
	Always going along with the majority.	A, levels 1–4	125	40%	25%	35%
		A, levels 5–8	173	47	21	32
		A, levels 9+	17	70	12	18
		B, levels 1–4	31	61	23	16
		B, levels 5–8	19	68	11	21
		B, levels 9+	10	80	10	10
	Being careful to stay on the good side of everyone, so everyone agrees that you are a great guy.	A, levels 1–4	124	45	18	37
		A, levels 5–8	173	45	22	33
		A, levels 9+	17	64	6	30
		B, levels 1–4	31	54	23	23
		B, levels 5–8	19	73	11	16
		B, levels 9+	10	80	10	10

"conforming" activities. Between 31 and 37 percent of Division A employees at levels 1–8 stated that going along with the majority, agreeing with the boss, and staying on everyone's good side brought approval; only once (level 5–8 responses to one of the three items) did a majority suggest that such actions would generate disapproval.

Furthermore, responses from Division A workers at levels 1–4 indicate that behaviors geared toward risk avoidance were as likely to be rewarded as to be punished. Only at job levels 9 and above was it apparent that the reward system was positively reinforcing behaviors desired by top management. Overall, the same "tendencies toward conservatism and apple-polishing at the lower levels" which divisional management had complained about during the interviews were those claimed by subordinates to be the most rational course of action in light of the existing reward system. Management apparently was not getting the behaviors it was *hoping* for, but it certainly was getting the behaviors it was perceived by subordinates to be *rewarding*.

An Insurance Firm

The Group Health Claims division of a large eastern insurance company provides another rich illustration of a reward system which reinforces behaviors not desired by top management.

Attempting to measure and reward accuracy in paying surgical claims, the firm systematically keeps track of the number of returned checks and letters of complaint received from policyholders. However, underpayments are likely to provoke cries of outrage from the insured, while overpayments often are accepted in courteous silence. Since it often is impossible to tell from the physician's statement which of two surgical procedures, with different allowable benefits, was performed, and since writing for clarifications will interfere with other standards used by the firm concerning "percentage of claims paid within two days of receipt," the new hire in more than one claims section is soon acquainted with the formal norm: "When in doubt, pay it out!"

The situation would be even worse were it not for the fact that other features of the firm's reward system tend to neutralize those described. For example, annual "merit" increases are given to all employees, in one of the following three amounts:

1. If the worker is "outstanding" (a select category, into which no more than two employees per section may be placed): 5 percent.
2. If the worker is "above average" (normally all workers not "outstanding" are so rated): 4 percent.
3. If the worker commits gross acts of negligence and irresponsibility for which he might be discharged in many other companies: 3 percent.

Now, since (a) the difference between the 5 percent theoretically attainable through hard work and the 4 percent attainable merely by living until the review data is small and (b) since insurance firms seldom dispense much of a salary increase in cash (rather, the worker's insurance benefits increase, causing him to be further overinsured), many employees are rather indifferent to the possibility of obtaining the extra 1 percent reward and, therefore, tend to ignore the norm concerning indiscriminant payments.

However, most employees are not indifferent to the rule which states that, should absences or latenesses total three or more in any six-month period, the entire 4 or 5 percent due at the next "merit" review must be forfeited. In this sense the firm may be described as *hoping* for performance, while *rewarding* attendance. What it gets, of course, is attendance. (If the absence-lateness rule appears to the reader to be stringent, it really is not. The company counts "times" rather than "days" absent, and a 10-day absence, therefore, counts the same as one lasting 2 days. A worker in danger of accumulating a third absence within six months merely has to remain ill [away from work] during his second absence until his first absence is more than six months old. The limiting factor is that at some point his salary ceases, and his sickness benefits take over. This usually is sufficient to get the younger workers to return; but, for those with 20 or more years' service, the company provides sickness benefits of 90 percent of normal salary, tax-free! Therefore. . . .)

CAUSES

Extremely diverse instances of systems which reward behavior A although the rewarder apparently hopes for behavior B have been given. These are useful to illustrate the breadth and magnitude of the phenomenon, but the diversity increases the difficulty of determining commonalities and establishing causes. However, four general factors may be pertinent to an explanation of why fouled-up reward systems seem to be so prevelant.

Fascination with an "Objective" Criterion

It has been mentioned elsewhere that:

Most "objective" measures of productivity are objective only in that their subjective elements are (a) determined in advance, rather than coming into play at the time of the formal evaluation, and (b) well concealed on the rating instrument itself. Thus, industrial firms seeking to devise objective rating systems first decide, in an arbitrary manner, what dimensions are to be rated, . . . usually including some items having little to do with organizational effectiveness while excluding others that do. Only then does [the] Personnel Division churn out official-looking documents on which all dimensions chosen to be rated are assigned point values, categories, or whatever [6, p. 92].

Nonetheless, many individuals seek to establish simple, quantifiable standards against which to measure and reward performance. Such efforts may be successful in highly predictable areas within an organization, but are likely to cause goal displacement when applied anywhere else. Overconcern with attendance and lateness in the insurance firm and with number of people placed in the vocational rehabilitation division may have been largely responsible for the problems described in those organizations.

Overemphasis on Highly Visible Behaviors

Difficulties often stem from the fact that some parts of the task are highly visible while other parts are not. For example, publications are easier to demonstrate than teaching, and scoring baskets and hitting home runs are more readily observable than feeding teammates and advancing base runners. Similarly, the adverse consequences of pronouncing a sick person well are more visible than those sustained by labeling a well person sick. Team-building and creativity are other examples of behaviors which may not be rewarded simply because they are hard to observe.

Hypocrisy

In some of the instances described the rewarder may have been getting the desired behavior, notwithstanding claims that the behavior was not desired. This may be true, for example, of management's attitude toward apple-polishing in the manufacturing firm (a behavior which subordinates felt was rewarded, despite management's avowed dislike of the practice). This also may explain politicians' unwillingness to revise the penalties for disobedience of ecology laws, and the failure of top management to devise reward systems which would cause systematic evaluation of training and development programs.

Emphasis on Morality or Equity, Rather than Efficiency

Some consideration of other factors prevents the establishment of a system which rewards behaviors desired by the rewarder. The felt obligation of many Americans to vote for one candidate or another, for example, may impair their ability to withhold support from politicians who refuse to discuss the issues. Similarly, the concern for spreading the risks and costs of wartime military service may outweigh the advantage to be obtained by committing personnel to combat until the war is over.

It should be noted that only with respect to the first two causes are reward systems really paying off for other than desired behaviors. In the case of the third and fourth causes the system *is* rewarding behaviors desired by the rewarder, and the systems are fouled up only from the standpoints of those who believe the rewarder's public statements (cause 3), or those who seek to maximize efficiency rather than other outcomes (cause 4).

CONCLUSIONS

Modern organization theory requires a recognition that the members of organizations and society possess divergent goals and motives. It, therefore, is unlikely that managers and their subordinates will seek the same outcomes. Three possible remedies for this potential problem are suggested.

Selection

It is theoretically possible for organizations to employ only those individuals whose goals and motives are wholly consonant with those of management. In such cases the same behaviors judged by subordinates to be rational would be perceived by management as desirable. State-of-the-art reviews of selection techniques, however, provide scant grounds for hope that such an approach would be successful (for example, see 12).

Training

Another theoretical alternative is for the organization to admit those employees whose goals are not consonant with those of management and then, through training, socialization, or whatever, alter employee goals to make them consonant. However, research on the effectiveness of such training programs, though limited, provides further grounds for pessimism (for example, see 3).

Altering the Reward System

What would have been the result if:

1. Nixon had been assured by his advisors that he could not win reelection except by discussing the issues in detail?
2. Physicians' conduct was subjected to regular examination by review boards for type 1 errors (calling healthy people ill) and to penalties (fines, censure, etc.) for errors of either type?

3. The President of XYZ Corporation had to choose between (*a*) spending $11 million for antipollution equipment and (*b*) incurring a 50–50 chance of going to jail for five years?

Managers who complain that their workers are not motivated might do well to consider the possibility that they have installed reward systems which are paying off for behaviors other than those they are seeking. This, in part, is what happened in Vietnam, and this is what regularly frustrates societal efforts to bring about honest politicians, civic-minded managers, etc. This certainly is what happened in both the manufacturing and the insurance companies.

A first step for such managers might be to find out what behaviors currently are being rewarded. Perhaps an instrument similar to that used in the manufacturing firm could be useful for this purpose. Chances are excellent that these managers will be surprised by what they find—that their firms are not rewarding what they assume they are. In fact, such undesirable behavior by organizational members as they have observed may be explained largely by the reward systems in use.

This is not to say that all organizational behavior is determined by formal rewards and punishments. Certainly it is true that in the absence of formal reinforcement some soldiers will be patriotic, some presidents will be ecology-minded, and some orphanage directors will care about children. The point, however, is that in such cases the rewarder is not *causing* the behaviors desired but is only a fortunate bystander. For an organization to *act* upon its members, the formal reward system should positively reinforce desired behaviors, not constitute an obstacle to be overcome.

It might be wise to underscore the obvious fact that there is nothing really new in what has been said. In both theory and practice these matters have been mentioned before. Thus in many states Good Samaritan laws have been installed to protect doctors who stop to assist a stricken motorist. In states without such laws it is commonplace for doctors to refuse to stop, for fear of involvement in a subsequent lawsuit. In college basketball additional penalties have been instituted against players who foul their opponents deliberately. It has long been argued by Milton Friedman and others that penalties should be altered so as to make it irrational to disobey the ecology laws, and so on.

By altering the reward system the organization escapes the necessity of selecting only desirable people or of trying to alter undesirable ones. In Skinnerian terms (as described in 11, p. 704), "As for responsibility and goodness—as commonly defined—no one . . . would want or need them. They refer to a man's behaving well despite the absence of positive reinforcement that is obviously sufficient to explain it. Where such reinforcement exists, 'no one needs goodness.'"

REFERENCES

1. Barnard, Chester I. *The functions of the executive.* Cambridge, Mass.: Harvard University Press, 1964.
2. Blau, Peter M., and W. Richard Scott, *Formal organizations.* San Francisco: Chandler, 1962.
3. Fiedler, Fred E. "Predicting the effects of leadership training and experience from the contingency model." *Journal of Applied Psychology* (1972) 56, 114–19.
4. Garland, L. H. "Studies of the accuracy of diagnostic procedures." *American Journal of Roentgenological, Radium Therapy and Nuclear Medicine* (1959) 82, 25–38.
5. Kerr, Steven. "Some modifications in MBO as an OD strategy." *Academy of Management Proceedings* (1973) 39–42.
6. Kerr, Steven. "What price objectivity? *American Sociologist* (1973) 8, 92–93.
7. Litwin, G. H., and R. A., Stringer, Jr. *Motivation and organizational climate.* Boston: Harvard University Press, 1968.
8. Perrow, Charles. The analysis of goals in complex organizations. In *Readings on modern organizations,* ed. A. Etzioni. Englewood Cliffs, N.J.: Prentice-Hall, 1969.
9. Scheff, Thomas J. Decision rules, types of error, and their consequences in medical diagnosis. In *Mathematical explorations in behavioral science.* ed. F. Massarik and P. Ratoosh. Homewood, Ill.: Irwin, 1965.
10. Simon, Herbert A. *Administrative behavior.* New York: Free Press, 1957.
11. Swanson, G. E. "Review symposium: Beyond freedom and dignity." *American Journal of Sociology* (1972) 78, 702–05.
12. Webster, E. *Decision making in the employment interview.* Montreal: Industrial Relations Center, McGill University, 1964.

The Effect of Performance on Job Satisfaction*

Edward E. Lawler III and Lyman W. Porter

The human relations movement with its emphasis on good interpersonal relations, job satisfaction, and the importance of informal groups provided an important initial stimulant for the study of job attitudes and their relationship to human behavior in organizations. Through the thirties and forties, many studies were carried out to determine the correlates of high and low job satisfaction. Such studies related job satisfaction to seniority, age, sex, education, occupation, and income, to mention a few. Why this great interest in job satisfaction? Undoubtedly some of it stemmed from a simple desire on the part of scientists to learn more about job satisfaction, but much of the interest in job satisfaction seems to have come about because of its presumed relationship to job performance. As Brayfield and Crockett have pointed out, a common assumption that employee satisfaction directly affects performance permeates most of the writings about the topic that appeared during this period of two decades.[1] Statements such as the following characterized the literature: "Morale is not an abstraction; rather it is concrete in the sense that it directly affects the quality and quantity of an individual's output," and "Employee morale—reduces turnover—cuts down absenteeism and tardiness; lifts production."[2]

It is not hard to see how the assumption that high job satisfaction leads to high performance came to be popularly accepted. Not only did it fit into the value system of the human relations movement but there also appeared to be some research data to support this point. In the Western Electric studies, the evidence from the Relay Assembly Test Room showed a dramatic tendency for increased employee productivity to be associated with an

---

* Reprinted from *Industrial Relations, a Journal of Economy and Society* (October 1967) 7, no. 1, 20–28.

[1] Arthur H. Brayfield and Walter H. Crockett, "Employee attitudes and employee performance," *Psychological Bulletin* (September 1955) 52, 396–424.

[2] Ibid.

increase in job satisfaction. Also, who could deny that in the Bank Wiring Room there was both production restriction and mediocre employee morale. With this background it is easy to see why both social scientists and managers believed that, if job dissatisfaction could be reduced, the human brake on production could be removed and turned into a force that would increase performance.

PREVIOUS RESEARCH

But does the available evidence support the belief that high satisfaction will lead to high performance? Since an initial study, in 1932, by Kornhauser and Sharp, more than 30 studies have considered the relationship between these two variables.[3] Many of the earlier studies seemed to have assumed implicitly that a positive relationship existed and that it was important to demonstrate that it in fact did exist. Little attention was given to trying to understand *why* job satisfaction should lead to higher performance; instead, researchers contented themselves with routinely studying the relationship between satisfaction and performance in a number of industrial situations.

The typical reader of the literature in the early fifties was probably aware of the fact that some studies had failed to find a significant satisfaction-performance relationship. Indeed, the very first study of the problem obtained an insignificant relationship.[4] However, judging from the impact of the first review of the literature on the topic, by Brayfield and Crockett, many social scientists, let alone practicing managers, were unaware that the evidence indicated how little relationship exists between satisfaction and performance.[5] The key conclusion that emerged from the review was that "there is little evidence in the available literature that employee attitudes bear any simple—or, for that matter, appreciable—relationship to performance on the job." (The review, however, pointed out that job satisfaction did seem to be positively related, as expected, to two other kinds of employee behavior, absenteeism and turnover.)

The review had a major impact on the field of industrial psychology and helped shatter the kind of naïve thinking that characterized the earlier years of the human relations movement. Perhaps it also discouraged additional research, since few post-1955 studies of the relationship between satisfaction and performance have been reported in scientific journals.

Another review, covering much of the same literature, was completed about the same time.[6] This review took a more optimistic view of the

---

[3] Arthur Kornhauser and A. Sharp, "Employee attitudes: Suggestions from a study in a factory," *Personnel Journal* (1932) *10*, 393–401.

[4] Ibid.

[5] Brayfield and Crocket, "Employee attitudes and employee performance," 396–424.

[6] Frederick Herzberg, Bernard Mausner, R. O. Peterson, and Dora F. Capwell, *Job attitudes: Review of research and opinion* (Pittsburgh: Psychological Service, 1957).

evidence: ". . . there is frequent evidence for the often suggested opinion that positive job attitudes are favorable to increased productivity. The relationship is not absolute, but there are enough data to justify attention to attitudes as a factor in improving the worker's output. However, the correlations obtained in many of the positive studies were low." [7] This review also pointed out, as did Brayfield and Crockett, that there was a definite trend for attitudes to be related to absenteeism and turnover. Perhaps the chief reasons for the somewhat divergent conclusions reached by the two reviews were that they did not cover exactly the same literature and that Brayfield and Crockett were less influenced by suggestive findings that did reach statistical significance. In any event, the one conclusion that was obvious from both reviews was that there was not the *strong, persuasive* relationship between job satisfaction and productivity that had been suggested by many of the early proponents of the human relations movement and so casually accepted by personnel specialists.

A more recent review of the literature by Vroom has received less attention than did the two earlier reviews,[8] perhaps because it is now rather generally accepted that satisfaction is not related to performance. However, before we too glibly accept the view that satisfaction and performance are unrelated, let us look carefully at the data from studies reviewed by Vroom. These studies show a median correlation of $+.14$ between satisfaction and performance. Although this correlation is not large, the consistency of the direction of the correlation is quite impressive. Twenty of the 23 correlations cited by Vroom are positive. By a statistical test such consistency would occur by chance less than once in a hundred times.

In summary, the evidence indicates that a low but consistent relationship exists between satisfaction and performance, but it is not at all clear *why* this relationship exists. The questions that need to be answered at this time, therefore, concern the place of job satisfaction both in theories of employee motivation and in everyday organizational practice. For example, should an organization systematically measure the level of employee satisfaction? Is it important for an organization to try to improve employee job satisfaction? Is there theoretical reason for believing that job satisfaction should be related to job behavior and if so, can it explain why this relationship exists?

WHY STUDY JOB SATISFACTION?

There are really two bases upon which to argue that job satisfaction is important. Interestingly, both are different from the original reason for studying job satisfaction, that is, the assumed ability of satisfaction to

---

[7] Ibid., 103.

[8] Victor H. Vroom, *Work and motivation* (New York: John Wiley & Sons, 1964).

influence performance. The first, and undoubtedly the most straightforward reason, rests on the fact that strong correlations between absenteeism and satisfaction, as well as between turnover and satisfaction, appear in the previous studies. Accordingly, job satisfaction would seem to be an important focus of organizations which wish to reduce absenteeism and turnover.

Perhaps the best explanation of the fact that satisfaction is related to absenteeism and turnover comes from the kind of path-goal theory of motivation that has been stated by Georgopoulos, Mahoney, and Jones; Vroom; and Lawler and Porter.[9] According to this view, people are motivated to do things which they feel have a high probability of leading to rewards which they value. When a worker says he is satisfied with his job, he is in effect saying that his needs are satisfied as a result of having his job. Thus, path-goal theory would predict that high satisfaction will lead to low turnover and absenteeism because the satisfied individual is motivated to go to work where his important needs are satisfied.

A second reason for interest in job satisfaction stems from its low but consistent *association* with job performance. Let us speculate for a moment on why this association exists. One possibility is that, as assumed by many, the satisfaction *caused* the performance. However, there is little theoretical reason for believing that satisfaction can cause performance. Vroom, using a path-goal theory of motivation, has pointed out that job satisfaction and job performance are caused by quite different things: ". . . job satisfaction is closely affected by the amounts of rewards that people derive from their jobs and . . . level of performance is closely affected by the basis of attainment of rewards. Individuals are satisfied with their jobs to the extent to which their jobs provide them with what they desire, and they perform effectively in them to the extent that effective performance leads to the attainment of what they desire."[10]

RELATIONSHIP BETWEEN SATISFACTION AND PERFORMANCE

Vroom's statement contains a hint of why, despite the fact that satisfaction and performance are caused by different things, they do bear some relationship to each other. If we assume, as seems to be reasonable in terms

---

[9] Basil S. Georgopoulos, G. M. Mahoney, and N. W. Jones, "A path-goal approach to productivity," *Journal of Applied Psychology* (1957) *41*, 345–53; Vroom, *Work and motivations;* Edward E. Lawler and Lyman W. Porter, "Antecedent attitudes of effective managerial performance," *Organizational Behavior and Human Performance* (May 1967) *2*, 122–43. See also Lyman W. Porter and Edward E. Lawler, *Managerial attitudes and performance* (Homewood, Ill.: Irwin, 1968).

[10] Vroom, *Work and motivation*, p. 246.

FIGURE 1   The Theoretical Model

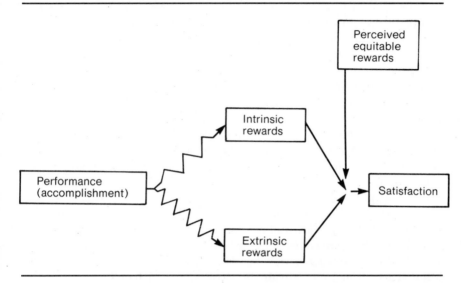

of motivation theory, that rewards cause satisfaction, and that in some cases performance produces rewards, then it is possible that the relationship found between satisfaction and performance comes about through the action of a third variable—rewards. Briefly stated, good performance may lead to rewards, which in turn lead to satisfaction; this formulation then would say that satisfaction, rather than causing performance, as was previously assumed, is caused by it. Figure 1 presents this thinking in a diagrammatic form.

This model first shows that performance leads to rewards, and it distinguishes between two kinds of rewards and their connection to performance. A wavy line between performance and extrinsic rewards indicates that such rewards are likely to be imperfectly related to performance. By extrinsic rewards is meant such organizationally controlled rewards as pay, promotion, status, and security—rewards that are often referred to as satisfying mainly lower level needs.[11] The connection is relatively weak because of the difficulty of tying extrinsic rewards directly to performance. Even though an

---

[11] Abraham H. Maslow, *Motivation and personality* (New York: Harper & Row, 1954). According to Maslow, needs are arranged in a hierarchy with physiological and security needs being the lowest level needs, social and esteem needs next, and autonomy and self-actualization needs the highest level.

organization may have a policy of rewarding merit, performance is difficult to measure, and in dispensing rewards like pay, many other factors are frequently taken into consideration. Lawler, for example, found a low correlation between amount of salary and superiors' evaluation for a number of middle and lower level managers.[12]

Quite the opposite is likely to be true for intrinsic rewards, however, since they are given to the individual by himself for good performance. Intrinsic or internally mediated rewards are subject to fewer disturbing influences and thus are likely to be more directly related to good performance. This connection is indicated in the model by a semiwavy line. Probably the best example of an intrinsic reward is the feeling of having accomplished something worthwhile. For that matter, any of the rewards that satisfy self-actualization needs or higher order growth needs are good examples of intrinsic rewards.

The model also shows that intrinsic and extrinsic rewards are not directly related to job satisfaction since the relationship is moderated by expected equitable rewards. This variable refers to the level or amount of rewards that an individual feels he *should* receive as the result of his job performance. Thus, an individual's satisfaction is a function both of the number and amount of the rewards he receives as well as what he considers to be a fair level of reward. An individual can be satisfied with a small amount of reward if he feels that it is a fair amount of reward for his job.[13]

This model would seem to predict that, because of the imperfect relationship between performance and rewards and the importance of expected equitable rewards, there would be a low but positive relationship between job satisfaction and job performance. The model also leads to a number of other predictions about the relationship between satisfaction and performance. If it turns out that, as this model predicts, satisfaction is dependent on performance, then it can be argued that satisfaction is an important variable from both a theoretical and a practical point of view despite its low relationship to performance. However, when satisfaction is viewed in this way, the reasons for considering it to be important are quite different from those that are proposed when satisfaction is considered to cause performance. But first, let us look at some of the predictions that are derivable from the model and at some data that were collected in order to test the predictions.

---

[12] Edward E. Lawler, "Managers' attitudes toward how their pay is and should be determined," *Journal of Applied Psychology* (August 1966) 50, 273–79.

[13] Lyman W. Porter, "A study of perceived need satisfaction in bottom and middle management jobs," *Journal of Applied Psychology* (January 1961) 45, 1–10.

RESEARCH DATA

Usable data were collected from 148 middle and lower level managers in five organizations. One of the organizations was a large manufacturing company; the others were small social service and welfare agencies. As determined from the demographic data collected from each manager, the sample was typical of other samples of middle and lower level managers, with one exception—31 of the managers were female.

Two kinds of data were collected for each manager. Superior and peer rankings were obtained on two factors: (1) how hard the manager worked and (2) how well the manager performed his job. Since a number of peers ranked each manager, the average peer's rankings were used for data analysis purposes. The rankings by the superiors and peers were in general agreement with each other, so the rankings met the requirements for convergent and discriminant validity. In addition to the superior and peer rankings each manager filled out an attitude questionnaire designed to measure his degree of satisfaction in five needed areas. This part of the questionnaire was identical to the one used in earlier studies by Porter.[14] It consists of 13 items in the following form:

> The opportunity for independent thought and action in my management position:
> (a) How much is there now?
> (min) 1 2 3 4 5 6 7 (max)
> (b) How much should there be?
> (min) 1 2 3 4 5 6 7 (max)

The answers to the first of these questions (a) for each of the 13 items was taken as the measure of need fulfillment or rewards received. The answer to the second of the questions (b) was taken as a measure of the individual's expected equitable level of rewards. The difference in answers between the second and first of these questions was taken as the operational measure of need satisfaction. That is, the larger the difference between "should" and "is now" in our findings, the greater the *dis*satisfaction.[15]

The 13 items, though presented in random order in the questionnaire, had been preclassified into five types of needs that have been described by Maslow: security, social, esteem, autonomy, and self-actualization.

---

[14] Ibid.

[15] A third question about the importance of the various types of needs was also included, but the results based on it are not reported in the findings presented in this article.

PREDICTIONS AND RESEARCH RESULTS

Let us now consider two specific predictions that our model suggests. The first is that an individual's degree of need satisfaction is related to his job performance as rated by his peers and by his superior. A second prediction is that this relationship is stronger for managers than for nonmanagers.

The basis for this second prediction can be found in the assumed connection between rewards and performance. It seems apparent that most organizations have considerably more freedom to reward their managers differentially than they do their often unionized rank-and-file employees (unless the latter are on incentive pay plans). Even in a nonunionized organization (such as a governmental unit), management jobs generally offer the possibility of greater flexibility in differential rewards, especially in terms of prestige and autonomy in decision making. Management jobs also typically provide greater opportunities to satisfy higher order intrinsic needs. As the model shows, satisfaction of these higher order needs is more closely tied to performance.

Satisfaction and Performance

Data collected from our sample of managers generally support the first two predictions. Job satisfaction (the sum of the difference scores for all 13 items) correlates significantly with both the superiors' rankings ($r = 0.32$, $p < 0.01$) and peers' rankings ($r = 0.30$, $p < 0.01$) of performance. Although the correlations are not large, they are substantially larger than the median correlation between satisfaction and performance at the level of rank-and-file workers ($r = 0.14$ as given in Vroom's review). It is possible that this higher relationship came about because we used a different measure of need satisfaction than has been typically used before or because we used a better performance measure. However, our belief is that it came about because the study was done at the management level in contrast to the previous studies which mainly involved nonmanagement employees. Neither our measure of job performance nor our measure of satisfaction would seem to be so unique that either could account for the higher relationship found between satisfaction and performance. However, future studies that use the same measure for both managers and nonmanagers are needed if this point is to be firmly established.

Satisfaction and Effort

An additional prediction from the model is that satisfaction should be more closely related to the rankings obtained on performance than to the rankings obtained on effort. The prediction is an important one for the model and stems from the fact that satisfaction is seen as a variable that is more directly dependent on performance than on effort. Others have pointed out that effort is only one of the factors that determines how effective an individual's performance will be. Ability factors and situational constraints are other obviously relevant determinants. It is also important to note that if we assume, as many previous writers have, that satisfaction causes performance then it would seem logical that satisfaction should be more closely related to effort than to performance. Satisfaction should influence an individual's performance by affecting his motivation to perform effectively, and this presumably is better reflected by effort than by job performance.

The results of the present study show, in fact, a stronger relationship between the superiors' rankings of performance and satisfaction ($r = 0.32$), than between the superiors' rankings of effort and satisfaction ($r = 0.23$). Similarly, for the peer rankings there is a stronger relationship between performance and satisfaction ($r = 0.30$), than between effort and satisfaction ($r = 0.20$).

Intrinsic and Extrinsic Rewards

The model suggests that intrinsic rewards that satisfy needs such as self-actualization are more likely to be related to performance than are extrinsic rewards, which have to be given by someone else and, therefore, have a weaker relationship between their reception and performance. Thus, the satisfaction should be more closely related to performance for higher than for lower order needs. Table 1 presents the data relevant to this point. There is a slight tendency for satisfaction of the higher order needs to show higher correlations with performance than does satisfaction with lower order needs. In particular, the highest correlations appear for self-actualization, which is, of course, the highest order need in the Maslow need hierarchy.

TABLE 1 Pearson Correlations between Performance and Satisfaction in Five Need Areas

	Rankings by	
Needs	Superiors	Peers
Security	0.21*	0.17†
Social	0.23*	0.26*
Esteem	0.24*	0.16†
Autonomy	0.18†	0.23*
Self-actualization	0.30*	0.28*

* $p < 0.01$
† $p < 0.05$

Overall, the data from the present study are in general agreement with the predictions based on the model. Significant relationships did appear between performance and job satisfaction. Perhaps even more important for our point of view, the relationship between satisfaction and performance was stronger than that typically found among blue-collar employees. Also in agreement with our model was the finding that satisfaction was more closely related to performance than to effort. The final prediction, which was supported by the data, was that the satisfaction of higher order needs would be the most closely related to performance. Taken together then, the data offer encouraging support for our model and in particular for the assertion of the model that satisfaction can best be thought of as depending on performance rather than causing it.

IMPLICATIONS OF THE FINDINGS

At this point we can ask the following question: What does the strength of the satisfaction-performance relationship tell us about an organization? For example, if a strong positive relationship exists we would assume that the organization is effectively distributing differential extrinsic rewards based on performance. In addition, it is providing jobs that allow for the satisfaction of higher order needs. Finally, the poorer performers rather than the better ones are quitting and showing high absenteeism, since, as we know, satisfaction, turnover, and absenteeism are closely related.

Now let us consider an organization where no relationship exists between satisfaction and performance. In this organization, presumably, rewards are not being effectively related to performance, and absenteeism and turnover in the organization are likely to be equally distributed among both the good and poor performers. Finally, let us consider the organization where satisfaction and performance bear a negative relationship to each other. Here absenteeism and turnover will be greatest among the best performers. Furthermore, the poor performers would be getting more rewards than the good performers.

Clearly, most organization theorists would feel that organizational effectiveness is encouraged by rewarding good performers and by restricting turnover to poorer performers. Thus, it may be desirable for organizations to develop a strong relationship between satisfaction and performance. In effect, the argument is that the less positive relationship between satisfaction and performance in an organization, the less effective the organization will be (ceteris paribus). If this hypothesis were shown to be true, it would mean that a measure of the relationship between satisfaction and performance would be a helpful diagnostic tool for examining organizations. It is hardly necessary to note that this approach is quite different from the usual human relations one of trying to maximize satisfaction, since here we are suggesting trying to maximize the relationship between satisfaction and performance, rather than satisfaction itself.

One further implication of the model appears to warrant comment. It well may be that a high general level of satisfaction of needs like self-actualization may be a sign of organization effectiveness. Such a level of satisfaction would indicate, for instance, that most employees have interesting and involving jobs and that they probably are performing them well. One of the obvious advantages of providing employees with intrinsically interesting jobs is that good performance is rewarding in and of itself. Furthermore, being rewarded for good performance is likely to encourage further good performance. Thus, measures of higher order need satisfaction may provide good evidence of how effective organizations have been in creating interesting and rewarding jobs, and, therefore, indirect evidence of how motivating the jobs themselves are. This discussion of the role of intrinsic rewards and satisfaction serves to highlight the importance of including measures of higher order need satisfaction in attitude surveys. Too often attitude surveys have focused only on satisfaction with extrinsic rewards, such as pay and promotion, and on the social relations which were originally stressed by the human relations movement.

In summary, we have argued that it is important to consider the satisfaction level that exists in organizations. For one thing, satisfaction is important because it has the power to influence both absenteeism and turnover. In addition, in the area of job performance we have emphasized that, rather than being a cause of performance, satisfaction is caused by it. If this is true, and we have presented some evidence to support the view that it is, then it becomes appropriate to be more concerned about which people and what kind of needs are satisfied in the organization, rather than about how to maximize satisfaction generally. In short, we suggest new ways of interpreting job satisfaction data.

The Subtle Significance
of Job Satisfaction*

Dennis W. Organ

Imagine that Michael Jordan were to become dissatisfied with the Chicago Bulls organization. Suppose, for example, Jordan felt that the team's management had reneged on some promise, or violated some understanding, or sullied his reputation. How would Jordan act out his dissatisfaction? Would he deliberately turn over the ball, let an opposing player score an easy uncontested basket, commit silly fouls to exit the game early?

I submit that it is virtually unthinkable that Jordan or any other professional athlete would respond this way, for two reasons. First, to do so would severely compromise the player's own interests—the "stats" would suffer, and, with that, the bargaining wedge for future contracts. Second, and more important, true professionals cannot bear the intrinsic pain of deliberately botching their individual performance. Whatever grievance Jordan might have against the Bulls, he would inflict unbearable grief on himself as he mentally replayed episodes of shoddy workmanship.

So, given the prohibitive personal and psychic costs of betraying one's craft, how does a professional act out dissatisfaction—aside from merely voicing it? Perhaps voicing dissatisfaction is as far as some would go. But athletes, like other professionals—including those in the clinical laboratory—have some other options. They can choose to define their obligations and their roles narrowly; they will do what they contractually must do. They will do what redounds directly to their self-interests, but contribute only grudgingly (if at all) in other ways. They can choose not to help teammates improve their skills, not to sacrifice leisure hours to "rubber chicken" banquets for community groups, not to take part in (or not even to attend) informal discussions off the playing arena, not to make suggestions for improving the organization, not to sign autographs. They can tie up valuable management time by pressing every imaginable petty grievance, sour the

---

* From *Clinical Laboratory Management Review* (Jan/Feb 1990) *4*, no. 1, 94–98. Copyright © 1990 by Clinical Laboratory Management Association, Inc.

whole atmosphere for players and staff, and undermine confidence in the organization.

Research now indicates that precisely these effects on Organizational Citizenship Behavior, rather than in-role performance or productivity as traditionally defined, are the casualty of dissatisfaction.

SATISFACTION CAUSES PRODUCTIVITY— AN APPEALING BUT DISCREDITED PREMISE

The notion that "a happy employee is a productive employee" lay for a long time at the center of one popular school of management thought. This concept of worker motivation, probably traceable to some distorted accounts of the legendary Hawthorne research of the 1920s and 1930s, certainly has its appeal. Most managers want productivity, and they prefer a satisfied work force over one that is dissatisfied. So practitioners espouse that whatever makes people happy is justifiable as "an investment in higher productivity." Not surprisingly, surveys have shown a strong tendency by human resource and line managers and union leaders to agree that an individual's job satisfaction translates into a corresponding level of productivity (1, 2).

Unfortunately, researchers began to discredit this theory almost from the start. Nearly 35 years ago, Brayfield and Crockett (3) reviewed an already large body of empirical study of the relationship between job attitudes and productivity. They concluded that no "appreciable" relationships existed. Periodic updates have found no reason to modify this general assessment.

THE PENDULUM TURNS

Interestingly, the findings of "rigorous research" have not disturbed practicing managers. Well into the 1970s, possibly into the early 1980s, most managers—either because they did not know about the results of behavioral research, or perhaps because they chose to believe evidence from their own experience—held to the premise that satisfaction does significantly affect productivity. In retrospect, it is doubtful if management science research alone would have ever seriously undermined that premise.

A much more powerful stimulus to revising management opinion was the combined form of double-digit inflation in the late 1970s and the recession of the early 1980s. Malaise about the state of the "body economic" saturated the financial tabloids and the after-dinner speeches of corporate CEOs. We must wake up, it was argued, to the dawning of a new era—one of global competition, deregulation, and accountability. "Country-club-style" management led to creeping costs—costs that only begat more costs rather than increasing output. The ethos of the day was for organizations to hack away the dead wood, downsize to a lean and mean profile, and get more bang for the buck. That meant *every* buck, including the one spent on amenities to make people happy or put into their pay checks.

Tough-minded management came to the fore. Its rationale was the rigorous research showing no consistent or "appreciable" effect of satisfaction on productivity. The old model that a happy worker is a productive worker was rejected as simplistic, if not soft-headed. The new model emphasized performance; let satisfaction fall where it may. The important consideration was not *how many* people were happy but *which* people. The underlying logic was to obtain results from those able and willing to supply them and to ensure that those people, and only those, had any reason for satisfaction.

The new, tough-minded management doctrine was evident in a variety of reforms in human resource practices. For example, many firms took steps to ensure that performance appraisals differentiated among people to a much greater extent. Supervisors could no longer rate a few people as, for example, a 5 on a 5-point scale and everyone else a 4. They had to use the 1s and 2s on the scale. Some programs required every manager to rank people from top to bottom. By definition every department had 50 percent of its people "below average." Moreover, performance measurement was not based on the subjective impressions of supervisors. Feverish activity went into the design of quantitative indicators of specific accomplishments. The message was clear and emphatic: "Let's see your stats as they relate to the bottom line." Merit-pay plans, although nominally in effect in most organizations for many years, acquired new and sharp teeth. Those in the top quartile of ratings and statistical categories received substantial raises; those in the bottom quartile were "zeroed out."

How did such reforms affect job satisfaction? For some, the effect was positive. Overall, as some research suggests (4, 5), the effect was reduced satisfaction. But so what? Job satisfaction doesn't affect a person's productivity, so it doesn't matter. Or does it?

SATISFACTION AND ORGANIZATIONAL CITIZENSHIP BEHAVIOR

Research currently distinguishes between *in-role* performance and productivity and *extra-role* contributions in the form of Organizational Citizenship Behavior (OCB). Individual in-role performance consists of well-specified job requirements—what the person must do according to the job description—and accomplishments (such as meeting certain quotas or statistical norms) that contractually qualify the individual for incremental rewards, such as bonus pay or prizes. Such performance is to some degree a function of attitude, but also of aptitude, expertise, work flow, dependence on others, and resources (such as equipment, budget, staff). Positive attitudes can add little to a person's in-role performance once the limits of those other constraints are reached.

Negative attitudes that might otherwise cause reduced effort for this kind of performance often will not have this effect—people can be disciplined (even terminated) for unsatisfactory in-role performance. And, negative attitudes toward management notwithstanding, someone who needs bonus pay and qualifies for it will perform accordingly.

But for the professional—not only the Michael Jordans but also the highly skilled specialists in the laboratory—there is an even more compelling reason why in-role performance will not suffer because of dissatisfaction. The reason is ego-involvement. For the ego-involved professional, poor or even mediocre performance is intrinsically painful. It arouses feelings of guilt, embarrassment, and self-reproach.

So neither satisfaction nor dissatisfaction will necessarily manifest itself by effects on individual in-role performance.

The problem is that in-role performance is never enough. As Daniel Katz noted:

> An organization which depends solely upon its blueprints of prescribed behavior is a very fragile system. . . . The patterned activity which makes up an organization is so intrinsically a cooperative set of interrelationships, that we are not aware of the cooperative nexus any more than we are of any habitual behavior like walking. Within every work group in a factory, within every division in a government bureau, or within any department of a university are countless acts of cooperation without which the system would break down. We take these everyday acts for granted . . . [6].

An effective organization depends on many forms of discretionary, voluntary contributions for which people seldom get direct credit. These contributions make up OCB. Satisfied people do more of these things (because OCB is primarily a function of attitude and not very dependent on ability or resources); dissatisfied people can choose to do less of them without incurring the risk of sanctions or lost benefits. Because OCB includes many humble and mundane gestures, cutting back on OCB does not hurt the ego as would inferior task performance.

Characteristics of OCB

The concept of OCB becomes less abstract, and much more intuitively familiar to the practicing manager, by understanding some of its characteristics.

Altruism consists of those voluntary actions that help another person with a work problem—instructing a new hire on how to use equipment, helping a co-worker catch up with a backlog of work, fetching materials that a colleague needs and cannot procure on his own.

Courtesy subsumes all of those foresightful gestures that help someone else prevent a problem—touching base with people before committing to action that will affect them, providing advance notice to someone who needs to know to schedule work.

Sportsmanship is a citizen-like posture of tolerating the inevitable inconveniences and impositions of work without whining and grievances—for example, the forbearance shown by a technician whose vacation schedule must yield to unexpected contingencies, or by the programmer who must temporarily endure cramped work quarters.

Conscientiousness is a pattern of going well beyond minimally required levels of attendance, punctuality, housekeeping, conserving resources, and related matters of internal maintenance.

Civic virtue is responsible, constructive involvement in the political process of the organization, including not just expressing opinions but reading one's mail, attending meetings, and keeping abreast of larger issues involving the organization.

At Indiana University, we have developed reliable research instruments for rating people's contributions in these forms. Two other categories for which we do not presently have measures, but which logically relate to OCB, are *Peacemaking*—actions that help to prevent, resolve, or mitigate unconstructive interpersonal conflict—and *Cheerleading*—the words and gestures of encouragement and reinforcement of co-workers' accomplishments and professional development.

A key point is that the person who shows these characteristics of OCB seldom sees it register in his or her individual productivity or "stats" (an exception, perhaps, would be an outstanding attendance record). More often, OCB contributes either to a colleague's performance or to improving the efficiency of the system. A manager, for example, has more time and stamina for important business when not mediating protracted grievances by a staff lacking in sportsmanship. The operator who ignores matters of courtesy generally does not sacrifice his or her individual productivity but creates snafus farther down the line, eventually hurting others' work.

The experienced administrator may, as Katz suggested, take OCB for granted. But if, for whatever reasons, OCB diminishes, the perceptive manager either sees or foresees the eventual effects. As Max Depree, chairman of Herman Miller, Inc., observed (7), one of the warning signs of a company in decline is a "general loss of grace and civility."

Research at Indiana University (8) and elsewhere confirms that OCB is where we must look for the effects of dissatisfaction. The effects are indirect and not generally visible in lower in-role performance. The loss is in those discretionary forms of citizenship on which effective systems depend.

Interdependence and OCB

Management theorists have always noted the essential condition of interdependence created by organization. Much of their creative energies have involved formulating principles, rules, and design structures that address this condition.

James D. Thompson (9) pointed out that formal structure suffices for only certain types of interdependence as they arise from the basic technology of organization. *Mediating technologies*—common to banks, telephone exchanges, libraries, and retail establishments—link clients or customers who wish to be interdependent. This technology creates what Thompson termed "pooled interdependence," which can be managed by standardized rules and procedures. *Long-linked technologies,* of which the archetype is the assembly line, give rise to serial or "linear interdependence." Detailed plans and forecasts are needed to cope with long-linked technologies.

Thompson's third form, *intensive technology,* perhaps best describes the clinical laboratory. Thompson defines this form to "signify that a variety of techniques is drawn upon in order to achieve a change in some specific object; but the selection, combination, and order of application are determined by feedback from the object itself" (9). This type of technology breeds complex, often unforeseeable, reciprocal interdependence. Thompson argued that formal structure, standardized procedures, and elaborate plans are not sufficient to manage this dependence. It requires "mutual adjustment," spontaneous give-and-take, informal helping, teamwork, and cooperation—in other words, OCB. OCB always matters, but especially when intensive technologies breed complex reciprocal interdependence among people, managers, and departments.

SATISFACTION: FAIRNESS, NOT HAPPINESS

So job satisfaction is important after all. Does this mean reverting to country-club-style management, with all its attendant concern for making people happy? The answer is "no" because recent research (10) suggests that happiness has little to do with job satisfaction. When people answer questions about their satisfaction—with work, pay, supervision, promotion—they think about fairness. They compare what they might reasonably have expected and what they actually experience.

Fairness certainly is an inherently subjective and complex issue. People have different ideas about what makes an arrangement fair or unfair. One person will think in terms of visible accomplishments; another will think in terms of loyalty and commitment (e.g., seniority). Still others think of ability, effort, external markets (such as supply and demand for specific expertise), precedent (the fact that certain groups "have always rated a premium"), or education. Seldom is there consensus about the relative weights of these criteria. Fortunately, most people have a reasonably high threshold for perceiving inequity. A system need not match any one person's preferred formula so long as the rank and file understand that an array of relevant criteria have been considered. Most employees expect the technically excellent performer to command a differential in pay or status; they just don't want other criteria of worthiness to be totally ignored. When differentials become marked, and when they are determined by unduly narrow conceptions or measures of contribution, the threshold of unfairness is breached. Dissatisfaction mounts, OCB suffers, and eventually, so does the organization.

Any discussion of fairness at work must reckon with procedural and distributive justice. The process in which decisions are made and benefits determined can affect satisfaction just as much as the decisions and benefits themselves. Studies of employee personnel systems and managerial leadership point to four critical factors in perceptions of fairness:

- *Feedback*—ample and prompt.
- *Recourse*—the option of appeal.
- *Fundamental respect for human dignity*—Even the most incompetent and incorrigible subordinate has the right to be addressed civilly.
- *Some form of input*—We do not mean pure democracy, but simply the opportunity to be heard. As one CEO put it, "having a voice does not mean having a vote."

CONCLUSION

Management research and theory have taken a long time and a torturous path in catching up with the insights of Chester Barnard. More than half a century ago, Barnard (11) noted the essential condition of the "*willingness* of persons to contribute efforts to the cooperative system." This quality of willingness "is something different from effectiveness, ability, or value of personal contributions. . . . [it] means self-abnegation." Willingness is characterized by "[an] indefinitely large range of variation in its intensity among individuals" and, within individuals, "it cannot be constant in degree." Finally, this "willingness to cooperate, positive or negative, is the expression of the net satisfactions and dissatisfactions experienced or anticipated."

Barnard underscored the very nature of organizations as cooperative systems. Rules, structures, policies, job descriptions, sanctions, incentives—they all play necessary roles in collaborative endeavors, but as derivatives of, not as substitutes for, the underlying disposition to cooperate. Such a disposition can be sustained only by a sense of the organization as a microcosm of a just world. Occasional inequities can be tolerated if there is faith that the system works fairly over the long run, with self-correcting tendencies. When faith yields to a narrowly defined, *quid pro quo* contractual relationship, the disposition to cooperate ebbs. Surveys show that most of the nation's labor force begins work with a fairly high degree of job satisfaction and that most of the people, most of the time, will describe themselves as "all in all, satisfied." There is a generally prevalent inclination to give the employer the benefit of the doubt—"I'll assume you're treating me fairly until you persuade me otherwise." So the disposition is generally present to render a substantial contribution via OCB. A good-faith effort by managers to provide a "square deal" will do much to ensure the quality of OCB.

REFERENCES

1. Gannon, M. J., and J. P. Noon. "Management's critical deficiency." *Business Horizons* (1971) *14*, 49–56.
2. Katzell, R. A., and D. Yankelovich. *Work, productivity, and job satisfaction.* New York: The Psychological Corporation, 1975.
3. Brayfield, A. H., and W. H. Crockett. "Employee attitudes and employee performance." *Psychological Bulletin* (1955) *52*, 396–424.
4. Baird L. S., and W. C. Hamner. "Individual versus system rewards: Who's dissatisfied, why and what is their likely response?" *Academy of Management Journal* (1979) *22*, 783–92.
5. Pearce, J. L. and L. W. Porter. "Employee responses to formal performance appraisal feedback." *Journal of Applied Psychology* (1986) *71*, 211–18.
6. Katz, D. "The motivational basis of organizational behavior." *Behavioral Science* (1964) *9*, 131–46.
7. Labich, K. "Hot company, warm culture." *Fortune* (February 27, 1989), 74–78.
8. Organ, D. W. *Organizational citizenship behavior.* Lexington Mass: Lexington Books, 1988.
9. Thompson, J. D. *Organizations in action.* New York: McGraw-Hill, 1967.
10. Organ, D. W., and J. P. Near. "Cognition vs. affect in measures of job satisfaction." *International Journal of Psychology* (1985) *20*, 241–53.
11. Barnard, C. I. *The functions of the executive.* Cambridge, Mass.: Harvard University Press, 1938.

Growth Needs and Intrinsic Work Motivation*

Craig C. Pinder

Imagine you are walking with a friend through your neighborhood on a warm summer evening. As you walk, you notice a nine-year-old boy pushing a lawn mower in erratic circles and strips around the grass on his parents' front yard. The boy has his head lowered between his straight, extended arms, and he is bent over at the waist as he runs and pushes the mower. Upon getting closer, you hear him making sounds like an engine—an airplane engine. You stop and ask the young man what he is doing, and learn that he is pretending to be a pilot flying an airplane. The sounds he was emitting, of course, were those made by the plane's motor. The young pilot seems friendly enough so you stop to chat for a while. The conversation reveals that the boy is having fun with his fantasy Beechcraft and that he did not consider his activity to be work. Further probing on your part informs you that the boy receives no pay or other form of direct compensation from his parents for cutting the grass (or flying his airplane). You part company, wishing him a safe flight.

Is the boy in this example working (cutting the lawn) or playing (flying his aircraft)? Or, does it matter at all what you call or how you classify his behavior? For the boy, the behavior clearly was playing. On the other hand, the boy's father would view it as work—a chore that he would now not have to perform himself. It may simply be a matter of one's perspective, as seemed to be the case when Tom Sawyer managed to lure his friends into whitewashing his Aunt Polly's fence.

We can look a bit deeper behind the reasons for our young pilot's behavior, asking, for example, what motivated him to behave the way he did. We can probably rule out existence and relatedness needs as explanations for the boy's action, because it did not seem that he was deriving any

* From Craig C. Pinder, *Work motivation: Theories, issues, and applications* (Glenview, Ill.: Scott, Foresman, 1984), 57–70. [Editor's note: All references in this reading may be found in Pinder's textbook, just cited.]

monetary rewards for his play, nor did he seem to be seeking any social interaction from it. If we assume that the boy's behavior was, in fact, motivated (as opposed to being simply random or compulsive), we are left with the conclusion that the boy must have been motivated largely by growth needs. What, you may ask, has *growth* got to do with the erratic flight of a low altitude lawn mower?

* * * * *

WHAT IS INTRINSIC MOTIVATION?

Current thinking in work motivation would view the boy's behavior as being *intrinsically* motivated. Or, we might say the boy was intrinsically motivated to do what he was doing. Intrinsically motivated behavior can be defined, loosely, as behavior that is performed for its own sake, rather than for the purpose of acquiring any material or social rewards. One scholar who has extensively investigated intrinsically motivated behaviors defines them as those "which a person engages in to feel competent and self determining" (Deci, 1975, p. 61). Consistent with this view, Wexley and Yukl (1977, p. 89) define intrinsic motivation in work settings as "a term used to describe effort that is expended in an employee's job to fulfull growth needs such as achievement, competence, and self-actualization." In short, these various definitions imply a motivational force that originates in what Maslow (1954) would call the higher order needs, or what Alderfer (1972) would classify as growth needs—a force directed toward behavior that is its own incentive.

The distinction between internal and external work motivation originated with Herzberg, Mausner, and Snyderman's (1959) study of the determinants of job satisfaction. And although the concepts of intrinsic and extrinsic motives, rewards, and outcomes have not always been consistently understood and used in recent years (Dyer and Parker, 1975), the distinction is important, and intrinsic motivation is a major factor in explaining much of the work behavior of many employees. In fact, it may be that intrinsic motivation (and hence the intrinsic rewards required to satisfy it) will become increasingly more important as the work force becomes more highly educated and less threatened by challenging jobs (Cooper, Morgan, Foley, and Kaplan, 1979).

Intrinsic and Extrinsic Outcomes

Insofar as we can distinguish between intrinsic and extrinsic motivation, we can also distinguish between intrinsic and extrinsic job outcomes (Lawler, 1969). Intrinsic outcomes relate to either the satisfaction or frustration of the higher level, or growth needs. Examples of intrinsic outcomes would include positive feelings of accomplishment or a sense of diminished self-esteem. Intrinsic outcomes occur, when they occur, immediately upon the performance of the acts that produce them. They are, in a sense, self-administered by the individual, rather than distributed by others.

Extrinsic outcomes tend to relate more to the gratification and frustration of the existence and relatedness needs. They include things such as pay, promotions, and social interaction with one's colleagues. Moreover, they tend to be mediated by outsiders, such as one's supervisor or peers.

There is some dispute about the precise dividing line between intrinsic and extrinsic outcomes (Dyer and Parker, 1975), so some writers discourage continued use of the distinction (e.g., Guzzo, 1979). This author's view is that some job outcomes can often appeal to both higher and lower level needs (e.g., pay increases can enhance one's feelings of self-esteem), and, although there may be some disagreement concerning where one draws the boundary, it is useful to refer to intrinsic outcomes as those job-related consequences that, at least in part, function either to gratify or frustrate a person's growth needs.

The Origins and Nature of Intrinsic Motivation

According to Deci (1975), there have been at least three general approaches taken by psychologists to understand intrinsically motivated behavior. One of these, represented by the work of Hebb (1955), posits that human beings seek preferred or *optimum* levels of arousal (where arousal is seen as the stimulation of the brain and central nervous system). Arousal levels result primarily from the stimulation that is found in the individual's environment. If the arousal level is too low in comparison with a person's desired level, the person will be motivated to behave in such a way as to increase it. For example, an employee who is used to a fairly hectic work pace, but who finds things slower than usual on a particular day, will be motivated to seek out other people for conversation, set new tasks to be accomplished, or do something, simply to "stir things up." On the other hand, if the person's level of arousal is sufficiently greater than the preferred level, the individual will attempt either to withdraw from the highly arousing circumstances, or take steps to slow things down toward the desired level (e.g., by turning off a noisy radio or moving into a job that is less demanding). In this view then, intrinsically motivated behavior is behavior intended to increase or decrease the physiological stimulation a person experiences, in order to bring it into line with desired levels.

A second approach (which is similar to the first), posits that people desire and behave to achieve an optimum level of uncertainty or *incongruity*, where incongruities consist of psychological inconsistencies in a person's beliefs, thoughts, perceptions, values, or behaviors (Zajonc, 1960). Unlike Festinger (1957) who posited that people find *cognitive dissonance* aversive, and that they are motivated to minimize the number of inconsistent cognitions they hold, this approach claims that individuals vary in the number and intensity of disparate beliefs, acts, and perceptions they prefer in their lives. When a person is experiencing either too little consistency ("Things just don't add up!") or too much consistency ("The world is in total harmony with itself"), behavior is instigated either to reduce or increase the level of congruity in the person's mind. Whereas the optimum arousal approach described above is physiological in orientation, the optimal congruity approach stresses the level of psychic comfort or discomfort a person experiences as a consequence of his or her acts and perceptions. The work of Hunt (1965) and Berlyne (1973) represents this second approach to explaining the origins of intrinsically motivated behavior.

The third approach to intrinsic motivation identified by Deci (1975) is best represented by White's (1959) concept of competence (or *effectance*) motivation, and de Charm's (1968) notion of personal causation.

According to White (1959), competence refers to a person's capacity to master and deal effectively with the surroundings—to be in charge of them. The exploratory behavior of children characterizes a desire to be competent, as do adult behaviors that are intended to enquire, to manipulate, and to learn about things. Competence motivation represents a need that is always available to instigate and direct behavior, although this need is less urgent (or prepotent, to use Maslow's term) than are the types of existence needs we have examined in a previous chapter. When it is aroused, however, competence motivation causes people to seek out challenging situations in their environments, and then to conquer those situations, leading to feelings of competence and efficacy.

Likewise, according to de Charms (1968), people desire to be the *origin* of their own behavior, rather than the *pawns* of circumstances beyond their control. People strive for personal causation, to be in charge of their own lives, and for the outcomes that accrue to them.

In short, then, Deci (1975) sees intrinsically motivated behaviors as those behaviors a person engages in to feel competent and self-determining. These behaviors consist of two general types—those intended to find or create challenge and those intended to conquer it. Hence, the adult who deliberately takes a clock apart merely to see how it works, or who learns a foreign language simply for the sake of learning it, are two other examples of intrinsically motivated behavior from this third perspective.

In summary then, there have been at least three conceptual interpretations of intrinsic motivation, each of them predicated on a different fundamental assumption regarding human nature: the first one is primarily biological/physiological; the second is cognitive/perceptual; and the third is based on a need fulfillment model of human functioning. Does this mean that there is no similarity or overlap among the three approaches?

Similarities among the Three Approaches.   Notice that the *challenge* associated with any of the exploratory behaviors mentioned in connection with the third approach (above) might serve to increase or decrease a person's level of arousal, and/or the level of consistency he experiences, suggesting that the three general approaches to understanding intrinsic motivation are somewhat compatible with one another.

For example, the man who disassembles a machine that does not need repair opens (literally) a great deal of new arousal as he perceives and manipulates the delicate internal mechanisms. Further, there is a strong chance that he may either confirm or disconfirm his prior beliefs about what he would find inside the machine, thereby either reducing or increasing the net level of congruity he holds in his mind about the way things operate. Finally, if he were successful at reassembling the machine, he is likely to experience feelings of mastery and competence. The point is that the three concepts of intrinsic motivation cited by Deci (1975) are compatible (or at least reconcilable) with one another, so one might conclude that, in a sense, a process of increasing incongruity, arousal, and challenge followed by attempts to reduce this incongruity, arousal, and challenge constitute the psychological mechanisms behind behaviors we refer to as intrinsically motivated behavior. Thus, Deci (1975, pp. 61–62) states:

> Only when a person is able to reduce incongruity . . . and only when a person is able to conquer the challenges which he encounters or creates will he feel competent and self-determining. He will feel satisfied when he is able to seek out pleasurable stimulation and deal effectively with overstimulation. In short, people seem to be engaged in the general process of seeking and conquering challenges which are optimal.

According to Deci (1975), the need to be competent and self-determining is innate among humans, although the specific types of behaviors required of an individual to satisfy it varies from one person to the next. Deci considers self-actualization to be one common manifestation of the need for competence and self-determination; he sees achievement motivation as another. In fact, achievement motivation has been one of the most thoroughly researched needs in psychology and is one that has special relevance to work behavior. Therefore, let's take a close look at this particular human need.

Achievement Motivation

Henry Murray generated numerous lists of human needs. One of these needs is referred to as the *need for achievement*, which he defined as a need to:

> accomplish something difficult. To master, manipulate, or organize physical objects, human beings, or ideas. To do this as rapidly and as independently as

possible. To overcome obstacles and attain a high standard. To excel oneself. To rival and surpass others. To increase self-regard by the successful exercise of talent. [Murray, 1938, p. 164.]

The overlap between this need and the notion of self-actualization from Maslow is apparent, although not complete. The essence of achievement motivation might be seen as a struggle against one's *own* standards of excellence, which clearly is consistent with the idea of becoming all that one is capable of becoming. But the element of achievement motivation having to do with mastering objects and overcoming obstacles and challenges is not necessarily part of self-actualization, although the two can, in practice, go hand in hand. Further, the aspects of the need for achievement pertaining to mastering and organizing the environment are clearly consistent with White's (1959) concept of competence motivation, and de Charms's (1968) notion that people prefer to be responsible for their outcomes rather than merely being pawns.

In short, these various growth needs are not identical, in large measure because they have been identified and studied by scholars working more or less independently of one another. But they do converge considerably in terms of the types of behaviors they instigate.

David McClelland, a student of Henry Murray, has devoted much of his career to developing our understanding of achievement motivation and to the role it plays in entrepreneurial behavior and the economic prosperity of nations (Stewart, 1982). His work is far too extensive to be summarized completely here, so the reader is referred to some of the original sources (e.g., McClelland, 1961, 1962, 1965; McClelland and Winter, 1969). But a number of features of this work of particular relevance to our understanding of employee work motivation will be discussed here.

The Origins of Achievement Motivation.   First, McClelland believes that all motives are learned from experiences in which certain cues in the environment are paired with positive or negative consequences. Accordingly, the need for achievement is learned when opportunities for competing with standards of excellence become associated with positive outcomes. Hence, childhood rearing practices that encourage youngsters to independently tackle challenges and to do well against them are critical. In fact, McClelland holds that child rearing practices are the most important determinants of the level of a person's achievement motivation (McClelland, 1961, pp. 340–50). However, McClelland has also shown that deliberate programs of training that involve the development of an achievement-oriented mentality can induce entrepreneurial behavior among adults where it did not previously exist (McClelland, 1965; McClelland and Winter, 1969). In other words, adults can be trained, it seems, to create and respond to opportunities to strive against challenges, and to behave in the ways described in the definition above. It is important to recognize that most of McClelland's research evidence pertains to boys and men, so his theory is limited to males. Attempts to generalize it to females have not yet been successful (Stein & Bailey, 1973).

Characteristics of Achievement-Motivated Behavior. It was stated in an earlier chapter that we can sometimes detect the existence of many particular needs in an individual by observing the person's behavior and drawing inferences from it. Accordingly, the behavior of achievement-motivated individuals is commonly characterized by three features. First, achievement-motivated people prefer tasks of *moderate* levels of difficulty. Second, achievement-motivated people prefer tasks for which successful performance depends upon their own efforts, rather than upon luck. Finally, achievement-motivated people demand feedback and knowledge about their successes and failures to a far greater degree than do people who are low in achievement motivation.

The preference for tasks of moderate levels of difficulty deserves special attention. According to Atkinson (1964), the total *achievement-oriented force* impacting a person who confronts a task is determined by three variables. Further, the three combine multiplicatively, so that if one of them is inactive, or "zero," there is no pyschological force to engage in the task.

The first factor is the strength of the person's underlying need for achievement. This remains constant from one day to the next, although, as suggested above, it can be developed among male adults using focused training procedures.

The second factor is the level of difficulty of the task, as the person perceives it. Whether a particular task will be viewed as easy or difficult depends on a host of variables, such as the individual's perception of his ability to perform the task, for example.

The third factor which determines the strength of achievement-oriented motivation is the degree of intrinsic reward (or feelings of accomplishment) the individual expects he will experience if he manages to accomplish the task. Naturally, achieving a difficult challenge will bring the person greater feelings of accomplishment than will achieving a task that is perceived as simple. Therefore, the value of this third factor is inversely related to the second factor—the perceived level of difficulty of the task. Symbolically:

$$T.A.F. = nACh \times P.S. \times I.S.$$
$$I.S. = (1 - P.S.)$$

where

    T.A.F. = Total achievement-motivated force.
    nAch = Strength of the person's underlying need for achievement.
    P.S. = The perceived probability of task success.
    I.S. = Intrinsic feeling of accomplishment.

To illustrate how this formula works, consider the net force operating on an employee if (*a*) he has a very low level of the need for achievement, or (*b*) if he perceives the task to be too difficult for him to succeed, or (*c*) he perceives the task as very easy. In all three cases, we would not expect much achievement motivation in the person contemplating the task. His level of effort toward performing the task would be determined by the strength of other needs and incentives he believed would result from task success (such as the recognition of a female he might be trying to impress.)

The Importance of Perceived Task Difficulty.   Notice that insofar as a person's level of underlying need strength is constant in the short run, the net level of achievement-related force acting on him to engage in a particular task will be determined by his perception of the level of difficulty of that task. The implication of this for the design of jobs and for the assignment of people to jobs is clear: In order to arouse motivational force associated with achievement needs, a supervisor must structure jobs and assign people to them so that employees see their chances of job performance as "50–50": not too low, but not too high. There must be a moderate level of challenge perceived. In practice, application of this principle can be difficult, because it requires that a supervisor be capable of accurately perceiving the difficulty level of a task as the employee sees it. So, a supervisor who overestimates or underestimates an employee's ability vis-à-vis a task will probably fail to arouse and take advantage of a certain amount of the natural achievement motivation of that worker. In theory, the principle is relatively simple; effectively applying it can be another matter.

COMBINING INTRINSIC AND EXTRINSIC MOTIVATION

Return for a moment to the hypothetical case of the boy and the lawn mower that opened this chapter. Consider what would happen if the boy's father elected to compensate him for cutting the lawn, using pay or some other form of extrinsic reward. Further, assume his father agreed to pay the boy some amount of money for cutting the grass each time he did it, thereby making the receipt of the money contingent upon his cutting the lawn. What would happen to the boy's net level of motivation to cut the lawn, and what would happen to the amount of fun the boy would have in cutting the grass/flying his imaginary airplane?

Both common sense and considerable research evidence (Lawler, 1971) support the proposition that compensation systems that tie pay and other rewards to the performance of an activity increase the level and rate of performance of that task. It would stand to reason, therefore, that paying the boy to fly his lawn mower would add considerable extrinsic motivation to the level of intrinsic motivation the boy already had for that task. In other words, the net level of motivation in the lad to cut the lawn should not be greater than before, because the extrinsic motivation provided by the money will somehow combine with his prior level of intrinsic motivation, resulting in a greater overall level of motivation than the boy had before he started to receive the pay. Again, common sense would support this reasoning, as do some formal theories of work motivation (e.g., Galbraith and Cummings, 1967; Porter and Lawler, 1968).

A series of experiments by Deci (e.g., 1971, 1972) and others (e.g., Condry, 1975; Greene and Lepper, 1974; Pritchard, Campbell and Campbell, 1977) has generated sufficient cause to believe, however, that intrinsic and extrinsic motivation may not always "add up" (in a pyschological sense) the way common sense suggests. Instead, it may be that, in some circumstances, the addition of an extrinsic, contingently paid incentive (such as money) to a work context, in which the employee is intrinsically motivated to do the work, may result in a loss of some (or all) of the employee's prior level of intrinsic motivation toward that task, and maybe toward other tasks perceived as similar.

The possibility that intrinsic and extrinsic incentives may not be additive has generated considerable research (see Notz, 1975; and Guzzo, 1979, for two reviews), although the evidence on the issue is mixed (e.g., Arnold, 1976; Hamner and Foster, 1975; Pinder, 1976). Sometimes extrinsic rewards have been shown to reduce intrinsic motivation; other times the opposite effect occurs—the contingent reward enhances intrinsic motivation. How can we explain the inconsistent results of studies into the matter?

Among others, Staw (1976) has reviewed the evidence on this so-called *overjustification hypothesis*, and has suggested that whether extrinsic rewards enhance or reduce intrinsic motivation depends on at least five factors:

1. The degree of saliency of the reward.
2. The prevailing norm regarding the appropriateness of payment for the activity in question.
3. The prior level of commitment of the person to the task.
4. The degree of choice the individual has to perform, or not to perform, the task.
5. The existence of potential adverse consequences.

So, according to Staw, extrinsic rewards are more likely to reduce subsequent levels of intrinsic motivation if the reward is highly salient, meaning that it is obvious to those who are to receive it and that it is understood that the reward will be received upon the performance of the act. The more salient the reward, the more likely it is to have an adverse impact on intrinsic motivation (Ross, 1975).

Second, Staw suggests that rewards that are normally provided for a behavior in our culture are less likely to reduce a person's intrinsic motivation to engage in that behavior. He notes that, in many of the studies in which rewards have been observed to reduce intrinsic motivation, those rewards were provided for the performance of acts that are not usually followed by reward (such as participating in games and puzzles in a laboratory setting). On the other hand, behaviors that are normally compensated in our culture (and that we might be inclined to classify as work) are less likely to be influenced by the provision of extrinsic outcomes. Hence, rewards may be more damaging to play behavior and learning behaviors than they are to work behavior.

Third, if the person is initially *very* committed to the task being rewarded, according to Staw, extrinsic rewards are less likely to dampen intrinsic motivation. Those studies that have demonstrated an adverse impact of extrinsic rewards have tended to involve tasks of only moderate prior levels of intrinsic motivation (cf. Arnold, 1976, with Pinder, 1976).

A fourth factor is the level of choice or compulsion a person feels with regard to performing the task. If the individual feels a high level of external pressure to engage in a task, she is more likely to believe that she is extrinsically motivated to behave in that manner, so little intrinsic rationale is available, and little damage can be done by the provision of extrinsic rewards. Finally, the perception that failure to perform the task might result in adverse consequences also contributes to the chances that the person will not attribute her own behavior to internal causes.

The point here is this: It is believed that people observe and rationalize their own behavior in a manner similar to that by which they observe the behavior of others and make attributions about the causes of that behavior. When an act is conducted in the context of a highly salient highly compelling set of extrinsic circumstances (such as the fear of threats or the inducement of rewards), individuals are more likely to attribute their own behavior to these external causes. Otherwise, when there are few apparent external forces to which their behavior can be attributed, the individuals are more likely to assume that they are behaving in a certain manner because they want to—they like doing so. It seems that the presence or absence of such external factors largely determines whether people make intrinsic or extrinsic attributions about their own acts, as well as the cultural appropriateness of those external factors (such as money). While research on this issue is far from conclusive, one thing is clear: Money is an interesting incentive and reward for a number of reasons, and it may not have the simple psychological effects on human motivation that appear at first glance.

Cognitive Evaluation Theory

Deci (1975; Deci and Porac, 1978) has developed a *Cognitive Evaluation Theory* in an attempt to reconcile the contradictory evidence pertaining to the relationship between intrinsic and extrinsic motivation. According to the theory, rewards can bear at least two fundamental features for the individual receiving them. The first of these is referred to as feedback, meaning that rewards given for performance of a task can convey information to the individual concerning how well she is doing at the task. A second feature of rewards can be the messages, if any, they have for the individual about why she is performing the task. Deci refers to these as *control perceptions* (i.e., "Why am I doing this job? For the reward, of course!").

Depending upon which of these two features of a reward system is more salient for an individual, it can serve either to enhance or reduce the person's intrinsic motivation toward it. If control perceptions are more salient, they may cause a shift in the person's perceived *locus of causality*, such that she attributes her reasons for engaging in the task to the external inducements surrounding it, rather than to any internal satisfaction provided by the task itself.

This notion draws on self-perception theory (Bem, 1967), which states that people examine their own behavior, much as they do the behavior of other people, and make attributions about their own motives for behaving as they do. In Deci's theory, control perceptions arising from a reward are said to shift from self-perceptions of intrinsic motivation ("I am cutting the lawn because it is fun") to extrinsic self-attributions ("I am doing it for the money"). As the perceived locus of causality shifts, the person's intrinsic motivation to do the task diminishes. Highly contingent rewards (such as in a piece rate or commission payment system) seem more likely to imply control perceptions, and thereby reduce intrinsic motivation, than less contingent pay systems (such as monthly salaries or hourly wages), largely because they are salient and undeniably connected with the behavior.

According to Deci, feedback perceptions may either enhance or reduce intrinsic motivation. If the feedback indicates to the person that he is doing well at a task, his feelings of competence are enhanced, and his intrinsic motivation for the task is increased (because, for Deci, competence and self-determination are the essence of intrinsic motivation). But if the person perceives that he is doing poorly as a result of the feedback implied by the rewards (or lack of rewards), his feelings of competence will be diminished, as will his intrinsic motivation, and the person will be less likely to engage in the task in the future without some form of extrinsic incentive.

A major shortcoming of Cognitive Evaluation Theory is that it fails to specify the conditions under which either of the two facets of reward (feedback or control) will be more salient for a particular individual in a given situation (Guzzo, 1979). In a recent statement of the theory, Deci and Porac (1978) state only that "'individual differences and situational factors' are related to the way people interpret the meaning of the rewards they receive" (pp. 163–64). Arnold's (1976) work suggests that, when an individual's prior level of intrinsic motivation for a task is very high, feedback perceptions may be more salient, although one experiment failed to confirm this hypothesis (Pinder, Nord, and Ramirez, 1984).

In sum, the relationship between intrinsic and extrinsic motivation is not as simple as originally assumed (Lepper and Green, 1978), and further study is needed before final conclusions are warranted. At present, however, there is some cause to believe that paying people, expecially children, for performing voluntary activities is probably detrimental to their continued intrinsic motivation to engage in these activities.

A major implication of the "Deci effect" for industrial work settings (if and when it occurs) is that contingent payment systems may offset or undermine the intrinsic motivation generated by managerial programs, such as job enrichment (Deci, 1975). At present, however, there seems to be little empirical evidence that this occurs in practice (Staw, 1977), in spite of our common, everyday encounters with surly employees who refuse to perform duties that are not strictly within the formal definitions of their jobs ("I'm not paid to do that!"). More research is needed to determine whether this phenomenon bears the same applied importance in work settings as it does in educational settings.

SUMMARY AND CONCLUSION

In brief, human needs for growth can exhibit themselves through a variety of behaviors for different individuals. It would seem that, as our society continues to enjoy relative economic abundance and high levels of education, growth needs will continue to account for a significant proportion of our overall motivation to work and to behave on the job as we do. Members of the older generation are often critical of younger employees, whom they perceive as irresponsible, or as lacking in the *work ethic*, when they observe them leaving jobs for no apparent reason, or complaining about not receiving enough challenge from their work. The point is that older employees in today's work force had their views about work and the value of holding a job formed during tougher economic times than have been experienced by most employees who are less than 40 years of age today. This generation gap in work values is understandable, although at times it contributes to considerable intergeneration conflict and intolerance.

* * * * *

Motivation, Leadership, and Organization: Do American Theories Apply Abroad?*

Geert Hofstede

A well-known experiment used in organizational behavior courses involves showing the class an ambiguous picture—one that can be interpreted in two different ways. One such picture represents either an attractive young girl or an ugly old woman, depending on the way you look at it. Some of my colleagues and I use the experiment, which demonstrates how different people in the same situation may perceive quite different things. We start by asking half of the class to close their eyes while we show the other half a slightly altered version of the picture—one in which only the young girl can be seen—for only five seconds. Then we ask those who just saw the young girl's picture to close their eyes while we give the other half of the class a five-second look at a version in which only the old woman can be seen. After this preparation we show the ambiguous picture to everyone at the same time.

The results are amazing—most of those "conditioned" by seeing the young girl first see only the young girl in the ambiguous picture, and those "conditioned" by seeing the old woman tend to see only the old woman. We then ask one of those who perceive the old woman to explain to one of those who perceive the young girl what he or she sees, and vice versa, until everyone finally sees both images in the picture. Each group usually finds it

* By permission of Geert Hofstede. Reprinted from *Organization Dynamics*, Summer 1980, pp. 42–63. © 1980, AMACOM, a division of American Management Associations. All rights reserved.

This article is based on research carried out in the period 1973–78 at the European Institute for Advanced Studies in Management, Brussels. The article itself was sponsored by executive search consultants Berndtson International S. A., Brussels. The author acknowledges the helpful comments of Mark Cantley, André Laurent, Ernest C. Miller, and Jennifer Robinson on an earlier version of it.

very difficult to get its views across to the other one and sometimes there's considerable irritation at how "stupid" the other group is.

CULTURAL CONDITIONING

I use this experiment to introduce a discussion on cultural conditioning. Basically, it shows that in five seconds I can condition half a class to see something different from what the other half sees. If this is so in the simple classroom situation, how much stronger should differences in perception of the same reality be between people who have been conditioned by different education and life experience—not for five seconds, but for 20, 30, or 40 years?

I define culture as the collective mental programming of the people in an environment. Culture is not a characteristic of individuals; it encompasses a number of people who were conditioned by the same education and life experience. When we speak of the culture of a group, a tribe, a geographical region, a national minority, or a nation, culture refers to the collective mental programming that these people have in common; the programming that is different from that of other groups, tribes, regions, minorities or majorities, or nations.

Culture, in this sense of collective mental programming, is often difficult to change; if it changes at all, it does so slowly. This is so not only because it exists in the minds of the people but if it is shared by a number of people, because it has become crystallized in the institutions these people have built together: their family structures, educational structures, religious organizations, associations, forms of government, work organizations, law, literature, settlement patterns, buildings, and even, as I hope to show, scientific theories. All of these reflect common beliefs that derive from the common culture.

Although we are all conditioned by cultural influences at many different levels—family, social, group, geographical region, professional environment—this article deals specifically with the influence of our national environment: that is, our country. Most countries' inhabitants share a national character that's more clearly apparent to foreigners than to the nationals themselves; it represents the cultural mental programming that the nationals tend to have in common.

NATIONAL CULTURE IN FOUR DIMENSIONS

The concept of national culture or national character has suffered from vagueness. There has been little consensus on what represents the national culture of, for example, Americans, Mexicans, French, or Japanese. We seem to lack even the terminology to describe it. Over a period of six years, I have been involved in a large research project on national cultures. For a set of 40 independent nations, I have tried to determine empirically the main criteria by which their national cultures differed. I found four such criteria, which I label dimensions; these are Power Distance, Uncertainty Avoidance, Individualism—Collectivism, and Masculinity—Femininity. To understand the dimensions of national culture, we can compare it with the dimensions of personality we use when we describe individuals' behavior. In recruiting, an organization often tries to get an impression of a candidate's dimensions of personality, such as intelligence (high–low); energy level (active–passive); and emotional stability (stable–unstable). These distinctions can be refined through the use of certain tests, but it's essential to have a set of criteria whereby the characteristics of individuals can be meaningfully described. The dimensions of national culture I use represent a corresponding set of criteria for describing national cultures.

Characterizing a national culture does not, of course, mean that every person in the nation has all the characteristics assigned to that culture. Therefore, in describing national cultures we refer to the common elements within each nation—the national norm—but we are not describing individuals. This should be kept in mind when interpreting the four dimensions explained in the following paragraphs.

The Research Data

The four dimensions of national culture were found through a combination of theoretical reasoning and massive statistical analysis, in what is most likely the largest survey material ever obtained with a single questionnaire. This survey material was collected between 1967 and 1973 among employees of subsidiaries of one large U.S.-based multinational corporation (MNC) in 40 countries around the globe. The total data bank contains more than 116,000 questionnaires collected from virtually everyone in the corporation, from unskilled workers to research Ph.D.s and top managers. Moreover, data were collected twice—first during a period from 1967 to 1969 and a repeat survey during 1971 to 1973. Out of a total of about 150 different survey questions (of the precoded answer type), about 60 deal with the respondents' beliefs and values; these were analyzed for the present study. The questionnaire was administered in the language of each country; a total of 20 language versions had to be made. On the basis of these data, each of the 40 countries could be given an index score for each of the four dimensions.

I was wondering at first whether differences found among employees of one single corporation could be used to detect truly national culture differences. I also wondered what effect the translation of the questionnaire could have had. With this in mind, I administered a number of the same questions in 1971–73 to an international group of about 400 managers from different public and private organizations following management development courses in

Lausanne, Switzerland. This time, all received the questionnaire in English. In spite of the different mix of respondents and the different language used, I found largely the same differences between countries in the manager group that I found among the multinational personnel. Then I started looking for other studies, comparing aspects of national character across a number of countries on the basis of surveys using other questions and other respondents (such as students) or on representative public opinion polls. I found 13 such studies; these compared between 5 and 19 countries at a time. The results of these studies showed a statistically significant similarity (correlation) with one or more of the four dimensions. Finally, I also looked for national indicators (such as per capita national income, inequality of income distribution, and government spending on development aid) that could logically be supposed to be related to one or more of the dimensions. I found 31 such indicators—of which the values were available for between 5 and 40 countries—that were correlated in a statistically significant way with at least one of the dimensions. All these additional studies (for which the data were collected by other people, not by me) helped make the picture of the four dimensions more complete. Interestingly, very few of these studies had even been related to each other before, but the four dimensions provide a framework that shows how they can be fit together like pieces of a huge puzzle. The fact that data obtained within a single MNC have the power to uncover the secrets of entire national cultures can be understood when it's known that the respondents form well-matched samples from their nations: They are employed by the same firm (or its subsidiary); their jobs are similar (I consistently compared the same occupations across the different countries); and their age categories and sex composition were similar—only their nationalities differed. Therefore, if we look at the differences in survey answers between multinational employees in countries A, B, C, and so on, the general factor that can account for the differences in the answers is national culture.

Power Distance

The first dimension of national culture is called *Power Distance*. It indicates the extent to which a society accepts the fact that power in institutions and organizations is distributed unequally. It's reflected in the values of the less powerful members of society as well as in those of the more powerful ones. A fuller picture of the difference between small Power Distance and large Power Distance societies is shown in Figure 1. Of course, this shows only the extremes; most countries fall somewhere in between.

Uncertainty Avoidance

The second dimension, *Uncertainty Avoidance*, indicates the extent to which a society feels threatened by uncertain and ambiguous situations, and tries to avoid these situations by providing greater career stability,

FIGURE 1   The Power Distance Dimension

Small Power Distance	Large Power Distance
Inequality in society should be minimized.	There should be an order of inequality in this world in which everybody has a rightful place; high and low are protected by this order.
All people should be interdependent.	A few people should be independent; most should be dependent.
Hierarchy means an inequality of roles, established for convenience.	Hierarchy means existential inequality.
Superiors consider subordinates to be "people like me."	Superiors consider subordinates to be a different kind of people.
Subordinates consider superiors to be "people like me."	Subordinates consider superiors as a different kind of people.
Superiors are accessible.	Superiors are inaccessible.
The use of power should be legitimate and is subject to the judgment as to whether it is good or evil.	Power is a basic fact of society that antedates good or evil. Its legitimacy is irrelevant.
All should have equal rights.	Power-holders are entitled to privileges.
Those in power should try to look less powerful than they are.	Those in power should try to look as powerful as possible.
The system is to blame.	The underdog is to blame.
The way to change a social system is to redistribute power.	The way to change a social system is to dethrone those in power.
People at various power levels feel less threatened and more prepared to trust people.	Other people are a potential threat to one's power and can rarely be trusted.
Latent harmony exists between the powerful and the powerless.	Latent conflict exists between the powerful and the powerless.
Cooperation among the powerless can be based on solidarity.	Cooperation among the powerless is difficult to attain because of their low-faith-in-people norm.

establishing more formal rules, not tolerating deviant ideas and behaviors, and believing in absolute truths and the attainment of expertise. Nevertheless, societies in which uncertainty avoidance is strong are also characterized by a higher level of anxiety and aggressiveness that creates, among other things, a strong inner urge in people to work hard. (See Figure 2.)

FIGURE 2 The Uncertainty Avoidance Dimension

Weak Uncertainty Avoidance	Strong Uncertainty Avoidance
The uncertainty inherent in life is more easily accepted and each day is taken as it comes.	The uncertainty inherent in life is felt as a continuous threat that must be fought.
Ease and lower stress are experienced.	Higher anxiety and stress are experienced.
Time is free.	Time is money.
Hard work, as such, is not a virtue.	There is an inner urge to work hard.
Aggressive behavior is frowned upon.	Aggressive behavior of self and others is accepted.
Less showing of emotions is preferred.	More showing of emotions is preferred.
Conflict and competition can be contained on the level of fair play and used constructively.	Conflict and competition can unleash aggression and should therefore be avoided.
More acceptance of dissent is entailed.	A strong need for consensus is involved.
Deviation is not considered threatening; greater tolerance is shown.	Deviant persons and ideas are dangerous; intolerance holds sway.
The ambiance is one of less nationalism.	Nationalism is pervasive.
More positive feelings toward younger people are seen.	Younger people are suspect.
There is more willingness to take risks in life.	There is great concern with security in life.
The accent is on relativism, empiricism.	The search is for ultimate, absolute truths and values.
There should be as few rules as possible.	There is a need for written rules and regulations.
If rules cannot be kept, we should change them.	If rules cannot be kept, we are sinners and should repent.
Belief is placed in generalists and common sense.	Belief is placed in experts and their knowledge.
The authorities are there to serve the citizens.	Ordinary citizens are incompetent compared with the authorities.

Individualism—Collectivism

The third dimension encompasses *Individualism* and its opposite, *Collectivism*. Individualism implies a loosely knit social framework in which people are supposed to take care of themselves and of their immediate families only, while collectivism is characterized by a tight social framework in which people distinguish between in-groups and out-groups; they expect their in-group (relatives, clan, organizations) to look after them, and in exchange for that they feel they owe absolute loyalty to it. A fuller picture of this dimension is presented in Figure 3.

FIGURE 3   The Individualism Dimension

Collectivist	Individualist
In society, people are born into extended families or clans who protect them in exchange for loyalty.	In society, everybody is supposed to take care of himself/herself and his/her immediate family.
"We" consciousness holds sway.	"I" consciousness holds sway.
Identity is based in the social system.	Identity is based in the individual.
There is emotional dependence of individual on organizations and institutions.	There is emotional independence of individual from organizations or institutions.
The involvement with organizations is moral.	The involvement with organizations is calculative.
The emphasis is on belonging to organizations; membership is the ideal.	The emphasis is on individual initiative and achievement; leadership is the ideal.
Private life is invaded by organizations and clans to which one belongs; opinions are predetermined.	Everybody has a right to a private life and opinion.
Expertise, order, duty, and security are provided by organization or clan.	Autonomy, variety, pleasure, and individual financial security are sought in the system.
Friendships are predetermined by stable social relationships, but there is need for prestige within these relationships.	The need is for specific friendships.
Belief is placed in group decisions.	Belief is placed in individual decisions.
Value standards differ for in-groups and out-groups (particularism).	Value standards should apply to all (universalism).

Masculinity

The fourth dimension is called *Masculinity* even though, in concept, it encompasses its opposite pole, *Femininity*. Measurements in terms of this dimension express the extent to which the dominant values in society are "masculine"—that is, assertiveness, the acquisition of money and things, and not caring for others, the quality of life, or people. These values were labeled "masculine" because, *within* nearly all societies, men scored higher in terms of the values' positive sense than of their negative sense (in terms of assertiveness, for example, rather than its lack)—even though the society as a whole might veer toward the "feminine" pole. Interestingly, the more an entire society scores to the masculine side, the wider the gap between its "men's" and women's" values (see Figure 4).

A SET OF CULTURAL MAPS OF THE WORLD

Research data were obtained by comparing the beliefs and values of employees within the subsidiaries of one large multinational corporation in 40 countries around the world. These countries represent the wealthy

FIGURE 4   The Masculinity Dimension

Feminine	Masculine
Men needn't be assertive, but can also assume nurturing roles.	Men should be assertive. Women should be nurturing.
Sex roles in society are more fluid.	Sex roles in society are clearly differentiated.
There should be equality between the sexes.	Men should dominate in society.
Quality of life is important.	Performance is what counts.
You work in order to live.	You live in order to work.
People and environment are important.	Money and things are important.
Interdependence is the ideal.	Independence is the ideal.
Service provides the motivation.	Ambition provides the drive.
One sympathizes with the unfortunate.	One admires the successful achiever.
Small and slow are beautiful.	Big and fast are beautiful.
Unisex and androgyny are ideal.	Ostentatious manliness ("machismo") is appreciated.

countries of the West and the larger, more prosperous of the Third World countries. The Socialist block countries are missing; but data are available for Yugoslavia (where the corporation is represented by a local, self-managed company under Yugoslavian law). It was possible, on the basis of mean answers of employees on a number of key questions, to assign an index value to each country on each dimension. As described in the box on Research Data, these index values appear to be related in a statistically significant way to a vast amount of other data about these countries, including both research results from other samples and national indicator figures.

Because of the difficulty of representing four dimensions in a single diagram, the position of the countries of the dimensions is shown in Figures 5, 6, and 7 for two dimensions at a time. The vertical and horizontal axes and the circles around clusters of countries have been drawn subjectively, in order to show the degree of proximity of geographically or historically related countries. The three diagrams thus represent a composite set of cultural maps of the world.

Of the three "maps," those in Figure 5 (Power Distance × Uncertainty Avoidance) and Figure 7 (Masculinity × Uncertainty Avoidance) show a scattering of countries in all corners—that is, all combinations of index values occur. Figure 6 (Power Distance × Individualism), however, shows one empty corner: The combination of Small Power Distance and Collectivism does not occur. In fact, there is a tendency for Large Power Distance to be associated with Collectivism and for Small Power Distance with Individualism. However, there is a third factor that should be taken into account here: national wealth. Both Small Power Distance and Individ-

The 40 Countries—Showing Abbreviations Used in Figures 5, 6, and 7

ARG	Argentina	HOK	Hong Kong	POR	Portugal
AUL	Australia	IND	India	SAF	South Africa
AUT	Austria	IRA	Iran	SIN	Singapore
BEL	Belgium	IRE	Ireland	SPA	Spain
BRA	Brazil	ISR	Israel	SWE	Sweden
CAN	Canada	ITA	Italy	SWI	Switzerland
CHL	Chile	JAP	Japan	TAI	Taiwan
COL	Colombia	MEX	Mexico	THA	Thailand
DEN	Denmark	NET	Netherlands	TUR	Turkey
FIN	Finland	NOR	Norway	USA	United States
FRA	France	NZL	New Zealand	VEN	Venezuela
GBR	Great Britain	PAK	Pakistan	YUG	Yugoslavia
GER	Germany (West)	PER	Peru		
GRE	Greece	PHI	Philippines		

FIGURE 5   The Position of the 40 Countries on the Power Distance and
Uncertainty Avoidance Scales

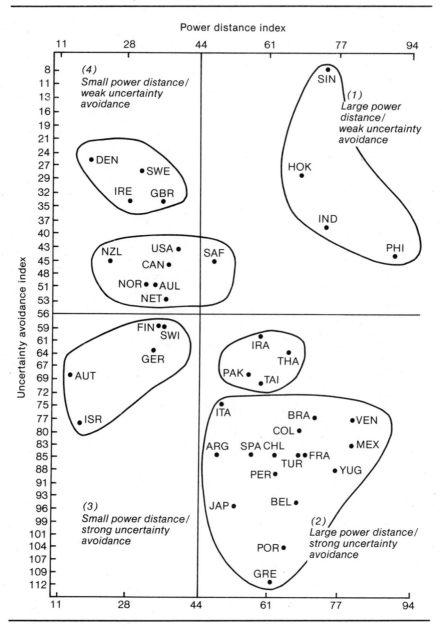

FIGURE 6   The Position of the 40 Countries on the Power Distance and
Individualism Scales

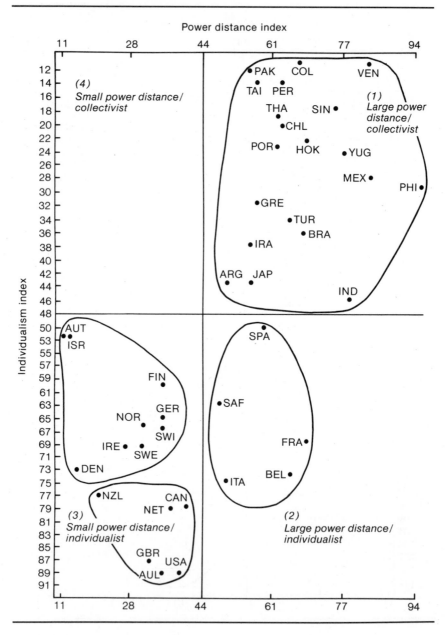

FIGURE 7 The Position of the 40 Countries on the Uncertainty Avoidance and Masculinity Scales

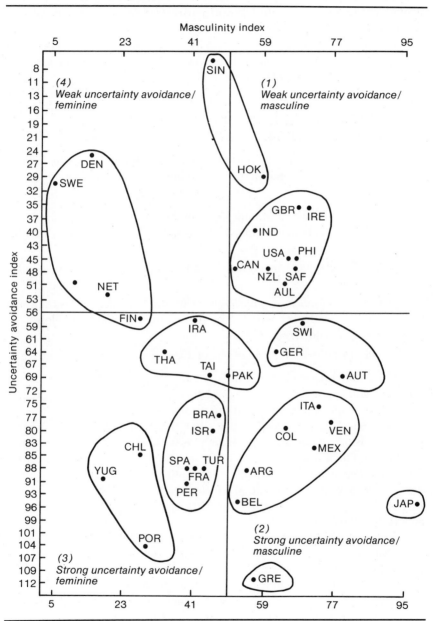

ualism go together with greater national wealth (per capita gross national product). The relationship between Individualism and Wealth is quite strong, as Figure 6 shows. In the upper part (Collectivist) we find only the poorer countries, with Japan as a borderline exception. In the lower part (Individualism), we find only the wealthier countries. If we look at the poorer and the wealthier countries separately, there is no longer any relationship between Power Distance and Individualism.

THE CULTURAL RELATIVITY
OF MANAGEMENT THEORIES

Of particular interest in the context of this discussion is the relative position of the United States on the four dimensions. Here is how the United States rates:

- On *Power Distance* at rank 15 out of the 40 countries (measured from below), it is below average but it is not as low as a number of other wealthy counties.
- On *Uncertainty Avoidance* at rank 9 out of 40, it is well below average.
- On *Individualism* at rank 40 out of 40, the United States is the single most individualist country of the entire set (followed closely by Australia and Great Britain).
- On *Masculinity* at rank 28 out of 40, it is well above average.

For about 60 years, the United States has been the world's largest producer and exporter of management theories covering such key areas as motivation, leadership, and organization. Before that, the centers of theorizing about what we now call "management" lay in the Old World. We can trace the history of management thought as far back as we want—at least to parts of the Old Testament of the Bible, and to ancient Greece (Plato's *The Laws* and *The Republic*, 350 B.C.). Sixteenth-century European "management" theorists include Niccolo Machiavelli (Italy) and Thomas More (Great Britain); early twentieth-century theorists include Max Weber (Germany) and Henry Fayol (France).

Today we are all culturally conditioned. We see the world in the way we have learned to see it. Only to a limited extent can we, in our thinking, step out of the boundaries imposed by our cultural conditioning. This applies to the author of a theory as much as it does to the ordinary citizen. Theories reflect the cultural environment in which they were written. If this is true, Italian, British, German, and French theories reflect the culture of Italy, Britain, Germany, and France of their day, and American theories reflect the culture of the United States of its day. Since most present-day theorists are middle-class intellectuals, their theories reflect a national intellectual middle-class culture background.

Now we ask the question: To what extent do theories developed in one country and reflecting the cultural boundaries of that country apply to other countries? Do American management theories apply in Japan? In India? No management theorist, to my knowledge, has ever explicitly addressed himself or herself to this issue. Most probably assume that their theories are universally valid. The availability of a conceptual framework built on four dimensions of national culture, in conjunction with the cultural maps of the world, makes it possible to see more clearly where and to what extent theories developed in one country are likely to apply elsewhere. In the remaining sections of this article I shall look from this viewpoint at most popular American theories of management in the areas of motivation, leadership, and organization.

MOTIVATION

Why do people behave as they do? There is a great variety of theories of human motivation. According to Sigmund Freud, we are impelled to act by unconscious forces within us, which he called our id. Our conscious conception of ourselves—our ego—tries to control these forces, and an equally unconscious internal pilot—our superego—criticizes the thoughts and acts of our ego and causes feelings of guilt and anxiety when the ego seems to be giving in to the id. The superego is the product of early socialization, mainly learned from our parents when we were young children.

Freud's work has been extremely influential in psychology, but he is rarely quoted in the context of management theories. The latter almost exclusively refer to motivation theories developed later in the United States, particularly those of David McClelland, Abraham Maslow, Frederick Herzberg, and Victor Vroom. According to McClelland, we perform because we have a need to achieve (the achievement motive). More recently, McClelland has also paid a lot of attention to the power motive. Maslow has postulated a hierarchy of human needs, from more "basic" to "higher": most basic are physiological needs, followed by security, social needs, esteem needs and, finally, a need for "self-actualization." The latter incorporates McClelland's theory of achievement, but is defined in broader terms. Maslow's theory of the hierarchy of needs postulates that a higher need will become active only if the lower needs are sufficiently satisfied. Our acting is basically a rational activity by which we expect to fulfill successive levels of needs. Herzberg's two-factor theory of motivation distinguishes between hygienic factors (largely corresponding to Maslow's lower needs—physiological, security, social) and motivators (Maslow's higher needs—esteem, self-actualization); the hygienic factors have only the potential to motivate negatively (demotivate—they are necessary but not sufficient conditions), while only the motivators have the potential to motivate positively. Vroom has formalized the role of "expectancy" in motivation; he opposes "expectancy" theories and "drive" theories. The former see people as being *pulled* by the expectancy of some kind of result from their acts, mostly consciously. The latter (in accordance with Freud's theories) see people as *pushed* by inside forces—often unconscious ones.

Let us now look at these theories through culture-conscious glasses. Why has Freudian thinking never become popular in U.S. management theory, as has the thinking of McClelland, Maslow, Herzberg, and Vroom? To what extent do these theories reflect different cultural patterns? Freud was part of an Austrian middle-class culture at the turn of the century. If we compare present-day Austria and the United States on our cultural maps, we find the following:

- Austria scores considerably lower on Power Distance.
- Austria scores considerably higher on Uncertainty Avoidance.
- Austria scores considerably lower on Individualism.
- Austria scores considerably higher on Masculinity.

We do not know to what extent Austrian culture has changed since Freud's time, but evidence suggests that cultural patterns change very slowly. It is, therefore, not likely to have been much different from today's culture. The most striking thing about present-day Austrian culture is that it combines a fairly high Uncertainty Avoidance with a very low Power Distance (see Figure 5). Somehow the combination of high Uncertainty Avoidance with high Power Distance is more comfortable (we find this in Japan and in all Latin and Mediterranean countries—see Figure 5). Having a powerful superior whom we can both praise and blame is one way of satisfying a strong need for avoiding uncertainty. The Austrian culture, however (together with the German, Swiss, Israeli, and Finnish cultures), cannot rely on an external boss to absorb its uncertainty. Thus, Freud's superego acts naturally as an inner uncertainty-absorbing device, an internalized boss. For strong Uncertainty Avoidance countries like Austria, working hard is caused by an inner urge—it is a way of relieving stress (see Figure 2). The Austrian superego is reinforced by the country's relatively low level of Individualism (see Figure 6). The inner feeling of obligation to society plays a much stronger role in Austria than in the United States. The ultra high Individualism of the United States leads to a need to explain every act in terms of self-interest, and expectancy theories of motivation do provide this explanation—we always do something *because* we expect to obtain the satisfaction of some need.

The comparison between Austrian and U.S. culture has so far justified the popularity of expectancy theories of motivation in the United States. The combination in the United States of weak Uncertainty Avoidance and relatively high Masculinity can tell us more about why the achievement motive has become so popular in that country. David McClelland, in his book *The Achieving Society*, sets up scores reflecting how strong achievement need is in many countries by analyzing the content of children's stories used in those countries to teach the young to read. It now appears that there is a strong relationship between McClelland's need for achievement country scores and the combination of weak Uncertainty Avoidance and strong Masculinity charted in Figure 7. (McClelland's data were collected for two historic years—1925 and 1950—but only his 1925 data relate to the cultural map in Figure 7. It is likely that the 1925 stories were more traditional, reflecting deep underlying cultural currents; the choice of stories in 1950 in most countries may have been affected by modernization currents in education, often imported from abroad.)

Countries in the upper righthand corner of Figure 7 received mostly high scores on achievement need in McClelland's book; countries in the lower lefthand corner of Figure 7 received low scores. This leads us to the conclusion that the concept of the achievement motive presupposes two cultural choices—a willingness to accept risk (equivalent to weak Uncertainty Avoidance; see Figure 2) and a concern with performance (equivalent to strong Masculinity; see Figure 4). This combination is found exclusively in countries in the Anglo-American group and in some of their former colonies (Figure 7). One striking thing about the concept of achievement is that the word itself is hardly translatable into any language other than English; for this reason, the word could not be used in the questionnaire of the multinational corporation used in my research. The English-speaking countries all appear in the upper righthand corner of Figure 7.

If this is so, there is reason to reconsider Maslow's hierarchy of human needs in the light of the map shown in Figure 7. Quadrant 1 (upper righthand corner) in Figure 7 stands for *achievement motivation*, as we have seen (performance plus risk). Quadrant 2 distinguishes itself from quadrant 1 by strong Uncertainty Avoidance, which means *security motivation* (performance plus security). The countries on the feminine side of Figure 7 distinguish themselves by a focusing on quality of life rather than on performance and on relationships between people rather than on money and things (see Figure 4). This means *social motivation*: quality of life plus security in quadrant 3, and quality of life plus risk in quadrant 4. Now, Maslow's hierarchy puts self-actualization (achievement) plus esteem above social needs above security needs. This, however, is not the description of a universal human motivation process—it is the description of a value system, the value system of the U.S. middle class to which the author belonged. I suggest that, if we want to continue thinking in terms of a hierarchy for countries in the lower righthand corner of Figure 7 (quadrant 2), security needs should rank at the top; for countries in the upper lefthand corner (quadrant 4), social needs should rank at the top; and for countries in the lower lefthand corner (quadrant 3) *both* security and social needs should rank at the top.

One practical outcome of presenting motivation theories is the movement toward humanization of work—an attempt to make work more intrinsically interesting to the workers. There are two main currents in humanization of work—one, developed in the United States and called *job enrichment*, aims at restructuring individual jobs. A chief proponent of job enrichment is Frederick Herzberg. The other current, developed in Europe and applied mainly in Sweden and Norway, aims at restructuring work into group work—forming, for example, such semiautonomous teams as those seen in the experiments at Volvo. Why the difference in approaches? What is seen as a "human" job depends on a society's prevailing model of humankind. In a more masculine society like the United States, humanization takes the form of masculinization, allowing individual performance. In the more feminine societies of Sweden and Norway, humanization takes the form of femininization—it is a means toward more wholesome interpersonal relationships in its deemphasis of interindividual competition.

LEADERSHIP

One of the oldest theorists of leadership in world literature is Machiavelli (1468–1527). He described certain effective techniques for manipulation and remaining in power (including deceit, bribery, and murder) that gave him a bad reputation in later centuries. Machiavelli wrote in the context of the Italy of his day, and what he described is clearly a large Power Distance situation. We still find Italy on the larger Power Distance side of Figure 5 (with all other Latin and Mediterranean countries), and we can assume from historical evidence that Power Distances in Italy during the sixteenth century were considerably larger than they are now. When we compare Machiavelli's work with that of his contemporary, Sir Thomas More (1478–1535), we find cultural differences between ways of thinking in different countries even in the sixteenth century. The British More described in *Utopia* a state based on consensus as a "model" to criticize the political situation of his day. But practice did not always follow theory, of course: More, deemed too critical, was beheaded by order of King Henry VIII, while Machiavelli the realist managed to die peacefully in his bed. The difference in theories is nonetheless remarkable.

In the United States a current of leardership theories has developed. Some of the best known were put forth by the late Douglas McGregor (Theory X versus Theory Y), Rensis Likert (System 4 management), and Robert R. Blake with Jane S. Mouton (the Managerial Grid ®). What these theories have in common is that they all advocate participation in the manager's decisions by his or her subordinates (participative management); however, the initiative toward participation is supposed to be taken by the manager. In a worldwide perspective (Figure 5), we can understand these theories from the middle position of the United States on the Power Distance side (rank 15 out of 40 countries). Had the culture been one of larger Power Distance, we could have expected more "Machiavellian" theories of leadership. In fact, in the management literature of another country with a larger Power Distance index score, France, there is little concern with participative management American style, but great concern with who has the power. However, in countries with smaller Power Distances than the United States (Sweden, Norway, Germany, Israel), there is considerable sympathy for models of management in which even the initiatives are taken by the subordinates (forms of industrial democracy) and with which there's little sympathy in the United States. In the approaches toward "industrial democracy" taken in these countries, we notice their differences on the second dimension, Uncertainty Avoidance. In weak Uncertainty Avoidance countries like Sweden, industrial democracy was started in the form of local experiments and only later was given a legislative framework. In strong Uncertainty Avoidance countries like Germany, industrial democracy was brought about by legislation first and then had to be brought alive in the organizations ("Mitbestimmung").

The crucial fact about leadership in any culture is that it is a complement to subordinateship. The Power Distance Index scores in Figure 5 are, in fact, based on the values of people as *subordinates*, not on the values of superiors. (Whatever a naïve literature on leadership may give us to understand, leaders cannot choose their styles at will; what is feasible depends to a large extent on the cultural conditioning of a leader's subordinates. Along these lines, Figure 8 describes the type of subordinateship that, other things being equal, a leader can expect to meet in societies at three different levels of Power Distance—subordinateship to which a leader must respond. The middle level represents what is most likely found in the United States.

Neither McGregor, nor Likert, nor Blake and Mouton allow for this type of cultural proviso—all three tend to be prescriptive with regard to a leadership style that, at best, will work with U.S. subordinates and with those in cultures—such as Canada or Australia—that have not too different Power Distance levels (Figure 5). In fact, my research shows that subordinates in larger Power Distance countries tend to agree more frequently with Theory X.

A U.S. theory of leadership that allows for a certain amount of cultural relativity, although indirectly, is Fred Fiedler's contingency theory of leadership. Fiedler states that different leader personalities are needed for "difficult" and "easy" situations, and that a cultural gap between superior and subordinates is one of the factors that makes a situation "difficult." However, this theory does not address the kind of cultural gap in question.

In practice, the adaptation of managers to higher Power Distance environments does not seem to present too many problems. Although this is an unpopular message—one seldom professed in management development

FIGURE 8   Subordinateship for Three Levels of Power Distance

Small Power Distance	Medium Power Distance (United States)	Large Power Distance
Subordinates have weak dependence needs.	Subordinates have medium dependence needs.	Subordinates have strong dependence needs.
Superiors have weak dependence needs toward their superiors.	Superiors have medium dependence needs toward their superiors.	Superiors have strong dependence needs toward their superiors.
Subordinates expect superiors to consult them and may rebel or strike if superiors are not seen as staying within their legitimate role.	Subordinates expect superiors to consult them but will accept autocratic behavior as well.	Subordinates expect superiors to act autocratically.
Ideal superior to most is a loyal democrat.	Ideal superior to most is a resourceful democrat.	Ideal superior to most is a benevolent autocrat or paternalist.
Laws and rules apply to all and privileges for superiors are not considered acceptable.	Laws and rules apply to all, but a certain level of privileges for superiors is considered normal.	Everybody expects superiors to enjoy privileges; laws and rules differ for superiors and subordinates.
Status symbols are frowned upon and will easily come under attack from subordinates.	Status symbols for superiors contribute moderately to their authority and will be accepted by subordinates.	Status symbols are very important and contribute strongly to the superior's authority with the subordinates.

courses—managers moving to a larger Power Distance culture soon learn that they have to behave more autocractically in order to be effective, and tend to do so; this is borne out by the colonial history of more Western countries. But is is interesting that the Western ex-colonial power with the highest Power Distance norm—France—seems to be most appreciated by its former colonies and seems to maintain the best postcolonial relationships with most of them. This suggests that subordinates in a large Power Distance culture feel even more comfortable with superiors who are real autocrats than with those whose assumed autocratic stance is out of national character.

The operation of a manager in an environment with a Power Distance norm lower than his or her own is more problematic. U.S. managers tend to find it difficult to collaborate wholeheartedly in the "industrial democracy" processes of such countries as Sweden, Germany, and even the Netherlands. U.S. citizens tend to consider their country as the example of democracy, and find it difficult to accept that other countries might wish to develop forms of democracy for which they feel no need and that make major inroads upon managers' (or leaders') prerogatives. However, the very idea of management prerogatives is not accepted in very low Power Distance countries. This is, perhaps, best illustrated by a remark a Scandinavian social scientist is supposed to have made to Herzberg in a seminar: "You are against participation for the very reason we are in favor of it—one doesn't know where it will stop. We think that is good."

One way in which the U.S. approach to leadership has been packaged and formalized is management by objectives (MBO), first advocated by Peter Drucker in 1955 in *The Practice of Management*. In the United States, MBO has been used to spread a pragmatic results orientation throughout the organization. It has been considerably more successful where results are objectively measurable than where they can only be interpreted subjectively, and, even in the United States, it has been criticized heavily. Still, it has been perhaps the single most popular management technique "made in U.S.A." Therefore, it can be accepted as fitting U.S. culture. MBO presupposes:

- That subordinates are sufficiently independent to negotiate meaningfully with the boss (not-too-large Power Distance).
- That both are willing to take risks (weak Uncertainty Avoidance).
- That performance is seen as important by both (high Masculinity).

Let us now take the case of Germany, a below-average Power Distance country. Here, the dialogue element in MBO should present no problem. However, since Germany scores considerably higher on Uncertainty Avoidance, the tendency toward accepting risk and ambiguity will not exist to the same extent. The idea of replacing the arbitrary authority of the boss with the impersonal authority of mutually agreed-upon objectives, however, fits the small Power Distance/strong Uncertainty Avoidance cultural cluster very well. The objectives become the subordinates' "superego." In a book of case studies about MBO in Germany, Ian R. G. Ferguson states that "MBO has acquired a different flavor in the German-speaking area, not least because in these countries the societal and political pressure towards increasing the value of man in the organization on the right to codetermination has become quite clear. Thence, MBO has been transliterated into Management by Joint Goal Setting (Führung durch Zielvereinbarung)." Ferguson's view of MBO fits the ideological needs of the German-speaking countries of the moment. The case studies in his book show elaborate formal systems with extensive ideological justification; the stress on *team* objectives is quite strong, which is in line with the lower individualism in these countries.

The other area in which specific information on MBO is available is France. MBO was first introduced in France in the early 1960s, but it became extremely popular for a time after the 1968 student revolt. People expected that this new technique would lead to the long–overdue democratization of organizations. Instead of DPO (Direction par Objectifs), the French name for MBO become DPPO (Direction *Participative* par Objectifs). So in France, too, societal developments affected the MBO system. However, DPPO remained, in general, as much a vain slogan as did Liberté, Egalité, Fraternité (Freedom, Equality, Brotherhood) after the 1789 revolt. G. Franck wrote, in 1973, ". . . I think that the career of DPPO is terminated, or rather that it has never started, and it won't ever start as long as we continue in France our tendency to confound ideology and reality. . . ." In a postscript to Franck's article, the editors of *Le Management* write: "French blue- and white-collar workers, lower-level and higher-level managers, and 'patrons' all belong to the same cultural system which maintains dependency relations from level to level. Only the deviants really dislike this system. The hierarchical structure protects against anxiety; DPO, however, generates anxiety. . . ." The reason for the anxiety in the French cultural context is that MBO presupposes a depersonalized authority in the form of internalized objectives; but French people, from their early childhood onward, are accustomed to large Power Distances, to an authority that is highly personalized. And in spite of all attempts to introduce Anglo-Saxon management methods, French superiors do not easily decentralize and do not stop short-circuiting intermediate hierarchical levels, nor do French subordinates expect them to. The developments of the 1970s have severely discredited DPPO, which probably does injustice to the cases in which individual French organizations or units, starting from less exaggerated expectations, have benefited from it.

In the examples used thus far in this section, the cultural context of leadership may look rather obvious to the reader. But it also works in more subtle, less obvious ways. Here's an example from the area of management decision making: A prestigious U.S. consulting firm was asked to analyze the decision-making processes in a large Scandinavian "XYZ" corporation. Their report criticized the corporation's decision-making style, which they characterized as being, among other things, "intuitive" and "consensus based." They compared "observations of traditional XYZ practices" with "selected examples of practices in other companies." These "selected examples," offered as a model, were evidently taken from their U.S. clients and reflect the U.S. textbook norm—"fact based" rather than intuitive management, and "fast decisions based on clear responsibilities" rather than the use of informal, personal contacts and the concern for consensus.

Is this consulting firm doing its Scandinavian clients a service? It follows from Figure 7 that where the United States and the Scandinavian culture are wide apart is on the Masculinity dimension. The use of intuition and the concern for consensus in Scandinavia are "feminine" characteristics of the culture, well embedded in the total texture of these societies. Stressing "facts" and "clear responsibilities" fits the "masculine" U.S. culture. From a neutral viewpoint, the reasons for criticizing the U.S. decision-making style are as good as those for criticizing the Scandinavian style. In complex decision-making situations, "facts" no longer exist independently from the people who define them, so "fact-based management" becomes a misleading slogan. Intuition may not be a bad method of deciding in such cases at all. And if the implementation of decisions requires the commitment of many people, even a consensus process that takes more time is an asset rather than a liability. But the essential element overlooked by the consultant is that decisions have to be made in a way that corresponds to the values of the environment in which they have to be effective. People in this consulting firm lacked insight into their own cultural biases. This does not mean that the Scandinavian corporation's management need not improve its decision making and could not learn from the consultant's experience. But this can be done only through a mutual recognition of cultural differences, not by ignoring them.

ORGANIZATION

The Power Distance × Uncertainty Avoidance map (Figure 5) is of vital importance for structuring organizations that will work best in different countries. For example, one U.S.-based multinational corporation has a worldwide policy that salary-increase proposals should be initiated by the employee's direct superior. However, the French management of its French subsidiary interpreted this policy in such a way that the superior's superior's superior—three levels above—was the one to initiate salary proposals. This way of working was regarded as quite natural by both superiors and subordinates in France. Other factors being equal, people in large Power Distance cultures prefer that decisions be centralized because even superiors have strong dependency needs in relation to their superiors; this tends to move decisions up as far as they can go (see Figure 8). People in small Power Distance cultures want decisions to be decentralized.

While Power Distance relates to centralization, Uncertainty Avoidance relates to formalization—the need for formal rules and specialization, the assignment of tasks to experts. My former colleague O. J. Stevens at INSEAD has done an interesting research project (as yet unpublished) with M.B.A. students from Germany, Great Britain, and France. He asked them to write their own diagnosis and solution for a small case study of an organizational problem—a conflict in one company between the sales and product development departments. The majority of the French referred the problem to the next higher authority (the president of the company); the Germans attributed it to the lack of a written policy, and proposed establishing one; the British attributed it to a lack of interpersonal communication, to be cured by some kind of group training.

Stevens concludes that the "implicit model" of the organization for most' French was a pyramid (both centralized and formal); for most Germans, a well-oiled machine (formalized but not centralized); and for most British, a village market (neither formalized nor centralized). This covers three quadrants (2, 3, and 4) in Figure 5. What is missing is an "implicit model" for quadrant 1, which contains four Asian countries, including India. A discussion with an Indian colleague leads me to place the family (centralized, but not formalized) in this quadrant as the "implicit model" of the organization. In fact, Indian organizations tend to be formalized as far as relationships between people go (this is related to Power Distance), but not as far as workflow goes (this is Uncertainty Avoidance).

The "well-oiled machine" model for Germany reminds us of the fact that Max Weber, author of the first theory of bureaucracy, was a German. Weber pictures bureaucracy as a highly formalized system (strong Uncertainty Avoidance), in which, however, the rules protect the lower-ranking members against abuse of power by their superiors. The superiors have no power by themselves, only the power that their bureaucratic roles have given them as incumbents of the roles—the power is in the role, not in the person (small Power Distance).

The United States is found fairly close to the center of the map in Figure 5, taking an intermediate position between the "pyramid," "machine," and "market" implicit models—a position that may help explain the success of U.S. business operations in very different cultures. However, according to the common U.S. conception of organization, we might say that *hierarchy is not a goal by itself* (as it is in France) and that *rules are not a goal by themselves*. Both are means toward obtaining results, to be changed if needed. A breaking away from hierarchic and bureaucratic traditions is found in the development toward matrix organizations and similar temporary or flexible organization systems.

Another INSEAD colleague, André Laurent, has shown that French managers strongly disbelieve in the feasibility of matrix organizations, because they see them as violating the "holy" principle of unit of command. However, in the French subsidiary of a multinational corporation that has a long history of successful matrix management, the French managers were quite positive toward it; obviously, then, cultural barriers to organizational innovation can be overcome. German managers are not too favorably disposed toward matrix organizations, either, feeling that they tend to frustrate their need for organizational clarity. This means that matrix organizations will be accepted *if* the roles of individuals within the organization can be defined without ambiguity.

The extreme position of the United States on the Individualism scale leads to other potential conflicts between the U.S. way of thinking about organizations and the values dominant in other parts of the world. In the U.S. Individualist conception, the relationship between the individual and the organization is essentially calculative, being based on enlightened self-interest. In fact, there is a strong historical and cultural link between Individualism and Capitalism. The capitalist system—based on self-interest and the market mechanism—was "invented" in Great Britain, which is still among the top three most Individualist countries in the world. In more Collectivist societies, however, the link between individuals and their traditional organizations is not calculative, but moral: It is based not on self-interest but on the individual's loyalty toward the clan, organization, or society—which is supposedly the best guarantee of that individual's ultimate interest. "Collectivism" is a bad word in the United States, but "individualism" is as much a bad word in the writings of Mao Tse-tung, who writes from a strongly Collectivist cultural tradition (see Figure 6 for the Collectivist scores of the Chinese majority countries Taiwan, Hong Kong, and Singapore). This means that U.S. organizations may get themselves into considerable trouble in more Collectivist environments if they do not recognize their local employees' needs for ties of mutual loyalty between company and employee. ("Hire and fire" is very ill perceived in these countries, if firing isn't prohibited by law altogether.) Given the value position of people in more Collectivist cultures, it should not be seen as surprising if they prefer other types of economic order to capitalism—if capitalism cannot get rid of its Individualist image.

CONSEQUENCES FOR POLICY

So far we have seriously questioned the universal validity of management theories developed in one country—in most instances here, the United States.

On a practical level, this has the least consequence for organizations operating entirely within the country in which the theories were born. As long as the theories apply within the United States, U.S. organizations can base their policies for motivating employees, leadership, and organization development on these policies. Still, some caution is due. If differences in environmental culture can be shown to exist between countries, and if these constrain the validity of management theories, what about the subcultures and countercultures within the country? To what extent do the familiar theories apply when the organization employs people for whom the theories were not, in the first instance, conceived—such as members of minority groups with a different educational level, or belonging to a different generation? If culture matters, an organization's policies can lose their effectiveness when its cultural environment changes.

No doubt, however, the consequences of the cultural relativity of management theories are more serious for the multinational organization.

The cultural maps in Figures 5, 6, and 7 can help predict the kind of culture difference between subsidiaries and mother company that will need to be met. An important implication is that identical personnel policies may have very different effects in different countries—and within countries for different subgroups of employees. This is not only a matter of different employee values; there are also, of course, differences in government policies and legislation (which usually reflect quite clearly the country's different cultural position). And there are differences in labor market situations and labor union power positions. These differences—tangible as well as intangible— may have consequences for performance, attention to quality, cost, labor turnover, and absenteeism. Typical universal policies that may work out quite differently in different countries are those dealing with financial incentives, promotion paths, and grievance channels.

The dilemma for the organization operating abroad is whether to adapt to the local culture or try to change it. There are examples of companies that have successfully changed local habits, such as in the earlier mention of the introduction of matrix organization in France. Many Third World countries want to transfer new technologies from more economically advanced countries. If they are to work at all, these technologies must presuppose values that may run counter to local traditions, such as a certain discretion of subordinates toward superiors (lower Power Distance) or of individuals toward in-groups (more Individualism). In such a case, the local culture has to be changed; this is a difficult task that should not be taken lightly. Since it calls for a conscious strategy based on insight into the local culture, it's logical to involve acculturated locals in strategy formulations. Often, the original policy will have to be adapted to fit local culture and lead to the desired effect. We saw earlier how, in the case of MBO, this has succeeded in Germany but generally failed in France.

A final area in which the cultural boundaries of home-country management theories are important is the training of managers for assignments abroad. For managers who have to operate in an unfamiliar culture, training based on home-country theories is of very limited use and may even do more harm than good. Of more importance is a thorough familiarization with the other culture, for which the organization can use the services of specialized cross-cultural training institutes—or it can develop its own program by using host-country personnel as teachers.

SELECTED BIBLIOGRAPHY

The first U.S. book about the cultural relativity of U.S. management theories is still to be written, I believe—which lack in itself indicates how difficult it is to recognize one's own cultural biases. One of the few U.S. books describing the process of cultural conditioning for a management readership is Edward T. Hall's *The silent language* (Fawcett, 1959, but reprinted since). Good reading also is Hall's article "The silent language in overseas business" (*Harvard Business Review*, May–June 1960). Hall is an anthropologist and, therefore, a specialist in the study of culture. Very readable on the same subject are two books by the British anthropologist Mary Douglas, *Natural symbols: Exploration in cosmology* (Vintage, 1973) and the reader *Rules and meanings: The anthropology of everyday knowledge* (Penguin, 1973). Another excellent reader is Theodore D. Weinshall's *Culture and management* (Penguin, 1977).

On the concept of national character, some well-written professional literature is Margaret Mead's "National character," in the reader by Sol Tax, *Anthropology today* (University of Chicago Press, 1962), and Alex Inkeles and D. J. Levinson's, "National character," in Lindzey and Aronson's *Handbook of social psychology*, second edition, volume 4, (Addison-Wesley, 1969). Critique on the implicit claims of universal validity of management theories comes from some foreign authors: An important article is Michel Brossard and Marc Maurice's "Is there a universal model of organization structure?" (*International Studies of Management and Organization*, Fall 1976). This journal is a journal of translations from non-American literature, based in New York, that often contains important articles on management issues by non-U.S. authors that take issue with the dominant theories. Another article is Gunnar Hjelholt's "Europe Is different," in Geert Hofstede and M. Sami Kassem's reader, *European contributions to organization theory* (Assen Netherlands: Von Gorcum, 1976).

Some other references of interest: Ian R. G. Ferguson's *Management by objectives in Deutschland*, (Herder and Herder, 1973) (in German); G. Franck's "Epitaphe pour la DPO," in *Le Management*, November 1973 (in French); and D. Jenkin's *Blue- and white-collar democracy*, (Doubleday, 1973).

Note: Details of Geert Hofstede's study of national cultures have been published in his book, *Culture's consequences: International differences in work-related values* (Beverly Hills: Sage Publications, 1980).

Part B   Interventions

INTRODUCTION

Having considered some of the more influential theoretical notions pertaining to the motivation of work behavior, we turn now to reflections on the sorts of programs used by organizations to harness individual motives to the goal of organizational effectiveness.

The article by Schuler and Jackson makes a strong case for the design of human resource management programs that fit a firm's competitive strategy. First, of course, top management must know what its strategy is. That strategy, in turn, determines the mix of role behaviors required of rank-and-file participants. Finally, to elicit those role behaviors demands a careful, deliberate, and internally consistent system of interventions in the form of compensation systems, job descriptions, promotion practices, management decision-making styles, and employee socialization. Schuler and Jackson illustrate in detail how strategies of innovation, quality enhancement, and cost reduction call for correspondingly different interventions via human resource management programs.

Lawrence Miller, a consultant who helps organizations design programs of employee behavior modification, provides a brief sketch of the essential steps in such programs. Behavior modification represents a practical application of operant concepts and methods, as developed and described in the writings of psychologist B. F. Skinner and the work of other "neo-behaviorist" psychologists. The techniques of behavior modification do not presuppose any particular classes of "motives" or other internal psychological states. Rather, they provide a straightforward self-correcting method of arranging the immediate antecedents and consequences of specific behaviors so as to strengthen those behaviors.

For most organizations, wage and salary programs continue to serve—for better or worse—as the primary source of employee motivation. The 1980s witnessed a renewed emphasis on the motivational potentialities of pay, along with vigorous efforts to experiment with variations on traditional methods of compensation. Feldman and Arnold describe five types of innovations in pay programs that became increasingly widespread by the end of the 1980s and showed every sign of continued expansion into the 1990s. Corey Rosen describes yet another compensation program—employee stock ownership plans, or ESOPs—that has become increasingly popular. The reader should know, however, that such plans have recently become controversial because of numerous instances in which they were used for reasons (i.e., to finance leveraged buyouts) not originally intended; we should certainly anticipate that some of the abuses of these programs will lead to modifications of some of the legal and financial aspects noted in Rosen's paper.

Our selections on organizational interventions appropriately concludes with an article by Staw that cautions us to rein in our expectations. Staw reviews evidence indicating that individual job satisfaction and individual job productivity are "sticky variables" that often fail to yield to the more popular forms of work motivation programs. He does not argue against interventions, but he explains why the improvement of work attitudes and performance requires *systems* of internally consistent programs—and, even then, we should not expect massive changes that can be sustained. Straw describes three philosophically different types of systems from which to choose.

11

Linking Competitive Strategies with Human Resource Management Practices*

Randall S. Schuler

Susan E. Jackson

Over the past several years there has been increased recognition that there is a need to match the characteristics of top managers with the nature of the business. According to Reginald H. Jones, former chairman and CEO of the General Electric Company:

> When we classified . . . [our] . . . businesses, and when we realized that they were going to have quite different missions, we also realized we had to have quite different people running them.[1]

Within academia there has been similar growing awareness of this need. Although this awareness is being articulated in several ways, one of the most frequent involves the conceptualization and investigation of the relationship between business strategy and the personal characteristics of top management.[2] Here, particular manager characteristics such as personality, skills, abilities, values, and perspectives are matched with particular types of business strategies. For example, a recently released study conducted by Hay Group Incorporated, in conjunction with the University of Michigan and the Strategic Planning Institute, reports that when a business is pursuing a growth strategy it needs top managers who are likely to abandon the status quo and adapt their strategies and goals to the marketplace. According to the study, insiders are slow to recognize the onset of decline and tend to persevere in strategies that are no longer effective; so, top managers need to be recruited from the outside.

Recruiting outsiders as part of strategy has been successful for Stroh Brewing Company, once a small, family-run brewery in Detroit. Some 20

* From Randall S. Schuler and Susan E. Jackson, *The Academy of Management Executive* (1987) *1*, no. 3, 207–19.

percent of its senior management team of 25 executives, including President Roger T. Fridholm, have been brought into Stroh since 1978. They've been instrumental in transforming it into the third-largest U.S. brewery.[3]

The result of such human resource staffing practices has been rather significant: Growth companies that staffed 20 percent of their top three levels with outsiders exceeded their expected return on investment by 10 percent. Those that relied on inside talent fell short of their goals by 20 percent. The same holds true for companies in declining industries: Companies with outsiders in one out of every five top managements jobs exceeded expected returns by 20 percent; those with a low proportion of outsiders fell 5 percent short.[4]

Outsiders, of course, are not always helpful. When a business is pursuing a mature strategy, what is needed is a stable group of insiders who know the intricacies of the business.

The results of the Hay study suggest that the staffing practices of top management be tied to the nature of the business because different aspects of business demand different behaviors from the individuals running them. The implication, then, is that selecting the right top manager is an important staffing decision.

Another perspective holds that top managers are capable of exhibiting a wide range of behavior, and all that is needed is to match compensation and performance appraisal practices with the nature of the business. Peter Drucker, commenting on the relationship between compensation and a strategy of innovation, observed that:

> I myself made this mistake [thinking that you can truly innovate within the existing operating unit] 30 years ago when I was a consultant on the first major organizational change in American history, the General Electric reorganization of the early 1950s. I advised top management, and they accepted it, that the general managers would be responsible for current operations as well as for managing tomorrow. At the same time, we worked out one of the first systematic compensation plans, and the whole idea of paying people on the basis of their performance in the preceding year came out of that.
>
> The result of it was that for 10 years General Electric totally lost its capacity to innovate, simply because tomorrow produces costs for 10 years and no return. So, the general manager—not only out of concern for himself but also out of concern for his group—postponed spending any money for innovation. It was only when the company dropped this compensation plan and at the same time organized the search for the truly new, not just for improvement outside the existing business, that GE recovered its innovative capacity, and brilliantly. Many companies go after this new and slight today and soon find they have neither.[5]

Similar results illustrating the power of performance appraisal and compensation to affect individual behavior have been reported in the areas of reinforcement, behavior modification, and motivation theories.[6] However, while there has been much written on matching the behavior of top managers with the nature of the business, less attention has been given to the other employees in the organization. Nevertheless, it seemed reasonable to assume that the rest of the work force would also have to be managed differently, depending on the business. This, then, became our focus of attention.

A critical choice we had to make in our study concerned which aspects of the business we were going to use. Consistent with previous studies, we decided to use the general notion of organizational strategy.[7] On the basis of previous studies that looked at strategy and human resource practices, we decided to adapt Porter's framework of competitive strategy.[8] Using the competitive strategy framework, we developed three archetypes of competitive strategy—PHRM practices combinations. These were derived from the literature, secondary sources, and our previous research. We then examined each of the three archetypes in depth, using additional secondary data and field results, and addressed issues regarding implementation and revision of the archetypes. All are presented in this article.

First, we shall review the nature and importance of competitive strategy, and then we shall describe the concept of needed role behavior that enabled us to link competitive strategies and HRM practices.

COMPETITIVE STRATEGIES

Crucial to a firm's growth and prosperity is the ability to gain and retain competitive advantage. One way to do this is through strategic initiative. MacMillan defines "strategic initiative" as the ability to capture control of strategic behavior in the industries in which a firm competes.[9] To the extent one company gains the initiative, competitors are obliged to respond and thereby play a *reactive* rather than proactive role. MacMillan argues that firms that gain a strategic advantage control their own destinies. To the extent a firm gains an advantage difficult for competitors to remove, it stays in control longer and therefore should be more effective.

The concept of competitive advantage is described by Porter as the essense of competitive strategy.[10] Emerging from his discussion are three competitive strategies that organizations can use to gain competitive advantage: innovation, quality enhancement, and cost reduction. The *innovation strategy* is used to develop products or services different from those of competitors; the primary focus here is on offering something new and different. Enhancing product and/or service quality is the primary focus of the *quality enhancement strategy*. In the *cost reduction strategy*, firms typically attempt to gain competitive advantage by being the lowest cost producer. Although we shall describe these three competitive strategies as pure types applied to single business units or even single plants or functional areas, some overlap can occur. That is, it is plausible to find business units, plants, or functional areas pursuing two or more competitive strategies simultaneously. This, and how to manage it, are discussed later.

COMPETITIVE STRATEGY:
NEEDED ROLE BEHAVIORS

Before developing a linkage between competitive strategy and HRM practices, there must be a *rationale* for that linkage. This rationale gives us a basis for predicting, studying, refining, and modifying both strategy and practices in specific circumstances.

Consistent with previous research, the rationale developed is based on what is needed from employees apart from the specific technical skills, knowledges, and abilities (SKAs) required to perform a specific task.[11] Rather than thinking about task-specific SKAs, then, it is more useful to think about what is needed from an employee who works with other employees in a social environment.[12] These needed employee behaviors are actually best thought of as needed role behaviors.[13] The importance of roles and their potential dysfunction in organizations, particularly role conflict and ambiguity, is well documented.[14]

Based on an extensive review of the literature and secondary data, several role behaviors are assumed to be instrumental in the implementation of the competitive strategies. Exhibit 1 shows several dimensions along which employees' role behaviors can vary. The dimensions shown are the ones for which there are likely to be major differences across competitive strategies. This can be illustrated by describing the various competitive strategies and their necessary organizational conditions in more detail, along with the needed role behaviors from the employees.

Innovation Strategy and Needed Role Behaviors

Because the imperative for an organization pursuing an innovation strategy is to be the most unique producer, conditions for innovation must be created. These conditions can be rather varied. They can be created either formally through official corporate policy or more informally. According to Rosabeth Moss Kanter:

> Innovation [and new venture development] may originate as a deliberate and official decision of the highest levels of management or there may be the more-or-less "spontaneous" creation of mid-level people who take the initiative to solve a problem in new ways or to develop a proposal for change. Of course, highly successful companies allow both, and even official top management decisions to undertake a development effort benefit from the spontaneous creativity of those below.[15]

To encourage as many employees as possible to be innovative, 3M has developed an informal doctrine of allowing employees to "bootleg" 15 percent of their time on their own projects. A less systematic approach to innovation is encouraging employees to offer suggestions for new and improved ways of doing their own job or manufacturing products.

EXHIBIT 1 Employee Role Behaviors for Competitive Strategies

1. Highly repetitive, predictable behavior ——— Highly creative, innovative behavior
2. Very short-term focus ——— Very long-term behavior
3. Highly cooperative, interdependent behavior ——— Highly independent, autonomous behavior
4. Very low concern for quality ——— Very high concern for quality
5. Very low concern for quantity ——— Very high concern for quantity
6. Very low risk taking ——— Very high risk taking
7. Very high concern for process ——— Very high concern for results
8. High preference to avoid responsibility ——— High preference to assume responsibility
9. Very inflexible to change ——— Very flexible to change
10. Very comfortable with stability ——— Very tolerant of ambiguity and unpredictability
11. Narrow skill application ——— Broad skill application
12. Low job (firm) involvement ——— High job (firm) involvement

Adapted from R. S. Schuler, "Human resource management practice choices," in *Readings in personnel and human resource management*, 3rd ed., ed. R. S. Schuler, S. A. Youngblood, and V. L. Huber, (St. Paul Minn.: West Publishing, 1988).

Overall, then, for firms pursuing a competitive strategy of innovation, the profile of employee role behaviors includes (1) a high degree of creative behavior, (2) a longer-term focus, (3) a relatively high level of cooperative, interdependent behavior, (4) a moderate degree of concern for quality, (5) a moderate concern for quantity, (6) an equal degree of concern for process and results, (7) a greater degree of risk taking, and (8) a high tolerance of ambiguity and unpredictability.[16]

The implications of pursuing a competitive strategy of innovation for managing people may include selecting highly skilled individuals, giving employees more discretion, using miminal controls, making a greater investment in human resources, providing more resources for experimentation, allowing and even rewarding occasional failure, and appraising performance for its long-run implications. As a consequence of these conditions, pursuing an innovation strategy may result in feelings of enhanced personal control and morale, and thus a greater commitment to self and profession rather than to the employing organization. Nevertheless, benefits may accrue to the firm as well as the employee, as evidenced by the success of such innovative firms as Hewlett-Packard, the Raytheon Corporation, 3M, Johnson & Johnson, and PepsiCo.

Thus, the innovation strategy has significant implications for human resource management. Rather than emphasizing managing people so they work *harder* (cost-reduction strategy) or *smarter* (quality strategy) on the same products or services, the innovation strategy requires people to work *differently*. This, then, is the necessary ingredient. [17]

Quality-Enhancement Strategy and Needed Role Behaviors

At Xerox, CEO David Kearns defines quality as "being right the first time every time." The implications for managing people are significant. According to James Houghton, chairman of Corning Glass Works, his company's "total quality approach" is about people. At Corning, good ideas for product improvement often come from employees, and in order to carry through on their ideas Corning workers form short-lived "corrective action teams" to solve specific problems.

> Employees [also] give their supervisors written "method improvement requests," which differ from ideas tossed into the traditional suggestion box in that they get a prompt formal review so the employees aren't left wondering about their fate. In the company's Erwin Ceramics plant, a maintenance employee suggested substituting one flexible tin mold for an array of fixed molds that shape the wet ceramic product baked into catalytic converters for auto exhausts.[18]

At Corning, then, quality improvement involves getting employees committed to quality and continual improvement. While policy statements emphasizing the "total quality approach" are valuable, they are also followed up with specific human resources practices: feedback systems are in place, teamwork is permitted and facilitated, decision making and responsibility are a part of each employee's job description, and job classifications are flexible.

Quality improvement often means changing the processes of production in ways that require workers to be more involved and more flexible. As jobs change, so must job classification systems. At Brunswick's Mercury Marine division, the number of job classifications was reduced from 126 to 12. This has permitted greater flexibility in the use of production processes and employees. Machine operators have gained greater opportunities to learn new skills. They inspect their own work and do preventive maintenance in addition to running the machines.[19] It is because of human resource practices such as these that employees become committed to the firm and hence, willing to give more. Not only is the level of quality likely to improve under these conditions, but sheer volume of output is likely to increase as well. For example, in pursuing a competitive strategy involving quality improvement. L.L. Bean's sales have increased tenfold while the number of permanent employees has grown only fivefold.[20]

The profile of employee behaviors necessary for firms pursuing a strategy of quality enhancement is (1) relatively repetitive and predictable behaviors, (2) a more long-term or intermediate focus, (3) a modest amount of cooperative, interdependent behavior (4) a high concern for quality, (5) a modest concern for quantity of output, (6) high concern for process (*how* the goods or services are made or delivered, (7) low risk-taking activity, and (8) commitment to the goals of the organization.

Because quality enhancement typically involves greater employee commitment and utilization, fewer employees are needed to produce the same level of output. As quality rises, so does demand, yet this demand can be met with proportionately fewer employees than previously. Thanks to automation and a cooperative workforce, Toyota is producing about 3.5 million vehicles a year with 25,000 production workers—about the same number as in 1966 when it was producing one million vehicles. In addition to having more productive workers, fewer are needed to repair the rejects caused by poor quality. This phenomenon has also occurred at Corning Glass, Honda, and L.L. Bean.

Cost-Reduction Strategy and Needed Role Behaviors

Often, the characteristics of a firm pursuing the cost-reduction strategy are tight controls, overhead minimization, and pursuit of economies of scale. The primary focus of these measures is to increase productivity, that is, output cost per person. This can mean a reduction in the number of employees and/or a reduction in wage levels. Since 1980, the textile industry's labor force decreased by 17 percent, primary metals, almost 30 percent, and steel, 40 percent. The result has been that, over the past four years, productivity growth in manufacturing has averaged 4.1 percent per year, versus 1.2 percent for the rest of the economy.[21] Similar measures have been taken at Chrysler and Ford and now are being proposed at GM and AT&T. Reflecting on these trends, Federal Reserve Governor Wayne D. Angell states, "We are invigorating the manufacturing sector. The period of adjustment has made us more competitive."[22]

In addition to reducing the number of employees, firms are also reducing wage levels. For example, in the household appliance industry where GE, Whirlpool, Electrolux, and Maytag account for 80 percent of all production, labor costs have been cut by shifting plants from states where labor is expensive to less costly sites. The result of this is that a new breed of cost-effective firms are putting U.S. manufacturing back on the road to profitability.[23]

Cost reduction can also be pursued through increased use of part-time employees, subcontractors, work simplification and measurement procedures, automation, work rule changes, and job assignment flexibility. Thus, there are several methods for reducing costs. Although the details are vastly different, they all share the goal of reducing output cost per employee.

In summary, the profile of employee role behaviors necessary for firms seeking to gain competitive advantage by pursuing the competitive strategy of cost reduction is as follows: (1) relatively repetitive and predictable behaviors, (2) a rather short-term focus, (3) primarily autonomous or individual activity, (4) modest concern for quality, (5) high concern for quantity of output (goods or services), (6) primary concern for results, (7) low risk-taking activity, and (8) a relatively high degree of comfort with stability.

Given these competitive strategies and the needed role behaviors, what HRM practices need to be linked with each of the three strategies?

TYPOLOGY OF HRM PRACTICES

When deciding what human resource practices to use to link with competitive strategy, organizations can choose from six human resource practice "menus." Each of the six menus concerns a different aspect of human resource management. These aspects are planning, staffing, appraising, compensating, and training and development.

A summary of these menus is shown in Exhibit 2. Notice that each of the choices runs along a continuum. Most of the options are self-explanatory, but a rundown of the staffing menu will illustrate how the process works. A more detailed description of all menus is provided elsewhere.[24]

Recruitment

In each of these areas, a business unit (or a plant) must make a number of decisions; the first choice involving where to recruit employees. Companies can rely on the internal labor market (e.g., other departments in the

EXHIBIT 2   Human Resource Management Practice Menus

Planning Choices

Informal ———	Formal
Short Term ———	Long Term
Explicit Job Analysis ———	Implicit Job Analysis
Job Simplification ———	Job Enrichment
Low Employee Involvement ———	High Employee Involvement

Staffing Choices

Internal Sources ———	External Sources
Narrow Paths ———	Broad Paths
Single Ladder ———	Multiple Ladders
Explicit Criteria ———	Implicit Criteria
Limited Socialization ———	Extensive Socialization
Closed Procedures ———	Open Procedures

Appraising Choices

Behavioral Criteria ———	Results Criteria
Purposes: Development, Remedial, Maintenance	
Low Employee Participation ———	High Employee Participation
Short-Term Criteria ———	Long-Term Criteria
Individual Criteria ———	Group Criteria

Compensating Choices

Low Base Salaries ———	High Base Salaries
Internal Equity ———	External Equity
Few Perks ———	Many Perks
Standard, Fixed Package ———	Flexible Package
Low Participation ———	High Participation
No Incentives ———	Many Incentives
Short-Term Incentives ———	Long-Term Incentives
No Employment Security ———	High Employment Security
Hierarchical ———	High Participation

Training and Development

Short Term ———	Long Term
Narrow Application ———	Broad Application
Productivity Emphasis ———	Quality of Work Life Emphasis
Spontaneous, Unplanned ———	Planned, Systematic
Individual Orientation ———	Group Orientation
Low Participation ———	High Participation

Adapted from R. S. Schuler, "Human resource management practice choices," in *Readings in personnel and human resource management*, 3rd ed., ed. R. S. Schuler, S. A. Youngblood, and V. L. Huber (St. Paul, Minn.: West Publishing, 1988).

firm and other levels in the organizational hierarchy), or they can rely on the external labor market exclusively. Although this decision may not be significant for entry-level jobs, it is very important for most other jobs. Recruiting internally essentially means a policy of promotion from within. While this policy can serve as an effective reward, it commits a firm to providing training and career development opportunities if the promoted employees are to perform well.

Career Paths

Here, the company must decide whether to establish broad or narrow career paths for its employees. The broader the paths, the greater the opportunity for employees to acquire skills that are relevant to many functional areas and to gain exposure and visibility within the firm. Either a broad or a narrow career path may enhance an employee's acquisition of skills and opportunities for promotion, but the time frame is likely to be much longer for broad skill acquisition than for the acquisition of a more limited skill base. Although promotion may be quicker under a policy of narrow career paths, an employee's career opportunities may be more limited over the long run.

Promotions

Another staffing decision to be made is whether to establish one or several promotion ladders. Establishing several ladders enlarges the opportunities for employees to be promoted and yet stay within a given technical specialty without having to assume managerial responsibilities. Establishing just one promotion ladder enhances the relative value of a promotion and increases the competition for it.

Part and parcel of a promotion system are the criteria used in deciding who to promote. The criteria can vary from the very explicit to the very implicit. The more explicit the criteria, the less adaptable the promotion system is to exceptions and changing circumstances. What the firm loses in flexibility, the employee may gain in clarity. This clarity, however, may benefit only those who fulfill the criteria exactly. On the other hand, the more implicit the criteria, the greater the flexibility to move employees around to develop them more broadly.

Socialization

After an employee is hired or promoted, he or she is next socialized. With minimal socialization, firms convey few informal rules and establish few procedures to immerse employees in the culture and practices of the organization. Although it is probably easier and cheaper to do this than to provide maximum socialization, the result is likely to be a more restricted psychological attachment and commitment by the employee to the firm, and perhaps less predictable behavior from the employee.

Openness

A final choice to be made in the staffing menu is the degree of openness in the staffing procedures. The more open the procedures, the more likely there is to be job posting for internal recruitment and self-nomination for promotion. To facilitate a policy of openness, firms need to make the relevant information available to employees. Such a policy is worthwhile; since it allows employees to select themselves into jobs, it is a critical aspect of attaining successful job-person fit. The more secret the procedures, the more limited the involvement of employees in selection decisions, but the faster the decision can be made.

A key aspect of the choices within the staffing activity or any other HRM activity is that different choices stimulate and reinforce different role behaviors. Because these have been described in detail elsewhere, their impact is summarized below.

HYPOTHESES OF COMPETITIVE STRATEGY-HRM ARCHETYPES

Based on the above descriptions of competitive strategies and the role behaviors necessary for each, and the brief typology of HRM practices, we offer three summary hypotheses.

Innovation Strategy

Firms pursuing the innovation strategy are likely to have the following characteristics: (1) jobs that require close interaction and coordination among groups of individuals, (2) performance appraisals that are more likely to reflect longer-term and group-based achievements, (3) jobs that allow employees to develop skills that can be used in other positions in the firm, (4) compensation systems that emphasize internal equity rather than external or market-based equity, (5) pay rates that tend to be low, but that allow employees to be stockholders and have more freedom to choose the mix of components (salary, bonus, stock options) that make up their pay package, and (6) broad career paths to reinforce the development of a broad range of skills. These practices facilitate cooperative, interdependent behavior that is oriented toward the longer term, and foster exchange of ideas and risk taking.[25]

Quality-Enhancement Strategy

In an attempt to gain competitive advantage through the quality-enhancement strategy, the key HRM practices include (1) relatively fixed and explicit job descriptions, (2) high levels of employee participation in decisions relevant to immediate work conditions and the job itself, (3) a mix of individual and group criteria for performance appraisal that is mostly short-term and results-oriented, (4) relatively egalitarian treatment of employees and some guarantees of employment security, and (5) extensive and continuous training and development of employees. These practices facilitate quality enhancement by helping to ensure highly reliable behavior from individuals who can identify with the goals of the organization and, when necessary, be flexible and adaptable to new job assignments and technological change.[26]

Cost-Reduction Strategy

In attempting to gain competitive advantage by pursuing a strategy of cost reduction, key human resource practice choices include (1) relatively fixed (stable) and explicit job descriptions that allow little room for ambiguity, (2) narrowly designed jobs and narrowly defined career paths that encourage specialization, expertise, and efficiency, (3) short-term, results-oriented performance appraisals, (4) close monitoring of market pay levels for use in making compensation decisions, and (5) minimal levels of employee training and development. These practices maximize efficiency by providing means for management to monitor and control closely the activities of employees.[27]

AN INNOVATIVE STRATEGY: ONE COMPANY'S EXPERIENCE

Frost, Inc., is one company that has made a conscious effort to match competitive strategy with human resource management practices. Located in Grand Rapids, Michigan, Frost is a manufacturer of overhead conveyor trolleys used primarily in the auto industry, with sales of $20 million.[28] Concerned about depending too heavily on one cyclical industry, President Charles D. "Chad" Frost made several attempts to diversify the business, first into manufacturing lawn mower components and later into material-handling systems, such as floor conveyors and hoists. These attempts failed. The engineers didn't know how to design unfamiliar components, production people didn't know how to make them, and sales people didn't know how to sell them. Chad Frost diagnosed the problem as inflexibility. "We had single-purpose machines and single-purpose people," he said, "including single-purpose managers."

Frost decided that automating production was the key to flexibility. Twenty-six old-fashioned screw machines on the factory floor were replaced with 11 numerical-controlled machines paired within 18 industrial robots. Frost decided to design and build an automated storage-and-retrieval inventory control system, which would later be sold as a proprietary product, and to automate completely the front office to reduce indirect labor costs. The new program was formally launched in late 1983.

What at first glance appeared to be a hardware-oriented strategy turned out to be an exercise in human resource management. "If you're going to reap a real benefit in renovating a small to medium-size company, the machinery is just one part, perhaps the easiest part, of the renovation process," says Robert McIntyre, head of Amprotech, Inc., an affiliate consulting company Frost formed early in the automation project to provide an objective, "outside" view. "The hardest part is getting people to change."

Frost was clearly embarking on a strategy of innovation. As it turns out, many of the choices the company made about human resource practices were intended to support the employee role behaviors identified as being crucial to the success of an innovation strategy.

For example, the company immediately set out to increase employee identification with the company by giving each worker 10 shares of the closely held company and by referring to them henceforth as "shareholder-employees." The share ownership, which employees can increase by making additional purchases through a 401(d) plan, are also intended to give employees a long-term focus, which is another behavior important for an innovation strategy to succeed. Additional long-term incentives consist of a standard corporate profit-sharing plan and a discretionary profit-sharing plan administered by Chad Frost.

Frost's compensation package was also restructured to strike a balance between results (productivity) and process (manufacturing). In Frost's case, the latter is a significant consideration, since the production process is at the heart of the company's innovation strategy. Frost instituted a quarterly bonus that is based on companywide productivity, and established a "celebration fund" that managers can tap at their discretion to reward significant employee contributions. The bonuses serve to foster other needed employee role behaviors. By making the quarterly bonus dependent on companywide productivity, the company is encouraging cooperative, interdependent behavior. The "celebration fund" meanwhile, can be used to reward and reinforce innovative behavior. (Even the form of the celebration can be creative. Rewards can range from dinner with Chad Frost to a weekend for an employee and spouse at a local hotel, to a belly dancing performance in the office.)

Frost encourages cooperative behavior in a number of other ways as well. Most offices (including Chad Frost's) lack doors, which is intended to foster openness of communication. Most executive perks have been eliminated, and all employees have access to the company's mainframe computer (with the exception of payrole information) by way of more than 40 terminals scattered around the front office and factory floor.

In our view, a vital component of any innovation strategy is getting employees to broaden their skills, assume more responsibilities, and take risks. Frost encourages employees to learn new skills by paying for extensive training programs, both at the company and at local colleges. It even goes further, identifying the development of additional skills as a prerequisite for advancement. This is partly out of necessity, since Frost has compressed its 11 previous levels of hierarchy into four. Because this has made it harder to reward employees through traditional methods of promotion, employees are challenged to advance by adding skills, assuming more responsibilities, and taking risks.

Honda's Quality-Enhancement Strategy

We can identify those human resource practices that facilitate product quality by examining Honda of America's Marysville, Ohio, plant.[29] With a current work force of approximately 4,500, this plant produces cars of quality comparable to those produced by Honda plants in Japan. Although pay rates (independent of bonuses) may be as much as 30–40 percent lower than rates at other Midwest auto plants, Honda has fewer layoffs and lower inventory rates of new cars than its competitors. How is this possible?

One possible explanation is that Honda knows that the delivery of quality products depends on predictable and reliable behavior from its employees. In the initial employee orientation session, which may last between three and four hours, job security is emphasized. Employees' spouses are encouraged to attend these sessions, because Honda believes that spouse awareness of the company and its demands on employees can help minimize absenteeism, tardiness, and turnover. Of course, something so critical to quality as reliable behavior is not stimulated and reinforced by only one human resource practice. For example, associates who have perfect attendance for four straight weeks receive a bonus of $56. Attendance also influences the size of the semiannual bonus (typically paid in spring and autumn). Impressive attendance figures also enhance an employee's chances for promotion. (Honda of America has a policy of promotion from within.)

In addition to getting and reinforcing reliable and predictable behavior, Honda's HRM practices encourage a longer-term employee orientation and a flexibility to change. Employment security, along with constant informal and formal training programs, facilitate these role behaviors. Training programs are tailored to the needs of the associates (employees) through the formal performance appraisal process, which is developmental rather than evaluational. Team leaders (not supervisors) are trained in spotting and removing peformance deficiencies as they occur. To help speed communication and remove any organizational sources of performance deficiencies, the structure of the organization is such that there are only four levels between associates and the plant manager.

At Honda, cooperative, interdependent behavior is fostered by egalitarian HRM practices. All associates wear identical uniforms with their first names embossed; parking spaces are unmarked, and there is only one cafeteria. All entry-level associates receive the same rate of pay except for a 60-cents-an-hour shift differential. The modern health center adjacent to the main plant is open to all. These practices, in turn, encourage all associates to regard themselves collectively as "us" rather than "us" versus "them." Without this underlying attitude, the flexible work rules, air-conditioned plant, and automation wouldn't be enough to sustain associate commitment and identification with the organization's goal of high quality.

The success of Honda's quality enhancement strategy goes beyond concern for its own HRM practices. It is also concerned with the human resource practices of other organizations, such as its suppliers. For example, Delco-Remy's practice of participative management style, as well as its reputation for producing quality products at competitive prices, was the reason why Delco was selected by Honda as its sole supplier of batteries.[30]

A Cost-Reduction Strategy at United Parcel Service

Through meticulous human engineering and close scrutiny of its 152,000 employees, United Parcel Service (UPS) has grown highly profitable despite stiff competition. According to Larry P. Breakiron, the company's senior vice president of engineering, "Our ability to manage labor and hold it accountable is the key to success."[31] In other words, in an industry where "a package is a package," UPS succeeds by its cost-reduction strategy.

Of all paths that can be taken to pursue a cost-reduction strategy, the one taken by UPS is the work standard/simplification method. This method has been the key to gains in efficiency and productivity increases. UPS's founder, James E. Casey, put a premium on efficiency. In the 1920s, Casey hired pioneers of time and motion study such as Frank Gilbreth and Fredrick Taylor to measure the time each UPS driver spent each day on specific tasks. UPS engineers cut away the sides of UPS trucks to study how the drivers performed, and then made changes in techniques to enhance worker effectiveness. The establishment of effective work standards has led not only to enormous gains in efficiency and cost reduction; it actually makes employees less tired at the end of the day. During the day, the employees engage in short-term, highly repetitive role behaviors that involve little risk taking. Because specialists identify the best way to accomplish tasks, employee participation in job decisions is unnecessary.

Through the use of time and motion studies, UPS has established very specific ways for workers to perform their jobs. The company also monitors closely the performance of the workers. More than 1,000 industrial engineers use time and motion study to set standards for a variety of closely supervised tasks. In return, the UPS drivers, all of whom are Teamsters, earn approximately $15 per hour—a dollar or so more than the drivers at other companies. In addition, employees who perform at acceptable levels enjoy job security.

IMPLEMENTATION ISSUES

These descriptions of Frost, Honda, and UPS illustrate how a few organizations systematically match their HRM practices not only with their articulated competitive strategies, but also with their perceptions of needed role behavior from their employees. Although only a beginning, the success of these firms suggests that HRM practices for all levels of employees are affected by strategic considerations. Thus, while it may be important to match the characteristics of top management with the strategy of the organization, it may be *as* important to do this for *all* employees.

Although the results of these examples generally support the three major hypotheses, they also raise several central issues: Which competitive strategy is best? Is it best to have one competitive strategy or several? What are the implications of a change of competitive strategy?

Which Competitive Strategy Is Best?

Of the three competitive strategies described here, deciding which is best depends on several factors. Certainly customer wants and the nature of the competition are key factors. If customers are demanding quality, a cost-reduction strategy may not be as fruitful as a quality improvement strategy. At the Mercury Marine division of Brunswick and at Corning Glass Works, the issues seem to be quality. According to McComas, "Customers, particularly industrial trial buyers, would have been no more inclined to buy their products even if the manufacturer could have passed along savings of, say, 10 percent or even 20 percent."[32]

If, however, the product or service is relatively undifferentiated, such as the overnight parcel delivery industry, a cost-reduction strategy may be the best way to gain competitive advantage. Even here, though, there is a choice. United Parcel Service, for example, is pursuing the cost-reduction strategy through work process refinements such as work clarification, standardization, measurement, and feedback. Roadway, in contrast, pursues the same strategy by combining employee independence and ownership (drivers own their own trucks, of various colors; UPS drivers do not own their brown trucks) with as much automation as possible.[33] The advantage of these latter approaches to cost reduction, compared with such approaches as wage concessions or work force reductions, is the amount of time required to implement them. Cost reduction through wage concessions or employee reductions, though painful, can be relatively straightforward to implement. As a consequence, it can be duplicated by others, essentially eliminating the competitive advantage gained by being able to offer lower prices. The adoption of two-tiered wage contracts within the airline industry is a good example: Soon after American Airlines installed a two-tier wage system for its pilots, Eastern, United, and Frontier Airlines negotiated similar contracts with their employees.

There may, however, be some external conditions that might permit the success of a strategy of cost reduction to last. After four straight years of losses and a shrinkage in the number of stores from nearly 3,500 in 1974 to a little more than 1,000 in 1982, the Great Atlantic & Pacific Tea Company (A&P) and the United Food and Commercial Workers (UFCW) saw the handwriting on the wall: Either reduce costs and be competitive, or go out of business. According to a *Business Week* article:

> In an experimental arrangement negotiated with the . . . UFCW at 60 stores in the Philadelphia area, workers took a 25 percent pay cut in exchange for an unusual promise: If a store's employees could keep labor costs at 10 percent of sales—by working more efficiently or by boosting store traffic—they'd get a cash bonus equal to 1 percent of the store's sales. They'd get a 0.5 percent bonus at 11 percent of sales or 1.5 percent at 9.5 percent of sales. It was a gamble in the low-margin supermarket business, but it worked.[34]

The result? An 81 percent increase in operating profits in 1984 and a doubling of A&P's stock price. Although the UFCW agreed with the incentive compensation scheme at A&P, the union appears unwilling to see this practice spread. Consequently, competitors of A&P, such as Giant Food, Inc., would have difficulty implementing the same scheme.[35]

By contrast, a quality improvement strategy, whether by automation or quality teams, is more time consuming and difficult to implement. As the U.S. auto industry has experienced, it is taking a long time to overcome the competitive advantage gained by the Japanese auto industry through quality improvement. The J. D. Powers 1986 Consumer Satisfaction Index of automobiles suggests, however, that Ford's dedicated approach to quality enhancement may be reaping benefits.

One Competitive Strategy or Several?

Although we focused on the pursuit of a common competitive strategy in our examples, this may be oversimplifying reality. For example, at Honda in Marysville, associates are encouraged to be innovative. Each year the group of associates that designs the most unique or unusual transportation vehicle is awarded a trip to Japan. At UPS, teamwork and cooperation are valued and at Frost, Inc., product and service quality are of paramount importance. Lincoln Electric is recognized as one of the lowest cost *and* highest quality producers of arc welders. While these examples indicate that organizations may pursue more than one competitive strategy at a time, it may be that organizations actually need to have multiple and concurrent competitive strategies. Using multiple strategies results in the challenge of stimulating and rewarding different role behaviors while at the same time trying to manage the conflicts and tensions that may arise as a consequence. This may be the very essence of the top manager's job. According to Mitchell Kapor of Lotus Development Corporation:

> To be a successful enterprise, we have to do two apparently contradictory things quite well: We have to stay innovative and creative, but at the same time we have to be tightly controlled about certain apects of our corporate behavior. But I think that what you have to do about paradox is embrace it. So we have the kind of company where certain things are very loose and other things are very tight. The whole art of management is sorting things into the loose pile or the tight pile and then watching them carefully.[36]

Perhaps, then, the top manager's job is facilitated by separating business units or functional areas that have different competitive strategies. To the extent that this separation is limited or that a single business unit has multiple strategies, effective means of confrontation and collaboration need to exist. However, even with this issue under control, there is another equally significant challenge.

Change of Competitive Strategies

By implication, changes in strategy should be accompanied by changes in human resources practices. As the products of firms change, as their customers' demands change, and as the competition changes, the competitive strategies of firms will change. Consequently, employees will face an ever-changing employment relationship. A significant implication of this is that employees of a single firm may be exposed to different sets of human resource practices during the course of employment. Thus, employees may be asked to exhibit different role behaviors over time and they may be exposed to several different conditions of employment. Although it remains to be seen whether all employees can adjust to such changes, it appears that many can and have. For those who wish not to, firms may offer outplacement assistance to another firm, or even to another division in the company. For those who have problems changing, firms may offer training programs to facilitate the acquisition of necessary skills and abilities as well as needed role behaviors.

Another implication is that all components of a system of human resource practices need to be changed and implemented simultaneously. The key human resource practices work together to stimulate and reinforce particular needed employee behaviors. Not to invoke a particular practice (e.g., high participation) implies invoking another (e.g., low participation) that is less likely to stimulate and reinforce the necessary employee behaviors. The likely result is that employees will experience conflict, ambiguity, and frustration.

CONCLUSION

The recent attack on U.S. firms for failing to keep costs down, not maintaining quality, and ignoring innovation are misdirected, given what many firms like Frost, Honda–Marysville, UPS, Corning Glass, A&P, 3M, and Brunswick are doing.[37] These firms and others are pursuing competitive strategies aimed at cost reduction, quality improvement, and innovation. The aim in implementing these strategies is to gain competitive advantage and beat the competition—both domestically and internationally. While cost and market conditions tend to constrain somewhat the choice of competitive strategy, the constraint appears to be one of degree rather than of kind. Consequently, we can find firms pursuing these three competitive strategies regardless of industry.

All firms are not seeking to gain competitive strategy. Not doing so, however, is becoming more of a luxury. For those attempting to do so, the experiences of other firms suggest that effectiveness can be increased by systematically melding human resource practices with the selected competitive strategy. Certainly, the success or failure of a firm is not likely to turn entirely on its human resource management practices, but the HRM practices are likely to be critical.[38]

ENDNOTES

The authors wish to thank John W. Slocum, Jr., C. K. Prahalad, and John Dutton for their many helpful suggestions, and the Human Resource Planning Society, the Center for Entrepreneurial Studies, New York University, and the University of Michigan for their financial support of this project.

1. C. Fombrun "An interview with Reginald Jones," *Organizational Dynamics* (Winter 1982), 46.
2. D. C. Hambrick and P. A. Mason "Upper echelons: The organization as a reflection of its top managers," *Academy of Management Review* (1984) 9, 193–206; A. K. Gupta, "Contingency linkages between strategy and general manager characteristics: A conceptual examination," *Academy of Management*

Review (1984) *9*, 399–412; A. K. Gupta and V. Govindarajan, "Build, hold, harvest: Converting strategic intentions into reality," *Journal of Business Strategy* (1984a) *4*, 34–47; A. K. Gupta and Govindarajan, "Business unit strategy, managerial characteristics, and business unit effectiveness at strategy implementation," *Academy of Management Journal* (1984b) *9*, 25–41; M. Gerstein and H. Reisman, "Strategic selection: Matching executives to business conditions," *Sloan Management Review* (Winter 1983), 33–49; D. Miller, M.F.R. Kets de Vries, and J. M. Toulouse, "Top executives' locus of control and its relationship to strategy-making, structure, and environment," *Academy of Management Journal* (1982) *25*, 237–53; A. D. Szilagyi and D. M. Schweiger, "Matching managers to strategies: A review and suggested framework," *Academy of Management Review* (1984) *9*, 626–37; and J. D. Olian and S. L. Rynes, "Organizational staffing: Integrating practice with strategy," *Industrial Relations*, (1984) *23*, 170–83.

3. Lee J. A. Byrne and A. Leigh Cowan, "Should companies groom new leaders or buy them?" *Business Week* (September 22), 94–95.

4. Ibid.

5. A. J. Rutigliano, "Managing the new: An interview with Peter Drucker," *Management Review* (January 1986), 38–41.

6. D. Q. Mills, *The new competitors* (New York: Free Press, 1985); and M. Beer, B. Spector, P. R. Lawrence, D. Q. Mills, and R. E. Walton, *Managing human assets* (New York: Macmillan, 1984); R. M. Kanter, "Change masters and the intricate architecture of corporate culture change," *Management Review* (October 1983), 18–28; and R. M. Kanter, *The change masters* (New York: Simon & Schuster, 1983).

7. J. L. Kerr, "Diversification strategies and managerial rewards: An empirical study" *Academy of Management Journal* (1985) *28*, 155–79; J. W. Slocum, W. L. Cron, R. W. Hansen, and S. Rawlings, "Business strategy and the management of plateaued employees" *Academy of Management Journal* (1985) *28*, 133–54; D. C. Hambrick and C. C. Snow, "Strategic reward systems," in *Strategy, organization design and human resources management* ed. C. C. Snow, (Greenwich, Conn.: JAI Press, 1987).

8. For detailed examples of how firms use their human resource practices to gain competitive advantage, see R. S. Schuler and I. C. MacMillan, "Gaining competitive advantage through human resource management practices," *Human Resource Management* (Autumn 1984), 241–55; R. S. Schuler, "Fostering and facilitating entrepreneurship in organizations: Implications for organization structure and human resource management practices," *Human Resource Management* (Winter 1986), 607–29; and M. E. Porter, *Competitive strategy* (New York: Free Press, 1980); and M. E. Porter, *Competitive advantage* (New York: Free Press, 1985).

9. For an extensive discussion of competitive initiative, competitive strategy, and competitive advantage, see I. C. MacMillan's "Seizing competitive initiative," *Journal of Business Strategy* (1983), 43–57.

10. See Endnote 18, Porter, 1980, 1985.

11. B. Schneider, "Organizational behavior," *Annual Review of Psychology* (1985) *36*, 573–611.

12. D. Katz and R. L. Kahn, *The social psychology of organizations*, 2nd ed. (New York: John Wiley & Sons, 1978).

13. J. C. Naylor, R. D. Pritchard, and D. R. Ilgen, *A theory of behavior in organizations* (New York: Academic Press, 1980); T. W. Dougherty and R. D. Pritchard, "The measurement of role variables: Exploratory examination of a new approach" *Organizational Behavior and Human Decision Processes* (1985) *35*, 141–55.

14. J. R. Rizzo, R. J. Hose, and S. I. Lirtzman, "Role conflict and ambiguity in complex organizations," *Administrative Science Quarterly* (1970) *14*, 150–63; S. E. Jackson and R. S. Schuler, "A meta-analysis and conceptual critique of research on role ambiguity and role conflict in work settings," *Organizational Behavior and Human Decision Processes* (1985) *36*, 16–78.

15. R. M. Kanter, "Supporting innovation and venture development in established companies," *Journal of Business Venturing* (Winter 1985), 47–60.

16. H. DePree, *Business as unusual* (Zeeland, Mich.: Herman Miller, 1986).

17. The following discussion is based on our survey and observations, and findings reported on by others. For a review of what others have reported, see R. S. Schuler's "Human resource management practice choices," *Human Resource Planning* (March 1987), 1–19.

18. M. McComas, "Cutting costs without killing the business," *Fortune* (October 13, 1986), 76.

19. For a detailed presentation of Marine Mercury's program to improve quality, see Endnote 18 above.

20. S. E. Prokesch, "Bean meshes man, machine," *The New York Times* (December 23, 1985), 19, 21.

21. S. E. Prokesch, "Are America's manufacturers finally back on the map?" *Business Week* (November 17, 1986), 92, 97.

22. Ibid., 92.

23. Ibid., 97. For more on Electrolux's human resource practices, see B. J. Feder's "The man who modernized Electrolux," *The New York Times* (December 31, 1986), 24.

24. Schuler, 1987.

25. E. E. Lawler III, "The strategic design of reward systems," in R. S. Schuler and S. A. Youngblood (Eds.), *Readings in personnel and human resource management*, 2nd ed., (St. Paul, Minn.: West Publishing, 1984), 253–69; and R. S. Schuler, "Human resource management practice choices," in R. S. Schuler, S. A. Youngblood, and V. L. Huber (Eds.) *Readings in personnel and human resource management*, 3rd ed., (St Paul, Minn.: West Publishing, 1988). Other factors that can influence the human resource practices are top management, hierarchical considerations, what other firms are doing, what the firm has done in the past, the type of technology, size and age of firm, unionization status, and the legal environment and its structure (see R. K. Kazanjian and R. Drazin, "Implementing manufacturing innovations: Critical choices of structure and staffing roles," *Human Resource Management*, (Fall 1986), 385–404).

26. P. F. Drucker, *Innovation and entrepreneurship* (New York: Harper & Row, 1985); K. Albrecht and S. Albrecht, *The creative corporation* (Homewood, Ill.: Dow Jones-Irwin, 1987).

27. P. F. Drucker, "Quality means a whole new approach to manufacturing," *Business Week* (June 8, 1987), 131–43; P. F. Drucker, "Pul-eeze! Will somebody help me?" *Time*, (February 2, 1987), 48–57; and R. L. Desatnick, *Managing to keep the customer* (San Francisco: Jossey-Bass, 1987).

28. This description is expanded upon in detail by S. Galante, "Frost, Inc.," *Human Resource Planning* (March 1987), 57–67.
29. For additional collaborating information, see J. Merwin, "A tale of two worlds," *Forbes* (June 16, 1986), 101–05; and S. Chira, "At 80, Honda's founder is still a fiery maverick," *The New York Times* (January 12, 1987), 35.
30. As reported in Schuler and MacMillan, "Gaining competitive advantage through human resource management practices," *Human Resource Management* (Autumn 1984), 249–50.
31. D. Machalaba, "United Parcel Service gets deliveries done by driving its workers," *The Wall Street Journal* (April 22, 1986), 1 and 23.
32. M. McComas, "Cutting costs without killing the business," *Fortune* (October 13, 1986), 77.
33. Ibid.
34. M. McComas, "How A&P fattens profits by sharing them," *Business Week* (December 22, 1986), 44. For an excellent discussion of the difficulties to be overcome in dealing with changing from human resource practices based on hierarchy or status to those based on performance or what's needed, see R. M. Kanter, "The new workforce meets the changing workplace: Strains, dilemmas, and contradictions in attempts to implement participative and entrepreneurial management," *Human Resource Management* (Winter 1986), 515–38.
35. For a discussion of relevant issues, see D. Q. Mills, "When employees make concessions," *Harvard Business Review* (May–June 1983), 103–13; and R. R. Rehder and M. M. Smith, "Kaizen and the art of labor relations," *Personnel Journal* (December 1986), 83–94.
36. *The Boston Globe* (January 27, 1985).
37. Recent attacks on public and private firms have been summarized by the use of the word "corpocracy." A description of corpocracy is found in M. Green and J. F. Berry's "Takeovers, a symptom of corpocracy," *The New York Times* (December 3, 1986).
38. The application of these human resource practices to strategy can be done by a firm on itself and even upon other firms that may be upstream or downstream of the local firm. For a further description, see Schuler and MacMillan (Endnote 30).

Behavior Management*

Lawrence M. Miller

The advantage of the behavior management approach to changing performance is well illustrated by an incident that occurred on an airplane a few years back. One of our consultants sat next to the president of a medium-sized corporation. They began talking, and the consultant described the type of service he performed. The president responded by noting that he could really use some help with his senior vice president. He described this vice president as having a very bad attitude, which had persisted for several months. Our consultant asked "What does this vice president do that causes you to feel that he has a bad attitude?" The president thought for a while and then responded, "Well, whenever I give him a report to read, I never hear back from him. And when I do, he's always so critical." It was agreed that there was nothing else that this vice president did to manifest his bad attitude and that if these behaviors were to change it would indicate an improvement in attitude. Our consultant then made some specific recommendations involving measurement and techniques of feedback that would be likely to alter the rates of the problem behaviors.

The president was able to understand and implement a few relatively quick and simple procedures to alter these specific behaviors. The problem of his vice president's "bad attitude" had become a simple and relatively easy matter to improve. This is the essence of the direct approach to behavior change in the workplace.

DIRECT, EXTERNAL APPROACH TO BEHAVIOR

The direct or external approach to changing behavior has gained increasing acceptance and adherence over the past 10 to 20 years. This direct approach is also referred to as the behavioral model, behaviorism, behavior

* From Lawrence M. Miller, *Behavior management* (New York: Wiley-Interscience, 1978), 52–66. Copyright © 1978. John Wiley & Sons, Inc. Reprinted by permission.

modification, or behavior management. All these terms refer to the behavior change techniques based on the effects of environmental events, stimuli, without reference to explanations of mental conditions, states, motivations, needs, or drives. Behavior management does not deny that internal states exist. Whether internal states exist or not is irrelevant. The question is, Can behavior be changed and predicted from changes in the external environment? The research overwhelmingly demonstrates that the answer is affirmative (*Journal of Applied Behavior Analysis*, 1967–77).

The differences between the direct and indirect approaches to improving human performance in organizations can be summarized in the following four points:

1. The *change in behavior is explained as a direct function of the changes* in the environment, rather than as a change in an internal motivation or need that in turn causes a change in behavior. Behavior management studies the specific conditions that exist in the individual's environment, alters those conditions, and measures the subsequent change in behavior.

2. *Evaluation of the effort to improve performance is based on the direct measurement of behavior and its results.* The indirect approaches have relied heavily on measures of attitude and satisfaction.

These internal conditions are generally assessed by the use of attitude questionnaires. Behavior management does not consider the responses to questionnaires significant when the goal behaviors of concern, such as rates of work, attendance, and on-time arrivals to work, can be measured directly.

Goals for behavior management are stated in terms of increasing or decreasing rates of behavior or the product of behavior. The ongoing measurement of behavior is an essential element of every behavior management effort. Because of this direct measurement and because goals are stated in terms of increasing or decreasing behavior, the evaluation mechanism is built into every project. Economic evaluation of these projects becomes relatively simple and direct.

3. *Behavior management is a technique of management.* Behavior management is not a theory to which managers should attempt to conform because it is a correct theory of human nature. It is a technique designed to assist the manager in achieving his goals and should be applied to aid the organization in accomplishing the specific goals that define its productivity. It may be applied to improve the quality of products, reduce absenteeism or turnover, and increase output measures, sales, new business development, and increase other specific contributions of managers and employees. The manager should have specific, measurable objectives in mind before implementing a behavior change effort.

4. *The direct approach is more acceptable and receives a more favorable response from the manager because it is focused on his objectives,* for it provides him with a procedure for directly affecting the achievement of his objectives and demonstrates observable results in a relatively short period of time. Because of these factors and the compatibility of the direct approach with the "business of managing," the manager is more favorably disposed toward performance improvement efforts.

Behavior management is a nontheory of behavior (Skinner, 1950). It is the study and application of what works. Its development is based on empirical research. It did not start with a grand theory of human nature. Simple questions were asked and tested. Why does one specific behavior increase or decrease? How is a behavior acquired, or why does a behavior decrease? Highly controlled laboratory studies were conducted to answer these questions. As these questions have been answered through data collection and analysis, a set of principles has developed. The goal of behavior management is to discover lawful relationships. Investigation has determined that some lawful relationships between environmental events and behavior do exist, much as the study of physics has determined that larger bodies tend ot attract smaller bodies.

Whereas the historical evolution of behavior management is undoubtedly of secondary interest to most managers, a brief review of its development may help in understanding its principles.

The development of the science of behavior involved dozens of individual researchers; however, the work of the following men represents the most essential contributions: John B. Watson, Edward L. Thorndike, and B. F. Skinner.

John B. Watson

John B. Watson, more than any other single individual, is responsible for the initiation of behaviorism and for its first applications to business. Watson believed that all behavior was explainable as a function of stimuli that preceded the behavior. The so-called Stimulus–Response (S–R) model is the result of Watson's work. Watson described the purpose of his work in the following passage:

> Behaviorism, as I tried to develop it in my lectures at Columbia in 1912 and in my earliest writings, was an attempt to do one thing—apply to the experimental study of man the same kind of procedure and the same language of description that many research men had found useful for so many years in the study of animals lower than man. We believed then, as we do now, that man is an animal different from other animals only in the types of behavior he displays (Watson, 1920).

Before Watson psychology had been dominated by the internal approach, and he challenged its advocates to demonstrate the effects of their work and to apply the methods of empirical science. Watson demonstrated that human behavior could be studied scientifically and that it occurred in predictable patterns relative to conditions in the environment.

Perhaps Watson's most famous experiment, the one that led him to some of his conclusions, involved Little Albert, an 11-month-old boy who had become friendly with a white rat (Watson, 1920). Although this experiment was highly questionable from an ethical point of view, it did demonstrate some important principles of behavior. Watson decided that he would try to condition the response of fear in poor Little Albert. He attempted to pair a number of different stimuli with the white rat to condition a fear of the rat. He tried scaring Little Albert with a mask, a dog, a monkey, burning newspapers, and other stimuli that might elicit the fear response. Albert was not impressed by any of these. Finally, Watson created a loud noise by hitting an iron bar with a hammer behind Little Albert's head. This succeeded in sending Albert into a screaming fit. Watson then paired the frightening stimulus of the loud noise with the white rat. Every time Albert was permitted to see his little white friend, he was startled by the loud noise. Eventually the sight of the white rat, by itself, created the fear and caused poor Little Albert to cry.

In addition to showing that fears may be caused by conditions of the environment, this experiment demonstrated the principle of generalization. The newly acquired fear of the white rat generalized to other furry objects. Albert was now afraid of a dog, a rabbit, and even a Santa Claus mask. At Albert's expense some of the most basic forms of emotional learning had been demonstrated. (In Watson's defense it must be reported that he demonstrated that Albert could be deconditioned or unlearn these same fears.)

Watson limited his investigation to the relationship between preceding stimuli and subsequent behavior. For this reason the relationship he described is referred to as the Stimulus–Response (S–R) model. He believed that all behavior could be explained in terms of eliciting stimuli that occurred some time before the behavior. Although this explanation is no longer considered sufficient to explain all forms of learning, it did lay the foundation for the empirical investigation of human learning.

Watson defined the "behaviorists' platform":

> The behaviorist asks why don't we make what we can observe the real field of psychology? Let us limit ourselves to things that can be observed, and formulate laws concerning only those things. Now what can we observe? We can observe behavior—what the organism does or says. And let us point out at once: that saying is doing—that is behaving. Speaking overtly or to ourselves (thinking) is just as objective a type of behavior as baseball (Watson, 1924).

Edward L. Thorndike

While Watson was pursuing the study of the effect of preceding stimuli on behavior, E. L. Thorndike was developing his Law of Effect (Thorndike, 1913). He placed small animals such as cats, dogs, and chickens in "puzzle boxes" from which they learned to escape. There was an exit door to the box that could be opened by manipulating a lever. The animals were deprived of food until they managed to open the door. They obtained food, their reinforcer, after they managed to manipulate the lever and open the door. Thorndike found that the animal's speed of opening the door increased following experience. The animals were learning. From these experiments Thorndike formulated his Law of Effect:

> When a modifiable connection between a situation and a response is made and is accompanied or followed by a satisfying state of affairs, that connection's strength is increased: when made and accompanied or followed by an annoying state of affairs, its strength is decreased.

Thorndike accepted Watson's stimulus–response relationship but added that these relationships are strengthened as a function of the consequences that follow the behavior. Thorndike also argued that the effects or consequences of a behavior are direct and do not need to be explained in terms of mediating processes such as thought. The behavior is increased or decreased as a direct effect of the consequence.

B. F. Skinner

B. F. Skinner has been acclaimed by the American Psychological Association as the most influential living psychologist, and he is without a doubt the most controversial.* Skinner's contributions to the development of psychology as a science and as a means of improving human behavior are tremendous but difficult to categorize. Many cannot be as clearly defined as his own science would require. Four of the more significant are (1) his development and articulation of a technology of empirical investigation of behavior, (2) his distinction between operant and respondent behavior, (3) his development of the concept of "contingencies of reinforcement," and (4) his advocacy of behavior change and cultural design based on the empirical analysis of behavior.

Empirical Investigation.   Skinner is the antitheorist. Whereas the results of his research may be termed a theory of behavior, he opposed the formulation of theories of human behavior. Skinner (1950) argues that the

---

* Author's note: Skinner died August 18, 1990.

empirical data from the direct observation of behavior and its environment are a sufficient source of knowledge and that no interpretative theories are necessary. Skinner defined terms empirically. For example, reinforcement is defined as the presentation or removal of a stimulus, resulting in an increase in the rate of a response. It is defined by its effect on the behavior; reinforcement increases the rate of behavior. It is impossible, therefore, to say that an event is reinforcing unless an increase in the rate of a behavior can be demonstrated.

Skinner developed the language of the empirical investigation of behavior. All sciences require clear definition of terms to enable investigation to proceed in an orderly fashion. The definition of the language of behaviorism is one of Skinner's most significant contributions.

Skinner also provided a framework for behavioral research. He divided his observations into those concerned with independent variables (factors that affect a behavior and that can be managed in such a way as to cause a change in behavior) and the dependent variables (the behaviors affected by the independent variable). Skinner is concerned with discovering the specific relationships or "functional relationships" between the dependent and independent variables.

The essential elements of Skinner's system are summarized in the following table:

Independent Variables
Type of reinforcement or punishment
Schedule of reinforcement or punishment
Dependent Variables
Rate of response
Rate of acquiring a new response
Rate of extinction

At least as great as any technical innovations Skinner may have contributed is the general approach toward his subject that he promoted. This "attitude of science" is the single most distinguishing feature of the direct approach to behavior change.

> Science is first of all a set of attitudes. It is a disposition to deal with the facts rather than with what someone has said about them. . . . Science is a willingness to accept facts even when they are opposed to wishes. . . . The opposite of wishful thinking is intellectual honesty. . . . Scientists have simply found that being honest—with oneself as much as with others—is essential to progress. Experiments do not always come out as one expects, but the facts must stand and the expectations fall. The subject matter, not the scientist, knows best (Skinner, 1953).

Operant and Respondent Behavior.   Skinner defined types of behavior according to the manner in which they are acquired and maintained. Respondent behaviors are those *elicited* by a stimulus and are acquired through the procedures of "classical conditioning," the pairing of an unconditioned stimulus with a conditioned stimulus. Operant behaviors are those that are *emitted* by the organism and that act on the environment. They result in reinforcement. In other words, in respondent behavior, the organism reacts to the environment, while in operant behavior the response acts on the environment.

Skinner defined and studied operant behavior. He argued that most of the behaviors performed by any organism, human or animal, are operant behaviors and may be explained by an analysis of the reinforcements that have resulted from the operant behavior's acting on the environment. For example, the behavior of coming to work results in social approval, payment of money, and other reinforcers that maintain the performance of this behavior. If the behavior of coming to work did not act on the environment, if there were no consequences resulting from it, the operant of coming to work would extinguish; that is, it would cease to occur.

The "Contingencies of Reinforcement."   The relationships between the behavior of an individual and the environment are described by Skinner as the contingencies of reinforcement:

> An adequate formulation of the interaction between an organism and its environment must always specify three things: (1) the occasion upon which a response occurs, (2) the response itself, and (3) the reinforcing consequences. The interrelationships among them are the "contingencies of reinforcement" (Skinner, 1969).

The contingencies between behavior and environment are often stated in terms of an if–then relationship. If A occurs, then B will follow. [See Figure 1.] If I finish this chapter on time, I can go to the beach this weekend. If you increase the number of customers on whom you call, then

FIGURE 1   The Contingencies of Reinforcement

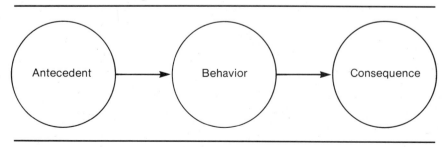

you will increase your commissions. If Johnny finishes his homework by eight o'clock, he may watch television for one hour.

Our world is composed of our behavior and the reaction of the environment to our behavior. These contingencies of reinforcement are the structure within which we live, the relationships that may explain our slow rate of learning, or feelings of depression, or our overeating. Skinner laid the foundation for the analysis of the contingencies of reinforcement.

Advocacy of Behavior Change and Cultural Design.   Many of Skinner's writings are not scientific. Most notably his well-known novel *Walden II* and his more recent *Beyond Freedom and Dignity* have gone beyond his data to propose applications of the science of behavior to social problems. Unfortunately, this advocacy has led to serious misunderstandings of the science of behavior and of his own positions in regard to this science. Skinner has devoted the greatest portion of his most recent book *About Behaviorism* to answering these criticisms and misunderstandings.

Skinner desired to create public debate on the social and cultural application of behavior change, and he has undoubtedly succeeded. If, however, the degree to which his recent writings have been misunderstood is an indication of his success at communicating his ideas, he has not been entirely successful. Perhaps the greatest controversy followed his publication of *Beyond Freedom and Dignity*. Contrary to the misinterpretation of many, Skinner does not argue against freedom. He is very much in favor of freedom and increasing individual freedom. He does, however, argue that the popular comprehension and the literature of freedom have hindered the progress of our culture. Skinner argues that mankind is not free in the sense of being autonomous and free from influence. On the contrary, Skinner argues that mankind's behavior is controlled by his environmental conditioning, and freedom must, therefore, be viewed in the context of this environmental control. He believes that mankind reacts negatively to aversive or negative contol such as would be imposed by a dictator. These forms of control characterized by the threat of punishment are the ones we fear. Forms of control based on positive reinforcement are the ones that we least notice and that are most desirable. Skinner argues that these forms, already present in our environment, should be carefully studied and used to create a society that results in the greatest benefit.

Skinner's outspoken advocacy of the application of his techniques to cultural design has created considerable debate because these techniques contradict the popular view and require a reexamination of accepted beliefs and habits. As has been the case at previous periods in human history, positions that contradict popular understandings of the human condition and that are supported by empirically gathered data have resulted in significant changes in the course of human history. The work of Galileo and Darwin resulted in similar controversy, change of traditional views, and eventual progress. Only future generations will be able to assess Skinner's final contribution to the understanding of the human condition.

DOES BEHAVIOR MANAGEMENT WORK IN ORGANIZATIONS?

Behavior management is the result of the trial-and-error applications of operant conditioning principles in the work setting. Does it work? This is the question that Skinner would hope we would ask. Behavior management has been systematically applied in the business and industrial settings only during the past few years. The contingencies of reinforcement have, however, been operating since the first person began working. All work behavior, regardless of the system or philosophy of management in effect, is explainable by analyzing the contingencies of reinforcement and may be changed by altering these contingencies.

The argument is often made that changing behavior in the work setting is not as simple as in the laboratory, classroom, or mental hospital. This is certainly true, and the complexity of the contingencies operating in the workplace is one of the primary reasons why application to organizations has not been more extensive. But behavior management has demonstrated its ability to change behavior, both in the workplace and other settings. It is the task of this book to present some of the results, as well as the principles and techniques of behavior management.

Behavior management systems are currently in use in more than 50 major corporations that I know of, and probably many more. Among the corporations now using these programs are the 3M Corporation, Western Electric, Westinghouse, Airco Alloys, Inc., Milliken & Company, General Mills, AT&T, Dart Industries, Inc., Pennwalt Corporation, Emery Air Freight, Questor Corporation, Ford Motor Company, American Can, Connecticut General Life Insurance Company, General Electric, Weyerhaeuser Company, and numerous others.

The application of behavior management to industrial organizations may be the best kept secret in management today. Most companies have no desire to advertise the techniques they are using or the results they have received. Nonetheless, a sampling of results leaves one wondering why there is not more discussion of these techniques in management publications and why more systematic research has not been conducted. The following are a few of the documented results witnessed during the past few years:

- One of the largest textile firms in the country has reported savings or earnings of approximately $20 million that can be directly attributed to behavior management programs.

- A midwestern plant of one of the major corporations listed in the preceding paragraph has reported that its cost accountants have attributed $600,000 in annual cost reductions to a behavior management effort that cost approximately $70,000 to implement.

- A textile-finishing plant that had been having a number of serious personnel problems implemented a six-month behavior management training program, and a year later the plant set a record for attendance—down to 0.9 percent absenteeism for eight weeks running. This same plant boosted quality savings to $25,000 per week over the same eight-week period.

- The City of Detroit garbage collectors instituted a behavior management program in which efficiency was reinforced with bonuses to the garbage collectors. The city saved $1,654,000 during the first year, after bonuses of $307,000 were paid to the collectors.

- ACDC Electronics Division of Emerson Electronics, instituting a program to improve attendance, met engineering specifications and production objectives. Profits increased 25 percent over forecast; costs were reduced by $550,000, and they received a return on investment, including consultant fees, of 1,900 percent.

- B. F. Goodrich Chemical Company started a program to meet production schedules and increased production by 300 pecent.

- Emery Air Freight has instituted numerous programs since 1969 and attributes direct savings of more than $3 million to behavior management.

- Waste in the spinning department of a carpet mill was identified as an area in need of improvement. By posting feedback data and providing verbal reinforcement and small tangible reinforcements, waste variance was reduced from $1,153 per week to $437 per week—an annualized savings of $37,232.

- A thorough analysis of the cost benefit of one behavior management program in one textile plant demonstrated improvements in plant turnover ($102,000 savings); finishing department efficiency ($32,895 savings); attendance ($26,457 savings); quality ($29,725 savings); sewing department efficiency ($15,158 savings); attendance in the sewing department ($27,333 savings); for a total plantwide annual savings of $233,369.

- A major textile firm began several programs with its trucking operations. One involved reducing the average time that loaded trailers wait for a tractor. The time was reduced from an average 67 minutes to between 35 to 40 minutes. This program is in operation in 42 plants and has reported savings in excess of $1 million.

The results here are only a small sample of those obtained. Each of these programs specified behaviors to be changed, altered specific environmental contingencies, and measured the changes in behavior and corresponding outcomes in terms of productivity, and so forth. In each of these programs environmental contingencies were complex, though the ones changed were relatively simple. While there may be a dozen consequences to our behavior (such as quitting a job or remaining on a job), one consequence may change the course of our actions (such as a raise or a compliment by our boss). It is not necessary to understand all the complexities of environmental influence to put the technology of behavior management to work. It is necessary only to identify clearly the behavior to be changed, the consequence to be altered, and measure the rate of the behavior before and after the consequence is changed. The result, in terms of an increase or decrease in the rate of behavior, indicates whether or not the procedure is working.

More than 20,000 managers and supervisors have been trained in the application of behavior management during the past five years by just one consulting firm specializing in it. All of these managers or supervisors have used behavior change projects as a routine part of their job. Most of these projects have followed a four-step process that has become known as the "cookbook" method of behavior management. This method, while deceptively simple, contains the basic ingredients of operant conditioning as applied to the work situation. These four steps are *pinpoint, record, consequate, evaluate* (Miller, 1974) and include the following:

- *Pinpoint:* The manager must identify and define the specific behavior or behaviors he wishes to change. A behavior is pinpointed when it may be accurately and reliably observed and recorded. For example, "working slowly" is not pinpointed. Completing "43 work units per eight-hour day" is. Similarly, "having a good attitude" is not pinpointed; "smiling at least once during each conversation with another person" is. The ability to specify behavior in pinpointed terms is both a necessary first skill for the manager who wishes to increase his ability to manage his employee's (or his own) behavior and a skill that requires a major change in the behavior pattern of most industrial supervisors.

- *Record:* The manager is asked to count the occurrence of the pinpointed behavior or some result of it. The frequency is to be recorded before any effort is made to change the behavior. This is for establishing baseline data. These data serve as the means of evaluating the behavior change strategy to be implemented after their establishment. The manager generally graphs these data to determine whether the frequency of the behavior is increasing, decreasing, or remaining the same. The establishment of baseline data before the initiation of a change procedure is a fundamental practice of the scientist that has been adopted with no great difficulty by the line manager and supervisor, who often have less than a high school education. The value of knowing where you have been, where you want to get to, and when you have arrived is understood by most individuals of good sense.

• *Consequate:* To consequate a behavior is to arrange for a consequence to follow it. The manager is encouraged to arrange a "reinforcing consequence," one that results in an increase in the rate of the desired performance. The reinforcing consequence most commonly used in behavior management is visualized feedback or knowledge of results. Managers often use the graph of the baseline data they have plotted to illustrate a goal level of performance and either post the graph in a visible location in the work area or personally show it to the worker whose performance is being recorded. The supervisor pairs verbal praise and approval with the visual feedback. This simple procedure has been used literally thousands of times to increase individual workers' productivity. Other reinforcers are raffle tickets, time off, job changes, letters of recognition, or anything else that may prove meaningful to the employee. A consequence may also include a "punisher," an event that results in the decreased rate of behavior. Managers have been taught the empirical meaning and effective use of punishment as a management procedure. Punishment, which is used only when reinforcement does not work, usually involves the least drastic punishing consequence available. A consequence may also involve the removal of a reinforcer that may be maintaining the performance of an undesirable behavior. The emphasis in most behavior management programs is on the use of "social" reinforcement. This includes the recognition by the manager of a job well done. When social reinforcement can be instituted in an organization on an ongoing basis, the organization is most likely to maintain high levels of performance. The use of tangible reinforcement, unless it becomes an institutionalized part of the compensation system, is not likely to be maintained over a long time, and performance is likely to drop as the procedure is discontinued.

concerned. Behavior management teaches the manager to measure performance on an ongoing basis, even when it is good, so that the conditions affecting it can be studied and managed. One of the primary effects of this evaluation is to provide built-in, or intrinsic, reinforcement for the manager. The manager or supervisor can obtain a great deal of satisfaction from observing the line on a graph go upward or downward as he alters the conditions that he believes affects that performance.

Behavior management is much more than these four simple steps. These steps are one method used to initiate behavior management at the level of the individual supervisor. Behavior management may also involve the alteration of a companywide system of compensation, objective setting, or information flow. When the principles of behavior management are fully understood by the manager, they become, not a technique to be called upon on difficult occasions, but a "way of life."

REFERENCES

Miller, Lawrence M. *Behavior management: New skills for business and industry.* Atlanta: Behavioral Systems, 1974.

Skinner, B. F. "Are theories of learning necessary?" *Psychological Review* (1950) 57, 193–216.

_____. *Science and human behavior.* New York: Free Press, 1953, pp. 12–13.

_____.*Contingencies of reinforcement: A theoretical analysis.* New York: Appleton-Century-Crofts, 1969, 7.

Thorndike, E. L. *The psychology of learning.* New York: Columbia University Teachers College, 1913.

Watson, John B. *Behaviorism.* New York: W. W. Norton, 1924, p. ix.

Watson, J. B., and R. Raynor. "Conditioning emotional reactions." *Journal of Experimental Psychology* (February 1920) 3, 1–14.

Recent Innovations
in Reward Systems*

Daniel C. Feldman
Hugh J. Arnold

There has been increased interest recently in the design of organizational reward systems. As a result, a number of innovative approaches have been developed to the administration of pay and other rewards for effective performance. This increased interest has largely arisen from recognition of the fact that pay, far from being an almost irrelevant factor in modern organizations, as suggested by theorists such as Maslow and Herzberg, is in fact an important determinant of the satisfaction and motivation of organization members. Edward Lawler has been a leading proponent of the importance of pay in organizations and has been in the forefront of the development and study of innovative approaches to pay. Lawler (1976) recently discussed five new approaches to the administration of pay in organizations which have been shown to be effective. These innovations are discussed below and their strengths and weaknesses are summarized in Table 1.

CAFETERIA FRINGE BENEFITS

Almost every organization rewards its members with some combination of pay and fringe benefits such as life insurance, health insurance, and pension plans. Quite commonly an organization has one standard fringe benefit package for nonsalaried employees, another for salaried employees, and a third for senior managers. The weakness of such approaches to fringe benefits is that they fail to take into account differences among individuals in the value and importance they place upon the different benefits available. Research consistently indicates that factors such as age, marital status, and

---

TABLE 1 Overview of Innovative Approaches to Pay

	Major Advantages	Major Disadvantages	Favorable Situational Factors
Cafeteria fringe benefits.	Increased pay satisfaction.	Cost of administration.	Well-educated, heterogeneous work force.
Lump-sum salary increases.	Increased pay satisfaction; greater visibility of pay increases.	Cost of administration.	Fair pay rates.
Skill-based evaluation.	More flexible and skilled work force; increased satisfaction.	Cost of training; higher salaries.	Employees who want to develop themselves; jobs that are interdependent.
Open salary information.	Increased pay satisfaction, trust, and motivation; better salary administration.	Pressure to pay all the same; complaints about pay rates.	Open climate; fair pay rates; pay based on performance.
Participative pay decisions.	Better pay decisions; increased satisfaction, motivation, and trust.	Time-consuming.	Democratic management climate; work force that wants to participate and that is concerned about organizational goals.

Source: Reprinted, by permission of the publisher, from E. E. Lawler III, "New approaches to pay: Innovations that work," *Personnel* (1976) 53, 11–23. Copyright © 1976 by AMACOM, a division of American Management Associations. All rights reserved.

number of children influence the extent to which individuals value different types of benefits (Glueck, 1978). For example, young, single members tend to value higher salaries and more vacations, and to be less concerned regarding things like insurance and pensions. Middle-aged members with young families value salaries and bonuses but tend to be less concerned with vacation time and more concerned with various types of insurance. Older members are concerned less with current salaries and more with pensions and retirement benefits.

A fringe benefit program that ignores these differences among people and treats all organization members identically fails to obtain the maximum payoff from the considerable monetary investment involved in such fringe benefit programs. If fringe benefit plans are to assist the organization by increasing the levels of satisfaction and motivation of their members, the plans must be capable of responding to the significant differences among individuals in the value they place on the benefits available.

An innovative approach to the resolution of this problem is known as a cafeteria-style fringe benefit program. The term *cafeteria* is employed as an analogy, since under such a plan the organization presents its employees with a whole range of alternative benefits and permits the employees to pick and choose those that they individually value most up to some set maximum value (the employee's total compensation level). At one extreme an individual could take his or her compensation entirely in the form of salary with no other benefits, while at the other extreme an individual could in any given year opt for a reduction in salary and an increase in other benefits, such as insurance or pension contributions. A variant of the cafeteria-style plan requires all employees to accept a minimal level of certain benefits such as health and life insurance and then permits free choice in allocation of compensation beyond these minimal levels.

The advantages of cafeteria-style benefit plans are twofold. First, they increase employees' perceptions of the value of their total compensation package. Second, they increase the likelihood that employees will be satisfied with their pay and benefits package. This increased satisfaction is associated with lower levels of turnover and absenteeism and greater ease in attracting new members.

Although cafeteria fringe benefits have significant advantages, they are obviously not without their drawbacks. First, they tend to create bookkeeping difficulties for the organization, which must keep track of exactly who has chosen which benefits and insure that the benefits are properly administered and dispensed. Fortunately, the use of computer systems greatly alleviates the difficulties encountered and brings the problems down to quite manageable proportions. Second, the uncertainty regarding exactly how many people will choose each benefit can make it difficult for the organization to price certain benefits, such as insurance, for which the cost to the organization is partially dependent upon the number of people choosing the benefit. This difficulty is particularly salient for smaller organizations and may result in some short-term costs to the organization in the early stages of a program until the numbers of employees choosing various options have stabilized and accurate pricing can be employed. Cafeteria-style fringe benefit programs have been successfully implemented and maintained in both large organizations (e.g., the Systems Division of the TRW Corporation, with 12,000 employees) and small organizations (e.g., the Educational Testing Service, with 3,000 employees).

SKILL-EVALUATION PAY PLANS

Basing a person's salary upon the job-related skills which he or she possesses was previously mentioned briefly under our discussion of alternative methods of pay administration. The most common approach to pay administration in the past has been to base an employee's pay upon what the job requires the individual to do (this is referred to as the job-requirement or job-evaluation approach to pay administration). Skill-evaluation pay plans, on the other hand, base the amount of pay not on what the current job requires of the employee but upon what that employee is capable of doing, as indicated by the range of job-related skills that the employee has demonstrated that he or she possesses. The wider the range of skills possessed, and hence the more jobs that a person is capable of performing, the higher the salary.

Skill-evaluation pay plans have been successfully implemented in organizations in Europe as well as in a number of North American plants operated by Procter & Gamble and General Foods. The plans have frequently been employed in plants organized and designed around work groups. In such situations group members are generally highly dependent upon one another for the effective performance of their group and a high level of rotation among jobs is common. A skill-evaluation pay plan is particularly well suited to such a situation since it increases the flexibility of the work force and encourages individuals to develop a broad perspective on the operation and effectiveness of the plant.

Where skill-evaluation pay plans are in effect, new organization members typically start at a basic pay rate and move up in salary as they demonstrate the skill to perform more and more jobs. Once all of the production jobs have been mastered the individual achieves the top or "plant" rate. Further salary increases can only be obtained by acquiring a specialty rate based upon the development of expertise in a skilled trade, such as electricity or plumbing.

Skill-based pay plans are successful in developing a highly skilled and flexible work force and have also been found to lead to feelings of personal growth and development among the individuals participating in them. They are also perceived to be a fair method of administering pay. On the negative side, such plans can be costly to the organization in two respects. First, they require that the organization provide individuals with formal training and other opportunities to learn, such as on-the-job practice. These training costs can frequently become quite high. Second, as the majority of employees develop a wide variety of skills, they must be paid accordingly, resulting in a highly paid work force. A final potential problem that needs to be noted can arise when individuals who have been encouraged to grow and develop their skills reach the top level and have nowhere further to go. Such individuals may become frustrated and unhappy if new avenues for development, such as interplant transfers or special assignments, are not identified.

LUMP-SUM SALARY INCREASES

Almost all organizations review the salaries of their members once a year to determine the amount by which the annual salary of each of their members will be increased. The amount of increase decided upon is then averaged over the number of pay periods in a year (e.g., 12 if members are paid monthly), and then each regular paycheck is incremented accordingly. Thus, it usually takes an employee an entire year actually to collect the full amount of the annual increase, and the increase is received in small installments. The advantages of this system from the organization's viewpoint are that the organization does not have to part with large amounts of cash at any one time and, further, the organization does not put itself in a position of having paid for services prior to their being rendered by the employee. At the same time, however, the practice of integrating annual increments into regular paychecks suffers both from the fact that it is an inflexible method of administering pay as a reward and from the fact that it serves to make even quite large annual salary increases relatively unnoticeable to the employee when they are averaged over many pay periods.

An alternative that a number of organizations have begun to experiment with is the administration of annual salary increases in a single lump sum. Under such a system the individual is informed of the amount of his or her annual salary increase and is then given the choice of how and when to receive the increase. The individual may choose to take the full amount immediately, to have the increment integrated into each regular paycheck, or to receive the increment in any combination of lump-sum payments and regular increments that may be convenient. Such a system has a number of advantages. First, it is an innovative approach to pay administration and can serve to encourage innovation and experimentation throughout the organization. Second, it makes the organization's pay system much more flexible and permits it to meet the unique needs of individual members, rather than treating everyone in an identical fashion. Finally, it serves to make pay increments much more visible as an organizational reward, and hence increases the likelihood that individuals will perceive a link between effective performance and the receipt of rewards. Naturally, the greater visibility afforded by lump-sum increases will only be viewed as desirable by organizations that have in place an equitable pay system that effectively links pay to performance. If an organization's pay system is inequitable or does not tie pay to performance, then the greater visibility afforded by lump-sum increases will be more likely to create than eliminate problems.

Like all innovative approaches to pay, lump-sum increases are not without their drawbacks. They clearly create bookkeeping and record-keeping difficulties of keeping track of who has chosen which specific mode of receiving salary increases. Again, computerization has made such problems eminently manageable. A more serious problem has to do with the cost to the organization of providing individuals with the full amount of their increase at a single time, prior to the individual actually having earned it. Most organizations that employ lump-sum increases deal with this problem by treating a lump-sum increase as a loan on which the employee is charged a low rate of interest until the work has been done to earn the increase. Individuals who quit prior to the end of the year for which they have received a lump-sum increment are expected to repay that portion they have not earned (e.g., one third of the total if they were to quit eight months after receiving the lump sum and hence four months or one third of a year prior to "earning" the full increment). There will naturally be some losses associated with such a program from employees who leave without repaying the unearned amount of their lump-sum increases.

Overall, the advantages of lump-sum increases in terms of increased flexibility and visibility of the reward system appear to outweigh quite clearly the potential disadvantages.

OPEN SALARY INFORMATION

Pay secrecy is standard practice in most organizations. The precise amount of money being earned by individual members is treated as confidential information. The most common rationale for maintaining secrecy is that members of the organization prefer a secrecy policy and would not like others to know how much they are making. However, such a justification is almost always an assumption or fabrication on the part of managers when they are asked to explain why pay is kept secret. It is extremely rare that an organization has systematically polled its members and discovered that they do indeed prefer pay secrecy. An alternative explanation for the prevalence of pay secrecy is that it permits managers to avoid having to explain and justify their pay decisions to their subordinates.

Although pay secrecy does have this advantage of making life easier and less demanding for the manager making pay decisions, it also has a number of disadvantages for the organization. Research indicates that when pay is secret individuals consistently and significantly overestimate the amount of pay being received by others at the same level in the organization. The research further shows that the degree to which people overestimate the pay of others at the same level is directly related to levels of dissatisfaction. The more a person overestimates the pay of others, the more dissatisfied that person becomes. When pay rates are kept secret, the organization is incapable of correcting such false impressions since the organization's policy is to withhold precisely that information necessary to correct the erroneous impressions.

A further disadvantage of pay secrecy is that it reduces the potential of pay to serve as a positive motivating force. As we pointed out earlier, if pay is to motivate effective performance, two factors must be present. First, individuals must perceive that pay is related to performance, and, second, an adequate level of trust must exist such that individuals trust that the organization will in the future reward them with more pay if they work hard now in order to perform effectively. Pay secrecy effectively undermines both of these essential factors. First, since pay is secret it is extremely difficult for the individual to determine whether or not the organization does or does not relate pay to performance. The individual has only his or her own personal experience to go on and is denied access to information regarding how the organization treats all the rest of its members. Second, a policy of pay secrecy is itself a manifestation of a low level of trust between the organization and its members. This low level of trust again impedes the capacity of the pay system to motivate effective performance.

The obvious alternative to pay secrecy is a policy of openness regarding pay. By sharing pay information openly, the organization can contribute to the creation of a climate of greater trust and can help clarify for employees the relationship between pay and performance. Both these factors can lead to increased motivation if it is in fact the case that the organization's pay system does relate pay to performance. If the pay system does not successfully tie pay to performance, then sharing pay information will make the inequities more obvious and clearly would not be expected to increase motivation.

A further potential advantage of an open pay system lies in the fact that it may encourage members to make better and more equitable pay decisions. When pay is secret there may be little motivation for the manager to give a lot of attention to pay decisions since he or she knows that there is little if any chance that those decisions will be challenged or questioned. On the negative side, however, an organization implementing an open pay policy must take care that managers do not respond by paying all of their subordinates equally in order to avoid having to explain and justify their decisions. Such a practice would obviously undermine any potential benefits to be gained from open pay information.

A decision to switch from a policy of pay secrecy to one of open salary information must obviously be handled with care. If an organization is characterized by a long history of pay secrecy and low levels of trust, an abrupt switch to open pay information may be neither feasible nor desirable. A gradual opening of pay information may be more effective in such situations, beginning, for example, with publication of salary ranges and averages for various positions and moving gradually over time to full, open salary information. An organization must also attend to difficulties in measuring performance when implementing open salary information. As jobs become more complex, the criteria for evaluating performance effectiveness frequently become more ambiguous. In such situations, a policy of full salary openness may not be desirable, since individuals may disagree about the quality of performance of different individuals.

What is critical for all types of jobs at all levels is for managers to rethink their policies regarding pay information. Keeping pay information secret because "we've always done it that way" or because it makes life easier for the managers who don't have to justify their decisions is scant justification for a policy that clearly undermines the potential of pay to serve as a positive motivator of effective performance.

PARTICIPATIVE PAY DECISIONS

A relatively recent innovation that has been tried by some organizations is to involve individuals in the process of setting salaries by permitting all members of the organization to participate directly in pay decisions. Several organizations that have permitted employees to participate directly in the design of salary or bonus systems found that the participatively designed systems resulted in improved attendance, reduced turnover, and higher levels of satisfaction (Lawler, 1976; Jenkins and Lawler, 1981). Other organizations that have permitted decisions regarding annual pay increments to be made by work peers have found that peer groups tend to make such decisions in a highly responsible manner and that such a system results in a high degree of satisfaction with pay and a high level of commitment to the organization.

Naturally, a participative approach to pay decisions is not without its potential difficulties, particularly in situations in which pay decisions are made by work peers and no clear-cut standards of performance (such as number of items produced and sales volume) are available. When the organization places no restriction on the total amount of money available for salary increases, peer groups frequently find it hard to say no to a raise for each member. On the other hand, when the organization does put a limit on total raises available and performance standards aren't clear-cut, there is a tendency for a peer group to decide on equal raises for everyone in order to avoid conflict and disagreement. Such an approach undermines the capacity of the pay system to motivate effective performance since all receive an equal increment regardless of their performance. Finally, as is the case with all types of participative management, the participative process itself is time-consuming and results in a reduction in the total time available for individuals to devote to their primary work responsibilities.

REFERENCES

Glueck, W. F. *Personnel: A diagnostic approach.* rev. ed. Dallas: Business Publications, 1978.

Jenkins, G. D., Jr., and E. E. Lawler III. Impact of employee participation in pay plan development. *Organizational Behavior and Human Performance* (1981) *28*, 111–128.

Lawler, E. E., III. New approaches to pay: Innovations that work. *Personnel,* (1976) *53* (5), 11–23.

14

Employee Stock Ownership Plans: A New Way to Work*

Corey Rosen

Since the Industrial Revolution, it has always been assumed that a few people would actually own the means of production and everyone else would work for them. Any other alternative, it seemed, was socialistic—or worse. In the last 10 years, however, more and more American businesses are taking a new approach—they're making their workers owners.

About 5,000 companies now have employee ownership plans, and a majority of the stock of at least 500 of these is owned by employees. These companies range from small businesses to industrial giants. A hypothetical executive might in any one day use several products made by employee-owned companies. He might, for instance, get up in the morning and have a glass of Juice Bowl orange juice, Starflower granola, Celestial Seasonings tea, and Rath bacon while perusing his *Milwaukee Journal*. Later, he might scan *U.S. News & World Report* and the *Daily Tax Report* from the Bureau of National Affairs. When he returns home, he might don his running shoes made out of Gore-Tex and go to sleep under his George Washington bedspread made by Bates Fabric. All of those products would be produced by companies substantially owned by their employees.

The perhaps surprising fact is that employee ownership has moved into the mainstream of American business. It has received the blessings of Congress through a whole series of tax breaks, and has been endorsed by such disparate figures as Russell Long (its most active proponent), Ted Kennedy, Ronald Reagan, and even Pope John Paul. Some companies are interested in employee ownership simply because it provides tax breaks, but most are attracted to the possibility of creating a new, and more productive, way to work. By making employees owners, the agrument goes, everyone becomes a capitalist, with the result that everyone works harder and more effectively. So far, the evidence seems to bear this theory out, but it also

* From *Business Horizons* (1983) 26, 48–54. Copyright © 1983 by the Foundation for the School of Business, Indiana University.

raises some very distinct warnings. Employee ownership can work very well indeed, it seems to be saying, but it is not magic, and only well-designed plans will live up to expectations.

HOW EMPLOYEE OWNERSHIP PLANS WORK

There are lots of ways to make employees owners, but a vehicle created by Congress in 1974 called an ESOP (employee stock ownership plan) is overwhelmingly the ownership plan of choice.

An ESOP works by creating an employee stock ownership trust (ESOT). The rules of the ESOP are drawn to meet all the requirements of ERISA (the Employee Retirement Income Security Act), which governs employee benefit plans generally. Plans meeting these rules are called "qualified," meaning that companies can take tax deductions or, in some cases, credits, for contributions to them, at least within certain limits.[1]

Companies contribute either stock or cash to buy stock for the trust, where it is allocated to employee accounts and held until the employee leaves the company or retires. Under the law, allocations can be made according to relative compensation or some more egalitarian formula, but they cannot be made in a way that would favor higher-paid employees proportionately more than lower-paid employees. The amount of stock allocated to employees is not yet theirs, however. In order to encourage employees to stay with the company, most plans use a gradual vesting schedule under which employees acquire an increasing right to the shares as the years go by. Typically, employees are not vested for the first 3 years, then vested 30 percent after the third year, 40 percent after the fourth, and so on up to 10. Generally, vesting must be completed by the 10th year (but it can sometimes be the 15th), though it can be completed as fast as a company wants.

In most cases, all full-time employees who have worked at least 1,000 hours in one year must be eligible to participate in the ESOP. It is possible, although generally not a good idea (as we shall see later), to limit the ESOP to just one class of employees, such as office workers, but only if such a limitation is not a way to reward more highly compensated employees. Employees covered by a collective bargaining agreement can also be excluded, but they must have the right to negotiate in.

The stock in the trust must have full voting rights in companies whose stock is publicly traded. In other companies, employees must be able to vote

---

[1] For more detailed information, see "ESOPs: An employer handbook" (Washington, D. C.: U.S. Senate Committee on Finance, 1979); "Employee ownership: A handbook" (Arlingon, Va.: National Center for Employee Ownership, 1982).

their allocated shares only on those issues which by state law or corporate charter require more than a majority vote. Companies can pass through full voting rights, however, and about 15 percent of them do.[2] Companies that do not have a ready market for their stock must also agree to buy the stock back from their departing employees within a reasonable period of time (generally five years), and with interest if the payment is not immediate. The company can, however, also exercise a right of first refusal on the stock to make sure it stays in friendly hands. In order to determine how much the stock being contributed or purchased is worth, closely held companies must have a regular outside valuation done.

Stock contributed to the trust is not taxable to the employee until it is distributed, at which time it can be rolled over into an IRA (in which case no taxes are paid until withdrawals are made), or can be treated according to capital gains or 10-year averaging for most of the amount.

ESOPs also are governed by two very special rules concerning how the company may use them. First, ESOPs are required to invest primarily in the stock of the employer. Second, ESOPs may borrow money. The first rule makes it practical to use an ESOP as a device to make employees owners. Other plans can invest in employer stock, too, but generally cannot hold more than 10 percent of their assets in such stock. If they do, they must be able to show that that decision is fiduciarially sound, which can be hard to do considering all the other investment possibilities. Yet if an employee benefit plan owns only a little employer stock and many other things, it will be hard to convince employees that they are really owners.

The second rule allows companies to use the ESOP to raise capital in a manner that can save tax dollars. Say the Modern Baking Company wants to borrow money for new pie-making machinery. Normally, it would go to the bank, borrow the dollars, and then deduct the interest when it repaid them. If Modern Baking were to use an ESOP, however, it would have the ESOT go to the bank (Modern Baker executives actually, acting for the ESOT) and borrow the money. The ESOT would then use the cash to buy new issues of company stock, meaning the company would get the cash it needs and the ESOT would provide ownership for employees. To repay the loan, the company would make *deductible* cash contributions to the trust. What that means is that the company is deducting, in effect, both the principal and the interest from the loan repayment. Moreover, with the same dollars it uses to finance growth, it is creating an employee benefit plan that (you've guessed it by now) provides the employees not just with a piece of the pie but the pie-making machinery.

---

[2] Thomas Marsh and Dale McAllister, "ESOPs tables: A survey of companies with employee stock ownership plans," *Journal of Corporation Law* (Spring 1981), 593–94.

SOME SPECIFIC USES OF THE ESOP

For most companies, an ESOP is basically an employee benefit plan. Since companies can contribute new issues of stock to the ESOP, it provides a way to provide a benefit without paying any cash up front. Even better, the company can take a tax deduction for the value of the stock it contributes. The company is betting, of course, that the extra productivity the plan generates will create enough growth so that, when employees start to leave the company, there will be cash to pay them off. Good plans anticipate this by making periodic cash contributions to the ESOP to enable it to buy the stock itself.

Another common use of ESOPs is creating a market for the stock of an owner in a closely held firm. Many smaller companies are closed or liquidated, even though they are profitable, simply because no one can be found who is willing to take all the risks that buying them would entail. Even where buyers can be found, owners often prefer to see their employees keep their business tradition going. ESOPs provide a mechanism for addressing this problem. The owner can make deductible cash contributions out of company earnings to allow the ESOP to purchase his or her stock. Alternatively, the ESOP can borrow the cash needed to buy out the owner. In either case, the sale is treated as a capital gain, even though normally a gradual sale of stock by an owner back to the company is treated as dividend income and taxed as ordinary income would be.

A third common use of an ESOP is in cases where employees want to buy a company outright, either because it is failing or because the parent firm wants to divest that operation. Employee buyouts have become increasingly common in recent years, although, contrary to popular impression, they are only a small part of the employee ownership movement. To accomplish a buyout, the employees form a new shell corporation, which sets up an ESOP. The ESOP borrows money to buy the assets of the old company. It then trades the assets for all the stock in the new firm and, presto, the employees own the company. As in any leveraged ESOP, the new company makes tax-deductible contributions to the trust to enable it to repay the loan. In some cases, employees may agree to wage concessions to help assure that their new firm will have the cash flow needed for repayment.

In a related use, ongoing, but distressed, companies are now beginning to trade stock for wage concessions. Pan Am, Conrail, McClouth Steel, and a number of other firms have used this approach. Essentially, the workers are saying that, if they make concessions, they are investing in the company and should, like any invester, get an ownership share.

ESOPs can also be used to acquire companies (the trust takes out a loan to acquire the assets of the target firm), to divest subsidiaries, to go private, or, as in the leveraging model described earlier, to raise capital. One special kind of ESOP, the so-called PAYSOP (payroll-based ESOP) also deserves mention. Starting this year [1983], employers can take a tax credit equal to 0.5 percent of payroll (0.75 percent in 1985–87) for contributions to a specially regulated ESOP. The plan, which generally must be separate from a conventional ESOP, must provide immediate vesting, must not distribute benefits for seven years, and must ignore compensation in excess of $100,000 when allocating stock. According to a recent survey, 70 percent of all major companies either have a PAYSOP or plan to install one.[3] These plans provide such a small amount of stock, however, that, in themselves, they really do not create what would normally be understood as employee ownership.

FINANCIAL DISADVANTAGES OF ESOPs

Despite their much-touted benefits, ESOPs have some significant financial limitations. First, the tax benefits are, obviously, of use only if a firm is making a profit or expects to make one soon. Unused deductions or credits can be carried forward 15 years; but, practically, the real dollar value of deductions used so far in the future is minimal.

Second, any of the ESOP tax benefits are up-front. Down the road, as employees start to leave, the company has a new liability. That means that if the company has not put aside the cash needed to repurchase this stock, it could be in trouble. The ability to put this cash aside will, of course, depend on the company's profitability. For this and the above reason, most ESOP consultants contend that ESOPs are appropriate only for financially healthy firms, and are best for ones with growth prospects.

Third, ESOPs cause a dilution in the equity of other owners where new treasury stock is issued to the trust. Whether this dilution causes a decline in shareholder values depends on whether the ESOP itself creates at least an equivalent amount of value. In a leveraged plan, for instance, the ESOP is being used to acquire new capital, meaning the shareholders now own a smaller percentage of a larger pie. In any ESOP, the extra productivity the ESOP can create can offset or more than offset the dilution effect. Whenever the ESOP passes through voting rights on the stock, however, there is necessarily a dilution in voting control. Whether or not that is an issue, of course, depends on the company.

Finally, ESOP legal fees are high, although model plans developed by the National Center for Employee Ownership and others may help keep costs down. Normally, an ESOP costs a minimum of $10,000 to $15,000 to install, with costs rising with the size of the company. Yearly valuations and

---

[3] *Bureau of National Affairs Tax Report* (October 21, 1982) no. 204: G-1.

administrative costs can add a few thousand dollars every year. Although some very small companies do have ESOPs, and are happy with them, firms with fewer than 10 employees need to consider the costs and benefits very carefully.

HOW ESOPs HAVE WORKED

All these financial considerations are of little consequence, though, if employee ownership fails its real test—improving employee performance. So far, the idea is still too new to have received the thorough testing needed to produce a definitive answer. The initial evidence, however, has been very striking.

A 1978 study by the Institute for Social Research at the University of Michigan, for instance, found that companies with employee ownership plans were 150 percent as profitable as comparable companies without them, and that the ratio was directly related to the amount of equity employees owned (the more they owned, the higher was the ratio).[4] A survey of more that 200 ESOP companies reported in the *Journal of Corporation Law* found that the ESOP firms had an average annual productivity growth rate of 1.52 percent greater than comparable conventional firms.[5] When one considers that average annual U.S. productivity for the period studied grew at only 0.2 percent per year (in the 1960s it was around 3 percent), the magnitude of the difference becomes apparent. Perhaps most impressive are data gathered at Cornell University, where William Whyte and his colleagues have been tracking the approximately 60 employee buyouts of distressed firms that have occurred since 1971. All but four of these are still in business, and most have become profitable.[6] Chicago and Northwestern Railroad, the first major buyout, saw its stock value go up over 100 times. Its first owner, Ben Heilman of Northwest Industries, had complained that the rate of return on the line was "disgusting."

A wide variety of case studies bear these data out, and no methodologically reliable study has yet been done which, on a case or survey basis, suggests that ownership does not contribute to productivity. Still, two major surveys and a handful of case studies cannot prove the point, although they certainly are suggestive.

---

[4] Michael Conte and Arnold Tannenbaum, *Employee ownership* (Ann Arbor: University of Michigan Survey Research Center, 1981).

[5] Marsh and McAllister, "ESOPs tables," 612–15.

[6] Correspondence with William F. Whyte, Cornell University School of Industrial and Labor Relations, 1981–82.

FOUR ESOP FABLES

Four companies—W. L. Gore and Associates, Allied Plywood, the Lowe's Companies, and Saratoga Knitting Mills—typify the positive uses of employee ownership plans.

W. L. Gore is a high-technology manufacturer of a variety of products, including Gore-Tex, a fabric coating that is commonly used in outdoor products. The company is 95 percent owned by employees, or, to be more precise, associates. According to Gore, there are no employees, since everyone owns stock and everyone participates in company affairs. In fact, the company uses what it calls a "lattice" organization in which anyone can communicate with anyone else, without having to go up and down the traditional corporate hierarchies. Employees vote all their stock and elect the board.

The high level of employee involvement may seem to some a recipe for chaos, but Gore has grown at an annual compound rate of 40 percent for the last several years and now employs 2,000 employees. It is currently building another seven plants around the world.

Allied Plywood, by contrast, is a small plywood distributor in northern Virginia. Ed Sanders, the company's founder, had built the company in the course of his business career. In the mid-1970s, he began to think about cashing in his stock and retiring. At first, he simply had the company redeem his stock, but, to his dismay, found that the IRS asked for 70 percent of the price (the top rate at the time). Fortunately, he chanced on a letter to the editor of the *Washington Post,* which described how a company could be sold to its employees through an ESOP. Since he had always considered his 20 employees almost part of the family, this seemed like an ideal approach. Sanders proceeded to set up the ESOP and make annual cash contributions to it. The ESOP took the contributions and bought his shares, with Sanders now paying just capital gains. In 1982, the ESOP took out a loan to buy the remaining 45 percent of the stock Sanders then owned, and the company became 100 percent employee-owned.

Since the ESOP was established, only one employee has left, and that was for personal reasons. Sales have increased, but the number of employees hasn't—a testimony to the fact that as owners the employees want to maximize company earning. Job satisfaction, according to a National Center for Employee Ownership survey, is very high. Perhaps most importantly, the company has been consistently profitable even in the midst of the construction industry depression.

The Lowe's Companies are a notable example of using an ESOP as an employee benefit plan. Lowe's set up an employee ownership plan in 1957. Although technically not an ESOP, the plan operated much like the ESOPs now in use. In 1978, in fact, the plan was formally converted to an ESOP.

Lowe's employs 7,000 people in a chain of home improvement and building supply stores throughout the Southeast. Under its ESOP, employees own 25 percent of the company—a figure Lowe's president Bob Strickland hopes will grow.

When the Lowe's employee ownership plan was started, the company had six stores. Today it has 205. When the plan started, there were five competitors. Three have since sold out, one is only one fourth the size of Lowe's, and the other has just started an ESOP. Lowe's success has filtered down to its employee owners. The company made news in 1975, for instance, when an 18-year employee who never made more than $125 per week cashed in his ESOP shares for $660,000. Six- and even a few seven-figure checks are a regular part of the ESOP program now.

Lowe's plan is not charity, however. Former president Carl Buchan started the plan because he wanted to "give employees a direct, personal self-interest in improving the company's earnings." Strickland says the concept has worked. Sales per employee are three times those of the big three retailers, while profits per employee are twice as high. Shrinkage is less than 0.5 percent. According to Strickland, Lowe's success is a direct function of its employee ownership plan.

Saratoga Knitting Mills, a manufacturer of tricot fabric for women's intimate apparel, presents a very different picture. The company had been a subsidiary of Cluett-Peabody, but in 1975 that conglomerate decided to shut down the mill, claiming its profit potential was inadequate. Together with some outside investors, the employees arranged for a buyout. The ESOP now owns 51 percent of the stock.

In 1975, the company had 64 employees. Today, its stock value has tripled and it employs 134. An ESOP-based acquisition is possible. Productivity is up, waste is down. Scrap loss, for instance, was cut from 1.5 percent to 0.28 percent.

AND SOME FOIBLES

These four cases illustrate the potential of employee ownership, but it should be understood that it would be equally easy to give examples of companies that either fail to realize that potential or simply abuse the idea. Of course, these companies are not eager to have their names in print, but their general characteristics can be identified.

At one company we have studied, for instance, employees own about 9 percent of the stock, but there are no voting or other participation rights associated with the stock. Employees do not think of themselves as owners; if anything, the ESOP has made them somewhat skeptical of management. When employees own so little stock, there simply is no reason to believe that there will be any change in their behavior. The typical ESOP in a closely held firm owns at least 20 percent of the company's stock. Our initial research is indicating that the threshold level at which ownership becomes real to employees is probably around this number in smaller firms. In larger companies, where a smaller percentage means more in terms of control and dollar values, a smaller percentage will probably do the trick. The typical Fortune 500 PAYSOP, however, where employees own less than 1 percent of the stock, will have no significant impact.[7]

Another company made its employees 100 percent owners, and constantly reminded them of this fact, but did not provide any ownership rights. One consultant has suggested that these plans be called "ESAPs"—employee stock appreciation plans—since that is what they really provide. The result was that employees became skeptical about management's motives. Although they appreciated the extra benefit the ESOP represented, they really did not feel like owners, and there was little evidence that they acted that way either. An even more dramatic case is South Bend Lathe, where employees bought the company through an ESOP but did not acquire voting rights for the stock. That was handled by a trust committee appointed by the management. A few years ago, workers at South Bend Lathe, upset about wages and other policies, went on strike.

The essential lesson these companies are teaching is that "ownership" is a very connotative word. Companies that want their employees to act like owners need to treat them like owners. If they simply want to provide an employee benefit plan, with the hopes that it will improve motivation in much the same way a profit-sharing plan might, then they should not call their employees owners. The term may be technically correct, but it is bound to cause confusion and even cynicism.

Treating employees like owners will mean different things in different companies. Voting rights may or may not be crucial, but a clear sense among employees that they have some control over what they do, and that their ideas are treated with respect, is crucial indeed. Companies that provide full participating rights, in our experience, are uniformly pleased with their decision, reporting that employees are responsible shareholders and that employee motivation is very high.

In fact, the joining of employee ownership and participation seems to provide a very effective combination. Although data on this point are scarce, our own experience, and that of consultants in the field, suggests that employee owners are much more ready to participate effectively at the job

---

[7] Corey Rosen, "Employee ownership in the Fortune 500," *Employee Benefit Plan Review Research Report No. 208* (May 1982), 1–5.

and company level. Since an overwhelming literature now confirms the productivity gains that can be made from worker participation, this is a very important connection.[8]

A third company had its stock valued at $10 per share. The owner then wanted to get a bank loan for the ESOP to buy his shares at $70 per share, claiming that this is what he could get on the open market. The bank turned him down. He was lucky they did, for the transaction would have been illegal. These kinds of manipulations of share values, as well as a variety of other practices, violate the basic principle of ESOP law—that the plan operate for "the exclusive benefit of the employees." "Exclusive" does not mean that other people cannot benefit, but whenever there is a conflict between the interests of the employees and some other party, however, the employees come first. Companies that set up plans solely for their tax benefits run a good risk of violating this principle.

Finally, there is the company that had installed an ESOP but most of whose employees didn't know it. As this article suggests, ESOPs are complicated. An effective and ongoing communications program is essential to making an ownership plan work.

The real question a company must ask itself in considering an ESOP, then, is, "Do we really want to share ownership with employees?" If the answer is yes, research and experience indicate that everyone can benefit. By sharing ownership (and, it appears, control as well), the company actually grows, making both management and workers better off.

THE FUTURE OF EMPLOYEE OWNERSHIP

For all its rapid growth, and for all the recent attention it has garnered, employee ownership is still just a footnote to the American economic system. For it to become a basic part of the way we do business, a number of things need to happen.

First, businesses need to be convinced that employee ownership contributes to the bottom line. The data so far are enticing, but not yet decisive. Moreover, most businesspeople still have only a vague familiarity with the concept. It will take, then, more positive results, more publicity, and, mostly, more word of mouth, before the idea really settles into the consciousness of American entrepreneurs and managers. Whether or not this will happen is still uncertain.

Second, business must feel pressure to change and innovate. It has only been recently that American businesses have had to reexamine some of their

---

[8] Carl Frieden, *Workplace democracy and productivity* (Washington, D.C.: Center for Economic Alternatives, 1980).

basic conceptions about management styles and employee relations. Whether the current openness to change remains will presumably depend upon the continued existence of external competitive threats. That, alas, seems likely.

Third, labor unions need to take a more positive approach. Until recently, most unions opposed employee ownership plans, contending that they clouded the union role, were too often used in desperate situations (an inaccurate perception, but a powerful one), and were a threat to pension plans. In the last year or two, however, some national unions, such as the UAW and the Communications Workers, have endorsed the idea and many others are reexamining their position. As unions look for a new relationship to management, it is conceivable that employee ownership could become part of their bargaining agenda. At this time, however, that still seems far off.

The final determinant of the future of employee ownership is whether employees will seek it. As far back as 1975, a Peter Hart opinion poll indicated that Americans would rather work for an employee-owned firm by a three to one margin. As the American worker becomes more educated, moreover, it seems reasonable to assume, as work psychologists have, that more will be demanded from work than just a salary. This trend might well be juxtaposed against an increasing interest in the workplace as a community, one to replace the communities a mobile America is losing. Since people desire to have some control over their communities, they might begin to demand more control over their workplace.

Whatever may come of these trends, employee ownership does seem to represent a very practical alternative for the American economy, one that deserves careful consideration.

Organizational Psychology and the Pursuit of the Happy/Productive Worker*

Barry M. Staw

What I am going to talk about in this article is an old and overworked topic, but one that remains very much a source of confusion and controversy. It is also a topic that continues to attract the attention of managers and academic researchers alike, frequently being the focus of both popular books and scholarly articles. The issue is how to manage an organization so that employees can be both happy and productive—a situation where workers and managers are both satisfied with the outcomes.

The pursuit of the happy/productive worker could be viewed as an impossible dream from the Marxist perspective of inevitable worker–management conflict. Such a goal could also be seen as too simple or naïve from the traditional industrial relations view of outcomes being a product of necessary bargaining and compromise. Yet, from the psychological perspective, the pursuit of the happy/productive worker has seemed a worthwhile though difficult endeavor, one that might be achieved if we greatly increase our knowledge of work attitudes and behavior. In this article, I will examine this psychological perspective and try to provide a realistic appraisal of where we now stand in the search for satisfaction and productivity in work settings.

APPROACHES TO THE HAPPY/PRODUCTIVE WORKER

One of the earliest pursuits of the happy/productive worker involved the search for a relationship between satisfaction and productivity. The idea was that the world might be neatly divided into situations where workers are

* From Barry M. Staw, *California Management Review* (Summer 1986) 27, no. 4, 40–53. © 1986, The Regents of the University of California.

This article is based on an invited address delivered at the 1985 American Psychological Association, Los Angeles, California.

either happy and productive or unhappy and unproductive. If this were true, then it would be a simple matter to specify the differences between management styles present in the two sets of organizations and to come up with a list of prescriptions for improvement. Unfortunately, research has never supported such a clear relationship between individual satisfaction and productivity. For over 30 years, starting with Brayfield and Crockett's classic review of the job satisfaction–performance literaure,[1] and again with Vroom's discussion of satisfaction–performance research,[2] organizational psychologists have had to contend with the fact that happiness and productivity may not necessarily go together. As a result, most organizational psychologists have come to accept the argument that satisfaction and performance may relate to two entirely different individual decisions—decisions to participate and to produce.[3]

Though psychologists have acknowledged the fact that satisfaction and performance are not tightly linked, this has not stopped them from pursuing the happy/productive worker. In fact, over the last 30 years, an enormous variety of theories have attempted to show how managers can reach the promised land of high satisfaction and productivity. The theories shown in Table 1 constitute only an abbreviated list of recent attempts to reach this positive state.

None of the theories in Table 1 have inherited the happy/productive worker hypothesis in the simple sense of believing that job satisfaction and performance generally co-vary in the world *as it now exists*. But, these models all make either indirect or direct assumptions that *it is possible* to achieve a world where both satisfaction and performance will be present. Some of the theories focus on ways to increase job satisfaction, with the implicit assumption that performance will necessarily follow; some strive to directly increase performance, with the assumption that satisfaction will result; and some note that satisfaction and performance will be a joint product of implementing certain changes in the organization.

Without going into the specifics of each of these routes to the happy/productive worker, I think it is fair to say that most of the theories in Table 1 have been oversold. Historically, they each burst on the scene with glowing

---

TABLE 1   Paths to the Happy/Productive Worker

Worker Participation	The Pursuit of Excellence
Supportive Leadership	Socio-Technical Systems
9–9 Systems	Organizational Commitment
Job Enrichment	High Performing Systems
Behavior Modification	Theory Z
Goal Setting	Strong Culture

and almost messianic predictions, with proponents tending to simplify the process of change, making it seem like a few easy tricks will guarantee benefits to workers and management alike. The problem, of course, is that as results have come in from both academic research and from wider practical application, the benefits no longer have appeared so strong nor widespread. Typically, the broader the application and the more well-documented the study (with the experimental controls and measures of expected costs and benefits), the weaker have been the empirical results. Thus, in the end, both managers and researchers have often been left disillusioned, skeptical that any part of these theories are worth a damn and that behavioral science will ever make a contribution to management.

My goal with this article is to *lower our expectations*—to show why it is so difficult to make changes in both satisfaction and performance. My intention is not to paint such a pessimistic picture as to justify not making any changes at all, but to innoculate us against the frustrations of slow progress. My hope is to move us toward a reasoned but sustainable pursuit of the happy/productive worker—away from the alternating practice of fanfare and despair.

CHANGING JOB ATTITUDES

Although organizational psychologists have accepted the notion that job satisfaction and performance do not necessarily co-vary, they have still considered job attitudes as something quite permeable or subject to change. This "blank slate" approach to job attitudes comes from prevailing psychological views of the individual, where the person is seen as a creature who constantly appraises the work situation, evaluates the merits of the context, and formulates an attitude based on these conditions. As the work situation changes, individuals are thought to be sensitive to the shifts, adjusting their attitudes in a positive or negative direction. With such an approach to attitudes, it is easy to see why job satisfaction has been a common target of organizational change, and why attempts to redesign work have evolved as a principal mechanism for improving job satisfaction.

Currently, the major debate in the job design area concerns whether individuals are more sensitive to objective job conditions or social cues. In one camp are proponents of job redesign who propose that individuals are highly receptive to concrete efforts to improve working conditions. Hackman and Oldham, for example, argue that satisfaction can be increased by improving a job in terms of its variety (doing a wider number of things), identity (seeing how one's various tasks make a meaningful whole), responsibility (being in charge of one's own work and its quality), feedback (knowing when one has done a good job), and significance (the meaning or relative importance of one's contribution to the organization or society in general).[4] In the opposing camp are advocates of social information processing. These researchers argue that jobs are often ambiguous entities subject to multiple interpretations and perceptions.[5] Advocates of social information processing have noted that the positive or negative labeling of a task can greatly determine one's attitude toward the job, and that important determinants of this labeling are the opinions of coworkers who voice positive or negative views of the work. These researchers have shown that it may be as easy to persuade workers that their jobs are interesting by influencing the *perception* of a job as it is to make objective changes in the work role.

The debate between job design and social information processing has produced two recent shifts in the way we think about job attitudes. First, organizational psychology now places greater emphasis on the role of cognition and subjective evaluation in the way people respond to jobs. This is probably helpful, because, even though we have generally measured job conditions with perceptual scales, we have tended to confuse these perceptions with objective job conditions. We need to be reminded that perceptions of job characteristics do not necessarily reflect reality, yet they can determine how we respond to that reality.

The second shift in thinking about job attitudes is a movement toward situationalism, stressing how even slight alterations in job context can influence one's perception of a job. It is now believed that people's job attitudes may be influenced not only by the objective properties of the work, but also by subtle cues given off by coworkers or supervisors that the job is dull or interesting. I think this new view is a mistake since it overstates the role of external influence in the determination of job attitudes. The reality may be that individuals are quite resistant to change efforts, with their attitudes coming more as a function of personal disposition than situational influence.

THE CONSISTENCY OF JOB ATTITUDES

Robert Kahn recently observed that, although our standard of living and working conditions have improved dramatically since World War II, reports of satisfaction on national surveys have not changed dramatically.[6] This implies that job satisfaction might be something of a "sticky variable," one that is not so easily changed by outside influence. Some research on the consistency of job attitudes leads to the same conclusion. Schneider and Dachler, for example, found very strong consistency in satisfaction scores over a 16-month longitudinal study (averaging 0.56 for managers and 0.58 for nonmanagers).[7] Pulakos and Schmitt also found that high school students' preemployment expectations of satisfaction correlated significantly with ratings of their jobs several years later.[8] These findings, along with the fact that job satisfaction is generally intertwined with both life satisfaction and mental health, imply that there is some ongoing consistency in job attitudes, and that job satisfaction may be determined as much by dispositional properties of the individual as any changes in the situation.

A Berkeley colleague, Joseph Garbarino, has long captured this notion of a dispositional source of job attitudes with a humorous remark, "I always told my children at a young age that their most important decision in life would be whether they wanted to be happy or not; everything else is malleable enough to fit the answer to this question." What Garbarino implies is that job attitudes are fairly constant, and, when reality changes for either the better or worse, we can easily distort that reality to fit our underlying disposition. Thus, individuals may think a great deal about the nature of their jobs, but satisfaction can result as much from the unique way a person views the world around him as from any social influence or objective job characteristics. That is, individuals predisposed to be happy may interpret their jobs in a much different way than those with more negative predispositions.

The Attitudinal Consistency Study

Recently, I have been involved with two studies attempting to test for dispositional sources of job attitudes. In the first study, Jerry Ross and I reanalyzed data from the National Longitudinal Survey, a study conducted by labor economists at Ohio State.[9] We used this survey to look at the stability of job attitudes over time and job situations. The survey's measures of attitudes were not very extensive but did provide one of the few available sources of data on objective job changes.

The National Longitudinal Survey data revealed an interesting pattern of results. We found that job satisfaction was fairly consistent over time, with significant relationships among job attitudes over three- and five-year time intervals. We also found that job satisfaction showed consistency *even when people changed jobs*. This later finding is especially important, since it directly contradicts the prevailing assumptions of job attitude research.

Most job design experiments and organizational interventions that strive to improve job attitudes change a small aspect of work, but look for major changes in job satisfaction. However, the National Longitudinal Survey data showed that when people changed their place of work (which would naturally include one's supervisor, working conditions, and procedures), there was still significant consistency in attitudes. One could, of course, argue that people leave one terrible job for another, and this is why such consistency in job attitudes arises. Therefore, we checked for consistency across occupational changes. The National Longitudinal Survey showed consistency not only across occupational changes but also when people changed *both* their employers and their occupations. This evidence of consistency tells us that people may not be as malleable as we would like to think they are, and that there may be some underlying tendency toward equilibrium in job attitudes. If you are dissatisfied in one job context, you are also likely to be dissatisfied in another (perhaps better) environment.

The Dispositional Study

The consistency data from the National Longitudinal Survey, while interesting, do not tell us what it is that may underlie a tendency to be satisfied or dissatisfied on the job. Therefore, Nancy Bell (a doctoral student at the Berkeley Business School), John Clausen (a developmental sociologist at Berkeley), and I undertook a study to find some of the dispositional sources of job satisfaction.[10] We sought to relate early personality characteristics to job attitudes later in life, using a very unusual longitudinal data source.

There are three longitudinal personality projects that have been running for over 50 years at Berkeley (the Berkeley Growth Study, the Oakland Growth Study, and the Guidance Study), and they have since been combined into what is now called the Intergenerational Study. Usually when psychologists speak of longitudinal studies, they mean data collected from one- or two-year intervals. These data span over 50 years. Usually, when psychologists refer to personality ratings, they mean self-reports derived from the administration of various questionnaires. Much of the Intergenerational Study data are clinical ratings derived from questionnaires, observation, and interview materials evaluated by a different set of raters for each period of the individual's life. Thus, these data are of unusual quality for psychological research.

Basically what we did with data from the Intergenerational Study was to construct an affective disposition scale that measured a very general positive–negative orientation of people. We then related this scale to measures of job attitudes at different periods in people's lives. The ratings used for our affective disposition scale included items such as "cheerful," "satisfied with self," and "irritable" (reverse coded), and we correlated this scale with measures of job and career satisfaction. The results were very provocative. We found that affective dispositions, from as early as the junior high school years, significantly predicted job attitudes during middle and late adulthood (ages 40–60). The magnitude of correlations was not enormous (in the 0.3 to 0.4 range). But, these results are about as strong as we usually see between two attitudes measured on the same questionnaire by the same person at the same time—yet, these data cut across different raters and over 50 years in time.

What are we to conclude from this personality research as well as our reanalyses of the National Longitudinal Survey? I think we can safely conclude that there is a fair amount of consistency in job attitudes and that there may be dispositional as well as situational sources of job satisfaction. Thus, it is possible that social information processing theorists have been on the right track in viewing jobs as ambiguous entities that necessitate interpretation by individuals. But, it is also likely that the interpretation of jobs (whether they are perceived as positive or negative) can come as much from internal, dispositional causes (e.g., happiness or depression) as external sources.

Consequently, efforts to improve job satisfaction via changes in job conditions will need to contend with stable personal dispositions toward work—forces that may favor consistency or equilibrium in the way people view the world around them.

THE INTRANSIGENCE OF JOB PERFORMANCE

Although we have not conducted research on the consistency of performance or its resistance to change, I think there are some parallels between the problems of changing attitudes and performance. Just as job attitudes may be constrained by individual dispositions, there are many elements of both the individual and work situation that can make improvements in job performance difficult.[11]

Most of the prevailing theories of work performance are concerned with individual motivation. They prescribe various techniques intended to stimulate, reinforce, or lure people into working harder. Most of these theories have little to say about the individual's limits of task ability, predisposition for working hard, or the general energy or activity level of the person. Somewhat naïvely, our theories have maintained that performance is under the complete control of the individual. Even though there are major individual differences affecting the quantity or quality of work produced, we have assumed that, *if the employee really wants to perform better, his or her performance will naturally go up.*

There already exist some rather strong data that refute these implicit assumptions about performance. A number of studies[12] have shown that mental and physical abilities can be reliable predictors of job performance, and it is likely that other dispositions (e.g., personality characteristics) will eventually be found to be associated with effective performance of certain work roles. Thus, influencing work effort may not be enough to cause wide swings in performance, unless job performance is somewhat independent of ability (e.g., in a low skill job). Many work roles may be so dependent on ability (such as those of a professional athlete, musician, inventor) that increases in effort may simply not cause large changes in the end product.

In addition to ability, there may also be other individual factors that contribute to the consistency of performance. People who work hard in one situation are likely to be the ones who exert high effort in a second situation. If, for example, the person's energy level (including need for sleep) is relatively constant over time, we should not expect wide changes in available effort. And, if personality dimensions such as dependability and self-confidence can predict one's achievement level over the lifecourse,[13] then a similar set of personal attributes may well constitute limitations to possible improvements in performance. Already, assessment centers have capitalized on this notion by using personality measures to predict performance in many corporate settings.

Performance may not be restricted just because of the individual's level of ability and effort, however. Jobs may *themselves* be designed so that performance is not under the control of the individual, regardless of ability or effort. Certainly we are aware of the fact that an assembly line worker's output is more a product of the speed of the line than any personal preference. In administrative jobs, too, what one does may be constrained by the work cycle or technical procedures. There may be many people with interlocking tasks so that an increase in the performance of one employee doesn't mean much if several tasks must be completed sequentially or simultaneously in order to improve productivity. Problems also arise in situations where doing one's job better may not be predicated upon a burst of energy or desire but upon increases in materials, financial support, power, and resources. As noted by Kanter, the administrator must often negotiate, hoard, and form coalitions to get anything done on the job, since there are lots of actors vying for the attention and resources of the organization.[14] Thus, the nature of the organization, combined with the abilities and efforts of individuals to maneuver in the organization, may serve to constrain changes in individual performance.

ASSESSING THE DAMAGE

So far I have taken a somewhat dark or pessimistic view of the search for the happy/productive worker. I have noted that, in terms of satisfaction and performance, it may not be easy to create perfect systems because both happiness and performance are constrained variables, affected by forces not easily altered by our most popular interventions and prescriptions for change. Should organizational psychologists, therefore, close up shop and go home? Should we move to a more descriptive study of behavior as opposed to searching for improvements in work attitudes and performance?

I think such conclusions are overly pessimistic. We need to interpret the stickiness of job attitudes and performance not as an invitation to complacency or defeat but as a realistic assessment that it will take very strong treatments to move these entrenched variables. Guzzo, Jackson, and Katzell have recently made a similar point after a statistical examination (called meta-analysis) of organizational interventions designed to improve productivity.[15] They noted that the most effective changes are often *multiple treatments*, where several things are changed at once in a given organization. Thus, instead of idealistic and optimistic promises, we may literally need to throw the kitchen sink at the problem.

The problem of course is that we have more than one kitchen sink! As noted earlier, nearly every theory of organizational behavior has been devoted to predicting and potentially improving job attitudes and performance. And simply aggregating these treatments is not likely to have the desired result, since many of these recommendations consist of conflicting prescriptions for change. Therefore, it would be wiser to look for compatible *systems* of variables that can possibly be manipulated in concert. Let us briefly consider three systems commonly used in organizational change efforts and then draw some conclusions about their alternative uses.

THREE SYSTEMS OF ORGANIZATIONAL CHANGE

The Individually Oriented System

The first alternative is to build a strong individually oriented system, based on the kind of traditional good management that organizational psychologists have been advocating for years. This system would emphasize a number of venerable features of Western business organizations, such as:

- Tying extrinsic rewards (such as pay) to performance.
- Setting realistic and challenging goals.
- Evaluating employee performance accurately and providing feedback on performance.
- Promoting on the basis of skill and performance, rather than personal characteristics, power, or connections.
- Building the skill level of the work force through training and development
- Enlarging and enriching jobs through increases in responsibility, variety, and significance.

All of the above techniques associated with the individually oriented system are designed to promote both satisfaction and productivity. The major principle underlying each of these features is to structure the work and/or reward system so that high performance is either intrinsically or extrinsically rewarding to the individual, thus creating a situation where high performance contributes to job satisfaction.

In practice, there can be numerous bugs in using an individually oriented system to achieve satisfaction and performance. For example, just saying that rewards should be based on performance is easier than knowing what the proper relationship should be or whether there should be discontinuities at the high or low end of that relationship. Should we, for instance, lavish rewards on the few highest performers, deprive the lowest performers, or establish a constant linkage between pay and performance? In terms of goal-setting, should goals be set by management, workers, or joint decision making, and what should the proper baseline be for measuring improvements? In terms of job design, what is the proper combination of positive social cues and actual job enrichment that will improve motivation and satisfaction?

These questions are important and need to be answered in order to "fine-tune" or fully understand an individually oriented system. Yet, even without answers to these questions, we already know that a well-run organization using an individually oriented system *can* be effective. The problem is we usually don't implement such a system, either completely or very well, in most organizations. Instead, we often compare poorly managed corporations using individually oriented systems (e.g., those with rigid bureaucratic structures) with more effectively run firms using another motivational system (e.g., Japanese organizations), concluding that the individual model is wrong. The truth may be that the individual model may be just as correct as other approaches, but we simply don't implement it as well.

The Group-Oriented System

Individually oriented systems are obviously not the only way to go. We can also have a group-oriented system, where satisfaction and performance are derived from group participation. In fact, much of organizational life could be designed around groups, if we wanted to capitalize fully on the power of groups to influence work attitudes and behavior.[16] The basic idea would be to make group participation so important that groups would be capable of controlling both satisfaction and performance. Some of the most common techniques would be:

- Organizing work around intact groups.
- Having groups charged with selection, training, and rewarding of members.
- Using groups to enforce strong norms for behavior, with group involvement in off-the-job as well as on-the-job behavior.
- Distributing resources on a group, rather than individual, basis.
- Allowing and perhaps even promoting intergroup rivalry so as to build within-group solidarity.

Group-oriented systems may be difficult for people at the top to control, but they can be very powerful and involving. We know from military research that soldiers can fight long and hard, not out of special patriotism but from devotion and loyalty to their units. We know that participation in various high-tech project groups can be immensely involving, both in terms of one's attitudes and performance. We also know that people will serve long and hard hours to help build or preserve organizational divisions or departments, perhaps more out of loyalty and altruism than self-interest. Thus, because individuals will work to achieve group praise and adoration, a group-oriented system, effectively managed, can potentially contribute to high job performance and satisfaction.

The Organizationally Oriented System

A third way of organizing work might be an organizationally oriented system, using the principles of Ouchi's Theory Z and Lawler's recommendations for developing high-performing systems.[17] The basic goal would be to arrange working conditions so that individuals gain satisfaction from contributing to the entire organization's welfare. If individuals were to identify closely with the organization as a whole, then organizational performance would be intrinsically rewarding to the individual. On a less-altruistic basis, individuals might also gain extrinsic rewards from association with a high-performing organization, since successful organizations may provide greater personal opportunities in terms of salary and promotion. Common features of an organizationally oriented system would be:

- Socialization into the organization as a whole to foster identification with the entire business and not just a particular subunit.

- Job rotation around the company so that loyalty is not limited to one subunit.

- Long training period, with the development of skills that are specific to the company and not transferable to other firms in the industry or profession, thus committing people to the employing organization.

- Long-term or protected employment to gain organizational loyalty, with concern for survival and welfare of the firm.

- Decentralized operations, with few departments or subunits to compete for the allegiance of members.

- Few status distinctions between employees so that dissension and separatism are not fostered.

- Economic education and sharing of organizational information about products, financial condition, and strategies of the firm.

- Tying individual rewards (at all levels in the firm) to organizational performance through various forms of profit sharing, stock options, and bonuses.

The Japanese have obviously been the major proponents of organizationally oriented systems, although some of the features listed here (such as profit sharing) are very American in origin. The odd thing is that Americans have consistently followed an organizationally oriented system for middle and upper management and for members of professional organizations such as law and accounting firms. For these high-level employees, loyalty may be as valued as immediate performance, with the firm expecting the individual to defend the organization, even if there does not seem to be any obvious self-interest involved. Such loyalty is rarely demanded or expected from the lower levels of traditional Western organizations.

EVALUATING THE THREE SYSTEMS

I started this article by noting that it may be very difficult to change job performance and satisfaction. Then I noted that recognition of this difficulty should not resign us to the present situation but spur us to stronger and more systemic actions—in a sense, throwing more variables at the problem. As a result, I have tried to characterize three syndromes of actions that might be effective routes toward the happy/productive worker.

One could build a logical case for the use of any of the three motivational systems. Each has the potential for arousing individuals, steering their behavior in desired ways, and building satisfaction as a consequence of high performance. Individually oriented systems work by tapping the desires and goals of individuals and by taking advantage of our cultural affinity for independence. Group-oriented systems work by taking advantage of our more social selves, using group pressures and loyalty as a means of enforcing desired behavior and dispensing praise for accomplishments. Finally, organizationally oriented systems function by building intense attraction to the goals of an institution, where individual pleasure is derived from serving the collective welfare.

If we have three logical and defensible routes toward achieving the happy/productive worker, which is the best path? The answer to this question will obviously depend on how the question is phrased. If "best" means appropriate from a cultural point of view, we will get one answer. As Americans, although we respect organizational loyalty, we often become suspicious of near-total institutions where behavior is closely monitored and strongly policed—places like the company town and religious cult. If we define "best" as meaning the highest level of current performance, we might get a different answer, since many of the Japanese-run plants are now outperforming the American variety. Still, if we phrase the question in terms of *potential* effectiveness, we may get a third answer. Cross-cultural comparisons, as I mentioned, often pit poorly managed individually oriented systems (especially those with noncontingent rewards and a bureaucratic promotion system) against more smoothly running group or organizationally oriented systems. Thus, we really do not know which system, managed to its potential, will lead to the greatest performance.

Mixing the Systems

If we accept the fact that individual, group, and organizationally oriented systems may each do *something* right, would it be possible to take advantage of all three? That is, can we either combine all three systems into some suprasystem or attempt to build a hybrid system by using the best features of each?

I have trepidations about combining the three approaches. Instead of a stronger treatment, we may end up with either a conflicted or confused environment. Because the individually oriented system tends to foster competition among individual employees, it would not, for example, be easily merged with group-oriented systems that promote intragroup solidarity. Likewise, organizationally oriented systems that emphasize how people can serve a common goal may not blend well with group-oriented sytems that foster intergroup rivalry. Finally, the use of either a group- or organizationally oriented reward system may diminish individual motivation, since it becomes more difficult for the person to associate his behavior with collective accomplishments and outcomes. Thus, by mixing the motivational approaches, we may end up with a watered-down treatment that does not fulfill the potential of *any* of the three systems.

In deciding which system to use, we need to face squarely the costs as well as benefits of the three approaches. For example, firms considering an individually oriented system should assess not only the gains associated with increases in individual motivation but also potential losses in collaboration that might result from interpersonal competition. Similarly, companies thinking of using a group-oriented system need to study the trade-offs of intergroup competition that can be a by-product of increased intragroup solidarity. And, before thinking that an organizationally oriented system will solve all the firm's problems, one needs to know whether motivation to achieve collective goals can be heightened to the point where it outweighs potential losses in motivation toward personal and group interests. These trade-offs are not trivial. They trigger considerations of human resource policy as well as more general philosophical issues of what the organization wants to be. They also involve technical problems for which current organizational research has few solutions, since scholars have tended to study treatments in isolation rather than the effect of larger systems of variables.

So far, all we can be sure of is that task structure plays a key role in formulating the proper motivational strategy. As an example, consider the following cases: a sales organization can be divided into discrete territories (where total performance is largely the sum of individual efforts), a research organization where several product groups are charged with making new developments (where aggregate performance is close to the sum of group efforts), and a high-technology company where success and failure is due to total collaboration and collective effort. In each of these three cases, the choice of the proper motivational system will be determined by whether one views individual, group, or collective effort as the most important element. Such a choice is also determined by the degree to which one is willing to sacrifice (or trade off) a degree of performance from other elements of the system, be they the behavior of individuals, groups, or the collective whole. Thus, the major point is that each motivational system has its relative strengths and weaknesses—that despite the claims of many of our theories of management, there is no simple or conflict-free road to the happy/productive worker.

CONCLUSION

Although this article started by noting that the search for the happy/productive worker has been a rather quixotic venture, I have tried to end the discussion with some guarded optimism. By using individual, group, and organizational systems, I have shown how it is *at least possible* to create changes that can overwhelm the forces for stability in both job attitudes and performance. None of these three approaches are a panacea that will solve all of an organization's problems, and no doubt some very hard choices must be made between them. Yet, caution need not preclude action. Therefore, rather than the usual academic's plea for further research or the consultant's claim for bountiful results, we need actions that are flexible enough to allow for mistakes and adjustments along the way.

REFERENCES

1. Brayfield, A. H. and W. H. Crockett. "Employee attitudes and employee performance." *Psychological Bulletin* (1955) *51*, 396–424.
2. Vroom, Victor H. *Work and motivation.* New York: John Wiley & Sons, 1969.
3. March, James G., and Herbert A. Simon. *Organizations.* New York: John Wiley & Sons, 1958.
4. Hackman, Richard J., and Greg R. Oldham. *Work redesign.* Reading, Mass: Addison-Wesley, 1980.
5. E.g., Salancik, Gerald R., and Jeffrey Pfeffer. "A social information processing approach to job attitudes and task design." *Administrative Science Quarterly* (1978) *23*, 224–53.
6. Robert Kahn (1985).
7. Schneider, Benjamin, and Peter Dachler. "A note on the stability of the job description index." *Journal of Applied Psychology* (1978) *63*, 650–53.
8. Pulakos, Elaine D., and Neal Schmitt. "A longitudinal study of a valance model approach for the prediction of job satisfaction of new employees." *Journal of Applied Psychology* (1983) *68*, 307–12.
9. Staw, Barry M., and Jerry Ross. "Stability in the midst of change: A dispositional approach to job attitudes." *Journal of Applied Psychology* (1985) *70*, 469–80.
10. Staw, Barry M., Nancy E. Bell, and John A. Clausen. "The dispositional approach to job attitudes: A lifetime longitudinal test." *Administrative Science Quarterly* (March 1986).
11. See: Peters, Lawrence H., Edward J. O'Connor, and Joe R. Eulberg. "Situational constraints: Sources, consequences, and future considerations." In *Research in personnel and human resources management*, vol. 3, Kendreth M. Rowland and Gerald R. Ferris, eds. (Greenwich, Conn.: JAI Press, 1985).
12. For a review, see Dunnette, Marvin D. "Aptitudes, abilities, and skills." In *Handbook of industrial and organizational psychology*, Marvin D. Dunnette, ed., (Chicago: Rand McNally, 1976).
13. As found by John Clausen, personal communications, 1986.
14. Kanter, Rosabeth M. *The change masters.* New York: Simon & Schuster, 1983.
15. Guzzo, Richard A., Susan E. Jackson, and Raymond A. Katzell. "Meta-analysis

analysis. In *Research in organizational behavior,* vol. 9, Barry M. Staw and Larry L. Cummings, eds. (Greenwich, Conn.: JAI Press, 1987).

16. See: Leavitt, Harold J. "Suppose we took groups seriously." In *Man and work in society,* E. L. Cass and F. G. Zimmer, eds. (New York: Van Nostrand, 1975).

17. Ouchi, William, *Theory Z: How American business can meet the Japanese challenge.* Reading, Mass: Addison-Wesley, 1981. Lawler, Edward E., III. "Increasing worker involvement to enhance organizational effectiveness." In *Change in organizations,* Paul Goodman, ed. (San Francisco: Jossey-Bass, 1982).

Organizations and People: Patterns of Conflict and Accommodation

INTRODUCTION

So far as is known, no work organization to date has completely reconciled its goals and operations with the needs and interests of all its participants. To begin, participants have discordant preference orderings among themselves, giving rise to political processes in which some gain at the expense of others. Also, the structural devices that create the very condition of organization impose constraints upon behavior, and these constraints are more onerous for some than others. Inevitably, instances of abuse will occur, some by accident and some by plan.

Increasingly, one hears these days of "job stress." Organ examines the varied meanings that people attach to this term and the implications for health, emotion, performance, and adaptation.

In a recent article for *Fortune*, Alan Farnham reports ominous trends in the state of employee trust in the leaders of their organizations. Farnham traces the decline in trust to what some believe is a disproportionate share of the loot by a few people in top positions, coupled with the increasing isolation of those affluent few from the hard realities of the day-to-day work experience of the rank and file. Fortunately, the author can report specific companies and top managers that have reversed this trend.

A continued cause of dismay to many observers of American business, in addition to the "trust gap," is another sort of gap—that between the earnings of men and women. Some analysts contend the differential results from an impersonal market, with too many women entering occupations for which there is little labor demand. Others say the cause is discrimination and argue for compensation based on the inherent "comparable worth of the jobs that people perform." Mahoney examines the economic, philosophical, and administrative aspects of this issue and assesses the prospects for its amicable resolution.

In the reckoning of some students of organization, turnover of personnel reflects poor management. Yet, ironically, while turnover may well indicate unresolved points of conflict between people and organizations,

Dalton and Todor argue that turnover is a constructive means of improving the fortunes of the individual as well as of the organization. They suggest that a certain degree of turnover is a sign of a healthy labor market, a means of diffusing innovations across firms, a boon to individual careers, and a necessary condition of social progress.

Absenteeism, like turnover, might at first glance be taken as evidence of unresolved conflicts between people and organizations. Gary Johns explains, however, why we must consider absence from work as a more complex phenomenon. Dissatisfaction with the work itself, to be sure, seems to account for some portion of job absences, but other factors appear to be involved. And, while absence from work is costly, it might provide the most available means by which some people are able to cope with their particular forms of work stress.

The Meaning of Stress*

Dennis W. Organ

Stress has become a modern watchword with a variety of meanings, both popular and scientific. Recent studies in the physiology of stress have important implications for executive behavior.

Everybody knows about it, everyone talks about it, and—judging by the number of paperback books and magazine articles currently devoted to the subject—everyone seems to be interested in it. People complain about the stress of work and the stress of retirement; the stress of poverty and the stress created by fame and riches; the stress of crowding and the stress of isolation; the stress of adolescence and the stress of the midlife crisis. To describe someone as "working under enormous stress" is at once to offer sympathy and to accord a measure of respect. To fail at a task *because* of stress is no shame; to succeed *in spite of* stress renders success all the more glorious. Any behavior, no matter how bizarre, cruel, or apparently irrational, is suddenly understandable if we imagine the behaver as operating under stress. Any act of love or benevolence is somehow tarnished if it did not create stress for the actor or was not born out of the very crucible of stress.

Stress, in sum, has become a watchword of the time, a sibilant one-syllable utterance that comes as close as any one word to expressing the subjective tone of a world view. But the term has developed an elasticity of meaning. The word functions more and more to express, rather than denote. Thus, the term becomes more susceptible to usage when it can be neither proved nor disproved, and when it is, therefore, neither meaningful nor helpful. This would not be cause for concern if stress were merely a vernacular term like *love, anger, ambition,* or *luck.* Certain words are useful precisely because they are preserved for signifying what is, after all, ineffable. *Stress,* however, is also a scientific term. Now there would be no problem if the scientific use of stress were strictly divorced from its vernacular usage; after all, one seldom experiences any problem distinguishing between the tension of a wire and the tension of studying for an exam, or between the pressure exerted by a liquid in a container and the pressure experienced when one is working on a tight schedule. In both cases the technical terms are precise, and the nontechnical meanings are vague and inchoate. One will at times belabor the analogies for literary or rhetorical effect, but no one seriously tries to apply the laws of physics to studying for an exam or working under a deadline. Unfortunately, the vernacular and technical meaning of "stress" have become thoroughly confused, possibly because they do overlap to some degree. The confusion has occasioned some serious misunderstanding about the relationships between stress and illness, stress and adaptation, stress and performance, and even stress and life.

VERNACULAR MEANINGS

In everyday discourse, "stress" has a pejorative connotation. If used in reference to something outside us, it generally means something to be avoided or, at best, a necessary evil: a critical, hard-driving boss; congested urban traffic; a final exam; preparing an income tax return on the night of April 14; enduring Howard Cosell's commentary while you watch the Cowboys and the Vikings. If used to describe a subjective feeling, the term is roughly synonymous with tension, dread, anxiety, or worry. Occasionally we do, of course, dilute the pejorative color of the term by associating it with achievements of one sort or another, as when a speaker welcomes the "edge" of stress (tension) before taking the podium, or the stress (pain) of training and preparing for the Boston Marathon. Yet even then the term is used in what is essentially as intrinsically negative sense, "good" only because it is inextricably linked to an eventual outcome (success, victory) which is sought. In brief, we use the term in everyday parlance to mean either a source or cause of discomfort, or the feelings of discomfort itself—that is, "distress."

Now there is nothing wrong or incorrect in using the word in this manner. In fact, the dictionary will confirm that this is a perfectly acceptable form of usage. It is wrong only when one substitutes this definition of stress for the precise technical meaning of stress in statements about relationships between stress and illness, performance, and adaptation. As a technical term in medical science, stress is not something "out there," nor is it a state of mind. Both external circumstances and internal emotional states can be *stressors*, or sources of stress (although neither the circumstances nor the emotion need be unpleasant, undesired, or negative in order to qualify as stressors). But stress itself, as a technical term, refers to a pattern of complex, albeit well-defined physiological reactions.

STRESS AS A PHYSIOLOGICAL STATE

Stress became a scientific construct when it was defined and elaborated in the research and writing of Professor Hans Selye. As a young medical student at the University of Prague in 1925, Selye was struck by the observation that certain symptoms seemed to correlate with illness of all types. A physician could not complete a diagnosis for a patient based on the evidence that he was suffering from headaches, loss of appetite, nausea, and weakness in the muscles; the doctor would need something more "specific" in order to determine what the underlying problem was. Selye wondered if there might not be something of significance to this observation, namely that the body has a stereotyped, nonspecific reaction to any demand placed upon it. He later discovered in experiments with laboratory animals that whether one subjected rats to extreme cold, injected chemical irritants into their tissue, or simply forcefully immobilized them, there were certain common reactions in the animal's physiological processes. Of course, there were specific effects associated with each particular treatment, but Selye was interested in the common denominators—the invariant response of the organism's body to any demand placed upon it. The common features constituted what Selye labeled the general adaptation syndrome, or G.A.S.—the symptoms by which a state of stress is manifested.

Selye's *The Stress of Life*, published in 1956 and written for non-technically trained audiences, makes it clear that one of the conspicuous agents in this syndrome is the pituitary, a cherry-sized organ resting at the base of the brain. When some external force (a germ, overload on a muscle group, extreme cold) threatens the body, the pituitary signals the alarm stage, the first of the three-stage G.A.S., by sending ACTH (the adrenocorticotrophic hormone) to the endocrine glands, including the adrenals. The adrenals, in response, secrete their hormones (adrenalin and noradrenalin, collectively called the catecholamines) into the bloodstream, and eventually these in collaboration with the sympathetic nervous system trigger a succession of changes in the body chemistry, including changes in the digestive organs, metabolism, and the level of fatty acids and clotting elements in the blood. These effects triggered by the adrenals constitute the second stage of Selye's G.A.S., the stage of resistance, during which the organism seemingly adapts to the demand placed upon it, enabling it to neutralize, isolate, or minimize the damage to the integrity of the organism as a whole. Given sufficiently long exposure to any of the noxious elements (severe cold, chemical irritant, electric shock), the third stage, exhaustion, follows as the adaptive energies of the organism are depleted.

For Selye, then, stress means the common denominator of all adaptive reactions by the body to stressors placed upon it. While Selye means demands of any kind, his interest is clearly in those demands which are clearly physical in nature. Psychologists have, on the other hand, been more interested in demands which are more subtle—demands originating from the social environment, demands cued by symbols, or demands exerted by the emotions and the psyche. Such demands are quite relevant to the concept of stress as defined by Selye because of the mediating role played by the hypothalamus, one of the lower centers of the brain. The hypothalamus regulates many functions of the body, including hunger and temperature; it regulates emotions; and, under conditions of emotional arousal (fear, anger, even ecstasy), sends messages to the pituitary which trigger the sequence of events described in Selye's endocrine studies. It is important, however, to note that any strong emotional response—whether interpreted as "good" or "bad," or even whether a person is consciously aware of or attending to the emotion—results in stress as defined by Selye.

But the emotion is the stressor, not the stress itself; the emotion is the source of the demand which triggers the stress response. The demand need not be emotional in nature to evoke the stress response. So when we speak of *psychological stress* in a way which is at all faithful to the technical meaning of stress, we mean demands or sources of stress that are psychological in nature—for example, anxiety, frustration, or approach-avoidance conflict. There are other demands on the body which evoke the stress response yet arouse no strong feelings at all, and we find that many instances of emotional arousal not ordinarily thought of as "stressful" (in the vernacular) do in fact lead to stress as defined by Selye.

STRESS AND FEELINGS

Consider the results of an experiment conducted by Dr. Lennart Levi of the Karolinska Institute in Stockholm.[1] On successive evenings he arranged for 20 female clerical workers to see four films. The first of these was a bland movie about the Swedish countryside. The other movies were selected for their presumed ability to arouse some strong emotion: *Paths of Glory*, a movie about the arbitrary execution of three men as scapegoats following a breakdown of a French army unit in World War I, was considered to be anger-provoking; *Charleys' Aunt*, a comedy, was expected to induce a pleasant emotional arousal; and *The Mask of Satan*, a horror film, was selected to arouse fear and anxiety. The films had their intended effects, as shown by the subjects' ratings and descriptions of the movies as well as their reports of their own reactions. The natural scenery film they judged to be rather boring; they felt aggressive and angry watching *Paths of Glory*; amused, happy, and laughing at *Charley's Aunt*; and frightened by *Mask of Satan*. In other words, subjects "felt" different emotions for the different movies. Levi found, however, in an analysis of subjects' urine samples following each movie that, except for the dull scenery film, the movies were equally stressful, regardless of whether the film provoked a "pleasant" or "unpleasant" emotion. All three of the movies inducing emotional arousal were associated with increased levels of adrenalin and noradrenalin in the urine, a tell-tale indicator of the stress syndrome defined by Selye.

---

[1] Lennart Levi, *Stress and distress in response to psychosocial stimuli* (New York: Pergamon Press, 1972), 55–73.

STRESS AND ILLNESS

Table 1 shows a list of changes or events that can occur in a person's life. With each event a number is associated that serves as a rough index of the relative degree of adjustment demanded by the event. The weighting scheme was derived through studies by Professors T. H. Holmes and R. H. Rahe and their colleagues at the University of Washington.[2] Their studies asked people of varying ages and from several different cultures to compare each event with each other in terms of the degree of adjustment required. It seems to be universally agreed that the death of a spouse requires more adjustment on the part of the surviving spouse than any other single event. The table provides a rough measure of the degree of adjustment required of a person by totaling the number of points associated with each change in a given period.

Holmes and his coworkers find that once a person "earns" 200 or more points in a single year, there is at least a 50–50 chance of experiencing a fairly serious breakdown in health in the following year. One who totals up 300 or more points in a year runs that risk factor up to a 75–80 percent chance. The illness brought on by such demands for adjustment can appear in almost every specific form: digestive ailments, respiratory problems, back trouble, kidney malfunction, injuries to the bones or muscles, almost any breakdown in the body's economy. What is the explanation for this relationship? Significant changes in one's immediate life environment trigger rapid succession of new situations with which one has to cope. The endocrine system—the intricate collaborative workings of the pituitary, the adrenals, the extra doses of hormones—provides the means for borrowing from the long-term store of adaptation energy in order to provide the sustained arousal and vigilance needed to cope with the novelty, uncertainty, or conflict occasioned by the new situations. But remember it is this encodrine system which provides the basis for resistance to any agent which threatens the body. We are constantly exposed to, even constantly transporting within us, microbes that can do damage to body tissues. Usually a healthy immune system defends against such bacteria. But if the endocrine system is constantly marshaling the body's energy for adjustment, the capacity for resisting those lurking microbes will be exhausted. Thus, wherever the body is most vulnerable, a breakdown can occur after a period of sufficiently great demands for social or psychological adjustment.[3]

One should take note of the fact that a number of events in Table 1 are "positive"; one ordinarily thinks of them as occasions for pleasure or celebration. The layman's definition of "stress" as something to be avoided,

---

[2] T. H. Holmes and R. H. Rahe, "The social readjustment rating scale," *Journal of Psychosomatic Research* (November 1968), 213–18.

[3] For a readable account of the effect of life changes on illness, see Alvin Toffler, *Future shock* (New York: Random House, 1970), 289–304.

TABLE 1 Social Readjustment Rating Scale

Life Event	Scale Value
Death of spouse	100
Divorce	73
Marital separation	65
Jail term	63
Death of a close family member	63
Major personal injury or illness	53
Marriage	50
Fired from work	47
Marital reconciliation	45
Retirement	45
Major change in health of family member	44
Pregnancy	40
Sex difficulties	39
Gain of a new family member	39
Business readjustment	39
Change in financial state	38
Death of a close friend	37
Change to a different line of work	36
Change in number of arguments with spouse	35
Mortgage over $10,000	31
Foreclosure of mortgage or loan	30
Change in responsibilities at work	29
Son or daughter leaving home	29
Trouble with in-laws	29
Outstanding personal achievement	28
Wife begins or stops work	26
Begin or end school	26
Change in living conditions	25
Revision of personal habits	24
Trouble with boss	23
Change in work hours or conditions	20
Change in residence	20
Change in schools	20
Change in recreation	19
Change in church activities	19
Change in social activities	18
Mortgage or loan less than $10,000	17
Change in sleeping habits	16
Change in number of family get-togethers	15
Change in eating habits	15
Vacation	13
Christmas	12
Minor violations of the law	11

SOURCE: L. O. Ruch and T. H. Holmes, "Scaling of life change: Comparison of direct and indirect methods," *Journal of Psychosomatic Research* (June 1971), 224.

something not preferred, hardly seems to apply to events such as marriage, birth of a child, promotion, outstanding personal achievement, sudden drastic improvement in financial position, moving to a bigger home in a better neighborhood, or graduation from college. Yet, to the extent that these events pose demands for adjustment, they are stressful in Selye's sense; and, if enough of these changes are bunched together, they can produce health problems.

One can also see in the "Type A" coronary-prone behavior pattern, described by Meyer Friedman and Ray H. Rosenman, how the linkage between stress, technically defined, and illness is somewhat different from the relationship involving the vernacular meaning of stress as distress. The Type A pattern is one of struggle against the limitations of time; of poised, combative, even hostile striving to compete against other people; of stretching one's self incessantly against self-imposed goals in leisure as well as work.[4]

In *The Hurricane Years*, Cameron Hawley has given us a personification of the Type A executive in the character of Judd Wilder. In the opening pages of the novel, Wilder, an advertising and promotion executive for a carpet company, is leaving the Pennsylvania turnpike and trying to return from New York with the proofs of the stockholders' report before 8:30 that evening. There is no particular urgency in getting the report back by that time; it is simply a goal Wilder has set for himself. Behind the wheel, he experiences a massive heart attack and is rushed to a county hospital. There he comes under the care of Dr. Aaron Kharr, who soon recognizes the behavior pattern characteristic of men like Wilder: ". . . inherently aggressive, competitive, energetic, and ambitious . . . naturally geared to operate at a high adrenaline level."

The incessant process of struggle provokes a chronically fast-paced tempo of the endocrine system with consequent chronically high levels of adrenal hormones in the blood. These hormones, which cannot be metabolized in the overt fight-or-flight response for which they were designed by evolution, cause clotting elements in the blood which speed up the formation of plaques in the arterial walls. Thus, Type A's have a much higher than average risk of premature coronary artery disease, even when other risk factors (such as high blood pressure, cigarette smoking, high-fat diet) are held constant.

Curiously, though, the Type A does not think of himself as "nervous," "under stress," or in any sense crippled by anxiety. Indeed, according to Friedman and Rosenman, anxiety is an unfamiliar state of mind to the extreme Type A. Also, Type A's seldom experience the subjective sense of

---

[4] Meyer Friedman and Ray H. Rosenman, *Type A behavior and your heart* (New York: Knopf, 1974).

fatigue.[5] The stress which is the bane of Type A's is not conscious discomfort or distress on an emotional dimension, but rather the response of the endocrine system to the unreasonable succession of demands they place upon themselves as they, like Judd Wilder, become "hooked on adrenaline."

STRESS AND PERFORMANCE

An issue long of interest to layman and scientist alike concerns the effect of stress on job performance. Some people believe that a lapse in performance is itself evidence of unusual stress experienced by the performer; others believe that stress is a direct contributor to improved, more effortful work on a job. Certainly stress, in the vernacular sense, is likely to impair performance of a complex task because of the distractions produced by worry or fear or other connotations inherent in the layman's definition of stress. However, if we define stress in the more precise, scientific manner as intended by Selye, we can discern no general relationship in the empirical data between stress and quality of performance. The reason for this is that the stress syndrome is in response to the total demand from all sources placed on the person. Part of that demand may be the very effort to maintain performance in the presence of simultaneously competing demands from the environment, such as unpredictable noise, information overload, fatigue from illness, or even distractions by sexually arousing stimuli.

Studies by Professor David Glass and his colleagues at Rockefeller University show that subjects working on a clerical task under conditions of randomly intermittent, irritating noise were able to stabilize at a performance level equivalent to subjects working under less-adverse conditions.[6] The evidence of stress induced by the noise came not in any differences in quantity or quality of work between groups but later, *after* the noise ended. Subjects who had coped with the simultaneous demands of performing as well as coping with the noise later showed less tolerance for the frustration of trying to solve what was (unbeknownst to them) actually an insoluble puzzle. Glass was not willing to go so far as to say that the stress of adaptation had *caused* the subsequent decline in frustration tolerance, but the link certainly suggests that stress is more often behaviorally reflected in situations temporally and spatially removed from the original sources of demand than it is shown directly or immediately in "performance." The adaptation energy extracted by a higher than normal level of endocrine activity must be replenished sooner or later, and the involuntary "letdown" which seems to

---

[5] See David C. Glass, *Behavior patterns, stress, and coronary disease* (Hillsdale, N.J.: Lawrence Erlbaum Associates, 1977), 42–50.

[6] David C. Glass and Jerome E. Singer, *Urban stress: Experiments in noise and social stressors* (New York: Academic Press, 1972).

be necessary for such replenishment may show up in such trivial, apparently unrelated symptoms as forgetting to lock the garage door, injuring oneself with a power saw, or inadvertently dumping cigarette ashes into one's full cup of coffee.

STRESS AND ADAPTATION

Actually, the replenishment of adaptation enengy referred to above is illusory, according to Selye. Selye believes that each person has a fixed, finite reservoir of adaptation energy to feed the endocrine system. One cannot increase this amount; all one can do is occasionally transfer some from long-term reserves to a smaller but more immediately available status— much like depositing some of your life's savings into current withdrawal accounts. That transfer, it appears, does require some temporary lapse in the form of rest or even "depression." But it is nonetheless a borrowing which can never be repaid.

Thus "adaptation" is costly. To the layman, someone adapting to a stressful condition is functioning in the condition so that it is no longer stressful; one "is getting used to it so it doesn't bother him anymore." For Selye, however, adaptation is the very stuff of which stress is made. It is precisely the process of getting used to it—whether "it" be cold temperatures, muscular strain, or a critical boss—which uses up some of the fixed store of adaptation energy.

IMPLICATIONS FOR MANAGERS

To eliminate stress means to eliminate all things which require adaptation, and that virtually means to eliminate life itself. Even to reduce stress to minimal practical levels means never to visit a stimulating city, never to gaze at an attractive woman, never to take up new activities, never to pursue one's dreams—if possible, even never to dream. Surely, such a life is hardly worth living, whatever it might promise in the form of longevity. As Selye puts it:

> Vitality is like a special kind of bank account which you can use up by withdrawals but cannot increase by deposits. Your only control over this most precious fortune is the rate at which you make your withdrawals. . . . The intelligent thing to do is to withdraw generously but never expend wastefully.

Selye concedes that there are probably vast differences among individuals in the amount of adaptation energy given to them to draw upon. And even his basic premise, that the amount of adaptation energy available to a person is a genetically predetermined constant, is a theoretical supposition not shared by all other experts. Nevertheless, his point of view is worth pondering, for it poses some serious philosophical implications.

Consider, for example, the adage that "anything worth doing at all is worth doing well." Quite a few people, many successful managers among them, seem to live and work implicitly by this principle. Yet managers often seem to agree with another notion that "80 percent of your success is determined by 20 percent of what you do." Selye's position would be that the crucially important 20 percent may be well worth the extravagant stores of endocrine-derived adaptation energy necessary to meet the demands posed by the 20 percent. For the remaining 80 percent, however, it would be wasteful, uneconomical, and downright inefficient to place the same demands upon one's self or upon others. The 80 percent is worth doing, and perhaps has to be done in some fashion in order for the other 20 percent to mean anything; but it does not necessarily have to be done immediately, perfectly, or even well. Yet it is curious that many managers who seem to be so judiciously and expertly selective in the expenditure of money and other finite physical resources can be so indiscriminate in disbursing the most precious finite resource of all—vitality.

The Trust Gap*

Alan Farnham

Today, as CEOs waken to the new dawn of participatory management and even slugabeds are heard to murmur "empowerment" in their sleep, there is reason to believe that their heretofore faithful retainers, the employees, would like nothing better than to push a butter knife slowly through the boss's well-intentioned heart.

Relations between employer and employed are not good, and at an especially dicey moment. Just when top management wants everyone to begin swaying to a faster, more productive beat, employees are loath to dance. Observes David Sirota, chairman of the corporate polling firm Sirota Alper & Pfau: "CEOs say, 'We're a team, we're all in this together, rah, rah, rah.' But employees look at the difference between their pay and the CEO's. They see top management's perks—oak dining rooms and heated garages, versus cafeterias for the hourly guys and parking spaces half a mile from the plant. And they wonder: 'Is this togetherness?'" As the disparity in pay widens, the wonder grows.

People below the acme of the corporate pyramid trust those on top just about as far as they can throw a Gulfstream IV, with shower. Hourly workers and supervisors indeed agree that "we're all in this together," but what "we're in" turns out to be a frame of mind that mistrusts senior management's intentions, doubts its competence, and resents its self-congratulatory pay.

Just about everyone who keeps tabs on employee opinion finds evidence of a trust gap. And it is widening. One example: The Hay Group, drawing on 10 years of survey data—hundreds of companies, thousands of employees—concluded in a 1988 study that the attitudes of middle managers and professionals toward the workplace are becoming more like those of hourly workers, historically the most disaffected group.

No one contends that relations between top management and everybody else are as acrid these days as, say, during the Pullman strike. Nor are today's complaints as dramatic as those of earlier generations (cave-ins,

---

* From *FORTUNE* (December 4, 1989), 56–78. Reprinted with permission.

manglings, people falling into vats and being rendered into Durham's Pure Leaf Lard). Today's grievances are less salty, more subtle. But they smoke and gutter all the same—some with a peculiar brilliance.

What's the problem? Is it just pay? Working conditions? Benefits not good enough? None of these rank high in the new pantheon of gripes. If that surprises you, you aren't alone. When Louis Harris & Associates polled office workers and their managers on behalf of the Steelcase office furniture company this year, they found a growing "perception gap" between what employees really want and what top management *thinks* they want.

Managers assume, for instance, that job security is of paramount importance to employees. In fact, among workers it ranks far below such ethereal-sounding desires as respect, a higher standard of management ethics, increased recognition of employee contributions, and closer, more honest communications between employees and senior management.

When Opinion Research Corporation of Chicago surveyed 100,000 middle managers, supervisors, professionals, salespeople, and technical, clerical, and hourly workers of Fortune 500 companies in 1988, it found the lines of communications fraying. With the exception of the sales group, employees believed top management now was less willing to listen to their problems than five years earlier. The groups also felt top management now accorded them less respect.

A. Foster Higgins & Co., an employee-benefits consulting firm, finds that only 45 percent of large employers make regular use of worker opinion surveys, probably the most obvious means of carrying employee messages upward. Says Richard Knapp, a principal of the firm: "Organizations audit their financial resources regularly but fail to take the temperature of their own employees." Such companies, he says, are "flying blind."

Why don't companies make greater use of surveys? Because, says Bruce Pfau, executive vice president of Sirota Alper & Pfau, some CEOs still believe that asking underlings questions is tantamount to letting them run the show. "It's a sort of an aristocratic attitude: 'Who are you to tell me what you want? You work for me.'"

Companies that do use surveys sometimes conceal results from employees or fail to explain how policy changes are related to survey findings. Failure to follow through deepens employee cynicism: "Management didn't want my opinion in the first place," employees think. "Now they're sorry they asked." In September, after studying Fortune 500 companies' use of a wide variety of from-the-bottom-up communications tools—including surveys, telephone hot lines, quality circles, suggestion programs, and exit interviews—Towers Perrin, another big consulting firm, concluded that the "open doors" of many corporations were only "slightly ajar."

Not listened to, employees return the compliment. Missives from the boardroom are met increasingly with disbelief, not just by "the little people" but by everyone below VP. The Hay Group calls these doubters "the fraternity of skeptics." Hay's director of management research, Ronald Grey, attributes the fraternity's growth to employees' mounting awareness of inconsistencies between what management says and what it does—between saying "People are our most important asset" and in the next breath ordering layoffs, or between sloganeering about quality while continuing to evaluate workers by how many pieces they push out the back door.

The result is a weird world in which top management thinks it's sending crucial messages, but employees never hear a word. According to a survey by the Forum Corporation, a consulting firm, 82 percent of Fortune 500 executives believe their corporate strategy is understood by "everyone who needs to know." Alas, Louis Harris research finds, less than a third of employees say management provides clear goals and direction. When the Hay Group asked what kind of information workers wanted more of from top management, the troops checked "reliable information on where the company is headed" and "how my job fits into the total."

Quinn Spitzer, a VP of the Kepner-Tregoe management consulting outfit, tells of visiting a big company and having an executive show him a summary of the corporate strategy. "I said, 'This is terrific. When we discuss this with the employees I think we can really make some headway.' I wasn't proposing to share it with people on the production line, but just with middle managers. He said, 'You can't discuss this—it's our strategy, it's confidential, and it's for the senior executive group.'"

Observes Ilene Gochman, vice president of Opinion Research: "The days when management could say, 'Trust us, this is for your own good,' are over. Employees have seen that if the company steams off on some new strategic tack and it doesn't work, employees lose their jobs, not management."

Left to guess their CEO's plan, many employees end up wondering whether the brass has one. Confidence in top management's competence is collapsing. Gochman found an across-the-board vote of declining confidence she calls "just unbelievable."

Employees aren't stupid. After holding focus groups with thousands of them, Gochman concludes that management's low ratings arise from workers' awareness of new challengers out there. "With all the downsizing, mergers, and acquisitions, they're looking more critically at the kinds of things top management is doing," she says. "Some companies have just turned themselves inside out, getting into businesses they never were in before. Respondents wonder, 'Can management pull it off?'" When CEOs screw up and then expect subordinates to make sacrifices, resentment breeds fast. Emotionally, cold fusion is a proven reality.

Competence may be hard to divine, but pay is known, and to the penny. The rate of increase in top management's compensation parted company from workers' in 1979 and hasn't looked back since. Chiefs who make 100 times the average Indian's pay are no longer rare. European and

Japanese CEOs, who seldom earn more than 15 times the employee average, look on in amazement. Says William Werther, a management professor at the University of Miami: "The gap is widening beyond what the guy at the bottom can even understand."

Bud Crystal, a compensation expert and professor at Berkeley's Haas School of Business, suggests the ghoulish possibility that departed middle managers may be providing the food for this feeding frenzy: "It may be financed from the bodies of middle management. By having a leaner, meaner organization with fewer levels, the CEO—on the seventh day he rested—takes half the savings and puts it in his pocket."

Donald Kanter, a Boston University marketing professor and coauthor of *The Cynical Americans*, finds that U.S. workers are willing to accept substantial differentials in pay between corporate highs and lows. Few believe CEOs should go shoeless or that they should receive less than a just reward. But more and more, the lows—and middles—are asking the question: Just how just is just?

Bruce Pfau notes, "Executives never ask us to find out what employees think about executive salaries." So he and his partners decided to finance their own study. Of 350 employees surveyed in a random national sample, two thirds thought CEOs got too big a share of corporate profits. Nearly half, however, believed their *own* share was "about right." And solid majorities believed the shares going to stockholders, to the community at large, and to reinvestment were also about right. In employees' eyes, top management alone is getting more than it deserves.

It doesn't help that the passengers aboard the gravy train look as if they all hail from the same gene pool. According to a *Wall Street Journal* survey, the average CEO of 850 of the largest U.S. companies is still a Protestant male with three or more kids. He served in the armed forces, plays golf, and has been married to the same stay-at-home woman for 20 years. He would hesitate to promote a homosexual into management. He prefers navy-blue suits with red power ties. In other words: He's somebody increasingly unlike the rest of the work force.

Cosseted, closeted, whisked by limousine from home to the office, CEOs live never less than one remove from everyday annoyances. Are you hot? They are delightfully cool. Cold? They are toasty. Pale? They, by chance, are freshly back from a conference in the islands. Prick them and a man comes in to bleed. Or so it looks to the rank and file.

Sometimes the distance between them and everybody else comes across in the chance remark: Citicorp Chairman John Reed brushed aside an importunate aide with, "Can't talk now; gotta meet Jimmy Connors." After Time, Inc. (parent of Fortune's publisher) acquired Warner Communications, Time's CEO, J. Richard Munro, repaired to his vacation home in upstate New York to rest. There a local reporter asked if he didn't stand to make a lot of money from the deal (some $12 million over the next 10 years). "That sounds like a lot of money unless you live in New York and live in the world I live in," Munro responded. "In New York City, it's like Monopoly money."

A ripsaw is cutting through the ties that bind: On the upstroke, economic differences are cleaving top from bottom, and on the down, shared associations are falling away. Says Miami's Werther: "There's very little common ground left in terms of the experience of the average worker and the CEO." The military draft, which Barbara Ehrenreich, author of *Fear of Falling*, calls "that one great class-mixing experience," is long gone. Meanwhile, American society, as well as its work force, becomes more polyglot.

Eventually top management is likely to reflect more accurately the makeup of society. But "eventually" can be a long time. "The real change," says Werther, "won't come until after the turn of the century. Then you'll get the people who were born in the Sixties." Until then, coming hard on the heels of today's CEOs are a generation of MBAs.

What doctors are to hospitals, what lawyers are to law firms, these larval CEOs may be to industry: a credentialed caste. Says Stanford business school professor Jeffrey Pfeffer of his own students: "A lot of them think that everybody who doesn't have an MBA from Stanford, or possibly Harvard, is some lower form of life."

What future does this trend suggest? One reminiscent of a bad B-movie: *Beneath the Planet of the MBAs*. Here an effete, luxury-loving, self-absorbed technocratic elite holds uneasy sway over a demoralized, poorly educated but well-built mass of workers. One day, during a squabble over whose office gets the Keith Haring print, the workers rise up. At fadeout, the MBAs are found strangled in their Hermès ties.

"Oh, come off it," you say. "A business enterprise needn't be one big happy family to succeed. Aren't plenty of slave ships making good time?" Some are. But companies seething with class discord pay a penalty in drag. "Forget ethics," says David Sirota. "These companies are dysfunctional. Top management isn't hearing what it needs to hear" about markets, competitors, problems, and opportunities. "They've walled themselves off."

These companies pay another price they typically don't care to discuss. Michael Crino, professor of management at Clemson University, explains: "If people feel somehow that their side of the scale isn't balanced with yours, they may go to extremes to balance it. If management is arrogant, if it keeps all the perks to itself when the company does well, then pushes all the disasters downhill when times are bad, then there are certain collateral behaviors you can expect to see." He means sabotage. Quiet desperation, it seems, went out with high-button greaves.

With computers on every desk, employees with scores to settle find the weapons of vengeance ready to hand. Says Crino: "They have the potential to do an ungodly amount of damage." He cites the example of an oil company employee who erased a database worth millions of dollars. Drilling and exploration were suspended until the file could be recreated.

Meanwhile, old-fashioned sabotage is alive and well. "People," says Crino philosophically, "still get a thrill out of physical destruction." A department store employee who believed herself unfairly discharged taped razor blades between her fingers, then slashed $20,000 in overcoats before she was caught. At a fast-food restaurant, a worker secretly relieved himself in customers' iced tea, then feigned innocence when they questioned the taste. Is sabotage increasing? Signs point that way. When Crino called companies that promise sabotage protection, he says, "They indicated they had lots of work."

Some companies have woken up to the hidden costs of the trust gap and are experimenting with ingenious ways of sewing corporate top and bottom back together. Few CEOs have mastered the aristo-bypass, but those who have offer the following advice.

Start with the obvious. Tie the financial interests of higher-ups and lower-downs closer together by making exposure to risk and to reward more equitable. When Nucor, a steel company in Charlotte, North Carolina, with $1.1 billion in sales, went through tough times, President Ken Iverson took a 60 percent cut in pay. "How often do you see that?" asks Jude Rich, president of Sibson & Company, a compensation consulting firm. "It makes a real difference if employees see that their CEO is willing to take it in the shorts along with them."

Herb Kelleher, CEO of Southwest Airlines, agrees. "If there's going to be downside," he says, "you should share it. When we were experiencing hard times two years ago, I went to the board and told them I wanted to cut my salary. I cut all the officers' bonuses 10 percent, mine 20 percent."

Consider instituting profit sharing, a Scanlon Plan, gain sharing, or some other program that lets employees profit from their efforts. Make sure, however, that incentive compensation is linked to performance over which the beneficiaries have control. "Corporatewide profit sharing à la Du Pont?" sneers Rich. "A waste of time."

Rethink perks. Says Richard Huseman, co-author of *Managing the Equity Factor* and professor of management at the University of Georgia: "Now that perquisites come under taxable income, they just don't have the same bang for executives as they used to. Yet they still have at least the same downside with the rank and file. At this point you can say they're more trouble than they're worth." Most companies, he says, would be better off sticking to financial rewards, which don't carry nearly the same visibility. Kelleher views perks mainly as focusing attention on the wrong things: "Having people competing for the corner office, the Oriental rug—it distracts you. We feel there's competition enough outside Southwest."

Look at the office layout with an eye toward equity. While touring Sweden, Frank Becker, a Cornell professor and expert on office design, was surprised to learn that same-size offices are the norm there. He asked his hosts how they could give the same amount of space to a secretary as to an engineer. "They looked at me like I was crazy," says Becker. "They said: 'How can we hire a secretary and expect her to be committed to our company when, by the size of the office we give her, we tell her she's a second-class citizen?'"

Union Carbide benefited from making its offices more uniform. The company's former headquarters at 270 Park Avenue, says Becker, was one of the most hierarchical, class-conscious office environments in Manhattan: "Every rank had a different kind of ashtray, a different kind of water pitcher, different offices, different furniture. When somebody moved, you had to change all aspects of his office. It was inefficient and expensive." And divisive.

When Carbide moved to Danbury, Connecticut, it asked what features employees wanted in the new building. None said Mark Cross wastebaskets. "The marble-top tables went by the wayside," says Jim Barton, Carbide's director of general services. "In terms of amenities, everybody had the choice of the same stuff. It was an egalitarian approach: 2,350 private offices, all the same size. No executive parking, No executive dining room." After the change, worker performance improved. "No matter how you measure it—flow of paperwork, time spent in the building by employees—we substantially increased productivity," says Barton. When Becker analyzed the results, he found higher occupant satisfaction than at any building he had studied in the United States.

In parceling out amenities, your principle first and last ought to be: Do no harm. A consultant friend of Herb Kelleher was retained by a company that wanted to know how it could create a more "familylike" atmosphere. The consultant told Kelleher, "They'd read all these management books. After five minutes in their plant, I said: Look, there are two things you can do right off. One, take down the signs that say NO UNIFORMED EMPLOYEES BEYOND THIS POINT; and two, stop having separate Christmas parties for the blacks and whites."

Make sure your door is really open. At Rubbermaid an employee badly needed to talk to CEO Stanley Gault. Trouble was, the man got off his shift at 5 A.M. Gault gave up an hour's sleep to be there. None of the CEOs Fortune interviewed for this article could recall employees ever abusing an open-door policy: They don't walk through your door unless they have to.

If you don't now survey employee attitudes, start. What you find can help identify problems before they become crises. Share findings, and make sure employees know how subsequent decisions may be related to them. For CEOs who fear surveys may whip up too rich a froth of expectation,

Richard Knapp of Foster Higgins offers reassurance: "Employees by and large are reasonable people. They understand you can't do everything they want. As long as they know their views are being considered and they get some feedback from you to that effect, you will be meeting their expectations."

Preston Trucking, a Maryland-based carrier with 1988 revenues of $594 million, uses surveys and other bottom-up communications tools to great effect. An employee suggestion program brought in 4,412 money-making ideas last year. Average value to the company: $300 each. This year Preston hopes to get about 5,800, or one from every employee.

Explain things—personally. While Foster Higgins finds 97 percent of the CEOs it surveyed believe communicating with employees has a positive impact on job satisfaction, and 79 percent think it benefits the bottom line, only 22 percent actually do it weekly or more often.

Says Mark Pastin, professor of management at Arizona State University: "You find CEOs who think the best thing about being CEO is that they don't have to mix it up with the riffraff." The head of an insurance company once came to Pastin with the complaint that employees weren't "getting" his corporate vision. Had he ever told it to them, asked Pastin? Well, yes, he'd sent out materials, the man replied. But had he *talked* to employees? "You mean, did I make a video?" asked the CEO hopefully. No, said Pastin, had he ever met with them, in a room, say? The CEO was appalled: "You mean, sit with them in little red plastic chairs and drink coffee out of Styrofoam cups?" He hadn't.

Bob Swanson, CEO of Genentech, the biotech pioneer, faces a special challenge: Since many of his new hires come straight from the most rarefied university laboratories, few know much about business. Some even harbor misgivings about working for a corporation. When Swanson meets with them, he explains, among other things, why it's okay to make a profit. He also imparts the company's goals and credo in a handy pocket-size brochure.

When in doubt, be open. Du Pont has trimmed its global work force by 37,000 since 1982 to 140,000, yet has retained a high level of loyalty and commitment. How? By playing straight with employees and not withholding bad news until the last minute. The company believes in giving as much advance warning as possible—two full years, in the case of one plant closing.

Jude Rich awards IBM high marks for showing "basic respect for the individual," especially for taking pains to outplace IBM people. "You don't hear people at IBM complaining about John Akers's salary," he says. The point here is simple reciprocity: If you behave generously toward employees, employees are more likely to respond in kind.

Analysts rate Southwest's employees the most productive of any airline. Why are they? Says Kelleher: "Because they know we aren't trying to milk them in order to swell the bottom line." Dallas ramp supervisor Dennis Wynn agrees. His baggage handlers regularly achieve a feat unheard of elsewhere in the industry: 10-minute turn-arounds of aircraft. "When that plane comes in at 1:50 and you take off 200 bags and put on 200 more, and it takes off at 2:00, nobody needs to tell you you did good," Wynn says. In seven years with Southwest, he has been out sick once, with ulcers ("too much Cajun food"). "But hey," he says, "if I'm a little sick, if it's sleeting, I can come to work."

Wynn gets no special bonus for these heroics, just as Preston Trucking's personnel get no bonus for the suggestions they submit. At both companies workers give their all primarily because they believe management gives them full attention and respect.

Every now and then workers return the favor. Last year Chuck Dunlap, manager of Preston's Kearny, New Jersey, dock, had a problem: He wanted to save money by closing down the dock on the Friday before Christmas. But his Teamsters contract didn't recognize Friday as a holiday; he could close the dock, but 35 drivers would still have to be paid. Dunlap asked shop steward Carl Conoscenti for help. "I'll handle it," said Carl. He told the drivers several things: One, that they were due the money; two, that nobody would think less of them for taking it; and three, nobody would *know* if they took it. None took it. "These are *Teamsters*," says Dunlap, arms raised in disbelief. "This is *New Jersey*."

Don't disdain the hokey. This Thanksgiving, as last, Allen Paulson, CEO of Gulfstream Aerospace, will don a chef's hat and serve turkey to his employees, wishing each one well by name. And on Valentine's Day, Herb Kelleher will send out 8,200 personalized Valentines. Corny? "Just hearing about it makes me wince," says Robert Levering, author of *A Great Place to Work*. But employees on the receiving end at these companies don't wince.

Why not? Because their employers have worked hard—for years, in some cases—to establish their sincerity. Preston, years ago, had terrible relations between management and labor. Then, one day, top management resolved to bury the hatchet. All sorts of reforms were announced, including the Four-to-One Rule: For every criticism a manager made about a driver's performance, he had to give him four compliments. You can imagine how this went over. "It was like a . . . like a *marriage encounter*," says Teamster Nick Costa, rolling his eyes. Eventually, though, drivers discovered that the rule really did reflect a change of heart.

In 1984, when Mike Warren signed on as CEO of Alabama Gas, the biggest natural-gas distributor in that state, he found relations with the company's unions in poor repair. To show workers he meant to put the bad old days behind, Warren got a 20-foot papier-mâché dinosaur, plunged a stake through its heart, and wheeled the corpse around from department to department.

"If all we'd done was go around with a papier-mâché dinosaur, they'd have seen through it immediately," Warren says. "The follow-through was crucial." He started eating dinner regularly with union leaders. If he was out driving and saw workers laboring in a ditch, he got out and visited with them. He surveyed employees and solicited their suggestions. Two years later the steel workers' union sent Warren a brontosaurus statuette inscribed "Dinosaur Killer of the Year." To Warren, their gesture said: Okay, now we believe you.

You can adopt whatever hokey touches suit your company, but CEOs agree that it is suicidal to start down this road unless you are absolutely sincere. Says Arizona State's Pastin: "Company picnics don't mean a damn unless other factors are present." Such as honest communications, respectful treatment, and equitable standards of gain and sacrifice.

Be aware that even more radical experiments are afoot. Should a CEO's compensation be set at some multiple of the average worker's? This controversial idea has been espoused by no less a troika than Peter Drucker, J. P. Morgan, and Socrates.

Drucker says Morgan discovered that the poorly performing clients of J. P. Morgan & Company had one characteristic in common: "Each company's top executive was paid more than 130 percent of the compensation of the people in the next echelon, and these, in turn, more than 130 percent of the compensation of those below them." Morgan concluded that disproportionately high executive salaries disrupted teamwork. Drucker, who believes Morgan's discovery still holds true, favors a 20-to-1 ratio between CEO and average worker pay. Socrates endorsed 5 to 1.

Management has not raced to embrace this idea. At present only a handful of U.S. companies use it, including Herman Miller, the $800 million furniture maker (which uses 20 to 1), and Vermont ice-cream maker Ben & Jerry's Homemade (5 to 1).

John Tepper Marlin, an economist who studied Ben & Jerry's corporate culture, considers the 5-to-1 ratio a mixed blessing. While the company gets high-caliber janitors—and while employee productivity runs high—the ice-cream maker has had trouble attracting experienced senior managers. A year ago Ben Cohen and Jerry Greenfield, who own 34 percent of the stock, resolved to get women into their top-management cadre by hiring a female chief financial officer. She would receive around $70,000 a year, plus three pints of ice cream daily. After a six-month nationwide hunt, they still couldn't find one, prompting employees to dub the woman B&J's "UFO" (unidentified female officer). The company ended up grooming controller Fran Rathke for the job.

A second radical experiment might be called sharing the sweat. It isn't immediately clear to everyone that CEOs work. Flying off in a sleek jet with an attentive aide to deliver a short talk may sound like work to you, but a cable overhauler could get used to it. Before a back injury forced Preston's Joe Ruggiero to switch from driving to an administrative job, he admits he thought guys in pink ties "just fooled around all day."

Some companies see an advantage to having top management every so often labor demonstrably. In October, Hyatt Hotels dispatched its entire headquarters staff to work for a day changing sheets, pouring coffee, running elevators. President Darryl Hartley-Leonard worked as a doorman at the Hyatt in Chicago. Bill Kurvers, the full-time door captain who worked alongside him, says, "He did very well, much to our surprise. It was a busy day—we could use all the help we could get." At first Hartley-Leonard refused tips. Fellow doormen quickly set him straight. What did he get from his experience, besides tips? Says Kurvers: "He got respect."

And something more, Hartley-Leonard explains: "It was the damnedest thing—employees came up to me and shook my hand. We didn't goof around at it, and it wasn't play-acting. You forget how captured you are in a line job." Anything else? "Jesus, my back aches." He describes the experience as a good reality check.

The officers of Southwest Airlines, Kelleher included, work at least once every quarter as baggage handlers, ticket agents, and flight attendants. "We're trying to create an understanding of the difficulties every person has on his job," explains Kelleher. "When you're actually dealing with customers, and you've done the job yourself, you're in a better position to appraise the effect of some new program or policy."

And don't forget those nice new MBAs! Lincoln Electric puts MBAs—even ones from Harvard—on its welding line for more than a ceremonial visit. Rob Shepard, a Harvard MBA who survived the training to become a special-projects coordinator, says: "Those eight weeks were as tough as anything I ever had in the Marine Corps." President Donald Hastings, himself a Harvard MBA who went through the drill, tells why Lincoln does it: "We want them to understand the difficulty of the factory environment and to have respect for the people out there. These MBAs have got a big target on their backs. People have to see they aren't just traders coming in from the financial world." Do they sweat? "Oh, gosh yes. Sweat just pouring off them."

Enlightenment has it costs. Preston lost nearly 25 percent of its managers when it adopted the ol' Four-to-One and began listening to drivers' complaints about supervisors. Even Kelleher says, in mock exasperation, "I don't mind their tracking dirt across my rug, but I just *wish* they'd stop calling me shithead in front of the customers."

Is trying to close a trust gap worth the trouble? Bob Swanson, pointing to Genentech's low turnover and the fat pile of résumés on his desk, thinks it is. Chuck Dunlap at Preston, whose drivers bring in business and turn down pay, thinks it is. Herb Kelleher, who leaves his Mercedes parked on the edge of the runway for weeks at a time without fear anyone will scratch a set of keys across the paint, thinks it is. The point, Hyatt's Hartley-Leonard observes, is that "employees *do* feel they're living in a society of equals." And that, as much of the American experience attests, is a pretty good feeling.

Approaches to the Definition of Comparable Worth*

Thomas A. Mahoney

Despite the flurry of current attention to the topic, comparable pay for jobs of comparable worth is not a new social or economic issue. Biblical discussion of the comparable worth and pay for harvesters working different amounts of time in the vineyard testifies to the continuing vitality of the issue for thousands of years. Comparable worth, then and now, is conceived as a measure of individuals and/or work, a criterion measure that in some sense "ought" to dictate actual income or compensation. As illustrated in the Biblical parable, the criterion of comparable worth applied by the employer conflicted with that applied by employees, and the compensation provided appeared unjustified to them. Search for a generally accepted criterion of worth continues today in the effort to achieve "comparable pay for jobs of comparable worth." (This phrase is chosen in preference to the more popular phrase of "equal pay for jobs of comparable worth" which, taken literally, would imply equal pay for all jobs whose worth can be compared.)

Judgments about the distribution of income and wealth are made in every society, and policies are formulated to achieve some desired distribution. These policies appear in statutes regarding taxation, welfare payments, other forms of transfer payments, and in social norms regarding individual charity. Various social criteria of justice regarding income and wealth distribution are incorporated in provisions for inheritance, minimal social welfare, and the variation of benefit levels with size of family, age, and other variables. These norms, expressed in custom and statute, vary over time and from one society to another. Social philosophy regarding the distribution of wealth and income in the United States is a continuing concern in political debates.

* From *Academy of Management Review* (1983) 8, 14–22. Reactions and comments by Sara Rynes were most helpful. A version of this paper was presented at the Academy of Management meeting, San Diego, 1981.

Social concerns for income distribution cannot be differentiated from considerations of employment compensation, because fully four fifths of personal income in the United States is derived from employment earnings. Nevertheless, with certain exceptions, the determination of employment compensation has been accomplished independently of the political process. Social norms regarding income distribution have been expressed primarily in statutes concerning income taxation and transfer payments, rather than direct regulation of compensation. This is not the case in all societies and need not continue in this country. Concerns for comparable worth, for example, are based in broad social concerns for income distribution and seek changes in income distribution through changes in the distribution of employment compensation.

Comparable worth issues of today derive in part from concern about the economic status of different groups in society, specifically the lower economic status of females compared with that of males (Grune, 1980). This differential in status appears particularly in what has been termed the *earnings gap* between men and women. Female earnings persistently average about 60 percent of male earnings. The male–female earnings gap has been subjected to various analyses seeking to identify causes of the gap and, where appropriate, policies that would eliminate that gap (England and McLaughlin, 1979; Ferber and Lowry, 1976; Fuchs, 1971; Mincer and Polachek, 1978; Oaxaca, 1973; Sawhill, 1973). Implicitly, the earnings gap has been judged socially undesirable. Analyses of the earnings gap attempt to apportion causal influence to different policies and actions in order to give a better understanding of the reasons for the gap and the likely consequences of policy changes.

One significant influence of the male–female earnings gap lies in the occupational distributions of male and female employment (Sanborn, 1964; Treiman and Terrell, 1975). Males and females are not represented equally in the various occupations, and male-dominated occupations are compensated at higher rates than are female-dominated occupations. Causes (and thus potential remedies) of these male–female occupational wage differentials are unclear. The "crowding hypothesis" illustrates one line of reasoning about male–female occupational distributions and wage differentials (England and McLaughlin, 1979). Occupational and industrial labor markets are segmented by sex, according to the crowding hypothesis, with the result that females are discouraged and restricted from entry to male-dominated occupations and are crowded into lower paid, female-dominated occupations. The consequence of this segmentation and crowding is that restricted supplies in male-dominated occupations permit upward wage pressure, and the competition of relative oversupply in female occupations holds down wages there. Correction of the earnings gap, according to proponents of the crowding hypothesis, will occur as barriers to occupational mobility are removed, thus permitting redistribution of occupational employment of males and females with the consequent narrowing of wage differentials.

Another line of reasoning attributes the wage differentials between male- and female-dominated occupations to discrimination in the setting of wage rates (Treiman, 1979). Probably because of custom and social tradition, women's work is undervalued in social attitudes. Social attitudes of the past condoned the payment of lower wages to women than to men regardless of the similarity of work assignments.

More critically, it is argued that social attitudes toward the evaluation of men's and women's work are generalized to the occupations typically performed by each sex. These attitudes are incorporated in existing wage structures and in systems of job evaluation that perpetuate bias in the evaluation of tasks performed in female-dominated occupations. Correction of the earnings gap, then, requires revaluation and realignment of the occupational wage structure, raising the rates of compensation for female-dominated occupations relative to male-dominated occupations. Concern for comparable worth derives from this line of reasoning. Some criterion of occupational worth other than traditional wage criteria is sought as the basis for realignment of the wage structure.

Although current concern for comparable worth arises in the context of relative compensation for male- and female-dominated occupations, comparable worth in truth is a more general issue pervading social and economic analysis. Assessments of comparable worth in male- and female-dominated occupations cannot fail to affect assessments of relative worth among any occupations regardless of sex composition. Thus, considerations of criteria of comparable worth naturally extend beyond the more limited range of concern for the male–female earnings gap.

CONCEPTS OF COMPARABLE WORTH

Three major streams of thought can be identified as contributing to the development of concepts of comparable worth. These are arbitrarily labeled (1) social philosophy, (2) economics, and (3) administrative theory. These traditions share many similar concerns and concepts, but they offer different approaches to the development of concepts of comparable worth.

Social Philosophy

This approach to the definition of worth derives from concepts of social comparison, reference groups, and distributive justice (Homans, 1961; Runciman, 1966). Basically, persons and groups that are equal in some critical sense ought to be treated equally, and persons and groups that are different ought to be treated proportionally differently. More specifically, different reward treatments (e.g., earnings) that are not proportional to differences in a critical comparison variable (e.g., skill) are violations of the norms of justice. As applied to the concept of comparable worth, the social philosophy tradition suggests that earnings from employment ought to be proportional to the contributions made through employment.

Although the general norm of proportionality enjoys widespread acceptance, there is less consensus on the operational definition of contributions. In general, the social philosophy tradition tends to emphasize aspects of work inputs, the labor service capabilities brought to and expended in work, and aspects of personal characteristics, such as education, skill, and experience. Thus, generalizing, persons or groups expending equal work capabilities ought to be paid equally, and pay differentials should be proportional to the expenditure of work capabilities.

Economics

Two streams of thought in economics are differentiated in terms of approach to the concept of comparable worth, the neoclassical and radical economics approaches. Neoclassical economics approaches the definition of worth in terms of individual valuations expressed in market exchanges. First, each individual buyer and seller assesses the worth of an exchange in terms of its opportunity costs and typically assigns different valuations to the exchange. (Indeed, without these different valuations of worth, no exchange would occur!) A more general concept of worth emerges as market price, the rate at which marginal exchanges occur at general equilibrium in a system of competitive markets. These rates of exchange directly express comparable worth to marginal buyers and sellers. Applied in the context of work and wages, comparable worth is defined as market wage rates realized in a system of competitive markets. The neoclassical tradition thus defines comparable worth as the outcome of a specified system of market exchanges, and it does not specify any particular wage structure or measure of work contributions in the definition (Hicks, 1966).

The tradition of radical economics takes issue with and modifies this approach to the definition of comparable worth (Edwards, Reich, and Gordon, 1975). Briefly, the tradition of radical economics challenges the assumptions of neoclassical economics and views that tradition as an apology for a capitalistic society (Bronfenbrenner, 1970). Considerable emphasis is placed on assertions that the process assumptions of general equilibrium and competitive markets are unrealizable in our society, and that there exist numerous sociopolitical barriers to mobility, competition, and freedom of access and exchange. Various social groups (e.g., females) may be denied entry to selected occupations for employment, thus restricting competition in those occupations and intensifying competition in other occupations (e.g., the crowding hypothesis). Significant wage differentials thus may be maintained between occupations that otherwise would disappear. The tradition of radical economics might accept the ideal definition of comparable worth from the neoclassical tradition, but it stresses the unworkability of this definition in society. Given the realities of sociopolitical structuring of economic opportunities in society, the radical economics tradition would be more inclined to align with the comparable worth concepts of the social philosophy tradition and to specify those contribution characteristics critical in assessing comparable worth.

Administrative Practice

Administrative practice in the establishment of wage rates typically addresses issues of worth within the context of a single employer or work group. Although most administrative practice developed pragmatically, various criteria of worth are evidenced in this practice and employed in the rationalization of practice.

Job evaluation is a major component of administrative practice and is the primary method of determining relative worth of different jobs in a single employing organization (Belcher, 1974; Lytle, 1954). The unit of analysis is the job, and the intent is to evaluate jobs in terms of relative worth to the employer. Evaluations typically are based on arbitrarily specified criteria of comparison that often reflect aspects of work inputs, rather than work outputs. Typical criteria for comparison include measures of skill requirements, level of responsibility, and physical and mental demands of the job, rather than direct measures of output. The specific criteria for job evaluation often vary from one employer and/or work group to another and, because they are arbitrarily specified, may conflict with normative criteria suggested in the tradition of social philosophy. The approaches of job evaluation and the tradition of social philosophy to assessment of worth are similar in many respects. Both are normative and prescriptive in approach, both employ arbitrary criteria of worth, and both often apply measures of occupational inputs, rationalized in job evaluation as proxies for outputs and in the tradition of social philosophy as direct measures of exchange. The two approaches differ critically, however, in defining the scope of the relevant social population, job evaluation often focusing on a subset of jobs within a single organization (i.e., clerical, production, or managerial) and the tradition of social philosophy tending to include all occupations of society as the relevant population.

A second criterion of worth employed in administrative practice is the concept of market wage derived from the tradition of economics. Some organizations employ surveys of market wages directly in the establishment of wage rates, but others employ market surveys in the validation of job evaluation systems. Job evaluation factors and factor weights must yield relative job evaluations consistent with relative wage rates observed in market surveys (Schwab, 1980). Administrative practice thus tends to employ both a normative criterion of job worth (job evaluation) and an empirical criterion (market surveys). The distinction between these two criteria appears most starkly when the results of job evaluation conflict with wage survey information. No consistent approach to resolving this conflict is apparent either in current practice or in rationalizations of practice.

COMMON DIMENSIONS

Although the various approaches to the definition of comparable worth appear to be quite different, several dimensions of comparison can be identified. Admittedly, the dimensions of comparisons are rather fuzzy, but they nevertheless are useful in highlighting similarities and differences in the broad, analytical approaches to comparable worth and thus in focusing the debate among advocates of each. These dimensions are displayed in Figure 1, which presents an overall summary of the different approaches.

Process—Outcome

Both the process and outcome of wage determination obviously are closely related. Approaches to the definition of comparable worth differ, however, in terms of relative emphasis on process and outcome in the judgment of job worth. Briefly, worth may be defined as (1) whatever outcomes result from a specified *process* of wage determination (process focus), without regard to the nature of those outcomes; or (2) in terms of comparison of the wage determination *outcomes* with some exogenous criterion of worth (outcome focus) without regard to the process producing those outcomes. Neoclassical economics, for example, defines occupational worth in terms of the process of market exchange. Assuming a system of competitive market exchanges, the resulting market wages are direct expressions of worth independent of any exogenous criteria of worth. Market determined wage rates reflect consumer valuations of the products and services of

FIGURE 1 Comparisons of Alternative Concepts of Comparable Worth

Comparative Dimensions	Traditions			
	Social Philosophy	Neoclassical Economics	Radical Economics	Administrative
Process/outcome focus	Outcome	Process	Outcome	Process/outcome
Level of analysis	Societal	Market	Societal/market	Firm/market
Person/job focus	Person	Job/person	Person	Job

labor as realized by employers, the comparative productivities of labor in satisfying consumer demands, and employee tastes and preferences for alternative jobs. Relative wages are presumed to change over time as influenced by market demand and supply, and, assuming a competitive market process, they will indicate change in job worth. Market wage surveys employed in wage determination employ this same definition of job worth, and survey results are treated as direct expressions of worth.

Alternatively, the approaches of social philosophy and radical economics tend to emphasize exogenous criteria of worth, rather than the process of wage determination. Thus, for example, relative education may be specified as an appropriate criterion for reward differentiation and may be imposed on the assessment of worth; similarly, sex may be rejected as inappropriate. Job evaluation approaches to wage determination also impose externally derived criteria of worth on the system of wage determination, criteria specified by an employer or negotiated through collective bargaining.

Level of Analysis

Three levels of analysis appear in the different approaches to determination of worth—a firm or micro level, a market level, and a societal or macro level. Although wage and earnings relationships at all three levels are interrelated, analytical approaches differ in terms of relative emphasis on the different levels. Also, the application of a single approach to determination of worth at one level of analysis may be inconsistent with application of that same approach at another level of analysis.

The approach of social philosophy, for example, considers macro or societal comparisons of worth to be of greatest significance as evidenced by continuing reference to the male–female earnings gap. The issue of comparable worth is important as it relates to this earnings gap. Although an earnings gap also might be evidenced at market and establishment levels of analysis, the broader societal earnings gap is of primary interest.

The principal level of analysis in the neoclassical approach is the labor market, and comparisons of worth at both firm (micro) and societal (macro) levels of analysis are derived from these market comparisons. The primary focus of radical economics is less clear; both labor market and societal concerns are considered. Societal influences are evidenced in the structuring of labor markets and market processes. Barriers to entry, mobility, and information in both capital and labor markets, for example, contribute to market segmentation and the channeling of competitive forces. Market rates are a joint influence of societal structuring of markets and competitive behaviors within markets. The primary concern, however, is with achieving appropriate societal wage outcomes.

Administrative approaches to wage determination are concerned, of course, with wage setting at the establishment level. They employ concepts reflective of both firm (micro) and market levels of analysis. The primary focus of job evaluation is on relative job comparisons within work groups and establishments, almost regardless of market and societal considerations except as reflected in judgments of worth and equity by employees of the organization. Acceptance by the affected work group is a critical requirement in a system of job evaluation. At the same time, comparability of the job evaluation results with surveys of market wages also figures as an alternative criterion of validity of the system. Thus, alternative levels of analysis are employed in administrative approaches to wage determination, and the relative concern for each varies from one organization to another.

Person—Job

A fundamental differentiation among conceptual approaches is the relative emphasis on person or job as the appropriate basis for determinations of worth. In its extreme form, this distinction appears in assertions that people equal in some critical respect ought to be paid equally and in contradictory assertions that jobs equal in some critical respect ought to be paid equally. In terms of economic analyses, this distinction can be related to the distinction between characteristics of labor supply and labor demand, a distinction that has plagued wage theory for years. Labor demand is conceptualized as demand for the output of labor services (marginal revenue product), yet labor supply is characterized in terms of input characteristics (skill and hours). Neoclassical economics equates demand and supply characteristics in the abstract as "standardized unit of labor," a concept that is virtually impossible to operationalize. Also, because market wage rates reflect marginal decisions in which demand and supply evaluations of worth are presumed to be equal, there is no necessity to differentiate between supply and demand characteristics at the margin.

Concepts of human capital developed and applied in economic analysis illustrate the distinction between job and person characteristics in terms of the concepts of labor demand and supply (Mincer, 1970). Worth based on demand for labor is expressed in characteristics of job performance. Worth thus is assumed to be associated with labor supply or personal characteristics associated with job performance. Certain labor supply characteristics, such as education, skill, and experience, are assumed to be more productive of desired job performances and deserving of relatively higher wages. Because these labor supply characteristics both command higher wage rates and are considered more productive, they are viewed as measures of human capital. Employees invest in human capital (e.g., education) as justified by the rates of return (wages) for such investments. Human capital concepts thus might be applied to comparable worth judgments in rationalizing personal characteristics of labor supply as the basis for judgments of worth. However, human capital concepts developed from empirical observation of wage differentials associated with personal characteristics also require rationalization or justification on grounds other than labor market wage determination. They require some rationalization of productivity assumptions external to the process of wage determination. Otherwise, all correlations of personal variables (e.g., sex) with wage differentials might be treated as evidence of human capital relationships. Human capital theory, although reliant on market concepts, is equally reliant on independent assumptions about imputations of productivity to personal characteristics of labor supply.

The traditions of social philosophy and radical economics tend to focus on labor supply or personal characteristics—a consequence, in part, of their concern for social group comparisons. Groups equal in terms of relevant personal input characteristics, such as education, ought to be paid equally. Part of the rationale for this focus is drawn from human capital concepts, but the rationale also is based on social comparison norms of cost, investment, and contribution. Persons making equal investments and contributions to work should be equally compensated.

The administrative approach of job evaluation focuses on the job as the basis of worth, and it considers personal characteristics only as required by the job. Although job evaluation measures tend to reflect measures of contribution and personal input to the job, the intent is to base assessments of worth on the job without differentiating among persons in the same job. One major exception to this approach occurs in the use of maturity curves in the payment of scientific and technical employees; the job in this instance is characterized in terms of qualifications of the incumbent, discipline, and years since graduation (Fuller, 1972). The use of wage survey data in wage determination also is intended to focus on job characteristics, rather than personal characteristics.

APPLICATIONS OF CONCEPTS

Applications of conceptual approaches to comparable worth have been varied, ranging from direct applications in wage determination and the formulation of public policy to less direct applications of the concepts in analyses attempting to explain wage phenomena. Direct applications of the concepts in wage determination are observed in job evaluation, wage negotiations, and arbitrators' rulings on wages, all of which employ concepts of comparability. They also figure prominently in recent court decisions and in efforts by the EEOC to develop guidelines for assessing wage discrimination and nondiscrimination under Title VII of the Civil Rights Act (Treiman and Hartmann, 1981).

The dimensions employed in assessing comparability in wage determination vary from one decision to another. Job evaluation, for example, specifies arbitrary, weighted criteria for use in the assessment of relative worth of jobs, and both criteria and weights may vary from one administrative unit to another. Although certain approaches, such as the Hay System, generally are standardized in all settings, other approaches based on empirical factor analyses and policy-capturing analyses may be unique to each application (Robinson, Wahlstrom, and Mecham, 1974). Typically the criteria employed in job evaluation concern dimensions of task requirements rationalized as measures of work contribution. These criteria are assumed to be reflective of both input and output valuations of worth; more onerous tasks both demand greater input contributions and are more productive of valued outputs.

Judgments of the validity of any system of job evaluation employ validity criteria drawn from one or another of the different conceptual approaches. One such criterion is derived from economics. It involves comparison of relative job evaluations with relative wage rates observed in market surveys (Fox, 1972). The job evaluation system is judged valid to the extent that relative market rates are duplicated for key jobs. Several approaches to statistical job evaluation, in fact, are derived from multivariate analysis of wage survey data, with both factors and weights identified empirically (Edwards, 1948). Predictably, this approach to validity assessment of job evaluation is criticized from the traditions of social philosophy and radical economics as merely perpetuating wage inequities established and maintained through discriminatory market institutions. Rather, comparable worth advocates seek an alternative criterion of worth (Treiman and Hartmann, 1981).

Another approach to assessment of the validity of job evaluation rests on its acceptance by those affected by the system—acceptance as demonstrated in terms of attitude surveys, recruiting and turnover experience, grievances, and collective wage negotiations. Acceptability of job evaluation presumably reflects acceptance of both criteria used to assess worth and the assessment of relative value resulting from the evaluation process (Livernash, 1957). Consistent with the tradition of social philosophy, the source of this criterion is found in the social norms and values of groups affected by the system. The scope of the relevant society is relatively confined, however, and norms of acceptability likely vary considerably from one group to another, thus accounting for the many variants of job evaluation observed in practice (Kerr and Fisher, 1950). The application of social norms of acceptability in job evaluation provides the potential for yielding consensus norms of comparable worth assessments in relatively confined societies that are contradictory when aggregated in a larger social setting.

The criteria of job worth expressed in public policy are derived from various influences. The Equal Pay Act of 1963, for example, requires that men and women be paid equally for doing equal work, and it defines equal work as requiring equal skill, effort, and responsibility performed under similar working conditions. Differential payments reflecting seniority, merit, quantity or quality of production, or any factor other than sex are permitted, however. The Equal Pay Act is applicable at the firm or employer level of analysis. It is concerned primarily with wage outcomes, rather than wage determination processes, and it tends to focus on job, rather than personal characteristics, characteristics similar to those often specified in job evaluation systems.

Most concern for comparable worth issues is derived from Title VII of the 1964 Civil Rights Act, which prohibits discrimination because of race, color, religion, sex, or national origin in all employment practices including compensation (Williams and McDowell, 1980). What constitutes discrimination in compensation is not specified, however. The current debate over comparable worth concepts reflects attempts to establish definitions and guidelines for nondiscriminatory compensation. A committee of the National Academy of Sciences (NAS), under contract with the EEOC, recently completed an investigation of the validity of compensation systems and methods for determining the relative worth of jobs (Treiman and Hartmann, 1981). The committee investigation analyzed male–female wage differentials in light of several of the criteria reviewed here and concluded that (1) market wages cannot be used as the sole standard for judging the relative worth of jobs and (2) policy interventions to alter market outcomes may be required in order to end discrimination. The committee recommended that some form of job evaluation might be developed for the determination of comparable worth, but it did not recommend any specific criteria for job evaluation. (The NAS committee also considered potential discrimination and bias in job description and job rating, issues not examined here as relevant to the definition of comparable worth.)

The NAS committee recommended a process for determining job worth that reflects several of the approaches to the determination of worth reviewed above. Briefly, the committee recommended that wage differentials paid to white males be accepted as market rates reflecting relative job worth. The same market influences cannot be expected to operate in the determination of wages for females, however. A form of job evaluation was recommended as a means of generalizing market influences to female wages. A method of job evaluation that reproduces relative wage differentials among jobs held by white males might be developed and then applied in the determination of worth of female jobs. Such a norm of comparable worth based solely on the earnings treatment of white males is not likely to satisfy comparable worth advocates of the social philosophy tradition. In fact, it is this norm that is challenged when it is argued that job characteristics common in female occupations are less common and undervalued in male occupations.

CONCLUDING OBSERVATION

One feature that appears in all of the approaches to the definition of worth and that has not been noted explicitly is the role of subjective taste, preference, and norms. Subjective social norms of justice figure prominently in the traditions of both social philosophy and radical economics. These norms dictate the criteria appropriate in the justification of relative earnings. Taste and preference also figure in the labor supply behaviors critical in determining worth in the neoclassical tradition and are expressed in marginal decisions. Although viewed as individual tastes, these preferences undoubtedly are influenced also by social norms and traditions. Further, the ultimate test of job evaluation lies in acceptance of the process by those affected and the compatability of results with their subjective norms of comparability. Judgments of worth ultimately are based on subjective norms, regardless of the tradition employed, and will vary with the subjective norms applied.

The scope of consensus of tastes or norms of relative worth is likely to vary inversely with the specificity of comparisons made. Although broad social consensus regarding the relative worth of male and female mail carriers is conceivable, it is unlikely that consensus regarding the relative worth of secretaries and welders or of two different secretarial positions can be achieved beyond the confines of a single firm or work group.

Finally, note the paradox of aggregation of judgments of relative worth. Judgments of relative worth of different jobs that are acceptable within small social settings may aggregate into measures of earnings at another level of analysis that conflict with broad social norms of worth. Analogously, it would appear unlikely that any specific norms or criteria of comparable worth applied uniformly across society would be accepted consensually within all industries, firms, and work groups. The search for consensual norms of job worth is most likely to be successful if confined to individual firms, regardless of implications for male–female earnings differentials throughout society. The current concern over comparable worth may be rooted in the male–female earnings gap in society, but comparable worth is a more general issue than merely male–female comparisons. It is an issue based on subjective judgments, an issue most likely to be resolved within relatively small groups of employees. Realizations of consensus on comparable worth thus are most likely within small employee groups. "Comparable pay for jobs of comparable worth" within these groups is not likely to impact significantly on the male–female earnings gap in society.

REFERENCES

Belcher, D. W. *Compensation administration.* Englewood Cliffs, N.J.: Prentice-Hall, 1974.

Bronfenbrenner, M. "Radical economics in America, 1970." *Journal of Economic Literature* (1970) 8, 747–66.

Edwards, P. M. "Statistical methods in job evaluation." *Advanced Management* (1948) 13 (4), 155–63.

Edwards, R. C.; M. Reich; and D. M. Gordon, eds. *Labor market segmentation.* Lexington, Mass.: D. C. Heath, 1975.

England, P., and S. D. McLaughlin. "Sex segregation of jobs and male–female income differentials." In *Discrimination in organizations.* ed. R. Alvarez, K. Lutterman, and Associates. San Francisco: Jossey-Bass, 1979, 189–213.

Ferber, M. A., and H. M. Lowry. "The sex differential in earnings: A reappraisal." *Industrial and Labor Relations Review* (1976) 29, 377–87.

Fox, W. M. Purpose and validity in job evaluation. *Personnel Journal* (1972) 51, no. 10, 432–37.

Fuchs, V. R. "Differences in hourly earnings between men and women." *Monthly Labor Review* (1971) 94, 9–15.

Fuller, L. E. "Designing compensation programs for scientists and professionals in business." In *Handbook of wage and salary administration.* ed. M. L. Rock. New York: McGraw-Hill, 1972, 824–35.

Grune, J. A. *Manual on pay equity: Raising wages for women's work.* Washington, D.C.: Conference on Alternative State and Local Policies, 1980.

Hicks, J. R. *The theory of wages.* New York: St. Martin's Press, 1966.

Homans, G. *Social behavior: Its elementary forms.* New York: Harcourt Brace Jovanovich, 1961.

Kerr, C., and L. H. Fisher. "Effect of environment and administration on job evaluation." *Harvard Business Review* (1950) 28, no. 3, 77–96.

Livernash, E. R. "The internal wage structure." In *New concepts in wage determination.* ed. G. W. Taylor and F. C. Pierson. New York: McGraw-Hill, 1957, 140–72.

Lytle, C. W. *Job evaluation methods.* New York: Ronald Press, 1954.

Mincer, J. "The distribution of labor incomes: A survey with special reference to the human capital approach." *Journal of Economic Literature* (1970) 8, 1–26.

Mincer, J., and S. Polachek. "Women's earnings reexamined." *Journal of Human Resources* (1978) 13, 119–35.

Oaxaca, R. "Male–female wage differentials in urban labor markets." *International Economic Review* (1973) *14*, 693–709.

Robinson, D. D.; O. W. Wahlstrom; and R. C. Mecham, "Comparison of job evaluation methods: A 'policy capturing' approach using the position analysis questionnaire." *Journal of Applied Psychology* (1974) *59*, 633–37.

Runciman, W. G. *Relative deprivation and social justice.* London: Routledge and Kegan Paul, 1966.

Sanborn, H. "Pay differences between men and women." *Industrial and Labor Relations Review* (1964) *17*, 534–50.

Sawhill, I. V. "The economics of discrimination against women." *Journal of Human Resources* (1973) *8*, no. 3, 383–95.

Schwab, D. P. "Job evaluation and pay setting: Concepts and practices." In *Comparable worth: Issues and alternatives.* ed. E. R. Livernash. Washington, D.C.: Equal Employment Advisory Council, 1980, 49–78.

Treiman, D. J. *Job evaluations: An analytical review.* Interim Report of the Committee on Occupational Classification and Analysis to the Equal Employment Opportunity Commission, National Research Council. Washington, D.C.: National Academy of Sciences, 1979.

Treiman, D. J., and H. I. Hartmann. eds. *Women, work, and wages: Equal pay for jobs of equal value.* Washington, D.C.: National Academy Press, 1981.

Treiman, D. J., and K. Terrell. "Women, work and wages—trends in the female occupational structure since 1940." In *Social indicator models.* ed. K. Land and S. Spilerman. New York: Russell Sage Foundation, 1975, 157–200.

Williams, R. E., and D. S. McDowell. "The legal framework." In *Comparable worth: Issues and alternatives.* ed. E. R. Livernash. Washington, D.C.: Equal Employment Advisory Council, 1980, 197–250.

Turnover Turned Over:
An Expanded and
Positive Perspective*

Dan R. Dalton

William D. Todor

The references to turnover in the organization literature began to appear around the year 1900 (104). Soon an emphasis emerged which considered both the costs of turnover and how these costs might be reduced (5, 6, 7, 24, 33, 83, 116). Nonorganizational scholars, notably economists, have also shared a concern with turnover (117). These early studies have much in common with current views of organizational turnover and its implications. Recent reviews of turnover (19, 51, 53, 102, 104, 115, 133) continue to emphasize the dysfunctional aspects of turnover on the organization.

These negative connotations have become axiomatic. In its most visible form turnover tends to be associated with short-term disturbances imposed on the organization: interruptions of normal operations, retraining, scheduling difficulties, etc. This lack of stability fosters responses which range from managerial irritation to organizational arrest.

However, before concluding that turnover is invariably undesirable, it should be placed into a larger perspective. How does turnover fit into the individual and societal context in which it is found?

Porter and Steers (102) suggest that turnover represents an interesting and important phenomenon to those concerned with studying the behavior of individuals in organizations. Turnover is referred to as a "relatively clear-cut act of behavior that has potentially critical consequences for both the person and the organization" (102, p. 151). However, these "critical consequences" need not be, and often are not, undesirable to the individual, the

* From *Academy of Management Review* (1979) *4*, 225–35. The authors wish to express their appreciation to Robert Dubin, Newton Margulies, Joseph W. McGuire, and Lyman W. Porter for their comments on this manuscript.

organization, or society. It is suggested here that turnover is a *positive* phenomenon. It is with this focus that turnover will be examined.

This investigation will be conducted from four perspectives: (*a*) organizational, (*b*) economic, (*c*) sociological, and (*d*) psychological/social psychological.

ORGANIZATIONAL PERSPECTIVE OF TURNOVER

Most organizational theorists have focused on the negative aspects of turnover. This view is related to an alleged inverse relationship between turnover and organizational effectiveness (104). Establishing empirical support for this view is problematic. Often the research is biased because it fails to consider the possible benefits of turnover.

For instance, there is evidence that describes the costs of turnover to the organization (39, 66, 86, 87, 132). These costs are generally for recruitment, replacement, and training of personnel. In a recent article, Mirvis and Lawler (86) measured the financial impact of employee attitudes. Among dimensions measured was the cost of turnover to the organization. An essential qualification can be made to these analyses as they do not consider both sides of the balance sheet. Investigations of this nature may mislead the reader because only the costs are reported. In order to accurately evaluate the consequences of turnover on organizational effectiveness, both the costs and the benefits should be assessed.

Accounting procedures aside, there is evidence that turnover does not decrease organizational effectiveness. Available research does not indicate a consistent relationship between measures of production and turnover (80, 89, 100).

Turnover Can Increase Effectiveness

There is evidence that turnover *increases*, not decreases, organizational effectiveness (47, 60, 131, 135, 140). Innovation has clear implications for organizational effectiveness. Mobility has been cited by many as a force by which innovation is moved from firm to firm (25, 46, 65). Grusky (46) has indicated that the process of mobility brings "new blood" and new ideas into the organization. This process vitalizes the organization and enables it to adapt more adequately to internal demand and ever-changing environmental pressures. Dubin (25) says one of the important consequences of the immobile work career is that which Thorstein Veblen has referred to as "trained incapacity." Dubin suggested that "trained incapacity" is the inability to conceive of, or utilize, new ideas. Immobility, then, is dysfunctional to innovation and may reduce organizational effectiveness.

Recent work in the area of institutional management (4, 98) has also posited the importance of personnel movement from firm to firm as a mechanism for the transfer of innovation. These movements are also essential to the development of interfirm organization, which is believed to be a critical element of institutional management (97).

Another key dimension in organizational effectiveness is the capacity and ease by which technological changes can be incorporated (26, 37, 38). Flexibility and adaptability are critical elements of organizational effectiveness (13, 29, 40, 88, 93, 114, 125, 126, 134). The influx of trained personnel is vital. Work force mobility may be fundamental to achieving this goal.

Lawler (66) has suggested that organizations should adopt a policy to reduce turnover. This position may be subject to several exceptions. In the case of seasonal industries and seasonal employment the costs of stability are enormous. For example, the expense of maintaining a year-round labor force in the fruit picking and canning industry would be prohibitive.

Variables Affecting Turnover

There are several variables which purportedly affect the level of turnover. The following illustrate some of the relationships which are common in the literature:

a. The level of pay is inversely related to turnover (11, 16, 18, 36, 58, 66, 77, 102).
b. Routinization is positively related to turnover (9, 44, 56, 102).
c. Accurate communication about the nature of the job is inversely related to turnover (44, 66, 102).
d. Centralization is inversely related to turnover (10, 44, 66, 80, 96, 102).
e. Integration is inversely related to turnover (66, 96, 102, 115).

These relationships suggest that an organization could reduce turnover by reviewing practices and procedures, and by modifying pay scales and structure. But at what cost? Mechanisms may be available to reduce turnover but organizations may be hesitant to utilize them. Perhaps the cost incurred to reduce turnover might exceed the cost of turnover itself. There is, for example, a characteristically high rate of turnover among waitresses. Perhaps by raising wages, the organizations could reduce the incidence of turnover. But is this strategy cost effective? It may be far less expensive to cope with turnover than to prevent it.

There are other areas in which organizations benefit from turnover. Private pension funds are based on nonturnover employees. Recent managerial opposition to the vesting of pension funds may have reflected a view that employee turnover would substantially reduce the future payout from such funds.

ECONOMIC PERSPECTIVE OF TURNOVER

Turnover is not an issue for the classical economist. In the analysis of the competitive firm, wages must equal marginal product. Since wages and marginal product are assumed to be equal in most firms, no one person nor firm should suffer from turnover (12). Unless the managers of a firm believed that the marginal productivity of a prospective employee was at least equal to the wage which would be paid, the employee would not be hired.

The assumptions which lead to this analysis are not entirely self-evident. It is not clear that all employees are rational nor all firms competitive in the classical sense. Also, firms or individuals may not have sufficient knowledge about marginal products or relative wages to operationalize this simple model.

There is evidence to support the marginal productivity theory. According to this theory, there is a close relationship between wage differentials and the allocation of labor to various employments. Wage differentials reflect present variations in the supply-demand proportions of labor for different types and/or locations of work. Being rational and income-maximizing, labor will respond to existing structure of wages (and nonmonetary incentives) by moving away from employments of less net attractiveness and toward employment of relatively greater attractiveness (41).

This assertion is subject to criticism. Individual rationality and the propensity to maximize income are questionable. Nonetheless, the Office of Research and Statistics of the U.S. Social Security Administration (90) concluded that there is a meaningful amount of purposive mobility in the economy. Moreover, it is possible for the labor market to make marginal adjustments that are envisaged in conventional economic theory of the labor market.

Gallaway (37) suggests empirical evidence concerning geographic mobility argues that behavior is reasonably consistent with the premises of conventional economic theory. Differential economic advantage may not be the only factor, but it is clearly an important one.

Wertheimer (136) supports this view. In his book, *The Monetary Rewards of Migration within the United States,* he says the income difference attributable to migration is positive for all categories of employment investigated. Furthermore, there is evidence that individuals do not leave an organization without having assessed the market (57, 82, 93). A large percentage of individuals have made arrangements for new employment before leaving (82).

The existence of opportunity knowledge suggests an important implication of turnover for the economy. Given that mobility results in net positive income to the migrators, it may be concluded that mobility increases net national product (35, 69) and contributes to the long-term growth rate of the economy (37, 38).

For a variety of economic, ethical, and social reasons, many people favor mitigation of income differences, and therefore find equalizing measures desirable. Again, horizontal and vertical mobility is a mechanism for decreasing income differences (35, 69).

Nonmobility in the labor force may result in "stickiness" in local labor markets. This tendency is especially problematic in declining labor markets. Rather than moving to more viable markets, some employees prefer to remain until such time as employment is finally terminated. This has two important consequences. *First*, this persistence increases short-run costs to employers in wages and benefits. *Second*, this lack of migration may generate a long-run cost to the community in terms of unemployment compensation and related support programs.

Two Labor Market Theories

Economics offers two theories closely aligned with turnover: the dual labor market and the theory of labor market segmentation. Virtually all labor market studies have shown that the labor force is segmented in some sense (91, 106). Segmentation separates labor into primary and secondary markets. Piore (99) discusses the character of these markets.

The *primary* market offers jobs which possess several of the following traits: (*a*) high wages, (*b*) good working conditions, (*c*) employment stability, (*d*) job security, (*e*) equity, (*f*) due process in the administration of work rules, and (*g*) chances for advancement.

The *secondary* market is decidedly different. Secondary jobs are less attractive with (*a*) lower wages, (*b*) poorer working conditions, (*c*) considerable variation in employment stability, (*d*) harsh and often arbitrary discipline, and (*e*) little opportunity for advancement.

This segmentation may have very important implications for turnover in organizations and society. Typically, the primary market is not characterized by ease of entry. Kerr (63) points out the many jobs in the primary market are distinguished by limited ports of entry and various sorting procedures. They require preparation and ritual. Proper educational and/or social levels must be attained in order to enter the primary labor market.

The relevance to turnover is clear. Individuals, by and large, begin their employment in the secondary market. Vertical mobility from the secondary market to the primary is difficult. Orderlies do not ordinarily become doctors and mail room clerks do not become accountants through vertical mobility. More often individuals must quit their jobs in the secondary market, attain the necessary educational and social prerequisites, and then enter the primary market. In order to bridge these labor market levels one must become a turnover "statistic." What are the implications of reducing this secondary-to-primary labor market turnover? Osterman (91) has suggested that movements between segments are important matters of public concern. Each of us could consider our employment history and cite many instances of turnover in the secondary market while striving to train for and enter the primary market.

The findings that turnover increases concomitantly with the educational level of the worker (14, 44, 96) may be partially explained by the dual market phenomenon. Education may ease entry into the primary market. If so, horizontal turnover may be necessary since it is not usually possible to enter the primary market vertically within the subject organization. The individual must leave the secondary, acquire the requisite education, and reenter the labor market in the primary sector.

To summarize from the economic perspective, turnover increases net national product, may reduce inequitable distribution of income, contributes to the long-term growth rate of the economy, and reduces market "stickiness" with its resultant dysfunctions. Additionally, turnover, in an economic context, becomes a necessary behavior for those who would aspire to enter the primary market.

SOCIOLOGICAL PERSPECTIVE OF TURNOVER

With respect to turnover, there may be a Smithian "invisible hand" prejudice operating. Increasing the satisfaction of an individual, and thereby preventing turnover, does not necessarily enhance the satisfaction of society. Adam Smith, writing in *An Inquiry into the Nature and Causes of the Wealth of Nations* (118), popularized the notion of the "invisible hand." Simply, this concept suggests that individual decisions are "led by an invisible hand to promote . . . the public interest." Adam Smith did *not* state that this was invariably true. However, he and his followers have contributed to a dominant tendency of thought—that is, a propensity to assume that decisions reached individually will, in fact, be in the best interests of an entire society.

This illustrates the fallacy of composition wherein premises assert something about the parts of the whole and the conclusion asserts what is true of the parts is necessarily true of the whole (79). Examples of this fallacy are clearly seen in the "paradox of thrift" (120) and the "tragedy of the commons" (74).

Society does not necessarily gain by the reduction of turnover in the organization. The reduction may, in fact, involve important dysfunctions to society. Society has a stake in the advancement, both social and economic, of its citizenry. One way this growth can be accomplished is through vertical mobility within the organization. Fortunately, vertical and horizontal mobility are not contradictory or mutually exclusive concepts (127). Hall (49) suggests horizontal and spatial mobility are generally closely related to vertical mobility. Job changes are important components of the vertical mobility process. This movement provides a legitimating mechanism for individuals to move toward those positions best suited to their abilities (109). Indeed, horizontal migration has become increasingly effective as a selection process by which individuals are channeled to places where their potential can be realized more fully (17).

Mobility is of importance, not only to the individual, but to the efficiency and well-being of society (71). Progress comes through movements to new jobs involving more skill, responsibility, and independence (107). Very often the firm does not have the growth potential or the positions available wherein the individual can prosper. Turnover may be an expected consequence of the limited opportunity for vertical mobility within an organization.

Notions of success and achievement are central to the study of mobility. When occupational achievement and open class ideology are present, mobility becomes a primary mechanism for distributing the labor force and providing progressive career stages (85, 94). Other studies have shown similar relations between levels of aspiration and turnover (23, 105). Also, individuals tend to change jobs as their perception of opportunity increases (18, 21, 36, 81, 96).

In fact, it may be that turnover in these cases does not arise merely as a reaction to lack of opportunity in the organization. Individuals may seek mobility as a proactive strategy. Increasingly, people seem to be planning, and actually having, careers involving multiple organizations and even multiple occupations (101). The "stepping stone" job strategy appears to be operational in some individuals (42, 60, 119).

In a survey of executives (reported in the *Los Angeles Times*, October 31, 1977), mobility was cited as essential for success in the business world. Two thirds of the respondents had worked for three or more organizations and only 14 percent had held their present positions for five or more years. Greater potential for advancement and increased scope of responsibility were identified as the primary motives for horizontal mobility.

It has been estimated that one third of the work force may be employed in career-type occupations and professions (137). Evidence supports the generalization that upward occupational achievement is more probable when one has high aspirations and a willingness to be horizontally as well as vertically mobile (127). It is no surprise that people with a high "career anchor" (129) commonly turn over. It may well be a sound strategy for advancement.

Mobility Reduces Inequality

Mobility may also serve to reduce inequality or inequity in social exchange (2, 3, 15, 54, 111, 130). Indeed the exchange approach in sociology might be described as the economic analysis of noneconomic social situations (31). From the perspective of any approach, perceived inequity and inequality may be reduced by mobility of the actors.

Society may be served by diverting migration away from large cities to less-crowded areas. This amounts to a reduction in ecological pressure (136). In all probability, any such migration results in turnover for some firm, somewhere.

Given turnover could be substantially reduced, what are the consequences and costs to society? Assume individuals are convinced (co-opted) to remain at their first job. What are the social costs of not advancing beyond that point in their career development; not having become a turnover "statistic"?

From a sociological perspective, the positive aspects of turnover are impressive. Horizontal mobility may be the means by which the social and economic growth of the citizenry may be accomplished. Occupational achievement, beneficial to society, is facilitated by those who are horizontally as well as vertically mobile. Mobility may reduce inequity in social exchange. Finally, turnover may be a mechanism to reduce ecological pressure.

PSYCHOLOGICAL/SOCIAL PSYCHOLOGICAL PERSPECTIVES OF TURNOVER

As living organisms, individuals are endowed with the ability to respond to both benign and noxious environmental stimuli (28, 56). Systems possessing the ability to react to their environments in a manner favorable to the viability of the organism have a quality referred to as "adaptability" (48). Coping and response to organizational stress have been addressed in the organizational literature (61). An individual's decision to initiate a particular movement (turnover) can be defined as an adjustment process in an adaptive system maintaining its homeostatic level (43). The literature is replete with references to the notion of movement as a response to stress (20, 43, 56, 67, 68, 70, 92, 121, 138, 139). Ritchey's (108) analysis adequately summarizes the view: When the stress threshold is exceeded, it produces the decision to move.

Organizations may not benefit from reducing turnover caused by environmental stress. Kurt Lewin's (72, 73) concept of force field analysis illustrates this point. Movement from a quasi-stationary equilibrium may be accomplished by increasing forces to move or by reducing resisting forces. The former *increases* while the latter *decreases* pressure on the individual. Organizations attempting to reduce turnover create forces resisting the decision to move. The original quasi-stationary equilibrium may be maintained but the total pressure on the individual will have increased. The individual may take other, perhaps counterproductive, actions to reduce the pressure. Turnover would have been a positive action in this case for the individual involved and the organization as well.

For the extreme case there is evidence that turnover may be the end product of the somatic conversion to stress (32, 61, 62, 124, 128). The organization should not deter turnover by employees inflicted with physical manifestations of stress. The health of the individual and the organization are clearly enhanced by withdrawal in these cases.

In the less-extreme case, the process of adjustment to employment by the individual may be dysfunctional to the organization (9, 75). Individuals may not leave the organization for a variety of reasons, including the fact that they may have been co-opted by the organization. The organization may succeed in reducing turnover. This, however, does not suggest that individuals will not display coping mechanisms and withdrawal behavior. The employee may resort to temporary withdrawals. As a response to role conflict or stress the employee may answer with alcoholism, drug abuse, accidents, or other nonproductive behaviors (52, 78). Chung (22) suggests that dissatisfied performers who do not leave the organization may express dissatisfaction with apathy, sabotage, absenteeism, and other counter-productive behaviors. It would be far better for the organization if these individuals would leave.

A Judgmental Error

Turnover may be a response to judgmental error by the employee. Proactive mobility excepted, some aspirants, while theoretically free to choose an occupation, have no means to ascertain occupational opportunities or have their occupational aptitudes evaluated (127). Individuals have little market information and few resources to sustain themselves while job searching (37, 108). An individual's choice of occupation may be influenced more by social space than by knowledge, experience, or a rational approach to the labor market (127). Dubin (26) points out that for the bulk of the population, the decision about type of work is made when the choice becomes necessary—namely, when the labor market is initially entered. This strategy leads to error. Individuals enter the labor market with little information and have a large degree of ignorance about future outcomes (30). Under these circumstances, turnover as a response to error in judgement is an inevitable and expected consequence of such work-search behavior.

This tendency may exist later in individuals' careers as well. Pavalko (95) refers to this phenomenon as the "career crunch," suggesting that expectations about present and future occupational activities are often inconsistent with the reality. When an alternative employment opportunity arises, an increase in turnover may be expected (8, 36, 66).

Too much commitment can be disadvantageous to an organization's flexibility (112). This can be true on several dimensions. Commitment can lead to an inviolate trust of past policies (112) or to the affirmation of past mistakes (64, 122, 123). It may be partially responsible for the phenomenon which Janis (59) has referred to as "groupthink." The infusion of new personnel may mitigate these tendencies. The cosmopolitan (45, 84) whose commitment is more focused on professional ability and not on the organization, might be a more valuable asset to the organization's flexibility and innovation than the individual not likely to turn over.

Turnover may be seen as a reaction to stress which may be far less destructive than its alternatives, a strategy by which initial job-entry errors are rectified, and a possible amelioration of the dysfunctions associated with overcommitment to an organization.

CONCLUSION

The emphasis has been on turnover with a positive focus from the perspective of several disciplines: (a) organizational, (b) economic, (c) sociological, and (d) psychological/social psychological. Any substantial reduction in the amount of turnover may have short-run positive consequences for the firm. However, the long-run implications may be dysfunctional to the individual, to the organization, and to society.

From the organizational standpoint, turnover costs may be misrepresented because of a failure to account for the benefits as well as the costs of turnover. There is evidence that turnover increases organizational effectiveness and innovation, assists the development of institutional management and interfirm cooperation, and augments technological change. Furthermore, the costs of reducing turnover may exceed the actual cost of turnover.

From an economic viewpoint, it has been suggested that mobility and migration are essential. In general, mobility increases net national product and contributes to the long-term growth rate of the economy. It serves to reduce the income disparity of individuals. Turnover may also be the main process by which individuals progress from the *secondary* to the *primary* job market.

Sociologically, mobility aids both the social and economic development of the individual. Mobility may provide a means to promote progression through career stages and a selective process whereby individuals are channeled to areas in which their potential can be more fully realized. Mobility may serve to reduce inequity and inequality in social exchange. Also, migration may be a strategy for reducing ecological pressure.

Finally, turnover may be a coping mechanism for the individual under stress. Blocking this process may invite absenteeism, apathy, sabotage, and other nonproductive or counterproductive behaviors. Turnover allows for the rectification of errors that occur in the job search process. In addition, the organization must be aware of the consequence of little or no turnover coupled with overcommitment to the organization.

To view turnover as a strictly positive or negative phenomenon seems somewhat shortsighted. Certainly, turnover has both positive and negative ramifications for the organization. What, then, is the appropriate level of turnover? Several factors should be considered.

First, the amount of turnover is most often expressed in terms of a percentage. This measure is difficult to interpret and may be misleading. For instance, an unusually high percentage of turnover would not be meaningful in a seasonal industry and/or seasonal employment. Also, high rates of turnover can be anticipated in industries in which the cost of preventing turnover exceeds the cost of turnover itself. Therefore, for those working as bank tellers, waitresses, and other, similar jobs, this tendency would be expected.

Second, raw turnover percentages are difficult to evaluate without considering the individual component. A relatively low percentage of turnover of 1 or 2 percent could have critical consequences for an organization if the individuals who have chosen to leave had essential or exclusive skills or information. Similarly, a rather large percentage turnover rate would have little impact if the individuals who leave are preceived to have little of such information. To compare one organization's 20 percent turnover rate with another's 35 percent rate on the basis of the raw percentage alone would be hazardous.

Third, in order to assess turnover accurately, both the costs and the benefits of turnover should be appraised. Estimating the impact of turnover on the organization by summing the costs of recruitment, training, etc. only reflects one side of the equation. It ignores the possibility that turnover has positive consequences for the organization, some of which have been the subject of preceding sections.

Fourth, turnover, to be evaluated accurately, should include a perspective broader than that of a single individual or even the single firm because it has consequences that transcend the organization or any of its members.

REFERENCES

1. Abbott, L. D. *Masterworks of economics*. New York: McGraw-Hill, 1973.
2. Adams, J. S. "Toward an understanding of inequity." *Journal of Abnormal Social Psychology* (1963) 67, 422–36.
3. Adams, J. S. "Inequality in social exchange." In *Advances in experimental social psychology*. ed. L. Berkowitz. New York: Academic Press, 1966.
4. Aldrich, H. E., and J. Pfeffer, "Environments of organizations." In *The annual review of sociology*. ed. Alex Inkeles, James Coleman, and Neil Smelser. Palo Alto, Calif.: Annual Reviews, Inc., 1976, 79–116.
5. Alexander, M. "Cost of hiring and firing men." *Engineering Magazine* (1915a) 48, 733–36.
6. Alexander, M. "Waste in hiring and discharging employees." *Scientific American* (1915b) 79, 102–03.
7. Alexander, M. "Hiring and firing: Its economic waste and how to avoid it." *Annals of the American Academy of Political and Social Science* (1916) 65, 128–44.

8. Anderson, B. W. Empirical generalizations on labor turnover." In *Labor and manpower*. ed. R. Pegnetter. Iowa City: University of Iowa Press, 1974.
9. Argyris, C. *Understanding organizational behavior*. Chicago: Dorsey Press, 1960.
10. Argyris, C. "Personality and organization theory revisited." *Administrative Science Quarterly* (1973) *18*, 141–67.
11. Armknecht, P. A., and J. F. Early. "Quits in manufacturing: A study of their cause." *Monthly Labor Review* (1972) *95*, 31–37.
12. Becker, G. S. *Human capital*. New York: National Bureau of Economic Research, 1975.
13. Bennis, W. G. "Toward a truly scientific management: The concept of organizational health." *General Systems Yearbook* (1962) *7*, 269–82.
14. Berg, I. *Education and jobs*. New York: Praeger, 1970.
15. Blau, P. M. *Exchange and power in social life*. New York: John Wiley & Sons, 1964.
16. Blau, P. M. *The organization of academic work*. New York: John Wiley & Sons, 1973.
17. Blau, P. M., and O. D. Duncan. *The American occupational structure*. New York: John Wiley & Sons, 1967.
18. Bowey, A. M. *A guide to manpower planning*. London: MacMillan, 1974.
19. Brayfield, A. H., and W. H. Crockett. "Employee attitudes and employee performance." *Psychological Bulletin* (1955) *52*, 396–424.
20. Brown, L. A., and E. G. Moore. "The intraurban migration process: A perspective." *General Systems Yearkbook* (1970) *15*, 109–22.
21. Burton, B. R., and J. E. Parker. "Interindustry variations in voluntary labor mobility." *Industrial Labor Relations Review* (1969) *22*, 199–216.
22. Chung, K. H. *Motivational theories and practices*. Columbus, Ohio: Grid, 1977.
23. Crockett, H. J. "The achievement motive and differential occupational mobility in the United States." *American Sociological Review* (1962) *27*, 191–204.
24. Dennison, H. S. "Methods of reducing the labor turnover." *U.S. Bureau of Labor Statistics Bulletin No. 202*. Washington, D.C.: U.S. Government Printing Office, 1916, 56–59.
25. Dubin, R. "Management in Britain—impressions of a visiting professor." *Journal of Management Studies* (1970) *7*, 183–98.
26. Dubin, R. "Work in modern society." In *Handbook of work, organization, and society*. ed. R. Dubin. Chicago: Rand McNally, 1976, 5–36.
27. Dubin, R.; R. A. Hedley; and T. C. Taveggia. "Attachment to work." In *Handbook of work, organization, and society*. ed. R. Dubin. Chicago: Rand McNally, 1976, 281–341.
28. Dubos, R. *Man adapting*. New Haven, Conn.: Yale University Press, 1965.
29. Duncan, R. B. "Multiple decision making structures in adapting to environmental uncertainty: The impact on organizational effectiveness." *Human Relations* (1973) *26*, 273–91.
30. Dunkerley, D. *Occupations and society*. London: Routledge & Kegan Paul, 1975.
31. Emerson, R. M. "Social exchange theory." In *The annual review of sociology*. ed. A. Inkeles, J. Coleman, and N. Smelser. Palo Alto, Calif.: Annual Reviews, Inc., 1976, 335–362.

32. Ferguson, D. "A study of neurosis and occupation." *British Journal of Industrial Medicine* (1973) *30*, 187–98.
33. Fisher, B. "Methods of reducing the labor turnover." *Annals of the American Academy of Political and Social Sciences* (1916) 65.
34. Fraser, R. "The incidence of neurosis among factory workers." *Industrial Health Research Board Report No. 90*, 1947.
35. Friedman, M. *Capitalism and freedom*. Chicago: University of Chicago Press, 1962.
36. Fry, F. L. "A behavioral analysis of economic variables affecting turnover." *Journal of Behavioral Economics* (1973) *2*, 247–95.
37. Gallaway, L. E. *Manpower economics*. Homewood, Ill.: Richard D. Irwin, 1971.
38. Gallaway, L. E. "The significance of the labor market." In *Readings in labor economics and labor relations*. ed. R. L. Rowan. Homewood, Ill.: Richard D. Irwin, 1977.
39. Gaudet, F. J. *The literature on labor turnover*. New York: Industrial Relations Press, 1960.
40. Georgopoulos, B. S., and A. S. Tannenbaum. "The study of organizational effectiveness." *American Sociological Review* (1957) *22*, 534–40.
41. Gitlow, A. L. *Labor and manpower economics*. Homewood, Ill.: Richard D. Irwin, 1971.
42. Glickman, A. S.; C. P. Hahn; E. A., Fleishman; and B. Baxter. *Top management development and succession*. New York: MacMillan, 1968.
43. Golant, S. M. "Adjustment process in a system: A behavioral model of human movement." *Geographical Analysis* (1971) *3*, 203–20.
44. Goodman, P. S.; P. Salipante; and H. Paransky. "Hiring, training, and retraining the hard core unemployed: A selected review." *Journal of Applied Psychology* (1973) *58*, 23–33.
45. Gouldner, A. W. "Cosmopolitans and locals: Towards an analysis of latent social role." *Administrative Science Quarterly* (1957) *12*, 281–306.
46. Grusky, O. "Administrative succession in formal organizations." *Social Forces* (1960) *39*, 105–15.
47. Guest, R. H. Managerial succession in complex organizations." *American Journal of Sociology* (1962) *68*, 47–56.
48. Hall, A. D., and R. E. Fagen, "Definition of a system." In *Modern systems research for the behavioral scientist*. ed. W. R. Buckley. Chicago: Aldine, 1968, 81–92.
49. Hall, R. H. *Occupations and the social structure*. Englewood Cliffs, N.J.: Prentice-Hall, 1969.
50. Hardin, G. "The tragedy of the commons." *Science* (1968) *162*, no. 2, 1243–48.
51. Herzberg, F.; B. Mausner; R. O. Peterson; and D. G. Capwell. *Job attitudes: Review of research and opinion*. Pittsburgh: Psychological Service of Pittsburgh, 1957.
52. Hill, J. M. "The representation of labour turnover as a social process." In *Labour turnover and retention*. ed. B. O. Pettman. Epping, Eng.: Gower, 1975, 77–98.
53. Hinrichs, J. R. "Psychology of men at work." In *Annual review of psychology*. ed. P. H. Mussen and M. R. Rosenzweig. Palo Alto, Calif.: Annual Reviews, Inc., 1970.
54. Homans, G. C. "Social behavior as exchange." *American Journal of Sociology* (1958) *62*, 597–606.

55. Homans, G. C. *Social behavior: Its elementary forms.* New York: Harcourt, Brace & World, 1961.
56. Howard, A., and R. A. Scott. "A proposed framework for the analysis of stress in the human organism." *Behavioral Science* (1965) *10*, 141–60.
57. Hyman, R. "Economic motivation and labor stability." *British Journal of Industrial Relations* (1970) *8*, 159–78.
58. Ingham, G. K. *Size of industrial organization and worker behavior.* Cambridge: Cambridge University Press, 1970.
59. Janis, I. L. *Victims of groupthink.* Boston: Houghton Mifflin, 1972.
60. Jennings, E. E. *The mobile manager.* Lansing: University of Michigan Press, 1967.
61. Kahn, R. L.; D. M. Wolfe; R. P. Quinn; J. D. Snoek; and R. A. Rosenthal, *Organizational stress: Studies in role conflict and ambiguity.* New York: John Wiley & Sons, 1964.
62. Kasl, S. V., and S. Cobb. Some psychological factors associated with illness behavior and selected illnesses." *Journal of Chronic Disease* (1964) *17*, 325–45.
63. Kerr, C. The balkanization of labor markets. In *Labor mobility and economic opportunity.* ed. E. Bakke. Cambridge, Mass.: MIT Press, 1954, 92–110.
64. Kiesler, C. A., and R. Mathog. "Resistance to influence as a function of number of prior consonant acts." In *The psychology of commitment.* ed. C. A. Kiesler. New York: Academic Press, 1971, 66–73.
65. Kirshenbaum, A. B., and A. Goldberg, "Organization behavior, career orientations, and propensity to move among professionals." *Sociology of Work and Occupations,* (1976) *3*, no. 3, 357–72.
66. Lawler, E. E. *Motivation in work organizations.* Monterey, Calif.: Brooks/Cole, 1973.
67. Lazarus, R. S.; J. Deese; and S. F. Oster. "The effects of psychological stress upon performance. In *Contemporary research in personality.* ed. I. G. Sarason. Princeton: D. Van Nostrand, 1962, 288–302.
68. Lee, D. H. The role of attitude in response to environmental stress. *Journal of Social Issues* (1966) *22*, 83–91.
69. Leftwich, R. *The price system and resource allocation.* New York: Holt, Rinehart & Winston, 1966.
70. Leslie, G. R., and A. H. Richardson, "Life cycle, career pattern, and the decision to move." *American Sociological Review* (1961) *26*, 894–902.
71. Levitan, S. A.; G. L. Mangun; and S. Marshall, *Human resources and labor markets.* New York: Harper & Row, 1976.
72. Lewin, K. *The conceptual representation and the measurement of psychological forces.* Durham, N.C.: Duke University Press, 1938.
73. Lewin, K. *Field theory in social science.* New York: Harper & Row, 1951.
74. Lloyd, W. F. "Two lectures on the checks of population," (pamphlet). Oxford: University of Oxford Press, 1833. In G. Hardin, "The tragedy of the commons." *Science* (1966) *162*, no. 2, 1243–48.
75. Lundquist, A. "Absenteeism and job turnover as a consequence of unfavorable job adjustment." *Acta Sociologica* (1959) *3*, no. 2, 119–31.
76. Lyons, T. F. *Nursing attitudes and turnover.* Ames: Industrial Relations Center, Iowa State University, 1968.
77. MacKay, D. I.; D. Boddy; J. Brack; J. A. Diack; and N. Jones. *Labor markets.* London: George Allen, 1971.

78. Mangione, T. W., and R. P. Quinn, "Job satisfaction, counterproductive behavior, and drug use at work." *Journal of Applied Psychology*, (1975), *60*, no. 1, 114–16.

79. Manicas, T., and A. N. Kruger, *Logic: The essentials.* New York: McGraw-Hill, 1976.

80. March, J. G., and H. A. Simon, *Organizations.* New York: John Wiley & Sons, 1958.

81. Marsh, R. M., and H. Mannari. "Lifetime commitment in Japan: Roles, norms and values." *American Journal of Sociology* (1971) *76*, 796–812.

82. Mattila, J. P. "Job quitting and frictional unemployment." *American Economic Review* (1974) *64*, 235–39.

83. Mayo, E. "Revery and industrial fatigue." *Personnel Journal* (1924) *8*, 273–81.

84. Merton, R. K. "Patterns of influence: Local and cosmopolitan influentials." In *Social theory and social structure.* ed. R. K. Merton. Glencoe, Ill.: Free Press, 1957.

85. Mills, C. W. *White collar.* New York: Oxford University Press, 1951.

86. Mirvis, P. M., and E. E. Lawler. "Measuring the financial impact of employee attitudes." *Journal of Applied Psychology* (1977) *62*, no. 1, 1–8.

87. Moffatt, G. W., and K. Hill. "Labor turnover in Australia: A review of research." *Personnel Practice Bulletin*, (1970), *26*, 142–49.

88. Mott, P. E. *The characteristics of effective organizations.* New York: Harper & Row, 1972.

89. Mueller, E. H. *The relationship between teacher turnover and student achievement.* Ph.D. dissertation, School of Education, University of Virginia. In *A study of turnover* J. Price. Ames: Iowa State University Press, 1977.

90. Office of Research and Statistics, Social Security Administration. "Interindustry Mobility in the United States, 1957–1960." *Research Report No. 18.* Washington, D.C.: U. S. Government Printing Office, 1967.

91. Osterman, P. "An empirical study of labor market segmentation." *Industrial and Labor Relations Review* (1975) *28*, no. 4, 508–23.

92. Parnes, H. S., and R. S. Spitz. "A conceptual framework for studying labor mobility." *Monthly Labor Review* (1969) *92*, 55–58.

93. Parsons, D. O. "Quit rates over time: A search and information approach." *American Economic Review* (1973) *63*, 390–401.

94. Parsons, T. "The professional and social structure. "*Social Forces*, (1939) *17*, 457–67.

95. Pavalko, R. M. *Sociology of occupations and professions.* Itasca, Ill.: F. E. Peacock, 1971.

96. Pettman, B. O. "Some factors influencing labor turnover: A review of research literature." *Industrial Relations*, (1973) *4*, 43–61.

97. Pfeffer, J., and H. Leblebici. "Executive recruitment and the development of interfirm organizations." *Administrative Science Quarterly* (1973) *17*, 218–28.

98. Pfeffer, J. "Beyond management and the worker: The institutional function of management." *Academy of Management Review* (1976) *1*, no. 2, 36–46.

99. Piore, M. J. "Notes for a theory of labor market stratification. "Department of Economics Working Paper No. 95, MIT, 1972. In P. Osterman, "An empirical study of labor market segmentation." *Industrial Relations Review* (1975) *28*, 508–23.

study of labor market segmentation." *Industrial Relations Review* (1975) *28*, 508–23.

100. Pomeroy, R., and H. Yahr. *Studies in public welfare.* New York: Center for the Study of Urban Problems, Graduate Division, Bernard Baruch College, City University, 1967. In *The study of turnover.* James Price. Ames: Iowa State University Press, 1977.

101. Porter, L. W.; E. E. Lawler; and J. R. Hackman, *Behavior in organizations.* New York: McGraw-Hill, 1975.

102. Porter, L. W., and R. M. Steers. "Organizational, work, and personal factors in employee turnover and absenteeism." *Psychological Bulletin* (1973) *80*, 151–76.

103. Price, J. L. *Organizational effectiveness: An inventory of propositions.* Homewood, Ill.: Richard D. Irwin, 1968.

104. Price, J. L. *The study of turnover.* Ames: Iowa State University Press, 1977.

105. Reismann, L. "Levels of aspiration and social class." *American Sociological Review* (1953) *18*, 233–42.

106. Reynolds, L. G. *The structure of labor markets.* New York: Harper & Row, 1951.

107. Reynolds, L. G. *Labor economics and labor relations.* Englewood Cliffs, N.J.: Prentice-Hall, 1964.

108. Ritchey, P. N. "Explanations of migration." In *The annual review of sociology.* ed. A. Inkeles, J. Coleman, and N. Smelser. Palo Alto, Calif.: Annual Reviews, Inc., 1976, 363–404.

109. Ritti, R. R. "Underemployment of engineers." *Industrial Relations* (1970) *9*, 437–52.

110. Rowan, R. L., ed. *Readings in labor economics and labor relations.* Homewood, Ill.: Richard D. Irwin, 1977.

111. Runciman, W. G. *Relative deprivation and social justice.* Berkeley: University of California Press, 1967.

112. Salancik, G. R. "Commitment and the control of organizational behavior and belief." In *New directions in organizational behavior.* ed. B. M. Staw and G. R. Salancik. Chicago: St. Clair, 1977, 1–54.

113. Sales, S. M., and J. House. "Job dissatisfaction as a possible contributor to risk of death from coronary disease." *Proceedings of the Annual Convention of the American Psychological Association* (1970), 593–94.

114. Schein, E. A. *Organizational psychology.* Englewood Cliffs, N.J.: Prentice-Hall, 1970.

115. Schuh, A. "The predictability of employee tenure: A review of the literature." *Personnel Psychology,* (1967) *20*, 133–52.

116. Sheridan, J. E. "Reducing labor turnover." *100%* (1916) *6*, 92–96.

117. Slichter, S. H. *The turnover of factory labor.* New York: Appleton, 1919.

118. Smith, A. [*An inquiry into the nature and causes of the wealth of nations*]. In *Masterworks of economics.* L. D. Abbott. New York: McGraw-Hill, 1973. (Originally published, 1776.)

119. Sofer, C. *Men in mid-career: A study of British managers and technical specialists.* Cambridge: Cambridge University Press, 1970.

120. Solman, L. C. *Macroeconomics.* Reading, Mass.: Addison-Wesley, 1977.

121. Speare, A. "Residential satisfaction as an intervening variable in residential mobility." *Demography* (1974) *11*, 173–88.
122. Staw, B. M. "Knee-deep in the big muddy: A study of escalating commitment to a chosen course of action." *Organizational Behavior and Human Performance*, (1976), *16*, 27–44.
123. Staw, B. M., and F. V. Fox. "Escalation: The determinants of commitment to a previously chosen course of action." *Human Relations* (1977), *30*, 431–50.
124. Staw, B. M., and G. R. Salancik. *New directions in organizational behavior.* Chicago: St. Clair, 1977.
125. Steers, R. M. "Problems in the measurement of organizational effectiveness." *Administrative Science Quarterly* (1975) *20*, 546–58.
126. Steers, R. M. "When is an organization effective?: A process approach to understanding effectiveness." *Organizational Dynamics* (Autumn 1976), 50–63.
127. Taylor, L. *Occupational sociology.* New York: Oxford University Press, 1968.
128. Taylor, P. J. "Sickness and absence resistance." *Transactions of the Society of Occupational Medicine* (1968), *18*, 96–100.
129. Tausky, C., and R. Dubin. "Career anchorage: Managerial mobility motivations." *American Sociological Review* (1965) *30*, 725–35.
130. Thibaut, J., and H. Kelley. *The social psychology of groups.* New York: John Wiley & Sons, 1959.
131. Torrence, P. "Some consequences of power differences on decision making in permanent and temporary three man groups." In *Small groups.* ed. A. P. Hare, E. F. Borgatta, and R. F. Bales. New York: Knopf, 1966, 600–09.
132. Tuchi, B. J., and B. E. Carr. "Labor turnover." *Hospitals,* (1971), *45*, 88–92.
133. Vroom, V. *Work and motivation.* New York: John Wiley & Sons, 1964.
134. Webb, R. J. "Organizational effectiveness and the voluntary organization." *Academy of Management Journal* (1974), *17*, 663–77.
135. Wells, W. P., and D. C. Pelz. *Scientists in organization.* New York: John Wiley & Sons, 1966.
136. Wertheimer, R. F. *The monetary rewards of migration within the United States.* Washington, D.C.: The Urban Institute, 1970.
137. Wilensky, H. L. "Work, careers, and social integration." *International Social Science Journal* (1960), *12*, 533–60.
138. Wolpert, J. "Behavioral aspects of the decision to migrate." *Regional Science Association,* (1965), *15*, 159–69.
139. Wolpert, J. "Migration as an adjustment to environmental stress." *Journal of Social Issues,* (1966), *22*, 92–102.
140. Ziller, R. C.; R. D., Behringer; and J. D. Goodchilds. "Group creativity under conditions of failure and variations in group stability." *Journal of Applied Psychology,* (1962), *46*, 43–49.

20

The Great Escape*

Gary Johns

On a typical day, between 2 and 4 percent of Americans fail to show up for work. This doesn't seem like a high absence rate, but in the long run it has major consequences for the national economy. For example, each year more time is lost from work due to absenteeism than through strikes and lockouts, with direct costs to business estimated at up to $30 billion. Also, cases that go to arbitration after an employee has been fired most commonly involve excessive absenteeism.

Absentees, managers, and researchers have very different perspectives on why people miss work. The usual excuse, the one listed in the personnel files, is illness. In reality, we don't know how much absence is due to legitimate illness, since personnel absence-control systems don't encourage the frank reporting of causes.

Even when researchers ask people in confidence why they are typically absent from work, the respondents usually mention some common medical difficulty. Although these explanations may be sincere, there is reason to doubt their precision. People tend to explain behavior that may be viewed negatively by others, such as absenteeism, in terms of factors beyond their control. And since sickness is a culturally accepted reason for staying home, one that is largely beyond a person's control, it is reasonable for people to explain their absences in medical terms. These explanations will usually be accepted by managers as long as they are not invoked too often.

If sickness were the real cause in most cases, we would expect absenteeism to decrease as medical care improves. A study by British researchers Peter Taylor and John Burridge of absence rates in the British Post Office between 1891 and 1980 dispelled this notion. Instead of decreasing, absence ascribed to illness increased over this period. Furthermore, in the years between 1960 and 1980, the medical diagnoses given for absenteeism changed sharply. Stomach and respiratory problems decreased, while psychological disorders and musculoskeletal conditions such as lower-back pain increased markedly. This suggests that workers and physicians explain ab-

* From *Psychology Today* (October 1987), 30–33.

sences in terms of medical conditions that are popular at the time and, therefore, more acceptable.

Several studies of the consequences of high blood pressure show that a diagnosis of illness can affect absenteeism about as strongly as the illness itself. In one study, physician R. Brian Haynes and his colleagues at the McMaster University Faculty of Health Sciences examined steelworkers at Dominion Steel in Hamiliton, Ontario. They found that the workers who had been diagnosed as hypertensive were absent considerably more than those who had hypertension but were unaware of their condition. When these workers were informed of their problem, their absenteeism increased to the same level as that of their previously diagnosed coworkers. Since the early stages of hypertension have no obvious symptoms, this increased rate of absence was almost certainly a psychological reaction by the workers to the information that they were sick, a fact that also provided a legitimate reason for missing work.

None of this implies that much absence isn't due to real illness. But there is considerable scope for two employees with the same physical condition to view it as a more or less legitimate reason to miss work. Clearly, many factors other than objective physical health affect absenteeism.

While people normally explain their absences in terms of sickness, managers and other employees often have less forgiving explanations: laziness, malingering, irresponsibility, a poor work ethic, or other deviant aspects of personality. Psychologist Lee Ross of Stanford University has noted that people tend to explain the behavior of others as an expression of personality. It seems that we discount the influence of situational factors on others' actions, especially when the behavior is unusual. Since most people don't miss much work, the frequent absentee is likely to be described in deviant terms.

Graduate student Paul Innes and I found, for example, that teachers in a Quebec school felt that their colleagues were more likely than themselves to abuse a sick-pay system. Psychologist Nigel Nicholson of the University of Sheffield learned much the same thing when he interviewed transport and industrial workers about absenteeism. The absence of coworkers was often explained in negative personal terms, even by men and women who were frequently absent themselves.

The subject of absenteeism evokes a Jekyll and Hyde response. The Dr. Jekyll persona permits workers to attribute much of their absence to "legitimate" medical causes. However, their Mr. Hyde reminds them that absenteeism is negative and possibly deviant. In the Quebec study, Innes and I found that the teachers underestimated how often they missed work and overestimated their coworkers' absenteeism. This and other research shows that when workers are asked to compare their own absence with that of coworkers, they consistently report that they are absent "somewhat less than average." They seem to resolve their Jekyll and Hyde conflict through a tightly coupled line of thought: "I'm usually absent because I'm sick, I'm absent less than others and their reasons are suspect anyway."

There hasn't been much research on the connection between personality, deviant or otherwise, and absenteeism. Some studies, however, have found that past absence is often a good predictor of current absence, that people who miss a lot of days in one job typically continue the pattern in new jobs and that truancy from school is followed by high absence rates at work. Psychologists regard such stability of behavior in the face of a changed environment as an indication that personality factors may be involved. But it could also result from ongoing problems, such as chronic ill health or persistent family troubles, that continue to interfere with steady attendance.

Absenteeism may also be interpreted in economic terms. Research shows that it tends to decrease when unemployment is high, as workers try to protect their jobs, and to increase when overtime pay is readily available. Absence rates also increase when workers, especially low-paid ones, get their money anyway through sick-pay plans. Feelings of unfairness can be partially redressed if the worker works fewer hours.

A number of firms have tried to combat absenteeism with plans that offer cash or other rewards for little or no absence. When plans are kept simple, they usually reduce absenteeism, although only a few have been evaluated over long periods of time or monitored for cost-effectiveness. More complicated plans provide employees with generous paid sick days and then offer "well pay" if employees don't use them. Since such plans have complex psychological effects, their consequences are much harder to predict. Logic suggests, however, that deferring well-pay benefits for a long time, perhaps until the employee retires, shouldn't work well. The reward is too far removed from the behavior to be effective.

At its broadest, the economic view of absenteeism is grounded in the old saying "time is money." Psychologist Stuart Youngblood, a management professor at Texas A&M University, studied how people's valuation of their time influences their absenteeism. He had workers at a Midwest public utility estimate how much they would pay for certain fringe benefits, and then asked them how much additional time they would work without pay to obtain the same benefits. This gave him an estimate of how highly people valued their nonwork time.

When he compared these estimates with records of absenteeism he found, logically enough, that those who placed a high value on their time off were usually absent more than those who valued it less. This suggests that flextime is one way to reduce absenteeism. . . . By giving employees some flexibility regarding when they begin to work, it allows them to work a full shift and still have the part of the day that is most valuable to them, early morning or late afternoon, for themselves.

If absentees usually explain their behavior medically, while others ascribe absences to personality flaws or economics, psychologists often look on absenteeism as a form of withdrawal from a dissatisfying job. Of all the possible sources of dissatisfaction, dislike of the work itself is the best predictor of absenteeism. Unhappiness with supervisors, coworkers, or other factors is much less critical. Studies also show that dissatisfaction is reflected more in how often people are absent than in the total number of days they miss. A dissatisfied worker is likely to take frequent one- or two-day breaks, rather than long layoffs. These "time-outs" apparently help employees escape boredom, stress and other disliked aspects of the job.

Although job dissatisfaction sometimes leads to absenteeism, the relationship between the two variables isn't very strong. Attitudes, such as those toward the job, may not be reflected in behavior such as absence or attendance if other factors constrain the behavior. For example, employees may dislike their jobs but feel that it is ethically wrong to miss work. Others may enjoy their jobs but genuinely feel that they are ill and can't come to work. With these conflicting pressures, it is no wonder that the connection between job dissatisfaction and absence is smaller than might be imagined.

The medical, deviance, economic, and withdrawal interpretations of absenteeism all suggest that it is due to private, individual factors. Some researchers now suggest that much absence is a matter of social control, a complex product of what coworkers, supervisors, and friends think and say about absenteeism. This, in turn, relates to variables, such as occupation, office or plant layout, absence-control systems, and the social mix of the work force. These combine to form a distinct "absence culture" for a particular work group, department, organization, or occupation.

Weak absence cultures exert little control; workers stay home in accordance with their own job attitudes and prevailing medical or economic conditions. Strong absence cultures may provide specific norms about how much or when absenteeism is expected. In some parts of the country, for example, going deer hunting on the first day of the open season is an acceptable reason for absence from work. In some organizations, informal strictures against staying home are so strong that white-collar workers come in even when they are really sick.

The concept of absence cultures can be extended to include entire countries. For the past few years, time lost due to absenteeism in the United States has averaged about 3 percent. Some countries, such as Japan and Switzerland, have traditionally had lower rates, while others, such as England and Italy, have had much higher rates. It seems unlikely that this disparity can be explained by national differences in health, deviance, job satisfaction, or economics. More likely, it reflects a differing social consensus about how much absence is acceptable.

Industrial-relations researchers Paul Edwards of the University of Warwick and Hugh Scullion of the University of Strathclyde contrasted absence patterns in British clothing-manufacturing plants with those in metalworking factories. In the clothing plants, the rate of absenteeism was very high despite the fact that workers were not paid for missed days. Close supervision, a tight piecework pay system, and rigid quality control put workers under considerable pressure. With a weak union and few means of collective protest, workers apparently saw absenteeism as a legitimate means of escaping the pressure. Even the managers didn't consider it much of a problem, since they were free to move workers around to cover for absentees.

In the metalworking plants, the rate of absenteeism was low despite a sick-pay plan and generally unpleasant working conditions. Counterbalancing this, the strong union contract called for enough employees that workers could move around the plant and still finish their work before the end of the shift. On one assembly line, workers were able to "double up" for coworkers who took extended breaks.

This high degree of control over shop-floor activities relieved the pressure of work and made absence for this purpose less necessary. Also, strong informal pressure by the workers themselves controlled excessive absenteeism. In one shop, for example, workers openly posted a scheduled rotation of unofficial half-day absences to keep the level manageable. Supervisors and shop stewards also worked together to put pressure on chronic absentees who abused the sick-pay system.

One manufacturing company I examined had four plants producing the same product in different parts of Canada. Their average rates of absence varied from 5 percent to 12 percent. Within the plants, absence rates in blue-collar departments ranged from near 0 percent to more than 20 percent. In one plant, the shipping department had absences well below the plant average. In another, absence in shipping was well above the plant average—a difference of 10 percent between one shipping department and another despite identical policies. Such contrasts provide strong circumstantial evidence for the operation of distinct absence cultures in different plants and even within the same plant.

Popular explanations for absenteeism often rely on circular reasoning. Employees are said to be absent because they are "absence prone," and proneness is defined as being absent a lot. As I have discussed, researchers are learning that absence is much more complex: It is the product of medical conditions, personality factors, job attitudes, economic consequences, and cultural dictates. These factors interact differently in each work setting to influence absence rates there.

Groups and Social Influence Processes in Organizations

INTRODUCTION

Very little of significance goes on in organizations on a purely individual basis. At every turn, a person confronts the fact of dependence upon others—for service, information, permission, good will. Dependence gives rise to interaction, and interaction creates a kaleidoscopic succession of overlapping social groups. In this section we examine some of the emergent processes and outcomes that result from living and working in group contexts.

Significantly, three of the five selections that follow have decision making as a focus, and the other two articles treat topics that have much relevance for decisions. Jerry Harvey, in an article that has appeared in every edition of this volume and which has become an acknowledged classic, describes the "Abilene Paradox," in which groups sometimes make very bad decisions that no one member of the group would ever have made or wanted to make. Harvey believes that "the inability to manage agreement is a major source of organizational dysfunction."

Conversely, according to Cosier and Schwenk, bad decisions also come out of groups when there is too much agreement. The authors take the position that not only should conflict not be suppressed, it should be *programmed* into the decision-making process—especially at the top management level in large corporations. They offer two methods, Devil's Advocacy and the Dialectic Method, for ensuring that the healthy conflict of ideas resonates throughout the decision-making process.

Andrew Grove, drawing from experience as CEO at Intel, explains why the decision-making process in a high-tech firm *necessarily* means that decisions are group products. Otherwise, people with the authority and responsibility to make major decisions are cut off from the base of technical knowledge needed to inform such decisions.

Brian Dumaine, in an article written for *Fortune*, examines a rapidly developing trend in business: the self-managing work team. As companies experience the need to downsize and eliminate layers of management, they find that one means of doing so is to eliminate first-line supervision (as traditionally conceived) and turn more operating, personnel, and planning decisions over to the work group. Dumaine reports some of the fantastic successes experienced by firms that have moved aggressively in this direction; but he also points out some of the dilemmas that follow, notably with respect to compensation.

As if it were not enough to appreciate the complexities of group dynamics in our own culture, Jon Alston explains how this complexity is overlaid by unspoken assumptions that vary from one culture to another. Looking at three examples from the Orient—mistakenly considered by many Westerners as a homogeneous culture—Alston shows how the Japanese *wa*, Chinese *guanxi*, and Korean *inhwa* concepts reflect contrasting philosophies of what interpersonal relationships are all about.

The Abilene Paradox:
The Management of Agreement*

Jerry B. Harvey

The July afternoon in Coleman, Texas (population 5,607) was particularly hot—104 degrees as measured by the Walgreen's Rexall Ex-Lax temperature gauge. In addition, the wind was blowing fine-grained West Texas topsoil through the house. But the afternoon was still tolerable—even potentially enjoyable. There was a fan going on the back porch; there was cold lemonade; and finally, there was entertainment. Dominoes. Perfect for the conditions. The game required little more physical exertion than an occasional mumbled comment, "Shuffle 'em," and an unhurried movement of the arm to place the spots in the appropriate perspective on the table. All in all, it had the makings of an agreeable Sunday afternoon in Coleman— that is, it was until my father-in-law suddenly said, "Let's get in the car and go to Abilene and have dinner at the cafeteria."

I thought, "What, go to Abilene? Fifty-three miles? In this dust storm and heat? And in an unairconditioned 1958 Buick?"

But my wife chimed in with, "Sounds like a great idea. I'd like to go. How about you, Jerry?" Since my own preferences were obviously out of step with the rest I replied, "Sounds good to me," and added, "I just hope your mother wants to go."

"Of course I want to go," said my mother-in-law. "I haven't been to Abilene in a long time."

So into the car and off to Abilene we went. My predictions were fulfilled. The heat was brutal. We were coated with a fine layer of dust that was cemented with perspiration by the time we arrived. The food at the cafeteria provided first-rate testimonial material for antacid commericials.

Some four hours and 106 miles later we returned to Coleman, hot and exhausted. We sat in front of the fan for a long time in silence. Then, both to be sociable and to break the silence, I said, "It was a great trip, wasn't it?"

---

* Reprinted by permission of the publisher from *Organizational Dynamics* (Summer 1974). Copyright © by AMACOM, a division of American Management Associations.

No one spoke.

Finally my mother-in-law said, with some irritation, "Well, to tell the truth, I really didn't enjoy it much and would rather have stayed here. I just went along because the three of you were so enthusiastic about going. I wouldn't have gone if you all hadn't pressured me into it."

I couldn't believe it. "What do you mean 'you all'?" I said. "Don't put me in the 'you all' group. I was delighted to be doing what we were doing. I didn't want to go. I only went to satisfy the rest of you. You're the culprits."

My wife looked shocked. "Don't call me a culprit. You and Daddy and Mama were the ones who wanted to go. I just went along to be sociable and to keep you happy. I would have had to be crazy to want to go out in heat like that."

Her father entered the conversation abruptly. "Hell!" he said.

He proceeded to expand on what was already absolutely clear. "Listen, I never wanted to go to Abilene. I just thought you might be bored. You visit so seldom I wanted to be sure you enjoyed it. I would have preferred to play another game of dominoes and eat the leftovers in the icebox."

After the outburst of recrimination we all sat back in silence. Here we were, four reasonably sensible people who, of our own volition, had just taken a 106-mile trip across a godforsaken desert in a furnace-like temperature through a cloud-like dust storm to eat unpalatable food at a hole-in-the-wall cafeteria in Abilene, when none of us had really wanted to go. In fact, to be more accurate, we'd done just the opposite of what we wanted to do. The whole situation simply didn't make sense.

At least it didn't make sense at the time. But since that day in Coleman, I have observed, consulted with, and been a part of more that one organization that has been caught in the same situation. As a result, they have either taken a side-trip, or, occasionally, a terminal journey to Abilene, when Dallas or Houston or Tokyo was where they really wanted to go. And for most of those organizations, the negative consequences of such trips, measured in terms of both human misery and economic loss, have been much greater than for our little Abilene group.

This article is concerned with that paradox—the Abilene Paradox. Stated simply, it is as follows: Organizations frequently take actions in contradiction to what they really want to do and, therefore, defeat the very purposes they are trying to achieve. It also deals with a major corollary of the paradox, which is that *the inability to manage agreement is a major source of organization dysfunction.* Last, the article is designed to help members of organizations cope more effectively with the paradox's pernicious influence.

As a means of accomplishing the above, I shall: (1) describe the symptoms exhibited by organizations caught in the paradox; (2) describe, in summarized case-study examples, how they occur in a variety of organizations; (3) discuss the underlying causal dynamics; (4) indicate some of the implications of accepting this model for describing organizational behavior; (5) make recommendations for coping with the paradox; and, in conclusion, (6) relate the paradox to a broader existential issue.

SYMPTOMS OF THE PARADOX

The inability to manage agreement, not the inability to manage conflict, is the essential symptom that defines organizations caught in the web of the Abilene Paradox. That inability effectively to manage agreement is expressed by six specific subsymptoms, all of which were present in our family Abilene group.

1. Organization members agree privately, as individuals, about the nature of the situation or problem facing the organization. For example, members of the Abilene group agreed that they were enjoying themselves sitting in front of the fan, sipping lemonade, and playing dominoes.

2. Organization members agree privately, as individuals, about the steps that would be required to cope with the situation or problem they face. For members of the Abilene group "more of the same" was a solution that would have adequately satisfied their individual and collective desires.

3. Organization members fail to accurately communicate their desires and/or beliefs to one another. In fact, they do just the opposite and thereby lead one another into misperceiving the collective reality. Each member of the Abilene group, for example, communicated inaccurate data to other members of the organization. The data, in effect, said, "Yeah, it's a great idea. Let's go to Abilene," when in reality members of the organization individually and collectively preferred to stay in Coleman.

4. With such invalid and inaccurate information, organization members make collective decisions that lead them to take actions contrary to what they want to do, and thereby arrive at results that are counterproductive to the organization's intent and purposes. Thus, the Abilene group went to Abilene when it preferred to do something else.

5. As a result of taking actions that are counterproductive, organization members experience frustration, anger, irritation, and dissatisfaction with their organization. Consequently, they form subgroups with trusted acquaintances and blame other subgroups for the organization's dilemma. Frequently, they also blame authority figures and one another. Such phenomena were illustrated in the Abilene group by the "culprit" argument that occurred when we had returned to the comfort of the fan.

6. Finally, if organization members do not deal with the generic issue—the inability to manage agreement—the cycle repeats itself with greater intensity. The Abilene group, for a variety of reasons, the most important of which was that it became conscious of the process, did not reach that point.

To repeat, the Abilene Paradox reflects a failure to manage agreement. In fact, it is my contention that the inability to cope with (manage) agreement, rather than the inability to cope with (manage) conflict, is the single most pressing issue of modern organizations.

OTHER TRIPS TO ABILENE

The Abilene Paradox is no respecter of individuals, organizations, or institutions. Following are descriptions of two other trips to Abilene that illustrate both the pervasiveness of the paradox and its underlying dynamics.

Case 1: The Boardroom

The Ozyx Corporation is a relatively small industrial company that has embarked on a trip to Abilene. The president of Ozyx has hired a consultant to help discover the reasons for the poor profit picture of the company in general and the low morale and productivity of the R&D division in particular. During the process of investigation, the consultant becomes interested in a research project in which the company has invested a sizable proportion of its R&D budget.

When asked about the project by the consultant in the privacy of their offices, the president, the vice president for research, and the research manager each describes it as an idea that looked great on paper but will ultimately fail because of the unavailability of the technology required to make it work. Each of them also acknowledges that continued support of the project will create cash flow problems that will jeopardize the very existence of the total organization.

Furthermore, each individual indicates he has not told the others about his reservations. When asked why, the president says he can't reveal his "true" feelings because abandoning the project, which has been widely publicized, would make the company look bad in the press and, in addition, would probably cause his vice president's ulcer to kick up or perhaps even cause him to quit, "because he has staked his professional reputation on the project's success."

Similarly, the vice president for research says he can't let the president or the research manager know his reservations, because the president is so committed to it that "I would probably get fired for insubordination if I questioned the project."

Finally, the research manager says he can't let the president or vice president know of his doubts about the project, because of their extreme commitment to the project's success.

All indicate that, in meetings with one another, they try to maintain an optimistic façade so the others won't worry unduly about the project. The research director, in particular, admits to writing ambiguous progress reports so the president and the vice president can "interpret them to suit themselves." In fact, he says he tends to slant them to the "positive" side, "given how committed the brass are."

The scent of the Abilene trail wafts from a paneled conference room where the project research budget is being considered for the following fiscal year. In the meeting itself, praises are heaped on the questionable project and a unanimous decision is made to continue it for yet another year. Symbolically, the organization has boarded a bus to Abilene.

In fact, although the real issue of agreement was confronted approximately eight months after the bus departed, it was nearly too late. The organization failed to meet a payroll and underwent a two-year period of personnel cutbacks, retrenchments, and austerity. Morale suffered, the most competent technical personnel resigned, and the organization's prestige in the industry declined.

Case 2: The Watergate

> Apart from the grave question of who did what, Watergate presents America with the profound puzzle of why. What is it that led such a wide assortment of men, many of them high public officials, possibly including the President himself, either to instigate or to go along with and later try to hide a pattern of behavior that by now appears not only reprehensible, but stupid? (*The Washington Star and Daily News*, editorial [May 27, 1973].)

One possible answer to the editorial writer's question can be found by probing into the dynamics of the Abilene Paradox. I shall let the reader reach his own conclusions, though, on the basis of the following excerpts from testimony before the Senate investigating committee on "The Watergate Affair."

In one exchange, Senator Howard Baker asked Herbert Porter, then a member of the White House staff, why he (Porter) found himself "in charge of or deeply involved in a dirty tricks operation of the campaign." In response, Porter indicated that he had had qualms about what he was doing, but that he ". . . was not one to stand up in a meeting and say that this should be stopped. . . . I kind of drifted along."

And when asked by Baker why he had "drifted along," Porter replied, "In all honesty, because of the fear of the group pressure that would ensue, of not being a team player," and ". . . I felt a deep sense of loyalty to him [the President] or was appealed to on that basis." (*Washington Post* [June 8, 1973], 20.)

Jeb Magruder gave a similar response to a question posed by committee counsel Dash. Specifically, when asked about his, Mr. Dean's, and Mr. Mitchell's reactions to Mr. Liddy's proposal, which included bugging the Watergate, Mr. Magruder replied, "I think all three of us were appalled. The scope and size of the project were something that at least in my mind were not envisioned. I do not think it was in Mr. Mitchell's mind or Mr. Dean's, although I can't comment on their states of mind at that time."

Mr. Mitchell, in an understated way, which was his way of dealing with difficult problems like this, indicated that this was not an "acceptable project." (*Washington Post*, [June 15, 1973], A14.)

Later in his testimony Mr. Magruder said, ". . . I think I can honestly say that no one was particularly overwhelmed with the project. But I think we felt that this information could be useful, and Mr. Mitchell agreed to approve the project, and I then notified the parties of Mr. Mitchell's approval." (*Washington Post* [June 15, 1973], A14.)

Although I obviously was not privy to the private conversations of the principal characters, the data seem to reflect the essential elements of the Abilene Paradox. First, they indicate agreement. Evidently, Mitchell, Porter, Dean, and Magruder agreed that the plan was inappropriate. ("I think I can honestly say that no one was particularly overwhelmed with the project.") Second, the data indicate that the principal figures then proceeded to implement the plan in contradiction to their shared agreement. Third, the data surrounding the case clearly indicate that the plan multiplied the organization's problems, rather than solved them. And finally, the organization broke into subgroups with the various principals, such as the President, Mitchell, Porter, Dean, and Magruder, blaming one another for the dilemma in which they found themselves, and internecine warfare ensued.

In summary, it is possible that because of the inability of White House staff members to cope with the fact that they agreed, the organization took a trip to Abilene.

ANALYZING THE PARADOX

The Abilene Paradox can be stated succinctly as follows: Organizations frequently take actions in contradiction to the data they have for dealing with problems and, as a result, compound their problems, rather than solve them. Like all paradoxes, the Abilene Paradox deals with absurdity. On the surface, it makes little sense for organizations, whether they are couples or companies, bureaucracies or governments, to take actions that are diametrically opposed to the data they possess for solving crucial organizational problems. Such actions are particularly absurd since they tend to compound the very problems they are designed to solve and thereby defeat the purposes the organization is trying to achieve. However, as Robert Rapaport and others have so cogently expressed it, paradoxes are generally paradoxes only because they are based on a logic or rationale different from what we understand or expect.

Discovering that different logic not only destroys the paradoxical quality but also offers alternative ways for coping with similar situations. Therefore, part of the dilemma facing an Abilene-bound organization may be the lack of a map—a theory or model—that provides rationality to the paradox. The purpose of the following discussion is to provide such a map.

The map will be developed by examining the underlying psychological themes of the profit-making organization and the bureaucracy and it will include the following landmarks: (1) Action Anxiety; (2) Negative Fantasies; (3) Real Risk; (4) Separation Anxiety; and (5) the Psychological Reversal of Risk and Certainty. I hope that the discussion of such landmarks will provide harried organizations' travelers with a new map that will assist them in arriving at where they really want to go and, in addition, will help them in assessing the risks that are an inevitable part of the journey.

ACTION ANXIETY

Action anxiety provides the first landmark for locating roadways that bypass Abilene. The concept of action anxiety says that the reason organization members take actions in contradiction to their understanding of the organization's problems lies in the intense anxiety that is created as they think about acting in accordance with what they believe needs to be done. As a result, they opt to endure the professional and economic degradation of pursuing an unworkable research project or the consequences of participating in an illegal activity, rather than act in a manner congruent with their beliefs. It is not that organization members do not know what needs to be done—they do know. For example, the various principals in the research organization cited *knew* they were working on a research project that had no real possibility of succeeding. And the central figures of the Watergate episode apparently *knew* that, for a variety of reasons, the plan to bug the Watergate did not make sense.

Such action anxiety experienced by the various protagonists may not make sense, but the dilemma is not a new one. In fact, it is very similar to the anxiety experienced by Hamlet, who expressed it most eloquently in the opening lines of his famous soliloquy:

> To be or not to be; that is the question:
> Whether 'tis nobler in the mind to suffer
> The slings and arrows of outrageous fortune

Or to take arms against a sea of troubles
And by opposing, end them? . . . (*Hamlet*, Act III, Scene)

It is easy to translate Hamlet's anxious lament into that of the research manager of our R&D organization as he contemplates his report to the meeting of the budget committee. It might go something like this:

To maintain my sense of integrity and self-worth or compromise it, that is the question. Whether 'tis nobler in the mind to suffer the ignominy that comes from managing a nonsensical research project, or the fear and anxiety that come from making a report the president and V.P. may not like to hear.

So, the anguish, procrastination, and counterproductive behavior of the research manager or members of the White House staff are not much different from those of Hamlet; all might ask with equal justification Hamlet's subsequent searching question of what it is that

makes us rather bear those ills we have than fly to others we know not of. (*Hamlet*, Act III, Scene II)

In short, like the various Abilene protagonists, we are faced with a deeper question: Why does action anxiety occur?

NEGATIVE FANTASIES

Part of the answer to that question may be found in the negative fantasies organization members have about acting in congruence with what they believe should be done.

Hamlet experienced such fantasies. Specifically, Hamlet's fantasies of the alternatives to current evils were more evils, and he didn't entertain the possibility that any action he might take could lead to an improvement in the situation. Hamlet's was not an unusual case, though. In fact, the "Hamlet syndrome" clearly occurred in both organizations previously described. All of the organization protagonists had negative fantasies about what would happen if they acted in accordance with what they believed needed to be done.

The various managers in the R&D organization foresaw loss of face, prestige, position, and even health as the outcome of confronting the issues about which they believed, incorrectly, that they disagreed. Similarly, members of the White House staff feared being made scapegoats, branded as disloyal, or ostracized as nonteam players if they acted in accordance with their understanding of reality.

To sum up, action anxiety is supported by the negative fantasies that organization members have about what will happen as a consequence of their acting in accordance with their understanding of what is sensible. The negative fantasies, in turn, serve an important function for the persons who have them. Specifically, they provide the individual with an excuse that releases him psychologically, both in his own eyes and frequently in the eyes of others, from the responsibility of having to act to solve organization problems.

It is not sufficient, though, to stop with the explanation of negative fantasies as the basis for the inability of organizations to cope with agreement. We must look deeper and ask still other questions: What is the source of the negative fantasies? Why do they occur?

REAL RISK

Risk is a reality of life, a condition of existence. John Kennedy articulated it in another way when he said at a news conference, "Life is unfair." By that I believe he meant we do not know, nor can we predict or control with certainty, either the events that impinge upon us or the outcomes of actions we undertake in response to those events.

Consequently, in the business environment, the research manager might find that confronting the president and the vice president with the fact that the project was a "turkey" might result in his being fired. And Mr. Porter's saying that an illegal plan of surveillance should not be carried out could have caused his ostracism as a nonteam player. There are too many cases when confrontation of this sort has resulted in such consequences. The real question, though, is not, Are such fantasized consequences possible? but, Are such fantasized consequences likely?

Thus, real risk is an existential condition, and all actions do have consequences that, to paraphrase Hamlet, may be worse than the evils of the present. As a result of their unwillingness to accept existential risk as one of life's givens, however, people may opt to take their organizations to Abilene rather than run the risk, no matter how small, of ending up somewhere worse.

Again, though, one must ask, What is the real risk that underlies the decision to opt for Abilene? What is at the core of the paradox?

FEAR OF SEPARATION

One is tempted to say that the core of the paradox lies in the individual's fear of the unknown. Actually, we do not fear what is unknown, but we are afraid of things we do know about. What do we know about that frightens us into such apparently inexplicable organizational behavior?

Separation, alienation, and loneliness are things we do know about—and fear. Both research and experience indicate that ostracism is one of the most powerful punishments that can be devised. Solitary confinement does not draw its coercive strength from physical deprivation. The evidence is overwhelming that we have a fundamental need to be connected, engaged, and related and a reciprocal need not to be separated or alone. Every one of us, though, has experienced aloneness. From the time the umbilical cord was cut, we have experienced the real anguish of separation—broken friendships, divorces, deaths, and exclusions. C. P. Snow vividly described the tragic interplay between loneliness and connection:

> Each of us is alone; sometimes we escape from our solitariness, through love and affection or perhaps creative moments, but these triumphs of life are pools of light we make for ourselves while the edge of the road is black. Each of us dies alone.

That fear of taking risks that may result in our separation from others is at the core of the paradox. It finds expression in ways of which we may be unaware, and it is ultimately the cause of the self-defeating, collective deception that leads to self-destructive decisions within organizations.

Concretely, such fear of separation leads research committees to fund projects that none of its members want and, perhaps, White House staff members to engage in illegal activities that they don't really support.

THE PSYCHOLOGICAL REVERSAL
OF RISK AND CERTAINTY

One piece of the map is still missing. It relates to the peculiar reversal that occurs in our thought processes as we try to cope with the Abilene Paradox. For example, we frequently fail to take action in an organizational setting because we fear that the actions we take may result in our separation from others, or, in the language of Mr. Porter, we are afraid of being tabbed as "disloyal" or are afraid of being ostracized as "nonteam players." But therein lies a paradox within a paradox, because our very unwillingness to take such risks virtually ensures the separation and aloneness we so fear. In effect, we reverse "real existential risk" and "fantasied risk" and by doing so transform what is a probability statement into what, for all practical purposes, becomes a certainty.

Take the R&D organization described earlier. When the project fails, some people will get fired, demoted, or sentenced to the purgatory of a make-work job in an out-of-the-way office. For those who remain, the atmosphere of blame, distrust, suspicion, and backbiting that accompanies such failure will serve only to further alienate and separate those who remain.

The Watergate situation is similar. The principals evidently feared being ostracized as disloyal nonteam players. When the illegality of the act surfaced, however, it was nearly inevitable that blaming, self-protective actions, and scapegoating would result in the very emotional separation from both the President and one another that the principals feared. Thus, by reversing real and fantasied risk, they had taken effective action to ensure the outcome they least desired.

One final question remains: Why do we make this peculiar reversal? I support the general thesis of Alvin Toffler and Philip Slater, who contend that our cultural emphasis on technology, competition, individualism, temporariness, and mobility has resulted in a population that has frequently experienced the terror of loneliness and seldom the satisfaction of engagement. Consequently, though we have learned of the reality of separation, we have not had the opportunity to learn the reciprocal skills of connection, with the result that, like the ancient dinosaurs, we are breeding organizations with self-destructive decision-making proclivities.

A POSSIBLE ABILENE BYPASS

Existential risk is inherent in living, so it is impossible to provide a map that meets the no-risk criterion, but it may be possible to describe the route in terms that make the landmarks understandable and that will clarify the risks involved. In order to do that, however, some commonly used terms such as *victim, victimizer, collusion, responsibility, conflict, conformity, courage, confrontation, reality,* and *knowledge* have to be redefined. In addition, we need to explore the relevance of the redefined concepts for bypassing or getting out of Abilene.

Victim and Victimizer

Blaming and fault-finding behavior is one of the basic symptoms of organizations that have found their way to Abilene, and the target of blame generally doesn't include the one who criticizes. Stated in different terms, executives begin to assign one another to roles of victims and victimizers. Ironic as it may seem, however, this assignment of roles is both irrelevant and dysfunctional, because once a business or a government fails to manage its agreement and arrives in Abilene, all its members are victims. Thus, arguments and accusations that identify victims and victimizers at best become symptoms of the paradox, and, at worst, drain energy from the problem-solving efforts required to redirect the organization along the route it really wants to take.

Collusion

A basic implication of the Abilene Paradox is that human problems of organization are reciprocal in nature. As Robert Tannenbaum has pointed out, you can't have an autocratic boss unless subordinates are willing to collude with his autocracy, and you can't have obsequious subordinates unless the boss is willing to collude with their obsequiousness.

Thus, in plain terms, each person in a self-defeating, Abilene-bound organization *colludes* with others, including peers, superiors, and subordinates, sometimes consciously and sometimes subconsciously, to create the dilemma in which the organization finds itself. To adopt a cliché of modern organization, "It takes a real team effort to go to Abilene." In that sense each person, in his own collusive manner, shares responsibility for the trip, so searching for a locus of blame outside oneself serves no useful purpose for either the organization or the individual. It neither helps the organization handle its dilemma of unrecognized agreement nor does it provide psychological relief for the individual, because focusing on conflict when agreement is the issue is devoid of reality. In fact, it does just the opposite, for it causes the organization to focus on managing conflict when it should be focusing on managing agreement.

Responsibility for Problem-Solving Action

A second question is, Who is responsible for getting us out of this place? To that question is frequently appended a third one, generally rhetorical in nature, with "should" overtones, such as, Isn't it the boss (or the ranking government official) who is responsible for doing something about the situation?

The answer to that question is no.

The key to understanding the functionality of the no answer is the knowledge that, when the dynamics of the paradox are in operation, the authority figure—and others—are in unknowing agreement with one another concerning the organization's problems and the steps necessary to solve them. Consequently, the power to destroy the paradox's pernicious influence comes from confronting and speaking to the underlying reality of the situation, and not from one's hierarchical position within the organization. Therefore, any organization member who chooses to risk confronting that reality possesses the necessary leverage to release the organization from the paradox's grip.

In one situation, it may be a research director's saying, "I don't think this project can succeed." In another, it may be Jeb Magruder's response to this question by Senator Baker:

> If you were concerned because the action was known to you to be illegal, because you thought it improper or unethical, you thought the prospects for success were very meager, and you doubted the reliability of Mr. Liddy, what on earth would it have taken to decide against the plan?

Magruder's reply was brief and to the point:

> Not very much, sir. I am sure that if I had fought vigorously against it, I think any of us could have had the plan cancelled. (*Time* [June 25, 1973], 12.)

Reality, Knowledge, Confrontation

Accepting the paradox as a model describing certain kinds of organizational dilemmas also requires rethinking the nature of reality and knowledge, as they are generally described in organizations. In brief, the underlying dynamics of the paradox clearly indicate that organization members generally know more about issues confronting the organization than they don't know. The various principals attending the research budget meeting, for example, knew the research project was doomed to failure. And Jeb Magruder spoke as a true Abilener when he said, "We knew it was illegal, probably, inappropriate." (*Washington Post* [June 15, 1973], A16.)

Given this concept of reality and its relationship to knowledge, confrontation becomes the process of facing issues squarely, openly, and directly in an effort to discover whether the nature of the underlying collective reality is agreement or conflict. Accepting such a definition of confrontation has an important implication for change agents interested in making organizations more effective. That is, organization change and effectiveness may be facilitated as much by confronting the organization with what it knows and agrees upon as by confronting it with what it doesn't know or disagrees about.

REAL CONFLICT AND PHONY CONFLICT

Conflict is a part of any organization. Couples, R&D divisions, and White House staffs all engage in it. However, analysis of the Abilene Paradox opens up the possibility of two kinds of conflict—real and phony. On the surface, they look alike, but, like headaches, have different causes and, therefore, require different treatment.

Real conflict occurs when people have real differences. ("My reading of the research printouts says that we can make the project profitable." "I come to the opposite conclusion.") ("I suggest we 'bug' the Watergate." "I'm not in favor of it.")

Phony conflict, on the other hand, occurs when people agree on the actions they want to take, and then do the opposite. The resulting anger, frustration, and blaming behavior generally termed *conflict* are not based on real differences. Rather, they stem from the protective reactions that occur when a decision that no one believed in or was committed to in the first place goes sour. In fact, as a paradox within a paradox, such conflict is symptomatic of agreement!

GROUP TYRANNY AND CONFORMITY

Understanding the dynamics of the Abilene Paradox also requires a "reorientation" in thinking about such concepts as "group tyranny"—the loss of the individual's distinctiveness in a group, and the impact of conformity pressures on individual behavior in organizations.

Group tyranny and its result, individual conformity, generally refer to the coercive effect of group pressures on individual behavior. Sometimes referred to as groupthink, it has been damned as the cause for everything from the lack of creativity in organizations ("A camel is a horse designed by a committee") to antisocial behavior in juveniles ("My Johnny is a good boy. He was just pressured into shoplifting by the kids he runs around with").

However, analysis of the dynamics underlying the Abilene Paradox opens up the possibility that individuals frequently perceive and feel as if they are experiencing the coercive organization conformity pressures when, in actuality, they are responding to the dynamics of mismanaged agreement. Conceptualizing, experiencing, and responding to such experiences as reflecting the tyrannical pressures of a group again serves an important psychological use for the individual: As was previously said, it releases him from the responsibility of taking action and, thus, becomes a defense against action. Thus, much behavior within an organization that heretofore has been conceptualized as reflecting the tyranny of conformity pressures is really an expression of collective anxiety and, therefore, must be reconceptualized as a defense against acting.

A well-known example of such faulty conceptualization comes to mind. It involves the heroic sheriff in the classic Western movies who stands alone in the jailhouse door and singlehandedly protects a suspected (and usually innocent) horsethief or murderer from the irrational, tyrannical forces of group behavior—that is, an armed lynch mob. Generally, as a part of the ritual, he threatens to blow off the head of anyone who takes a step toward the door. Few ever take the challenge, and the reason is not the sheriff's six-shooter. What good would one pistol be against an armed mob of several hundred people who *really* want to hang somebody? Thus, the gun in fact serves as a face-saving measure for people who don't wish to participate in a hanging anyway. ("We had to back off. The sheriff threatened to blow our heads off.")

The situation is one involving agreement management, for a careful investigator canvassing the crowd under conditions in which the anonymity of the interviewees' responses could be guaranteed would probably find: (1) that few of the individuals in the crowd really wanted to take part in the hanging; (2) that each person's participation came about because he perceived, falsely, that others wanted to do so; and (3) that each person was afraid that others in the crowd would ostracize or in some other way punish him if he did not go along.

DIAGNOSING THE PARADOX

Most individuals like quick solutions, "clean" solutions, "no-risk" solutions to organization problems. Furthermore, they tend to prefer solutions based on mechanics and technology, rather than on attitudes of "being." Unfortunately, the underlying reality of the paradox makes it impossible to provide either no-risk solutions or action technologies divorced from existential attitudes and realities. I do, however, have two sets of suggestions for dealing with these situations. One set of suggestions relates to diagnosing the situation, the other to confronting it.

When faced with the possibility that the paradox is operating, one must first make a diagnosis of the situation, and the key to diagnosis is an answer to the question: Is the organization involved in a conflict-management or an agreement-management situation? As an organization member, I have found it relatively easy to make a preliminary diagnosis about whether an organization is on the way to Abilene or is involved in legitimate, substantive conflict by responding to the Diagnostic Survey (see Figure 1). If the answer to the first question is "not characteristic," the organization is probably not in

FIGURE 1   Organization Diagnostic Survey

Instructions: For each of the following statements please indicate whether it *is* or *is not* characteristic of your organization.

1. There is conflict in the organization.
2. Organization members feel frustrated, impotent, and unhappy when trying to deal with it. Many are looking for ways to escape. They may avoid meetings at which the conflict is discussed, they may be looking for other jobs, or they may spend as much time away from the office as possible by taking unneeded trips or vacation or sick leave.
3. Organization members place much of the blame for the dilemma on the boss or other groups. In "back room" conversations among friends the boss is termed incompetent, ineffective, "out of touch," or a candidate for early retirement. To his face, nothing is said, or, at best, only oblique references are made concerning his role in the organization's problems. If the boss isn't blamed, some other group, division, or unit is seen as the cause of the trouble: "We would do fine if it were not for the damn fools in Division X."
4. Small subgroups of trusted friends and associates meet informally over coffee, lunch, and so on to discuss organizational problems. There is a lot of agreement among the members of these subgroups about the cause of the troubles and the solutions that would be effective in solving them. Such conversations are frequently punctuated with statements beginning with, "We should do . . ."
5. In meetings where those same people meet with members from other subgroups to discuss the problem they "soften their positions," state them in ambiguous language, or even reverse them to suit the apparent positions taken by others.
6. After such meetings, members complain to trusted associates that they really didn't say what they wanted to say, but also provide a list of convincing reasons why the comments, suggestions, and reactions they wanted to make would have been impossible. Trusted associates commiserate and say the same was true for them.
7. Attempts to solve the problem do not seem to work. In fact, such attempts seem to add to the problem or make it worse.
8. Outside the organization individuals seem to get along better, be happier, and operate more effectively than they do within it.

Abilene or conflict. If the answer is "characteristic," the organization has a problem of either real or phony conflict, and the answers to the succeeding questions help to determine which it is.

In brief, for reasons that should be apparent from the theory discussed here, the more times "characteristic" is checked, the more likely the organization is on its way to Abilene. In practical terms, a process for managing agreement is called for. And finally, if the answer to the first question falls into the "characteristic" category and most of the other answers fall into the category "not characteristic," one may be relatively sure the organization is in a real conflict situation and some sort of conflict management intervention is in order.

COPING WITH THE PARADOX

Assuming a preliminary diagnosis leads one to believe he and/or his organization is on the way to Abilene, the individual may choose to actively confront the situation to determine directly whether the underlying reality is one of agreement or conflict. Although there are, perhaps, a number of ways to do it, I have found one way in particular to be effective—confrontation in a group setting. The basic approach involves gathering organization members who are key figures in the problem and its solution into a group setting. Working within the context of a group is important, because the dynamics of the Abilene Paradox involve collusion among group members; therefore, to try to solve the dilemma by working with individuals and small subgroups would involve further collusion with the dynamics leading up to the paradox.

The first step in the meeting is for the individual who "calls" it (i.e., the confronter) to own up to his position first and be open to the feedback he gets. The owning-up process lets the others know that he is concerned lest the organization may be making a decision contrary to the desires of any of its members. A statement like this demonstrates the beginning of such an approach:

> I want to talk with you about the research project. Although I have previously said things to the contrary, I frankly don't think it will work, and I am very anxious about it. I suspect others may feel the same, but I don't know. Anyway, I am concerned that I may end up misleading you and that we may end up misleading one another, and, if we aren't careful, we may continue to work on a problem that none of us wants and that might even bankrupt us. That's why I need to know where the rest of you stand. I would appreciate any of your thoughts about the project. Do you think it can succeed?

What kinds of results can one expect if he decides to undertake the process of confrontation? I have found that the results can be divided into *two* categories, at the technical level and at the level of existential experience. Of the two, I have found that, for the person who undertakes to initiate the process of confrontation, the existential experience takes precedence in his ultimate evaluation of the outcome of the action he takes.

The Technical Level

If one is correct in diagnosing the presence of the paradox, I have found the solution to the technical problem may be almost absurdly quick and simple, nearly on the order of this:

"Do you mean that you and I and the rest of us have been dragging along with a research project that none of us has thought would work? It's crazy. I can't believe we would do it, but we did. Let's figure out how we can cancel it and get to doing something productive." In fact, the simplicity and quickness of the solution frequently don't seem possible to most of us, since we have been trained to believe that the solution to conflict requires a long, arduous process of debilitating problem solving.

Also, since existential risk is always present, it is possible that one's diagnosis is incorrect; and the process of confrontation lifts to the level of public examination real, substantive conflict, which may result in heated debate about technology, personalities, and/or administrative approaches. There is evidence that such debates, properly managed, can be the basis for creativity in organizational problem solving. There is also the possibility, however, that such debates cannot be managed; and, substantiating the concept of existential risk, the person who initiates the risk may get fired or ostracized. But that again leads to the necessity of evaluating the results of such confrontation at the existential level.

Existential Results

Evaluating the outcome of confrontation from an existential framework is quite different from evaluating it from a set of technical criteria. How do I reach this conclusion? Simply from interviewing a variety of people who have chosen to confront the paradox and listening to their responses. In short, for them, psychological success and failure apparently are divorced from what is traditionally accepted in organizations as criteria for success and failure.

For instance, some examples of success are described when people are asked, "What happened when you confronted the issue?" They may answer this way:

> I was told we had enough boat rockers in the organization, and I got fired. It hurt at first, but in retrospect it was the greatest day of my life. I've got another job and I'm delighted. I'm a free man.

Another description of success might be this:

> I said I don't think the research project can succeed and the others looked shocked and quickly agreed. The upshot of the whole deal is that I got a promotion and am now known as a "rising star." It was the high point of my career.

Similarly, those who fail to confront the paradox describe failure in terms divorced from technical results. For example, one may report:

> I didn't say anything and we rocked along until the whole thing exploded and Joe got fired. There is still a lot of tension in the organization, and we are still in trouble, but I got a good performance review last time. I still feel lousy about the whole thing, though.

From a different viewpoint, an individual may describe his sense of failure in these words:

> I knew I should have said something and I didn't. When the project failed, I was a convenient whipping boy. I got demoted; I still have a job, but my future here is definitely limited. In a way I deserve what I got, but it doesn't make it any easier to accept because of that.

Most important, the act of confrontation apparently provides intrinsic psychological satisfaction, regardless of the technological outcomes for those who attempt it. The real meaning of that existential experience, and its relevance to a wide variety of organizations, may lie, therefore, not in the scientific analysis of decision making but in the plight of Sisyphus. That is something the reader will have to decide for himself.

THE ABILENE PARADOX AND THE MYTH OF SISYPHUS

In essence, this paper proposes that there is an underlying organizational reality that includes both agreement and disagreement, cooperation and conflict. However, the decision to confront the possibility of organization agreement is all too difficult and rare, and its opposite, the decision to accept the evils of the present, is all too common. Yet those two decisions may reflect the essence of both our human potential and our human imperfectibility. Consequently, the choice to confront reality in the family, the church, the business, or the bureaucracy, though made only occasionally, may reflect those "peak experiences" that provide meaning to the valleys.

In many ways, they may reflect the experience of Sisyphus. As you may remember, Sisyphus was condemned by Pluto to a perpetuity of pushing a large stone to the top of a mountain, only to see it return to its original position when he released it. As Camus suggested in his revision of the myth, Sisyphus's task was absurd and totally devoid of meaning. For most of us, though, the lives we lead pushing papers or hubcaps are no less absurd, and in many ways we probably spend about as much time pushing rocks in our organizations as Sisyphus did in his.

Camus also points out, though, that on occasion as Sisyphus released his rock and watched it return to its resting place at the bottom of the hill, he was able to recognize the absurdity of his lot, and, for brief periods of time, transcend it.

So it may be with confronting the Abilene Paradox. Confronting the absurd paradox of agreement may provide, through activity, what Sisyphus gained from his passive but conscious acceptance of his fate. Thus, through the process of active confrontation with reality, we may take respite from pushing our rocks on their endless journeys and, for brief moments, experience what C. P. Snow termed "the triumphs of life we make for ourselves" within those absurdities we call organizations.

SELECTED BIBLIOGRAPHY

Chris Argyris in *Intervention theory and method: A behavioral science view* (Addison-Wesley, 1970) gives an excellent description of the process of "owning up" and being "open," both of which are major skills required if one is to assist his organization in avoiding or leaving Abilene.

Albert Camus in *The myth of Sisyphus and other essays* (Vintage Books, Random House, 1955) provides an existential viewpoint for coping with absurdity, of which the Abilene Paradox is a clear example.

Jerry B. Harvey and R. Albertson in "Neurotic organizations: Symptoms, causes and treatment," Parts I and II, *Personnel Journal* (September and October 1971) provide a detailed example of a third-party intervention into an organization caught in a variety of agreement-management dilemmas.

Irving Janis in *Victims of groupthink* (Houghton Mifflin, 1972) offers an alternative viewpoint for understanding and dealing with many of the dilemmas described in "The Abilene Paradox." Specifically, many of the events that Janis describes as examples of conformity pressures (i.e., group tyranny) I would conceptualize as mismanaged agreement.

In his *The pursuit of loneliness* (Beacon Press, 1970), Philip Slater contributes an in-depth description of the impact of the role of alienation, separation, and loneliness (a major contribution to the Abilene Paradox) in our culture.

Richard Walton in *Interpersonal peacemaking: Confrontation and third party consultation* (Addison-Wesley, 1969) describes a variety of approaches for dealing with conflict when it is real, rather than phony.

Agreement and Thinking Alike: Ingredients for Poor Decisions*

Richard A. Cosier

Charles R. Schwenk

There is an old story at General Motors about Alfred Sloan. At a meeting with his key executives, Sloan proposed a controversial strategic decision. When asked for comments, each executive responded with supportive comments and praise. After announcing that they were all in apparent agreement, Sloan stated that they were not going to proceed with the decision. Either his executives didn't know enough to point out potential downsides of the decision, or they were agreeing to avoid upsetting the boss and disrupting the cohesion of the group. The decision was delayed until a debate could occur over the pros and cons.

There is growing evidence that suggests conflict and dissent are what organizations really need to succeed.[1] Corporate decisions should be made after thoughtful consideration of counterpoints and criticism. People with different viewpoints must be encouraged to provide thoughts on important decisions. Widespread agreement on a key issue is a red flag, not a condition of good health.

Some contemporary managers, however, recognize the benefits of conflict. Gavin Rawl, chief executive officer at Exxon, follows a policy of "healthy disrespect," according to *Business Week*.

> Even as he rose through the Exxon hierarchy, however, Rawl always had a healthy disrespect for bureaucracy. The company was obsessed with consensus. Proposals would wend their way through a maze of committees and task forces, through layers of staff. As senior vice president Charles R. Sitter says: "In a large organization, good ideas have lots of foster parents, and the bad decisions produce lots of orphans." Consensus, after all, is safer: The footprints are covered.[2]

* From *Academy of Management EXECUTIVE* (1990) 4, no. 1, 69–74. © Academy of Management Executive.

Another example is the flamboyant Scott McNealy, Sun Microsystems' chief executive officer. McNealy encourages noisy, table-pounding meetings and debate among senior executives. Dissent and opinion is a natural part of the "controlled chaos."[3]

These managers, like others, have recognized the need to allow different view points and critical thinking into organizational decisions. The type of conflict that is encouraged involves different interpretations of common issues or problems.[4] This "cognitive conflict" was noted as functional many years ago by psychologist Irving Janis. Janis, in his famous writings on groupthink, pointed out that striving for agreement and preventing critical thought frequently leads to poor decisions, such as those made during the Bay of Pigs invasion and the defense of Pearl Harbor.

Cognitive conflict can arise in two ways: (1) It can reflect true disagreement among managers and surface through an open environment which encourages participation or (2) It can be programmed into the decision-making processes and forced to surface, regardless of managers' true feelings. Although both methods may be effective, the second is decidedly less common. Given the potential benefits of programmed conflict in organizational decision making, companies would do well to implement it. While elements of both methods of conflict generation are reviewed, means for encouraging programmed conflict is a major focus in this article.

ALLOWING TRUE DISAGREEMENT

Allowing disagreement to surface in organizations is exemplified by Jack Welch at General Electric. *Business Week* observed:

> Welch, though, is convinced he can reach his aims. Like a man obsessed, he is driving G.E. through drastic fundamental change. Once formal, stable, gentlemanly, the new G.E. is tough, aggressive, iconoclastic. "It's a brawl," says Frank P. Doyle, senior vice president for corporate relations. "It's argumentative, confrontational." Working there can be a shock to newcomers. "There's a much higher decibel level here. I told Jack what passes for conversation here would be seen as a mugging by RCA people," Doyle says.[5]

The planning process involves scrutiny and criticism at G.E. Suggestions are expected and frequently offered and people are encouraged by Welch to speak their minds. This is consistent with organizational case studies that note the value of "forthright discussion" versus behind-the-scenes politicking in determining organizational strategy. In one case, the vice president for manufacturing and finance at a company showing strong performance stated:

> You don't need to get the others behind you before the meeting. If you can · explain your view [at the meeting], people will change their opinions. Fore-

front [the fictitious name of the company] is not political at this point. But, you must give your reasons or your ideas don't count. (VP of manufacturing.)

There is some open disagreement—it's not covered up. We don't gloss over the issues, we hit them straight on. (VP of finances.)[6]

Several studies on strategic decision making show that, in general, successful companies advocate open discussions, surfacing of conflict, and flexibility in adopting solutions. Other studies, however, suggest that strategy is facilitated by consensus. This contradiction raised an important issue. Consensus may be preferred for smaller, nondiversified, privately held firms competing in the same industry, while larger firms dealing with complex issues of diversification may benefit from the dissent raised in open discussions. Larger firms in uncertain environments need dissent, while smaller firms in more simple and stable markets can rely on consensus. In addition, Dess concludes, "organizations competing within an industry experiencing high growth may benefit from a relatively high level of disagreement in assessing the relative importance of company objectives and competitive methods."[7]

Examples of the benefits of conflict in tactical problem-solving (short-term) situations are also common. Bausch and Lomb have established "tiger teams" composed of scientists from different disciplines. Team members are encouraged to bring up divergent ideas and offer different points of view. Xerox uses round table discussions composed of various functional experts to encourage innovation. Compaq expects disagreement during all stages of new product development. Stuart Gannes, writing in *Fortune,* explains, "But at Compaq, instead of just arguing over who is right, we tear down positions to reasons. And when you get to reasons you find facts and assumptions."[8] Apple Computer, Ford Motor Company, Johnson and Johnson, and United Parcel Service are other examples of companies that tolerate conflict and debate during decisions.

In general, successful leaders seem to encourage managers to speak their minds. While this allows conflict into decision making, it carries a potential high cost. Positions are frequently tied to people and competitive "zero-sum" situations in which perceived winners and losers are likely to develop. Clearly, "losers" are less likely in future discussions to give their opinions.

Also, unprogrammed conflict is likely to be emotional and involve personal feelings. Lingering dislikes and rivalries are possible after higher emotional interchanges. Coalitions form and long-term divisiveness ensues. Corporate time and money may have to be diverted from problem solving to resolving emotional conflicts between managers.

What may, in fact, be needed is programmed conflict that raises different opinions *regardless of the personal feelings of the managers.* Although research exists supporting some options for programmed conflict, few, if any, examples exist in the corporate world.

PROGRAMMED CONFLICT

The Devil's Advocate

What can leaders do to experience the benefits associated with conflict in decision making, while minimizing the cost? Two options with potential are the devil's advocate and dialectic methods for introducing programmed conflict into organizational decisions.

The usefulness of the devil's advocate technique was illustrated several years ago by psychologist Irving Janis when discussing famous fiascos. Janis attributes groupthink—the striving for agreement instead of the best decision in a group—to decisions such as were made during The Bay of Pigs and Pearl Harbor.[9] Watergate and Vietnam are also often cited as examples. Janis recommends that everyone in the group assume the role of a devil's advocate and question the assumptions underlying the popular choice. Alternatively, an individual or subgroup, could be formally designated as the devil's advocate and present a critique of the proposed course of action. This avoids the tendency of agreement interfering with problem solving. Potential pitfalls are identified and considered before the decision is final.

While Janis's observations are generally well known and accepted, corporate implementation of devil's advocacy as a formal element in decision making is rare. This is despite of recent research that supports the benefits of devil's advocacy.[10] The conflict generated by the devil's advocate may cause the decision maker to avoid false assumptions and closely analyze the information. The devil's advocate raises questions that force an in-depth review of the problem-solving situation.

EXHIBIT 1   A Devil's Advocate Decision Program

---

1. A proposed course of action is generated.

    ↓

2. A devil's advocate (individual or group) is assigned to criticize the proposal.

    ↓

3. The critique is presented to key decision makers.

    ↓

4. Any additional information relevant to the issues is gathered.

    ↓

5. The decision to adopt, modify, or discontinue the proposed course of action is taken.

    ↓

6. The decision is monitored.

A devil's advocate decision program (DADP) can take several forms. However, all options require that an individual or group be assigned the role of critic. It needs to be clear that the criticism must not be taken personally, but is part of the organizational decision process.

The devil's advocate is assigned to identify potential pitfalls and problems with a proposed course of action. The issue could relate to strategic planning, new product development, innovation, project development, or of other problems not amenable to programmed solutions. A formal presentation to the key decision makers by the devil's advocate raises potential concerns. Evidence needed to address the critique is gathered and the final decision is made and monitored. This DADP is summarized in Exhibit 1.

It is a good idea to rotate people assigned to devil's advocate roles. This avoids any one person or group being identified as the critic on all issues. The devil's advocate role may be advantageous for a person and the organization. Steve Huse, chairperson and CEO of Huse Food Group, states that the devil's advocate role is an opportunity for employees to demonstrate their presentation and debating skills. How well someone understands and researches issues is apparent when presenting a critique.[11] The organization avoids costly mistakes by hearing viewpoints that identify pitfalls instead of foster agreement.

Often, a devil's advocate is helpful in adopting expert advice from computer-based decision support systems. Behavioral scientists Cosier and Dalton suggest that computer-based decisions may be more useful if exposed to a critique than simply accepted by managers.[12]

The Dialectic

While the DADP lacks an "argument" between advocates of two conflicting positions, the dialetic method (DM) programs conflict into decisions, regardless of managers' personal feelings, by structuring a debate between conflicting views.

The dialectic philosophy, which can be traced back to Plato and Aristotle, involves synthesizing the conflicting views of a thesis and an antithesis. More recently, it played a principle role in the writings of Hegel, who described the emergence of new social orders after a struggle between opposing forces. While most of the world's modern legal systems reflect dialectic processes, Richard O. Mason was one of the first organization theorists to apply the dialectic to organizational decisions.[13] He suggested that the decision maker consider a structured debate reflecting a plan and a counterplan before making a strategic decision. Advocates of each point of view should present their assumptions in support of the argument.

The benefits of DM are in the presentation and debate of the assumptions underlying proposed courses of action. False or misleading assump-

EXHIBIT 2   The Dialectic Decision Method

---

1. A proposed course of action is generated.

   ↓

2. Assumptions underlying the proposal are identified.

   ↓

3. A conflicting counterproposal is generated based on different assumptions.

   ↓

4. Advocates of each position present and debate the merits of their proposals before key decision makers.

   ↓

5. The decision to adopt either position, or some other position (e.g., a compromise) is taken.

   ↓

6. The decision is monitored.

---

tions become apparent and decisions based on these poor assumptions are avoided. The value of DM, shown in Exhibit 2, for promoting better understanding of problems and higher levels of confidence in decisions is supported by research.[14]

Critics of DM point to the potential for it to accentuate who won the debate, rather than the best decision. Compromise, instead of optimal decisions, is likely. Managers will require extensive training in dialectic thinking and philosophy. Supporters of DADP argue that a critique focuses the decision maker on issues, while the dialectic focuses more on the process of structural debate. Nevertheless, Cosier and Dalton suggest that DM may be the best method to use under the worst decision-making condition—high uncertainty and low information availability. The dialectic may be a good way to define problems and generate needed information for making decisions under uncertainty. When information is available and causal relationships are known, computer-assisted or devil's advocate methods are preferred.

PROGRAMMED AND UNPROGRAMMED CONFLICT

It is not a major breakthrough in management advice to suggest that conflict can improve decisions, although it is useful to remind managers of the need to allow dissent. It is, however, uncommon for managers to formally program conflict into the decision-making process. Thus, regardless of personal feelings, programmed conflict requires managers to challenge, criticize, and generate alternative ideas. Compared to conflict that is allowed to naturally surface, programmed conflict may reduce negative emotional by-products of conflict generation since dissent is no longer "personal." It also insures that a comprehensive decision framework is applied to important problems and issues.

Two options for implementing programmed conflict are based on the devil's advocate (DADP) and dialectic (DM) methods. We challenge managers to formally encourage controversy and dissent when making important choices under uncertain conditions. Encouraging "yes sayers" and complacency promotes poor decisions and lack of innovative thinking in organizations.

ENDNOTES

1. Conflict has been frequently presented as a positive force in textbooks. See, for example, Peter P. Schoderbek, Richard A. Cosier, and John C. Aplin. *Management* (San Diego: Harcourt Brace Jovanovich, 1988), 511–12.

2. "The rebel shaking up Exxon," *Business Week* (July 18, 1988), 107.

3. "Sun Microsystems turns on the afterburners," *Business Week* (July 18, 1988), 115.

4. Tjosvold uses the term *controversy* to describe this type of conflict. He differentiates controversy from conflicts of interest, which involves the actions of one person blocking the goal attainment of another person. See Dean Tjosvold, "Implications of controversy research for management," *Journal of Management*, (1985) *11*, 22–23.

5. "Jack Welch: How good a manager?" *Business Week*, (December 14, 1987), 94.

6. Kathleen M. Eisenhardt and L. J. Bourgeois III, "Politics of strategic decision making in high-velocity environments," *Academy of Management Journal* (1988) *31*, 751–52.

7. Gregory G. Dess, "Consensus on strategy formulation and organizational performance: Competitors in a fragmented industry," *Strategic Management Journal* (1987) *8*, 274.

8. Stuart Gannes, "America's fastest-growing companies," *Fortune* (May 23, 1988), 29.

9. See Irving L. Janis, *Victims of groupthink* (Boston: Houghton-Mifflin, 1972).

10. See, for example, Richard A. Cosier, "Methods for improving the strategic decision: Dialectic versus the devil's advocate," *Strategic Management Journal* (1982) *16*, 176–84.

11. Steve Huse, chairperson and CEO of Huse Food Group Inc., shared these observations in an interview with the senior author.

12. A model is developed which recommends methods of presenting information based upon conditions of uncertainty and information availability in Richard A. Cosier and Dan R. Dalton, "Presenting information under conditions of uncertainty and availability: Some recommendations," *Behavioral Science* (1988) *33*, 272–81.

13. Richard O. Mason, "A dialectical approach to strategic planning," *Management Science* (1969) *15*, B403–B414.

14. Ian I. Mitroff and J. R. Emshoff, "On strategic assumption-making: A dialectical approach to policy and planning," *Academy of Management Review*, (1979) *4*, 1–12.

Decisions, Decisions*

Andrew S. Grove

Making decisions—or, more properly, participating in the process by which they are made—is an important and essential part of every manager's work from one day to the next. Decisions range from the profound to the trivial, from the complex to the very simple: Should we buy a building or should we lease it? Issue debt or equity? Should we hire this person or that one? Should we give someone a 7 percent or a 12 percent raise? Can we deposit a phosphosilicate glass with 9 percent phosphorus content without jeopardizing its stability in a plastic package? Can we appeal this case on the basis of Regulation 939 of the Internal Revenue Code? Should we serve free drinks at our departmental Christmas party?

In traditional industries, where the management chain of command was precisely defined, a person making a certain kind of decision was a person occupying a particular position in the organization chart. As the saying went, authority (to make decisions) went with responsibility (position in the management hierarchy). However, in businesses that mostly deal with information and know-how, a manager has to cope with a new phenomenon. Here a rapid divergence develops between power based on position and power based on knowledge, which occurs because the base of knowledge that constitutes the foundation of the business changes rapidly.

What do I mean? When someone graduates from college with a technical education, at that time and for the next several years, that young person will be fully up to date in the technology of the time. Hence, he possesses a good deal of knowledge-based power in the organization that hired him. If he does well, he will be promoted to higher and higher positions; and, as the years pass, his position power will grow but his intimate familiarity with current technology will fade. Put another way, even if today's veteran manager was once an outstanding engineer, he is not now the technical expert he was when he joined the company. At Intel, anyway, we managers get a little more obsolete every day.

---

* From Andrew S. Grove, *High output management* (New York: Vintage Books, 1985), 88–101. Copyright © 1983 by Andrew S. Grove.

So a business like ours has to employ a decision-making process unlike those used in more conventional industries. If Intel used people holding old-fashioned position power to make all its decisions, decisions would be made by people unfamiliar with the technology of the day. And, in general, the faster the change in the know-how on which the business depends or the faster the change in customer preferences, the greater the divergence between knowledge and position power is likely to be. If your business depends on what it *knows* to survive and prosper, what decision-making mechanism should you use? The key to success is again the middle manager, who not only is a link in the chain of command but also can see to it that the holders of the two types of power mesh smoothly.

IDEAL MODEL

Illustrated in Figure 1 is an ideal model of decision making in a know-how business. The first stage should be *free discussion,* in which all points of view and all aspects of an issue are openly welcomed and debated. The greater the disagreement and controversy, the more important becomes the word *free.* This sounds obvious, but it's not often the practice. Usually, when a meeting gets heated, participants hang back, trying to sense the

FIGURE 1   The Ideal Decision-Making Process

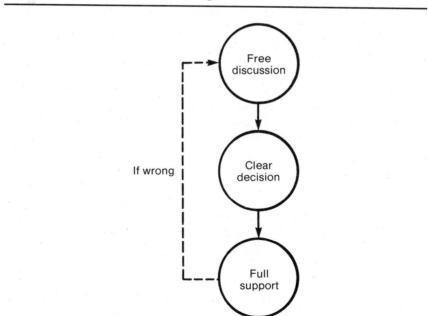

direction of things, saying nothing until they see what view is likely to prevail. They then throw their support behind that view to avoid being associated with a losing position. Bizarre as it may seem, some organizations actually encourage such behavior. Let me quote from a news account relating to the woes of a certain American automobile company: "In the meeting in which I was informed that I was released, I was told, 'Bill, in general, people who do well in this company wait until they hear their superiors express their view and then contribute something in support of that view.'" This is a terrible way to manage. All it produces is bad decisions, because if knowledgeable people withhold opinions, whatever is decided will be based on information and insight less complete than it could have been otherwise.

The next stage is reaching a *clear decision.* Again, the greater the disagreement about the issue, the more important becomes the word *clear.* In fact, particular pains should be taken to frame the terms of the decision with utter clarity. Again, our tendency is to do just the opposite: When we know a decision is controversial we want to obscure matters to avoid an argument. But the argument is not avoided by our being mealy-mouthed, merely postponed. People who don't like a decision will be a lot madder if they don't get a prompt and straight story about it.

Finally, everyone involved must give the decision reached by the group *full support.* This does not necessarily mean agreement: So long as the participants commit to back the decision, that is a satisfactory outcome. Many people have trouble supporting a decision with which they do not agree, but that they need to do so is simply inevitable. Even when we all have the same facts and we all have the interests of an organization in mind, we tend to have honest, strongly felt, real differences of opinion. No matter how much time we may spend trying to forge agreement, we just won't be able to get it on many issues. But an organization does not live by its members agreeing with one another at all times about everything. It lives instead by people committing to support the decisions and the moves of the business. All a manager can expect is that the commitment to support is honestly present, and this is something he can and must get from everyone.

The ideal decision-making model seems an easy one to follow. Yet I have found that it comes easily to only two classes of professional employees—senior managers who have been in the company for a long time, who feel at home with the way things are done, and who identify with the values of the organization; and the new graduates that we hire because they used the model as students doing college work. This is the way a team of students working on a laboratory experiment will resolve its differences; so for the young engineer the Intel model is a continuation of what he was used to. But for middle managers, the decision-making model is easier to accept intellectually than it is to practice. Why? Because they often have trouble expressing their views forcefully, a hard time making unpleasant or difficult decisions, and an even harder time with the idea that they are expected to support a decision with which they don't agree. It may take a while, but the logic of the ideal scheme will eventually win everyone over.

Another desirable and important feature of the model is that any decision be worked out and reached at the *lowest competent level*. The reason is that this is where it will be made by people who are closest to the situation and know the most about it. And by "know" I don't just mean "understand technically." That kind of expertise must be tempered with judgment, which is developed through experience and learning from the many errors one has made in one's career. Thus, ideally, decision making should occur in the middle ground, between reliance on technical knowledge on the one hand, and on the bruises one has received from having tried to implement and apply such knowledge on the other. To make a decision, if you can't find people with both qualities, you should aim to get the best possible mix of participants available. For experience, we at Intel are likely to ask a person in management senior to the other members of the group to come to the meeting. But it is very important that everybody there voice opinions and beliefs as *equals* throughout the free discussion stage, forgetting or ignoring status differentials.

A journalist puzzled by our management style once asked me, "Mr. Grove, isn't your company's emphasis on visible signs of egalitarianism, such as informal dress, partitions instead of offices, and the absence of other obvious perks like reserved parking spaces, just so much affectation?" My answer was that this is not affectation but a matter of survival. In our business we have to mix knowledge-power people with position-power people daily, and together they make decisions that could affect us for years to come. If we don't link our engineers with our managers in such a way as to get good decisions, we can't succeed in our industry. Now, status symbols most certainly do not promote the flow of ideas, facts, and points of view. What appears to be a matter of style really is a matter of necessity.

THE PEER-GROUP SYNDROME

The model is also hard to implement because anybody who makes a business decision also possesses emotions, such as pride, ambition, fear, and insecurity. These tend to come to the surface quickly when people who are not used to working with one another are asked to make a decision. This means we need to think about what keeps decision making from happening smoothly along the lines we've advocated.

The most common problem is something we call the *peer-group syndrome*. A number of years ago, at Intel's very first management training session, we tried some role-playing to show people what can occur when a group of peers meets to solve a problem or make a decision. We sat the people around a table to tackle what was then a live issue for them in their real jobs. Everyone was an organizational equal. The chairman of the meeting was one level higher, but was purposely sent out of the room so he couldn't hear what was to happen. Observers in the audience couldn't believe their eyes and ears as the mock meeting proceeded. The managers working on the problem did nothing but go around in circles for some 15 minutes, and none of them noticed they weren't getting anywhere. When the chairman was brought back in, he sat down and listened for a while and couldn't believe things either. We watched him lean forward as if he were trying to glean more from the conversation. We then saw a black cloud form over his head; finally he slapped the table and exclaimed, "What's going on here? You people are talking in circles and getting nowhere." After the chairman intervened, the problem was resolved in very short order. We named this the *peer-plus-one* approach, and have used it since then to aid decision making where we must. Peers tend to look for a more senior manager, even if he is not the most competent or knowledgeable person involved, to take over and shape a meeting.

Why? Because most people are afraid to stick their necks out. This is how John, an Intel software engineer, sees things:

> One of the reasons why people are reluctant to come out with an opinion in the presence of their peers is the fear of going against the group by stating an opinion that is different from that of the group. Consequently, the group as a whole wanders around for a while, feeling each other out, waiting for a consensus to develop before anyone risks taking a position. If and when a group consensus emerges, one of the members will state it *as a group opinion* ("I think *our* position seems to be . . ."), not as a personal position. After a weak statement of the group position, if the rest of the mob buys in, the position becomes more solid and is restated more forcefully.

Note the difference between the situation described earlier by the auto executive and the one John describes. In the former instance, the people were expected to wait for their supervisor to state his opinion first. In the latter, members of the group were waiting for a consensus to develop. The dynamics were different, but the bottom line in both is that people didn't really speak their minds freely. That certainly makes it harder for a manager to make the right decisions.

You can overcome the peer-group syndrome if each of the members has self-confidence, which stems in part from being familiar with the issue under consideration and from experience. But in the end self-confidence mostly comes from a gut-level realization that nobody has ever died from making a wrong business decision, or taking inappropriate action, or being overruled. And everyone in your operation should be made to understand this.

If the peer-group syndrome manifests itself, and the meeting has no formal chairman, the person who has the most at stake should take charge. If that doesn't work, one can always ask the senior person present to assume control. He is likely to be no more expert in the issues at hand than other members of the group—perhaps less expert—but he is likely to act as a godfather, a repository of knowledge about how decisions should be made, and give the group the confidence needed to make a decision.

One thing that paralyzes both knowledge and position power possessors is the fear of simply *sounding dumb*. For the senior person, this is likely to keep him from asking the question he should ask. The same fear will make other participants merely think their thoughts privately rather than articulate them for all to hear; at best they will whisper what they have to say to a neighbor. As a manager, you should remind yourself that, each time an insight or fact is withheld and an appropriate question is suppressed, the decision-making process is less good than it might have been.

A related phenomenon influences lower-level people present in the meeting. This group has to overcome the fear of being *overruled,* which might mean embarrassment: if the rest of the group or a senior-level manager vetoed a junior person or opposed a position he was advocating, the junior manager might lose face in front of his peers. This, even more than fear of sanctions or even of the loss of job, makes junior people hang back and let the more senior people set the likely direction of decision making.

But some issues are so complex that those called on to make a decision honestly aren't really sure how they feel. When knowledge and position power are separated, the sense of uncertainty can become especially acute, because the knowledge people are often not comfortable with the purely business-related factors that might influence a decision. What is often heard is, "We don't know what the company [or division or department] wants of us." Similarly, managers holding position power don't know what to do because they realize they don't know enough about the technical details to arrive at the correct decision. We must strive not to be done in by such obstacles. We are all human beings endowed with intelligence and blessed with willpower. Both can be drawn upon to help us overcome our fear of sounding dumb or of being overruled, and lead us to initiate discussion and come out front with a stand.

STRIVING FOR THE OUTPUT

Sometimes no amount of discussion will produce a consensus, yet the time for a decision has clearly arrived. When this happens, the senior person (or "peer-plus-one") who until now has guided, coached, and prodded the group along has no choice but to make a decision himself. If the decision-making process has proceeded correctly up to this point, the senior manager will be making the decision having had the full benefit of free discussion wherein all points of view, facts, opinions, and judgments were aired without position-power prejudice. In other words, it is legitimate—in fact, sometimes unavoidable—for the senior person to wield position-power authority if the clear decision stage is reached and no consensus has developed.

It is not legitimate—in fact, it is destructive—for him to wield that authority any earlier. This is often not easy. We Americans tend to be reluctant to exercise position power deliberately and explicitly—it is just "not nice" to give orders. Such reluctance on the part of the senior manager can prolong the first phase of the decision-making process—the time of free discussion— past the optimum point, and the decision will be put off.

If you either enter the decision-making stage too early or wait too long, you won't derive the full benefit of open discussion. The criterion to follow is this: don't push for a decision prematurely. Make sure you have heard and considered the real issues, rather than the superficial comments that often dominate the early part of a meeting. But if you feel that you have already heard everything, that all sides of the issue have been raised, it is time to push for a consensus—and failing that, to step in and make a decision. Sometimes free discussion goes on in an unending search for consensus. But, if that happens, people can drift away from the near consensus when they are close to being right, diminishing the chances of reaching the correct decision. So moving on to make the decision at the right time is crucial.

Basically, like other things managers do, decision making has an *output* associated with it, which in this case is the decision itself. Like other managerial processes, decision making is likelier to generate high-quality output in a timely fashion if we say clearly at the outset that we expect exactly that. In other words, one of the manager's key tasks is to settle six important questions in advance:

- What decision needs to be made?
- When does it have to be made?
- Who will decide?
- Who will need to be consulted prior to making the decision?
- Who will ratify or veto the decision?
- Who will need to be informed of the decision?

Let me illustrate how these six questions came into play in a recent decision I was involved in. Intel had already decided to expand its Philippine manufacturing plant, roughly doubling its capacity. The next question was where. Only limited space was available next to the existing plant. But, other things being equal, building there was the most desirable thing to do because overhead and communications could be shared, transportation costs between the two plants would amount to virtually nothing, and our employees could be transferred from one plant to the other very easily. The alternative consisted of buying a less-expensive plot of land quite some distance away. The land would be not only cheaper but more plentiful, which would allow us to build a relatively inexpensive one- or two-story building. Buying the lot near the existing plant meant that we would have had to build a high-rise to get the amount of floor space we needed, and a high-rise semiconductor manufacturing plant would not be the most efficient. That made us hesitate. But it would be nice to have a second building next to the one we already own. Back and forth and so on and so forth went the discussion.

Let's apply our six questions here. It is clear *what* decision needed to be made: we either build a multistory building next to our existing plant, or we build a one- or two-story building at a new outlying location. As for the question *when:* according to our long-range plans, we needed the new plant in two to two and a half years; if we apply time offsets, we must make the decision within a month. This answers the *when.*

Who will decide? Our facilities/construction people or the Intel group that manages the manufacturing plants? The answer is not easy. The first organization is more sensitive to matters pertaining to the costs and difficulties of construction, and will probably lean toward the new location. The plant management group, knowing that operational benefits will come from having the two plants side by side, will probably opt for the high-rise. So the decision-making body is composed of our construction manager for our Far East locations; his supervisor, the construction manager for the corporation; the manager of the Far East manufacturing plant network; and his supervisor, the senior manufacturing manager. The meeting gave us parallel levels of managers from the two organizations. The sensitivities of two interest groups coming to bear on a single decision is quite common in real corporate life. In such meetings, it is important to give to the two sides roughly equal representation, because only from such balance will an even-handed decision emerge. All of these individuals have consulted their staffs prior to the decision and gathered all relevant knowledge and views on the subject.

Who will ratify or veto the decision? The first common person to whom the senior managers of both organizations report is myself. Also, this was a big enough deal that the president of the company should be involved. Moreover, I was somewhat familiar with the locations in the Philippines and how a plant like the one we have there operates. So I was chosen as the person to veto or ratify the decision of the meeting.

Who will need to be informed of this decision? I chose Gordon Moore, our chairman of the board. He's not directly involved with manufacturing plants like the one contemplated, but we don't build a new one in the Far East every day, so he should know about what happened.

This is how the decision was made. After studying maps, construction plans and costs, land costs, and traffic patterns, and considering several times everything we thought was important, the group decided to build next to our existing plant but to accept only as much manufacturing area as four stories would yield. The cost would have escalated had we exceeded that. This, with all relevant background, was presented to me at the [earlier] meeting. . . . I listened to the presentation of the alternatives the group considered and to the reasons why they preferred their choice to these, and, after asking a series of questions and probing both the group's information and its thinking process, I ratified the decision. Subsequently I informed Gordon Moore of the outcome, and as you are reading this, the plant is either under construction or already operating.

Employing consistent ways by which decisions are to be made has value beyond simply expediting the decision making itself. People invest a great deal of energy and emotion in coming up with a decision. Then somebody who has an important say-so or the right to veto it may come across the decision later. If he does veto it, he can be regarded as a Johnny-come-lately who upsets the decision-making applecart. This, of course, will frustrate and demoralize the people who may have been working on it for a long time. If the veto comes as a surprise, however legitimate it may have been on its merits, an impression of political maneuvering is inevitably created. Politics and manipulation or even their appearance should be avoided at all costs. And I can think of no better way to make the decision-making process straightforward than to apply *before the fact* the structure imposed by our six questions.

One last thing: If the final word has to be dramatically different from the expectations of the people who participated in the decision-making process (had I chosen, for example, to cancel the Philippine plant project altogether), make your announcement but don't just walk away from the issue. People need time to adjust, rationalize, and in general put their heads back together. Adjourn, reconvene the meeting after people have had a chance to recover, and solicit their views of the decision at that time. This will help everybody accept and learn to live with the unexpected.

If good decision making appears complicated, that's because it is and has been for a long time. Let me quote from Alfred Sloan, who spent a lifetime preoccupied with decision making: "Group decisions do not always come easily. There is a strong temptation for the leading officers to make decisions themselves without the sometimes onerous process of discussion." Because the process is indeed onerous, people sometimes try to run away from it. A middle manager I once knew came straight from one of the better business schools and possessed what we might call a "John Wayne" mentality. Having become frustrated with the way Intel made decisions, he quit. He joined a company where his employers assured him during the interview that people were encouraged to make individual decisions which they were then free to implement. Four months later, he came back to Intel. He explained that if he could make decisions without consulting anybody, so could everybody else.

24

Who Needs a Boss?*

Brian Dumaine

Many American companies are discovering what may be *the* productivity breakthrough of the 1990s. Call the still-controversial innovation a self-managed team, a cross-functional team, a high-performance team, or, to coin a phrase, a superteam. Says Texas Instruments CEO Jerry Junkins: "No matter what your business, these teams are the wave of the future." Corning CEO Jamie Houghton, whose company has 3,000 teams, echoes the sentiment: "If you really believe in quality, when you cut through everything, it's empowering your people, and it's empowering your people that leads to teams."

We're not talking here about the teamwork that's been praised at Rotary Club luncheons since time immemorial, or the quality circles so popular in the 1980s, where workers gathered once a week to save paper clips or bitch about the fluorescent lights. What makes superteams so controversial is that they ultimately force managers to do what they had only imagined in their most Boschian nightmares: give up control. Because if superteams are working right, *mirabile dictu*, they manage themselves. No boss required. A superteam arranges schedules, sets profit targets, and—gulp—may even know everyone's salary. It has a say in hiring and firing team members as well as managers. It orders material and equipment. It strokes customers, improves quality, and, in some cases, devises strategy.

Superteams typically consist of between three and 30 workers—sometimes blue collar, sometimes white collar, sometimes both. In a few cases, they have become a permanent part of the work force. In others, management assembles the team for a few months or years to develop a new product or solve a particular problem. Companies that use them—and they work as well in service or finance businesses as they do in manufacturing—usually see productivity rise dramatically. That's because teams composed of people with different skills, from different parts of the company, can swoop around bureaucratic obstacles and break through walls separating different functions to get a job done.

---

* From *Fortune* (May 7, 1990), 52–60.

Ten years ago there were practically no superteams. Only a handful of companies—Procter & Gamble, Digital Equipment, TRW—were experimenting with them. But a recent survey of 476 Fortune 1,000 companies, published by the American Productivity & Quality Center in Houston, shows that while only 7 percent of the work force is organized in self-managed teams, half the companies questioned say they will be relying significantly more on them in the years ahead. Those who have already taken the plunge have seen impressive results:

- At a General Mills cereal plant in Lodi, California, teams—such as the one pictured on *Fortune*'s cover—schedule, operate, and maintain machinery so effectively that the factory runs with no managers present during the night shift.

- At a weekly meeting, a team of Federal Express clerks spotted—and eventually solved—a billing problem that was costing the company $2.1 million a year.

- A team of Chaparral Steel millworkers traveled the world to evaluate new production machinery. The machines they selected and installed have helped make their mill one of the world's most efficient.

- 3M turned around one division by creating cross-functional teams that tripled the number of new products.

- After organizing its home office operations into superteams, Aetna Life & Casualty reduced the ratio of middle managers to workers—from 1 to 7 down to 1 to 30—all the while improving customer service.

- Teams of blue-collar workers at Johnsonville Foods of Sheboygan, Wisconsin, helped CEO Ralph Stayer make the decision to proceed with a major plant expansion. The workers told Stayer they could produce more sausage, faster than he would have ever dared to ask. Since 1986, productivity has risen at least 50 percent.

Like latter-day Laocoöns, the companies using superteams must struggle with serpentine problems. How do you keep a team from veering off track? How should it be rewarded for inventing new products or for saving money? How much spending authority should a team have? What happens to the opportunity for team members to advance as the corporate hierarchy flattens? How should disputes among its members be resolved? Answers vary from company to company. Read on to see how some organizations are coping.

Superteams aren't for everyone. They make sense only if a job entails a high level of dependency among three or more people. Complex manufacturing processes common in the auto, chemical, paper, and high-tech industries can benefit from teams. So can complicated service jobs in insurance, banking, and telecommunications. But if the work consists of simple assembly line activity like stuffing pimentos into olives, teams probably don't make sense. Says Edward Lawler, a management professor at the University of Southern California: "You have to ask 'How complex is the work?' The more complex, the more suited it is for teams."

Lawler is getting at the heart of what makes superteams tick: cross-functionalism, as the experts inelegantly put it. The superteam draws together people with different jobs or functions—marketing, manufacturing, finance, and so on. The theory is that, by putting their heads together, people with different perspectives on the business can solve a problem quickly and effectively.

Contrast that to the Rube Goldberg approach a hierarchical organization would usually take. A person with a problem in one function might have to shoot it up two or three layers by memo to a vice president who tosses it laterally to a vice president of another function who then kicks it down to the person in his area who knows the answer. Then it's back up and down the ladder again. Whew.

Federal Express has been particularly successful using superteams in its back-office operations in Memphis. Two years ago, as part of a companywide push to convert to teams, Fedex organized its 1,000 clerical workers into superteams of 5 to 10 people, and gave them the training and authority to manage themselves. With the help of its teams, the company cut service glitches, such as incorrect bills and lost packages, by 13 percent in 1989.

At lunch with one team, this reporter sat impressed as entry-level workers, most with only high school educations, ate their chicken and dropped sophisticated management terms like *kaizen*, the Japanese art of continuous improvement, and *pareto*, a form of problem solving that requires workers to take a logical step-by-step approach. The team described how one day during a weekly meeting, a clerk from quality control pointed out a billing problem. The bigger a package, he explained, the more Fedex charges to deliver it. But the company's wildly busy delivery people sometimes forgot to check whether customers had properly marked the weight of packages on the air bill. That meant that Fedex, whose policy in such cases is to charge customers the lowest rate, was losing money.

The team switched on its turbochargers. An employee in billing services found out which field offices in Fedex's labyrinthine 30,000-person courier network were forgetting to check the packages, and then explained the problem to the delivery people. Another worker in billing set up a system to examine the invoices and make sure the solution was working. Last year alone the team's ideas saved the company $2.1 million.

In 1987, Rubbermaid began to develop a so-called auto office, a plastic, portable device that straps onto a car seat; it holds files, pens, and other articles and provides a writing surface. The company assembled a cross-functional team composed of, among others, engineers, designers, and marketers, who together went into the field to ask customers what features they wanted. Says Rubbermaid vice president Lud Huck: "A designer, an engineer, and a marketer all approach research from a different point of view."

Huck explains that, while a marketer might ask potential customers about price, he'd never think to ask important design questions. With contributions from several different functions, Rubbermaid brought the new product to market last year. Sales are running 50 percent above projections.

Companies making the move to superteams often discover middle managers who feel threatened, and refuse—even for a millisecond—to think outside their narrow functional specialties, or chimneys, as they're labeled at some companies. Understandable, since the managers probably made it to where they are by being marketing whizzes or masters of the bean-counting universe. Why help some poor slob in engineering? For superteams to work, functional chimneys must be broken down and middle managers persuaded to lend their time, people, and resources to other functions for the good of the entire corporation.

Robert Hershock, a group vice president at 3M, is an expert chimney breaker. In 1985 he introduced teams to his division, which makes respirators and industrial safety equipment, because it was desperately in need of new products. The old boss had simply told his underlings what to develop. R&D would sketch it up and deliver the concept to sales for comment, leaving manufacturing and marketing scrambling to figure out how to make or position the new offering. Says Hershock: "Every function acted as if it didn't need anyone else."

He formed an operating team made up of himself and six top managers, each from a different function. With suggestions from all interested parties, he hoped to chart new-product strategies that everyone could get behind. Under the operating team he established 10 self-managed "action teams," each with 8 to 10 people, again from different functions. They were responsible for the day-to-day development of new products.

It wasn't all sweetness and light. Hershock says one manager on the operating team dragged his feet all the way. "He'd say he wasn't in favor of this or that," recalls Hershock. "He'd say to his people, 'Meet with the action teams because Hershock said so, but don't commit to anything. Just report back to me what was said.'" Hershock worked to convince the man of the benefits of the team approach, but to no avail. Eventually the manager went to Hershock and said, "I didn't sleep all weekend. I'm upset." The manager found a good job in another division. "You need to have a sense of who's not buying in and let the teams kick people off who aren't carrying their weight," Hershock concludes. Today his division is one of 3M's most innovative and fastest growing.

It's easier to build superteams into a new office or factory than to convert an old one to them. When an operation is just starting up, a company can screen people carefully for educational skills and the capacity to work on a team, and can train them without worrying about bad old work habits like the "it's not my problem" syndrome. Nonetheless, General Mills is organizing superteams in all its existing factories. Randy Darcy, director of manufacturing, says transforming an old plant can take several years, versus only a year to 18 months for a new plant. Says Darcy: "It costs you up front, but you have to look at it as a capital project. If you consider the productivity gains, you can justify it on ROE."

Can you ever. General Mills says productivity in its plants that use self-managed teams is as much as 40 percent higher than at its traditional factories. One reason is that the plants need fewer middle managers. At one of General Mills' cereal plants in Lodi, workers on the night shift take care of everything from scheduling to maintenance. The company has also found that superteams sometimes set higher productivity goals than management does. At its Carlisle, Pennsylvania, plant, which makes Squeezit juice, superteams changed some equipment and squeezed out a 5 percent production increase in a plant management thought was already running at full capacity.

But you will never get large productivity gains unless you give your teams real authority to act. This is a theme that Johnsonville's Stayer, who teaches a case on teams at the Harvard business school, preaches with messianic zeal. "The strategic decision," he explains, "is who makes the decision. There's a lot of talk about teamwork in this country, but we're not set up to generate it. Most quality circles don't give workers responsibility. They even make things worse. People in circles point out problems, and it's someone else's problem to fix."

In 1986, a major food company asked Johnsonville to manufacture sausage under a private label. Stayer's initial reaction was to say no, because he thought the additional volume would overload his plant and force his people to work grueling hours. But before declining, he assembled his 200 production workers, who are organized in teams of 5 to 20, and asked them to decide whether *they* wanted to take on the heavier workload. Stayer discussed the pros: Through economies of scale, the extra business would lower costs and thus boost profits; since everyone's bonus was based on profitability, everyone would make more money. And the cons: long hours, strained machinery, and the possibility of declining quality.

After the teams deliberated for 10 days, they came back with an answer: "We can do it. We'll have to work seven days a week at first, but then the work will level off." The teams decided how much new machinery they would need and how many new people; they also made a schedule of how much to produce per day. Since Johnsonville took on the new project, productivity has risen over 50 percent in the factory. Says Stayer: "If I had tried to implement it from above, we would have lost the whole business."

Some large organizations still feel a need to exercise oversight of superteams' activities. What to do with a team that louses up quality or orders the wrong machinery? James Watson, a vice president of Texas Instruments' semiconductor group, may have the answer. At one of TI's chip factories in Texas, Watson helped create a hierarchy of teams that, like a shadow government, works within the existing hierarchy.

On top is a steering team consisting of the plant manager and his heads of manufacturing, finance, engineering, and human resources. They set strategy and approve large projects. Beneath the steering team, TI has three other teams: corrective-action teams, quality-improvement teams, and effectiveness teams. The first two are cross-functional and consist mainly of middle managers and professionals like engineers and accountants. Corrective-action teams form to tackle short-lived problems and then disband. They're great for those times when, as the technophantasmic novelist Thomas Pynchon writes, there's fecoventilatory collision: the s— hits the fan.

By contrast, TI's quality-improvement teams work on long-term projects, such as streamlining the manufacturing process. The corrective-action and quality-improvement teams guide and check effectiveness teams, which consist of blue-collar employees who do day-to-day production work, and professional workers.

What's to keep this arrangement from becoming just another hierarchy? "You have to keep changing and be flexible as business conditions dictate," says Watson. He contends that one of the steering team's most important responsibilities is to show a keen interest in the teams beneath it. "The worst thing you can do to a team is to leave it alone in the dark. I guarantee that if you come across someone who says teams didn't work at his company, it's because management didn't take interest in them." Watson suggests that the steering team periodically review everyone's work, and adds, "It doesn't have to be a big dog-and-pony show. Just walk around and ask, 'How are you doing?'"

Last spring a group of executives from a Fortune 500 manufacturer traveled to Midlothian, Texas, to learn how Chaparral Steel managed its teams. Efficient superteams have helped make Chaparral one of the world's most productive steel companies. During the tour, one executive asked a Chaparral manager, "How do you schedule coffee breaks in the plant?"

"The workers decide when they want a cup of coffee," came the reply.

"Yes, but who tells them when it's okay to leave the machines?" the executive persisted.

Looking back on the exchange, the Chaparral manager reflects, "The guy left and still didn't get it."

Why do Chaparral workers know when to take a coffee break? Because they're trained to understand how the whole business operates. Earl Engelhardt, who runs the company's educational program, teaches mill hands "The Chaparral Process," a course that not only describes what happens to a piece of steel as it moves through the company but also covers the roles of finance, accounting, and sales. Once trained, a worker understands how his job relates to the welfare of the entire organization. At team meetings, many of which are held in the company's modest boardroom, talk is of backlogs and man-hours per ton. Financial statements are posted monthly in the mill, including a chart tracking operating profits before taxes—the key measure for profit sharing.

In the early 1980s, the company sent a team leader and three mill-workers, all of whom had been through "The Chaparral Process," to Europe, Asia, and South America to evaluate new mill stands. These large, expensive pieces of equipment flatten and shape hot steel as it passes through the mill, much as the rollers on old washing machines used to wring clothes. After team members returned from their first trip, they discussed the advantages and disadvantages of various mill stands with other workers and with top management. Then they narrowed the field and flew off again. Eventually the team agreed on the best mill stand—in this case a West German model—and top management gave its blessing.

The team then ordered the mill stands and oversaw their installation, even down to negotiating the contracts for the work involved. At other companies it can take as long as several years to buy and install such a complicated piece of equipment. The Chaparral team got the job done in a year. Perhaps even more amazing, the mill stands—notoriously finicky pieces of machinery—worked as soon as they were turned on.

There remains considerable debate among employees, managers, and consultants over the best way to compensate team members. Most companies pay a flat salary. And instead of handing out automatic annual raises, they often use a pay-for-skills system that bases any increase not on seniority but on what an employee has learned. If, say, a steelworker learns how to run a new piece of equipment, he might get a 5 percent raise.

While the young and eager tend to do well with pay-for-skills, some old-school blue-collar workers like Chaparral Steel's Neil Parker criticize aspects of the system. Says he: "New guys come in who are aggressive, take all the courses, and get promoted ahead of guys who have been here years longer and who showed up for overtime when the company really needed us. It's not fair." As Parker suggests, pay-for-skills does set up a somewhat Darwinian environment at the mill, but that's just the way Chaparral's management likes it.

When teams develop a hot new product, like Rubbermaid's auto office, or save money, like the Federal Express team that caught $2.1 million in billing errors, you would think they would clamor for rewards. Not necessarily. In many cases, surprisingly, a little recognition is reward enough. The Fedex team members seem perfectly content with a gold quality award pin and their picture in the company newsletter. Says one: "We learn more in teams, and it's more fun to work in teams. It's a good feeling to know someone is using your ideas."

In his book *Managing New Products*, Thomas Kuczmarski, a consultant to many of the Fortune 500 industrials, argues that recognition isn't enough. "In most companies multidisciplinary teams are just lip service because companies don't provide the right motivation and incentive. Most top managers think people should just find 20 percent more time to work on a new team project. It's a very naïve and narrow-minded approach." His modest proposals: If a new product generates $1 million in profits, give each of the five team members $100,000 the first year. Or have each member write a check for $10,000 in return for 2 percent of the equity in the new product. If it flies they're rich; if it flops they lose their money.

Kuczmarski admits that no major corporation has adopted his provocative system, although he says a few are on the verge of doing so. One objection: Jack Okey, a Honeywell team manager, flatly states that it would be bad for morale to have, say, a junior engineer making more than a division vice president. "If you want to be an entrepreneur, there are plenty of entrepreneurial opportunities outside the company. You can have entrepreneurial spirit without entrepreneurial pay."

Perhaps. Awards dinners and plaques for jobs well done are common in the world of teams, but Texas Instruments vice president James Watson thinks more can be done. He cites the example from Japan, where there is a nationwide competition among manufacturers' teams. Sponsored by the Union of Japanese Scientists and Engineers, the competition pits teams selected by their companies against one another. Once a year the teams travel to Tokyo to make presentations before judges, who decide which performs best at everything from solving quality problems to continuously improving a manufacturing process. The winners get showered with prizes and media coverage.

Sometimes, despite everyone's best efforts, teams get hung up. Leonard Greenhalgh, a professor of management at Dartmouth's Tuck School, says the most common problem is the failure by team members to understand the feelings and needs of their coworkers. At GTE's training center in Connecticut, Greenhalgh had middle managers do role-playing to bring out how such problems can creep up. In a fictionalized case, a team of six pretended they were Porsche managers who had to set next year's production schedule. Each was given a different function and agenda. The Porsche sales manager, for instance, wanted to manufacture more of the popular Carrera convertibles, but the general counsel thought it a bad idea because of the liability problems generally associated with convertibles.

The GTE managers spent several hours arriving at a consensus. Says Greenhalgh: "Typically, a team lacks skills to build a strong consensus. One coalition tries to outvote the other or browbeat the dissenters." To make sure everyone is on board, says Greenhalgh, it's important that each team member feel comfortable airing his opinions. But that can take some training for all group members in how to respond. For instance, the GTE managers learned it's better not to blurt out an intimidating, "I disagree," but rather, "That's an interesting way to look at it; what about this?"

Companies using teams sometimes run into another problem: With fewer middle-manager positions around, there's less opportunity for advancement. The experts say they need to emphasize that because team members have more responsibility, their work is more rewarding and challenging. Harvard business school professor Anne Donnellon, who is doing a major new study of teams, sees this approach already working at some Fortune 500 companies: "People are adjusting to career-ladder shortening. If a team is operating well, I hear less talk about no opportunity for promotion and more about the product and the competition. They're focusing on getting the work done. After all, people want rewarding work."

If you've done all you can think of, and your team is still running on only three cylinders, you might consider something as prosaic as changing the office furniture. Aetna Life recently reorganized its home office operations into self-managed teams—combining clerks, technical writers, underwriters, and financial analysts—to handle customer requests and complaints. To facilitate teamwork, Aetna is using a new line of "team" furniture designed by Steelcase.

The furniture establishes small areas that the folks at Steelcase call neighborhoods. A central work area with a table lets teams meet when they need to, while nearby desks provide privacy. Says William Watson, an Aetna senior vice president: "I can't tell you how great it is. Everyone sits together, and the person responsible for accounting knows who prepares the bills and who puts the policy information in the computers to pay the claims. You don't need to run around the building to get something done."

The most important thing to remember about teams is that organizing them is a long, hard process, not a quick fix that can change your company in a few weeks. Says Johnsonville's Stayer: "When I started this business of teams, I was anxious to get it done and get back to my real job. Then I realized that, hey, this *is* my real job"—letting the teams loose. For those up to the challenge, there will be real results as well.

Wa, Guanxi, and *Inhwa:* Managerial Principles in Japan, China, and Korea*

Jon P. Alston

Japanese, Chinese, and Korean business organizations do not run on the same managerial principles. Each society has its separate, distinctive philosophy that guides business managers. These philosophies lead to specific behavior appropriate to the setting; as a result, knowledge of their principles is not only helpful, it is critical to success in dealings with managers from those countries.

Although each of the three principles is unique, each also resembles the others to some degree. Each can be summarized in one word. In Japan, business relations operate within the context of *wa*, which stresses group harmony and social cohesion. In China, business behavior revolves around *Guanxi*, or personal relations. For Korea, activities involve concern for *inhwa*, or harmony based on respect of hierarchical relationships, including obedience to authority.

WA

Wa refers to the value the Japanese place on group loyalty and consensus. It translates as the search for or the existence of mutual cooperation so a group's members can devote their total energies to attaining group goals. To achieve *wa*, members of the group are expected to submerge their individual (selfish) goals in favor of the group's. *Wa*, however, is not one-sided. Individual members profit only after the group has profited from their activities, but they must be rewarded nevertheless.

---

* From *Business Horizons* (March–April 1989), 26–31.

Wa takes place within a group context. The Japanese seldom interact with one another or with foreigners as individuals. Individuals are always members and representatives of one group or another. *Wa* relates individuals to groups. That is why most activities in Japan occur within a group and why group memberships are so important. Consequently, few Japanese are able to define themselves apart from their group memberships.

A Japanese worker, for example, will not respond to the question, "What do you do?" with the answer, "I am an engineer," or "I am a computer programmer." Instead he will say, "I work for Toyota" or "I am Toyota." His specific position is less important than his group membership. In artistic circles, actors and artists often take their teacher's name to show their membership in their mentor's school and loyalty to their teacher.

Wa demands that members of a group, whether a work team, a corporation, or a nation, cooperate with and trust each other. There are few practices in Japanese corporations that do not encourage a sense of *wa* among their workers (Alston, 1986, 40–43).

Wa is so pervasive that the Japanese prefer, and usually insist, that all business dealings take place among friends. That is one reason why proper introductions are so important when business relationships are initiated. The Japanese do not like to deal with strangers. As a result, few business contacts begin with direct business discussions. A Japanese will first want to place the stranger within some group context. Business cards *(meishi)* are always exchanged and carefully studied when the Japanese meet someone. Americans doing business with Japanese counterparts need business cards that explain in detail their business ranks. Otherwise, the Japanese will not know how to relate to this seemingly isolated individual.

The establishment of close friendships with coworkers is also necessary, because *wa* demands that members of a group achieve total agreement through consensus. This demands constant discussions and compromises. However, these discussions take place within an atmosphere of friendliness and cooperation as demanded by *wa*. As a result, the Japanese prefer to maintain the illusion of surface agreement until a consensus has been reached—a fact not often realized by foreigners, especially Americans. At times, telling the truth might upset someone and threaten the group's *wa*. There is no "laying one's cards on the table" in Japan until a close understanding between parties has been reached, if even then.

The willingness to subordinate the truth to group harmony is illustrated in the term *makoto*, which is equivalent to the English word "sincerity." However, the Japanese define this word as part of the process of insuring harmony and goodwill irrespective of the truth. Being sincere in Japan means being emotionally supportive; in the United States, the same term means being honest and open in intent. An American who is being sincere will be blunt and totally frank, even if an exposition of the facts upsets the other person. In Japan, being sincere means having concern for the emotional, rather than the factual. That is why Americans often mistake a Japanese "yes" for a "no."

Wa also involves a specific time dimension. The group's survival and eventual success are keyed to a long-term perspective. Once accepted, members of the group are permanent members—hence the ideal of lifetime employment found in Japanese corporations. The Japanese evaluate activities, such as possible business ventures, in light of how they will affect the long-term development of the group's *wa*.

The establishment of personal relationships, bringing together two groups with common interests, allows the Japanese to view contracts as personal agreements that should be changed when conditions change. A change will be reciprocated in the future, but contracts are seen as fluid. A change in the cost of raw material will prompt a supplier to ask that the contractual price at delivery be changed, since higher costs might preclude a profit. The other party is expected to agree to the increase, if possible, on the assumption that the supplier will in the future offer discounts or preferential treatment.

In addition, *wa* demands that strangers already have established some type of social relationship, no matter how tenuous, before they meet. Such a relationship is formed through a mediator. Few business contacts proceed smoothly unless proper introductions have been made by a third party who is respected by both parties.

Mediators are important because criticisms of colleagues and fellow group members threaten the group's *wa*. When criticism is necessary, a third party may be able to pass on criticisms and negative news that friends may not be able to state more overtly. If a clearer discussion of demands is needed, the mediator may pass a "letter of understanding" from one person to another. Such a memo can state a position or demands in blunter terms than those proper during conversations. Then, too, the memo's bluntness is decreased because the message was only indirectly passed from one party to the other. In this way detailed positions, demands, or interpretations of proposals are exchanged without threatening the group's *wa*.

If a mediator or message is inconvenient, the Japanese use informal meetings to discuss formal matters. When a meeting's setting is informal, serious discussions can be disguised as entertainment. That is why the Japanese spend a large part of their time entertaining clients and potential clients. Discussions at a bar can be semiserious and hint at disagreements that would be unwelcome in more formal settings.

Entertaining is seldom a waste of time among the Japanese. It is during a meal or drinking session that personal relations are established and *wa*-threatening discussions can take place (although they cannot be too blunt, challenging, or negative in content). Americans should prepare themselves for numerous suppers and bar-hopping excursions to allow *wa* to develop and be sustained.

GUANXI

Guanxi is one of the major dynamics in Chinese society. The term refers to special relationships two persons have with each other. It can be best translated as friendship with overtones of unlimited exchange of favors (Pye, 1982, 88). Two persons sharing a *Guanxi* relationship assume that each is fully committed to the other. They have agreed to exchange favors in spite of official commands to act neutrally. Whenever scarce resources exist in China, they are allocated by *Guanxi*, rather than official bureaucratic dictates.

Within this context, *Guanxi* bonds two persons through the exchange of favors rather than through sentiment. The *Guanxi* relationship does not have to involve friends, although that is preferred. Instead, the relationship is basically utilitarian rather than emotional. The moral dimension operating here is that a person who does not follow a rule of equity and refuses to return favor for favor loses face and becomes defined as untrustworthy.

Unlike *wa*, *Guanxi* has no group connotation; the relationship is total and personal. Each partner is now obligated to help the other, generally in an unlimited manner. The Chinese place great emphasis on rank, but *Guanxi* operates on the individual level.

This individualistic aspect of *Guanxi*, apart from the primary stress on family ties, allows Chinese workers to easily change employment. *Guanxi* relations that are no longer profitable or based on equal exchanges are easily broken. As a result, the economies in Taiwan and Hong Kong experience a large rate of both job mobility and entrepreneurship. Employees move whenever they see an advantage in doing so. Given the value of self-employment in Chinese society (illustrated by the saying "it is better to be the bill of a chicken than the anus of an ox"), *Guanxi* ties have to be continuously reinforced; when persons move from one company to another, *Guanxi* ties need to be established with the new personnel. This individualistic component of *Guanxi* allows for rapid changes in relations. The foreigner who lets his *Guanxi* relations lapse will find he has to deal with officials who may be totally uninterested in his projects.

A singular feature of *Guanxi* is that the exchanges tend to favor the weaker member. *Guanxi* links two persons, often of unequal ranks, in such a way that the weaker partner can call for special favors for which he does not have to equally reciprocate. An unequal exchange gives face (respect, honor) to the one who voluntarily gives more than he receives.

A consequence of this aspect of *Guanxi* is that claims of inadequacy should be seen as subtle demands that the other (and more powerful) person has the obligation to be magnanimous. During negotiations, Chinese officials expect that the (foreign) party will cede certain points because the latter is so much stronger and wealthier.

The power given to the weaker party reflects the Confucian principle of family loyalty, in which family ties demand the exchange of aid. A practical example of the prevalence of family-based *Guanxi* is found in government-controlled firms that have been given semi-independence since the mid-1980s. Many of these business concerns are headed by relatives of high-ranking party officials. These officials offered business licenses only to relatives or close friends. The following quotes from a recently published report illustrate the importance of *Guanxi* (*The Wall Street Journal*, 1988):

> The only people who can get licenses are those with good . . . connections. . . . Then they cannot *fail* to make money because they have a monopoly over trade in many goods, such as imported cars. Behind every big profiteer is a big protector. . . . The children of some leaders use the cover of their parents to profiteer. Who dares touch the tiger's bottom?

A practical consequence of *Guanxi* is that personal loyalties are often more important than organizational affiliation or legal standards. An American wishing to expedite his goods through Chinese customs might (and often does) have to wait days, even weeks, before all appropriate documents are cleared or stamped. However, an importer who has a *Guanxi* relationship with a government official or customs officer can expect a more immediate and positive response.

As a result, a person's rank or organizational position may not be indicative of his or her power. A person of low rank, in government or elsewhere, may in fact be very influential because of *Guanxi* relationships with those in higher positions. The implications of this are plain. Americans wishing to deal with Chinese must develop *Guanxi* relations themselves or know persons who enjoy *Guanxi* with those in central positions.

The development of one's own *Guanxi* relations is preferable, because these informal affiliations are more important than more formal ones. Representatives of foreign businesses must, therefore, expect a long stay in China to develop *Guanxi* relations and to discover who has *Guanxi* with powerful officials. Business with China cannot be done through cables and telexes. Export/import matters involve a relatively small number of persons, and a small group of Chinese officials make all major decisions. The challenge is to discover these influential persons and establish *Guanxi* with them or their associates; otherwise, the chances of business success are low. In essence, the Chinese bureaucracy inhibits action while *Guanxi* facilitates action. As an American states:

The informal *(Guanxi)* structure is there for a reason: the official system does not work. The unofficial system is a legitimate solution that creates jobs and allows business to function (Copeland and Griggs, 1985, 176).

In addition, the importance of *Guanxi* means that day-to-day policy is based on perceived personal interest and can change drastically. In many respects, *Guanxi* is antibureaucratic and pro-person. Unfortunately, policies change as quickly as personnel, so it is anyone's guess how long a specific policy will be maintained. Contracts, for example, are binding only as long as the circumstances at the time and the signers of the agreements remain constant. Changes in either supercede all prior agreements.

This fact has a positive element, in that Chinese managers can be highly adaptable and entrepreneurial. *Guanxi* provides a balance to the cumbersome Chinese bureaucracy by giving individuals a way to circumvent rules when personal feelings or relations interpose. As L. S. T. Tai (1988) suggests:

> A key to success in doing business in China is personal connections *(Guanxi).* The right connections can bring cheap and reliable material supplies, tax concessions, approval to sell goods domestically or for export, and provision of assistance when problems arise. But connections alone are not sufficient.

By the same token, decision making in China is slow, even when the cumbersome bureaucracy is circumvented by *Guanxi*. Decisions are made from top to bottom in China, and the superior in each *Guanxi* link must agree to a specific proposal. This practice, which can lead to extremely slow decision making for important decisions, causes much frustration for those who expect consistency of policy and universal rules' application from Chinese bureaucrats. In fact, policies change as powerful persons jockey for power, forcing their *Guanxi* associates to also change their behavior.

INHWA

A key principle of Korean business behavior is *inhwa*, which, like the Japanese *wa*, is defined as harmony. However, the Korean term does not emphasize the group element as in *wa*. Rather, *inhwa* stresses harmony between unequals. *Inhwa* links persons who are unequal in rank, prestige, and power (De Mente, 1988, 88, 131). This term requires that subordinates be loyal to their superiors and that superiors be concerned with the well-being of subordinates.

The concept is derived from Confucianism, which in this context emphasizes the regulation of unequals. It follows from the Confucian ideal that a person owes total loyalty to parents and authority figures, notably rulers, elders, and organizational leaders. In the modern world, *inhwa* demands that an individual offer loyalty to hierarchical rankings. Workers owe their employers and supervisors (and other superiors) the same loyalty they owe their parents and family elders. When Koreans state that all members of a company form a "family," the implication is that the leaders are to be obeyed as if they were family elders.

As a result of this, Korean corporate management is categorized as "clan management," a situation facilitated by the fact that many of Korea's senior managers in a specific firm are related by family ties. Roughly one third of all executive officers in Korea's largest business groups are family members of fellow employees or employers.

Inhwa ties form first-line loyalties in the same way that family ties supercede all others in Korea. As a result, Koreans prefer to develop personal ties with strangers before they conclude a deal with them. The paramount importance of personal relations means that business relations, like those in Japan, should be between "friends" or on a personal footing.

The *inhwa* relationship binds two or more persons, usually of unequal rank, without reference to organizational or other group memberships. This emphasis on the individual makes the Koreans relatively individualistic, much like the Chinese. There is little organizational loyalty in Korea, and workers switch employers whenever it is beneficial. The Korean adage that "one Korean is stronger than three" implies that *inhwa* relationships cannot be taken for granted after being established.

Korean negotiators also show a corresponding individualism. In a series of experiments, John Graham and associates found that Koreans were three times as likely as the Japanese to say "no." They were also more likely to interrupt and issue commands.

Foreign business persons must establish their own personal networks in government circles as well. Government officials "direct" much of Korea's economy, and few major contracts will be made unless one or more government offices support the venture. The problem for an American is that these *inhwa* relationships are long-term and take time and patience to develop and cultivate.

In addition, once *inhwa* relationships have been established, they must be constantly maintained and strengthened. Since contracts are interpreted through the personal relationships of the signers, rather than through the agreement per se, the contract is only as good as the personal relations that made it possible. Lawyers and other intermediaries should not take over from the original participants.

Korean contracts are not merely documents stating mutual obligations and rights. They are declarations of intentions backed by the integrity of the signers. The intentions of the parties are more important than contractual clauses. For this reason, renegotiation and redoing of contracts are expected behaviors. Koreans do not consider a contract binding if conditions or interests change.

Since the emotional dimension is more important than the specific contents of a contract, foreigners need to meet frequently with their Korean colleagues to develop ties of friendship. This feeling must be carefully cultivated after a formal partnership has been achieved.

No one should sign a contract with a Korean unless he or she is prepared to maintain that relationship over the length of the contract, often beyond. An agreement is only as good as long as the persons who negotiated are in power and interested in the project. Otherwise, the contract could be in danger (Leppert). A valuable ploy after a contract is signed is to perform favors for the main Korean parties so they do in fact maintain a proprietary interest in the project.

The *inhwa* relationship is intrinsically an unequal one, but personal relations occur only with those who have some claim of equality—especially age and prestige. Senior Korean officials will not deal comfortably with a junior member of an American negotiating team no matter how expert he may be. Koreans are extremely sensitive about titles and status, and those Americans who wish to deal with senior Korean officials should have senior rank themselves.

Another aspect of *inhwa* is that each party has responsibility to support the other person and make him happy. The latter results in *kibun*, which is defined as "feelings." No one who is part of an *inhwa* relationship dares upset the other. As a result, Koreans do not like to bear bad news. Often, bad news will not be delivered until the late afternoon (if at all), so the recipient will not have his whole day disrupted. Listen very carefully if a Korean hints at business difficulties near the end of a business day! At any rate, Koreans who have established personal relations with others avoid passing on upsetting information.

As a result, like the Japanese, Koreans seldom criticize or give negative information outright. This practice may result in misleading information, as the Korean businessman tries to avoid delivering bad news. He may not even announce a delay in a delivery date, since doing so is too painful. Americans doing business in Korea must listen carefully and probe for hidden meanings when their *inhwa*-related friends report.

Non-Asians often overlook the sometimes major differences among specific Asian countries. The understanding of intra-Asian differences begins with an awareness of how each culture's concepts, even though they might be related, differ from one another. Using the same key vocabularies, the non-Asian can begin the arduous task of discovering the significant differences as well as similarities among Asian cultures.

REFERENCES

Alston, Jon P. *The American samurai: Blending American and Japanese managerial practice.* New York and Berlin: Walter de Gruyter, 1986.

Copeland, Lennie, and Lewis Griggs. *Going international.* New York: Random House, 1985, 176.

De Mente, Boye. *Korean etiquette and ethics in business.* Lincolnwood, Ill.: NTC Books, 1988.

Graham, John; Nigel Campbell; and Hans Gunther Meissner. "Culture, negotiations, and international cooperative ventures." *International Business Education and Research Program, Working Paper #8*, Graduate School of Business Administration, University of Southern California (date unknown), 14.

Leppert, Paul. *Doing business with the Koreans.* Chula Vista, Calif.: Patton Pacific Press, 1987, 83.

Pye, Lucien. *Chinese commercial negotiating style.* Cambridge, Mass.: Oelgeschlager, Gunn & Hain, 1982.

Tai, Lawrence S. T. "Doing business in the People's Republic of China." *Management International Review* (1988), *1*, 8.

Ignatius, Idi. "China's restructuring is enriching peasants but not city dwellers." *The Wall Street Journal* (October 21, 1988), A-8.

Leadership

INTRODUCTION

Upon leaders falls the not always enviable task of fusing organizational purpose with the drives of individuals and groups. This task has, over the years, attracted the attention of legions of scholars and researchers. Of late, however, we hear among the scholars growing disenchantment with the fund of knowledge yielded by leadership research; and such expressions of disappointment arise at precisely the time when strong leadership is said to be most needed in our organizations and institutions.

In this section, we look at the question of leadership from several different perspectives. Kerr and Jermier find the concept "substitutes for leadership" to have some value in explaining why the effects of the same leader behavior vary from one situation to another, as well as accounting for why leader behavior sometimes has little or no effect. Miles notes that different motives may underlie what superficially seems to be the same leader style (i.e., a participative approach), and his discussion suggests that the inner purpose of the leader will determine whether the outward style is efficaceous.

Luthans grapples with a poignant question for our times: Are "successful" leaders also "effective" leaders? He finds evidence that managers on the fast promotion tracks are seldom the same individuals who build productive groups with sound human resource practices. "Success" as a leader appears to be more a function of networking and politicking, rather than a natural result of developing competent, committed subordinates.

Jackofsky, Slocum, and McQuaid examine corporate leadership in the context of cultural values, looking at leadership styles of CEOs in five different cultures. In general, they find results suggesting that leadership is constrained by the larger culture, and that, when leadership goes against the grain of that culture, the result is often the downfall of the leader.

Kotter addresses an issue that, while of longstanding interest, has come increasingly to the fore in musings on leadership: Are leadership and management synonymous? Are the distinctions among them merely hair-splitting semantics? Kotter develops a persuasive framework for separating these functions, and explains why the challenges of the 1990s will make the distinctions between them increasingly obvious.

Pfeffer urges us to consider a more disturbing question: Do we give leaders too much credit, as well as too much blame, for what happens to organizations? Pfeffer argues, on the one hand, that the latitude of action by leaders is much less than we often assume, and, on the other hand, that external forces neither controlled nor understood by leaders account for most of the variance in a firm's performance. Is leader effectiveness little more than a defense mechanism in our attempt to cope with a complex and unpredictable reality?

26

Substitutes for Leadership:
Their Meaning and Measurement*

Steven Kerr
John M. Jermier

Current theories and models of leadership seek to explain the influence of the hierarchical superior upon the satisfaction and performance of subordinates. While disagreeing with one another in important respects, these theories and models share an implicit assumption that, while the style of leadership likely to be effective may vary according to the situation, *some* leadership style will be effective *regardless* of the situation. It has been found, however, that certain individual, task, and organizational variables act as "substitutes for leadership," negating the hierarchical superior's ability to exert either positive or negative influence over subordinate attitudes and effectiveness. This paper identifies a number of such substitutes for leadership, presents scales of questionnaire items for their measurement, and reports some preliminary tests.

A number of theories and models of leadership exist, each seeking to most clearly identify and best explain the presumedly powerful effects of leader behavior or personality attributes upon the satisfaction and performance of hierarchical subordinates. These theories and models fail to agree in many respects, but have in common the fact that none of them systematically accounts for very much criterion variance. It is certainly true that data indicating strong superior-subordinate relationships have sometimes been reported. In numerous studies, however, conclusions have had to be based on statistical, rather than practical, significance, and hypothesis support has rested upon the researcher's ability to show that the trivially low correlations obtained were not the result of chance.

Current theories and models of leadership have something else in common: a conviction that hierarchical leadership is always important. Even situational approaches to leadership share the assumption that, while the

* From *Organizational Behavior and Human Performance* (1978), 22, 375–403. Copyright © 1978 by Academic Press, Inc. All rights of reproduction in any form reserved.

style of leadership likely to be effective will vary according to the situation, *some* leadership style will *always* be effective *regardless* of the situation. Of course, the extent to which this assumption is explicated varies greatly, as does the degree to which each theory is dependent upon the assumption. Fairly explicit is the Vertical Dyad Linkage Model developed by Graen and his associates (Graen, Dansereau, and Minami, 1972; Dansereau, Cashman, and Graen, 1973), which attributes importance to hierarchical leadership without concern for the situation. The Fiedler (1964, 1967) Contingency Model also makes the general assumption that hierarchical leadership is important in situations of low, medium, and high favorableness, though predictions about relationships between LPC and performance in Octants VI and VII are qualified (Fiedler and Chemers, 1974, p. 82). Most models of decision-centralization (e.g., Tannenbaum & Schmidt, 1958; Heller and Yukl, 1969; Vroom and Yetton, 1973; Bass and Valenzi, 1974) include among their leader decision-style alternatives one whereby subordinates attempt a solution by themselves, with minimal participation by the hierarchical superior. Even in such cases, however, the leader is responsible for initiating the method through delegation of the problem and is usually described as providing (structuring) information.

The approach to leadership which is least dependent upon the assumption articulated above, and which comes closest to the conceptualization to be proposed in this paper, is the Path-Goal Theory (House, 1971; House and Mitchell, 1974). Under circumstances when both goals and paths to goals may be clear, House and Mitchell (1974) point out that "attempts by the leader to clarify paths and goals will be both redundant and seen by subordinates as imposing unnecessary, close control." They go on to predict that "although such control may increase performance by preventing soldiering or malingering, it will also result in decreased satisfaction."

This prediction is supported in part by conclusions drawn by Kerr, Schriesheim, Murphy, and Stogdill (1974) from their review of the consideration-initiating structure literature and is at least somewhat consistent with results from a few recent studies. A most interesting and pertinent premise of the theory, however, is that even unnecessary and redundant leader behaviors will have an impact upon subordinate satisfaction, morale, motivation, performance, and acceptance of the leader (House and Mitchell, 1974; House and Dessler, 1974). While leader attempts to clarify paths and goals are, therefore, recognized by Path-Goal Theory to be unnecessary and redundant in certain situations, in no situation are they explicitly hypothesized by path-goal (or any other leadership theory) to be irrelevant.

This lack of recognition is unfortunate. As has already been mentioned, data from numerous studies collectively demonstrate that in many situations these leader behaviors *are* irrelevant, and hierarchical leadership (as operationalized in these studies) per se does not seem to matter. In fact, leadership variables so often account for very little criterion variance that a few writers have begun to argue that the leadership construct is sterile altogether, that "the concept of leadership itself has outlived its usefulness" (Miner, 1975, p. 200). This view is also unfortunate, however, and fails to take note of accurate predictions by leadership theorists even as such theorists fail to conceptually reconcile their inaccurate predictions.

What is clearly needed to resolve this dilemma is a conceptualization adequate to explain both the occasional successes and frequent failures of the various theories and models of leadership.

SUBSTITUTES FOR LEADERSHIP

A wide variety of individual, task, and organizational characteristics have been found to influence relationships between leader behavior and subordinate satisfaction, morale, and performance. Some of these variables (e.g., job pressure and subordinate expectations of leader behavior) act primarily to influence which leadership style will best permit the hierarchical superior to motivate, direct, and control subordinates. The effect of others, however, is to act as "substitutes for leadership," tending to negate the leader's ability to either improve or impair subordinate satisfaction and performance.

Substitutes for leadership are apparently prominent in many different organizational settings, but their existence is not explicated in any of the dominant leadership theories. As a result, data describing formal superior-subordinate relationships are often obtained in situations where important substitutes exist. These data logically ought to be, and usually are, insignificant, and are useful primarily as a reminder that when leadership styles are studied in circumstances where the choice of style is irrelevant, the effect is to replace the potential power of the leadership construct with the unintentional comedy of the "Law of the instrument."[1]

What is needed, then, is a taxonomy of situations where we should not be studying "leadership" (in the formal hierarchical sense) at all. Development of such a taxonomy is still at an early stage, but Woodward (1973) and Miner (1975) have laid important groundwork through their classifications of control, and some effects of nonleader sources of clarity have been considered by Hunt (Note 2) and Hunt and Osborn (1975). Reviews of the leadership literature by House and Mitchell (1974) and Kerr et al. (1974) have also proved pertinent in this regard, and suggest that individual, task, and organizational characteristics of the kind outlined in Table 1 will help to determine whether or not hierarchical leadership is likely to matter.

---

[1] Abraham Kaplan (1964, p. 28) has observed: "Give a small boy a hammer, and he will find that everything he encounters needs pounding."

TABLE 1   Substitutes for Leadership

| | Will Tend to Neutralize | |
Characteristic	Relationship-Oriented, Supportive, People-Centered Leadership (consideration, support, and interaction facilitation)	Task-Oriented, Instrumental, Job-Centered Leadership (initiating structure, goal emphasis, and work facilitation)
Of the subordinate:		
1. Ability, experience, training, knowledge.		X
2. Need for independence.	X	X
3. "Professional orientation."	X	X
4. Indifference toward organizational rewards.	X	X
Of the task:		
5. Unambiguous and routine.		X
6. Methodologically invariant.		X
7. Provides its own feedback concerning accomplishment.		X
8. Intrinsically satisfying.	X	
Of the organization:		
9. Formalization (explicit plans, goals, and areas of responsibility).		X
10. Inflexibility (rigid, unbending rules and procedures).		X
11. Highly specified and active advisory and staff functions.		X
12. Closely knit, cohesive work groups.	X	X
13. Organizational rewards not within the leader's control.	X	X
14. Spatial distance between superior and subordinates.	X	X

Conceptual Domain of Substitutes for Leadership

Since Table 1 is derived from previously conducted studies, substitutes are only suggested for the two leader behavior styles which dominate the research literature. The substitutes construct probably has much wider applicability, however, perhaps to hierarchical leadership in general.

It is probably useful to clarify some of the characteristics listed in Table 1. "Professional orientation" is considered a potential subsitite for leadership because employees with such an orientation typically cultivate horizontal, rather than vertical, relationships, give greater credence to peer review processes, however informal, than to hierarchical evaluations, and tend to develop important referents external to the employing organization (Filley, House, and Kerr, 1976). Clearly, such attitudes and behaviors can sharply reduce the influence of the hierarchical superior.

"Methodologically invariant" tasks may result from serial interdependence, from machine-paced operations, or from work methods which are highly standardized. In one study (House, Filley, and Kerr, 1971, p. 26), invariance was found to derive from a network of government contracts which "specified not only the performance requirements of the end product but also many of the management practices and control techniques that the company must follow in carrying out the contract."

Invariant methodology relates to what Miner (1975) describes as the "push" of work. Tasks which are "intrinsically satisfying" (another potential substitute listed in Table 1) contribute in turn to the "pull" of work. Miner believes that for "task control" to be effective, a force comprised of both the push and pull of work must be developed. At least in theory, however, either type alone may act as a substitute for hierarchical leadership.

Performance feedback provided by the work itself is another characteristic of the task which potentially functions in place of the formal leader. It has been reported that employees with high growth-need strength in particular derive beneficial psychological states (internal motivation, general satisfaction, work effectiveness) from clear and direct knowledge of the results of performance (Hackman and Oldham, 1976; Oldham, 1976). Task-provided feedback is often: (1) the most immediate source of feedback given the infrequency of performance appraisal sessions (Hall and Lawler, 1969); (2) the most accurate source of feedback given the problems of measuring the performance of others (Campbell, Dunnette, Lawler, and Weick, 1970); and (3) the most self-evaluation evoking and intrinsically motivating source of feedback given the controlling and informational aspects of feedback from others (DeCharms, 1968; Deci, 1972, 1975; Greller and Herold, 1975). For these reasons, the formal leader's function as a provider of role structure through performance feedback may be insignificant by comparison.

Cohesive, interdependent work groups and active advisory and staff personnel also have the ability to render the formal leader's performance feedback function inconsequential. Inherent in mature group structures are stable performance norms and positional differentiation (Bales and Strodtbeck, 1951; Borgatta and Bales, 1953; Stogdill, 1959; Lott and Lott, 1965; Zander, 1968). Task-relevant guidance and feedback from others may be provided directly by the formal leader, indirectly by the formal leader through the primary work group members, directly by the primary work group members, by staff personnel, or by the client. If the latter four instances prevail, the formal leader's role may be quite trivial. Cohesive work groups are, of course, important sources of affiliative need satisfaction.

Programming through impersonal modes has been reported to be the most frequent type of coordination strategy employed under conditions of low-to-medium task uncertainty and low task interdependence (Van de Ven, Delbecq, and Koenig, 1976). Thus, the existence of written work goals, guidelines, and ground rules (organizational formalization) and rigid rules and procedures (organizational inflexibility) may serve as substitutes for leader-provided coordination under certain conditions. Personal and group coordination modes involving the formal leader may become important only when less-costly impersonal strategies are not suitable.

ELABORATION OF THE CONSTRUCT

Table 1 was designed to capsulize our present knowledge with respect to possible substitutes for hierarchical leadership. Since present knowledge is the product of past research, and since past research was primarily unconcerned with the topic, the table is probably oversimplified and incomplete in a number of respects. Rigorous elaboration of the substitutes construct must necessarily await additional research, but we would speculate that such research would show the following refinements to be important.

Distinguishing between "Substitutes" and "Neutralizers"

A *neutralizer* is defined by Webster's as something which is able to "paralyze, destroy, or counteract the effectiveness of" something else. In the context of leadership, this term may be applied to characteristics which make it effectively *impossible* for relationship and/or task-oriented leadership to make a difference. Neutralizers are a type of moderator variable when uncorrelated with both predictors and the criterion, and act as suppressor variables when correlated with predictors but not the criterion (Zedeck, 1971; Wherry, 1946).

A *substitute* is defined to be "a person or thing acting or used in place of another." In context, this term may be used to describe characteristics which render relationship and/or task-oriented leadership not only impossible but also *unnecessary*.[2] Substitutes may be correlated with both predictors and the criterion, but tend to improve the validity coefficient when included in the predictor set. That is, they will not only tend to affect which leader behaviors (if any) are influential, but will also tend to impact upon the criterion variable.

The consequences of neutralizers and substitutes for previous research have probably been similar, since both act to reduce the impact of leader behaviors upon subordinate attitudes and performance. For this reason it is not too important that such summaries of previous research as Table 1 distinguish between them. Nevertheless, an important theoretical distinction does exist. It is that substitutes do, but neutralizers do not, provide a "person or thing acting or used in place of" the formal leader's negated influence. The effect of neutralizers is therefore to create an "influence vacuum," from which a variety of dysfunctions may emerge.

As an illustration of this point, look again at the characteristics outlined in Table 1. Since each characteristic has the capacity to counteract leader influence, all 14 may clearly be termed neutralizers. It is *not* clear, however, that all 14 are substitutes. For example, subordinates' perceived "ability, experience, training, and knowledge" tend to impair the leader's influence, but may or may not act as substitutes for leadership. It is known that individuals who are high in task-related self-esteem place high value upon nonhierarchical control systems which are consistent with a belief in the competence of people (Korman, 1970). The problem is that subordinate perceptions concerning ability and knowledge may not be accurate. Actual ability and knowledge may, therefore, act as a substitute, while false perceptions of competence and unfounded self-esteem may produce simply a neutralizing effect.

"Spatial distance," "subordinate indifference toward organizational rewards," and "organizational rewards not within the leader's control" are other examples of characteristics which do not render formal leadership unnecessary, but merely create circumstances in which effective leadership may be impossible. If rewards are clearly within the control of some other person, this other person can probably act as a substitute for the formal leader, and no adverse consequences (except probably to the leader's morale) need result. When no one knows where control over rewards lies, however, or when rewards are linked rigidly to seniority or to other factors beyond anyone's control, or when rewards are perceived to be unattractive altogether, the resulting influence vacuum would almost inevitably be dysfunctional.

---

[2] This potentially important distinction was first pointed out by M. A. Von Glinow in a doctoral seminar.

Distinguishing between Direct and Indirect
Leader Behavior Effects

It is possible to conceptualize a *direct effect* of leadership as one which occurs when a subordinate is influenced by some leader behavior *in and of itself.* An *indirect effect* may be said to result when the subordinate is influenced by the *implications* of the behavior for some future consequence. Attempts by the leader to influence subordinates must always produce direct and/or indirect effects or, when strong substitutes for leadership exist, no effect.

This distinction between direct and indirect effects of leader behavior has received very little attention, but its importance to any discussion of leadership substitutes is considerable. For example, in their review of path-goal theory, House and Dessler (1974, p. 31) state that "subordinates with high needs for affiliation and social approval would see friendly, considerate leader behavior as an immediate source of satisfaction" (direct effect). As Table 1 suggests, it is conceivable that fellow group members could supply such subordinates with enough affiliation and social approval to eliminate dependence on the leader. With other subordinates, however, the key "may be not so much in terms of what the leader does but may be in terms of how it is *interpreted* by his members" (Graen et al., 1972, p. 235). Graen et al. concluded from their data that "consideration is interpreted as the leader's evaluation of the member's role behavior . . ." (p. 233). For these subordinates, therefore, consideration seems to have been influential primarily because of its perceived implications for the likelihood of receiving future rewards. In this case the effect is an indirect one, for which group member approval and affiliation probably cannot substitute.

In the same vein, we are told by House and Dessler (1974, pp. 31–32) that:

> Subordinates with high needs for achievement would be predicted to view leader behavior that clarifies path-goal relationships and provides goal-oriented feedback as satisfying, Subordinates with high needs for extrinsic rewards would be predicted to see leader directiveness or coaching behavior as instrumental to their satisfaction if such behavior helped them perform in such a manner as to gain recognition, promotion, security, or pay increases.

It is apparent from House and Dessler's remarks that the distinction between direct and indirect effects need not be limited to relationship-oriented behaviors. Such characteristics of the task as the fact that it "provides its own feedback" (listed in Table 1 as a potential substitute for task-oriented behavior) may provide achievement-oriented subordinates with immediate satisfaction (direct effect), but fail to negate the superior's ability to help subordinates perform so as to obtain future rewards (indirect effect). Conversely, subordinate experience and training may act as substitutes for the indirect effects of task-oriented leadership, by preventing the leader from improving subordinate performance, but may not offset the direct effects.

Identifying Other Characteristics and Other Leader Behaviors

Any elaboration of the substitutes construct must necessarily include the specification of other leader behaviors, and other characteristics which may act as substitutes for leader behaviors. As was mentioned earlier, most previous studies of leadership were concerned with only two of its dimensions. This approach is intuitively indefensible. Richer conceptualizations of the leadership process already exist and almost inevitably underscore the importance of additional leader activities. As these activities are delineated in future research, it is likely that substitutes for them will also be identified.

Table 2 is offered as a guide to research. It portrays a state of increased sophistication of the substitutes construct, assuming future development along lines suggested in this section. Substitutes would be differentiated from neutralizers, and direct effects of leadership empirically distinguished from indirect effects. The columns on the right are intended to represent as-yet-unexplored leader behaviors, and the dotted lines on the bottom indicate the presence of additional characteristics which may act either as neutralizers or as true substitutes for leadership.

Distinguishing between Cause and Effect in Leader Behavior

Another area where the substitutes construct appears to have implications for leadership research concerns the question of causality. It is now evident from a variety of laboratory experiments and longitudinal field studies that leader behavior may result from, as well as cause, subordinate attitudes and performance. It is possible to speculate upon the effect that leadership substitutes would have on the relative causal strength of superior- and subordinate-related variables. This paper has tried to show that such substitutes act to reduce changes in subordinates' attitudes and performance which are *caused* by leader behaviors. On the other hand, there seems no reason why leadership substitutes should prevent changes in leader behavior which *result* from different levels of subordinate performance, satisfaction, and morale. The substitutes for leadership construct may, therefore, help to explain why the direction of causality is sometimes predominantly from leader behavior to subordinate outcomes, while at other times the reverse is true.

Specification of Interaction Effects among Substitutes and Neutralizers

From the limited data obtained thus far, it is not possible to differentiate at all among leadership substitutes and neutralizers in terms of relative strength and predictive capability. We have received some indication that the strength of a substitute, as measured by its mean level, is not strongly

TABLE 2 Substitutes for Leadership: A Theoretical Extension

| | Will Act as a Substitute for | | | | | |
| | Relationship-Oriented, Supportive, People-Centered Leadership (consideration, support, and interaction facilitation) | | Task-Oriented, Instrumental, Job-Centered Leadership (initiating structure, goal emphasis, and work facilitation) | | (other leader behaviors . . .) | |
Characteristic	Directly	Indirectly	Directly	Indirectly	Directly	Indirectly
Substitutes						
Of the subordinate:						
1. Ability.	X			X	?	?
3. "Professional" orientation.		X		X	?	?
Of the task:						
5. Unambiguous and routine.			X	X	?	?
7. Provides its own feedback concerning accomplishment.			X		?	?
8. Intrinsically satisfying.	X				?	?
Of the organization:						
12. Closely knit, cohesive work groups.	X		X	X	?	?
Neutralizers						
4. Indifference toward organizational rewards.		X		X	?	?
13. Organizational rewards not within the leader's control.		X		X	?	?

related to its predictive power. Substitutes for leadership as theoretically important as intrinsic satisfaction, for example, apparently need only be present in moderate amounts. Other, less important substitutes and neutralizers, might have to be present to a tremendous degree before their effects might be felt. Clearly, the data reported in this study are insufficient to determine at what point a particular substitute becomes important, or at what point several substitutes, each fairly weak by itself, might combine to collectively impair hierarchical leader influence. Multiplicative functions involving information on the strength and predictive power of substitutes for leadership should be able to be specified as evidence accumulates.

CONCLUSIONS

The research literature provides abundant evidence that, for organization members to maximize organizational and personal outcomes, they must be able to obtain both guidance and good feelings from their work settings. Guidance is usually offered in the form of role or task structuring, while good feelings may stem from "stroking" behaviors,[3] or may be derived from intrinsic satisfaction associated with the task itself.

The research literature does *not* suggest that guidance and good feelings must be provided by the hierarchical superior; it is only necessary that they somehow be provided. Certainly the formal leader represents a potential source of structuring and stroking behaviors, but many other organization members do, too, and impersonal equivalents also exist. To the extent that other potential sources are deficient, the hierarchical superior is clearly in a position to play a dominant role. In these situations the opportunity for leader downward influence is great, and formal leadership ought to be important. To the extent that other sources provide structure and stroking in abundance, the hierarchical leader will have little chance to exert downward influence. In such cases it is of small value to gain entree to the organization, distribute leader behavior questionnaires to anything that moves, and later debate about which leadership theory best accounts for the pitifully small percentage of variance explained, while remaining uncurious about the large percentage unexplained.

Of course, few organizations would be expected to have leadership substitutes so strong as to totally overwhelm the leader, or so weak as to require subordinates to rely entirely on him. In most organizations it is likely that, as was true here, substitutes exist for some leader activities but not for others. Effective leadership might, therefore, be described as the ability to supply subordinates with needed guidance and good feelings which are not

---

[3] *Stroking* is used here, as in transactional analysis, to describe "any type of physical, oral, or visual recognition of one person by another" (Huse, 1975, p. 288).

being supplied by other sources. From this viewpoint it is inaccurate to inform leaders (say, in management development programs) that they are incompetent if they do not personally provide these things regardless of the situation. While it may (or may not) be necessary that the organization as a whole function in a "9–9" manner (Blake and Mouton, 1964), it clearly is unnecessary for the manager to behave in such a manner unless no substitutes for leader-provided guidance and good feelings exist.

Dubin (1976, p. 33) draws a nice distinction between "proving" and "improving" a theory, and points out that, "if the purpose is to prove the adequacy of the theoretical model . . . data are likely to be collected for values on only those units incorporated in the theoretical model. This usually means that, either experimentally or by discarding data, attention in the empirical research is focused solely upon values measured on units incorporated in the theory."

In Dubin's terms, if we are really interested in improving, rather than proving, our various theories and models of leadership, a logical first step is that we stop assuming what really needs to be demonstrated empirically. The criticality of the leader's role in supplying necessary structure and stroking should be evaluated in the broader organizational context. Data pertaining to both leadership and possible substitutes for leadership (Table 1) should be obtained, and both main and interaction effects examined. A somewhat different use of information about substitutes for leadership would be as a "prescreen," to assess the appropriateness of a potential sample for a hierarchical leadership study.

What this all adds up to is that, if we really want to know more about the sources and consequences of guidance and good feelings in organizations, we should be prepared to study these things *whether or not* they happen to be provided through hierarchical leadership. For those not so catholic, whose interest lies in the derivation and refinement of theories of formal leadership, a commitment should be made to the importance of developing and operationalizing a *true* situational theory of leadership, one which will explicitly limit its propositions and restrict its predictions *to those situations* where hierarchical leadership theoretically ought to make a difference.

REFERENCES

Bales, R., and F. Strodtbeck. "Phases in group problem solving." *Journal of Abnormal and Social Psychology* (1951) *46*, 485–95.

Bass, B., and E. Valenzi. "Contingent aspects of effective management styles." In *Contingency approaches to leadership*. ed. J. G. Hunt and L. L. Larson. Carbondale: Southern Illinois University Press, 1974.

Blake, R., and J. Mouton. *The managerial grid*. Houston: Gulf, 1964.

Borgatta, E., and R. Bales. "Task and accumulation of experience as factors in the interaction of small groups." *Sociometry* (1953) *16*, 239–52.

Campbell, J.; E. Dunnette; E. Lawler; and K. Weick. *Managerial behavior, performance and effectiveness.* New York: McGraw-Hill, 1970.

Dansereau, F.; J. Cashman; and G. Graen. "Instrumentality theory and equity theory as complementary approaches in predicting the relationship of leadership and turnover among managers." *Organizational Behavior and Human Performance* (1973) *10*, 184–200.

DeCharms, R. *Personal causation.* New York: Academic Press, 1968.

Deci, E. "Intrinsic motivation, extrinsic reinforcement, and inequity." *Journal of Personality and Social Psychology* (1972) *22*, 113–20.

Deci, E. *Intrinsic motivation.* New York: Plenum, 1975.

Dubin, R. "Theory building in applied areas." In *Handbook of industrial and organizational psychology.* ed. M. Dunnette. Skokie, Ill.: Rand McNally, 1976.

Fiedler, F. E. "A contingency model of leadership effectiveness." In *Advances in experimental social psychology.* ed. L. Berkowitz. New York: Academic Press, 1964.

Fiedler, F. E. *A theory of leadership effectiveness.* New York: McGraw-Hill, 1967.

Fiedler, F. E., and M. M. Chemers. *Leadership and effective management.* Glenview, Ill.: Scott, Foresman, 1974.

Filley, A. C.; R. J. House; and S. Kerr. *Managerial process and organizational behavior.* 2nd ed. Glenview, Ill.: Scott, Foresman, 1976.

Graen, G.; F. Dansereau, Jr.; and T. Minami. "Dysfunctional leadership styles." *Organizational Behavior and Human Performance* (1972) *7*, 216–36.

Greller, M., and D. Herold. "Sources of feedback: A preliminary investigation." *Organizational Behavior and Human Performance* (1975) *13*, 244–56.

Hackman, R., and G. Oldham. "Motivation through the design of work: Test of a theory." *Organizational Behavior and Human Performance* (1976) *16*, 250–79.

Hall, D., and E. Lawler. "Unused potential in R and D labs." *Research Management* (1969) *12*, 339–54.

Heller, F. A., and G. Yukl. "Participation, managerial decision making, and situational variables." *Organizational Behavior and Human Performance* (1969) *4*, 227–34.

House, R. J. "A path-goal theory of leadership effectiveness. *Administrative Science Quarterly* (1971) *16*, 321–38.

House, R. J., and G. Dessler. "The path-goal theory of leadership: Some post hoc and a priori tests." In *Contingency approaches to leadership.* ed. J. G Hunt and L. L. Larson. Carbondale: Southern Illinois University Press, 1974.

House, R. J.; A. C. Filley; and S. Kerr. "Relation of leader consideration and initiating structure to R and D subordinates' satisfaction." *Administrative Science Quarterly* (1971) *16*, 19–30.

House, R. J., and T. R. Mitchell. "Path-goal theory of leadership." *Journal of Contemporary Business* (1974) *3*, 81–97.

Hunt, J. G., and R. N. Osborn. "An adaptive-reactive theory of leadership: The role of macro variables in leadership research." In *Leadership frontiers*. ed. J. G. Hunt and L. L. Larson. Carbondale: Southern Illinois University Press, 1975.

Huse, E. F. *Organization development and change*. St Paul: West, 1975.

Kaplan, Abraham. *The conduct of inquiry*. San Francisco: Chandler, 1964.

Kerr, S.; C. Schriesheim; C. J. Murphy; and R. M. Stogdill. "Toward a contingency theory of leadership based upon the consideration and initiating structure literature." *Organizational Behavior and Human Performance* (1974) *12*, 62–82.

Korman, A. "Toward a hypothesis of work behavior." *Journal of Applied Psychology* (1970) *54*, 31–41.

Lott, A., and B. Lott. "Group cohesiveness as interpersonal attraction: A review of relationships with antecedent and consequent variables." *Psychological Bulletin* (1965) *64*, 259–302.

Miner, J. "The uncertain future of the leadership concept: An overview." In *Leadership frontiers*. ed. J. G. Hunt and L. L. Larson. Carbondale: Southern Illinois University Press, 1975.

Oldham, G. "Job characteristics and internal motivation: The moderating effect of interpersonal and individual variables." *Human Relations* (1976) *29*, 559–70.

Stogdill, R. *Individual behavior and group achievement*. New York: Oxford University Press, 1959.

Tannenbaum, R., and W. Schmidt. "How to choose a leadership pattern." *Harvard Business Review* (1958) *36*, 95–101.

Van de Ven, A.; A. Delbecq; and R. Koenig. "Determinants of coordination modes within organizations." *American Sociological Review* (1976) *41*, 322–38.

Vroom, V., and P. Yetton. *Leadership and decision making*. Pittsburgh: University of Pittsburgh Press, 1973.

Wherry, R. "Test selection and suppressor variables." *Psychometrika* (1946) *11*, 239–47.

Woodward, J. "Technology, material control, and organizational behavior." In *Modern organizational theory*. ed. A. Negandhi. Kent: Kent State University, 1973.

Zander, A. "Group aspirations." In *Group dynamics: Research and theory*. 3rd ed. ed. D. Cartwright and A. Zander. New York: Harper & Row, 1968.

Zedeck, S. "Problems with the use of 'moderator' variables." *Psychological Bulletin* (1971) *76*, 295–310.

ENDNOTES

1. Bish, J., and C. Schriesheim. *An exploratory analysis of Form XII of The Ohio State Leadership Scales*. Paper presented at the National Academy of Management Conference, 1974.

2. Hunt, J. *Different nonleader clarity sources as alternatives to leadership.* Paper presented at the Eastern Academy of Management Conference, 1975.

3. Schriesheim, C. *The development and validation of instrumental and supportive leadership scales and their application to some tests of path-goal theory of leadership hypotheses.* Unpublished doctoral dissertation. The Ohio State University, 1978.

4. Wigdor, L. *Effectiveness of various management and organizational characteristics on employee satisfaction and performance as a function of the employee's need for job independence.* Unpublished doctoral dissertation. City University of New York, 1969.

Human Relations or Human Resources?*

Raymond E. Miles

The proselyting efforts of the advocates of participative management appear to have paid off. The typical modern manager, on paper at least, broadly endorses participation and rejects traditional, autocratic concepts of leadership and control as no longer acceptable or, perhaps, no longer legitimate.

However, while participation has apparently been well merchandised and widely purchased, there seems to be a great deal of confusion about what has been sold and what has been bought. Managers do not appear to have accepted a single, logically consistent concept of participation. In fact, there is reason to believe that managers have adopted two different theories or models of participation—one for themselves and one for their subordinates.

These statements reflect both my analysis of the development of the theory of participative management and my interpretation of managers' attitudes toward these concepts.

My views are based in part on a number of recent surveys of managers' beliefs and opinions. The most recent of these studies, which I conducted, was begun with a group of 215 middle and upper level managers in West Coast companies, and has been continued with a sample of over 300 administrators from public agencies.[1] This study was designed to clarify further certain aspects of managers' attitudes uncovered by earlier research under

---

[1] See Raymond E. Miles, "Conflicting elements in managerial ideologies," *Industrial Relations* (October 1964), 77–91. The subsequent research with public administrators is still being conducted, and reports have not yet been published.

the direction of Dale Yoder of Stanford[2] and Professors Mason Haire, Edwin Ghiselli, and Lyman Porter of the University of California, Berkeley.[3]

This series of studies involved the collection of questionnaire data on managers' opinions about people and on their attitudes toward various leadership policies and practices. Several thousand managers in all, both here and abroad, have participated.

This article is not intended to summarize all of the findings on managers' leadership attitudes available from these studies. Rather, my primary purpose is to construct a theoretical framework that may explain some of the principal dimensions of managers' views and some of the implications of their beliefs and opinions, drawing on the research simply to illustrate my views.

PARTICIPATIVE THEORIES

While the suggestion that managers have accepted a two-sided approach to participation may be disturbing, it should not be too surprising. Management theorists have frequently failed to deal with participation in a thorough and consistent manner. Indeed, from an examination of their somewhat ambivalent treatment of this concept, it is possible to conclude that they have been selling two significantly different models of participative management.

> One of the scholars' models, which we will designate the *human relations* model, closely resembles the concept of participation which managers appear to accept for use with their own subordinates.

> The second, and not yet fully developed, theory, which I have labeled the *human resources* model, prescribes the sort of participative policies that managers would apparently like their superiors to follow.

I shall develop and examine these two models, compare them with managers' expressed beliefs, and consider some of the implications of managers' dual allegiance to them.

---

[2] See Dale Yoder, "Management theories as managers see them," *Personnel* (July–August 1962), 25–30; "Management policies for the future," *Personnel Administration* (September–October 1962), 11–14 ff; Dale Yoder et al., "Managers' theories of management," *Journal of the Academy of Management* (September 1963), 204–11.

[3] See Mason Haire, Edwin Ghiselli, and Lyman W. Porter, "Cultural patterns in the role of the manager," *Industrial Relations* (February 1963), 95–117, for a report on the Berkeley studies.

Both the *human relations* and the *human resources* models have three basic components:

1. A set of assumptions about people's values and capabilities.
2. Certain prescriptions as to the amount and kind of participative policies and practices that managers should follow, in keeping with their assumptions about people.
3. A set of expectations with respect to the effects of participation on subordinate morale and performance.

This third component contains the model's explanation of how and why participation works—that is, the purpose of participation and how it accomplishes this purpose. In outline form, the models may be summarized as shown in Exhibit 1.

EXHIBIT 1   Two Models of Participative Leadership

Human Relations	*Human Resources*
Attitudes toward People	
1. People in our culture share a common set of needs—to belong, to be liked, to be respected.	1. In addition to sharing common needs for belonging and respect, most people in our culture desire to contribute effectively and creatively to the accomplishment of worthwhile objectives.
2. They desire individual recognition but, more than this, they want to feel a useful part of the company and their own work group or department.	2. The majority of our work force is capable of exercising far more initiative, responsibility, and creativity than their present jobs require or allow.
3. They will tend to cooperate willingly and comply with organizational goals if these important needs are fulfilled.	3. These capabilities represent untapped resources which are presently being wasted.
Kind and Amount of Participation	
1. The manager's basic task is to make each worker believe that he is a useful and important part of the department "team."	1. The manager's basic task is to create an environment in which his subordinates can contribute their full range of talents to the accomplishment of organizational goals. He must attempt to uncover and tap the creative resources of his subordinates.

EXHIBIT 1   *(concluded)*

Human Relations	Human Resources
2. The manager should be willing to explain his decisions and to discuss his subordinates' objections to his plans. On routine matters, he should encourage his subordinates to participate in planning and choosing among alternative solutions to problems.	2. The manager should allow, and encourage, his subordinates to participate not only in routine decisions but in important matters as well. In fact, the more important a decision is to the manager's department, the greater should be his effort to tap the department's resources.
3. Within narrow limits, the work group or individual subordinates should be allowed to exercise self-direction and self-control in carrying out plans.	3. The manager should attempt to continually expand the areas over which his subordinates exercise self-direction and self-control as they develop and demonstrate greater insight and ability.

Expectations

1. Sharing information with subordinates and involving them in departmental decision making will help satisfy their basic needs for belonging and for individual recognition.	1. The overall quality of decision making and performance will improve as the manager makes use of the full range of experience, insight, and creative ability in his department.
2. Satisfying these needs will improve subordinate morale and reduce resistance to formal authority.	2. Subordinates will exercise responsible self-direction and self-control in the accomplishment of worthwhile objectives that they understand and have helped establish.
3. High employee morale and reduced resistance to formal authority may lead to improved departmental performance. It should at least reduce intradepartment friction and thus make the manager's job easier.	3. Subordinate satisfaction will increase as a by-product of improved performance and the opportunity to contribute creatively to this improvement.

Note: It may fairly be argued that what I call the *human relations* model is actually the product of popularization and misunderstanding of the work of pioneers in this field. Moreover, it is true that some of the early research and writings of the human relationists contain concepts which seem to fall within the framework of what I call the *human resources* model. Nevertheless, it is my opinion that, while the early writers did not advocate the *human relations* model as presented here, their failure to emphasize certain of the *human resources* concepts left their work open to the misinterpretations which have occurred.

HUMAN RELATIONS MODEL

This approach is not new. As early as the 1920s, business spokesmen began to challenge the classical autocratic philosophy of management. The employee was no longer pictured as merely an appendage to a machine, seeking only economic rewards from his work. Managers were instructed to consider him as a "whole man" rather than as merely a bundle of skills and aptitudes.[4] They were urged to create a "sense of satisfaction" among their subordinates by showing interest in the employees' personal success and welfare. As Bendix notes, the "failure to treat workers as human beings came to be regarded as the cause of low morale, poor craftsmanship, unresponsiveness, and confusion."[5]

The key element in the *human relations* approach is its basic objective of making organizational members *feel* a useful and important part of the overall effort. This process is viewed as the means of accomplishing the ultimate goal of building a cooperative and compliant work force. Participation, in this model, is a lubricant which oils away resistance to formal authority. By discussing problems with his subordinates and acknowledging their individual needs and desires, the manager hopes to build a cohesive work team that is willing and anxious to tangle with organizational problems.

One further clue to the way in which participation is viewed in this approach is provided in Dubin's concept of "privilege pay."[6] The manager "buys" cooperation by letting his subordinates in on departmental information and allowing them to discuss and state their opinions on various departmental problems. He "pays a price" for allowing his subordinates the privilege of participating in certain decisions and exercising some self-direction. In return he hopes to obtain their cooperation in carrying out these and other decisions for the accomplishment of departmental objectives.

Implicit in this model is the idea that it might actually be easier and more efficient if the manager could merely make departmental decisions without bothering to involve his subordinates. However, as the advocates of this model point out, there are two parts to any decision—(1) the making of the decision and (2) the activities required to carry it out. In many instances, this model suggests, the manager might do better to "waste time" in discussing the problem with his subordinates, and perhaps even to accept sug-

---

[4] See Reinhard Bendix, *Work and authority in industry* (New York: John Wiley & Sons, 1956), 287–340.

[5] Ibid., p. 294.

[6] Robert Dubin, *The world of work* (Englewood Cliffs: N.J., Prentice-Hall, 1958), 243–44. It should be noted that Dubin treats the concept of privilege pay within a framework which goes beyond the *human relations* approach and, in some respects, is close to the *human resources* model.

gestions that he believes may be less efficient, in order to get the decision carried out.

In sum, the *human relations* approach does not bring out the fact that participation may be useful for its own sake. The possibility that subordinates will, in fact, bring to light points which the manager may have overlooked, if considered at all, tends to be mentioned only in passing. This is treated as a potential side benefit which, while not normally expected, may occasionally occur. Instead, the manager is urged to adopt participative leadership policies as the least-cost method of obtaining cooperation and getting his decisions accepted.

In many ways the *human relations* model represents only a slight departure from traditional autocratic models of management. The method of achieving results is different, and employees are viewed in more humanistic terms, but the basic roles of the manager and his subordinates remain essentially the same. The ultimate goal sought in both the traditional and the *human relations* model is compliance with managerial authority.

HUMAN RESOURCES MODEL

This approach represents a dramatic departure from traditional concepts of management. Though not yet fully developed, it is emerging from the writings of McGregor, Likert, Haire, and others as a new and significant contribution to management thought.[7] The magnitude of its departure from previous models is illustrated first of all in its basic assumptions concerning people's values and abilities, which focus attention on all organization members as reservoirs of untapped resources. These resources include not only physical skills and energy but also creative ability and the capacity for responsible, self-directed, self-controlled behavior. Given these assumptions about people, the manager's job cannot be viewed merely as one of giving direction and obtaining cooperation. Instead, his primary task becomes that of creating an environment in which the total resources of his department can be utilized.

The second point at which the *human resources* model differs dramatically from previous models is in its views on the purpose and goal of participation. In this model the manager does not share information, discuss departmental decisions, or encourage self-direction and self-control merely to improve subordinate satisfaction and morale. Rather, the purpose of these

---

[7] See particularly Douglas McGregor, *The human side of enterprise* (New York: McGraw-Hill, 1960); Rensis Likert, *New patterns of management* (New York: McGraw-Hill, 1961); and Mason Haire, "The concept of power and the concept of man," in *Social science approaches to business behavior*, ed. George Strother (Homewood, Ill.: Irwin/Dorsey, 1962), pp. 163–83.

practices is to improve the decision making and total performance efficiency of the organization. The *human resources* model suggests that many decisions may actually be made more efficiently by those directly involved in and affected by the decisions.

Similarly, this model implies that control is often most efficiently exercised by those directly involved in the work in process, rather than by someone or some group removed from the actual point of operation. Moreover, the *human resources* model does not suggest that the manager allow participation only in routine decisions. Instead, it implies that the more important the decision, the greater is his *obligation* to encourage ideas and suggestions from his subordinates.

In the same vein, this model does not suggest that the manager allow his subordinates to exercise self-direction and self-control only when they are carrying out relatively unimportant assignments. In fact, it suggests that the area over which subordinates exercise self-direction and control should be continually broadened in keeping with their growing experience and ability.

The crucial point at which this model differs dramatically from other models is in its explanation of the causal relationship between satisfaction and performance. In the *human relations* approach, improvement in subordinate satisfaction is viewed as an intervening variable which is the ultimate cause of improved performance. Diagrammatically, the causal relationship can be illustrated as in Exhibit 2.

In the *human resources* model the causal relationship between satisfaction and performance is viewed quite differently. Increased subordinate satisfaction is not pictured as the primary cause of improved performance; improvement results directly from creative contributions which subordinates make to departmental decision making, direction, and control. Subordinates' satisfaction is viewed instead as a by-product of the process—the

EXHIBIT 2   Human Relations Model

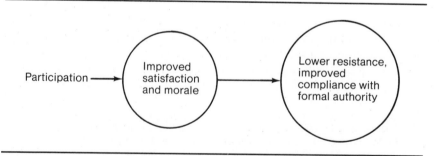

EXHIBIT 3   Human Resources Model

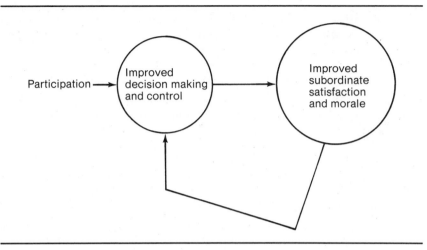

result of their having made significant contributions to organizational success. In diagram form the *human resources* model can be illustrated as in Exhibit 3.

The *human resources* model does not deny a relationship between participation and morale. It suggests that subordinates' satisfaction may well increase as they play more and more meaningful roles in decision making and control. Moreover, the model recognizes that improvements in morale may not only set the stage for expanded participation but create an atmosphere which supports creative problem solving. Nevertheless, this model rejects as unsupported the concept that the improvement of morale is a necessary or sufficient cause of improved decision making and control. Those improvements come directly from the full utilization of the organization's resources.

MANAGERS' OWN VIEWS

Which approach to participative management do managers actually follow? It was suggested earlier that managers' views appear to reflect both models. When they talk about the kind and amount of participation appropriate for their subordinates, they express concepts that appear to be similar to those in the *human relations* model. On the other hand, when they consider their own relationships with their superiors, their views seem to flow from the *human resources* model. A brief review of the relevant findings suggests some of the bases for this interpretation.

Participation for Subordinates

When we look at managers' views on the use of participative policies and practices with the subordinates who report to them, two points seem clear:

1. Managers generally accept and endorse the use of participative concepts.
2. However, they frequently doubt their subordinates' capacity for self-direction and self-control, and their ability to contribute creatively to departmental decision making.

In the Stanford studies, an overwhelming majority of managers indicated their agreement with statements emphasizing the desirability of subordinate participation in decision making.[8] In the Berkeley studies, a majority of the managers in each of 11 countries, including the United States, indicated their agreement with such concepts as sharing information with subordinates and increasing subordinate influence and self-control.[9] Similarly, in my recent studies, managers overwhelmingly endorsed participative leadership policies.

On the other hand, while managers appear to have great faith in participative policies, they do not indicate such strong belief in their subordinates' capabilities. For example, the Berkeley group in its international study found that managers tended to have a "basic lack of confidence in others" and typically did not believe that capacity for leadership and initiative was widely distributed among subordinates.[10] In my own study, managers in every group to date have rated their subordinates and rank-and-file employees well below themselves, particularly on such important managerial traits as *responsibility, judgment,* and *initiative.*

But if managers do not expect creative, meaningful contributions from their subordinates, why do they advocate participative management? A reasonable answer seems to be that they advocate participative concepts as a means of improving subordinate morale and satisfaction. This interpretation gains support from my recent studies. Here, managers were asked to indicate their agreement or disagreement with statements predicting improved morale and satisfaction and statements predicting improved performance as the result of following various participative leadership policies. In connection with each of these policies, managers indicated consistently greater

---

[8] Yoder et al., "Managers' theories of management," 204–11.

[9] Haire, Ghiselli, and Porter, "Cultural patterns," 95–117.

[10] Ibid.

agreement with the predictions of improved morale than with the predictions of improved performance.

The fact that managers appear to have serious doubts about the values and capabilities of those reporting to them seems to rule out their acceptance of the *human resources* model for use with their subordinates. On the other hand, the fact that they do endorse participation and seem quite certain about its positive impact on morale suggests a close relationship between their views and those expressed in the *human relations* model. Moreover, the types of participative policies which managers most strongly advocate seem to support this interpretation.

In my research, managers indicate strongest agreement with policies that advocate sharing information and discussing objectives with subordinates. However, they tend to be somewhat less enamored with the policies which suggest increasing subordinate self-direction and self-control. This pattern of participation seems much closer to that of the *human relations* approach than to the pattern advocated in the *human resources* model.

Participation for Themselves

When I examined managers' views toward their relationships with their own superiors, a much different pattern of responses became evident:

1. Managers in my studies tend to see little, if any, difference between their own capabilities and those of their superiors. In fact, they tend to rate themselves equal to, if not higher than, their superiors on such traits as *creativity, ingenuity, flexibility,* and *willingness to change.*
2. When asked to indicate at which levels in their organizations they feel each of the participative policies would be most appropriate, managers invariably feel most strongly that the full range of participative policies should be used by their own superiors.

More importantly, they also tend to be most certain that these participative policies will result in improved organizational performance *at their own level.*

Thus, when managers discuss the type of participative policies which their superiors should follow with managers at their own level, they appear to espouse the *human resources* model. They see themselves as reservoirs of creative resources. Moreover, the fact that they frequently view themselves as more flexible and willing to change than their superiors suggests that they feel their resources are frequently wasted. Correspondingly, they expect improvement in organizational performance to result from greater freedom for self-direction and self-control on their part.

REASONS BEHIND VIEWS

If the evidence of the current survey does represent managers' attitudes toward participative leadership, one serious question immediately comes to mind. How can managers desire one type of authority and control relationship with their superiors and at the same time advocate another type with their subordinates? A general answer, of course, is that this pattern of attitudes is just human nature. We tend not only to think more highly of ourselves than we do of others but also to want more than we are willing to give. There are, however, other logical, more specific explanations for managers' reluctance to accept the *human resources* model for use with their subordinates.

In the first place, the *human relations* model has been around much longer, and an exceptionally good selling job has been done in its behalf. The causal relationship among participation, satisfaction, and performance, despite a lack of empirical validation, has become common wisdom. The *human resources* model, on the other hand, has not been as fully or systematically developed, and has not been the subject of as hard a sell. Managers may "feel" some of the concepts expressed in the *human resources* model and intuitively grasp some of their implications for their relationships with their superiors, but little pressure has been put on them to translate their attitudes into a systematic model for use with their subordinates.

A second explanation for managers' failure to accept the *human resources* model for use with their subordinates is that they are simply reluctant to "buy" a theory that challenges concepts to which they are deeply and emotionally attached. There is no question that the *human resources* model does attack a number of traditional management concepts. Two of the bedrock concepts that are directly challenged deal with: (1) the origins and applicability of management prerogatives and (2) the source and limits of control.

The *human resources* model recognizes no definable, immutable set of management prerogatives. It does not accept the classical division between those who think and command and those who obey and perform. Instead, it argues that the solution to any given problem may arise from a variety of sources, and that to think of management (or any other group) as sufficient in and of itself to make all decisions is misleading and wasteful.

This approach does not directly challenge the "legal" right of management to command. It suggests, however, that there is a higher "law of the situation" that thoughtful managers will usually observe, deferring to expertise wherever it may be found. In this model the manager's basic obligation is not to the "management team" but to the accomplishment of departmental and organizational objectives. The criterion of success, therefore, is not the extent to which orders are carried out but the results obtained.

Admitting that he may not have all the answers is as difficult for the manager as for any of the rest of us. He has been taught to hide his deficiencies, not to advertise them. Holding on to information, maintaining close control, and reserving the right to make all decisions are ways by which the manager can ensure his importance. Further, many organizations have reinforced this type of behavior either *(a)* by failing to emphasize the manager's obligation to develop and utilize his human resources or *(b)* by failing to reward him when he does make this effort.

In the area of control the *human resources* model challenges the traditional concept that control is a scarce resource. In traditional theory there is presumed to be a virtually fixed amount of control. This fixed amount can be distributed in a variety of ways, but control given to one group must eventually be taken away from another. Given this concept, the manager is reluctant to allow his subordinates any real degree of self-control—what he gives up to them, he loses himself. In fact, it is frequently this basic fear of losing control which limits the amount of participation that managers are willing to allow.

The *human resources* model does not accept this lump-of-control theory. Instead, it argues that the manager increases his total control over the accomplishment of departmental objectives by encouraging self-control on the part of his subordinates. Control is thus an additive and an expanding phenomenon. Where subordinates are concerned with accomplishing goals and exercising self-direction and self-control, their combined efforts will far outweigh the results of the exercise of any amount of control by the manager.

Moreover, the fact that subordinates desire to exercise greater self-control does not mean that they reject the manager's legitimate concern for goal accomplishment. Rather, there is evidence that they in fact seek a partnership that will allow them to play a larger role, yet also will allow for a corresponding increase in management's control activity.[11]

In all, the fact that managers are reluctant to adopt a model which forces them to rethink, and perhaps restructure, their perceptions of their own roles and functions is not surprising. It is also not surprising that some writers in this field have hesitated to advocate a model which challenges such deeply held concepts. The *human relations* approach is easy to "buy," since it does not challenge the manager's basic role or status. It is correspondingly easy to sell, since it promises much and actually demands little. The *human resources* model, on the other hand, promises much but also demands a great deal from the manager. It requires that he undertake the

---

[11] See Clagget C. Smith and Arnold Tannenbaum. "Organizational control structure: A comparative analysis," *Human Relations* (November 1963), 299–316.

responsibility of utilizing all the resources available to him—his own and those of his subordinates. It does not suggest that it will make his job easier; it only acknowledges his obligation to do a much better job.

LOGICAL IMPLICATIONS

The nature of the evidence to date does not warrant any firm or sweeping conclusions. Nevertheless, it does suggest enough support for the interpretations made here to make it worthwhile, and perhaps imperative, to draw some logical implications from the fact that managers seem to have adopted two apparently conflicting attitudes regarding participative management.

The first implication, and the easiest one to draw, is that, given managers' present attitudes, the *human resources* model has little chance of ever gaining real acceptance as a guide to managers' relationships with their subordinates. Managers at every level view themselves as capable of greater self-direction and self-control, but apparently do not attribute such abilities to their subordinates. As long as managers throughout the organizational hierarchy remain unaware that the kind of participation *they* want and believe *they* are capable of handling is also the kind their subordinates want and feel they deserve, there would seem to be little hope for the *human resources* approach being actually put into practice.

A second, and somewhat more complex, implication of managers' current views is that real participation will seldom be found in modern organizations. Participation, in the *human relations* model, is viewed as an "ought" rather than a "must." The manager is under no basic obligation to seek out and develop talent, or to encourage and allow participation; it is something which he "probably should do" but not something for which he is made to feel truly responsible. Viewing participation in this fashion, the manager often junks it when problems arise or pressure builds up from above—the very times when it might be expected to produce the greatest gains.

A third implication, closely related to the second, is that the benefits which the *human resources* approach predicts from participative management will not accrue as long as managers cling to the *human relations* view. From the *human relations* model, a manager may draw a rule for decision making which says that he should allow only as much participation, self-direction, and self-control as is required to obtain cooperation and reduce resistance to formal authority. In the area of job enlargement, for example, the manager following the *human relations* model would be tempted to enlarge his subordinates' jobs just enough to improve morale and satisfaction, with little real concern for making full use of their abilities. This limited approach borders on pseudoparticipation and may be interpreted by subordinates as just another manipulative technique.

The *human resources* model, on the other hand, does not hold the manager to so limited a decision rule. In fact, it affirms that he is obligated to develop and encourage a continually expanding degree of responsible participation, self-direction, and self-control. The only limiting factors legitimate in this approach are the basic requirements of capacity to perform and the need for coordination. The manager following the *human resources* model would, therefore, continually expand subordinates' responsibility and self-direction up to the limits of their abilities, and/or to the point at which further expansion would produce a wasteful overlap among the responsibilities of members of his department. Even these limits, however, are far from absolute. The *human resources* model suggests that, with subordinates' broadened abilities and expanded information, voluntary cooperation can erase much of the need for specific job boundaries.

A fourth and final implication can be drawn from managers' confused and conflicting attitudes toward participative management. Managers' attitudes, as suggested earlier, in part reflect the ambivalent and inconsistent treatment which scholars have given to participative leadership concepts and are not likely to change until theorists firm up their own thinking.

SOME FINAL COMMENTS

It must be clear at this point that I feel that management scholars should focus their attention on developing and promoting the application of the *human resources* approach. While I cannot, at this stage, base my preference for the *human resources* model on solid empirical evidence, there is one strong argument for its potential usefulness. It is the fact that managers up and down the organizational hierarchy believe their superiors should follow this model.

Critics of the *human resources* approach have argued that (1) its costs outweigh its benefits because in its final form the *human resources* model prescribes management by committee at every level, which results in wasted effort and the inability to act in crisis situations; and (2) this approach is unsuitable for organizations or organizational groups whose members have neither the desire nor the ability to meet its challenge.

In answer to the first charge, this approach does imply a need for additional information flow to subordinates at all levels, and I admit that collecting and disseminating information increases costs.

However, information collected and *used* at lower levels may be less costly than information collected for use at upper levels that is subsequently ignored or misused. Further, and more important, the application of the *human resources* model does not require—in fact, would make unnecessary—committee-type sharing of routine departmental tasks.

This model would suggest that subordinates are generally willing to go along with their superiors' decisions on more or less routine matters, particularly when they are well informed and feel free to call important points to their bosses' attention. Moreover, this approach implies that many matters are to be delegated directly to one or more subordinates who, in most instances, will coordinate their own activities. At the same time, this model emphasizes that full and extended discussion by the whole department will be utilized where it can do the most good—on complex and important problems that demand the full talent and complete concern of the group. One could argue that under these circumstances crises should arise less often and consensus should be more quickly reached when they do arise.

There is no quick and easy answer to the second charge that the *human resources* model is more adaptable to and more easily applied with some groups than with others. Note, however, that it is the *human relations* approach, and not the *human resources* model, which promises quick and easy application. The latter cannot be put into full-blown practice overnight in any situation, particularly where subordinates have been conditioned by years of traditional or pseudoparticipative techniques of leadership. It involves a step-by-step procedure wherein the manager expands subordinates' responsibilities and participation in keeping with their developing abilities and concerns. High expectations and full support, coupled with an open recognition of the inevitability of occasional shortcomings, are required to achieve successful application.

Finally, there is a familiar ring to the critics' charge that many organization members are either unwilling or unable to contribute creatively, or to accept any real measure of responsibility. In fact, this charge brings us back once again to the heart of the conflict in managers' attitudes toward participation—their own view that subordinates are suited only for the *human relations* type of participation, while they themselves are well suited for the full range of participation suggested in the *human resources* model.

Successful versus Effective
Real Managers*

Fred Luthans

What do *successful* managers—those who have been promoted relatively quickly—have in common with *effective* managers—those who have satisfied, committed subordinates and high-performing units? Surprisingly, the answer seems to be that they have little in common. Successful managers in what we define as "real organizations"—large and small mainstream organizations, mostly in the mushrooming service industry in middle America—are not engaged in the same day-to-day activities as effective managers in these organizations. This is probably the most important, and certainly the most intriguing, finding of a comprehensive four-year observational study of managerial work that is reported in a recent book by myself and two colleagues, titled *Real Managers*.[1]

The startling finding that there is a difference between successful and effective managers may merely confirm for many cynics and "passed over" managers something they have suspected for years. They believe that, although managers who are successful (i.e., rapidly promoted) may be astute politicians, they are not necessarily effective. Indeed, the so-called successful managers may be the ones who do not in fact take care of people and get high performance from their units.

Could this finding explain some of the performance problems facing American organizations today? Could it be that the successful managers, the politically savvy ones who are being rapidly promoted into responsible positions, may not be the effective managers, the ones with satisfied, committed subordinates turning out quantity and quality performance in their units?

This article explores the heretofore assumed equivalence of "successful managers" and "effective managers." Instead of looking for sophisticated technical or governmental approaches to the performance problems facing today's organizations, the solution may be as simple as promoting effective

* From *The Academy of Management EXECUTIVE* (1988) *II*, no. 2, 127–32.

managers and learning how they carry out their jobs. Maybe it is time to turn to the real managers themselves for some answers.

And who are these managers? They are found at all levels and in all types of organizations, with titles such as department head, general manager, store manager, marketing manager, office manager, agency chief, or district manager. In other words, maybe the answers to the performance problems facing organizations today can be found in their own backyards, in the managers themselves in their day-to-day activities.

THE CURRENT VIEW OF MANAGERIAL WORK

Through the years management has been defined as the famous French administrator and writer Henri Fayol said, by the functions of planning, organizing, commanding, coordinating, and controlling. Only recently has this classical view of managers been challenged.[2] Starting with the landmark work of Henry Mintzberg, observational studies of managerial work have found that the normative functions do not hold up. Mintzberg charged that Fayol and others' classical view of what managers do was merely "folklore."[3]

On the basis of his observations of five CEOs and their mail, Mintzberg concluded that the manager's job consisted of many brief and disjointed episodes with people inside and outside the organization. He discounted notions such as reflective planning. Instead of the five Fayolian functions of management, Mintzberg portrayed managers in terms of a typology of roles. He formulated three interpersonal roles (figurehead, leader, and liaison); three informational roles (monitor or nerve center, disseminator, and spokesman), and four decision-making roles (entrepreneur, disturbance handler, resource allocator, and negotiator). Although Mintzberg based this view of managers on only the five managers he observed and his search of the literature, he did ask, and at least gave the beginning of an answer to, the question of what managers really do.

The best known other modern view of managerial work is provided by John Kotter. His description of managers is based on his study of 15 successful general managers. Like Mintzberg, Kotter challenged the traditional view by concluding that managers do not so simply perform the Fayolian functions, but rather spend most of their time interacting with others. In particular, he found his general managers spent considerable time in meetings getting and giving information. Kotter refers to these get-togethers as "network building." Networking accomplishes what Kotter calls a manager's "agenda"—the loosely connected goals and plans addressing the manager's responsibilities. By obtaining relevant and needed information from his or her networks, the effective general manager is able to implement his or her agenda. Like Mintzberg, Kotter's conclusions are based on managerial work from a small sample of elite managers. Nevertheless, his work represents a progressive step in answering the question of what managers do.

DETERMINING WHAT REAL MANAGERS DO

The next step in discovering the true nature of managerial work called for a larger sample that would allow more meaningful generalizations. With a grant from the Office of Naval Research, we embarked on such an effort.[4] We used trained observers to freely observe and record in detail the behaviors and activities of 44 "real" managers.[5] Unlike Mintzberg's and Kotter's managers, these managers came from all levels and many types of organizations (mostly in the service sector—such as retail stores, hospitals, corporate headquarters, a railroad, government agencies, insurance companies, a newspaper office, financial institutions, and a few manufacturing companies).

We reduced the voluminous data gathered from the free observation logs into managerial activity categories using the Delphi technique. Delphi was developed and used during the heyday of Rand Corporation's "Think Tank." A panel offers independent input and then the panel members are given composite feedback. After several iterations of this process, the data were reduced into the 12 descriptive behavioral categories shown in Exhibit 1. These empirically derived behavioral descriptors were then conceptually collapsed into the four managerial activities of real managers:

1. *Communication.* This activity consists of exchanging routine information and processing paperwork. Its observed behaviors include answering procedural questions, receiving and disseminating requested information, conveying the results of meetings, giving or receiving routine information over the phone, processing mail, reading reports, writing reports/memos/letters, routine financial reporting and bookkeeping, and general desk work.

2. *Traditional Management.* This activity consists of planning, decision making, and controlling. Its observed behaviors include setting goals and objectives, defining tasks needed to accomplish goals, scheduling employees, assigning tasks, providing routine instructions, defining problems, handling day-to-day operational crises, deciding what to do, developing new procedures, inspecting work, walking around inspecting the work, monitoring performance data, and doing preventive maintenance.

3. *Human Resource Management.* This activity contains the most behavioral categories: motivating/reinforcing, disciplining/punishing, managing conflict, staffing, and training/developing. The disciplining/punishing category was subsequently dropped from the analysis because it was not generally permitted to be observed. The observed behaviors for this activity include allocating formal rewards, asking for input, conveying appreciation, giving credit where due, listening to suggestions, giving positive feedback, group support, resolving conflict

EXHIBIT 1   The Activities of Real Managers

Descriptive categories derived from free observation	Real managers' activities

Exchanging information

Paperwork

→ Communication

Planning

Decision making → Traditional management

Controlling

Interacting with outsiders

→ Networking

Socializing/politicking

Motivating/reinforcing

Disciplining/punishing

Managing conflict → Human resource management

Staffing

Training/developing

between subordinates, appealing to higher authorities or third parties to resolve a dispute, developing job descriptions, reviewing applications, interviewing applicants, filling in where needed, orienting employees, arranging for training, clarifying roles, coaching, mentoring, and walking subordinates through a task.

4. *Networking.* This activity consists of socializing/politicking and interacting with outsiders. The observed behaviors associated with this activity include non-work-related "chit chat"; informal joking around; discussing rumors, hearsay, and the grapevine; complaining, griping, and putting others down; politicking and gamesmanship; dealing with customers, suppliers, and vendors; attending external meetings; and doing/attending community service events.

These four activities are what real managers do. They include some of the classic notions of Fayol (the traditional management activities) as well as the more recent views of Mintzberg (the communication activities) and Kotter (the networking activities). As a whole, however, especially with the inclusion of human resource management activities, this view of real managers' activities is more comprehensive than previous sets of managerial work.

After the nature of managerial activity was determined through the free observation of the 44 managers, the next phase of the study was to document the relative frequency of these activities. Data on another set of 248 real managers (not the 44 used in the initial portion of this study) were gathered. Trained participation observers filled out a checklist based on the managerial activities at a random time once every hour over a two-week period. We found that the real managers spend not quite a third of their time and effort in communication activities, about a third in traditional management activities, a fifth in human resource management activities, and about a fifth in networking activities. This relative frequency analysis based on observational data of a large sample provides a more definitive answer to the question of what real managers do than the normative classical functions and the limited sample of elite managers used by Mintzberg and Kotter.

HOW THE DIFFERENCE BETWEEN SUCCESSFUL AND EFFECTIVE REAL MANAGERS WAS DETERMINED

Discovering the true nature of managerial work by exploding some of the myths of the past and extending the work of Mintzberg and Kotter undoubtedly contributes to our knowledge of management. However, of more critical importance in trying to understand and find solutions to our current performance problems is singling out successful and effective managers to see what they really do in their day-to-day activities. The successful-versus-effective phase of our real managers study consisted of analyzing the existing data based on the frequencies of the observed activities of the real managers. We did not start off with any preconceived notions or hypotheses concerning the relationships between successful and effective managers. In fact, making such a distinction seemed like "splitting hairs" because the two words are so often used interchangeably. Nevertheless, we decided to define success operationally in terms of the speed of promotion within an organization. We determined a success index on a sample of the real managers in our study. It was calculated by dividing a manager's level in his or her organization by his or her tenure (length of service) there.[6] Thus, a manager at the fourth level of management, who has been with his or her organization for 5 years, would be rated more successful than a manager at the third level who has been there for 25 years. Obviously, there are some potential problems with such a measure of success, but for our large sample of managers this was an objective measure that could be obtained.

The definition and measurement of effectiveness is even more elusive. The vast literature on managerial effectiveness offered little agreement on criteria or measures. To overcome as many of the obstacles and disagreements as possible, we used a combined effectiveness index for a sample of the real managers in our study that represented the two major—and generally agreed upon—criteria of both management theory/research and practice: (1) getting the job done through high quantity and quality standards of performance, and (2) getting the job done through *people*, which requires their satisfaction and commitment.[7]

We obviously would have liked to use "hard measures" of effectiveness such as profits and quantity/quality of output or service, but again, because we were working with large samples of real managers from widely diverse jobs and organizations, this was not possible.

WHAT DO SUCCESSFUL REAL MANAGERS DO?

To answer the question of what successful real managers do, we conducted several types of analysis—statistical (using multiple regression techniques), simple descriptive comparisons (e.g., top third of managers as measured by the success index vs. bottom third), and relative strength of correlational relationships.[8] In all of these analyses, the importance that networking played in real manager success was very apparent. Of the four real manager activities, only networking had a statistically significant relationship with success. In the comparative analysis we found that the most successful (top third) real managers were doing considerably more networking and slightly more routine communication than their least successful (bottom third) counterparts. From the relative strength of relationship analysis we found that networking makes the biggest relative contribution to manager success and, importantly, human resource management activities makes the least relative contribution.

What does this mean? It means that in this study of real managers, using speed of promotion as the measure of success, it was found that successful real managers spent relatively more time and effort socializing, politicking, and interacting with outsiders than did their less-successful counterparts. Perhaps equally important, the successful real managers did not give much time or attention to the traditional management activities of planning, decision making, and controlling or to the human resource management activities of motivating/reinforcing, staffing, training/developing, and managing conflict. A representative example of this profile would be the following manager's prescription for success:

> I find that the way to get ahead around here is to be friendly with the right people, both inside and outside the firm. They get tired of always talking shop, so I find a common interest—with some it's sports, with others it's our kids—

and interact with them on that level. The other formal stuff around the office is important, but I really work at this informal side and have found it pays off when promotion time rolls around.

In other words, for this manager and for a significant number of those real managers we studied, networking seems to be the key to success.

WHAT DO EFFECTIVE REAL MANAGERS DO?

Once we answered the question of what successful managers do, we turned to the even more important question of what effective managers do. It should be emphasized once again that, in gathering our observational data for the study, we made no assumptions that the successful real managers were (or were not) the effective managers. Our participant observers were blind to the research questions and we had no hypothesis concerning the relationship between successful and effective managers.

We used the relative strength of correlational relationship between the real managers' effectiveness index and their directly observed day-to-day activities and found that communication and human resource management activities made by far the largest relative contribution to real managers' effectiveness and that traditional management and—especially—networking made by far the least relative contribution.[9]

These results mean that if effectiveness is defined as the perceived quantity and quality of the performance of a manager's unit and his or her subordinates' satisfaction and commitment, then the biggest relative contribution to real manager effectiveness comes from the human-oriented activities—communication and human resource management. A representative example of this effectiveness profile is found in the following manager's comments:

> Both how much and how well things get done around here, as well as keeping my people loyal and happy, has to do with keeping them informed and involved. If I make a change in procedure or the guys upstairs give us a new process or piece of equipment to work with, I get my people's input and give them the full story before I lay it on them. Then I make sure they have the proper training and give them feedback on how they are doing. When they screw up, I let them know it, but when they do a good job, I let them know about that, too.

This manager, like our study of real managers in general, found that the biggest contribution to effectiveness came from communicating and human resource management activities.

Equally important, however, was the finding that the least relative contribution to real managers' effectiveness came from the networking activity. This, of course, is in stark contrast to our results of the successful real manager analysis. Networking activity had by far the strongest relative relationship to success, but the weakest with effectiveness. On the other hand, human resource management activity had a strong relationship to effectiveness (second only to communication activity), but had the weakest relative relationship to success. In other words, the successful real managers do not do the same activities as the effective real managers (in fact, they do almost the opposite). These contrasting profiles may have significant implications for understanding the current performance problems facing American organizations. However, before we look at these implications and suggest some solutions, let's take a look at those real managers who are both successful *and* effective.

WHAT DO MANAGERS WHO ARE BOTH SUCCESSFUL AND EFFECTIVE DO?

The most obvious concluding question is what those who were found to be both successful and effective really do. This "combination" real manager, of course, is the ideal—and has been *assumed* to exist in American management over the years.

Since there was such a difference between successful and effective managers in our study, we naturally found relatively few (less than 10 percent of our sample) that were both among the top third of successful managers and the top third of effective managers. Not surprisingly, upon examining this special group, we found that their activities were very similar to real managers as a whole. They were not like either the successful or effective real managers. Rather, it seems that real managers who are both successful and effective use a fairly balanced approach in terms of their activities. In other words, real managers who can strike the delicate balance between all four managerial activities may be able to get ahead as well as get the job done.

Important is the fact that we found so few real managers that were both successful and effective. This supports our findings on the difference between successful and effective real managers, but limits any generalizations that can be made about successful and effective managers. It seems that more important in explaining our organizations' present performance problems, and what to do about them, are the implications of the wide disparity between successful and effective real managers.

IMPLICATIONS OF THE SUCCESSFUL VERSUS EFFECTIVE REAL MANAGERS FINDINGS

If, as our study indicates, there is indeed a difference between successful and effective real managers, what does it mean and what should we do about it? First of all, we need to pay more attention to formal reward systems to ensure that effective managers are promoted. Second, we must learn how effective managers do their day-to-day jobs.

The traditional assumption holds that promotions are based on performance. This is what the formal personnel policies say, this is what new management trainees are told and this is what every management textbook states *should* happen. On the other hand, more "hardened" (or perhaps more realistic) members and observers of *real* organizations (not textbook organizations or those featured in the latest best sellers or videotapes) have long suspected that social and political skills are the real key to getting ahead, to being *successful*. Our study lends support to the latter view.

The solution is obvious, but may be virtually impossible to implement, at least in the short run. Tying formal rewards—and especially promotions—to performance is a must if organizations are going to move ahead and become more productive. At a minimum, and most pragmatically in the short run, organizations must move to a performance-based appraisal system. Managers that are *effective* should be *promoted*. In the long run, organizations must develop cultural values that support and reward effective performance, not just successful socializing and politicking. This goes hand in hand with the current attention given to corporate culture and how to change it. An appropriate goal for cultural change in today's organizations might simply be to make effective managers successful.

Besides the implications for performance-based appraisals and organizational culture that came out of the findings of our study is a lesson that we can learn from the effective real managers themselves. This lesson is the importance they give and effort they devote to the human-oriented activities of communicating and human resource management. How human resources are managed—keeping them informed, communicating with them, paying attention to them, reinforcing them, resolving their conflicts, training/developing them—all contribute directly to managerial effectiveness.

The disparity our study found between successful and effective real managers has important implications for the performance problems facing today's organizations. While we must move ahead on all fronts in our search for solutions to these problems, we believe the activities basic to the effective real managers in our study—communication and human resource management—deserve special attention.

ENDNOTES

1. The full reference for the book is Fred Luthans, Richard M. Hodgetts, and Stuart Rosenkrantz, *Real managers* (Cambridge, Mass.: Ballinger, 1988). Some of the preliminary material from the real managers study was also included in the presidential speech given by Fred Luthans at the 1986 Academy of Management

meeting. Appreciation is extended to the co-authors of the book, Stu Rosenkrantz and Dick Hodgetts, to Diane Lee Lockwood on the first phase of the study, and to Avis Johnson, Hank Hennessey, and Lew Taylor on later phases. These individuals, especially Stu Rosenkrantz, contributed ideas and work on the backup for this article.

2. The two most widely recognized challenges to the traditional view of management have come from Henry Mintzberg, *The nature of managerial work* (New York: Harper & Row, 1973); and John Kotter, *The general managers* (New York: Free Press, 1982). In addition, two recent comprehensive reviews of the nature of managerial work can be found in the following references: Colin P. Hales, "What do managers do? A critical review of the evidence," *Journal of Management Studies* (1986) *23*, 88–115; and Stephen J. Carroll and Dennis J. Gillen, "Are the classical management functions useful in describing managerial work?" *Academy of Management Review* (1987) *12*, 38–51.

3. See Henry Mintzberg's article, "The manager's job: Folklore and fact," *Harvard Business Review* (July–August 1975) *53*, 49–61.

4. For those interested in the specific details of the background study, see Luthans, Hodgetts and Rosenkrantz (Endnote 1 above).

5. The source that details the derivation, training of observers, procedures, and reliability and validity analysis of the observation system used in the real managers study is Fred Luthans and Diane L. Lockwood's "Toward an observation system for measuring leader behavior in natural settings," in *Leaders and managers; International perspectives of managerial behavior and leadership*, ed. J. Hunt, D. Hosking, C. Schriesheim, and R. Stewart, (New York: Pergamon Press, 1984) 117–41.

6. For more background on the success portion of the study and the formula used to calculate the success index, see Fred Luthans, Stuart Rosenkrantz, and Harry Hennessey, "What do successful managers really do? An observational study of managerial activities," *Journal of Applied Behavioral Science* (1985) *21*, 255–70.

7. The questionnaire used to measure the real managers' unit quantity and quality of performance was drawn from Paul E. Mott's *The characteristics of effective organizations* (New York: Harper & Row, 1972). Subordinate satisfaction was measured by the Job Diagnostic Index found in P. C. Smith, L. M. Kendall, and C. L. Hulin's *The measurement of satisfaction in work and retirement* (Chicago: Rand-McNally, 1969). Subordinate commitment is measured by the questionnaire in Richard T. Mowday, L. W. Porter, and Richard M. Steers' *Employee-organizational linkage: The psychology of commitment, absenteeism, and turnover* (New York: Academic Press, 1982). These three standardized questionnaires are widely used research instruments with considerable psychometric backup and high reliability in the sample used in our study.

8. For the details of the multiple regression analysis and simple descriptive comparisons of successful versus unsuccessful managers, see Endnote 6 above. To determine the relative contribution the activities identified in Exhibit 1 made to success, we calculated the mean of the squared correlations (to approximate variance explained) between the observed activities of the real managers and the success index calculated for each target manager. These correlation squared

means were then rank ordered to obtain the relative strength of the managerial activities' contribution to success.

9. The calculation for the relative contribution the activities made to effectiveness was done as described for success in Endnote 8. The statistical and top third-bottom third comparison that was done in the success analysis was not done in the effectiveness analysis. For comparison of successful managers and effective managers, the relative strength of relationship was used; see *Real managers* (Endnote 1 above) for details.

Cultural Values and the CEO: Alluring Companions?*

Ellen F. Jackofsky
John W. Slocum, Jr.
Sara J. McQuaid

One hundred fifty years ago, William Procter and James Gamble delivered their handmade candles and soap by wheelbarrow. Their emphasis even then on innovative marketing, competitive strategies, and uncompromised honesty are hallmarks of the multinational Procter & Gamble Company today. IBM's Tom Watson, Jr., believed in constructive rebellion, claiming, "You can make a wild duck tame, but you can't make a tame duck wild again." Today the wild duck is a symbol of IBM's unwavering respect for creative nonconformists—that is, as long as they fly in the same direction. A founder of more recent vintage, Apple Computer's Steven Jobs is the quintessential rugged individualist whose fresh approach, willingness to take risks, and originality are evident in the company's name, as well as every product it makes.

These descriptions illustrate how a founder's values permeate a corporation and affect its direction. When leadership changes, the new leader often carries on traditions while bringing along a new set of values that are also gradually integrated into the company's culture. An awareness of different companies' values can facilitate a firm in its business transactions and help stave off conflict. The abundance of such corporate raiders as T. Boone Pickens and Carl Icahn, and the impact raiders have had on Phillips Oil, TWA, CBS, Gulf Oil, and other companies' human resources, are clear evidence of a clash of values.

The current emphasis on corporate culture both in academic journals and the popular press underscores the need for practicing managers to appreciate its influence. Yet little attention has been paid to the influence of *national* culture on corporations outside the United States. Viewing the world as "global village" requires that managers become more knowledge-

---

* From *The Academy of Management EXECUTIVE* (1988) *II*, no. 1, 39–49.

able about international business—yet many managers simply conduct international business as though they were dealing with fellow Americans. Culture shock, not to mention lost business, has often been the result. This article presents a framework for anticipating societal values that ultimately impact the behaviors of chief executive officers. Analyses of CEOs from five different cultures will illustrate how the framework can be used by managers involved in international business.

Although biographies, stories, and legends about company founders are abundant, surprisingly little consideration has been given to the importance of the current CEO to the firm. What has been written usually focuses on CEO succession or demographic statistics. Clearly, other variables—including personality characteristics, organizational design, environment, and business strategy—influence CEO behavior, but it is our contention that value systems necessarily come first and may actually determine these other factors and govern their impact on the CEO.

The potential for cultural differences among organizations is well known. The dominant values of a particular national culture are reflected in the constraints imposed on an organization by its environment (e.g., government, customers, and suppliers). In addition, the founders of an organization impose certain learned, cultural values on the organization from its beginning. Finally, organization members other than the founders behave in a manner consistent with the values of the "dominant elites" (the founders or current CEO).

Culture and value systems are closely related. Individuals learn such values as respect for privacy or freedom of speech from their society. Although individuals differ in how they translate these values into action, in general we can begin to understand the behavior of CEOs by understanding the values their cultures hold dear.

CULTURAL VALUES

A Dutch social scientist, Geert Hofstede, has proposed a paradigm to study the impact of societal culture on individuals.[1] To develop his classification system, he studied the values and beliefs of 116,000 IBM employees based in 40 countries around the world. He has been criticized for not including various types and sizes of firms. Critics point out, for example, that, because IBM has a culture of its own, it is difficult to discern whether a German CEO's behavior is characteristic of the German culture or of the culture of IBM. Yet his framework has held up surprisingly well when generalized to other contexts.

Hofstede's typology includes four cultural dimensions along which societies can be ordered: power distance, uncertainty avoidance, individualism-collectivism, and masculinity-femininity. Each dimension lies on a continuum ranging from low to high. The first, power distance (POW), refers

EXHIBIT 1   The Power Distance Dimension (POW)

Low (Austria, Israel, Denmark Sweden, Norway):	High (Philippines, Mexico, Venezuela, India, Brazil):
• Less centralization.	• Great centralization.
• Flatter organization pyramids.	• Tall organization pyramids.
• Fewer supervisory personnel.	• More supervisory personnel.
• Smaller wage differentials.	• Large wage differentials.
• Structure in which manual and clerical work are equally valued.	• Structure in which white-collar jobs are valued more than blue-collar jobs.

to the extent to which a culture encourages unequal distributions of power among people. In low power distance societies like the United States, Sweden, and Austria, more interaction takes place among people of different social classes and members of lower status can more easily move into higher-status positions. High power distance—or elitist—societies, such as the Philippines, Mexico, and India, force people of lower status to keep their distance from those of higher status, and hinder their advancement into the upper classes. Although an unequal distribution of power between managers and subordinates is the essence of organization, the processes by which these differences are manifested vary widely. In low power distance societies, managers and subordinates are highly interdependent and prefer a Theory Y style of leadership. Status differences between them are minimized. In high power distance societies, a more autocratic management style is not only more common; it is expected by subordinates, because it accentuates the differences in business relationships.

Hofstede's second dimension, uncertainty avoidance (UNC), refers to the extent to which people of a society feel threatened by unstable and ambiguous situations and try to avoid them. Hofstede contends that cultures use techniques to cope with uncertainty in much the same way organizations do. According to Hofstede, differences between companies operating in low and high uncertainty avoidance societies are quite pronounced. For example, in a low uncertainty avoidance society, organizations have fewer written rules and procedures, impose less structure on the activities of employees, encourage people to be generalists, rather than specialists, and attract managers with a propensity for risk taking. In high uncertainty avoidance societies, the opposite is true.

Individualism-collectivism (IND) is the third continuum in Hofstede's scheme. Individualist societies like Canada, New Zealand, Great Britain, and the United States are loosely knit social structures that expect people to

EXHIBIT 2   The Uncertainty Avoidance Dimension (UNC)

Low (Denmark, Sweden, Great Britain, United States, India):	High (Greece, Portugal, Japan, Peru, France):
• Less structuring of activities.	• More structuring of activities.
• Fewer written rules.	• More written rules.
• More generalists.	• More specialists.
• Variability.	• Standardization.
• Greater willingness to take risks.	• Less willingness to take risks.
• Less ritualistic behavior.	• More ritualistic behavior.

EXHIBIT 3   The Individualism-Collectivism Dimension (IND)

Low (Venezuela, Columbia, Taiwan, Mexico, Greece):	High (United States, Australia, Great Britain, Canada, the Netherlands):
• Organization as "family."	• Organization is more impersonal.
• Organization defends employee interests.	• Employees defend their own self-interests.
• Practices are based on loyalty, sense of duty, and group participation.	• Practices encourage individual initiative.

take care of themselves and their immediate families. People are masters of their own fate. Collectivist societies like Mexico, Turkey, and Japan are more tightly knit and emphasize in-group loyalty and dependence on others. People expect that the group (their clan, organization, or extended family) will protect and care for them. A strong spirit of cooperation characterizes collectivist societies; "every man for himself" might be a precept of the individualist society.

The level of individualism or collectivism in a culture will affect an organization's members in a variety of ways. Managers operating in cultures that place a high value on individualism frequently move from company to company. They believe that the corporation is not responsible for the welfare of its employees, they engage in networking activities, and they generally believe that individuals, as opposed to groups, make higher-quality decisions. In cultures that value collectivism, people are attracted to larger companies. They attach importance to structure, rather than to autonomy, they value team, rather than individual, achievement, and they consider the organization to be like a family.

The fourth dimension, masculinity-femininity (MAS), refers to the extent to which a culture values assertiveness, competitiveness, and the acquisition of tangible things as opposed to passivity, cooperation, and an emphasis on feelings, rather than goods. In masculine societies like Japan, Austria, and Italy, people believe that a job should provide opportunities for growth, challenge, recognition, and advancement. Feminine cultures like Sweden, Norway, and Portugal, accentuate good working conditions, security, the open expression of emotion, and the use of intuition, rather than hard facts, as a problem-solving mode. Masculine societies are characterized by fewer jobs for women and more industrial conflict. Work, as opposed to family, is the central life interest. Exhibits 1 through 4 summarize the main points on each continuum.

Because of the difficulties in representing the various combinations of these four value dimensions in a single diagram, Hofstede constructed "cultural maps" of the 40 countries, forming "country clusters." The clusters are summarized in Exhibit 5. This exhibit reveals, for example, that the United States (Cluster 7) is characterized by lower-than-average power distance and uncertainty avoidance values, higher-than-average masculinity values, and high individualism. In fact, the United States was the most individualistic culture in Hofstede's study. Some of today's American management heroes, such as Lee Iacocca of Chrysler, H. Ross Perot of EDS and GM, Sam Walton of Wal-Mart Stores, John Opel of IBM, Steven Jobs (formerly of Apple Computer), John Emery of Emery Air Freight, and John Byrne of GEICO Corporation reflect these values through their emphasis on the individual as problem solver (or wild duck) and their willingness to work side by side with their employees, take measurable risks, and provide employees with challenging and fulfilling work environments.

EXHIBIT 4   The Masculinity-Femininity Dimension (MAS)

Low (Sweden, Denmark, Thailand, Finland, Yugoslavia):

- Sex roles are minimized.
- Organizations do not interfere with people's private lives.
- More women in more qualified jobs.
- Soft, yielding, intuitive skills are rewarded.
- Social rewards are valued.

High (Japan, Austria, Venezuela, Italy, Mexico):

- Sex roles are clearly differentiated.
- Organizations may interfere to protect their interests.
- Fewer women are in qualified jobs.
- Aggression, competition, and justice are rewarded.
- Work is valued as a central life interest.

EXHIBIT 5   Country Clusters and Their Value Systems

Cluster 1:
  High power distance.
  High uncertainty avoidance.
  Medium to high individualism.
  Medium masculinity.
  —Belgium, France,* Argentina,
    Brazil, Spain.

Cluster 2:
  High power distance.
  High uncertainty avoidance.
  Low individualism.
  Low or high masculinity.
  —Columbia, Mexico, Venezuela
    (high masculinity).
  —Chile, Peru, Portugal (low
    masculinity).

Cluster 3:
  Medium power distance.
  High uncertainty avoidance.
  Medium individualism.
  High masculinity.
  —Japan.*

Cluster 4:
  High power distance.
  Low to medium uncertainty
    avoidance.
  Low individualism.
  Medium masculinity.
  —Pakistan, Taiwan,* Thailand,
    Hong Kong, India, Philippines,
    Singapore.

Cluster 5:
  High power distance.
  High uncertainty avoidance.
  Low individualism.
  Medium masculinity.
  —Greece, Turkey, Iran.

Cluster 6:
  Low power distance.
  Medium to high uncertainty
    avoidance.
  Medium individualism.
  Medium to high masculinity.
  —Austria, Israel, West Germany,*
    Switzerland.

Cluster 7:
  Low to medium power distance.
  Low to medium uncertainty
    avoidance.
  High individualism.
  High masculinity.
  —Australia, Canada, United States,
    New Zealand, Ireland, Great
    Britain.

Cluster 8:
  Low power distance.
  Low to medium uncertainty
    avoidance.
  Medium to high individualism.
  Low masculinity.
  —Denmark, Sweden,* Finland,
    Norway, the Netherlands.

* Countries examined in this article.

From Hofstede's *Culture's consequences: International differences in work-related values* (Beverly Hills, Calif: Sage Publications, 1980).

MANAGERIAL ROLES

To use Hofstede's four dimensions in analyzing how CEOs behave, it is helpful to delineate specifically what a CEO does. Henry Mintzberg proposed that managerial roles can be divided into three major groupings: interpersonal, informational, and decision-making.[2] The interpersonal role set, arising directly from a manager's formal authority, includes three roles: (1) the figurehead role, which involves representing the organization in formal ceremonies; (2) the liaison role, which involves interacting with those outside the organization who may affect its success; and (3) the leadership role, which involves directing and coordinating the activities of subordinates. These interpersonal roles provide a foundation for the informational set of roles.

Informational roles include (1) the monitor role, which involves scanning the environment for information the organization may need; (2) the disseminator role, which involves sharing information with and distributing it to subordinates; and (3) the spokesperson role, which involves transmitting information to others in an official capacity. This ability to gather and transmit information provides the manager with the resources needed to make decisions, the third role set.

Through these decision-making roles, the manager commits the organization to action. The manager is (1) an entrepreneur, when initiating innovative products or ideas; (2) a disturbance handler, when responding to threats and conflicts that are usually beyond the company's direct control; (3) a resource allocator, when deciding who will get which resources and how much they will get; and (4) a negotiator, when dealing with others to obtain competitive advantages for the firm.

Exhibit 6 illustrates the way these roles may encompass the complete managerial experience.

Mintzberg's intention was to classify the activities of managers by identifying closely related behaviors. The roles are essentially sets of interrelated behaviors characteristic of all managers. Individual managers will enact

---

EXHIBIT 6   Mintzberg's CEO Roles

Interpersonal roles:	Informational roles:	Decision-making roles:
1. Figurehead.	1. Monitor.	1. Entrepreneur.
2. Liaison.	2. Disseminator.	2. Disturbance handler.
3. Leadership.	3. Spokesperson.	3. Resource allocator.
		4. Negotiator.

From Henry Mintzberg's *The nature of managerial work* (New York: Harper & Row, 1973).

and interpret them differently, depending on their personalities, the structure of the firm, its strategy, the competitiveness of the environment and, we contend, societal values. Our major thesis is that societal values are reflected through the expression of CEO roles as classified in Mintzberg's scheme.

COLLECTING THE EVIDENCE

We collected anecdotal evidence of the potential relationships between cultural values and CEO roles, as available in published sources between 1977 and 1986. To do this, we conducted two computerized searches.[3] First we scanned articles printed in English during those years that contained the terms "CEO," "Director," or "President" in their titles. This search generated more than 150 articles, many of which were too brief to provide rich enough information.

Since it was neither practical nor possible to gather data from all 40 countries, we chose one country within those clusters whose value systems were the most pronounced; that is, countries ranked among the upper or lower 10 countries on each of the four value systems. For example, Japan ranks as the society highest in masculinity and fourth highest in uncertainty avoidance. Thus, we chose to study Japanese CEOs to show how those particular value systems were manifested through the CEOs' various roles. We eliminated from consideration those countries whose value systems are in a state of transition (like Finland, Iran, Italy, and South Africa), since their values are constantly changing. To establish validity, we also stipulated that data had to be available from at least two sources. We then consulted *Ward's Business Directory* to determine which companies from those countries had the highest sales in 1985.

Finally, we conducted another search on those top companies and their CEOs. We assumed that published data would be available about the CEOs of the largest companies but that information about smaller companies would be difficult to acquire, given our requirement that the articles be in English. Although the result is that our examples favor large corporations and the information about their CEOs reflects neither all of Hofstede's values nor all of Mintzberg's roles, we feel they provide a fascinating illustration of our general thesis. Sometimes, however, a CEO's behavior was inconsistent with the cultural values of his nation. This underscores the point that culture is not the only determinant of behavior.

Ultimately, we examined cultural values and CEO roles in five countries, each from a different cluster. Examples of countries from Clusters 2 and 5 were not available, given the limitations discussed above. We also chose not to analyze a country from Cluster 7. The latter contains the United States, from which examples are drawn throughout the article.

FRANCE: UNIONS, SOCIALISM, AND FALLS
FROM GRACE

France (Cluster 1) was classified by Hofstede as high in power distance and uncertainty avoidance, medium to high in individualism, and medium in masculinity. The literature search of CEOs in France uncovered information about Bernard Hanon of Renault and Jean-Paul Parayre of Peugeot SA. Both were CEOs of their respective companies and were ultimately forced out of their positions when the Socialist government imposed national austerity measures as a result of a general recession.

Hanon began his term as CEO of Renault in 1981, having been with the company for 26 years. He assumed the top position when Renault (along with the entire French auto industry) was faltering. During his regime, conditions at Renault worsened, as the company fell from first to sixth place in sales among European automobile companies. In 1985, he was unceremoniously dumped when France's Socialist government decreed that his leadership was not going to pull the company out of the mire.

Hanon's leadership of the state-owned company was tough-minded and autocratic (high POW), but as a decision maker he was extremely conservative (high UNC). For example, Hanon supported designing the new R-5 small car along the lines of the old model. The changes in the car would be mostly under the hood where the buyer could not see them. The subsequent launch of the Supercinq was unsuccessful because it was not sufficiently different in image or styling from the original. His decision to redesign conservatively the Supercinq exemplified the cultural value of uncertainty avoidance. In his decision-making role, his unwillingness to take a risk was also consistent with the uncertainty avoidance value. These decisions cost Renault billions of francs. Hanon did make an effort to show some spunk when he tried to reduce costs by cutting his labor force by 9,000 jobs, but he was thwarted by the government and France's strong unions.

When he was forced to resign as CEO of Renault, his supporters argued that he was made the scapegoat in a situation largely beyond his control. In an atmosphere of political unrest, he tried to perpetuate Renault's image as a model of industrial relations (high UNC) as well as take steps (including cutting staff) to reverse its downward trend. As "disturbance handler," then, he was less than effective. But his downfall was at least partially attributed to the power of France's labor unions, which opposed his attempt to reduce the number of jobs at Renault so drastically. In fact, strong labor unions, which thrive in a we-they atmosphere, epitomize the cultural value of high power distance.

While Bernard Hanon's administration was high in both power distance and uncertainty avoidance, Jean-Paul Parayre seemed to thrive on risk and uncertainty. When Parayre took over Peugeot in 1977, he was the first person to hold the CEO post without being a family member or long-time employee of the company. A respected civil servant before joining Peugeot, Parayre was the very image of the French technocrat: urbane and self-assured (high POW). His eventual demise as CEO was, like Hanon's, partially a result of his power struggle with the French labor unions (high POW), which came about when two of the acquisitions made under his influence (Citroën and Chrysler's European operations) suffered large financial setbacks. Yet during the Citroën takeover, Parayre boasted that he was responsible for decentralizing its management structure (low POW). The incongruity between the French value of high power distance and Parayre's decision to decentralize may have contributed to the difficulties in making the acquisition successful.

However, this low power distance decision seems to be an anomaly. One of the reasons for Parayre's rapid rise in government was his appetite for power. For instance, in his first job as a highway engineer, Parayre was asked to join the staff of a politician who later became France's prime minister. Because of his managerial acumen, he was later asked to join the Ministry for Industrial and Scientific Development, specifically to head the department overseeing the automotive sector of the economy. Parayre's extraordinary performance as spokesperson and negotiator so impressed the Peugeot family that they asked him to leave government service and join them. Only 37 when be began his automotive career, he rose quickly to the top. He was appointed CEO at the age of 40; to appoint a man so young to the key position of such a traditional company was unheard of. That he eventually fell from his perch was unfortunate and perhaps due more to the situation than to the man.

The administrations of Hanon and Parayre reflect the cultural values of France in many ways. Clear evidence of high power distance in French society is demonstrated by the active involvement of labor unions in both eventual departures. In their interpersonal roles, both men confirmed this high power distance value through their tough-minded and autocratic styles. High uncertainty avoidance was evident in Hanon's hesitation in introducing the changed automotive styling. However, while Hanon's personal style was very much in line with the French cultural profile, Parayre's was not. From accounts of his boldness and risk-taking nature, his behavior was probably influenced more by personality characteristics than by cultural values. One could argue that those instances in which his personality clashed with the French value system were the very ones that contributed to his demise.

GERMANY: DON'T "MALIBU" THE BEETLE

The Federal Republic of Germany was our chosen country from Cluster 6. This cluster has a value system of low power distance, medium to high uncertainty avoidance, medium individualism, and high masculinity. Carl H. Hahn of Volkswagen, Karlheinz Kaske of Siemens, and Heinz Nixdorf of Nixdorf Computer, A. G., are our CEO examples.

According to VW's determined boss, Carl Hahn, the company's competitive edge comes from its strong German engineering tradition. Under Hahn's leadership, VW plans to stick to its practice of changing styling only when needed (high UNC). He believes that VW's history of producing cars with high quality, ease of handling, and longevity is its major selling point. Hahn attributed VW's $144 million loss in the United States in 1983 to "Malibuing" the Beetle. Others in the company attributed the loss to Hahn's "screwing around with the Mona Lisa"—a good example of how CEO behavior that contradicts the German cultural value of high uncertainty avoidance was seen as inappropriate.

To ensure its competitive edge, VW invested more than $194 million to build one of the world's most highly automated final assembly plants in Wolfsburg. The plant was designed according to tight engineering specifications. There are few wage differentials between hierarchical levels (low POW).

To encourage VW's growth internationally, Hahn's strategy, as resource allocator, was to divisionalize the company (to include the upscale Audi division) so that it would not be overly dependent on any one car and could withstand sudden currency changes (high UNC).

When VW decided to manufacture its "Golf" car in the United States, it purchased and refurbished a Chrysler plant in Westmoreland, Pennsylvania. VW chose this strategy because it feared currency devaluations and possible U.S. protectionist policies. Although the plant was losing money, Hahn announced that the company would phase out production at parts plants in other U.S. locations and centralize all U.S. operations in the Westmoreland plant. Another decision—to build cars in Spain—hinged on whether or not the Spanish-built cars could be manufactured to the rigorous German quality standards (high MAS and high UNC). A master negotiator, Hahn has plans to expand and modernize production facilities as far afield as China and the Soviet Union (high MAS).

Siemens, A. G., is West Germany's second-largest company and the world's fifth-largest high-tech electrical and electronic equipment manufacturer. Siemen's president, Karlheinz Kaske, runs the company with typical German engineering thoroughness and a pedantic approach to management. Even though the company is diversified, with six relatively autonomous product groups, Kaske has developed a highly centralized organization (high POW). The company produces a myriad of products, including microcomputers, telecommunications equipment, industrial and office systems, and medical electronics, yet many of its products are low volume, and sales outside Germany are slow. Identifying and weeding out marginal performers while concentrating on the most salable products are two of Kaske's priorities. To compete in the office-automation market, Kaske has merged his telecommunications and computer divisions. Yet, according to outsiders, the company's major problem is its stubborn conservatism, which borders on inflexibility, coupled with a reluctance to take risks (high UNC). In addition, Kaske discourages his managers from making major decisions or questioning his judgment (high POW). Kaske, trained as a physicist, tenaciously clings to old managerial practices. The company's inability to translate technology into salable products reflects its obsession with perfection and product overdesign (high UNC). For example, in the computer-aided tomography (CAT scanner) market dominated by GE, Siemens took so long to get a prototype to production, the product arrived late in the marketplace. Siemens was also a pioneer in the ultrasonic imaging market, but lost its edge when it tried to engineer the product to meet every possible exigency (high UNC). Although Siemens is better off today than it was five years ago, it is still a bureaucratic monster that squanders more capital than it invests. Kaske's leadership style (high POW) is in direct opposition to the German value system, which again may be a partial explanation for some of his difficulties.

On the other hand, Heinz Nixdorf, founder of Nixdorf Computer, is more in tune with the German low power distance value. Nixdorf's leadership style is reflected in the belief that, if all employees are treated equally (with no status distinctions between managers and workers), they bring much needed stability to the company, which makes for good relationships with customers. He hates status symbols, so everyone has the same office furniture (low POW). He also believes that one of the best features of German industry is its ability to train workers (high UNC). Every year he hires about 500 new apprentices for a three-year training program, which costs approximately $20,000 per apprentice. This indicates that in his resource allocation role he believes his employees are his most important asset. Most of Nixdorf's employees—even trainees—work a 38.5 hour week and get paid to spend two of those hours in the company sports center. Only 9 percent of the more than 20,000 employees are unionized, which may reflect the country's low rating on power distance.

Customers are equally important. Nixdorf's strategy is to provide tailor-made problem-solving packages for clients in the high-tech market through state-of-the-art telecommunications equipment and point-of-sale terminals. In the next four years, he predicts the company will double its sales and eventually become Europe's leading computer company, employing over 70,000 people. To accomplish these goals, he will have to sell some equity, but he has little intention of relinquishing control of the company (high UNC). Investors will be able to buy only nonvoting shares.

Several commonalities in these three CEO's behaviors reflect German values. First, they each have an unambiguous leadership style. Extensive rules and regulations have been developed to cope with any exigency (high

UNC). Second, the managers who report to them have well-defined job responsibilities and are held accountable for financial results. Success is determined by career advancement, challenging jobs, and opportunities for recognition as a leader in the field (high MAS). Third, the German tradition of decision making based on demonstrable facts is manifested in their reliance on engineering principles and their search for the "one best way." Finally, their emphasis on stable employment, educational training, and the firm's performance standards directly reflects German society. The only apparent anomaly was Kaske's relatively high power distance as manifested in his centralization policies and autocratic leadership; as in the case of France's Parayre, Kaske may be influenced by other factors that outweigh cultural values.

SWEDEN: FROM GROCERIES TO ONE-ARMED ROBOTS

We chose Sweden to represent Hofstede's eighth cluster. The nation scores at the extremes of each of the four value dimensions: high in individualism, and low in power distance, uncertainty avoidance, and masculinity (it was the lowest for masculinity of the 40 countries in Hofstede's sample). Pehr Gyllenhammar of Volvo and Percy Barnevik of ASEA, a manufacturer of electrical equipment, exemplify these values.

In his leadership role, Pehr Gyllenhammar is highly individualistic. His response to a 1983 board rejection of his proposal to sell Volvo stock in the United States directly demonstrates this: he replaced three of the outside directors with Volvo executives (high IND). His aggressiveness is also apparent in his emphatic "No!" when asked whether he was discouraged after his company suffered large losses because of the oil market decline; he doesn't believe in short-term thinking.

This attitude has been well received in Sweden, a country of fairly high individualism and low uncertainty avoidance. Gyllenhammar led Volvo through a steady period of growth through automobile sales and, at the same time, directed the company into diverse markets, ranging from groceries to high tech. Although the car business is the cash cow responsible for 90 percent of profits, he considers the market peaked. The real profits, he believes, will come from diversification (low UNC). His latest efforts have been in the biotechnology industry, although it is there that Gyllenhammar suffered one of his greatest setbacks. A month after he negotiated a $528 million joint venture with Fermenta, a Swedish biotech and chemical company, the CEO of that company resigned in disgrace. Volvo cancelled its plans with that company, and was obligated to pay $35 million of debt to the former CEO because of an outside agreement. Gyllenhammar continued to try to erase this blow to his prestige through other biotech acquisitions.

Despite Gyllenhammar's forcefulness, he maintains a people-oriented leadership style (low MAS). His experiments, designed to eliminate the boredom of assembly line work, are known worldwide, although the resulting reduction in efficiency has created cost problems. His job enrichment program at Volvo's Kalmar plant in the early 1970s resulted in the flattening of the organization's hierarchy, the reduction of status differences between levels of employees, and increased decision making at lower levels within the company. These achievements are consistent with the Swedish values of low power distance and low masculinity. Gyllenhammar's popularity seems to stem more from the company's generous labor settlements than from its increasing profits, an indication of the country's low masculinity value. He enjoys celebrity status and regularly appears on television (fulfilling his figurehead and spokesperson roles), and some reporters have suggested that he is gathering support to run for political office. In general, Gyllenhammar conforms well to Swedish cultural values of individualism, risk-taking inclination, and concern for others. As evidence of his instinct for survival and willingness to take risks, he has been dubbed the "emperor" by certain Volvo insiders.

The other Swedish CEO we studied was Percy Barnevik of ASEA, which recently received international attention for its leadership role in the field of robotics. In 1982, when the company inaugurated its new plant in Belgium, the ribbon-cutting ceremony was performed by a one-armed robot. When the robot reached for a bouquet of flowers to present to the official, it knocked over the vase. Barnevik countered that such an incident will never happen again because now his robots can "see" by laser!

Prior to the high-tech era in ASEA's history, the company was a conservative manufacturer of electrical equipment. With Barnevik as CEO, a new strategy has emerged that emphasizes change (low UNC) and aggressiveness (high IND). Strategically, Barnevik has ruthlessly streamlined the company's Swedish holdings, getting rid of several unprofitable businesses while making others autonomous profit centers. A mere six weeks after becoming CEO, he changed the structure of the company, converting it from a directionless, top-heavy conglomerate into 40 separate profit centers. He also decentralized responsibility for accounting and profits (low POW).

Barnevik made another integrative and progressive move for ASEA into the high-tech specialty area of long-distance power transmission of high voltage direct current (HVDC). As a result of its aggressive policy in this area, ASEA has acquired 53 percent of the world's market for HVDC technology (high IND). Because of its use in long-distance cables, industry specialists predict rapid growth for HVDC, which now accounts for only 2 percent of power line sales worldwide.

Available evidence concerning CEO roles in Sweden is consistent with Hofstede's conclusions about Sweden's individualism and uncertainty avoidance. The strategies of both Gyllenhammar of Volvo and Barnevik of ASEA reflect individual initiative (high IND) and high risk taking (low UNC). Although there was no evidence indicating the masculinity value in Barnevik's case, it is clear that Gyllenhammar manages with a people-oriented style (low MAS). Barnevik's decentralization policy is evidence of low power distance. Gyllenhammar built his reputation largely through his efforts in job enrichment, a program also characterized by low power distance.

Taiwan: The Billionaire Buddhist

Taiwan represents Cluster 4. In general, Cluster 4 countries have high power distance, low to medium uncertainty avoidance, medium masculinity, and low individualism. Since Taiwan has particularly low individualism, we will focus on that value system.

Narratives, while limited, were found for Y. C. Wang, founder of Formosa Plastics Group, who is Taiwan's leading industrialist and one of the world's wealthiest men. He made the major share of his fortune producing polyvinyl chloride (a relatively old type of plastic). Most of it is exported.

In keeping with traditional Buddhist culture, Wang and his family are a close, collective unit. This close unit extends beyond the immediate family and into the business realm. Wang and his family's share of his three largest companies is worth about $550 million (other holdings place him well into the billionaire category) but he places a high value on traditionalism. He is proud of his humble beginnings and tells stories about his meager childhood. He is orderly, hard working, and gives unrelenting attention to detail, and expects his executives and production workers alike to emulate his example of hard work and long hours. Wang has never lost his entrepreneurial spirit and makes a point of knowing every detail of his operations, "breathing the same trench air that his troops breathe." This attitude is the very essence of low individualism: the CEO and his organization are highly dependent on one another.

Taiwan's people espouse the *jen* philosophy. While the United States perception is that personality is separate from society and culture, the *jen* philosophy states that to describe a person, one must describe not only the personality but the intimate social and cultural environment that makes his or her existence meaningful. Wang is devoted to this philosophy. In fact, in a 1983 speech at the Wharton School, he expressed concern over the "moral decadence" of the West. He said, "It is most alarming that one tends to relax his determination and hardworking habit after one has reached a certain degree of comfort in life."

Wang's business strategy centers on vertical integration. He is expanding his companies methodically, acquiring businesses that extend from those that already exist. For example, the initial chemical the company produced, polyvinyl chloride, is used to produce PVC pipe, and Wang's group is now the world's largest producer and processor of PVC.

Taiwan's culture is characterized by a collective identity (low IND) where individual views are sublimated to those of the collective whole.

Wang's emphasis on tradition, family, company, and his organizational conglomerate is entirely consistent with this *jen* philosophy.

Japan: Patience and Perseverance

Japan stands alone in Cluster 3. Its values include medium power distance and individualism, and high uncertainty avoidance and masculinity. It was, in fact, the most masculine country of those surveyed. The fascination with Japan regarding its extraordinary ascent in the world economy since World War II has produced a wealth of literature, including considerable information about Japanese CEOs. One study compared 229 American and 291 Japanese CEOs on a variety of managerial issues, including the management of their environments, production technology, management strategy, and organization structure. Interviews are also available with a wide variety of CEOs, including Ichiro Isoda of Sumitomo Bank, Takashi Ishihara of Nissan, and Yoshihiro Inayama of Nippon Steel. We will use these three CEOs as primary examples; but, instead of highlighting them individually, we have summarized their behaviors and considered them in light of the Japanese cultural values of high uncertainty avoidance and masculinity.

Japanese CEOs are infinitely patient, choosing to spend resources on strategic, rather than tactical, planning. In the decision-making roles, their attitude is that it is better to take no action at all than to risk failure (high UNC). In fact, Japanese CEOs would rather increase market share than emphasize short-term profits. For example, Ishihara has said that the accumulation of resources over the long term was what enabled Nissan to become a major competitor in the automobile industry.

The Japanese culture rewards perseverance. Many products have 12-to-20-year life cycles. Of course, new product ratios, and the ability to adapt to changes in the environment, are competitive realities. As a result, Japanese CEOs collect a large amount of information, which is then used in group decision making. Since information is widely dispersed in large Japanese companies, the role of the CEO as disseminator of information, both formally and informally, is believed necessary for quality decisions. While decision making by consensus and promotion by seniority permit CEOs to know their business intimately, they can also lead to inflexibility and a lack of imagination. This has sometimes hindered Japanese companies operating in unstable environments, such as securities markets.

Lifetime commitment is also highly valued in Japan (high UNC). Most CEOs have spent their entire working lives with the same company (Ishihara and Inayama have each been with their companies for about 50 years, and Isoda has been with Sumitomo Bank for 35 years). They are dependent on their companies not only for their working lives but for their leisure pursuits as well (high MAS). Because of their long tenure, most CEOs have worked in a variety of capacities for their companies, and work becomes a central life interest. This commitment to work reinforces organizational goals, values, and the ability to think multidimensionally.

In his leadership role, Isoda believes in giving his managers latitude while requiring strict accountability (high MAS). For example, when he assumed the CEO position in 1974, the bank was in serious financial trouble. One of its major customers, Ataka (a large trading company), was on the brink of bankruptcy. Isoda went to another large trading company and helped arrange a friendly merger, but had to absorb a $1 billion loss. Similarly, when Toyo Kogyo (manufacturer of the Mazda) experienced a major sales slump in the 1970s, Isoda sent in senior managers from his bank to occupy key managerial positions until a technical tie-up with Ford Motor Company could be reached. Isoda's decisions in these two instances were aided by members of his executive council. He has said he requires his executive council to know more about the company than he does. He ensures that they do through relentless questioning about all aspects of the bank's functioning (high UNC).

Japanese CEO behaviors reflect both high masculinity and high uncertainty avoidance. Masculinity is reflected in their great interest in work and emphasis on excelling, the establishment of clear lines of authority and responsibility, decisions supported by a great deal of information, and the intrusion of the company into the personal lives of employees. Uncertainty avoidance is evident through the use of groups in making strategic decisions, the discouraging of conflict and competition within companies, and through rites and rituals.

WHAT DOES IT ALL MEAN?

Through these brief vignettes, we have tried to analyze the relationships between cultural values and selected CEO roles. Because of the exploratory nature of this approach and the dearth of information on CEOs, our conclusions remain tentative. It was often difficult to separate the behavior of the CEO from the behavior of the firm, although clearly the two are not identical. Mintzberg's work remains one of the few available paradigms with which to study CEO behaviors, and yet very little systematic research has actually focused on the CEO. The information that does exist focuses on outcomes of CEO behaviors (such as return on investment, return on equity, and market share), rather than on behavioral processes of CEOs (such as networking, agenda setting, and leadership style).

University of Southern California management professor Warren Bennis has said that "the CEO is the single most important factor in a company's stock price." Although to some this may be a classic overstatement, the fact remains that the "CEO factor" must be reckoned with when one is dealing with companies, especially those of other cultures.[4] Yet figuring out the "CEO factor" is such an imprecise process, some analysts dismiss it altogether as too philosophical. Too many intangibles, such as personality, presence, ability to communicate and inspire loyalty, and even physical appearance factor into the equation. Perhaps these intangibles are the reason why we see so little comparative research on CEOs.

Despite the imprecision and inevitable inconsistencies between CEO roles and cultural values, we believe that each culture embodies distinctive attributes and that these are manifested in the behavior of CEOs. We recognize that other factors may be as important as culture in determining the behaviors of specific individuals; our intent was simply to highlight the cultural values as one of the most important forces.

To the extent that behaviors reflect values held by members of a society, an understanding of these values can aid our interpretation of critical CEO actions. For example, some have suggested that the decade of the 1990s in the United States will be one of increasingly transient employment. In response to this situation, Paul Hirsch forecasts that American CEOs will act as free agents.[5] Since the United States is a society high in individualism and low in uncertainty avoidance, free-agency status for CEOs is consistent with the society's cultural values.

National cultural values could affect our understanding of alternative forms of organizing, a major decision-making role performed by CEOs. The rise of *Chaebols* (conglomerates that are owned and managed by families) in Korea reflects values indigenous to that culture.[6] The Korean value of strong family involvement is reflected in the large percentage of blood relatives who have top-management positions in *Chaebols* of family origin. This is in contrast to the Japanese, whose conglomerates, though much like the Korean *Chaebols*, assign elites who are not necessarily blood relatives to departments of importance. A strong sense of loyalty to and dependence on those in authority is reflected in the close relationship between the *Chaebols* and government. This relationship is not actually a partnership; it is characterized by the government's using a firm hand to set the policies that management follows.

Our discussion may also provide insight into the kinds and types of information multinational corporations need for strategic planning. Strategic plans formulated at headquarters may not be well understood by managers in different countries because these managers interpret information through different perceptual filters. Headquarters' concerns for information systems designed to foster cooperation and integration may not be consistent with the national values of the CEO in the local firms. Important information may be ignored at the local level or not transmitted to headquarters simply because CEOs at the local level make different assumptions based on their values.

Finally, one of the CEO's major decision-making roles involves the art of negotiation.[7] An important aspect of negotiating is understanding how issues are interpreted. Since effective negotiators have the ability to see the world through the eyes of other parties, they must deal with foreign companies in a way that is congruent with the cultural values of the country. To plunge headlong into a country with different value systems without proper insight into those differences can result in strategic blunders. One way to ease the tensions created by such potentially explosive conditions is to understand and adjust for the impact of cultural values on chief executive officers.

ENDNOTES

Support for this project was granted from the Bureau of Business Research, Edwin L. Cox School of Business, Southern Methodist University, Dallas, Texas. The authors would like to acknowledge the constructive comments offered by Nancy Adler, Don Hambrick, Mike Harvey, Don Hellriegel, Geert Hofstede, and Michael Wooton on earlier drafts of this paper.

1. Geert Hofstede's work is documented in his book *Culture's consequences: International differences in work-related values* (Beverly Hills, Calif.: Sage Publications, 1980). For briefer treatments of his study, see the following by Hofstede: "Motivation, leadership, and organization: Do American theories apply abroad?" *Organizational Dynamics* (Summer 1980) 8, 42–63; "Dimensions of national cultures in fifty countries and three regions," in J. Deregowski, D. Dzivrawiec, and R. Anuis, eds., *Explications in cross-cultural psychology* (Liste, Netherlands: Suets & Zeitlinger, 1983), 335–55; and "The cultural relativity of the quality of life concept," *Academy of Management Review* (1984) 9, 389–98.

2. Henry Mintzberg, *The nature of managerial work* (New York: Harper & Row, 1973). See also, Mintzberg's The *structuring of organizations* (Englewood Cliffs, N.J.): Prentice-Hall, 1979); "Power and organization life cycles," *Academy of Management Review* (1984) 9, 207–25; and Henry Mintzberg and J. Waters, "Tracking strategy in an entrepreneurial firm," *Academy of Management Journal* (1982) 25, 465–99.

3. For a detailed description of the methodology, see Ellen F. Jackofsky and John W. Slocum, Jr.," CEO roles across cultures," in Donald Hambrick, ed., *Executive effects: Concepts and methods for the study of top managers* (Greenwich, Conn.: JAI Press, in press.).

4. The "CEO factor" is discussed in S. Jansson's "How CEOs affect their Companies' P/E multiples," *Institutional Investor* (December 1984), 99–104.

5. Paul Hirsch, *Pack your own parachute* (Reading, Mass.: Addison-Wesley, 1987).

6. S. Yoo and S. M. Lee, "Management style and practice of Korean Chaebols," *California Management Review* (Summer 1987), 95–109.

7. S. Schneider, "Strategy formulation: The impact of national culture," unpublished working paper, INSEAD, 1987.

30

Management and Leadership*

John P. Kotter

The word *leadership* is used in two very different ways in everyday conversation. Sometimes it refers to a process that helps direct and mobilize people and/or their ideas; we say, for example, that Fred is providing leadership on the such and such project. At other times it refers to a group of people in formal positions where leadership, in the first sense of the word, is expected; we say that the leadership of the firm is made up of 10 people, including George, Alice, and so on.

In this book, I will use the word almost exclusively in the first sense. The second usage contributes greatly to the confusion surrounding this subject, because it subtly suggests that everyone in a leadership position actually provides leadership.[1] This is obviously not true; some such people lead well, some lead poorly, and some do not lead at all. Since most of the people who are in positions of leadership today are called managers, the second usage also suggests that leadership and management are the same thing, or at least closely related. They are not.

Leadership is an ageless topic. That which we call management is largely the product of the last 100 years,[2] a response to one of the most significant developments of the twentieth century: the emergence of large numbers of complex organizations.[3] Modern management was invented, in a sense, to help the new railroads, steel mills, and auto companies achieve what legendary entrepreneurs created them for. Without such management, these complex enterprises tended to become chaotic in ways that threatened their very existence. Good management brought a degree of order and consistency to key dimensions, like the quality and profitability of products.

In the past century, literally thousands of managers, consultants, and management educators have developed and refined the processes which make up the core of modern management. These processes, summarized briefly, involve:[4]

---

* From John P. Kotter, *A force for change: How leadership differs from management* (New York: Free Press, 1990), 3–18.

1. Planning and budgeting—setting targets or goals for the future, typically for the next month or year; establishing detailed steps for achieving those targets, steps that might include timetables and guidelines; and then allocating resources to accomplish those plans.

2. Organizing and staffing—establishing an organizational structure and set of jobs for accomplishing plan requirements, staffing the jobs with qualified individuals, communicating the plan to those people, delegating responsibility for carrying out the plan, and establishing systems to monitor implementation.

3. Controlling and problem solving—monitoring results versus plan in some detail, both formally and informally, by means of reports, meetings, etc.; identifying deviations, which are usually called "problems"; and then planning and organizing to solve the problems.

These processes produce a degree of consistency and order. Unfortunately, as we have witnessed all too frequently in the last half century, they can produce order on dimensions as meaningless as the size of the typeface on executive memoranda. But that was never the intent of the pioneers who invented modern management. They were trying to produce consistent results on key dimensions expected by customers, stockholders, employees, and other organizational constituencies, despite the complexity caused by large size, modern technologies, and geographic dispersion. They created management to help keep a complex organization on time and on budget. That has been, and still is, its primary function.[5]

Leadership is very different. It does not produce consistency and order, as the word itself implies; it produces movement. Throughout the ages, individuals who have been seen as leaders have created change, sometimes for the better and sometimes not.[6,7] They have done so in a variety of ways, though their actions often seem to boil down to establishing where a group of people should go, getting them lined up in that direction and committed to movement, and then energizing them to overcome the inevitable obstacles they will encounter along the way.

What constitutes good leadership has been a subject of debate for centuries. In general, we usually label leadership "good" or "effective" when it moves people to a place in which both they and those who depend upon them are genuinely better off, and when it does so without trampling on the rights of others.[8] The function implicit in this belief is *constructive or adaptive change.*

Leadership within a complex organization achieves this function through three subprocesses which, as we will see in further detail later on in this book, can briefly be described as such:[9] .

1. Establishing direction—developing a vision of the future, often the dis-

tant future, along with strategies for producing the changes needed to achieve that vision.

2. Aligning people—communicating the direction to those whose cooperation may be needed so as to create coalitions that understand the vision and that are committed to its achievement.

3. Motivating and inspiring—keeping people moving in the right direction despite major political, bureaucratic, and resource barriers to change by appealing to very basic, but often untapped, human needs, values, and emotions.

Exhibit 1 compares these summaries of both management and leadership within complex organizations.[10]

Management and leadership, so defined, are clearly in some ways similar. They both involve deciding what needs to be done, creating networks of people and relationships that can accomplish an agenda, and then trying to ensure that those people actually get the job done. They are both, in this sense, complete action systems; neither is simply one aspect of the other. People who think of management as being only the implementation part of leadership ignore the fact that leadership has its own implementation processes: aligning people to new directions and then inspiring them to make it happen. Similarly, people who think of leadership as only part of the implementation aspect of management (the motivational part) ignore the direction-setting aspect of leadership.

But despite some similarities, differences exist which make management and leadership very distinct. The planning and budgeting processes of management tend to focus on time frames ranging from a few months to a few years, on details, on eliminating risks, and on instrumental rationality. By contrast, as shown in the chapters that follow, that part of the leadership process which establishes a direction often focuses on longer time frames, the big picture, strategies that take calculated risks, and people's values. In a similar way, organizing and staffing tend to focus on specialization, getting the right person into or trained for the right job, and compliance; while aligning people tends to focus on integration, getting the whole group lined up in the right direction, and commitment. Controlling and problem solving usually focus on containment, control, and predictability; while motivating and inspiring focus on empowerment, expansion, and creating that occasional surprise that energizes people.

But even more fundamentally, leadership and management differ in terms of their primary function. The first can produce useful change, the second can create orderly results which keep something working efficiently. This does not mean that management is never associated with change; in tandem with effective leadership, it can help produce a more orderly change process. Nor does this mean that leadership is never associated with order;

EXHIBIT 1   Comparing Management and Leadership

	Management	Leadership
Creating an agenda	Planning and budgeting—establishing detailed steps and timetables for achieving needed results, and then allocating the resources necessary to make that happen.	Establishing direction—developing a vision of the future, often the distant future, and strategies for producing the changes needed to achieve that vision.
Developing a human network for achieving the agenda	Organizing and staffing—establishing some structure for accomplishing plan requirements, staffing that structure with individuals, delegating responsibility and authority for carrying out the plan, providing policies and procedures to help guide people, and creating methods or systems to monitor implementation.	Aligning people—communicating the direction by words and deeds to all those whose cooperation may be needed so as to influence the creation of teams and coalitions that understand the vision and strategies, and accept their validity.
Execution	Controlling and problem solving—monitoring results vs. plan in some detail, identifying deviations, and then planning and organizing to solve these problems.	Motivating and inspiring—energizing people to overcome major political, bureaucratic, and resource barriers to change by satisfying very basic, but often unfulfilled, human needs.
Outcomes	Produces a degree of predictability and order, and has the potential of consistently producing key results expected by various stakeholders (e.g., for customers, always being on time; for stockholders, being on budget).	Produces change, often to a dramatic degree, and has the potential of producing extremely useful change (e.g., new products that customers want, new approaches to labor relations that help make a firm more competitive).

to the contrary, in tandem with effective management, an effective leadership process can help produce the changes necessary to bring a chaotic situation under control. But leadership by itself never keeps an operation on time and on budget year after year. And management by itself never creates significant useful change.

Taken together, all of these differences in function and form create the potential for conflict. Strong leadership, for example, can disrupt an orderly planning system and undermine the management hierarchy, while strong management can discourage the risk taking and enthusiasm needed for leadership. Examples of such conflict have been reported many times over the years, usually between individuals who personify only one of the two sets of processes: "pure managers" fighting it out with "pure leaders."[11]

But despite this potential for conflict, the only logical conclusion one can draw from an analysis of the processes summarized in Exhibit 1 is that they are both needed if organizations are to prosper. To be successful, organizations not only must consistently meet their current commitments to customers, stockholders, employees, and others, they must also identify and adapt to the changing needs of these key constituencies over time. To do so, they must not only plan, budget, organize, staff, control, and solve problems in a competent, systematic, and rational manner so as to achieve the results expected on a daily basis, they also must establish, and reestablish, when necessary, an appropriate direction for the future, align people to it, and motivate employees to create change even when painful sacrifices are required.

Indeed, any other combination than strong management and strong leadership has the potential for producing highly unsatisfactory results. When both are weak or nonexistent, it is like a rudderless ship with a hole in the hull. But adding just one of the two does not necessarily make the situation much better. Strong management without much leadership can turn bureaucratic and stifling, producing order for order's sake. Strong leadership without much management can become messianic and cult-like, producing change for change's sake—even if movement is in a totally insane direction. The latter is more often found in political movements than in corporations,[12] although it does occur sometimes in relatively small entrepreneurial businesses.[13] The former, however, is all too often seen in corporations today, especially in large and mature ones.

With more than enough management but insufficient leadership, one would logically expect to see the following: (1) a strong emphasis on shorter time frames, details, and eliminating risks, with relatively little focus on the long term, the big picture, and strategies that take calculated risks; (2) a strong focus on specialization, fitting people to jobs, and compliance to rules, without much focus on integration, alignment, and commitment; (3) a strong focus on containment, control, and predictability, with insufficient emphasis on expansion, empowerment, and inspiration. Taken together, it is logical to expect this to produce a firm that is somewhat rigid, not very innovative, and thus incapable of dealing with important changes in its market, competitive, or technological environment. Under these circumstances, one would predict that performance would deteriorate over time, although slowly if the firm is large and has a strong market position. Customers would be served less well because innovative products and lower prices from innovative manufacturing would be rare. As performance sinks, the cash squeeze would logically be felt more by investors who get meager or no returns and by employees who eventually are forced to make more sacrifices, including the ultimate sacrifice of their jobs.

This scenario should sound familiar to nearly everyone. Since 1970, literally hundreds of firms have had experiences that are consistent with it. No one can measure the overall impact of all this. But in the United States this problem has surely contributed to the fact that real wages were basically flat from 1973 to 1989, that stock prices when adjusted for inflation were less in late 1988 than in 1969, and that consumers have turned increasingly to less expensive or innovative foreign goods, leaving the country with a crippling trade deficit. And recent evidence suggests that the problem is still a long way from solved.

During 1988, senior executives in a dozen successful U.S. corporations were asked to rate all the people in their managerial hierarchies on the dimensions of both leadership and management.[14] The scale they were given ranged from "weak" to "strong", and their responses were grouped into four categories: people who are weak at providing leadership but strong at management, those who are strong at leadership but not at management, those who are relatively strong at both, and those who do not do either well. The executives were then asked if the specific mix of talent their companies had in each of these four categories was what they needed to prosper over the next 5 to 10 years. They could respond: we have about what we need; we have too few people in this category; or we have too many people like this. A summary of their responses is shown in Exhibit 2.

Half of those polled reported having too many people who provide little if any management or leadership. Executives in professional service busi-

EXHIBIT 2   How Executives in a Dozen Successful U.S. Firms Rate the People in Their Managerial Hierarchies

		Weak	Strong
Leadership	Strong	Nearly half say they have "too few"* people like this	Virtually all report "too few" people in this quadrant
	Weak	Half say they have "too many" people like this	Nearly two-thirds report "too many" people here
		Weak	**Strong**
		Management	

* Respondents were given three choices: (1) too few, (2) too many, (3) about right. The category having the largest number of responses is shown in the chart.

nesses, such as investment banking and consulting, were particularly likely to say this. The other half reported having very few people in this category, which, as one would expect, they said was just fine.

Nearly half reported having too few people who provide strong leadership but weak management. However, those who answered this way typically noted that such people were very valuable as long as they could work closely with others who were strong at management. Most of the remaining respondents reported having about the right number of people in this category for future needs, sometimes commenting that this "right number" was "very few." These respondents tended to be pessimistic about strong leaders/weak managers; they felt such people usually created more problems than they solved.

Nearly two thirds of those surveyed said they had too many people who are strong at management but not at leadership. Some even reported having "far too many." The other third split their responses between "too few" and "about right." Those saying too few usually worked for professional service firms.

Over 95 percent reported having too few people who are strong at both leadership and management. Everyone thought they had some people like that: not super humans who provide outstanding management and excellent leadership but mortals who are moderately strong on one of the two dimensions, and strong or very strong on the other. But the respondents felt they needed more, often many more, to do well over the next decade.

This survey is interesting, not because it proves anything by itself, but because the results are so consistent with a variety of other evidence. . . . As a whole, the data strongly suggests that most firms today have insufficient leadership, and that many corporations are "over-managed" and "under-led."

An even larger survey conducted a few years earlier provides some insight about why this leadership problem exists.[15] Nearly 80 percent of the 1,000 executives responding to that survey questionnaire said they felt their firms did less than a very good job of recruiting, developing, retaining, and motivating people with leadership potential (see Exhibit 3). These same executives also reported that their companies were not successful in this regard because of a large number of inappropriate practices (see Exhibit 4). For example, 82 percent of the respondents said that "the quality of career planning discussions in their firms" was less than adequate to support the objective of attracting, retaining, and motivating a sufficient number of people who could help with the leadership challenges. Seventy-seven percent said the same thing about "the developmental job opportunities available" and "the information available to high potentials on job openings in the company." Fully 93 percent indicated that "the way managers are rewarded for developing subordinates" with leadership potential was less than adequate to support the need for spotting high-potential people, identifying

EXHIBIT 3   Attracting, Developing, Retaining, and Motivating People
with Leadership Potential: Results from a Questionnaire of
1,000 Executives

1. How good a job is your company doing with respect to recruiting and hiring a
   sufficient number of people into the firm who have the potential some day of
   providing leadership in important management positions?
   Very good or execellent   27%
   Poor or fair   30%

2. How good a job is your firm doing with respect to developing these high-
   potential employees?
   Very good or excellent   19%
   Poor or fair   42%

3. How good a job is your company doing with respect to retaining and
   motivating these high-potential people?
   Very good or excellent   20%
   Poor or fair   43%

EXHIBIT 4   Adequacy of Practices Affecting a Firm's Leadership Capacity:
Results from the Questionnaire

The questionnaire asks 46 questions about practices that affect the firm's capacity
to attract, develop, retain, and motivate sufficient leadership. In summary, people
responded:

1. The vast majority of practices (80%) are more than adequate.*
   % answering this way = 0.2

2. The vast majority of practices (80%) are adequate.†
   % answering this way = 3.3

3. A bare majority of the practices (51%) are adequate.†
   % answering this way = 23.7

* response of 1 on a 4-point scale.
† A response of 1 or 2 on a 4-point scale.

their development needs, and then meeting those needs. Eighty-seven
percent reported the same problem with "the number and type of lateral
transfers made for developmental reasons across divisions." Seventy-nine
percent said the same thing about "the mentoring, role modeling, and
coaching provided," 75 percent about "the way feedback is given to subordinates regarding developmental progress," 69 percent about "the way re-

sponsibilities are added to the current job of high potentials for development purposes," 66 percent about "formal succession planning reviews," 65 percent about "the firm's participation in outside management training programs," and 60 percent about "the opportunities offered to people to give them exposure to higher levels of management."[16]

Equally interesting is what was not said. Those surveyed did not say their firms had insufficient leadership because there are not enough people on earth with leadership potential. Instead, they put the blame on themselves for not finding, retaining, developing, or supporting people with such potential. Some of those surveyed readily admitted that their firms often scared off such individuals, while others believed that they took talented young people with leadership potential and systematically turned them into cautious managers. These rather critical results would not be particularly surprising if they came from a disenfranchised group of lower- or middle-level managers. But this was not a survey of those groups. It was a poll of senior executives.

There are probably a variety of reasons why so many firms do not appear to have the practices needed to attract, develop, retain, and motivate enough people with leadership potential. But the most basic reason is simply this: Until recently, most organizations did not need that many people to handle their leadership challenges.

Modern business organizations are the product of the last century. They were created, for the most part, by strong entrepreneurial leaders,[17] like Andrew Carnegie, Pierre Du Pont, and Edward Filene. As these enterprises grew and became more complex, what we now call management was invented to make them function on time and on budget. As the most successful of these enterprises became larger, more geographically dispersed, and more technologically complicated, especially after World War II, they demanded many more people who could help provide that management.

A huge educational system emerged in response to this need, offering seminars, undergraduate degrees in management, and MBAs.[18] But the favorable economic climate for U.S. businesses after World War II allowed such a degree of stability that most firms didn't need much leadership—until the 1970s. Then suddenly, after 25 to 30 years of relatively easy growth, especially in the United States, the business world became more competitive, more volatile, and tougher. A combination of faster technological change, greater international competition, market deregulation, over-capacity in capital-intensive industries, an unstable oil cartel, raiders with junk bonds, and a demographically changing work force all contributed to this shift. The net result is that doing what was done yesterday, or doing it 5 percent better, is no longer a formula for success. Major changes are more and more necessary to survive and compete effectively in this new environment. More change always demands more leadership (see Exhibit 5). But firms are having difficulty adapting their practices to this new reality.

EXHIBIT 5 The Relationship of Change and Complexity to the Amount of Leadership and Management Needed in a Firm

	Low	**High**
High	Considerable leadership but not much management required (start-up businesses).	Considerable leadership and management required (most businesses and other organizations today).
Low	Little management or leadership required (most organizations until this century).	Considerable management but little leadership required (many successful corporations in the 1950s and 1960s).

Amount of change needed in the operation (due to environmental instability, rapid growth, etc.)

The complexity of the operation (due to size, technology, geographical dispersion, the number of products or services, etc.)

412

Examples of this shift can be found nearly everywhere. Consider the case of a small- to medium-sized plant owned by a successful U.S. firm like Honeywell. In 1970, this facility employed 100 people, was 20 years old, and produced control systems for manufacturing settings. Although the facility made nearly two dozen products, one of these accounted for half the volume. That product, relatively unique in the marketplace, was protected by a number of patents. Although the plant's products were sold in over 50 countries, U.S. sales accounted for 70 percent of total volume. In the U.S. market, the plant's main product line held a 34 percent market share in its specific niche; the number two competitor controlled about 24 percent.

An examination of the demands placed on the plant manager back in 1970 reveals the following. First and foremost, he was expected to meet monthly, quarterly, and yearly targets for production, costs, and a number of other quantifiable measures. These targets were established after some negotiation by his boss and were based heavily on historical data. To meet these targets, he allocated his time over the course of the year in roughly the following way:

- **5–10%**—working with his staff to produce the monthly, quarterly, and yearly plans to meet the targets.

- **20–30%**—working with his staff to make sure he had the appropriate organization in place to implement the plans, which in turn involved hiring, firing, performance appraisals, coaching, etc.

- **40–50%**—having daily production meetings, weekly budget review meetings, and the like to spot deviations from plan as quickly as possible and to solve them.

- **20–25%**—all other activities, such as assisting the sales force by meeting an important customer, or deciding if a new technology should be used in one part of the manufacturing process.

In other words, he spent the vast majority (75 to 80 percent) of his time *managing* the plant, with a heavy emphasis on the control aspects of management.

If a visitor to this plant in 1970 returned 15 years later, he would have found a very different facility. In 1985, the plant had more engineers and technicians and fewer foremen and middle managers. Although the number of employees was almost the same, the output was double the 1970 levels. The plant's product line was much more volatile; products introduced within the past five years accounted for nearly 35 percent of its volume versus 15 percent in 1970. The products themselves were more technologically complex, and the technology was changing faster than it had 15 years earlier. The plant's products were being sold in even more countries, and a greater volume was sold outside the United States. Worldwide market share for the plant's niche was about 14 percent, versus 29 percent in the United States, and its number one competitor, with nearly 22 percent of the world market, was now a Japanese company.

In this environment, the demands placed on the 1985 plant manager were in some ways similar, but in many ways different, from those found in 1970. The head of this facility in 1985 was still being asked to meet certain quantifiable targets on a monthly, quarterly, and yearly basis. That, in turn, still required producing plans, maintaining an organization, and many controlling efforts to keep things "on track." But the targets themselves were more complex and volatile due to market conditions; thus, the process of achieving them was more complicated. More importantly, in addition to all these activities, there was a whole new dimension to the job, one that was time-consuming and difficult, yet essential.

In 1985, the plant manager was being asked to match his Japanese rival by finding a way to increase certain quality measures not by 1 or 5 or 10 percent but by 100 percent. He was also asked to help the corporate manufacturing staff evaluate a number of options for moving some production out of the country, to find a way to incorporate a completely new technology into the heart of the manufacturing process, to reduce the time required to introduce new products by 50 percent, and to shrink inventories by at least a third. All of this, in turn, required much more from his staff—in terms of time, energy, creativity, and the willingness to make sacrifices and take risks. That created a huge challenge: to somehow get his people energized and committed to helping with the big cost and quality and technology issues. And all of this created change, far more than in 1970, which in turn was bumping up against a corporate bureaucracy designed for a more stable environment. It also led to the sorts of uncertainties that threatened vested interests.

The 1985 plant manager coped with these demands by allocating his time in the following way:

- **30–50%**—engaging in the same types of planning, organizing, and controlling activities as did his predecessor 15 years earlier, but using a less authoritarian style and delegating more (i.e., managing).

- **50–60%**—(a) trying to establish a clear sense of direction for the changes needed in quality, costs, inventories, technologies, and new product introductions; (b) trying to communicate that direction to all his people and to get them to believe that the changes are necessary; and (c) finally, trying to energize and motivate his people to overcome all the bureaucratic, political, and resource barriers to change (i.e., leading).

- **0–10%**—participating in other activities.

By almost all standards, the plant manager's job in 1985 was more difficult than it was in 1970, primarily because the firm's business environment was more difficult. In 1985, this person not only had to manage the plant by planning, budgeting, organizing, staffing, and controlling, he also had to provide substantial leadership on dozens of critical business issues. And he was not alone in this respect.

In 1970, in a business environment that was both favorable and changing relatively slowly, sufficient leadership could be supplied by the CEO and several other people. By 1985, in a much tougher and rapidly changing environment, hundreds of individuals, both above and below the plant manager level, were also needed to provide leadership for developing and implementing new marketing programs, new approaches to financing the business, new MIS systems, new labor relations practices, and much more. Doing all this well required skills and strategies that most people did not need in the relatively benign 1950s, 1960s, and early 1970s. It required more than technical and managerial ability. Some of these people had these new skills, but many did not.

This story is interesting because the type of environmental changes involved are not at all unusual. These same kinds of changes can be found in a wide variety of industries and in a large number of countries in addition to the United States (see Exhibit 6).

A simple military analogy sums all this up well. A peacetime army can usually survive with good administration and management up and down the hierarchy, coupled with good leadership concentrated at the very top. A wartime army, however, needs competent leadership at all levels. No one

EXHIBIT 6   Results of a Poll of Mid-level Executives from 42 Countries and 31 Industries*

1. For the industry you know best, how different is the business environment today (1988) versus that of 25 years ago (1963)?

1	2	3	4	5
Not different				Extremely different

Mean response:
4.4

2. If the business environment in the industry you know best is significantly different today than it was 25 years ago, how is it different?

Nearly 90 percent report:

- More competitive
- More technological change
- Faster changing

* Survey of 135 people conducted in September 1988.

yet has figured out how to manage people effectively into battle. From 1946 into the 1970s, the world economy was, for the most part, at peace. It is no longer. But precious few corporations now have the leadership necessary to win the battles they face in this economic war.

There are a number of reasons why firms, even some very good ones, have had difficulty adapting to the new business environment. The most obvious relates to the inherent difficulty of the task. All available evidence suggests that finding people with leadership potential and then nurturing that potential is much tougher than finding people with managerial potential and then developing those skills. [19]

Experts have been of limited help, even though a few predicted the environmental changes before the fact, usually in the mid- to late-1960s. [20] The biggest recommendation to evolve from this work has been a vague notion that we need to *manage* differently in the future. Individuals have stressed long-term planning, matrix structures, motivational systems, and much more. . . . [But] none of the ideas have worked well, and for reasons that are predictable in light of the real difference between management and leadership.

Starting in the early 1980s some people reacted to all this by emphasizing leadership. What is needed to cope with major change, they argued correctly, is not management, but something else. Their descriptions of this "something else" were often vague. But worse yet, most suggested that this other thing—leadership—was needed instead of management. That is, they offered a prescription that was not only wrong, but dangerous.

Strong leadership with weak management is no better, and sometimes actually worse, than the reverse. In such a situation (1) an emphasis on long-term vision but little short-term planning and budgeting, plus (2) a strong group culture without much specialization, structure, and rules, plus (3) inspired people who are not inclined to use control systems and problem-solving disciplines, all conspire to create a situation that can eventually get out of control, even wildly out of control. Under such circumstances, as many small entrepreneurial firms have learned the hard way, critical deadlines, budgets, and promises can go unmet, threatening the very existence of the organization.

The most extreme, and dangerous, examples of this phenomenon are of the Jim Jones variety. In such cases, a charismatic person emerges when a group of people are experiencing considerable pain. This person is not a good manager and, in fact, does not like good managers because they are too rational and controlling. The charismatic has a flawed vision, one that does not try to create real value for both the group and its key outside constituencies. But the lack of a rational management process—that is as powerful as the leadership—means the bad vision is not publicly discussed and discredited. The strong charisma creates commitment and great motivation to move in the direction of the vision. Eventually, this movement leads to tragedy; followers trample other people and then walk off a cliff.

Seeking out, canonizing, and turning over the reigns of power to this type of charismatic nonmanager is never the solution to a leadership crisis. But to move beyond this seductively dangerous prescription will require a much clearer sense of what leadership really means in complex organizations, what it looks like, and where it comes from. Given the inherent complexity of the subject matter and the barriers prohibiting rigorous empirical work on such a broad topic, satisfying such a purpose is an extraordinarily difficult task. Nevertheless, that task sets the agenda for this book, and the comparative analysis of leadership vis-à-vis the more clearly understood process of management will be the primary vehicle for achieving that agenda.

ENDNOTES

1. A sizable amount of the literature on leadership is based on studies of people in supervisory or managerial jobs, people who may or may not have been providing effective leadership. See Bass, *Handbook of leadership: A survey of theory and research*, New York: Free Press, 1981; and Yukl, *Leadership in organizations*, Englewood Cliffs, N.J. Prentice-Hall, 1989.

2. This is not to suggest that management, at least in an elementary form, did not exist centuries earlier. It surely did; and generals, kings, and high priests undoubtedly knew something about it. But the management they knew and used was the product of a vastly less complicated age. Compared to today, the organizations they managed were technologically simple and usually small—in other words, not very complex.

3. Chandler, *The visible hand*, Cambridge, Mass.: Belknap Press of Harvard University Press, 1977.

4. Summarized here are the elements of management most commonly included in both (*a*) the many books on that subject published in this century, and (*b*) a 1987 survey conducted by this author that asked 200 executives to describe the actions of someone they knew who was effectively managing whatever he or she was responsible for.

5. Although not the only function, that seems to be the most common one mentioned in the hundreds of books on management that have been published in the past 60 to 70 years.

6. Burns, *Leadership*, New York: Harper & Row, 1978.

7. Levinson and Rosenthal end their study of CEOs with the following conclusion, "Strong leaders are necessary, particularly for organizations that must undergo significant change. Not good managers or executives, but strong leaders." See Levinson and Rosenthal, *CEO: Corporate leadership in action*, York: Basic Books, 1984, p. 289.

8. Determining what "generally better off" and "trampling on the rights of others" mean, in practice, can be most difficult and has led to endless philosophical discussions. For the purposes of this book, effectiveness is measured by the cumulative after-the-fact opinions of all those affected by a leadership process.

9. The list is generally consistent with other important works on leadership in modern organizations—books by Bennis and Nanus, *Leaders: The strategies for taking charge*, New York: Harper & Row, 1985; and Peters and Austin, *A passion for excellence: The leadership difference*, New York: Random House, 1985, for example. But this specific way of thinking about leadership comes from the studies on which the book is based.

10. The distinction between leadership and management is similar in some ways to what Burns (endnote 6) and Bass, *Leadership and performance beyond expectations*, New York: Free Press, 1985, have called transformational leadership versus transactional leadership. The book by Burns and a 1977 article by Zaleznik, "Managers and leaders: Are they different?" *Harvard Business Review* (1977) 55, 67–87, are the first two works of which I am aware that begin to explore these differences.

11. For a fascinating analysis of the pure types and their potential for conflict, see Zaleznik (endnote 10), pp. 67–80.

12. This occurred in China during the "Cultural Revolution."

13. Very visible examples, although not extreme ones, include Apple before John Sculley became CEO and People Express during its final year of operation.

14. Approximately 200 executives were polled during 1987 either with a questionnaire or in an hour-long interview. The dimensions of "management" and "leadership" were not defined for them, but before they were asked to rate their fellow managers on those dimensions, they were first asked to describe in detail the actions of someone they knew who provided effective management and then to describe likewise the actions of someone who has provided effective leadership.

15. Further details on this survey can be found in Kotter, *The leadership factor* New York: Free Press, 1988.

16. *Ibid*, Chapter 6.

17. By "entrepreneurial," I mean leaders who focused their energies on taking advantage of opportunities to build businesses.

18. The sheer amount of management education offered today is at least 30 times greater than that offered 50 years ago.

19. Kotter (endnote 15) Chapter 3.

20. Beckhard, *Organizational development*, Reading, Mass.: Addison-Wesley, 1969.

31

The Ambiguity of Leadership*

Jeffrey Pfeffer

Problems with the concept of leadership are addressed: (a) the ambiguity of its definition and measurement, (b) the issue of whether leadership affects organizational performance, and (c) the process of selecting leaders, which frequently emphasizes organizationally irrelevant criteria. Leadership is a process of attributing causation to individual social actors. Study of leaders as symbols and of the process of attributing leadership might be productive.

Leadership has for some time been a major topic in social and organizational psychology. Underlying much of this research has been the assumption that leadership is causally related to organizational performance. Through an analysis of leadership styles, behaviors, or characteristics (depending on the theoretical perspective chosen), the argument has been made that more effective leaders can be selected or trained or, alternatively, the situation can be configured to provide for enhanced leader and organizational effectiveness.

Three problems with emphasis on leadership as a concept can be posed: (a) ambiguity in definition and measurement of the concept itself; (b) the question of whether leadership has discernible effects on organizational outcomes; and (c) the selection process in succession to leadership positions, which frequently uses organizationally irrelevant criteria and which has implications for normative theories of leadership. The argument here is that leadership is of interest primarily as a phenomenological construct. Leaders serve as symbols for representing personal causation of social events. How and why are such attributions of personal effects made? Instead of focusing on leadership and its effects, how do people make inferences about and react to phenomena labelled as leadership (5)?

* From *Academy of Management Review* (1977) 2, no. 1, 104–12. An earlier version of this paper was presented at the conference, Leadership: Where Else Can we Go? Center for Creative Leadership, Greensboro, North Carolina, June 30–July 1, 1975.

THE AMBIGUITY OF THE CONCEPT

While there have been many studies of leadership, the dimensions and definition of the concept remain unclear. To treat leadership as a separate concept, it must be distinguished from other social influence phenomena. Hollander and Julian (24) and Bavelas (2) did not draw distinctions between leadership and other processes of social influence. A major point of the Hollander and Julian review was that leadership research might develop more rapidly if more general theories of social influence were incorporated. Calder (5) also argued that there is no unique content to the construct of leadership that is not subsumed under other, more general models of behavior.

Kochan, Schmidt, and DeCotiis (33) attempted to distinguish leadership from related concepts of authority and social power. In leadership, influence rights are voluntarily conferred. Power does not require goal compatibility—merely dependence—but leadership implies some congruence between the objectives of the leader and the led. These distinctions depend on the ability to distinguish voluntary from involuntary compliance and to assess goal compatibility. Goal statements may be retrospective inferences from action (46, 53) and problems of distinguishing voluntary from involuntary compliance also exist (32). Apparently there are few meaningful distinctions between leadership and other concepts of social influence. Thus, an understanding of the phenomena subsumed under the rubric of leadership may not require the construct of leadership (5).

While there is some agreement that leadership is related to social influence, more disagreement concerns the basic dimensions of leader behavior. Some have argued that there are two tasks to be accomplished in groups—maintenance of the group and performance of some task or activity—and thus leader behavior might be described along these two dimensions (1,6,8,25). The dimensions emerging from the Ohio State leadership studies—consideration and initiating structure—may be seen as similar to the two components of group maintenance and task accomplishment (18).

Other dimensions of leadership behavior have also been proposed (4). Day and Hamblin (10) analyzed leadership in terms of the closeness and punitiveness of the supervision. Several authors have conceptualized leadership behavior in terms of the authority and discretion subordinates are permitted (23, 36, 51). Fiedler (14) analyzed leadership in terms of the least-preferred-coworker scale (LPC), but the meaning and behavioral attributes of this dimension of leadership behavior remain controversial.

The proliferation of dimensions is partly a function of research strategies frequently employed. Factor analysis on a large number of items describing behavior has frequently been used. This procedure tends to produce as many factors as the analyst decides to find, and permits the development of a large number of possible factor structures. The resultant factors must be named and further imprecision is introduced. Deciding on a summative concept to represent a factor is inevitably a partly subjective process.

Literature assessing the effects of leadership tends to be equivocal. Sales (45) summarized leadership literature employing the authoritarian-democratic typology and concluded that effects on performance were small and inconsistent. Reviewing the literature on consideration and initiating structure dimensions, Korman (34) reported relatively small and inconsistent results, and Kerr and Schriesheim (30) reported more consistent effects of the two dimensions. Better results apparently emerge when moderating factors are taken into account, including subordinate personalities (50), and situational characteristics (23, 51). Kerr et al. (31) list many moderating effects grouped under the headings of subordinate considerations, supervisor considerations, and task considerations. Even if each set of considerations consisted of only one factor (which it does not), an attempt to account for the effects of leader behavior would necessitate considering four-way interactions. While social reality is complex and contingent, it seems desirable to attempt to find more parsimonious explanations for the phenomena under study.

THE EFFECTS OF LEADERS

Hall asked a basic question about leadership: Is there any evidence on the magnitude of the effects of leadership (17, p. 248)? Surprisingly, he could find little evidence. Given the resources that have been spent studying, selecting, and training leaders, one might expect that the question of whether or not leaders matter would have been addressed earlier (12).

There are at least three reasons why it might be argued that the observed effects of leaders on organizational outcomes would be small. First, those obtaining leadership positions are selected, and perhaps only certain, limited styles of behavior may be chosen. Second, once in the leadership position, the discretion and behavior of the leader are constrained. And third, leaders can typically affect only a few of the variables that may impact organizational performance.

Homogeneity of Leaders

Persons are selected to leadership positions. As a consequence of this selection process, the range of behaviors or characteristics exhibited by leaders is reduced, making it more problematic to empirically discover an effect of leadership. There are many types of constraints on the selection process. The attraction literature suggests that there is a tendency for persons to like those they perceive as similar (3). In critical decisions such as the selections of persons for leadership positions, compatible styles of behavior probably will be chosen.

Selection of persons is also constrained by the internal system of influence in the organization. As Zald (56) noted, succession is a critical decision, affected by political influence and by environmental contingencies faced by the organization. As Thompson (49) noted, leaders may be selected for their capacity to deal with various organizational contingencies. In a study of characteristics of hospital administrators, Pfeffer and Salancik (42) found a relationship between the hospital's context and the characteristics and tenure of the administrators. To the extent that the contingencies and power distribution within the organization remain stable, the abilities and behaviors of those selected into leadership positions will also remain stable.

Finally, the selection of persons to leadership positions is affected by a self-selection process. Organizations and roles have images, providing information about their character. Persons are likely to select themselves into organizations and roles based upon their preferences for the dimensions of the organizational and role characteristics as perceived through these images. The self-selection of persons would tend to work along with organizational selection to limit the range of abilities and behaviors in a given organizational role.

Such selection processes would tend to increase homogeneity more within a single organization than across organizations. Yet many studies of leadership effect at the work group level have compared groups within a single organization. If there comes to be a widely shared, socially constructed definition of leadership behaviors or characteristics which guides the selection process, then leadership activity may come to be defined similarly in various organizations, leading to the selection of only those who match the constructed image of a leader.

Constraints on Leader Behavior

Analyses of leadership have frequently presumed that leadership style or leader behavior was an independent variable that could be selected or trained at will to conform to what research would find to be optimal. Even theorists who took a more contingent view of appropriate leadership behavior generally assumed that, with proper training, appropriate behavior could be produced (51). Fiedler (13), noting how hard it was to change behavior, suggested changing the situational characteristics, rather than the person, but this was an unusual suggestion in the context of prevailing literature, which suggested that leadership style was something to be strategically selected according to the variables of the particular leadership theory.

But the leader is embedded in a social system, which constrains behavior. The leader has a role set (27), in which members have expectations for appropriate behavior and persons who make efforts to modify the leader's behavior. Pressures to conform to the expectations of peers, subordinates, and superiors are all relevant in determining actual behavior.

Leaders, even in high-level positions, have unilateral control over fewer resources and fewer policies than might be expected. Investment decisions may require approval of others, while hiring and promotion decisions may be accomplished by committees. Leader behavior is constrained by both the demands of others in the role set and by organizationally prescribed limitations on the sphere of activity and influence.

External Factors

Many factors that may affect organizational performance are outside a leader's control, even if he or she were to have complete discretion over major areas of organizational decisions. For example, consider the executive in a construction firm. Costs are largely determined by operation of commodities and labor markets; and demand is largely affected by interest rates, availability of mortgage money, and economic conditions, which are affected by governmental policies over which the executive has little control. School superintendents have little control over birth rates and community economic development, both of which profoundly affect school system budgets. While the leader may react to contingencies as they arise, or may be a better or worse forecaster, in accounting for variation in organizational outcomes, he or she may account for relatively little compared to external factors.

Second, the leader's success or failure may be partly due to circumstances unique to the organization but still outside his or her control. Leader positions in organizations vary in terms of the strength and position of the organization. The choice of a new executive does not fundamentally alter a market and financial position that has developed over years and affects the leader's ability to make strategic changes and the likelihood that the organization will do well or poorly. Organizations have relatively enduring strengths and weaknesses. The choice of a particular leader for a particular position has limited impact on these capabilities.

Empirical Evidence

Two studies have assessed the effects of leadership changes in major positions in organizations. Lieberson and O'Connor (35) examined 167 business firms in 13 industries over a 20-year period, allocating variance in sales, profits, and profit margins to one of four sources: year (general economic conditions), industry, company effects, and effects of changes in the top executive position. They concluded that compared to other factors, administration had a limited effect on organizational outcomes.

Using a similar analytical procedure, Salancik and Pfeffer (44) examined the effects of mayors on city budgets for 30 U.S. cities. Data on expenditure by budget category were collected for 1951–68. Variance in amount and proportion of expenditure was apportioned to the year, the city, or the mayor. The mayoral effect was relatively small, with the city accounting for most of the variance, although the mayor effect was larger for expenditure categories that were not as directly connected to important interest groups. Salancik and Pfeffer argued that the effects of the mayor were limited both by absence of power to control many of the expenditures and tax sources, and by construction of policies in response to demands from interests in the environment.

If leadership is defined as a strictly interpersonal phenomenon, the relevance of these two studies for the issue of leadership effects becomes problematic. But such a conceptualization seems unduly restrictive, and it is certainly inconsistent with Selznick's (47) conceptualization of leadership as strategic management and decision making. If one cannot observe differences when leaders change, then what does it matter who occupies the positions or how they behave?

Pfeffer and Salancik (41) investigated the extent to which behaviors selected by first-line supervisors were constrained by expectations of others in their role-set. Variance in task and social behaviors could be accounted for by role-set expectations, with adherence to various demands made by role-set participants a function of similarity and relative power. Lowin and Craig (37) experimentally demonstrated that leader behavior was determined by the subordinate's own behavior. Both studies illustrate that leader behaviors are responses to the demands of the social context.

The effect of leadership may vary depending upon level in the organizational hierarchy, while the appropriate activities and behaviors may also vary with organizational level (26, 40). For the most part, empirical studies of leadership have dealt with first-line supervisors or leaders with relatively low organizational status (17). If leadership has any impact, it should be more evident at higher organizational levels or where there is more discretion in decisions and activities.

THE PROCESS OF SELECTING LEADERS

Along with the suggestion that leadership may not account for much variance in organizational outcomes, it can be argued that merit or ability may not account for much variation in hiring and advancement of organizational personnel. These two ideas are related. If competence is hard to judge, or if leadership competence does not greatly affect organizational outcomes, then other, person-dependent criteria may be sufficient. Effective leadership styles may not predict career success when other variables, such as social background, are controlled.

Belief in the importance of leadership is frequently accompanied by belief that persons occupying leadership positions are selected and trained according to how well they can enhance the organization's performance. Belief in a leadership effect leads to development of a set of activities oriented toward enhancing leadership effectiveness. Simultaneously, persons managing their own careers are likely to place emphasis on activities and developing behaviors that will enhance their own leadership skills, assuming that such a strategy will facilitate advancement.

Research on the bases of hiring and promotion has been concentrated in examination of academic positions (e.g., 7, 19, 20). This is possibly the result of availability of relatively precise and unambiguous measures of performance, such as number of publications or citations. Evidence on criteria used in selecting and advancing personnel in industry is more indirect.

Studies have attempted to predict either the compensation or the attainment of general management positions of MBA students, using personality and other background information (21, 22, 54). There is some evidence that managerial success can be predicted by indicators of ability and motivation, such as test scores and grades, but the amount of variance explained is typically quite small.

A second line of research has investigated characteristics and backgrounds of persons attaining leadership positions in major organizations in society. Domhoff (11), Mills (38), and Warner and Abbeglin (52) found a strong preponderance of persons with upper-class backgrounds occupying leadership positions. The implication of these findings is that studies of graduate success, including the success of MBAs, would explain more variance if the family background of the person were included.

A third line of inquiry uses a tracking model. The dynamic model developed is one in which access to elite universities is affected by social status (28) and, in turn, social status and the attendance at elite universities affect later career outcomes (9, 43, 48, 55).

Unless one is willing to make the argument that attendance at elite universities or coming from an upper-class background is perfectly correlated with merit, the evidence suggests that succession to leadership positions is not strictly based on meritocratic criteria. Such a conclusion is consistent with the inability of studies attempting to predict the success of MBA graduates to account for much variance, even when a variety of personality and ability factors are used.

Beliefs about the bases for social mobility are important for social stability. As long as persons believe that positions are allocated on meritocratic grounds, they are more likely to be satisfied with the social order and with their position in it. This satisfaction derives from the belief that occupational position results from application of fair and reasonable criteria, and that the opportunity exists for mobility if the person improves skills and performance.

If succession to leadership positions is determined by person-based criteria, such as social origins or social connections (16), then efforts to enhance managerial effectiveness with the expectation that this will lead to career success divert attention from the processes of stratification actually operating within organizations. Leadership literature has been implicitly aimed at two audiences. Organizations were told how to become more effective, and persons were told what behaviors to acquire in order to become effective and, hence, advance in their careers. The possibility that neither organizational outcomes nor career success are related to leadership behaviors leaves leadership research facing issues of relevance and importance.

THE ATTRIBUTION OF LEADERSHIP

Kelly conceptualized the layman as:

> an applied scientist, that is, as a person concerned about applying his knowledge of causal relationships in order to *exercise control* of his world (29, p. 2.)

Reviewing a series of studies dealing with the attributional process, he concluded that persons were not only interested in understanding their world correctly, but also in controlling it.

> The view here proposed is that attribution processes are to be understood not only as a means of providing the individual with a veridical view of his world, but as a means of encouraging and maintaining his effective exercise of control in that world (29, p. 22).

Controllable factors will have high salience as candidates for causal explanation, while a bias toward the more important causes may shift the attributional emphasis toward causes that are not controllable (29, p. 23). The study of attribution is a study of naïve psychology—an examination of how persons make sense out of the events taking place around them.

If Kelley is correct that individuals will tend to develop attributions that give them a feeling of control, then emphasis on leadership may derive partially from a desire to believe in the effectiveness and importance of individual action, since individual action is more controllable than contextual variables. Lieberson and O'Connor (35) made essentially the same point in introducing their paper on the effects of top management changes on organizational performance. Given the desire for control and a feeling of personal effectiveness, organizational outcomes are more likely to be attributed to individual actions, regardless of their actual causes.

Leadership is attributed by observers. Social action has meaning only through a phenomenological process (46). The identification of certain organizational roles as leadership positions guides the construction of meaning in the direction of attributing effects to the actions of those positions. While Bavelas (2) argued that the functions of leadership, such as task accomplishment and group maintenance, are shared throughout the group, this fact provides no simple and potentially controllable focus for attributing causality. Rather, the identification of leadership positions provides a simpler and more readily changeable model of reality. When causality is lodged in one or a few persons, rather than being a function of a complex set of interactions among all group members, changes can be made by replacing or influencing the occupant of the leadership position. Causes of organizational actions are readily identified in this simple causal structure.

Even if, empirically, leadership has little effect, and even if succession to leadership positions is not predicated on ability or performance, the belief in leadership effects and meritocratic succession provides a simple causal framework and a justification for the structure of the social collectivity. More importantly, the beliefs interpret social actions in terms that indicate potential for effective individual intervention or control. The personification of social causality serves too many uses to be easily overcome. Whether or not leader behavior actually influences performance or effectiveness, it is important because people believe it does.

One consequence of the attribution of causality to leaders and leadership is that leaders come to be symbols. Mintzberg (39), in his discussion of the roles of managers, wrote of the symbolic role, but more in terms of attendance at formal events and formally representing the organization. The symbolic role of leadership is more important than implied in such a description. The leader as a symbol provides a target for action when difficulties occur, serving as a scapegoat when things go wrong. Gamson and Scotch (15) noted that, in baseball, the firing of the manager served a scapegoating purpose. One cannot fire the whole team; yet, when performance is poor, something must be done. The firing of the manager conveys to the world and to the actors involved that success is the result of personal actions, and that steps can and will be taken to enhance organizational performance.

The attribution of causality to leadership may be reinforced by organizational actions, such as the inauguration process, the choice process, and providing the leader with symbols and ceremony. If leaders are chosen by using a random number table, persons are less likely to believe in their effects than if there is an elaborate search or selection process followed by an elaborate ceremony signifying the changing of control, and if the leader then has a variety of perquisites and symbols that distinguish him or her from the rest of the organization. Construction of the importance of leadership in a given social context is the outcome of various social processes, which can be empirically examined.

Since belief in the leadership effect provides a feeling of personal control, one might argue that efforts to increase the attribution of causality to leaders would occur more when it is more necessary and more problematic to attribute causality to controllable factors. Such an argument would lead to the hypothesis that the more the *context* actually effects organizational outcomes, the more efforts will be made to ensure attribution to *leadership*. When leaders really do have effects, it is less necessary to engage in rituals indicating their effects. Such rituals are more likely when there is uncertainty and unpredictability associated with the organization's operations. This results both from the desire to feel control in uncertain situations and from the fact that, in ambiguous contexts, it is easier to attribute consequences to leadership without facing possible disconfirmation.

The leader is, in part, an actor. Through statements and actions, the leader attempts to reinforce the operation of an attribution process which tends to vest causality in that position in the social structure. Successful leaders, as perceived by members of the social system, are those who can separate themselves from organizational failures and associate themselves with organizational successes. Since the meaning of action is socially constructed, this involves manipulation of symbols to reinforce the desired process of attribution. For instance, if a manager knows that business in his or her division is about to improve because of the economic cycle, the leader may, nevertheless, write recommendations and undertake actions and changes that are highly visible and that will tend to identify his or her behavior closely with the division. A manager who perceives impending failure will attempt to associate the division and its policies and decisions with others, particularly persons in higher organizational positions, and to disassociate himself or herself from the division's performance, occasionally even transferring or moving to another organization.

CONCLUSION

The theme of this article has been that analysis of leadership and leadership processes must be contingent on the intent of the researcher. If the interest is in understanding the causality of social phenomena as reliably and accurately as possible, then the concept of leadership may be a poor place to begin. The issue of the effects of leadership is open to question. But examination of situational variables that accompany more or less leadership effect is a worthwhile task.

The more phenomenological analysis of leadership directs attention to the process by which social causality is attributed and focuses on the distinction between causality as perceived by group members and causality as assessed by an outside observer. Leadership is associated with a set of myths reinforcing a social construction of meaning which legitimates leadership role occupants, provides belief in potential mobility for those not in leadership roles, and attributes social causality to leadership roles, thereby providing a belief in the effectiveness of individual control. In analyzing leadership, this mythology and the process by which such mythology is created and supported should be separated from analysis of leadership as a social influence process, operating within constraints.

REFERENCES

1. Bales, R. F. *Interaction process analysis: A method for the study of small groups.* Reading, Mass.: Addison-Wesley, 1950.
2. Bavelas, Alex. "Leadership: Man and function." *Administrative Science Quarterly* (1960), *4*, 491–98.
3. Berscheid, Ellen, and Elaine Walster. *Interpersonal attraction.* Reading, Mass.: Addison-Wesley, 1969.
4. Bowers, David G., and Stanley E. Seashore. "Predicting organizational effectiveness with a four-factor theory of leadership." *Administrative Science Quarterly* (1966) *11*, 238–63.
5. Calder, Bobby J. "An attribution theory of leadership." In *New directions in organizational behavior.* ed. B. Staw and G. Salancik. Chicago: St. Clair Press, 1976.
6. Cartwright, Dorwin C., and Alvin Zander. *Group dynamics: Research and theory.* 3d ed. Evanston, Ill.: Row, Peterson, 1960.
7. Cole, Jonathan R., and Stephen Cole. *Social stratification in science.* Chicago: University of Chicago Press, 1973.
8. Collins, Barry E., and Harold Guetzkow. *A social psychology of group processes for decision making.* New York: Wiley, 1964.
9. Collins, Randall. "Functional and conflict theories of stratification." *American Sociological Review* (1971) *36*, 1002–19.
10. Day, R. C., and R. L. Hamblin. "Some effects of close and punitive styles of supervision." *American Journal of Sociology* (1964) *69*, 499–510.
11. Domhoff, G. William. *Who rules America?* Englewood Cliffs, N.J.: Prentice-Hall, 1967.
12. Dubin, Robert. "Supervision and productivity: Empirical findings and theoretical considerations." In *Leadership and productivity.* ed. R. Dubin, G. C. Homans, F. C. Mann, and D. C. Miller. San Francisco: Chandler Publishing, 1965, 1–50.
13. Fiedler, Fred E. "Engineering the job to fit the manager." *Harvard Business Review* (1965) *43*, 115–22.
14. Fiedler, Fred E. *A theory of leadership effectiveness.* New York: McGraw-Hill, 1967.
15. Gamson, William A., and Norman A. Scotch. "Scapegoating in baseball." *American Journal of Sociology* (1964) *70*, 69–72.
16. Granovetter, Mark. *Getting a job.* Cambridge, Mass.: Harvard University Press, 1974.

17. Hall, Richard H. *Organizations: Structure and process.* Englewood Cliffs, N.J.: Prentice-Hall, 1972.
18. Halpin, A. W., and J. Winer. "A factorial study of the leader behavior description questionnaire." In *Leader behavior: Its description and measurement.* ed. R. M. Stogdill and A. E. Coons. Columbus, Ohio: Bureau of Business Research, Ohio State University, 1957, 39–51.
19. Hargens, L. L. "Patterns of mobility of new Ph.D.'s among American academic institutions." *Sociology of Education,* (1969) *42*, 18–37.
20. Hargens, L. L., and W. O. Hagstrom. "Sponsored and contest mobility of American academic scientists." *Sociology of Education* (1967) *40*, 24–38.
21. Harrell, Thomas W. "High earning MBA's." *Personnel Psychology* (1972) *25*, 523–30.
22. Harrell, Thomas W., and Margaret S. Harrell. "Predictors of management success." *Stanford University Graduate School of Business, Technical Report No. 3 to the Office of Naval Research.*
23. Heller, Frank, and Gary Yukl. "Participation, managerial decision making and situational variables." *Organizational Behavior and Human Performance* (1969) *4*, 227–41.
24. Hollander, Edwin P., and James W. Julian. "Contemporary trends in the analysis of leadership processes." *Psychological Bulletin* (1969), *71*, 387–97.
25. House, Robert J. "A path goal theory of leader effectiveness." *Administrative Science Quarterly* (1971) *16*, 321–38.
26. Hunt, J. G. "Leadership-style effects at two managerial levels in a simulated organization." *Administrative Science Quarterly* (1971) *16*, 476–85.
27. Kahn, R. L.; D. M. Wolfe; R. P. Quinn; and J. D. Snoek. *Organizational stress: Studies in role conflict and ambiguity.* New York: Wiley, 1964.
28. Karabel, J., and A. W. Astin. "Social class, academic ability, and college 'quality'." *Social Forces,* (1975) *53*, 381–98.
29. Kelley, Harold H. *Attribution in social interaction.* Morristown, N.J.: General Learning Press, 1971.
30. Kerr, Steven, and Chester Schriesheim. "Consideration, initiating structure and organizational criteria—An update of Korman's 1966 review." *Personnel Psychology* (1974) *27*, 555–68.
31. Kerr, S.; C. Schriesheim; C. J. Murphy; and R. M. Stogdill. "Toward a contingency theory of leadership based upon the consideration and initiating structure literature." *Organizational Behavior and Human Performance,* (1974) *12*, 62–82.
32. Kiesler, C., and S. Kiesler, *Conformity.* Reading, Mass.: Addison-Wesley, 1969.
33. Kochan, T. A.; S. M. Schmidt; and T. A. DeCotiis. "Superior-subordinate relations: Leadership and headship." *Human Relations* (1975), *28*, 279–94.
34. Korman, A. K. "Consideration, initiating structure, and organizational criteria—A review." *Personnel Psychology* (1966) *19*, 349–62.
35. Lieberson, Stanley, and James F. O'Connor. "Leadership and organizational performance: A study of large corporations." *American Sociological Review* (1972) *37*, 117–30
36. Lippitt, Ronald. "An experimental study of the effect of democratic and authoritarian group atmospheres." *University of Iowa Studies in Child Welfare* (1940) *16*, 43–195.

37. Lowin, A., and J. R. Craig. "The influence of level of performance on managerial style: An experimental object-lesson in the ambiguity of correlational data." *Organizational Behavior and Human Performance.* (1968) 3, 440–58.
38. Mills, C. Wright. "The American business elite: A collective portrait." In *Power, politics, and people.* ed. C. W. Mills. New York: Oxford University Press, 1963, 110–39.
39. Mintzberg, Henry. *The nature of managerial work.* New York: Harper & Row, 1973.
40. Nealey, Stanley M., and Milton R. Blood. "Leadership performance of nursing supervisors at two organizational levels." *Journal of Applied Psychology* (1968) 52, 414–42.
41. Pfeffer, Jeffrey, and Gerald R. Salancik. "Determinants of supervisory behavior: A role set analysis." *Human Relations* (1975) 28, 139–54.
42. Pfeffer, Jeffrey, and Gerald R. Salancik. "Organizational context and the characteristics and tenure of hospital administrators." *Academy of Management Journal* (1977) 20.
43. Reed, R. H., and H. P. Miller. "Some determinants of the variation in earnings per college men." *Journal of Human Resources* (1970) 5, 117–90.
44. Salancik, Gerald R., and Jeffrey Pfeffer. "Constraints on administrator discretion: The limited influence of mayors on city budgets." *Urban Affairs Quarterly* [in press when this reading was originally published].
45. Sales, Stephen M. "Supervisory style and productivity: Review and theory." *Personnel Psychology* (1966) 19, 275–86.
46. Schutz, Alfred. *The phenomenology of the social world.* Evanston, Ill.: Northwestern University Press, 1967.
47. Selznick, P. *Leadership in administration.* Evanston, Ill.: Row, Peterson, 1957.
48. Spaeth, J. L., and A. M. Greeley. *Recent alumni and higher education.* New York: McGraw-Hill, 1970.
49. Thompson, James D. *Organizations in action.* New York: McGraw-Hill, 1967.
50. Vroom, Victor H. "Some personality determinants of the effects of participation." *Journal of Abnormal and Social Psychology* (1959) 59, 322–27.
51. Vroom, Victor H., and Phillip W. Yetton. *Leadership and decision making* Pittsburgh: University of Pittsburgh Press, 1973.
52. Warner, W. L., and J. C. Abbeglin. *Big business leaders in America.* New York: Harper & Row, 1955.
53. Weick, Karl E. *The social psychology of organizing.* Reading, Mass.: Addison-Wesley, 1969.
54. Weinstein, Alan G., and V. Srinivasan. "Predicting managerial success of master of business administration (MBA) graduates." *Journal of Applied Psychology* (1974) 59, 207–12.
55. Wolfle, Dael. *The uses of talent.* Princeton: Princeton University Press, 1971.
56. Zald, Mayer N. "Who shall rule? A political analysis of succession in a large welfare organization." *Pacific Sociological Review* (1965) 8, 52–60.

Organizations: Structure, Strategy, Culture, and Environment

INTRODUCTION

We concluded the previous section with Pfeffer's argument that leaders—even those of the highest rank—receive too much credit and too much blame for what happens to organizations. The argument is that the larger organization—for example, its structure and culture—constrains the range of any leader's options, while inexorable outside forces determine much of an organization's outcomes.

In this section we examine the "big picture" of the internal structure of organizations, going beyond the level of individual and small group behavior, and we take some account of external environmental forces that shape organizational destinies.

A selection from the work of Mariann Jelinek describes the various "basic conformations" or types of formal structure that may characterize organizations. To some extent, structure evolves through experience; yet to some extent structure is also a matter of deliberate choice. In either case, structure depends on the stage of development of the organization, strategies for survival and growth, product line, and technology.

Miles, Snow, Meyer, and Coleman discuss the importance of a judicious fit between overall strategy, technology, process, and structure. They proceed to identify three types of viable strategy-structure combinations, each suited to a particular environmental opportunity. A fourth type, the "Reactor," is predicted to fail because of the lack of alignment between distinctive strategy and structure.

In recent years, we have witnessed something of a backlash against an overweening concern for formal structure. Some influential voices have expressed the view that an organization's "culture" matters much more than structural form in enabling a firm to compete in the marketplace. Kenneth Labich gives us a close-up look at the "warm culture" of one particular organization, Herman Miller, Inc. Kerr and Slocum, on the other hand, describe in more general terms how reward systems do much to define and reinforce a firm's culture, as they develop models of two contrasting types: A "clan culture" and a "market culture." The authors suggest, based on the results of their study, that strategy dictates the appropriate culture for organizational effectiveness.

One of the major issues of the day with respect to external forces is the public's expectation that a corporation discharge its "social responsibility." Unfortunately, we find no agreement on just how to define corporate social responsibility. Dalton and Cosier examine some of the logical problems arising from each of several popular definitions, yet still arrive at the conclusion that corporate officers must take some of the risks appropriate to managing both legally and responsibly.

We conclude this volume with a selection by Miles and Snow, which speculates about the nature of the new forms of organization already taking shape in response to global and turbulent market environments. The discussion forces us to rethink much of what we traditionally associate with the concept of organization. The "dynamic network" of the future—and the rather near future, at that—will call for radically different theoretical models to describe and predict their behavior.

Organization Structure: The Basic Conformations*

Mariann Jelinek

A key issue in organization design is the choice of the main structural conformation. There are varieties of each form, and a range of possible styles within the forms. Nevertheless, the choice of one or another of the basic configurations is the selection of certain capabilities and benefits—and certain disadvantages and potential problems as well. The choice implies constraints of a fundamental nature.

What are the main options, and what are their associated constraints? What are the forms' strengths and weaknesses, and the trade-offs involved in choice of one as against another? These topics will be the subject of this paper. In passing, we shall also make reference to various dimensions of structure and other organizational factors, such as strategy and environment, which affect the organization designer's choice. We will deal with the basic organizational configurations as they evolved historically—although clearly no organization is compelled to repeat this historical sequence.

THE SIMPLE ORGANIZATION OR "AGENCY" FORM

The simple organization is one with little or no structure; it typically consists of the boss (owner, leader, or manager) and the employees or workers. An example would be a workshop in which a master craftperson supervised a number of apprentices or helpers. Direction or coordination is provided by personal supervision, and each worker acts as the *agent* or extension of the boss. More extensive examples would include most large organizations before the evolution of formal, bureaucratic means of organizing. For example, kings directed extensive establishments personally, and each subordinate's authority and power derived directly from a relationship

---

* This selection was specially written by Mariann Jelinek for inclusion in *Organizations by design*, ed. Mariann Jelinek, Joseph A. Litterer, and Raymond E. Miles (Homewood, Ill.: Irwin/Business Publications, 1981), where it first appeared. © 1981, Mariann Jelinek.

with the king, whose agent the subordinate was. More modern examples of the larger sort are difficult to identify, with the possible exception of some religious, cult, or political groups. Here, too, the subordinates' power and authority derive directly from the leader; it is as agents of the leader, doing whatever is required, that the subordinates act. Typically, such a subordinate owes responsibility only to the leader personally, rather than for a position, and duties are defined by the leader's requests.

Many organizations begin as simple organizations. An entrepreneur with an idea hires others to assist in its realization. Typically, each employee does what the entrepreneur directs, and, particularly at initial stages, there is little or no formality. Anyone can be asked to do whatever needs doing; the work is the responsibility of all organization members, under the personal direction of the entrepreneur. As Mintzberg (1979) has pointed out, such organizations are flexible, but decidedly limited in their capacity to cope with complexity. They tend to operate simple technologies in simple environments, in order that needed coordination can take place through the leader—whose capacity to process information is necessarily limited.

DIVIDING THE WORK

Most organizations quickly become more formalized than the simple agency model. As an early step in formalization, work is explicitly divided. Thus the interest of Adam Smith (1776) and Charles Babbage (1832) in the steps or functions that went into pin making: formally dividing the work, and assigning different individuals responsibility for different parts, substitutes this structure for a portion of the control exercised by the leader in the agency or simple form. People no longer must be told what to do; instead, they're assigned to do one specific portion of the work regularly. Their responsibility is limited to that portion of the work.

As Smith and Babbage noted, dividing the work permits significant advantages because it facilitates specialization. Among the results are increases in efficiency, speed, and expertise; reduced waste; less time to learn the job (because less must be learned, and more frequent repetition speeds the process); and less time lost in changing from one tool or operation to another. The same advantages accrue whether the work to be subdivided is pin making, assembling an automobile or refrigerator, teaching or engineering: Specialization permits development of in-depth knowledge, experience, and facility *within a limited area*. Thus a large and complex task is often better accomplished by dividing it into smaller, more comprehensible pieces. In particular, where the range of skills required in a large task differ markedly, or where the strength or time requirements of different portions of the task differ, division of labor offers advantages.

The consequences of division of work are not wholly positive, however. Once the work is divided, people tend to orient themselves toward their portion of the work, rather than toward other portions, or toward the task as a whole. This orientation so colors department members' perceptions, for instance, that they quite naturally seek to make their own work easier and more meaningful, to acquire a larger share of resources, and to exercise more control over the flow of work to them and from them to others. Essentially, people behave in ways consistent with the structuring of tasks. Division of the work makes one portion of it central to them, and they proceed to behave in just that fashion—as if their portion of the work were central. These tendencies are called "suboptimization," the optimizing of a portion of the work, rather than the whole. They constitute one potentially dysfunctional consequence of dividing the work.

FUNCTIONAL FORM

The systematic division of work, typically reflected in departments, is fairly obvious. Somewhat less obvious is the basis for dividing it. How should the work be divided? There are numerous ways of dividing the work, and, given the potential consequences, the designer should choose knowledgeably from among the options. The basis on which work is divided will implicitly set the various departments' goals, and define members' perceptions. If we note that "function" means "a portion of the tasks or activities necessary" (Litterer, 1973), we will have a starting place. By functional form, we mean an organizational structure that divides the work among departments or units, each responsible for a portion of it. Some common bases for dividing work among functional departments would include (see Figures 1–5):

Business function: Manufacturing, sales, personnel, R&D departments.

Managerial function: Controller, planning, operations.

Technical function or process: Painting, welding, stamping, assembly.

Similar tools or techniques: Typing, operations research, computer center.

Time: Day shift, evening shift.

Shared product or purpose: Maintenance, editorial department, police.

Geographic location: Kalamazoo plant, New England region.

Client served: Consumer sales, government contracts, industrial equipment.

Some of these distinctions rest upon the activities of the manufacturing process, others on the output or client, still others on characteristics like time or location. It is important to note that the distinctions are not precise and mutually exclusive. Indeed, they are often used in combinations, particularly in more complex organizational forms. When someone refers to a

FIGURE 1   Functional Departments—Manufacturing Firm—Highly Centralized

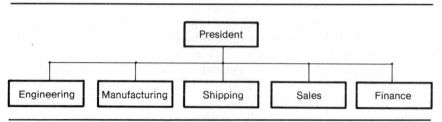

FIGURE 2   Functional Departments—School

FIGURE 3   Functional Departments—Hospital

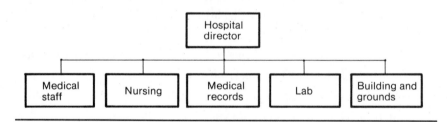

"functional organization structure," she or he means an organization in which each department performs only a portion of the needed activities of the organization, with coordination occurring at top levels. It is often provided by the president (as in Figures 1, 4A, and 4B, for instance)—making the functional form a logical successor to the agency organization, for the top manager still maintains a large amount of control. Functional organization identifies key aspects of the task, and clearly assigns responsibility for them. It permits and encourages specialization around these key tasks. Its disadvantages, beyond suboptimization, include potential difficulties in work flow

FIGURE 4A Departments by Managerial Function and Process

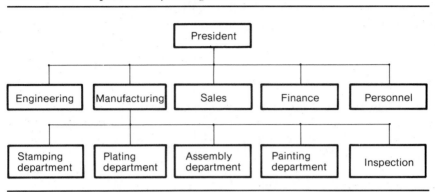

FIGURE 4B Departments by Process—City Government

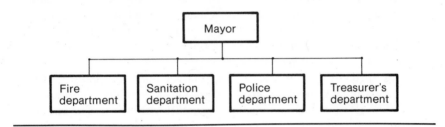

FIGURE 5 Departments by Clients Served

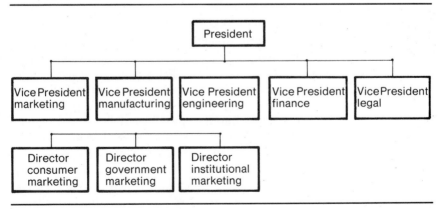

between and among departments, and information overload as top managers become overwhelmed with too many coordinating decisions. This form of organization *specializes;* its main problem is *reintegration* of the specialized, differentiated activities.

DIVISIONAL STRUCTURE

While product departments were mentioned above, most typically product organization occurs in larger organizations that have evolved several distinctly different products or product lines. It usually implies product coordination at least one level *below* top management. Historically, the divisional structure evolved first at Du Pont and General Motors, to meet a specific set of needs. Du Pont, which was reorganized from a cluster of family-owned predecessor firms in 1902, was soon expanded further by acquisition into the largest explosives manufacturing company in the United States. Du Pont had some 31 factories producing three main product lines—dynamite, black powder, and smokeless military gunpowder. The products were sufficiently different in raw materials, manufacture, and marketing to multiply complexities further. A great many new administrative mechanisms—like uniform and systematic information on costs and revenues, and rational allocation procedures—had to be evolved to make possible the coordination of so many activities.

Because of the differences in the product lines, the basic structure selected was organization into three operating departments, one for each product line. Within each, a functional structure was set up. The operating departments shared a common accounting system, and a common system for evaluating unit performance (return on investment). Resources for investment were allocated from the top. It was clear from the outset, however, that running so large and so complex an organization would require more managerial capacity than just a single chief executive. To coordinate and manage the firm as a whole—in contrast to the individual departments within it—an executive committee made up of the operating department heads was formed. This structure explicitly recognized the need for both product line, or operating responsibilities, and for organizationwide, coordinative responsibilities. It was only thus, by explicitly monitoring and managing relationships among the product lines, that the company as a whole could avoid the inefficiencies that had plagued the predecessor companies. The explicit charge of the executive committee was to coordinate and integrate activities for the firm as a whole. (See Figure 6 for a simplified organization chart.) Over time, the distinction between product line operations and the overall management of the firm was more strongly drawn, and more clearly reflected in structure by ensuring that the operating department heads were not the majority membership of the executive committee. Instead, corpo-

FIGURE 6   Du Pont's Organization prior to 1911 (much simplified)

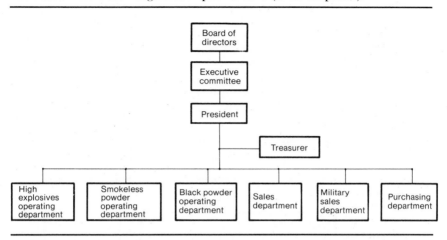

SOURCE: Adapted from Alfred D. Chandler, Jr., and Stephen Salisbury, *Pierre S. Du Pont and the making of the modern corporation* (New York: Harper & Row, 1976).

rate-level executives were appointed. This separation of tasks allowed the company to concentrate on new products, to allocate investment among the competing activities of the various product lines rationally, and to attend to financing new capital for expansion.

Du Pont's original structure made use of product-line form (the operating departments), functional departmentalization (within the main operating departments), and of staff as well as line managers. These innovations were essentially structural means to divide the work *of management*, distinguishing various product operations from corporate management, and from the specialized ancillary support functions not concerned directly with operations. By providing structural legitimacy for all of these functions, Du Pont's divisional structure achieved a high order of performance in a vastly more complex business situation than had existed before.

GENERAL MOTORS

General Motors, too, evolved a divisional structure in response to product-line differences. However, the genesis was different from Du Pont's. GM was founded by William C. Durant, who assembled it from widely diverse companies manufacturing everything from entire automobiles—such as Cadillac, Buick, Oakland, and even Cartercar—to components, tractors, an early refrigerator, and other things. Each had originally been an independent firm. There was no overall structure, to begin with, and no communication among different portions of the company. Aside from

FIGURE 7   Simplified Organization Chart, General Motors, 1924

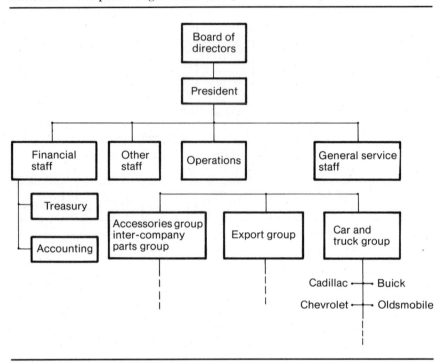

SOURCE: Adapted from Alfred D. Chandler, Jr., and Stephen Sallsbury, *Pierre S. Du Pont and the making of the modern corporation* (New York: Harper & Row, 1976).

the name, the various factories shared little. In the absence of controls or coordination, the various lines competed with one another, not only for financial resources within the firm, but outside it, in the marketplace as well.

GM's product line, even after some eliminations, contained 10 car models and seven brands. All but two were losing money in 1921. Since the products competed directly (as smokeless powder and dynamite did not, at Du Pont), coordination was even more essential. The problem at GM was to retain the advantages of decentralized independence—which permitted each division to specialize itself to concentrate on a specific market niche—while coordinating the whole firm. The design problem was to combine centralized control on financial and policy matters (to coordinate among divisions) with decentralized operations (to ensure timely and adequate operating decisions). Under Durant, the executive committee had consisted of the heads of the operating divisions (much like Du Pont's first structure), and had exercised little or no control. After Durant's bankruptcy, the firm was reorganized with a new executive committee. The division heads were retained in an advisory capacity, but were not executive committee members. A central financial staff, answerable to the executive committee, directed accounting and reporting procedures to ensure complete and comparable data. The divisions and their products were reduced, streamlined, and positioned so that each division was responsible for a single product-line and a specific price range designated by the executive committee.

This basic structure reflected the philosophy of the company (see Figure 7): Divisions should be autonomous and operate independently within broad policy boundaries laid down by the corporation. Policy should be a corporate responsibility, aimed at corporate coordination. The corporation would direct the reporting and accounting procedures, and would allocate financial resources. This philosophy, and this structure, continues to the present day with relatively little change. GM grew to be the largest producer of automobiles in the world with this structure.

ADMINISTRATIVE STRUCTURES

As organizations grew more complex, greater use was made of formal arrangements, written records and procedures, and explicit assignment of responsibilities. This formality offered many advantages, as Max Weber noted. Weber described a completely specified organization, which he called "bureaucracy" (from the French word for office, *bureau*). Weber's description was "an ideal type," or a model abstracted from the compromises required in the real world. By ignoring such compromises, the ideal type highlights the characteristics of bureaucracy. A bureaucracy, according to Weber, was rules based, in stark contrast to the earlier agency forms [that were] based on the leader's preference. As a result, the bureaucratic form provided a notable advance in efficiency, reliability, and predictability. The chief characteristics of the bureaucracy were:

1. Tasks are assigned to specific organization units and members as official duties, attached to *positions* (not individuals).

2. Authority is hierarchical, with higher positions holding greater authority, responsibility, and control. Power is concentrated at the top.

3. Formal rules govern behavior, ensuring uniformity in order to facilitate coordination.

4. Organization membership is a full-time commitment, typically a career for life.

5. Training and expertise are the basis for recruitment. There is a high degree of specialization.

6. Promotion is by seniority and merit.

7. Official activities are carefully segregated from private life; people act in accordance with their roles, not their preferences.

8. Files record and summarize all organizational activities.

Weber was aware of some drawbacks to this sort of organization, but he emphasized the advantages of the form in contrast to earlier methods of organizing. Predictability, reliability, increased output, lessened friction, discretion, and reduced material and personal costs were all advantages he cited as deriving from the technical superiority of the bureaucratic form.

THE DEGREE OF FORMALITY

The advantages of bureaucracy are so great that virtually every modern organization is, to some degree, "bureaucratic." This formality may be limited to an explicit division of labor, allowing and encouraging specialization, for instance. It may even be required by law: for example, hospitals are required to hire only specialists (medical doctors and trained nurses and technicians) to perform medical services. Even in private enterprises manufacturing proprietary materials for profit, such degrees of formality as explicit and accurate records of costs and revenues, payments and taxes, inspections, and injuries are required. These are all examples of formality. Such measures as the number of specialist job categories, differing from one another so incumbents are not immediately interchangeable, provide one indication of the degree of formality in an organization. Another measure is the degree to which procedures are specified in advance. If most activity within the organization is governed by protocol or procedure, and there is a set response to most situations, we can identify the organization as quite formal. Such organizations typically also have many levels of hierarchy, and require that situations that fall outside the set rules of operation be referred upward, to superiors. So, too, with conflict or differences between different departments or units. Such an organization is often referred to as "mechanistic" (Burns and Stalker, 1961) because it is expected to operate like a machine.

At its extreme, the "machine bureaucracy" centralizes power and decision making, reserving them to the top executive. At the extreme, such an organization is rigid and highly formal—everthing is specified, and organization members are allowed virtually no discretion. The underlying assumption is that tasks, environment, and circumstances will always remain the same. Of course, the extreme is far more rigid and specific than real-world organization structures would be. Nevertheless, it is clear that a range of bureaucratization is possible. To the degree that an organization does rely on rules, specify the duties of members, rely on specialists, and so on, it is bureaucratic. To the extent that decision making is delegated downward, initiative is permitted or encouraged, and informal arrangements vary the procedures, the organization is less bureaucratic. Virtually every organization of any size, public or private, is to some degree bureaucratic. This ubiquity testifies loudly to the advantages that Weber noted. These benefits are counterbalanced by costs—red tape, alienation, rigidity, inefficiency when rules fail to deal adequately with reality: in short, all that we imply by the stereotype "bureaucratic." The designer must recognize both costs and benefits.

In contrast to the highly bureaucratic, highly formal organization are informal or "organic" organizations (Burns and Stalker, 1961). These organizations rely on expertise and problem solving, rather than "the rules" or hierarchy, to accomplish tasks. People do what must be done, results matter more than rules, and tasks may frequently change, depending on the job at hand. Rather than relying on rules or procedures, such organizations may well rely on external training—as, for instance, when professional engineers, accountants, or architects are hired, then expected to work with relatively few formal rules. Instead, professional training and discretion are invoked. Of course, professional organizations are not the only organic organizations. Any organization that is relatively informal and operates in a flexible fashion may be identified as organic; professional organizations are merely one frequently encountered type of organic organization.

Organic, informal organization is very attractive, to most of us. Many of us like to imagine ourselves operating with few rules or constraints. We see ourselves as capable and responsible organization members, easily able to choose appropriate actions, and always in agreement with organizational goals. The difficulties of organic organizations are the obverse of those of bureaucracy: The informality and lack of rules that allows freedom of action also make for unpredictability; inefficiency, as people may "reinvent the wheel"; and inconsistency, as decisions are made one way this week and another next. The lack of structure also fails to provide guidance for some who need direction. In short, organic organizations, too, have liabilities, and the designer must be aware of these as well as the undeniable advantages in choosing an appropriate degree of formality.

LINE AND STAFF

Bureaucracy, with its carefully delineated hierarchy of authority and control assumes that any higher organization member is more knowledgeable and has more responsibility than any lower member. Increasing complexity—as at Du Pont and GM—quickly led to the recognition of several sorts of authority, however. While some executives were directly responsible for operations, if the organization as a whole was to be coordinated and run effectively, various administrative mechanisms had to be explicitly managed. Thus, for instance, accounting procedures and reporting systems had to be designed, managed, maintained, and their results interpreted. This was clearly a specialist activity, and just as clearly ancillary to the main activities of the firm. While essential to large-scale, complex operations, it was not part of operations. The solution was to divide the work—to specifically designate responsibility for the new technical requirements to specialists who held no other responsibility, while operating departments and members were designated as "line" activities. Organizationally, since support activity was all-pervasive yet not part of the central activity of manufacturing, these structural units were distinguished as "staff."

Staff units are specialized support activities which are traditionally expected to advise (but not to command) line managers and members. In current organizations, this exclusively "advisory" role frequently breaks down—especially where staff units must approve budgetary expenses, for instance. Nevertheless, the traditional model is still typically invoked. Staff units are usually responsible for the development of specialized expertise and technical data, longer range activities concerning the coordination of the firm as a whole, and the like. The advantages of separating staff activities is akin to that of specialization in general—it encourages the development of greater expertise in the designated area. The disadvantages are also related to specialization. Because the staff unit concentrates only on its specialty, which may be quite arcane and esoteric to other organization members, staff personnel may become cut off from organizational reality and from other organization members. Difficulties include getting staff recommendations, accepted by line personnel, ensuring realistic staff recommendations, and resolving jurisdictional disputes between line and staff.

These difficulties, and the need for greater responsiveness to both the needs of external environmental segments and internal coordination, led to the next organizational form, simultaneous organization.

SIMULTANEOUS FORMS

The functional and divisional organizational forms were designed with an eye to separating the work into distinct pieces, generally eliminating overlap, and assigning relatively clear responsibility for activities along whatever underlying dimension was selected. In contrast, *simultaneous* organizational forms, of which the most familiar is the matrix, seek to design along multiple dimensions at the same time. The aim is to gain the benefits of several sorts of specialization, several emphases for attention at once. In order to do so, simultaneous organizations arrange people according to two (or occasionally more) basic divisions of work.

Simultaneous organization evolved first under the Defense Department and received major impetus at NASA, the National Aeronautics and Space Administration, and in the aerospace industry. The typical predecessor arrangements were functional departmentalization, with coordination occurring at the top (as in Figure 1). This structure did serve to encourage needed specialization and technical expertise, by grouping technical specialists together. This grouping facilitated their communication with one another around work problems, thus providing a highly experienced technical resource pool. The structure was not adequate for coordinating the highly complex projects of aerospace work, however. The required communications across functional departments and technical specialties were not occurring smoothly, resulting in delays and increased costs. The design solution was to reorganize along both technical specialties and projects, simultaneously. Project teams, drawn from numerous departments as needed, worked together on a given project. Meanwhile, all project members were still members of their functional departments, with access to their resources of technical expertise. (See Figure 8). Each project member was responsible both to the functional department head, and to the project head; both evaluated the member.

Critical characteristics of the matrix form include simultaneous attention to two or more essential organizational tasks (here, the development and maintenance of specialized technical expertise, and the coordination of diverse specialists around a common temporary task). Functional departments are oriented toward the acquisition, maintenance, and development of specialized *resources*—people and equipment, for instance. Project teams are oriented toward the production of *output*. As a result, relationships, authority patterns, and evaluation all become highly complex and usually negotiated—because there are no clear and simple answers. The multiple dimensions of organization foster an ongoing tension—which can be highly creative, if appropriately balanced—between the underlying *resource* orientation and the desired *output* orientation.

FIGURE 8 Matrix Organization in Manufacturing

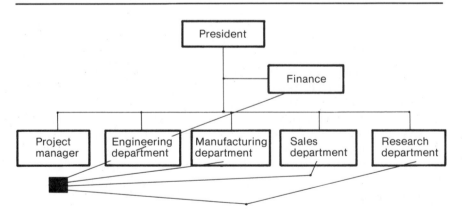

Note: Team members are drawn from various departments as needed, and report to *both* the project manager and their home department head.

The matrix form encourages a far more useful view of organizational realities, because it legitimates the sort of bargaining and negotiation that is essential when many goals—for instance, both output and resource goals—are to be met at once. It also encourages a general managerial viewpoint well down in the organization, where members see these alternate dimensions interacting and begin quite early in their careers to understand the trade-offs required.

Matrix forms, like functional and departmental forms, evolve in response to the problems around them, as managers seek new answers. In the case of the matrix, the first step was temporary teams, and temporary assignments. Later steps simply recognized that the organization faced an ongoing stream of such temporary projects. Thus, while any individual project was temporary, another would take its place for firms involved in project work. For such organizations, a permanent project orientation (with projects changing) and a permanent functional organization (with appropriate resources maintained) were needed.

The advantage of simultaneous organizations like the matrix is their ability to maximize along several dimensions. Because project teams can be easily constituted and dissolved, the simultaneous form can be highly responsive to change as well. Because of this responsiveness, and because of the technical support the departmental structure provides, organization members often find they can "have their cake and eat it, too," gaining benefits of motivation, involvement, and worthwhile participation. Disadvantages include substantial managerial overhead—particularly in the early stages (which may last for two or three years) while participants learn to negotiate and bargain instead of referring all conflicts up the hierarchy for resolution. The complexity and uncertainty of authority and responsibility lines can trouble some members, as can the need for high-order interpersonal skills.

CONCLUSIONS

Choice among organizational forms is contingent upon many factors. No single form—functional, product or geographic division, combination, or simultaneous—is "best" for all circumstances. The best choice is the one that best balances the costs and benefits for maximum gain, in the context of clear thinking about present and future organizational needs. Critical organizational dimensions must be addressed, as must the organization's ability to bear the costs and tolerate the disadvantages of any particular form. Stability is economically efficient, but may impose heavy costs in terms of lost flexibility, creativity, and involvement. Innovative simultaneous organizations emphasize responsiveness, but may impose substantial costs in terms of duplication, inefficiencies, and sheer complexity. Not all people tolerate well an ambiguous structure that requires multiple reporting relationships and bargaining. Each of the major design options—simple organizations, organization by functional components, by product, by division, mixed forms, and simultaneous forms—meets a particular set of needs. Each emphasizes some strengths at the price of some weaknesses. Design is the art of balancing these factors to choose appropriately.

REFERENCES

Babbage, Charles. *On the economy of machinery and manufacturers*. London: Charles Knight, 1832.

Burns, T., and G. M. Stalker. *The management of innovation*. London: Tavistock Publications, 1961.

Chandler, Alfred D. *Strategy and structure*. Cambridge, Mass.: MIT Press, 1962.

Chandler, Alfred D., and Steven Salisbury. *Pierre S. Du Pont and the making of the modern corporation*. New York: Harper & Row, 1977.

Jelinek, Mariann. "Organizational design." In *Organizational behavior*. 2d ed. ed. Don Hellriegel and John W. Slocum, Jr. St. Paul: West Publishing, 1979, chap. 4.

Litterer, Joseph A. *The analysis of organizations*. 2d ed. New York: John Wiley & Sons, 1973.

Mintzberg, Henry. *The structuring of organizations*. Englewood Cliffs, N.J.: Prentice-Hall, 1979.

Sloan, Alfred P. *My years at General Motors*. ed. John McDonald and Catherine Stevens. Garden City, N.Y.: Doubleday Anchor, 1972.

Smith, Adam. *The wealth of nations*. London: Straham and Candell, 1776.

Organizational Strategy, Structure, and Process*

Raymond E. Miles,

Charles C. Snow,

Alan D. Meyer,

and Henry J. Coleman, Jr.

Organizational adaptation is a topic that has received only limited and fragmented theoretical treatment. Any attempt to examine organizational adaptation is difficult, since the process is highly complex and changeable. The proposed theoretical framework deals with alternative ways in which organizations define their product-market domains (strategy) and construct mechanisms (structures and processes) to pursue these strategies. The framework is based on interpretation of existing literature and continuing studies in four industries (college textbook publishing, electronics, food processing, and health care).

An organization is both an articulated purpose and an established mechanism for achieving it. Most organizations engage in an ongoing process of evaluating their purposes—questioning, verifying, and redefining the manner of interaction with their environments. Effective organizations carve out and maintain a viable market for their goods or services. Ineffective organizations fail this market-alignment task. Organizations also constantly modify and refine the mechanism by which they achieve their purposes—rearranging their structure of roles and relationships and their managerial processes. Efficient organizations establish mechanisms that complement their market strategy, but inefficient organizations struggle with these structural and process mechanisms.

For most organizations, the dynamic process of adjusting to environmental change and uncertainty—of maintaining an effective alignment with

---

* From *Academy of Management Review* (1978) 3, no. 3, 546–62.

the environment while managing internal interdependencies—is enormously complex, encompassing myriad decisions and behaviors at several organization levels. But the complexity of the adjustment process can be penetrated: by searching for patterns in the behavior of organizations, one can describe and even predict the process of organizational adaptation. This article presents a theoretical framework that managers and students of management can use to analyze an organization as an integrated and dynamic whole—a model that takes into account the interrelationships among strategy, structure, and process. For a complete discussion of the theoretical framework and research studies, see (15). Specifically, the framework has two major elements: *(a)* a general model of the process of adaptation, which specifies the major decisions needed by the organization to maintain an effective alignment with its environment, and *(b)* an organizational typology, which portrays different patterns of adaptive behavior used by organizations within a given industry or other grouping. But as several theorists have pointed out, organizations are limited in their choices of adaptive behavior to those which top management believes will allow the effective direction and control of human resources (4, 5, 6). Thus, the theoretical framework to prevailing theories of management is also related. An increased understanding of the adaptive process, of how organizations move through it, and of the managerial requirements of different adjustment patterns can facilitate the difficult process of achieving an effective organization-environment equilibrium.

In the following sections, a typical example of organizational adaptation drawn from one of our empirical research studies is first presented. Second, a model of the adaptive process that arose from this research is described and discussed. In the third section, four alternative forms of adaptation exhibited by the organizations in our studies are described. Finally, the relationship between the organizational forms and currently available theories of management is discussed.

AN EXAMPLE OF ORGANIZATIONAL ADAPTATION

As an example of the problems associated with the adaptive process, consider the experience of a subsidiary of one of the companies in our studies.

> Porter Pump and Valve (PPV) is a semiautonomous division of a medium-sized equipment-manufacturing firm, which is in turn part of a large, highly diversified conglomerate. PPV manufactures a line of heavy-duty pumps and components for fluid-movement systems. The company does most of its own castings, makes many of its own parts, and maintains a complete stock of replacement parts. PPV also does special-order foundry work for other firms as its production schedule allows.

Until recently, Porter Pump and Valve had defined its business as providing quality products and service to a limited set of reliable customers. PPV's general manager, a first-rate engineer who spent much of his time in the machine shop and foundry, personified the company's image of quality and cost efficiency. In the mid-70s, corporate management became concerned about both the speed and direction of PPV's growth. The management and staff at corporate headquarters began considering two new product and market opportunities, both in the energy field. Fluid-movement systems required for nuclear power generation provided one of these opportunities, and the development of novel techniques for petroleum exploration, well recovery, and fluid delivery provided the second. PPV had supplied some components to these markets in the past, but it was now clear that opportunities for the sale of entire systems or large-scale subsystems were growing rapidly.

PPV's initial moves toward these new opportunities were tentative. The general manager discovered that contract sales required extensive planning, field-contact work, and careful negotiations—activities not within his primary area of interest or experience. Finally, in an effort to foster more rapid movement into these new markets, executives in the parent organization transferred the general manager to a head-office position and moved into the top spot at PPV a manager with an extensive background in both sales and engineering and who was adept at large-scale contract negotiations.

Within a year of the changeover in general managers, PPV landed several lucrative contracts, and more appeared to be in the offing. The new business created by these contracts, however, placed heavy coordination demands on company management, and, while the organization's technology (production and distribution system) has not been drastically revised over the past two years, workflow processes and the operational responsibilities of several managers have changed markedly. Materials control and scheduling, routine tasks in the past, are now complex activities, and managers of these operations meet regularly with the executive planning committee. Moreover, a rudimentary matrix structure has emerged in which various line managers undertake specific project responsibilities in addition to their regular duties. Key personnel additions have been made to the marketing department and more are planned, with particular emphasis on individuals who are capable of performing field planning and supervising and who can quickly bring new fluid systems to full operation. Budgets of some of the older departments are being cut back, and these funds are being diverted to the new areas of activity.

As illustrated, Porter Pump and Valve experienced changes in its products and markets, in the technological processes needed to make new products and serve new markets, and in the administrative structure and processes required to plan, coordinate, and control the company's new operations. None of the usual perspectives which might be used to analyze such organizational changes—for example, economics, industrial engineering, marketing, or policy—appears to address all of the problems experienced by Porter Pump and Valve. Therefore, how can the adaptive process which occurred at PPV be described in its entirety?

THE ADAPTIVE CYCLE

We have developed a general model of the adaptive process, which we call the *adaptive cycle*. Consistent with the strategic-choice approach to the study of organizations, the model parallels and expands ideas formulated by theorists, such as Chandler (9), Child (10), Cyert and March (11), Drucker (12, 13), Thompson (18), and Weick (19, 20). Essentially, proponents of the strategic-choice perspective argue that organizational behavior is only partially preordained by environmental conditions and that the choices which top managers make are the critical determinants of organizational structure and process. Although these choices are numerous and complex, they can be viewed as three broad "problems" of organizational adaptation: the *entrepreneurial problem*, the *engineering problem*, and the *administrative problem*. In mature organizations, management must solve each of these problems simultaneously; but for explanatory purposes, these adaptive problems can be discussed as if they occurred sequentially.

The Entrepreneurial Problem

The adaptive cycle, though evident in all organizations, is perhaps most visible in new or rapidly growing organizations (and in organizations which recently have survived a major crisis). In a new organization, an entrepreneurial insight, perhaps only vaguely defined at first, must be developed into a concrete *definition of an organizational domain: a specific good or service and a target market or market segment.* In an ongoing organization, the entrepreneurial problem has an added dimension. Because the organization has already obtained a set of "solutions" to its engineering and administrative problems, its next attempt at an entrepreneurial "thrust" may be difficult. In the example of Porter Pump and Valve, the company's attempt to modify its products and markets was constrained by its present production process and by the fact that the general manager and his staff did not possess the needed marketing orientation.

In either a new or ongoing organization, the solution to the entrepreneurial problem is marked by management's acceptance of a particular product-market domain, and this acceptance becomes evident when management decides to commit resources to achieve objectives relative to the domain. In many organizations, external and internal commitment to the entrepreneurial solution is sought through the development and projection of an organizational "image," which defines both the organization's market and its orientation toward it (e.g., an emphasis on size, efficiency, or innovation).

Although we are suggesting that the engineering phase begins at this point, the need for further entrepreneurial activities clearly does not disappear. The entrepreneurial function remains a top-management responsibility, although, as Bower (7) has described, the identification of a new opportunity and the initial impetus for movement toward it may originate at lower managerial levels.

The Engineering Problem

The engineering problem involves the creation of a system which *operationalizes management's solution to the entrepreneurial problem.* Such a system requires management to select an appropriate technology (input–transformation–output process) for producing and distributing chosen products or services and to form new information, communication, and control linkages (or modify existing linkages) to ensure proper operation of the technology.

As solutions to these problems are reached, initial implementation of the administrative system takes place. There is no assurance that the configuration of the organization, as it begins to emerge during this phase, will remain the same when the engineering problem finally has been solved. The actual form of the organization's structure will be determined during the administrative phase as management solidifies relations with the environment and establishes processes for coordinating and controlling internal operations. Referring again to Porter Pump and Valve, the company's redefinition of its domain required concomitant changes in its technology— from a pure mass-production technology to more of a unit or small-batch technology (21).

The Administrative Problem

The administrative problem, as described by most theories of management, is primarily that of reducing uncertainty within the organizational system, or, in terms of the present model, of rationalizing and stabilizing those activities which successfully solved problems faced by the organization during the entrepreneurial and engineering phases. Solving the administrative problem involves more than simply rationalizing the system already developed (uncertainty reduction); it also involves formulating and implementing those processes which will enable the organization to continue to evolve (innovation). This conception of the administrative problem, as a pivotal factor in the cycle of adaptation, deserves further elaboration.

Rationalization and Articulation.   In the ideal organization, management would be equally adept at performing two somewhat conflicting functions: It would be able to create an administrative system (structure and processes) that could smoothly direct and monitor the organization's current activities without, at the same time, allowing the system to become so ingrained that future innovation activities are jeopardized. Such a perspective requires the administrative system to be viewed as both a *lagging* and *leading* variable in the process of adaptation. As a lagging variable, it must rationalize, through the development of appropriate structures and processes, strategic decisions made at previous points in the adjustment process. As a leading variable, the administrative system must facilitate the organization's future capacity to adapt by articulating and reinforcing the paths along which innovative activity can proceed. At Porter Pump and Valve, management modified its planning, coordination, and control processes substantially in order to pursue the company's newly chosen areas of business (the "lagging" aspect of administration). At the same time, key personnel were added to the marketing department; their duties included product development, market research, and technical consulting. These activities were designed to keep PPV at the forefront of new product and market opportunities (the "leading" aspect of administration).

THE STRATEGIC TYPOLOGY

If one accepts the adaptive cycle as valid, the question becomes: How do organizations move through the cycle? That is, using the language of our model, what strategies do organizations employ in solving their entrepreneurial, engineering, and administrative problems? Our research and interpretation of the literature show that there are essentially three *strategic types* of organizations: Defenders, Analyzers, and Prospectors. Each type has its own unique strategy for relating to its chosen market(s), and each has a particular configuration of technology, structure, and process that is consistent with its market strategy. A fourth type of organization encountered in our studies is called the Reactor. The Reactor is a form of strategic "failure," in that inconsistencies exist among its strategy, technology, structure, and process.

Although similar typologies of various aspects of organizational behavior are available (1, 2, 3, 15, 16, 17), our formulation specifies relationships among strategy, technology, structure, and process to the point where entire organizations can be viewed as integrated wholes in dynamic interaction with their environments. Any typology is unlikely to encompass every form of organizational behavior—the world of organizations is much too changeable and complex to permit such a claim. Nevertheless, every organization that we have observed appears, when compared to other organizations in its industry, to fit predominantly into one of the four categories, and its behavior is generally predictable given its typological classification. The "pure" form of each of these organization types is described below.

Defenders

The Defender (i.e., its top management) deliberately enacts and maintains an environment for which a stable form of organization is appropriate. Stability is chiefly achieved by the Defender's definition of, and solution to, its entrepreneurial problem. Defenders define their *entrepreneurial* problem as *how to seal off a portion of the total market in order to create a stable domain*, and they do so by producing only a limited set of products directed at a narrow segment of the total potential market. Within the limited domain, the Defender strives aggressively to prevent competitors from entering its "turf." Such behaviors include standard economic actions like competitive pricing or high-quality products; but Defenders also tend to ignore developments and trends outside of their domains, choosing instead to grow through market penetration and perhaps some limited product development. Over time, a true Defender is able to carve out and maintain a small niche within the industry which is difficult for competitors to penetrate.

Having chosen a narrtow product-market domain, the Defender invests a great deal of resources in solving its *engineering* problem: *how to produce and distribute goods or services as efficiently as possible.* Typically, the Defender does so by developing a single core technology that his highly cost-efficient. Technological efficiency is central to the Defender's success since its domain has been deliberately created to absorb outputs on a predictable, continuous basis. Some Defenders extend technological efficiency to its limits through a process of vertical integration—incorporating each stage of production from raw materials supply to distribution of final output into the same organizational system.

Finally, the Defender's solution to its administrative problem is closely aligned with its solutions to the entrepreneurial and engineering problems. The Defender's *administrative problem—how to achieve strict control of the organization in order to ensure efficiency*—is solved through a combination of structural and process mechanisms that can be generally described as "mechanistic" (8). These mechanisms include a top-management group heavily dominated by production and cost-control specialists, little or no scanning of the environment for new areas of opportunity, intensive planning oriented toward cost and other efficiency issues, functional structures characterized by extensive division of labor, centralized control, communications through formal hierarchical channels, and so on. Such an administrative system is ideally suited for generating and maintaining efficiency, and the key characteristic of stability is as apparent here as in the solution to the other two adaptive problems.

Pursued vigorously, the Defender strategy can be viable in most industries, although stable industries lend themselves to this type of organization more than turbulent industries (e.g., the relative lack of technological change in the food-processing industry generally favors the Defender strat-

TABLE 1   Characteristics of the Defender

Entrepreneurial Problem	*Engineering Problem*	*Administrative Problem*
Problem: How to "seal off" a portion of the total market to create a stable set of products and customers.	**Problem:** How to produce and distribute goods or services as efficiently as possible.	**Problem:** How to maintain strict control of the organization in order to ensure efficiency.
Solutions: 1. Narrow and stable domain. 2. Aggressive maintenance of domain (e.g., competitive pricing and excellent customer service). 3. Tendency to ignore developments outside of domain. 4. Cautious and incremental growth primarily through market penetration. 5. Some product development but closely related to current goods or services.	**Solutions:** 1. Cost-efficient technology. 2. Single core technology. 3. Tendency toward vertical integration. 4. Continuous improvements in technology to maintain efficiency.	**Solutions:** 1. Financial and production experts most powerful members of the dominant coalition; limited environmental scanning. 2. Tenure of dominant coalition is lengthy; promotions from within. 3. Planning is intensive, cost oriented, and completed before action is taken. 4. Tendency toward functional structure, with extensive division of labor and high degree of formalization. 5. Centralized control and long-looped vertical information systems. 6. Simple coordination mechanisms and conflict resolved through hierarchical channels. 7. Organizational performance measured against previous years; reward system favors production and finance.

TABLE 1   *(concluded)*

Entrepreneurial Problem	Engineering Problem	Administrative Problem
Costs and benefits: It is difficult for competitors to dislodge the organization from its small niche in the industry, but a major shift in the market could threaten survival.	**Costs and benefits:** Technological efficiency is central to organizational performance, but heavy investment in this area requires technological problems to remain familiar and predictable for lengthy time periods.	**Costs and benefits:** Administrative system is ideally suited to maintain stability and efficiency but it is not well suited to locating and responding to new product or market opportunities.

SOURCE: Raymond E. Miles and Charles C. Snow, *Organizational strategy, structure, and process* (New York: McGraw-Hill, 1978), Table 3–1.

egy, compared with the situation in the electronics industry). This particular form of organization is not without its potential risks. The Defender's *primary risk* is that of *ineffectiveness*—being unable to respond to a major shift in its market environment. The Defender relies on the continued viability of its single, narrow domain, and it receives a return on its large technological investment only if the major problems facing the organization continue to be of an engineering nature. If the Defender's market shifts dramatically, this type of organization has little capacity for locating and exploiting new areas of opportunity. In short, the Defender is perfectly capable of responding to today's world. To the extent that tomorrow's world is similar to today's, the Defender is ideally suited for its environment. Table 1 summarizes the Defender's salient characteristics and the major strengths and weaknesses inherent in this pattern of adaptation.

Prospectors

In many ways, Prospectors respond to their chosen environments in a manner that is almost the opposite of the Defender. In one sense, the Prospector is exactly like the Defender: there is a high degree of consistency among its solutions to the three problems of adaptation.

Generally speaking, the Prospector enacts an environment that is more dynamic than those of other types of organizations within the same industry. Unlike the Defender, whose success comes primarily from efficiently serving a stable domain, the Prospector's prime capability is that of finding and exploiting new product and market opportunities. For a Prospector, maintaining a reputation as an innovator in product and market development may be as important as, perhaps even more important than, high profitability. In fact, because of the inevitable "failure rate" associated with sustained product and market innovation, Prospectors may find it difficult consistently to attain the profit levels of the more efficient Defender.

Defining its *entrepreneurial* problem as *how to locate and develop product and market opportunities*, the Prospector's domain is usually broad and in a continuous state of development. The systematic addition of new products or markets, frequently combined with retrenchment in other parts of the domain, gives the Prospector's products and markets an aura of fluidity uncharacteristic of the Defender. To locate new areas of opportunity, the Prospector must develop and maintain the capacity to survey a wide range of environmental conditions, trends, and events. This type of organization invests heavily in individuals and groups who scan the environment for potential opportunities. Because these scanning activities are not limited to the organization's current domain, Prospectors are frequently the creators of change in their respective industries. Change is one of the major tools used by the Prospector to gain an edge over competitors, so Prospector managers typically perceive more environmental change and uncertainty than managers of the Defender (or the other two organization types).

To serve its changing domain properly, the Prospector requires a good deal of flexibility in its technology and administrative system. Unlike the Defender, the Prospector's choice of products and markets is not limited to those which fall within the range of the organization's present technological capability. The Prospector's technology is contingent upon both the organization's current *and* future product mix: entrepreneurial activities always have primacy, and appropriate technologies are not selected or developed until late in the process of product development. Therefore, the Prospector's overall engineering problem is *how to avoid long-term commitments to a single type of technological process*, and the organization usually does so by creating multiple, prototypical technologies which have a low degree of routinization and mechanization.

Finally, the Prospector's *administrative* problem flows from its changing domain and flexible technologies: *how to facilitate, rather than control, organizational operations*. That is, the Prospector's administrative system must be able to deploy and coordinate resources among numerous decentralized units and projects, rather than to plan and control the operations of the entire organization centrally. To accomplish overall facilitation and coordination, the Prospector's structure-process mechanisms must be "organic" (8). These mechanisms include a top-management group dominated by marketing and research and development experts, planning that is broad, rather than intensive, and oriented toward results not methods, product or project structures characterized by a low degree of formalization, decentralized control, lateral as well as vertical communications, and so on. In contrast to the Defender, the Prospector's descriptive catchword throughout its administrative as well as entrepreneurial and engineering solutions is "flexibility."

TABLE 2 Characteristics of the Prospector

Entrepreneurial Problem	*Engineering Problem*	*Administrative Problem*
Problem:	**Problem:**	**Problem:**
How to locate and exploit new product and market opportunities.	How to avoid long-term commitments to a single technological process.	How to facilitate and coordinate numerous and diverse operations.
Solutions:	**Solutions:**	**Solutions:**
1. Broad and continuously developing domain.	1. Flexible, prototypical technologies.	1. Marketing and research and development experts most powerful members of the dominant coalition.
2. Monitors wide range of environmental conditions and events.	2. Multiple technologies.	2. Dominant coalition is large, diverse, and transitory; may include an inner circle.
3. Creates change in the industry.	3. Low degree of routinization and mechanization; technology embedded in people.	3. Tenure of dominant coalition not always lengthy; key managers may be hired from outside as well as promoted from within.
4. Growth through product and market development.		4. Planning is comprehensive, problem oriented, and cannot be finalized before action is taken.
5. Growth may occur in spurts.		

5. Tendency toward product structure with low division of labor and low degree of formalization.
6. Decentralized control and short-looped horizontal information systems.
7. Complex coordination mechanisms and conflict resolved through integrators.
8. Organizational performance measured against important competitors; reward system favors marketing and research and development.

Costs and benefits:
Administrative system is ideally suited to maintain flexibility and effectiveness but may underutilize and misutilize resources.

Costs and benefits:
Technological flexibility permits a rapid response to a changing domain, but the organization cannot develop maximum efficiency in its production and distribution system because of multiple technologies.

Costs and benefits:
Product and market innovation protect the organization from a changing environment, but the organization runs the risk of low profitability and overextension of its resources.

SOURCE: Raymond E. Miles and Charles C. Snow, *Organizational strategy, structure, and process* (New York: McGraw-Hill, 1978), Table 4-1.

Of course, the Prospector strategy also has its costs. Although the Prospector's continuous exploration of change helps to protect it from a changing environment, this type of organization runs the *primary risk* of *low profitability and overextension of resources*. While the Prospector's technological flexibility permits a rapid response to a changing domain, complete efficiency cannot be obtained because of the presence of multiple technologies. Finally, the Prospector's administrative system is well suited to maintain flexibility, but it may, at least temporarily, underutilize or even misutilize physical, financial, and human resources. In short, the Prospector is effective—it can respond to the demands of tomorrow's world. To the extent that the world of tomorrow is similar to that of today, the Prospector cannot maximize profitability because of its inherent inefficiency. Table 2 summarizes the Prospector's salient characteristics and the major strengths and weaknesses associated with this pattern of adaptation.

Analyzers

Based on our research, the Defender and the Prospector seem to reside at opposite ends of a continuum of adjustment strategies. Between these two extremes, a third type of organization is called the Analyzer. The Analyzer is a unique combination of the Prospector and Defender types and represents a viable alternative to these other strategies. A true Analyzer is an organization that attempts to minimize risk while maximizing the opportunity for profit—that is, an experienced Analyzer combines the strengths of both the Prospector and the Defender into a single system. This strategy is difficult to pursue, particularly in industries characterized by rapid market and technological change, and thus the word that best describes the Analyzer's adaptive approach is "balance."

The Analyzer defines its *entrepreneurial* problem in terms similar to both the Prospector and the Defender: *how to locate and exploit new product and market opportunities while simultaneously maintaining a firm core of traditional products and customers*. The Analyzer's solution to the entrepreneurial problem is also a blend of the solutions preferred by the Prospector and the Defender: the Analyzer moves toward new products or new markets but only after their viability has been demonstrated. This periodic transformation of the Analyzer's domain is accomplished through imitation—only the most successful product or market innovations developed by prominent Prospectors are adopted. At the same time, the majority of the Analyzer's revenue is generated by a fairly stable set of products and customer or client groups—a Defender characteristic. Thus, the successful Analyzer must be able to respond quickly when following the lead of key Prospectors while at the same time maintaining operating efficiency in its stable product and market areas. To the extent that it is successful, the

Analyzer can grow through market penetration as well as product and market development.

The duality evident in the Analyzer's domain is reflected in its *engineering* problem and solution. This type of organization must learn *how to achieve and protect an equilibrium between conflicting demands for technological flexibility and for technological stability*. This equilibrium is accomplished by partitioning production activities to form a dual technological core. The stable component of the Analyzer's technology bears a strong resemblance to the Defender's technology. It is functionally organized and exhibits high levels of standardization, routinization, and mechanization in an attempt to approach cost efficiency. The Analyzer's flexible technological component resembles the Prospector's technological orientation. In manufacturing organizations, it frequently includes a large group of applications engineers (or their equivalent) who are rotated among teams charged with the task of rapidly adapting new product designs to fit the Analyzer's existing stable technology.

The Analyzer's dual technological core thus reflects the engineering solutions of both the Prospector and the Defender, with the stable and flexible components integrated primarily by an influential applied research group. To the extent that this group is able to develop solutions that match the organization's existing technological capabilities with the new products desired by product managers, the Analyzer can enlarge its product line without incurring the Prospector's extensive research and development expenses.

The Analyzer's administrative problem, as well as its entrepreneurial engineering problems, contains both Defender and Prospector characteristics. Generally speaking, the *administrative* problem of the Analyzer is *how to differentiate the organization's structure and processes to accommodate both stable and dynamic areas of operation*. The Analyzer typically solves this problem with some version of a matrix organization structure. Heads of key functional units, most notably engineering and production, unite with product managers (usually housed in the marketing department) to form a balanced dominant coalition similar to both the Defender and the Prospector. The product manager's influence is usually greater than the functional manager's, since his or her task is to identify promising product-market innovations and to supervise their movement through applied engineering and into production in a smooth and timely manner. The presence of engineering and production in the dominant coalition is to represent the more stable domain and technology which are the foundations of the Analyzer's overall operations. The Analyzer's matrix structure is supported by intensive planning between the functional divisions of marketing and production, broad-gauge planning between the applied research group and the product managers for the development of new products, centralized control

TABLE 3 Characteristics of the Analyzer

Entrepreneurial Problem	Engineering Problem	Administrative Problem
Problem: How to locate and exploit new product and market opportunities while simultaneously maintaining a firm base of traditional products and customers.	**Problem:** How to be efficient in stable portions of the domain and flexible in changing portions.	**Problem:** How to differentiate the organization's structure and processes to accommodate both stable and dynamic areas of operation.
Solutions: 1. Hybrid domain that is both stable and changing. 2. Surveillance mechanisms mostly limited to marketing; some research and development. 3. Steady growth through market penetration and product-market development.	**Solutions:** 1. Dual technological core (stable and flexible component). 2. Large and influential applied engineering group. 3. Moderate degree of technical rationality.	**Solutions:** 1. Marketing and engineering most influential members of dominant coalition, followed closely by production. 2. Intensive planning between marketing and production concerning stable portion of domain; comprehensive planning among marketing, engineering, and product managers concerning new products and markets. 3. "Loose" matrix structure combining both functional divisions and product groups.

4. Moderately centralized control system with vertical and horizontal feedback loops.
5. Extremely complex and expensive coordination mechanisms; some conflict resolution through product managers, some through normal hierarchical channels.
6. Performance appraisal based on both effectiveness and efficiency measures, most rewards to marketing and engineering.

Costs and benefits:
Administrative system is ideally suited to balance stability and flexibility; but if this balance is lost, it may be difficult to restore equilibrium.

Costs and benefits:
Dual technological core is able to serve a hybrid stable-changing domain, but the technology can never be completely effective or efficient.

Costs and benefits:
Low investment in research and development, combined with imitation of demonstrably successful products, minimizes risk, but domain must be optimally balanced at all times between stability and flexibility.

SOURCE: Raymond E. Miles and Charles C. Snow, *Organizational strategy, structure, and process* (New York: McGraw-Hill, 1978), Table 5–1.

mechanisms in the functional divisions and decentralized control techniques in the product groups, and so on. In sum, the key characteristic of the Analyzer's administrative system is the proper differentiation of the organization's structure and processes to achieve a balance between the stable and dynamic areas of operation.

As is true for both the Defender and Prospector, the Analyzer strategy is not without its costs. The duality in the Analyzer's domain forces the organization to establish a dual technological core, and it requires management to operate fundamentally different planning, control, and reward systems simultaneously. Thus, the Analyzer's twin characteristics of stability and flexibility limit the organization's ability to move fully in either direction were the domain to shift dramatically. Consequently, the Analyzer's *primary risks* are both *inefficiency and ineffectiveness* if it does not maintain the necessary balance throughout its strategy-structure relationship. Table 3 summarizes the Analyzer's salient characteristics and the major strengths and weaknesses inherent in this pattern of adaptation.

Reactors

The Defender, the Prospector, and the Analyzer can all be proactive with respect to their environments, though each is proactive in a different way. At the extremes, Defenders continually attempt to develop greater efficiency in existing operations, while Prospectors explore environmental change in search of new opportunities. Over time, these action modes stabilize to form a pattern of response to environmental conditions that is both *consistent* and *stable*.

A fourth type of organization, the Reactor, exhibits a pattern of adjustment to its environment that is both *inconsistent* and *unstable;* this type lacks a set of response mechanisms which it can consistently put into effect when faced with a changing environment. As a consequence, Reactors exist in a state of almost perpetual instability. The Reactor's "adaptive" cycle usually consists of responding inappropriately to environmental change and uncertainty, performing poorly as a result, and then being reluctant to act aggressively in the future. Thus, the Reactor is a "residual" strategy, arising when one of the other three strategies is improperly pursued.

Although there are undoubtedly many reasons why organizations become Reactors, we have identified three. First, *top management may not have clearly articulated the organization's strategy.* For example, one company was headed by a one-man Prospector of immense personal skills. A first-rate architect, he led his firm through a rapid and successful growth period during which the company moved from the design and construction of suburban shopping centers, through the construction and management of apartment complexes, and into consulting with municipal agencies concerning urban planning problems. Within 10 years of its inception, the company was a loose but effective collection of semiautonomous units held together by this particular individual. When this individual was suddenly killed in a plane crash, the company was thrown into a strategic void. Because each separate unit of the company was successful, each was able to argue strongly for more emphasis on its particular domain and operations. Consequently, the new chief executive officer, caught between a number of conflicting but legitimate demands for resources, was unable to develop a unified, cohesive statement of the organization's strategy; thus, consistent and aggressive behavior was precluded.

A second and perhaps more common cause of organizational instability is that *management does not fully shape the organization's structure and process to fit a chosen strategy.* Unless all of the domain, technological, and administrative decisions required to have an operational strategy are properly aligned, strategy is a mere statement, not an effective guide to behavior. One publishing company wished, in effect, to become an Analyzer—management had articulated a direction for the organization which involved operating in both stable and changing domains within the college textbook publishing industry. Although the organization was comprised of several key Defender and Prospector characteristics, such as functional structures and decentralized control mechanisms, these structure-process features were not appropriately linked to the company's different domains. In one area where the firm wished to "prospect," for example, the designated unit had a functional structure and shared a large, almost mass-production technology with several other units, thereby making it difficult for the organization to respond to market opportunities quickly. Thus, this particular organization exhibited a weak link between its strategy and its structure-process characteristics.

The third cause of instability—and perhaps ultimate failure—is *a tendency for management to maintain the organization's current strategy-structure relationship despite overwhelming changes in environmental conditions.* Another organization in our studies, a food-processing company, had initially been an industry pioneer in both the processing and marketing of dried fruits and nuts. Gradually, the company settled into a Defender strategy and took vigorous steps to bolster this strategy, including limiting the domain to a narrow line of products, integrating backward into growing and harvesting, and assigning a controller to each of the company's major functional divisions as a means of keeping costs down. Within recent years, the company's market has become saturated, and profit margins have shrunk on most of the firm's products. In spite of its declining market, the organization has consistently clung to a Defender strategy and structure, even to the point of creating *ad hoc* cross-divisional committees whose sole purpose was to find ways of increasing efficiency further. At the moment, management recognizes that the organization is in trouble, but it is reluctant to make the drastic modifications required to attain a strategy and structure better suited to the changing market conditions.

Unless an organization exists in a "protected" environment, such as a monopolistic or highly regulated industry, it cannot continue to behave as a Reactor indefinitely. Sooner or later, it must move toward one of the consistent and stable strategies of Defender, Analyzer, or Prospector.

MANAGEMENT THEORY LINKAGES TO ORGANIZATIONAL STRATEGY AND STRUCTURE

Organizations are limited in their choices of adaptive behavior to those which top management believes will allow the effective direction and control of human resources. Therefore, top executives' theories of management are an important factor in analyzing an organization's ability to adapt to its environment. Although our research is only in its preliminary stage, we have found some patterns in the relationship between management theory and organizational strategy and structure.

A theory of management has three basic components: (a) a set of assumptions about human attitudes and behaviors, (b) managerial policies and actions consistent with these assumptions, and (c) expectations about employee performance if these policies and actions are implemented (see Table 4). Theories of management are discussed in more detail in Miles (14).

During the latter part of the 19th century and the early decades of the 20th, mainstream management theory, as voiced by managers and by management scholars, conformed to what has been termed the *Traditional* model. Essentially, the Traditional model maintained that the capability for effective decision making was narrowly distributed in organizations, and this approach thus legitimized unilateral control of organizational systems by top management. According to this model, a select group of owner-managers was able to direct large numbers of employees by carefully standardizing and routinizing their work and by placing the planning function solely in the hands of top managers. Under this type of management system, employees could be expected to perform up to some minimum standard, but few would be likely to exhibit truly outstanding performance.

Beginning in the 1920s, the Traditional model gradually began to give way to the *Human Relations* model. This model accepted the traditional notion that superior decision-making competence was narrowly distributed among the employee population but emphasized the universality of social needs for belonging and recognition. This model argued that impersonal treatment was the source of subordinate resistance to managerial directives, and adherents of this approach urged managers to employ devices to enhance organization members' feelings of involvement and importance in order to improve organizational performance. Suggestion systems, employee counseling, and even company unions had common parentage in this philosophy. The great Depression and World War II both acted to delay the development and spread of the Human Relations model, and it was not until the late 1940s and early 50s that it became the prime message put forth by managers and management scholars.

Beginning in the mid-50s, a third phase in the evolution of management theory began, with the emergence of the *Human Resources* model, which argued that the capacity for effective decision making in the pursuit of organizational objectives was widely dispersed and that most organization members represented untapped resources which, if properly managed, could considerably enhance organizational performance. The Human Resources approach viewed management's role not as that of a controller (however benevolent) but as that of a facilitator—removing the constraints that block organization members' search for ways to contribute meaningfully in their work roles. In recent years, some writers have questioned the extent to which the Human Resources model is applicable, arguing for a more "contingent" theory emphasizing variations in member capacity and motivation to contribute and the technological constraints associated with broadened self-direction and self-control. The Human Resources model probably still represents the leading edge of management theory, perhaps awaiting the formulation of a successor model.

Linking the Strategic Typology to Management Theory

Are there identifiable linkages between an organization's strategic type and the management theory of its dominant coalition? For example, do top executives in Defenders profess Traditional beliefs about management and those in Prospectors a Human Resources philosophy? The answer to this question is, in our opinion, a bit more complex than simply yes or no.

One of our studies investigated aspects of the relationship between organizational strategy-structure and management theory. Although the results are only tentative at this point, relatively clear patterns emerged. In general, Traditional and Human Relations managerial beliefs are more likely to be found in Defender and Reactor organizations, while Human Resources beliefs are more often associated with Analyzer and Prospector organizations. But this relationship appears to be *constrained in one direction;* it seems highly unlikely that a Traditional or Human Relations manager can function effectively as the head of a Prospector organization. The prescriptions of the Traditional model simply do not support the degree of decentralized decision making required to create and manage diversified organizations. It is quite possible for a Human Resources manager to lead a Defender organization. Of course, the organization's planning and control processes under such leadership would be less centralized than if the organization were managed according to the Traditional model. Using the Human

TABLE 4 Theories of Management

Traditional Model	Human Relations Model	Human Resources Model
Assumptions:	**Assumptions:**	**Assumptions:**
1. Work is inherently distasteful to most people.	1. People want to feel useful and important.	1. Work is not inherently distasteful. People want to contribute to meaningful goals which they have helped establish.
2. What workers do is less important than what they earn for doing it.	2. People desire to belong and to be recognized as individuals.	2. Most people can exercise far more creative, responsible self-direction and self-control than their present jobs demand.
3. Few want or can handle work which requires creativity, self-direction, or self-control.	3. These needs are more important than money in motivating people to work.	
Policies:	**Policies:**	**Policies:**
1. The manager's basic task is to closely supervise and control his (her) subordinates.	1. The manager's basic task is to make each worker feel useful and important.	1. The manager's basic task is to make use of his (her) "untapped" human resources.
2. He (she) must break tasks down into simple, repetitive, easily learned operations.	2. He (she) should keep his (her) subordinates informed and listen to their objections to his (her) plans.	2. He (she) must create an environment in which all members may contribute to the limits of their ability.
3. He (she) must establish detailed work routines and procedures and enforce these firmly but fairly.	3. The manager should allow his (her) subordinate to exercise some self-direction and self-control on routine matters.	3. He (she) must encourage full participation on important matters, continually broadening subordinate self-direction and control.

Expectations:

1. People can tolerate work if the pay is decent and the boss is fair.

2. If tasks are simple enough and people are closely controlled, they will produce up to standard.

Expectations:

1. Sharing information with subordinates and involving them in routine decisions will satisfy their basic needs to belong and to feel important.

2. Satisfying these needs will improve morale and reduce resistance to formal authority—subordinates will willingly cooperate and produce.

Expectations:

1. Expanding subordinate influence, self-direction, and self-control will lead to direct improvements in organizational performance.

2. Work satisfaction may improve as a "by-product" of subordinates making full use of their resources.

SOURCE: Raymond E. Miles, *Theories of management* (New York: McGraw-Hill, 1975), Figure 3–1.

Resources philosophy, heads of functional divisions might either participate in the planning and budgeting process or they might simply be delegated considerable autonomy in operating their cost centers. (In Defender organizations operated according to the Human Resources philosophy, human capabilities are aimed primarily at cost efficiency, rather than product development.)

The fit between management theory and the strategy, structure, and process characteristics of Analyzers is perhaps more complex than with any of the other types. Analyzers, as previously described, tend to remain cost efficient in the production of a limited line of goods or services while attempting to move as rapidly as possible into promising new areas opened up by Prospectors. Note that the organization structure of the Analyzer does not demand extensive, permanent delegation of decision-making authority to division managers. Most of the Analyzer's products or services can be produced in functionally structured divisions similar to those in Defender organizations. New products or services may be developed in separate divisions or departments created for that purpose and then integrated as quickly as possible into the permanent technology and structure. It seems likely to us, although our evidence is inconclusive, that various members of the dominant coalition in Analyzer organizations hold moderate but different managerial philosophies, that certain key executives believe it is their role to pay fairly close attention to detail while others appear to be more willing to delegate, for short periods, moderate amounts of autonomy necessary to bring new products or services on line rapidly. If these varying managerial philosophies are "mismatched" within the Analyzer's operating units—if, for example, Traditional managers are placed in charge of innovative subunits— then it is unlikely that a successful Analyzer strategy can be pursued.

Holding together a dominant coalition with mixed views concerning strategy and structure is not an easy task. It is difficult, for example, for managers engaged in new product or service development to function within planning, control, and reward systems established for more stable operations, so the Analyzer must be successfully differentiated into its stable and changing areas and managed accordingly. Note that experimentation in the analyzer is usually quite limited. The exploration and risk associated with major product or service breakthroughs are not present (as would be the case in a Prospector), and thus interdependencies within the system may be kept at a manageable level. Such would not be the case if Analyzers attempted to be both cost-efficient producers of stable products or services and active in a major way in new product and market development. Numerous organizations are today being led or forced into such a mixed strategy (multinational companies, certain forms of conglomerates, many organizations in high-technology industries, etc.), and their struggles may well produce a new organization type and demands for a supporting theory of management.

Whatever form this new type of organization takes, however, clearly its management-theory requirements will closely parallel or extend those of the Human Resources model (15).

CONCLUSIONS

Our research represents an initial attempt: *(a)* to portray the major elements of organizational adaptation, *(b)* to describe patterns of behavior used by organizations in adjusting to their environments, and *(c)* to provide a language for discussing organizational behavior at the total-system level. Therefore, we have offered a theoretical framework composed of a model of the adaptive process (called the adaptive cycle) and four empirically determined means of moving through this process (the strategic typology). In addition, we have related this theoretical framework to available theories of management (Traditional, Human Relations, Human Resources). Effective organizational adaptation hinges on the ability of managers to not only envision and implement new organizational forms but also to direct and control people within them.

We believe that managers' ability to meet successfully environmental conditions of tomorrow revolves around their understanding of organizations as integrated and dynamic wholes. Hopefully, our framework offers a theory and language for promoting such an understanding.

REFERENCES

1. Anderson, Carl R., and Frank T. Paine. "Managerial perceptions and strategic behavior." *Academy of Management Journal* (1975) *18*, 811–23.
2. Ansoff, H. Igor. *Corporate strategy.* New York: McGraw-Hill, 1965.
3. Ansoff, H. Igor, and Richard Brandenburg. "A language for organizational design." *Management Science* (1971) *17*, B717–B731.
4. Ansoff, H. Igor, and John M. Stewart. "Strategies for a technology-based business." *Harvard Business Review* (1967) *45*, 71–83.
5. Argyris, Chris. "On organizations of the future." *Administrative and Policy Study Series* 1, no. 03–006. Beverly Hills, Calif.: Sage Publications, 1973.
6. Beer, Michael, and Stanley M. Davis. "Creating a global organization: Failures along the way." *Columbia Journal of World Business* (1976) *11*, 72–84.
7. Bower, Joseph L. *Managing the resource allocation process.* Boston: Division of Research, Harvard Business School, 1970.
8. Burns, Tom, and G. M. Stalker. *The management of innovation.* London: Tavistock, 1961.
9. Chandler, Alfred D., Jr. *Strategy and structure.* Garden City, N.Y.: Doubleday, 1962.
10. Child, John. "Organizational structure, environment, and performance—The role of strategic choice." *Sociology* (1972) *6*, 1–22.

11. Cyert, Richard, and James G. March. *A behavioral theory of the firm.* Englewood Cliffs, N.J.: Prentice-Hall, 1963.
12. Drucker, Peter F. *The practice of management.* New York: Harper & Row, 1954.
13. Drucker, Peter F. *Management: Tasks, responsibilities, practices.* New York: Harper & Row, 1974.
14. Miles, Raymond E. *Theories of management.* New York: McGraw-Hill, 1975.
15. Miles, Raymond E., and Charles C. Snow. *Organizational strategy, structure, and process.* New York: McGraw-Hill, 1978.
16. Rogers, Everett M. *Communication of innovations: A cross-cultural approach.* 2d. ed. New York: Free Press, 1971.
17. Segal, Morley. "Organization and environment: A typology of adaptability and structure." *Public Administration Review* (1974) 35, 212–20.
18. Thompson, James D. *Organizations in action.* New York: McGraw-Hill, 1967.
19. Weick, Karl E. *The social psychology of organizing.* Reading, Mass.: Addison-Wesley, 1969.
20. Weick, Karl E. "Enactment processes in organizations." In *New directions in organizational behavior.* ed. Barry M. Staw and Gerald R. Salanick. Chicago: St. Clair, 1977, 267–300.
21. Woodward, Joan. *Industrial organization: Theory and practice.* London: Oxford University Press, 1965.

34

Hot Company, Warm Culture*

Kenneth Labich

Would this happen at your company? A young woman, a line worker in an assembly plant, shows up at the chairman's office in a sour mood. Not only does she get in to see the boss, but he sits there and takes it when she snaps at him: "Don't you know that two production managers were just fired?"

At most American companies, even some that mouth the participatory management principles currently in vogue, our young friend would not have made it past the security guards, let alone into the inner sanctum. But at Herman Miller, Inc., the big office furniture manufacturer, chairman Max DePree welcomed just such an employee. Not only did he look into her complaint, he agreed that an injustice had been committed and rectified it. The two managers were offered their jobs back; the vice president who had fired them was asked to resign. Says DePree, 64, with unmistakable sincerity: "It was a tragic but wonderful series of events. I consider it an enormous honor that I was approached with some expectation of fair play."

Such expectations require uncommon trust, and DePree and his forebears atop Herman Miller have built a thriving enterprise in large part because of sturdy bridges between management and employees. All hands are dedicated to fine design and insist on top quality, but they also know where profits come from. And they glare like tigers when the talk turns to their nearby archrival Steelcase, Inc.

Max's father, D. J. DePree, who founded the company in Zeeland, Michigan, in 1923, set the kinder, gentler tone with profit-sharing and employee-incentive programs long before they were fashionable. His sons, first Hugh, 73, and then Max, refined the process as they took the enterprise public and began to prosper with the expanding office furniture industry. Along the way, top executives have continued to nurture employees' commitment to the company. The latest sign of bonding is the institution of "silver parachutes" for all employees. In the event of a hostile takeover, plant workers who lose their jobs would receive big checks right along with

---

* From *Fortune* (February 27, 1989), 74–78.

the executives. Not surprisingly, there has never been any genuine effort to unionize the Herman Miller work force.

Since 1968, the company's key products have been components of the so-called Action Office—desk consoles, flexible panels, cabinets, chairs, and the like—that can be moved around easily to form an open environment while still providing some privacy for individual workstations. Herman Miller, named after D. J.'s father-in-law, who provided startup capital, will have revenues of over $800 million this year. That makes it one of the largest and most influential players, second in world sales only to privately held Steelcase.

Herman Miller and its unusually egalitarian culture attract attention. The company placed ninth overall in *Fortune's* 1989 survey of America's most admired corporations, nestled among household names like Exxon, Boeing, and PepsiCo. In terms of management excellence, the company placed even higher, rating sixth with the executives and industry analysts who contribute to the annual poll. Says James O'Toole, a professor at the University of Southern California and author of *Vanguard Management:* "If every company in America were managed like Herman Miller, we would not be concerned about the Japanese right now."

A couple of years ago Herman Miller's too-good-to-be-true management style got a shot of unpleasant reality. The company had become so intent on refining its internal dynamics that it began to lose some of its feel for the ever more competitive office furniture market. Earnings declined, and Wall Street was displeased. Like managers at less beneficent companies, Herman Miller executives made tough decisions, cut costs, and muscled up the distribution system. And, would you believe it, the crisis actually strengthened the carefully crafted links to employees.

At the heart of Herman Miller's management system are what Max DePree calls covenantal relationships between top management and all employees. He defines the company's central mission as "attempting to share values, ideals, goals, respect for each person, the process of our work together." In contrast, he says, many companies settle for contractual relationships, which he says "deal only with precedent and status."

Don't be put off by the rhetoric: The atmosphere at Herman Miller is electric, the sense of shared experiences is palpable, and the corporate ethos is user-friendly. It's the kind of outfit where people debate as passionately about fine points of Bauhaus architecture as about how to improve return on equity, where no one cares where an idea came from, as long as it works.

When top managers look to hire key employees, they focus more on character and the ability to get along with people than traditional résumé milestones. The senior vice president for research was once a high school football coach. A marketing senior vice president is a former dean of the agriculture school at Michigan State. DePree recruited Michele Hunt, a young black woman from the state's Department of Corrections, where she was training to become a prison warden. Now in charge of human resources and employee relations, she may be the only U.S executive to hold the title vice president for people.

Some imaginative personnel practices evolved over years of dealing with such enormously gifted but extremely high-strung designers as Charles Eames, George Nelson, Gilbert Rohde, and Robert Propst. The collaboration has produced some artistically triumphant work and vaulted Herman Miller into the top ranks of the industrial design world. Says Colin Forbes, chairman of the international design firm Pentagram: "At this level there are only a handful of companies: Braun and Olivetti in Europe, IBM and Herman Miller in the U.S."

The company cultivates that lofty reputation, crucial when selling to finicky architects and facility managers, by funneling unusually large amounts of money into design research (between 2 percent and 3 percent of revenues most years) and then taking pains to protect the integrity of the creative work that comes out the other end. Says Rob Harvey, a vice president: "Designers will put up with a lot of crap along the way if you let them express their creativity."

At times the system defies traditional business school logic. Bill Stumpf, one of the company's most prolific designers, had scored the office-design equivalent of a grand-slam home run in the 1970s with an outrageously successful desk chair called the Ergon. Herman Miller has sold millions of the designed-for-the-body chairs, and they were still a hot item in the early 1980s when Stumpf and designer Don Chadwick proposed a new desk chair called the Equa. All agreed that the new product, which uses a flexible fiberglass-like material, was a winner. Problem was, no matter how the engineers and production managers massaged the numbers, the Equa wound up costing about the same as the Ergon. Many if not most companies would have quickly scrapped the project, rather than risk cannibalizing their own missionary, but Herman Miller plunged ahead and continues to sell both chairs successfully.

Top management has long pondered how to deal ethically with employees up and down the corporate ladder. Several years ago the DePrees informed senior executives that, in order to ensure the fullest career development of promising managers, Max would be the last member of the family to head Herman Miller. To make absolutely sure the deal would stick, the next generation of DePrees would not even be permitted to work at the company.

So when Max decided to step down as chief executive last year to teach, Richard Ruch, 58, became the first outsider to run the business. He inherited some baggage that certain top bosses might find disturbing. Max DePree, who retains the chairman's title, limited the chief executive's salary to a figure 20 times the average wage of a line worker in the factory. "One of the real keys to leadership is making sure you don't find yourself defending the wrong things, such as your own inflated salary," he says. In 1989, Ruch can earn up to $470,000, including bonus.

Ruch, who has worked at Herman Miller for 33 years, professes no qualms about his salary limitations and is enthusiastic about letting workers in on business decisions. "It's almost always worth the trouble to tell people why you're doing something, and it's a wonderful way to get them committed to the company's goals," he says. "I am an absolute believer."

He had better be. Since 1950, Herman Miller has used a so-called Scanlon plan, named after the MIT lecturer, who pioneered participative management, whereby every employee receives a quarterly bonus based on various benchmarks, including cost-saving suggestions.

At Herman Miller all employees are organized into work teams. The team leader evaluates his workers every six months, and then each turns around and evaluates the leader. On the plant floor teams elect representatives to caucuses that meet periodically with line supervisors to discuss production shifts and grievances. If workers at these caucuses don't like what they hear, they can bypass the supervisor and go directly to the next executive level.

Everyone at Herman Miller knows the limits of this brand of management. Diane Bunse, a shift manager, describes the process as "participative, not permissive." Max DePree explains that Herman Miller is not a democracy: "Having a say does not mean having a vote." So managers have to be both firm in decision making and sympathetic in explaining why. Says Edward Simon, Jr., president and chief operating officer: "To be successful here, you have to know how to dance."

Some executives never do pick up the beat, and even successful Herman Miller leaders at times find themselves frustrated by the time and effort required to consult employees. Says Philip Mercorella, president of a subsidiary company that makes furniture and equipment for the health care industry: "Every once in a while, I fall off the wagon and have one of my ogre attacks."

But top management takes great pains to root out authoritarian tendencies and to arrest any other habits that could erode the warm, fuzzy Herman Miller culture. In his book *Leadership Is an Art*, DePree presents the warning signs of a company in decline. Among them: "dark tension" among key managers; no one taking enough time for rituals, such as retirement and holiday parties; people failing to tell or to understand historic company anecdotes, what he calls tribal stories; the issuing of an excessive number of manuals; a general loss of grace and civility.

DePree concedes he put together his list in the most painful way: analyzing his own company's distress. The trouble began in the early 1980s, as more and more players began to jump into the office furniture marketplace. Herman Miller executives can hardly ignore their biggest rival: Steelcase, the industry giant with about $1.6 billion in annual sales, is based

21 miles away. When a couple of Herman Miller executives recently sat down to talk business at a lounge in the local airport, they first carefully checked out the place for Steelcase employees who might be close enough to overhear.

With the office furniture maket growing at about a 20 percent annual pace and providing some companies with gross profit margins over 40 percent, scores of startup manufacturers joined in. As long as demand stayed high, the new entrants had little impact on established companies like Herman Miller. But in the mid-1980s the typhoon of cost cutting and restructuring hit corporate America. Fewer middle managers meant fewer offices, and hence much slower growth in the office furniture market. Severe price cutting began as competitors tried to cling to their market shares.

Herman Miller was especially vulnerable. The company had relied on the electronics business for 30 percent of its customers. When that industry slumped, Herman Miller lost its bearing.

Into this tight market the company tried to launch a major, next-generation product line called Ethospace, a system using rigid steel frames that can hold everything from filing cabinets to heating units. The problem: Ethospace cost about 20 percent more than the old Action office, and customers balked. These factors hurt Herman Miller's earnings, which declined about 8 percent in fiscal 1986 and another 12 percent in 1987.

Investor's Snapshot

Herman Miller	
Sales (latest four quarters)	$764.8 million
Change from year earlier	up 18.4%
Net profit	$47.5 million
Change	up 24.3%
Return on common stockholders' equity	18.4%
Five-year average	19.5%
Stock price range (last 12 months)	$19.00–$26.75
Recent share price	$21.00
Price/earnings multiple	11
Total return to investors (12 months to 1/26)	−3.5%

The reverses stunned Herman Miller's managers, and they decided to fight back. The first step was to woo several big financial institutions away from competitors. Equally important was to hook up with big dealers in key cities. In exchange for financing and marketing help, these important middlemen agreed to limit their sales to only, or almost only, Herman Miller products. Says David L. Armstrong, senior vice president for marketing: "It's the sort of thing you do when you're in a market-share war—and this is a brass-knuckle war."

While the skirmishes were taking place in the marketplace, the company's top managers worried about what had been going on inside Herman Miller. Their diagnosis: far too much navel-gazing. Immediately the company set about raising what it called the business literacy of its employees. Bonuses, previously based on a formula that included meeting production goals and employee cost-saving suggestions, would now also depend on the results of satisfaction surveys filled out by customers and on the company's return on assets.

After all the external and internal strife, Herman Miller is sitting pretty. "The company is taking the right steps to make itself stronger in a difficult environment," says Loran R. Braverman, who follows the company for Merrill Lynch. Earnings were up 34 percent in fiscal 1988. John Walthausen, a senior research analyst at First Albany Corporation, has spotted increasing acceptance of the new Ethospace line.

That would suit the company's planners just fine, but they aren't taking chances. They see more turbulence ahead for the office furniture industry as the sturdiest players dominate the market and the spindliest close shop. As the shakeout unfolds, Herman Miller may consider an acquisition or two (don't expect anything hostile). But growth is more likely to come from the health care field or overseas markets. The management philosophy that makes it all happen has come through a tough test stronger than ever.

Managing Corporate Culture through Reward Systems*

Jeffrey Kerr
John W. Slocum, Jr.

The concept of corporate culture has captured the imagination of executives and researchers alike.[1] For executives struggling to manage organizational change, corporate culture has become an important tool. They realize that significant strategic or structural realignment cannot occur if it is not supported by the organization's values and behavioral norms.[2] Yet, culture has proved to be a subtle, intangible phenomenon—pervasive but difficult to manage or influence. Many managers have found that culture cannot be manipulated directly.[3]

Most have an intuitive understanding of culture. Anthropologist Clyde Kluckhohn has defined culture as "the set of habitual and traditional ways of thinking, feeling and reacting that are characteristic of the way a particular society meets its problems at a particular point in time" (p. 86).[4] A corporation's culture simultaneously determines and reflects the values, beliefs, and attitudes of its members. These values and beliefs foster norms that influence employees' behavior. While most managers are aware of their companies' cultures, they are unsure about how it is maintained, transmitted, or influenced.

We believe that the reward system represents a particularly powerful means for influencing an organization's culture. Much of the substance of culture is concerned with controlling the behaviors and attitudes of organization members, and the reward system is a primary method of achieving

* From *Academy of Management EXECUTIVE* (1987) *1*, no. 2, 99–108. © Academy of Management Executive.

Portions of this article were presented at the American Institute for Decision Sciences meeting in Toronto, November 1984. The authors acknowledge contributions on earlier drafts of this manuscript made by Michael Beer, Bill Joyce, Lynn Isabella, Ralph Kilmann, Edward Lawler, and Randy Schuler.

Support for this project was given through a research grant to the authors from the Center for Enterprising, Cox School of Business, Southern Methodist University.

control. The reward system defines the relationship between the organization and the individual member by specifying the terms of exchange: It specifies the contributions expected from members and expresses values and norms to which those in the organization must conform, as well as the response individuals can expect to receive as a result of their performance.

The reward system—who gets rewarded and why—is an unequivocal statement of the corporation's values and beliefs. As such, the reward system is the key to understanding culture. An analysis of reward systems can provide executives with a basis for effectively managing long-term cultural change. In this article, we will describe the reward systems operating in a sample of firms and show how these systems reinforced and influenced cultural values and norms. We will then link reward systems and culture to the corporate strategies pursued by top managers in these firms.[5]

EXAMINING REWARD SYSTEMS

Reward systems are concerned with two major issues: performance and rewards. Performance includes defining and evaluating performance and providing employees with feedback. Rewards include bonus, salary increases, promotions, stock awards, and perquisites.

Of course, large corporations with several different businesses may have multiple reward systems. And while they may share some fundamental philosophies and values, they may differ according to the particular business setting, competitive situation, and product life cycle. Thus, multiple reward systems can support multiple cultures (or subcultures) within one organization.

Subcultures are a natural by-product of the tendency of organizations to differentiate. As organizations grow with respect to the number of products, services, and divisions, subcultures may reflect a number of distinct work and social environments. Through increasing differentiation, opportunity for the emergence of countercultures is also increased. Countercultures are shared values and beliefs that are in direct opposition to the patterns of the dominant culture. To the extent that divisional reward systems reinforce these distinct behavioral norms and belief systems, subcultures and countercultures are likely to be articulated and even reinforced.

TWO KINDS OF REWARD SYSTEMS

From these interviews [described in detail in the box on the next page], we identified two distinct reward systems: the hierarchy-based system and the performance-based system. Eight firms were classified as hierarchy-based and six as performance-based. Of course, the descriptions of reward systems and cultures that follow are composites representing "pure" types. Actual reward systems and cultures showed some variation but conformed to these general types.

Data-Collection Methods

We studied the reward systems of 14 companies in the Northeast and Midwest regions of the United States. All but one of the companies were included in *Fortune's* listing of the top 500 corporations. Sales ranged from $125 million to over $8 billion. The companies ranged from single-product industrial firms to multidivisional conglomerates.

Initial contact in each firm was made with the top human resources (HR) manager. HR managers were key informants and provided the names and titles of other managers in their firms who might be willing to participate in the study. To ensure the selection of knowledgeable managers, we asked that only those who had been with the company for at least five years and had received significant rewards (e.g., salary increases, bonuses, perquisites) be included. In addition, at least one manager interviewed in each firm was responsible for authorizing rewards for subordinates. Thus, both sides of the reward relationship—allocating and receiving—were represented in the sample.

In all, 75 interviews were conducted. Interview time per manager ranged from one hour to five or six hours. The average interview took 90 minutes and was conducted in the manager's office. We interviewed, on average, 5 managers from each firm, with as many as 10 managers interviewed in one firm. The interviewee

group included 5 chief executive officers, 7 group-level executives, 5 line vice presidents (manufacturing, production), 6 staff vice presidents, 25 division general managers, and 27 director-level managers.

Initial interviews in each firm concentrated on gathering objective data on the managerial reward system. These focused on performance definition and evaluation, feedback processes, and the administration of rewards (bonus, salary, stock, perquisites, and promotion). The first interviews were structured so that comparable data would be obtained. Subsequent interviews gathered subjective data on the firm's history, founders or dominant leaders, traditions, values, and norms. These interviews were necessarily open-ended and exploratory.

In addition to interview data, company documents, such as annual reports, 10-K reports, and company histories (when available), were also examined. Some firms provided documentation on the reward system itself. The 10-K and annual reports gave an overview of the firm's products, corporate and business strategy, and past economic performance. The company histories provided insight into the origins of the firm, which included their stated values and traditions. Data from these sources served as a check on the information gathered through the interviews.

The Corporate Hierarchy

In the hierarchy, superiors defined and evaluated the performance of subordinates. Performance was defined qualitatively as well as quantitatively. Nonquantifiable aspects of the subordinate's role were sometimes considered to be more important than quantifiable ones. Superiors were free to define those aspects of a manager's role that would be considered important. Thus, performance criteria could vary according to who one was working for.

Managers' jobs were broadly and subtly defined. Managers were accountable for how they conducted their interpersonal relationships, as well as the consequences of their actions. Numbers (e.g., return on investment) did not tell the whole story, and more subtle aspects of performance were sometimes viewed as more important. Superiors played a critical role in career mobility and success with the firm. They were the source of training, socialization, feedback, and rewards and were to be studied, emulated, and satisfied if subordinates expected to succeed.

Superiors interpreted the performance of subordinates according to subjective criteria. Even in quantified areas, superiors did not hesitate to interpret numerical outcomes in the context of their own knowledge of the situation. Factors such as interdivisional cooperation, long-term relations with customers, leadership style, and development of junior managers were evaluated, despite obvious difficulties in quantifying them. Such evaluation communicated the importance of the hierarchy and the subordinates' dependence on superiors. The subjective nature of evaluation allowed for the inclusion of qualitative performance criteria and reinforced the message that managers had to be concerned with more than the numbers. Subjective evaluation permitted consideration of the long-term consequences of managerial action. This implied an ongoing commitment to the activity or business in question.

In this system, formal performance appraisals took place once a year. Informal feedback, however, was quite frequent. A high level of interaction existed between superiors and subordinates. Feedback occurred on the job, in the dining room, during executive retreats, or at the country club and was oriented more toward employee development than toward evaluation. Since performance definition and evaluation were subjective, the quality of performance could be known only through superiors. The high level of interaction coupled with a developmental approach communicated the organization's commitment to the individual manager's success and future. This was conducive to the development of mentoring relationships and to extensive socialization of younger managers. The sense of dependency and vulnerability was balanced by a message of concern for the individual as a valued resource whose development was important to the organization.

Bonuses were based on corporate performance. The system rewarded the team, not individuals. This provided a basic rationale for cooperative, rather than competitive, behavior. The fact that potential bonus payouts increased by level emphasized the importance of long-term commitment to the organization (tenure was a precondition for promotion) and conformity to its norms. Bonus was a relatively small proportion of total compensation, ranging from 20 percent to 30 percent, while salary was the largest part of compensation. By severely limiting bonus for the individual star, the system removed the incentive for behaviors that benefited single managers, rather than the entire organization. The bonus system also reinforced the subordinate's dependence on superiors' judgment, because they determined bonus amounts.

Salary increases generally were determined through a formal salary plan, such as the Hay system. Two major factors in the size of a salary increase were tenure (time in grade) and performance (subjective evaluation by superiors). The tenure component gave structure to salary decisions. Policies specified the range of possible increases within job classifications.

Perquisites were even more constrained by policy than were raises and were carefully monitored. Status symbols, such as locations of offices, furniture, club memberships, first-class travel, and so forth, were considered important symbols of rank. Superiors sometimes insisted that managers use them, even if they did not want them. Perquisites communicated the importance of rank, tenure, and commitment, as well as a sense of ritual and tradition. Receiving a particular type of desk upon promotion, being told (not asked) to join a prestigious men's club because everyone of a given rank had always done so, being met at airports by local managers, attending specific executive development programs, were all rituals symbolizing a unique and shared tradition and history. Even for those not eligible for such perquisites, the fact that they existed provided a feeling of belonging not simply to an economic entity but to a social system.

In contrast to perquisites, stock awards were not structured in any obvious way. Managers had little knowledge about how and why awards were made. Awards were not directly related to individual or even corporate performance. Generally, the higher the managerial rank, the greater the eligibility for stock awards. The lack of information about stock awards meant that subordinates could not influence their distribution in any way. This lack of clarity imparted a sense of mysterious ritual to the reward. The message was that subordinates must trust superiors to do the right thing for them. Receiving stock awards symbolized acceptance into the inner circle. Therefore, managers had to be well aware of the total set of company values and norms and how to conform to them. Any deviation might be serious enough to reduce or temporarily eliminate a manager's stock awards.

Promotion from within was the standard policy in hierarchical firms. Promotions were relatively frequent (every two to four years) and were often motivated more by the individual's need for development (i.e., exposure to new functional areas) than by the organization's need to fill a slot. Many promotions did not entail significant increases in authority, responsibility, or salary. Commitment to employee development and cross-fertilization often resulted in lateral or diagonal movement, rather than vertical movement.

Managers were transferred on a regular basis across divisions or functional boundaries, in keeping with the emphasis on developing general managers with strong internal networks throughout the company. Promotion practices expressed concern for the lifetime career of employees. They contributed to a tight, homogeneous organization with common language, experience, and values. Lack of movement signaled a disinvestment in the individual and a loss of interest on the part of the organization.

Clan Culture.   We can characterize the kind of culture that emerged from the hierarchy-based reward system as a clan. William Ouchi has used the term *clan* to describe a control system based on socialization and internalized values and norms. Exhibit 1 summarizes the major features of the clan culture. In this culture, individuals in the organization are like a fraternal group. Everyone recognizes an obligation that goes beyond the simple exchange of labor for salary. It is tacitly understood that required contributions to the organization may exceed any contractual agreements. The individual's long-term commitment to the organization (loyalty) is exchanged for the organization's long-term commitment to the individual (security). This relationship is predicated on mutual interests.

The clan culture accomplishes this unity through a long and thorough socialization process. Members progress through the ranks by pursuing traditional career paths in the company. Older members of the clan serve as mentors and role models for younger members. It is through these relationships that the values and norms of the firm are maintained over suc-

---

EXHIBIT 1   Characteristics of a Clan Culture

The relationship between individual and organization:
• Fraternal relationship.
• Mutual long-term commitment.
• Rests on mutual interests, a shared fate.
• Sense of tradition, history, company, style.
• Hierarchy structures relationship.

The relationship among organization members:
• Pride in membership.
• Sense of interdependence, identification with peers.
• Extensive collegial network.
• Pressure from peers to conform.
• Stresses collective, rather than individual initiative, ownership.

The process of acculturation:
• Long, thorough socialization.
• Superiors are mentors, role models, agents of socialization.
• "Rich" normative structure governs wide range of behaviors.

---

cessive generations of managers. The clan is aware of its unique history and often documents its origins and celebrates its traditions in various ceremonies. Statements of its credo or publicly held values are reinforced. Members have a shared image of the organization's "style" and manner of conduct.

In the clan culture, members share a sense of pride in fraternity and in membership. The socialization process results in strong identification among members and a strong sense of interdependence. The up-through-the-ranks career pattern results in an extensive network of colleagues whose paths have crossed and who have shared similar experiences. Communication, coordination, and integration are facilitated by shared goals, perceptions, and behavioral tendencies.

In addition, pressure to conform is considerable. The very richness of the culture creates an environment in which few areas are left totally free from normative pressures. The culture does not usually generate risk taking or behavior or innovation, nor does it generate in members feelings of personal ownership for a division, product, or ideas. Not surprisingly, the culture is not conducive to entrepreneurial activity.

THE PERFORMANCE-BASED REWARD SYSTEM

In contrast to the hierarchy, the performance-based system objectively defined and measured performance and explicitly linked rewards to performance—which was almost completely defined quantitatively. Qualitative aspects of performance were generally ignored. Specific rewards or proportions of rewards were directly related to specific performance criteria (e.g., bonus based partly on return on assets, and partly on pretax profits, and so forth). In this way, managers exerted influence by objectively weighting the various components of the subordinate's job.

This reward system sent the message that the manager's job was specifically defined. Performance in divergent roles was assessed by a few basic financial outcomes. Accountability was primarily for results and not for the methods by which results were achieved. The message was that the numbers were paramount. Evaluations frequently were based on a formula in which the manager's financial results served as inputs. Nonquantifiable aspects of performance were generally not evaluated. Because of the quantitative emphasis, performance evaluation necessarily focused on the immediate time frame, with little consideration of long-term consequences.

This type of evaluation communicated to managers their independence from subjective judgments of superiors, since manager results could be understood by examining financial outcome. Superiors had few channels through which to express concern for stylistic aspects of a subordinate's performance. The system clearly told managers to focus on those performance elements that could be quantified. Because activities that might contribute to long-term competitiveness were sometimes hard to quantify, such activities were not formally incorporated into the reward system.

Performance feedback under this system was erratic. Some companies held one or more formal performance appraisal sessions while others held none. Informal interactions between superior and subordinate were infrequent. Feedback was oriented more toward evaluation than toward employee development. Because performance was defined and measured quantitatively, the subordinate manager was not dependent on the superior for interpretation.

The low level of superior-subordinate interaction and the evaluative, as opposed to developmental, approach to feedback served to emphasize autonomy. Concern was not expressed for subordinate development or long-term career progress. The reward system was not conducive to a mentoring relationship, nor was it likely to contribute to the transference of subtle norms and values. Socialization was not an important function of this system.

Bonuses were a very significant part of compensation. Bonus maximums ranged from 40 percent of salary to "no limit." In some firms, there was no cap on what a manager could earn in bonus if the financial criteria were met. Bonus was based almost exclusively on the performance of the division over which the manager had authority; the performance of other divisions or the entire corporation, whether better or worse, had almost no effect on the individual's bonus. Each division was a profit center and generated its own bonus pool. Actual bonus payment was determined by formula, and the resulting figure was rarely altered by superiors.

The bonus system communicated that the manager was an independent operator whose fate was somewhat independent of superiors and other divisions as well. No economic rationale for cooperative behavior between or among divisions existed. The potentially large size of bonuses communicated the value placed on the "star" performer, rather than the team player. The bonus system also deemphasized rank as an important source of rewards.

Salary increases and stock rewards were indirectly based on managerial performance. Salary increases were affected by the external labor market, the cost of living, and the manager's overall performance. Stock arrangements were frequently negotiated when a manager joined the firm. These rewards were loosely related to performance, and actual amounts were subjectively determined by superiors. This practice opposed the overall emphasis on objectivity, but stock awards and salary increases had a relatively lower value in the reward systems of these organizations. Significant performance feedback was conveyed in a manager's bonus. Perhaps superiors operating under this system needed to have some mechanisms available to them to express subjective perceptions of subordinate performance. The flexibility of salary increases and stock awards, relative to the bonus formula, may have satisfied that need.

Perquisites were almost nonexistent in the performance-based system. Symbols of rank and status were not emphasized, because the manager's level was not emphasized. While this communicated a sense of egalitarianism, it also lessened the sense of community and singularity. If reward rituals (predicted on tenure and hierarchical position) convey the existence of an in-group, then the absence of such rituals weakens the feeling of participation in a tradition and membership in a special group.

Promoting from within was not a norm in this system. It was common to find high-ranking managers brought in from the outside. Many had been with their companies only a few years. Promotions were generally motivated by the organization's need to fill a vacancy, rather than the individual's need for exposure. Relative to the hierarchy-based system, promotion occurred infrequently and was usually vertical (and within the same division or function).

The practice of hiring from outside conveyed to members that the organization's commitment to them was not necessarily long-term. Individuals repeatedly could be passed over for promotion when more attractive candidates from other firms or industries were identified. These organizations were indicating that they did not necessarily value tenure or the socialized individual and did not expect a long-term commitment from members. Under such conditions, we found a mutually exploitive relationship. The individual was utilized to fill a role or perform a particular function until he or she was needed elsewhere or was replaced by a more qualified person. This relationship engendered a similar response from individuals, who exploited the organization until better rewards could be gotten elsewhere.

The performance-based system provided few mechanisms for integration between divisions. Vertical promotions, rather than cross-divisional movement, tended to facilitate specialization. A wide network of managers who had worked together, known each other, and understood each other's responsibilities was not fostered, and promotional practices encouraged divisional independence and uniqueness. These organizations did not seek an integrated system based on shared language, norms, and goals.

Market Culture.   William Ouchi has used the term *market* to describe a system of control in which behaviors are constrained by negotiated terms of exchange. Exhibit 2 lists the major characteristics of the market culture. In this culture, the relationship between individual and organization is contractual. Obligations of each party are specified in advance. The individual is responsible for some level of performance, and the organization promises a given level of rewards in return. Increased levels of performance are exchanged for increased rewards as specified in a negotiated schedule. Neither party recognizes the right of the other to demand more than was originally

EXHIBIT 2   Characteristics of a Market Culture

The relationship between individual and organization:
• Contractual relationship.
• Mutual short-term commitment.
• Rests on self-interest, utilitarianism.
• Terms of exchange structure relationship.

The relationship among organization members:
• Independence from peers.
• Limited interaction.
• Little pressure from peers to conform.
• Stresses individual initiative, ownership.

The process of acculturation:
• Little socialization.
• Superiors are distant; are negotiators, resource allocators.
• "Lean" normative structure governing few behaviors.

---

specified. The organization does not promise (or imply) security; the individual does not promise (or imply) loyalty. The contract, renewed annually if each party adequately performs its obligations, is utilitarian, since each party uses the other as a means of furthering its own goals. Rather than promoting a feeling of membership in a social system, the market culture encourages a strong sense of independence and individuality in which everyone pursues his or her own interests.

The market culture does not exert a great deal of normative pressure on its members. Members do not share a common set of expectations regarding management style or philosophy. There is little pressure from peers to conform to specific behavior or attitudes. Much of superiors' interactions with subordinates consist of negotiating performance-reward agreements and/or evaluating requests for resource allocations. A superior's influence on subordinate rewards is limited. Superiors are less effective as role models or mentors, and the absence of long-term commitment by both parties weakens the acculturation process.

Relations among peers are also distant. Little evidence of economic independence gives little rationale for cooperating with peers. Managers do not interact frequently with counterparts in other divisions, nor do they develop an extensive network of colleagues in the company. Vertical career paths result in little understanding of or identification with other divisions.

The market culture is not designed to generate loyalty, cooperation, or a sense of belonging to a social system. Members do not feel constrained by norms, values, or allegiance to an accepted way of doing and thinking. But the market culture does generate personal initiative, a strong sense of ownership and responsibility for operations and decisions, and an entrepreneurial approach to management. The individual is free to pursue goals with a minimum of organizational constraints.

REWARD SYSTEMS, CULTURE, AND STRATEGY

It is important to recognize that a given culture and its associated reward system is neither good nor bad, effective nor ineffective, except in terms of its support for the total organizational system of which it is part. The hierarchy-based and the performance-based systems each identify and reward a set of complex behaviors. The difference lies in the cultural values that are expressed through the reward system. To the extent that it is congruent with organizational strategy, structure, and process, the reward system will effectively contribute to organizational goals. Thus, the clan culture may be ineffective in an environment that requires innovation, aggressiveness, and a strong desire for individual achievement. Similarly, the entrepreneurship, autonomy, and short-term focus of the market culture may be dysfunctional in mature capital-intensive industries, where system-wide integration is critical.

MATCHING ORGANIZATION STRATEGY
WITH REWARD SYSTEMS

We analyzed our sample of firms according to two environmental factors: type of industry and growth strategy. To analyze the corporate growth strategies of our firms, we used Milton Leontiades's steady state-evolutionary distinction.[6] Steady state firms grow through internally generated diversification or through increased penetration of existing markets. They are internally focused and concerned with the development of new products and technologies and with integration across business units. Evolutionary firms grow primarily through acquisitive diversification. They actively pursue new markets and industries and are receptive to mergers and joint ventures.

Each firm's history was examined to ascertain the extent of its external activity (acquisitions, mergers, joint ventures, divestitures). If, within the previous three years, a firm engaged in no external activities that resulted in entering a previously unoccupied industry, it was classified as steady state. In addition, we looked at each firm's 20-year history to determine the consistency of its strategy.

Exhibit 3 shows each firm's industry, growth strategy, and reward system. First, we looked at the relationship between growth strategy and reward systems. All but one firm pursuing a steady state strategy utilized a hierarchy-based reward system. Every firm pursuing an evolutionary strategy utilized a performance-based system.

EXHIBIT 3   Type of Industry and Growth Strategy of 14 Firms

Steady State Strategy	Evolutionary Strategy
Aluminum (H)	Diversified food products and restaurants (P)
Forest products (H)	
Power generation utility (H)	Diversified consumer and industrial products (P)
Integrated chemicals producer (H)	Diversified consumer and industrial products (P)
Mining and related machinery (P)	Diversified consumer products and services (P)
Machine tools (H)	Diversified consumer products and services (P)
Building and home improvement products (H)	Diversified industrial services (P)
Pharmaceuticals (H)	

(H) indicates a hierarchy-based reward system.
(P) indicates a performance-based reward system.

It is also clear that evolutionary firms are more diverse enterprises than steady state firms. In fact, except for the food products company, the firms pursuing an evolutionary strategy were generally considered to be conglomerates. In contrast, the firms in this steady state group tend to be focused on particular industries or technologies. Most are capital-intensive industries that require long-term commitment and a high degree of vertical integration. Forest products, aluminum, power generation, pharmaceuticals, and machine tools are all mature businesses that, to be effective, require massive investment in plant and equipment, research and development, and distribution systems.

Successfully competing in a mature industry requires long-term commitment to the business and a highly integrated organization. The steady state strategy, with its internal market focus, concern for integration, and growth through market penetration, fits the demand of a mature business. The strategy does not rely on acquisitions or divestitures, and companies survive by committing substantial physical, financial, and managerial resources to a stable set of businesses.

The steady state strategy requires a reward system that encourages stability, cooperation, and a long-term systemwide perspective from its managers. Coordination and control are more important than aggressiveness and entrepreneurship. The hierarchy-based reward system provides this kind of support. Its subjective, qualitative character allows for the inclusion of long-term performance criteria that would be difficult to quantify. Frequent contact between superiors and subordinates encourages the transference of subtle values to a younger generation of managers. Cross-divisional promotions foster integration and understanding of the total system. Promotion from within and bonus based on corporate performance reinforce long-term commitment and a sense of community.

How does corporate culture fit with strategy and reward systems design? A clan culture comprises a set of values and norms that are highly consistent with the demands of a steady state strategy. The need for integration and a systemwide perspective is addressed by the fraternal values, the sense of mutual interest, pride in membership, and an extensive collegial network. Long-term commitment is supported by a sense of history and tradition. The role of superiors as models and mentors emphasizes the importance of continuity and experience. Peer pressure and the rich normative structure underscore the need to perform in ways that are consistent and widely shared among members. The star is not valued as highly as the team player. In other words, the clan culture provides a foundation of values, norms, and attitudes that encourage behaviors consistent with the steady state strategy. Corporate culture and reward system design function as complementary elements in directing members toward achieving the strategic goals of the firm.

The demands of the evolutionary strategy are quite different. The effectiveness of this strategy depends on corporate managers choosing acquisitions carefully and knowing when to divert businesses from the portfolio. It frequently requires that management make business decisions in areas that are partially or even completely unfamiliar to them. Because the strategy hinges on changes in the portfolio of businesses, commitment to a particular business or technology is not as highly valued as it is in firms that have chosen a steady state strategy.

The evolutionary strategy requires a reward system that permits managers to make evaluations and reward decisions that are equitable and defensible to division managers despite their lack of familiarity with these divisions. The reward system should allow corporate managers to make comparisons across unrelated businesses. The large bonus component, based on divisional results, creates a sense of ownership in division management. The autonomy inherent in this system encourages an entrepreneurial orientation. The system tends not to foster cooperation among divisions. Such cooperation is not critical when divestment of divisions occurs with some regularity. In short, the performance-based system rewards independence and entrepreneurship, the star performer versus the team player, and does not require extensive involvement from corporate-level managers in the reward process.

Exhibit 2 shows that the values of the market culture fit closely with both the evolutionary strategy and the performance-based reward systems. The relatively low level of commitment to businesses is reflected in the contractual relationship between organization and individual. The need for autonomous, entrepreneurial relations between divisions is reflected in limited peer interaction, weak peer pressure, and a lean normative structure. We would not expect conformity to be highly valued in an organization that pursued diversity. We would not expect loyalty and commitment to be highly valued in an environment where divestment of divisions and/or their managements was a distinct possibility and part of overall corporate strategy. The performance-based reward system clearly expresses and reinforces a market culture. Clearly, corporate culture is the foundation for normative behaviors that support the overall corporate strategy.

ENGINEERING CULTURAL CHANGE

Reward systems express and reinforce the values and norms that comprise corporate culture. A careful consideration of reward system design can help decision makers successfully modify the organization's culture. Reward systems are, in effect, powerful mechanisms that can be used by managers to communicate desired attitudes and behaviors to organization members. We believe that, over time, cultures are amenable to change through the clear communication of performance criteria and the consistent application of rewards.

At the same time, we hope some sense of the complexity of culture has come through, along with a healthy respect for the difficulty of the task of changing a company's values, norms, and attitudes. Large organizations are like societies; their cultures are reinforced and modified over years. Culture itself is rooted in the countless details of organization life. How decisions are made, how conflict is resolved, how careers are managed—each small incident serves to convey some aspect of the organization's culture to those involved. Given the pervasiveness of culture, it is not surprising that managers are frequently frustrated in their attempts to change it.

There is some basis for optimism, however. Culture does not develop in a vacuum. It is an integral part of the company's fabric. Even with little or no attention paid to it, an organization's culture is likely to evolve in conjunction with the day-to-day activities of the company. Thus, except in unusual circumstances, the manager's task usually is not to create a basic congruence among rewards, culture, and business strategy, but to focus and fine-tune the natural interaction of these elements.

ENDNOTES

1. Several major popular books about culture have been written in the past five years. Some of the most recent include Edgar Schein's *Organizational culture*

and leadership and Ralph Kilmann et al.'s *Gaining control of the corporate culture* (both published by Jossey-Bass, San Francisco, 1985). Recent academic reviews of this literature include "Concepts of culture and organizational analysis," by Linda Smircich, *Administrative Science Quarterly* (1983) *28,* 339–58; "The uniqueness paradox in organizational stories," by Joann Martin et al., *Administrative Science Quarterly* (1983) *28,* 438–53; and "On studying organizational cultures," by Andrew Pettigrew, *Administrative Science Quarterly* (1979) *24,* 570–81.

2. The difficulty of changing an organization's culture so that it is more closely aligned with the firm's strategy has been explored by Howard Schwartz and Stanley Davis in "Matching corporate culture and business strategy," *Organizational Dynamics* (Summer 1981), 30–48; by Paul Shrivastava in "Integrating strategy formulation with organizational culture," *Journal of Business Strategy* (Winter 1984), 103–10; and by Jay Barney in "Organizational culture: Can it be a source of sustained competitive advantage?" *Academy of Management Review* (1986) *11,* 656–65.

3. For examples of how culture either facilitated or impeded change, see Thomas Moore's "Culture shock rattles the TV networks," *Fortune* (April 14, 1986); Harold Seneker's "Why CEOs pop pills (and sometimes quit)," *Fortune* (July 12, 1978); John Main's "Waking up AT&T: There's life after culture shock," *Fortune* (December 24, 1984); and John Solomon and J. Bussey's "Cultural change: Pressed by rivals, Procter & Gamble Company is altering its ways," *The Wall Street Journal* (May 20, 1985).

4. Anthropologist Clyde Klukhohn's work cited in the text is titled "The study of culture," in D. Lerner and H. Lasswell (eds.), *The policy sciences* (Stanford, Calif.: Stanford University Press, 1951).

5. For an excellent description of how diversification strategies affect managerial behavior, see Jeffrey Kerr's "Diversification strategies and managerial rewards: An empirical study," *Academy of Management Journal* (1985) *28,* 155–79.

6. See Milton Leontiades's *Strategies for diversification and change* (Boston: Little, Brown, 1980).

The Four Faces of Social Responsibility*

Dan R. Dalton
Richard A. Cosier

Imagine that your company is considering introducing a new plastic container to the market. Your company considers itself to be socially responsible; therefore, an extensive impact assessment program is undertaken. One of your environmentally minded employees suggests that people might light the containers and then cook their meals over the fire. Although the idea sounds bizarre, you don't want to take any chances, so for over a month you cook hamburgers over a fire made from your plastic bottles. Rats are fed this hamburger, then carefully monitored for negative side effects. Tests indicate that these rats suffer no ill effects.

Of course you also perform an extensive series of tests involving energy usage, disposal, and recycling opportunities. Then you invite the public to carefully scheduled hearings across the country in order to encourage consumer inputs. Finally, you market the new product and land a major soft drink company as a customer.

Sound as if your company has fulfilled its responsibilities and forestalled any possible objections? In the mid-1970s, Monsanto went through this very process in developing Cycle-Safe bottles and spent more than $47 million to market the product. But in 1977, the FDA banned the bottle because, when stored at 120 degrees for an extended period of time, molecules strayed from the plastic into the contents. Rats, fed with doses that were equivalent to consuming thousands of quarts of soft drink over a human lifetime, developed an above-normal number of tumors.

Monsanto felt that it was providing a product that did something for society—a plastic bottle that could be recycled. But social responsibility is unavoidably a matter of degree and interpretation. Forces outside of the

---

* From *Business Horizons* (1982) 25, 19–27. Copyright © 1982 by the Foundation for the School of Business, Indiana University.

TABLE 1   The Four Faces of Social Responsibility

	Illegal	Legal
Irresponsible	A	C
Responsible	B	D

business are liable to interpret a product to be socially unacceptable, even when the company has undertaken an extensive impact analysis.

A precise evaluation of what is socially responsible is difficult to establish, and of course, many definitions have been suggested. Joseph McGuire, in *Business and Society*, provided a persuasive focus when he stated that the corporation "must act 'justly' as a proper citizen should." Large corporations have not only legal obligations but also certain responsibilities to society which extend beyond the parameters set by law. As the Monsanto case illustrates, the line between legality and responsibility is sometimes very fine.

Peter Drucker offers a useful way to distinguish between behaviors in organizations; the first is what an organization does *to* society, the other what an organization can do *for* society. This suggests that organizations can be evaluated on at least two dimensions with respect to their performance as "citizens": legality and responsibility. Table 1 illustrates the various combinations of legality and responsibility which may characterize an organization's performance.

These combinations are the *four faces of social responsibility*. Each cell of the table represents a strategy which could be adopted by an organization. It is unfortunate, but we think true, that no matter which strategy is chosen, the corporation is subject to some criticism.

ILLEGAL AND IRRESPONSIBLE

In modern society, this strategy, if not fatal, is certainly extremely high risk. In an age of social consciousness, it is difficult to imagine an organization that would regularly engage in illegal and irresponsible behavior. What, for example, would be the consequences of an organization's blatantly refusing to employ certain minority groups or deliberately and knowingly using a carcinogenic preservative in foodstuff? Besides the fact that such behavior is patently illegal, it is offensive and irresponsible.

There are, however, instances of illegal and irresponsible corporate conduct which are not so easily condemned.

You Can Hardly Blame Them

Most of us have value systems. They vary, to be sure, from individual to individual and from corporation to corporation. They do, however, have common elements: They are tempered by temptation, consequence, and risk. Sometimes, when faced with high temptation, low consequence, and low risk, our value systems are not the constraining force they could be. This may be the human condition and insufficient justification for the excesses which often accompany individual and corporate decision making. Nonetheless, an appreciation of these factors often makes those decisions entirely understandable.

Suppose that the state in which you live invokes a regulation that all motor vehicles operated on a public thoroughfare must be equipped with an "X" type pollution-control device. This law, for the sake of discussion, is retroactive. All automobiles registered in the state must be refitted with such a device, which costs $500. All automobiles are subject to periodic inspection to assure compliance with the law. Assume that the maximum fine (consequence) for violating this statute is $50. Assume, furthermore, that there is 1 chance in 100 that you will be inspected and found in violation. The analytical question is simply stated: Would you have the device installed? If you do, it will cost $500. If you do not, the cost will be $500 plus a $50 fine, but only *if* you are caught. Many, if not most, of us surely would not install the device. Strictly speaking, our behavior is both illegal and irresponsible. Our failure to comply exacerbates a societal problem—namely, polluting the air. Our reluctance under the described circumstances, however, is understandable: temptation along with low consequence and low risk.

Compare this situation with that of a large organization faced with the decision to install pollution abatement equipment in one of its plants. Suppose, in this case, the total cost of the installation is $500,000; the maximum fine for noncompliance is $10,000; the chance of being caught is 1 in 100. We ask the same question: Would you comply? We have actually been charitable with the balance of costs and probabilities in this example. The Occupational Safety and Health Administration (OSHA), which was given the charter for establishing and enforcing occupational safety and health standards, has a limited number of inspectors and approximately 5 million organizations subject to its mandate. It has been estimated that an organization could plan on being inspected about every 77 years, or approximately as often as you could expect to see Halley's comet.[1] Furthermore, $10,000 is a very large fine by OSHA standards. The fundamental point, of course, is that the temptation to ignore the law ($500,000) is large, the ($10,000) low, and the risk (once every 77 years) very small. You cannot be surprised when an organization does not comply any more than you would be surprised that the individual with the polluting car did not comply.

It can be argued that the organization has the greater responsibility. Certainly, a polluting smokestack is more visible, literally and figuratively, than an automobile's exhaust. However, we daresay that the marginal pollution attributable to automobiles far exceeds that of smokestacks in most (if not all) regions. Illegal? Yes. Irresponsible? Yes. Understandable?

Whether or not the behavior is "understandable," the result, at a minimum, is bad publicity. The observation that a corporation is likely to be criticized for operating in that illegal/irresponsible area is obvious. There has, however, been testimony and documentation that the weight of potential litigations in a classic cost/benefit analysis is far less than the cost of recalling or correcting the alleged deficiencies. While we have suggested that behavior in this area is high risk, there is precious little evidence that it is suicidal.

ILLEGAL/RESPONSIBLE

Being in this cell raises very interesting issues. Monsanto found itself in this cell in the Cycle-Safe incident. The FDA ruled its product illegal, even though Monsanto felt socially responsible. Many times, however, organizations find themselves in this area because of jurisdictional disputes. Suppose that, prior to the Civil Rights Act of 1964 and attendant legislation, an organization chose to embark on a program to employ women in equal capacities as male employees. At the time, this would have been forward-looking and extremely responsible corporate behavior. Unfortunately, much of the behavior involved in implementing that strategy would have been unquestionably illegal. During that period, "protective legislation" was very common. This legislation, designed to "protect" women, restricted working hours, overtime, the amount of weight that could be lifted, and types of jobs (bartending, for example) available to women. These and similar matters were eventually adjudicated largely at the federal court level.

Grover Starling cites an interesting jurisdictional paradox. It seems that the Federal Meat Inspection Service ordered an Armour meat-packing plant to create an aperture in a conveyor line so that inspectors could remove samples for testing. Accordingly, the company did so. The Occupational

---

[1] "Why nobody wants to listen to OSHA," *Business Week*, (June 14, 1976), 76, from Randall S. Schuler, *Personnel and human resource management* (St. Paul: West Publishing, 1981).

Safety and Health Administration soon arrived and demanded that the aperture be closed. It seems that an aperture on that line constituted a safety hazard. Predictably, each agency threatened to close down the plant if it refused to comply with its orders.[2] This example demonstrates how an organization could be operating in a fundamentally desirable manner (safely) and yet run afoul of legislation at some level. An organization might adopt a program to train underprivileged children, for example, and find itself in violation of a minimum wage law.

One potential strategy for dealing with problems in this cell is challenging the law. Laws can be, and are regularly, deliberately violated for no other reason than to challenge their application. You cannot get a hearing in a state or federal court on a "what-if" basis. In order to get a hearing, someone must be in jeopardy. A classic example is the famous *Gideon* v. *Wainwright* case where the Supreme Court ruled that a suspect has the right to counsel and that the state must provide such counsel if the accused could not afford it. This case could not have been decided without an issue—a man convicted without benefit of counsel. Gideon had to be in jeopardy. Courts do not rule on hypothetical cases.

The public is often critical of the corporate use of the courts. It is true that the courts, aside from their jurisprudential charter, are often used as a delay mechanism. There are, for example, legendary antitrust cases which have been in the courts for years. The courts have ruled against the acquisition, but organizations, through a series of legal maneuvers, have managed to stall the actual separations. In the meantime, presumably, the benefits of the acquisition continue to accrue. Interestingly, everyone's "pursuit of justice" is someone else's "delay." Even in *Gideon* v. *Wainwright*, we have little doubt that the prosecuting attorney's office saw the several appeals as both a nuisance and a delay.

Again, organizations can find themselves in a dilemma. An organization in the illegal/responsible cell faces a paradox. It is likely to be criticized whether it lives within the law or, potentially, challenges it.

IRRESPONSIBLE/LEGAL

Historically, there have been astonishing excesses in this area. Some of them would have been laughable if they had not been so serious. For example, prior to the Pure Food and Drug Act, the advertising for a diet pill promised that a person taking this pill could eat virtually anything at any time and still lose weight. Too good to be true? Actually, the claim was quite true; the product lived up to its billing with frightening efficacy. It seems that the primary active ingredient in this "diet supplement" was tapeworm

---

[2] Grover Starling, *The changing environment of business* (Boston: Kent Publishing, 1980).

larvae. These larvae would develop in the intestinal tract and, of course, be well fed; the pill-taker would in time, quite literally, starve to death.

In another case, which can only be described as amazing, an "anti-alcoholic elixir" was guaranteed to prevent the person who received the "potion" from drinking to excess. It was *very* effective. The product contained such a large dose of codeine that the people taking it became essentially comatose. The good news, of course, is that they certainly did not drink very much. And at the time, this product was not illegal.

There are more current examples with which we are all familiar—black lung disease in miners and asbestos poisoning, among others. Certainly, it was not always illegal to have miners working in mines without sufficient safety equipment to forestall black lung; nor was it illegal to have employees regularly working with asbestos without adequate protection. It can be argued that these consequences were not anticipated and that these situations were not deliberately socially irresponsible. It is, however, less persuasive to make that argument with respect to the ages and extended working hours of children in our industrial past.

But enough of the past. Do major organizations continue to engage in behaviors which, while not illegal, may be completely irresponsible? Among several examples that come to mind, one is, we think, appropriate for discussion but likely to be highly contentious—the manufacture and distribution of cigarettes. Obviously, cigarette manufacturing is not illegal. Is it irresponsible?

We noted earlier that knowledge of the effects of certain drugs may have been lacking in the past. We mentioned codeine-based elixirs. There are others. Some compounds contained as much as three grams of cocaine per base ounce. One asthma reliever was nearly pure cocaine. Even so, perhaps their effects were little understood and little harm was thought to have been done. Can the same be said of the tobacco industry? Is there anyone who is not aware of the harmful effects of smoking? True, there are warning labels which imply that the purchaser knows what he or she is taking. But how many people would endorse the use of codeine or cocaine or any other harmful substance, even with an appropriate warning label? Comparing apples and oranges? Perhaps, but 50 years from now, writers may talk about the manufacture of tobacco products and use terms such as *astonishing, amazing,* and *laughable* as we have to describe other legal, but irresponsible, behaviors.

Certainly, issues other than health are contained in this category. Suppose an organization is faced with more demand for its product than it can meet. Naturally, the organization does not care to encourage competition and would prefer to meet the demand itself if possible. Unfortunately, its plants are already operating 24 hours per day, 7 days a week. There is simply no further capacity. Management decides to build a new plant, which can be completed in no less than four years.

In the meantime, it is discovered that an existing, abandoned plant can be acquired and refitted in six months. Now, this plant will not be efficient and will be only marginally profitable at best. It will, however, serve to meet the escalating demand until such time as the new plant is ready for full operation, some four years hence.

Jury-rigging this abandoned plant, however, involves several problems. Foremost among them is the fact that the community does not have the infrastructure to serve the plant and the expected influx of employees. School systems will have to be expanded; housing will have to be built; recreational services improved. For the sake of this discussion, suppose that the temporary plant will employ 1,200 persons. It would be reasonable to estimate that this would mean the addition of 3,000 to 3,500 persons in the community. But, remember, this plant will be closed as soon as the new plant in another location is operational.

What is your decision? Do you authorize the refitting of this temporary plant? Certainly, if you notify the community that the plant is temporary, you will pay certain costs. The community would be understandably unlikely to make permanent improvements. Local banks would be somewhat less than enthusiastic about financing building projects, home mortgages, or consumer loans of any description. The simple solution is obvious—don't tell.

The point is that to deliberately use this plant as a stop-gap measure knowing full well that it will be temporary is not illegal. We are aware of no legislation which would prevent this action. There remain, however, some obvious social ramifications of this strategy. The ultimate closing of this plant is likely to reduce this community to a ghost town; there will be widespread unemployment; property values will fall precipitously; the tax base will be destroyed.

Once again, operating in this area is subject to criticism, underscoring our earlier point that being a "law-abiding" corporate citizen is not nearly enough; while organizations may not violate a single law, they may not be socially responsible. What of gambling casinos dealing not only in games of chance but also offering endless free liquor and decolletage? How about the manufacturers of handguns? Automobiles with questionable, if not lethal, fuel systems? Can a society hold organizations to a standard higher than that demanded by law?

LEGAL/RESPONSIBLE

It would seem that we have finally arrived at a strategy for which an organization cannot be criticized. An organization in this sector is a law-abiding corporate citizen and engages in behaviors which exceed those required by law—voluntary socially oriented action. Alas, even this proactive strategy is subject to four severe criticisms.

- Such behavior amounts to a unilateral, involuntary redistribution of assets.
- These actions lead to inequitable, regressive redistribution of assets.
- An organization engaging in these behaviors clearly exceeds its province.
- Social responsibility is entirely too expensive and rarely subjected to cost/benefit analysis.

Involuntary Redistribution

Probably the chief spokesperson of this position is Nobel laureate and economist Milton Friedman. He points out that today, unlike 100 years ago, managers do not "own" the business. They are employees, nothing more and nothing less. As such their primary responsibility is to the owner—the stockholders. Their relationship is essentially a fiduciary one. Friedman argues that the primary charter of the manager, therefore, is to conduct the business in accordance with the wishes of the employer, given that these wishes are within the limits embodied in the law and ethical custom. Any social actions beyond that amount to an involuntary redistribution of assets. To the extent that these actions reduce dividends, stockholders suffer; to the extent that these actions raise prices, consumers suffer; to the extent that such actions reduce potential wages and benefits, employees suffer. Should any or all of these interested parties care to make philanthropic contributions to fund socially desirable projects, they may do so. Without their consent, however, such redistributions are clearly unilateral and involuntary.

Inequitable, Regressive Redistributions

This tendency can be referred to as a reverse Robin Hood effect.[3] Mr. Hood and his band of merry men stole from the rich and gave to the poor, but many programs under the loose rubric of social responsibility have not followed this redistribution pattern. In fact, it can be argued that many programs actually rob the poor to serve the rich. Obviously, the more wealthy persons are, the more regressive this social responsibility "tax."

Many projects which are not commercially feasible are supported by the largest of organizations under the banner of social responsibility. Opera and dance companies, for example, may be subsidized by corporate contributions. Public television is heavily financed by corporate sponsors. The reason that these subsidies are essential to the operation of these programs is that

---

[3] Discussion based largely on Dean Carson, "Companies as heroes?" . . . *New York Times* (1977).

public demand for these products is altogether insufficient to defray their costs. Presumably, the money to finance these ventures comes from somewhere in the organizational coffers. Consumers, employees, and others "contribute," as we previously noted, to the availability of these funds.

Who, however, is the primary beneficiary of these subsidized programs? For the most part, it seems fair to suggest that those who regularly attend ballets, operas, dance companies, live theater, symphonies, and watch similar programming on public television are relatively more affluent. It would appear that real income is transferred from the poorer to the richer in this exercise of social responsibility.

Exceeding Province

One, if not the foremost, justification for government involvement in private affairs is market failure. When the market cannot provide, for whatever reasons, that which the public demands, then government is (or should be) enfranchised to supply or finance that product or service. National defense, health and safety, and welfare are a few of the services which the private sector is unable to supply. It may be that libraries, museums, parks and recreation, operas, symphonies, and support for other performing arts are in this category as well. The objection which is central here is that it is not the province of private organizations to decide which of these projects should be funded and to what extent. Such support should not be a function of the predilections of corporate officials; this is the charter of government.

The issue clearly goes beyond fighting over who is going to play with what toys. In theory, public officials are subject to review by the citizenry. If the public does not approve of the manner in which funds are being prioritized for social concerns, they may petition their various legislatures. Failing in this, they may not support the reelection of the appropriate public officials. The public, on the other hand, does not vote or in any other manner approve or endorse highly ranking officers of corporations. By what right should corporations decide what is "good" and what is "right?" It may well be that a given corporate image of righteousness is somewhat different from your own.

The potential for corporate influence in this public area is enormous. Theodore Levitt, while (we hope) overstating the case somewhat, presents a clear view of the potential of business statesmanship:

> Proliferating employee welfare programs, its serpentine involvement in community, government, charitable, and educational affairs, its prodigious currying of political and public favor through hundreds of peripheral preoccupations, all these well-intended but insidious contrivances are greasing the rails for our collective descent into a social order that would be as repugnant to the corporations themselves as to their critics. The danger is that all things will turn the corporation into a 20th century equivalent of the medieval Church.

The corporation would eventually invest itself with all-embracing duties, obligations, and finally powers—ministering to the whole man and molding him and society in the image of the corporation's narrow ambitions and its essentially unsocial needs.[4]

A grim scenario, to be sure. The fundamental point remains. Critics argue that any of these voluntary socially responsible behaviors simply exceed the province of the corporation.

Expense of Social Responsibility

A final objection to the general issue of social responsibility, whether mandated by regulation or voluntarily pursued by organizations, is that it is oppressively expensive. The necessity to comply with ever-stricter environmental standards, for example, has literally forced the closing of hundreds of industrial locations across the country. Furthermore, it has been argued that these regulations have seriously affected domestic industry's ability to compete in international markets.

No one would argue that expense alone is sufficient to discard programs of environmental protection, employee safety, consumer protection, or a host of other socially responsive concerns. However, it can be argued that these programs should be subjected to a cost/benefit analysis. Quite often, this is not done. An automobile, for example, could be manufactured so soundly that driver deaths in accidents could be practically eliminated on our highways. But at what cost? We do not intend to address the question of what a human life is worth. Obviously, its value is incalculable. The fact remains that we live in a finite world; resources are limited. When we choose to make expenditures in one area, we necessarily restrict or eliminate expenditures in another. At what point do safety programs become overly paternalistic? At some time, employees, for example, must bear a certain responsibility for their own safety. The same can be said for those who operate motor vehicles on public highways.

While this principle seems clear, it is often not considered. What expense is justifiable to renovate and refit public buildings to render them essentially fireproof? Or, if not fireproof, at least such that the loss of human life by fire is remote? The hard fact is that very few people die each year in fires in multistoried buildings. Who is going to pay for such judicious safety? And for the benefit of how many?

The same approach can be pursued with respect to airliner safety. Fortunately, very few people lose their lives each year in commercial airplanes. There is no doubt that airplanes could be manufactured so that

---

[4] Theodore Levitt, "The dangers of social responsibility," *Harvard Business Review* (1958), 44.

they would be even safer in accidents. Again, at what cost? We do not wish to appear insensitive; the loss of a human life is a tragedy, especially if it could have been prevented. "Safety at any cost," however, is simply not viable in a society restricted by finite resources.

The objection regarding the expense of social responsibility is easily restated. Aside from its absolute expense, which can be formidable, critics argue that social responsibility is often not accompanied by sufficient benefits to justify its cost.

Once again, even while being both legal and responsible, an organization is likely to receive severe criticism.

We have suggested that every cell (Illegal/irresponsible, illegal/responsible, legal/irresponsible, legal/responsible) is subject to criticism. Furthermore, the cell that your organization occupies may be determined by individuals outside of your firm—federal agencies or consumer groups, to name a few. It may be a classic expression of the aphorism, "You're damned if you do, you're damned if you don't." Inasmuch as all strategies are subject to criticism, where should the organization operate? Which is the optimum strategy?

We think there are three fundamental principles which should be considered by an organization with respect to choosing a strategy for social responsibility: *primum non nocere*, organizational accountability, and the double standard.

Primum Non Nocere

This notion was first explicated over 2,500 years ago in the Hippocratic oath. Freely translated, it means "Above all, knowingly do no harm." This would seem to be a sound principle for both legality and responsibility. Organizations should not engage in any behavior if they know that harm will be done as a result. This is not meant to be literally interpreted. Certainly, knowing that some individuals will injure themselves is insufficient to bar the manufacture and distribution of, for example, steak knives. This, like any principle, should be tempered with good sense.

Organizational Accountability

An organization should be responsible for its impacts, *to* or *for* society, whether they are intended or not. Ordinarily, in the course of providing a good or a service, costs are incurred. Presumably, the price of the product or service is, at least in part, a function of the costs of its manufacture or delivery. The difference between the cost and the price is profit—the *sine qua non* of private enterprise. This would be acceptable, except for one oversight—very often society underwrites portions of the cost. Historically, given that the production of energy through sulphurous coal leads to higher levels of air pollution, the costs of producing electricity have been artificially low. That pollution is a cost. Sooner or later, someone has to pay to clean it up. But who? The consumer did not have to pay a premium for the electricity to enter a "clean-up" fund. The power company made no such contribution.

Today, we could argue that cigarette manufacturing enterprises enjoy a certain cost reduction. The manufacturer and the smoker can be thought of as enjoying a subsidy. Arguably, the retail price of cigarettes does not approach that necessary to cover its total costs. Where, for instance, is the fund that will eventually be called upon to pay for the medical costs allegedly associated with smoking? The point is that someone should be accountable for these behaviors.

Double Standard

Traditionally, the concept of a double standard has had a negative connotation. In the area of social corporate responsibility, we think it is reasonable, even commendable. As we have continuously noted, there are no rules that apply to organizations about what, where, when, how much, and how often they can engage in behaviors *for* society, but a certain power-responsibility equation has been suggested.[5] Essentially, this equation argues that the social responsibility expected of an organization should be commensurate with the size of the social power it exercises. Large companies—AT&T, General Motors, Exxon, IBM, General Electric, Du Pont—whose operations can literally dominate entire regions of the country have a greater responsibility than smaller organizations with less influence.

The larger an organization becomes, the more actual and potential influence it commands over society. Society, necessarily, takes a greater interest in the affairs of such organizations. Society has correspondingly less expectation of social responsibility from smaller organizations.

This is the nature of the double standard to which we have referred. While any double standard is somewhat unfair, it highlights an observation made by Drucker. He argues that the quest for social responsibility is not a result of hostility towards the business community. Rather, the demand for social responsibility is, in large measure, the price of success. Success and influence may well lead to a greater responsibility to society. A double standard, to be sure, but perhaps a reasonable one.

---

[5] Y. N. Chang and Filemon Campo-Flores, *Business policy and strategy* (Santa Monica, Calif.: Goodyear Publishing, 1980).

SO WHICH STRATEGY?

We believe that organizations should adopt a strategy reflected in cell D—legal and responsible. Remember, however, that the classification of cell D will be determined by the public (or government acting "for" the public). Organizations have to anticipate, and in some cases, influence the public reaction—be proactive. However, a proactive stance involves some risk. As we noted earlier, critics abound regardless of the cell in the table occupied by the organization. A certain risk, nevertheless, is necessary for any business to succeed. Drucker rightly states that to try to eliminate risk in business is futile. Risk is inherent in the commitment of present resources to future expectations. The attempt to eliminate risk may result in the greatest risk of all—rigidity.

We would argue that merely being a law-abiding corporate citizen is something less than social responsibility. It may be that large organizations must "do something." Affirmative action is a compelling analogy. It is not enough not to discriminate. Organizations must do something proactively to further the goals of equal employment opportunity. Perhaps this is true for other issues of corporate social responsibility as well. There may be an expectation that organizations must do something to further benefit society beyond following its formal laws.

Basically, some action is better than no action. Throughout the course of history, inaction has never advanced mankind. In our view, errors of commission are far better than those of omission. If our ancestors had heeded the critics who were opposed to doing something, we might all still be drawing on cave walls. This issue is not entirely philosophical; there are important pragmatic considerations as well, as evidenced in the remarks of Du Pont chairperson Irving S. Shapiro:

> I think we're a means to an end, and while producing goods and providing jobs is our primary function, we can't live successfully in a society if the hearts of its cities are decaying and its people can't make the whole system work. . . . It means that, just as you want libraries, and you want schools, and you want fire departments and police departments, you also want businesses to help do something about unsolved social problems.[6]

Occasionally, it is argued that true social responsibility does not exist. Organizations do not operate out of social responsibility—but good business. Many instances of activities which could be referred to as "responsible" are public relations strategies which are sound business; it pays to advertise. Truly philanthropic efforts occur without fanfare. Some argue that only when organizations anonymously contribute their executives and other resources

---

[6] Irving S. Shapiro, "Today's executive: Private steward and public servant," *Harvard Business Review* (1978), 101.

to socially responsible programs do you have true responsiveness. Perhaps. But we choose not to define social responsibility as philanthropy. We have no objection to enlightened self-interest.

Assuming that society is not totally victimized by actions justified under the banner of social responsibility, then corporations, even pursuing their interests, present a win-win situation. If restoring land to its natural state after mining is *only* done because it is good business, fine. Society benefits. The same can be said for many, if not most, socially responsible behaviors by organizations. We are less concerned with *why* it is done than with the fact that it *is* done. We think it can be best done legally and responsibly.

Organizations: New Concepts for New Forms*

Raymond E. Miles
Charles C. Snow

These are turbulent times in the world of organizations. Following a decade of declining productivity and failed organizations, many U.S. companies in the eighties have been forced to rethink their competitive approaches. Rapid technological change, as well as shifting patterns of international trade and competition, have put intense strain on these organizations' ability to keep pace with a set of new and often unpredictable competitors. One prominent executive, describing the current business landscape, says, "Not only is it a competitive jungle out there, new beasts are roaming around that we can't even identify."

Two major outcomes of the search for new competitive approaches are already apparent:

- First, the search is producing a new organizational form—a unique combination of strategy, structure, and management processes that we refer to as the *dynamic network*. The new form is both a cause and a result of today's competitive environment: The same "competitive beast" that some companies do not understand has been the solution to other companies' competitive difficulties.

- Second, as is always the case, the new organizational form is forcing the development of new concepts and language to explain its features and functions and, in the process, is providing new insights into the workings of existing strategies and structures. In the future, many organizations will be designed using such concepts as vertical disaggregation, internal and external brokering, full-disclosure information systems, and market substitutes for administrative mechanisms.

* From California Management Review (Spring 1986) *XXVIII*, no. 3, 62–73. © 1986, The Regents of the University of California.

In the following sections, we describe these new concepts and the dynamic network forms. We then examine their implications for management practice, organizational redesign, and government policy in trade and industry issues.

BUILDING BLOCKS OF CURRENT THEORY: STRATEGIC CHOICE AND FIT

Based on research conducted during the late sixties and seventies, there is now widespread agreement that most industries can contemporaneously support several different competitive strategies. Sociologists, for example, have described "generalist" organizations that are able to survive in a variety of environments alongside "specialist" organizations that thrive only in narrower segments or niches.[1] Economists have shown that in a given industry some firms compete primarily on the basis of cost leadership, some differentiate their product or service in the eyes of consumers, and others simply focus on a particular market segment.[2]

The most common competitive strategies, sometimes referred to as *generic strategies*, have been labelled Prospectors, Defenders, and Analyzers.[3] Prospectors are "first-to-the-market" with a new product or service and differentiate themselves from their competitors by using their ability to develop innovative technologies and products. Alternatively, Defenders offer a limited, stable product line and compete primarily on the basis of value and/or cost. Analyzers pursue a "second-in" strategy whereby they imitate and improve upon the product offerings of their competitors. Thus, they are frequently able to sell widely because of their ability to rationalize other firms' product designs and methods of production.

The Prospector–Defender–Analyzer typology, besides indicating overall strategic orientation, also specifies the major organizational and managerial features needed to support these competitive strategies. Defenders, for example, rely heavily on the functional organization structure developed around the turn of the century and its accompanying managerial characteristics of centralized decision making and control, vertical communications and integration, and high degrees of technical specialization.[4] Prospectors, on the other hand, use more flexible structures, such as autonomous work groups or product divisions in which planning and control are highly decentralized. These structures, pioneered in the twenties and thirties and refined in the fifties, facilitate market responsiveness but at the expense of overall specialization and efficiency. Finally, Analyzers often employ a "mixed" structure, such as the matrix, wherein project, program, or brand managers act as integrators between resource groups and program units. Matrix structures, which were widely adopted in the sixties, blend features of both the functional and divisional structures and thus are designed to be simultaneously efficient and flexible.[5]

Current theory in the area of strategy, structure, and process is founded largely on the twin concepts of strategic choice and fit. Managers make strategic choices based on their perceptions of the environment and of their organizations' capabilities. The success of these choices rests on how well competitive strategy matches environmental conditions and whether organization structure and management processes are properly fitted to strategy. Historically, strategy and structure have evolved together. Each advance in structural form was stimulated by the limitations of the previous form, and, because each new form built on the previous form, it helped to clarify the strengths and limitations of its predecessor. Also, each development in structure permitted new competitive strategies to be pursued. Saying all of this in different language, ways of doing business traditionally have been highly contingent on ways of organizing, and major competitive breakthroughs have been achieved by firms that invented, or were quick to apply, new forms of organization and management.[6]

BUILDING BLOCKS OF NEW THEORY: DYNAMIC NETWORKS AND INDUSTRY SYNERGY

New organizational forms arise to cope with new environmental conditions. However, no new means of organizing or managing arrives full-blown; usually it results from a variety of experimental actions taken by innovative companies. The competitive environment of the eighties is pushing many companies into this innovative mode, and the United States is on the verge of another breakthrough in organizational form. In order to describe this emerging form, illustrate its distinctive competence, and discuss the contributions it makes to the understanding of previous organizational forms, we must broaden the current theoretical framework summarized above to include new ways of looking at individual organizations and how they interact with each other in their respective industries.

Signs of the new organizational form—such as increased use of joint ventures, subcontracting and licensing activities occurring across international borders, and new business ventures spinning off of established companies—are already evident in several industries, so the realization of this new form simply awaits articulation and understanding. As noted, we have chosen to call this form the *dynamic network* to suggest that its major components can be assembled and reassembled in order to meet complex and changing competitive conditions.[7] Briefly, the characteristics of the dynamic network are as follows (see Figure 1):

- *Vertical disaggregation*—Business functions, such as product design and development, manufacturing, marketing, and distribution, typically conducted within a single organization, are performed by

FIGURE 1   A Dynamic Network

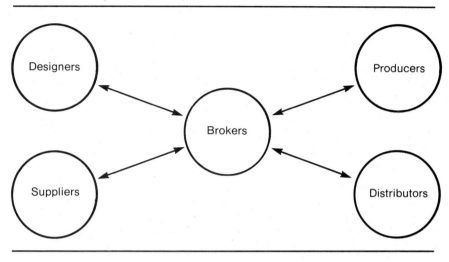

independent organizations within a network. Networks may be more or less complex and dynamic depending on competitive circumstances.

- *Brokers*—Because each function is not necessarily part of a single organization, business groups are assembled by or located through brokers. In some cases, a single broker plays a lead role and subcontracts for needed services. In other cases, linkages among equal partners are created by various brokers specializing in a particular service. In still others, one network component uses a broker to locate one or more other functions.

- *Market mechanisms*—The major functions are held together in the main by market mechanisms, rather than plans and controls. Contracts and payment for results are used more frequently than progress reports and personal supervision.

- *Full-disclosure information systems*—Broad-access computerized information systems are used as substitutes for lengthy trust-building processes based on experience. Participants in the network agree on a general structure of payment for value added and then hook themselves together in a continuously updated information system so that contributions can be mutually and instantaneously verified.

In order to understand all of its ramifications, the dynamic network must be viewed simultaneously from the perspective of its individual components and from the network as a whole. For the individual firm (or component), the primary benefit of participation in the network is the opportunity to pursue its particular distinctive competence. A properly constructed network can display the technical specialization of the functional structure, the market responsiveness of the divisional structure, and the balanced orientation characteristic of the matrix. Therefore, each network component can be seen as complementing, rather than competing with, the other components. Complementarity permits the creation of elaborate networks designed to handle complex situations, such as international construction projects, which cannot be accomplished by a single organization. It also permits rapid adjustment to changing competitive conditions, such as those found in many consumer goods industries (such as apparel or electronics).

Viewing the network as a whole, each firm's distinctive competence is not only enhanced by participation in the network, it is held in check by its fellow network members. That is, if a particular component performs its role poorly or somehow takes unfair advantage of another component, then it can be removed from the network (due to the independence that allows the network to reshape itself whenever necessary). However, removal of a component means that the initiating component and/or the responsible broker must find a replacement part or encourage one of the remaining components to perform the missing function. In either case, the network as a whole is likely to operate temporarily at undesirable levels. Thus, there is complementarity present in every well-conceived network that encourages each participant, singly and in combination, to perform capably and responsibly.

With this grasp of the means and motivation underlying the dynamic network form, it is possible to create a theoretical analog that enhances understanding of the role played by existing organizational forms within their own industries. We refer to this phenomenon as *industry synergy*. This concept comes from our belief that there is symmetry between the characteristics and operations of the dynamic network and the features and behavior of the firms within an industry (or major industry segment).

As noted earlier, most industries are able to support companies pursuing different competitive strategies. Each strategy type both contributes to, and benefits from, the demand for goods and services in the industry, shaping its contribution around its own distinctive competence. Each firm, according to current theory, competes symbiotically with other firms in the industry for a share of the total market. However, when viewed from the industry perspective, each firm also has a synergistic role to play that might be described as *implicit interdependence* among competitors. For example, in order to maintain its long-run viability, the total industry must meet the dual objectives of innovation and efficiency, suggesting that there may be an ideal mix of competitive strategies required by every healthy industry.[8] Using the language introduced earlier, every industry to some extent *re-*

quires the presence of Prospectors, Defenders, and Analyzers. Prospectors generate the technological and product innovations that push the industry forward, Analyzers rationalize some of these innovations for marketability and ease of manufacture, and Defenders lower costs to the minimum in certain product areas to facilitate mass consumption. In a manner analogous to the complementarity of the network form, each of these strategy types requires the presence of the others in order to perform its own role to the fullest. In turn, the industry's long-run aggregate performance is better than it otherwise would be if any one of the generic competitive strategies was missing.

DYNAMIC SYNERGY

Although no definitive research can be cited as evidence, it appears from case studies and observation that the mix of strategic roles required for industry synergy changes as the industry evolves. Several different patterns can be ascertained. First, and perhaps most obviously, embryonic industries are heavily populated with firms pursuing the Prospector strategy. A current example is the bioengineering "industry," in which many relatively small firms are experimenting with different technologies and product-service configurations. Less obvious is the claim that such industries are likely to remain latent until firms begin playing Analyzer and Defender roles. In the early days of the automobile industry, growth was not especially dramatic as various companies experimented with steam, electric, and internal combustion technologies, as well as various distribution methods. Rapid growth occurred only after Henry Ford played a Defender role by installing an assembly line for manufacturing a single type of car on a standardized basis and by forming a distribution network of franchise dealers that sold cars to the mass market. Similarly, one would predict that, in today's bioengineering industry, growth gains will be greatest when some large established company acquires one or more small R&D firms and begins to produce standardized products in large volume.

A second pattern of strategic mix involves mature industries. Here one would expect fewer participants than in new industries and a much greater proportion of firms using the efficiency-oriented Defender strategy. However, in order to prevent the industry from heading into decline, a few firms must behave as Prospectors (probably in limited areas). An example is the major home appliance industry. Over the last 15 years, dramatic gains in market share have been made by White Consolidated Industries, a company that relies exclusively on the Defender approach. Although much of the industry appears to have the characteristics of a commodity business, with advanced automated production systems churning out standardized products on a cost-effective basis, portions of the industry deal with innovative products and technologies (e.g., the "smart" kitchen). In these innovative areas, the leadership role is played by companies such as General Electric. To maintain its health, a mature industry requires the successful performance of both kinds of strategic roles.

Finally, there are industries in transition, for which the desired mix of competitive strategies is more varied and changing. One example is the electronics industry (including computers and semiconductors). Neither a new nor a mature industry, electronics is in the growth stage, but its segments are growing at much different rates. Consequently, over the next several years, there is the potential for this industry to achieve great success if it develops a comprehensive mix of competitive strategies. However, there is also the possibility that this industry will not realize its potential if the strategic mix becomes too narrow.

Consider the following scenario. Hewlett-Packard, a company that has traditionally competed as a Prospector across most of the markets in which it operates, recently has attempted to play an uncustomary role in its computer business. Within its Business Computers Group, Hewlett-Packard has tried to achieve the standardization, coordination, and integration most characteristic of the Analyzer, and it is having difficulty grafting this approach onto its present organization and management culture. If the approaches taken in the reorganization of its computer business are forced onto other HP businesses, then it is possible that across the entire company Hewlett-Packard will dilute its strength as *both* a Prospector and an Analyzer. Similarly, Intel, which has traditionally prided itself on its high-technology production competence, has recently begun to design, produce, and market business computer network systems. It, too, must be careful not to dilute its primary distinctive competence as it moves into new businesses requiring different technical and organizational abilities. If, as these examples suggest, certain companies do not maintain their primary distinctive competence, then the industry as a whole may not exhibit the comprehensive mix of competitive strategies needed to achieve long-term success.

In sum, a healthy industry's needs for innovation and efficiency are met through the complementary efforts of firms pursuing different strategies, each of which is based on a primary distinctive competence. By regularly being "first-to-the-market," Prospectors sustain technological innovation and are the principal contributors to the design of new products and services. By competing primarily as efficient producers, Defenders uphold quality levels while driving down the costs of standardized goods and services. The most important role played by Analyzers is that of transferring information throughout the industry, especially as it concerns the standardization of technology and product design. By sorting through the experiments conducted by Prospectors to determine those technologies, products, and services most amenable to rationalization, Analyzers establish a new plateau from which the next round of innovation can be launched. Subsequently, by developing successful approaches to mass production and marketing of new products, the Analyzer sets broad efficiency targets that Defenders try to surpass.

DIFFUSION OF THE DYNAMIC NETWORK FORM

Returning to the dynamic network shown in Figure 1, it can be argued that Prospectors essentially play the *designer* role within an industry, Analyzers play the *marketing/distribution* role (and also contribute as information brokers), and Defenders perform the *producer* role. By relating the components of the network form to the synergistic roles played by firms within an industry, it is possible to forecast where and how rapidly the network form may emerge.

Aspects of the new form can be identified even in capital-intensive industries where large investments, relatively indivisible production functions, and other factors make it difficult for companies to move toward the network structure. Often firms in these industries have a limited range of distinctive competence, even though they may perform all of the activities associated with a given business. In the petroleum industry, for example, most of the major firms have sought vertical integration as a means of assuring an uninterrupted flow of operations, ranging from the acquisition of raw materials to the sale of consumer petroleum products. Yet, these companies are not all equally skilled at performing each step of the exploration (supply), refining (production), product development (design), and marketing/distribution process. Thus, even though vertical disaggregation may be feasible in this industry, it is unlikely to occur in the short run. Presumably, if vertical disaggregation were easier to implement, some of the major firms would divest their less central functions and focus only on those value-added activities most closely associated with their abilities. Our prediction is that Defender companies would choose to perform the producer role, Prospectors would select the designer role, and so on.

In labor-intensive industries, where vertical disaggregation is less costly and easier to administer, the network form is gaining in popularity much more rapidly. In fact, one of our studies uncovered the partial use of the network structure over 20 years ago.[9] During the sixties and seventies, developments in the college textbook publishing industry caused many of the major firms to reevaluate their publishing activities and to modify their organization structures. For example, virtually every publishing company got out of the printing and binding business and simply contracted for these services as needed. Also, several companies allowed key editors to form their own publishing firms, which then became subsidiaries of the parent companies. These subsidiaries usually engaged in new publishing approaches, thereby developing an expertise that the parent company could tap into whenever appropriate. Lastly, some publishers drastically cut back their in-house operations in art, graphics, and design, choosing instead to subcontract this work to smaller, specialized groups that comprised a cottage industry around the major publishers. Thus, in the space of 10 years or so, several of the major college textbook publishers in effect developed networks in which portions of the producer and designer roles were moved out of the original companies into smaller specialty firms. The major companies simply retained those functions that were closest to their traditional distinctive competence (such as McGraw-Hill in product development and Prentice-Hall in sales).

As the United States continues to become more of a service economy, the case of textbook publishing (and many other examples) may well suggest the pattern by which other labor-intensive industries move toward the dynamic network model. The rationale for "people" and service businesses to adopt this structure is clearcut. The dynamic network is a far more flexible structure than any of the previous forms, it can accommodate a vast amount of complexity while maximizing specialized competence, and it provides much more effective use of human resources that otherwise have to be accumulated, allocated, and maintained by a single organization. The practice of leasing entire work forces, already in use in construction, hotel management, and retail sales, is a network characteristic that will become even more prevalent in the future. As managers gain experience and confidence in these network designs and practices, the dynamic network form will spread accordingly.

IMPLICATIONS

A new organizational form is both a cause and a result of the changing nature of competition. As organizations formulate new strategies to meet new competitive conditions, they find that their structures and management systems also require modification. Simultaneously, as new organizational forms become better understood and more widely used, new competitive strategies are easier to implement. The dynamic network form, as indicated earlier, has appeared as a means of coping with the business environment of the seventies and eighties. Its arrival now has implications for the way managers view the future directions of their companies, for the approaches used to manage existing structures, and for the way in which public policy is used to restore competitive vigor.

Strategists

Strategic planners have a growing literature to call upon as they formulate objectives and strategies for their companies. Frameworks are available to help strategists determine their companies' distinctive competence, generate strategic options, analyze competitors' behavior, and so on. However, all of these frameworks ignore or underemphasize the concept of industry synergy and the key industry roles defined by the network model. From these concepts, several recommendations for the strategic decision maker can be derived. First, the strategist must examine the industry's current mix of competitive strategies as a means of forecasting the industry's prospects for long-term viability. A healthy industry must at a minimum have firms with the ability to perform the designer and producer roles. Next, the strategist must try to anticipate how the industry's strategic mix might change over time. All firms are generally aware that, as an industry matures, the mix of competitive strategies is likely to shift from a high proportion of Prospectors to a high proportion of Defenders. Therefore, the astute strategist can develop moves within this overall scenario that are not obvious at first glance. For example, it might be advantageous to become the first Defender in an embryonic industry. Or it might be desirable to be the last Prospector in a mature industry. Basically, the strategist can be prepared to offer "nonobvious" strategies by thinking in terms of strategic roles and synergies at the industry level. Finally, the strategist must be ready to show the organization how it can change directions in order to take advantage of new opportunities or to counter competitive threats. The logic of the dynamic network model indicates that this flexibility can be achieved largely through vertical disaggregation. Thus, an organization may be able to obtain competitive advantage by performing only those activities closest to its distinctive competence, contracting with other components of a network for goods or services on an *ad hoc* basis, and perhaps serving as a broker in yet other areas. IBM used this approach in developing its personal computer (the PC jr.). Initially lagging behind its competitors, IBM quickly assembled a network of designers, suppliers, producers, and marketers to put together its first product offering. Later, after it had established itself in the market, IBM reintegrated portions of the network into its primary operating system.

Policymakers

The concepts of industry synergy and dynamic network can be used to examine aspects of international competition and their implications for public policy. The U.S. economy is becoming increasingly connected to world markets, so dynamic networks in many industries now operate across national boundaries. This fact complicates the recommendations made above to strategists. For example, in the case of a purely domestic industry, long-term viability rests on member firms playing a heterogeneous set of roles, such as designer, producer, and marketer/distributor. In the case of an international industry, however, one or more of these roles may be best suited to foreign firms. Presently, some large U.S. industries have the bulk of their manufacturing and assembly operations located overseas. The domestic portion of the industry is quite homogeneous, with a few firms performing the designer role and the remainder performing the marketing/ distribution role. In these situations, long-term industry health is an international concern, and individual firm strategists must take this into account as they try to anticipate the industry's strategic mix over time. Further, calls for a national industrial policy to revitalize declining industries will fail, according to the logic of the dynamic network model, if they implicitly rely on an improper role for American firms. The realities of international competition indicate that many American "producers" should rethink their industry role and attempt to find a more valuable location in an international network. Apparently, this is happening in the steel industry. Several American firms have achieved recent success by reorienting their plants toward customized products and applications instead of commodity products.[10] These companies cannot compete well in most commodity steel markets, so it is to their advantage to play a designer role in the industry and leave the producer role to foreign competitors.

Managers and Organization Designers

The final set of implications applies to managers, especially those in a position to redesign their organizations. Executives who perceive the network form as a competitive advantage for their companies now have an explicit model to guide their redesign efforts. On the other hand, some companies cannot or will not vertically disaggregate and completely adopt the new form. Nevertheless, these companies desire the benefits of the network approach. Managers of these companies need ideas for, and the means of, altering their existing organizations so as to simulate desirable features of the dynamic network.

In companies whose distinctive competence is best served by traditional organization structures, there may still be pressure to demonstrate more flexible, innovative behavior. The network model suggests that these companies can be more innovative by setting up special units focused on innovation, in which brokers bring resources together and later transfer results to the larger operating system. A number of mechanisms for supplementing existing structures are available, including internal venturing or "intrapreneurship," external coventuring, idea markets, and innovator roles, such as idea champions, sponsors, and orchestrators. Taken together, these structures, processes, and interpersonal roles comprise an innovating organization that operates parallel to the main system.[11] Developed and used in companies, such as IBM, Texas Instruments, Minnesota Mining and Manufacturing, and others, these innovating mechanisms can be employed by more traditional firms to keep pace with developments in their industries. Some companies may choose to internally generate more ideas and innovations, while others may rely on external coventuring schemes to create needed innovations. In either case, advances made by the innovating system are integrated into the larger organization only after their utility has been clearly demonstrated.

CONCLUSIONS

Current "merger mania" notwithstanding, it seems likely that the eighties and nineties will be known as decades of large-scale disaggregation and redeployment of resources in the United States and of a reshaping of strategic roles across the world economy. By the turn of the century, we expect U.S. firms to be playing producer roles primarily in high-technology goods and service industries (agriculture may be regarded as a high-tech industry). These industries are characterized by sophisticated products and delivery systems for which the United States has a worldwide competitive advantage. In more mature industries, especially those containing a large proportion of commodity products or services, we would expect U.S. firms to play primarily designer and distributor roles, with production limited to special-needs products and prototype designs to be licensed for production abroad. Of course, the United States will play a major marketer/distributor role in most industries throughout this period.

These shifting alignments will create both competitive challenges and opportunities for managers and policymakers. The greatest barrier to success will be outmoded views of what an "organization" must look like and how it must be managed. Future forms will all feature some of the properties of the dynamic network form, particularly heavy reliance on self-managed work groups and a greater willingness to view organizational boundaries and membership as highly flexible. We anticipate, ultimately, that key business units—such as a design engineering group or prototype-production team— will be autonomous building blocks to be assembled, reassembled, and redeployed within and across organizational and national boundaries as product or service life cycles demand.

REFERENCES

1. Hannan, Michael T., and John H. Freeman. "The population ecology of organizations." *American Journal of Sociology* (March 1977) 82, 929–64;   and Aldrich, Howard E. *Organizations and environments.* Englewood Cliffs, NJ: Prentice-Hall, 1979.
2. Porter, Michael E., *Competitive strategy.* New York: Free Press, 1980.
3. Miles, Raymond E., and Charles C. Snow. *Organizational strategy, structure, and process.* New York: McGraw-Hill, 1978.
4. Chandler, Alfred D., Jr. *Strategy and structure.* New York: Doubleday, 1962.
5. Davis, Stanley M., and Paul R. Lawrence. *Matrix.* Reading, Mass.: Addison-Wesley, 1977.

6. Miles, Raymond E., and Charles C. Snow. "Fit, failure, and the hall of fame." *California Management Review* (Spring 1984) *XXVI*, 10–28.
7. Ibid.
8. Economists do not agree on a single definition of industry health. Classical equilibrium theory states that firms in a competitive industry should not make profits in excess of the normal bank rate of return. Another economic theory, however, says that excess profits are required for industry innovation. Yet another theory maintains that excess profits may be rightfully earned by firms that minimize buyers' search and information-processing costs (by consistently offering high-quality products, etc.). Our criteria of long-run industry health are taken from Paul R. Lawrence and Davis Dyer, *Renewing American industry* (New York: Free Press, 1983).
9. Miles and Snow, *Organizational strategy, structure, and process*, chapter 10.
10. Goldhar, Joel D., and Mariann Jelinek. "Plan for economies of scope." *Harvard Business Review* (November/December 1983) *61*, 141–48.
11. See Galbraith, Jay R. "Designing the innovating organization," *Organizational Dynamics* (Winter 1982), 5–25; and Gifford Pinchot, III, *Intrapreneuring.* New York: Harper & Row, 1985.